English with an Acce

Since its original publication in 1997, *English with an Accent* has inspired generations of scholars to investigate linguistic discrimination, social categorization, social structures, and power. This new edition is an attempt to retain the spirit of the original while enriching and expanding it to reflect the greater understanding of linguistic discrimination that it has helped create.

This third edition has been substantially reworked to include:

- An updated concept of social categories, how they are constructed in interaction, and how they can be invoked and perceived through linguistic cues or language ideologies
- Refreshed accounts of the countless social and structural factors that go into linguistic discrimination
- Expanded attention to specific linguistic structures, language groups, and social domains that go beyond those provided in earlier editions
- New dedicated chapter on American Sign Language and its history of discrimination
- QR codes linking to external media, stories, and other forms of engagement beyond the text
- A revamped website with additional material

English with an Accent remains a book that forces us to acknowledge and understand the ways language is used as an excuse for discrimination. The book will help readers to better understand issues of cross-cultural communication, to develop strategies for successful interactions across social difference, to recognize patterns of language that reflect implicit bias, and to gain awareness of how mistaken beliefs about language create and nurture prejudice and discrimination.

Rusty Barrett is Professor of Linguistics at the University of Kentucky. His research is in Mayan linguistics, linguistic anthropology, and sociolinguistics. He is author of *From Drag Queens to Leathermen: Language, Gender, and Gay Male Subcultures*, co-author of *Other People's English: Code Meshing, Code Switching and African American Literacy*, and co-editor of the *Oxford Handbook of Language and Sexuality*.

Jennifer Cramer is Professor of Linguistics at the University of Kentucky. Her research is in perceptual dialectology, with a specific focus on dialect variation in Kentucky. She is the author of *Contested Southernness: The Linguistic Production and Perception of Identities in the Borderlands*, co-author of *Linguistic Planets of Belief: Mapping Language Attitudes in the American South*, and co-editor of *Cityscapes and Perceptual Dialectology: Global Perspectives on Non-linguists' Knowledge of the Dialect Landscape*.

Kevin B. McGowan is Associate Professor of Linguistics at the University of Kentucky and Director of the University of Kentucky Phonetics Lab. He is a phonetician, and his research primarily focuses on speech perception and the ways in which the creation and perception of social identities influence our ability to understand each other.

"The third edition of *English with an Accent* presents an extraordinary new resource created from a time-honored classic, taking the pieces of the original and elegantly intersecting them with 21st-century language practice. The original material is still there; however, it has been rewoven to include a broader semiotic realm, a deeper representation of language variation across multiple modalities, a richer set of theoretical and methodological approaches, and a new coherence rooted in the fact that language variation is simultaneously arbitrary and powerfully meaningful. As such, this edition sets a new standard for the presentation and discussion of linguistic discrimination."

Robin Queen, University of Michigan

"With crisp prose and cogent arguments, the authors recreate the eye-opening impact of *English with an Accent* in light of recent movements for social justice, crafting activities, exercises, and discussion questions that directly help readers engage in questions of how language socialization works and how it affects our personal lives as well as our society's future."

Kirk Hazen, West Virginia University

"Be prepared to get comfortable with being uncomfortable. This edition of *English with an Accent* hits home and will keep you engaged and engrossed in issues that society too often doesn't understand in any meaningful and life-altering way. Well, the road to enlightenment is clearly provided here."

Sonja Lanehart, University of Arizona

"Since its first publication, *English with An Accent* has inspired conversations that grapple with and challenge the ways people use language to recognize, categorize, and rank social differences. This latest version builds on this important foundation while providing significant updates to the coverage of topics and theory. Written in an engaging, provocative style, this new edition by Barrett, Cramer, and McGowan is comprehensive and accessible. It will leave readers with greater insight into and critical awareness of the subtle role language variation plays in the maintenance of power today and the marginalization and on-going subordination of particular social groups, in the U.S. and elsewhere."

Barbra A. Meek, University of Michigan

English with an Accent

Language, Ideology, and Discrimination in the United States

Third edition

Rusty Barrett, Jennifer Cramer, and Kevin B. McGowan

LONDON AND NEW YORK

Cover image: Jacob Floyd Ross

Third edition published 2023
by Routledge
4 Park Square, Milton Park, Abingdon, Oxon, OX14 4RN

and by Routledge
605 Third Avenue, New York, NY 10158

Routledge is an imprint of the Taylor & Francis Group, an informa business

First edition published by Routledge 1997
Second edition published by Routledge 2012

British Library Cataloguing-in-Publication Data
A catalogue record for this book is available from the British Library

Library of Congress Cataloging-in-Publication Data
Names: Barrett, Rusty, author. | Cramer, Jennifer, author. | McGowan, Kevin B., author.
Title: English with an accent : language, ideology, and discrimination in the United States / Rusty Barrett, Jennifer Cramer, and Kevin B. McGowan.
Description: Third edition. | Abingdon, Oxon ; New York, NY : Routledge, 2023. | Includes bibliographical references and index.
Summary: "Since its original publication in 1997, English with an Accent has inspired generations of scholars to investigate linguistic discrimination, social categorization, social structures, and power. This new edition is an attempt to retain the spirit of the original while enriching and expanding it to reflect the greater understanding of linguistic discrimination that it has helped create"— Provided by publisher.
Identifiers: LCCN 2022027712 (print) | LCCN 2022027713 (ebook) | ISBN 9781138041905 (hardback) | ISBN 9781138041936 (paperback) | ISBN 9781003332886 (ebook)
Subjects: LCSH: English language—Variation—United States. | English language—Social aspects—United States. | English language—Political aspects—United States. | Discrimination in language—United States. | Speech and social status—United States. | Language and culture—United States.
Classification: LCC PE2808.8 .B37 2023 (print) | LCC PE2808.8 (ebook) | DDC 306.440973—dc23/eng/20220718
LC record available at https://lccn.loc.gov/2022027712
LC ebook record available at https://lccn.loc.gov/2022027713

ISBN: 978-1-138-04190-5 (hbk)
ISBN: 978-1-138-04193-6 (pbk)
ISBN: 978-1-003-33288-6 (ebk)

DOI: 10.4324/9781003332886

Typeset in Times New Roman
by Apex CoVantage, LLC

Access the companion website: www.routledge.com/cw/barrett

For everyone who knows what it is like to feel your intelligence questioned, your grammar corrected, or your dreams denied simply because you happen to speak in a particular way.

Contents

List of figures xi
List of tables xv
The International Phonetic Alphabet xvi
Preface to the third edition xvii

1 The pronunciation of difference 1
Reproducing inequality 1
Discourse structural racism 4
Language ideologies 7
Red Summer 13
Where we are headed 17
Discussion questions 19

2 Language, categorization, and social identities 21
Fifty shades of grue 21
Only skin deep 24
Sorting humanity 27
Categories and cognition 32
Is that a sandwich? 34
Some basic semiotics 35
Language and racialization 38
Discussion questions 41

3 Things linguists know about language 42
Facts about language 42
Linguistic potential 43
Variety is the spice of life! 47
Are you a robot? 49
So-called Standard English 54
Communicative effectiveness depends on variation 58
Discussion questions 62

4 Language subordination 64
Reading a textbook: roles and responsibilities 64
Rejecting the gift: the individual's role in the communicative process 65
Hesitance and uncertainty? 67
Standard language ideology 70
Confronting ideologies 75
Discussion questions 77

5 Place-based variation in the American context 79
The social meaning of place 79
Regional varieties of American English 81
Spread the word 84
Vowels on the move 87
Regional variation in morphology and syntax 92
OMG! There's, like, so much more variation! 97
Structured variation: the hidden life of language 99
Discussion questions 100

6 Language, racialization, and racism 102
No MSG 102
Race, ethnicity, and linguistic variation 107
Ethnicity-indexing variation: words and sounds 109
Ethnicity-indexing variation: sentences and meanings 111
No MSG, no lazy grammar 117
Language, interaction, and ethnic inequality 120
Language, race, appropriation, and whiteness 123
Language is love 128
Discussion questions 129

7 Language diversity in the United States 130
Estados Unidos no tiene un idioma oficial 130
Language abundance 134
Stolen childhoods 146
Language ideologies and English public space 152
Embracing bilingualism 158
Discussion questions 159

8 American Sign Language and deaf culture 161
How people communicate 161
What it means to be hearing 162
Deaf culture 164
Sign languages and American Sign Language 166
Martha's Vineyard Sign Language 170
Oralism vs. manualism 174

Language ideology and deaf culture 180
Ideologies within the deaf community 184
Discussion questions 185

9 Putting language on the map 186
How we see the language around us 186
Perceptual dialectology 188
Linguistic landscapes 192
The linguistic perception of the American South 195
Kountry Livin' 197
What it means to sound Southern 202
Perceptions meet strategies of condescension 205
Discussion questions 208

10 A history of 'r' in the United States 210
Meaningful, important, and arbitrary 210
The remarkable letter 'r' 213
Rhotics: variety, terminology, and symbols 213
American [ɹ] is wei(r)d 218
Where did American [ɹ] come from? 219
From non-rhotic to rhotic: American sound change in the first half of the 20th century 224
Non-rhotic in Manhattan 225
Discussion questions 229

11 The communicative burden in education 231
The medium of instruction 231
Invisible ideologies go to school 233
The setting of goals 234
Whose language? 236
Appropriacy arguments 238
Languagelessness 241
Education as cultural assimilation 243
How teachers talk 248
How graduate students talk 249
What the science tells us 256
Discussion questions 256

12 Language use, media stereotypes, and fake news 258
Storytellers, Inc. 258
Teaching children how to discriminate 258
Building on stereotypes 262
Disney's worldview 266
Information literacy: beyond cartoons 273

Echo chambers and filter bubbles 278
Bad is stronger than good 280
Discussion questions 280

13 Language in the workplace 281
Unwelcoming environments 281
Sorry not sorry 282
"This is America, speak English!" 284
"Nobody can understand those people" 287
"You sound so insecure when you talk the way I do" 289
"You're so much prettier when you're not angry" 294
White men talking 298
Discussion questions 300

14 Examining the American judicial system and housing 302
Language(s) and the law 302
Lost in translation 303
Linguists as experts 306
American housing problems 310
Heard but not seen 315
I had you at "hello" 316
A human failing 317
Discussion questions 319

Epilogue: Teach your children well 320
Honesty & equality & respect & linguistic diversity 320
You've got to be carefully taught 320
Our hope for you, dear reader 322

Bibliography 324
Index 341

Figures

1.1	A rally seeking justice for Trayvon Martin and Byron Carter (a 20-year-old African American man killed by the police), Austin, Texas, July 2013	3
1.2	"No Dogs, Negroes, Mexicans" Texas Restaurant Sign, circa 1940s	15
1.3	"I am a man" mural commemorating the 1968 sanitation workers protest in Memphis, designed by Marcellous Lovelace and installed by BLK75	16
1.4	Hollywood Protective Society sign protesting the opening of a Japanese Presbyterian Church in their neighborhood	18
2.1	Map showing the distribution of SCD, including regions outside of Africa among populations categorized as white or Asian	26
2.2	Eighteenth century painting depicting 16 different *castas*, referred to when categorizing individuals	28
2.3	Bhagat Singh Thind, who was denied citizenship twice by the courts, was eventually granted US citizenship in 1936 and earned a doctorate in Theology, in his uniform during World War I	30
3.1	Hawg pilot from World War II	50
3.2	Top ten "ugliest" and "sexiest" accent rankings compared	51
3.3	Some people just can't contain themselves when it comes to correcting other people's grammar!	57
3.4	Companies like Grammarly.com depend on the fear that one's language might cause rejection by potential employers, teachers, or significant others	61
4.1	The balancing act of the communicative burden	67
4.2	Spectrogram of the English word "eye" spoken in modal voicing (left) and creaky voicing (right)	68
5.1	Dialect regions as defined by *The Atlas of North American English*	81
5.2	The states that make up the American South	82
5.3	Geographic distribution of the pen/pin merger	83
5.4	Taste of Dahntahn, a restaurant in Pittsburgh	84
5.5	English vowels and sample words	87
5.6	"I'm kind of a big dill" shirt	88
5.7	Patterns of the Northern Cities Shift	89
5.8	Geographic distribution of Northern Cities Shift	89
5.9	Patterns of the Southern Vowel Shift	90
5.10	Patterns of the California Vowel Shift	91

5.11	Geographic distribution of *um* and *uh* based on geolocated American Twitter data from October 2013–November 2014 (hotspot map produced with local spatial autocorrelation, using getis-ord gi*, 25 nearest neighbor binary spiral weights matrix)	97
5.12	The use of quotative discourse markers over time in California	99
6.1	Chinese restaurants still promote "No MSG" food	103
6.2	Magic Washer advertisement	104
6.3	The hoodie has come to index racist stereotypes of young Black men as dangerous	119
6.4	Young men arrested during the zoot suit riots in Los Angeles, 1943	120
6.5	Anti-Italian cartoon from *Life* magazine	124
6.6	1894 advertisement for Aunt Jemima pancake flour	126
7.1	A map of the states of Mexico before the Texas Revolution (1835–1836)	132
7.2	For population 5 years and older: a) Language other than English spoken at home; b) Percent of the population speaking a language other than English at home who spoke English less than "very well"	135
7.3	Overt housing and zoning discrimination and language ideologies limit access for those who do not speak English, pushing languages into "ethnic enclaves" like New York's Chinatown	137
7.4	American girl holding a doll (left), Ghanaian girls holding dolls (right)	138
7.5	Hatzalah ambulance in Brooklyn	144
7.6	States with laws making English their official language (in black) and states that are officially multilingual to some degree (in dark gray)	145
7.7	Polling place in New York City	147
7.8	"Tom Torlino, Navajo, before and after," black and white photographic portrait of a Navajo by J. N. Choate,	149
7.9	Speakers of Native American languages in 2010	150
7.10	The sombrero and fake moustache is the ("brownface") fashion equivalent to Mock Spanish; here, the former president of the University of Louisville (while still president) poses with his staff	155
8.1	Sign language depicted on the wall of the Washington School for the Deaf in Vancouver, WA	162
8.2	The anatomy of the human ear	163
8.3	Children at St. Rita's School in Cincinnati, OH, sign the National Anthem in 1918	166
8.4	The signs for letters of the English alphabet used to spell out English words in signed English and ASL	168
8.5	The ASL signs for *onion* (left) and *apple* (right) represent a minimal pair, contrasting only in terms of location of the sign	169
8.6	The Latin alphabet in British Sign Language	171
8.7	Map of Cape Cod and vicinity	172
8.8	Deaf President Now students protest the selection of another hearing president at Gallaudet University	182
9.1	Two maps: occupied housing units in the Northeast lacking a telephone in 1960	188
9.2	Mental map of the campus of the University of Michigan	189
9.3	Dialect mental map drawn by a resident of Louisville, Kentucky	190
9.4	Scores for "correctness" of English spoken in different areas	191

9.5 Trash can in Seattle, Washington, labeled in English, Spanish, Chinese, and Vietnamese 193
9.6 Signs in English and Native American languages – a) Osage/English bilingual stop sign, Pawhuska, OK, 2018; b) Women's restroom in English and Chickasaw, Sulphur, OK, 2011; c) Cherokee-English street sign, Tahlequah, OK, 2010; d) Family restroom sign in Lushootseed and English at the wəłəbʔaltxʷ/Intellectual House at the University of Washington, Seattle, 2018 195
9.7 Dialect map from a resident of Louisville, Kentucky in which only one large "Southern Twang" region is included 198
9.8 Dialect map from a resident of Louisville, Kentucky in which numerous dialect regions are included but "Black English" is written as an afterthought off the map in the bottom righthand corner 198
9.9 Ramsey's Restaurant celebrating *Corn Daze and 'maters* 199
9.10 The Florence Y'all Water Tower 200
9.11 Description of the Florence Y'alls logo, courtesy of the Florence Y'alls 201
9.12 The Korner Kountry Kitchen in Brookville, Indiana 203
9.13 Southerners who claim different stereotyped traits of being Southern divided by whether they evaluate their own speech as accented 204
10.1 The human vocal tract labeled to indicate places of importance to speech articulation 215
10.2 Bunched (left) and retroflex (right) are two common articulations of English approximant [ɹ] 216
10.3 Percent overall non-rhotic responses in three classes of NYC department store 226
10.4 Five decades of film and the rate of change from non-rhotic to rhotic, by actor's original rhoticity status whether rhotic or non-rhotic 227
10.5 Percent syllable-final r-maintenance by age, location, and race 228
11.1 Percentage of fourth graders who scored less than "basic" reading skills, by race and income 234
11.2 How do we recognize a child's emotional states? Our judgments are often filtered through stereotyped assumptions about expected behaviors associated with the child's ethnic background 242
11.3 In 1884, the Carlisle (Pennsylvania) Indian School had 375 students 244
11.4 April Lou, a teacher at PS 1 in New York with six immigrant children from Hong Kong and Taiwan. The children are holding up signs with their original name and the English name they were given for use in official school records 246
11.5 Pickets out front of Los Angeles Police headquarters protesting arrest of Mexican American student leaders, 1968 247
11.6 Student evaluation of lecturer's ethnicity and accent based on a recorded science lecture 252
11.7 Proportion accuracy transcribing Chinese-accented speech when shown a Chinese face, silhouette, or white face for listeners with More and Less experience listening to Mandarin-accented English 254
12.1 How do you imagine the sound of a bald eagle's cry? 259
12.2 Words gained by 3- and 5-year-olds exposed to novel words (experimental) compared to a control group 262

12.3 Comparing compliments received by female characters across three Disney film ages, appearance vs. skill 268
12.4 Percentage of animated characters with mixed, negative, or positive motivations, grouped by English accent 269
13.1 Flight attendants for Pacific Southwest Airlines modeling the uniforms worn in the 1970s, which typically included miniskirts or other revealing features to highlight women's sexuality 290
13.2 Women working in customer service positions are more likely to be subjected to sexual harassment because they may be victimized by customers in addition to co-workers 297
14.1 Comparing rate of absence of -s in third person present tense, possessives, and plural nouns of Rachel Jeantel to Foxy Brown and Tinky Gates, two African American teens analyzed in Rickford (1992) 308
14.2 The timeline for the establishment of HUD and the Fair Housing Act 313
14.3 Minority rental unit seekers told about and shown fewer units available than their white counterparts 314
14.4 Appointments to see apartments confirmed, by race and ethnicity 318
15.1 Protesters at the 2017 Women's March on Washington 321

Tables

2.1 Basic color terms in English, Shona (Zimbabwe), K'iche' (Guatemala), and Bassa (Liberia, Sierra Leone) 23
2.2 Different categories for race in Brazil, the United States, and early Spanish colonies 27
2.3 Racial categories used in the US Census over time 31
3.1 Number of Google hits for grammar terms 54
4.1 The processes of language subordination 73
5.1 Historical weakening of English strong verbs 95
6.1 English borrowings from Yiddish 110
6.2 Some everyday words with additional meanings in African American English (AAE) 110
6.3 Inversion across varieties of English 113
6.4 Some of the aspectual categories in Navajo 113
6.5 Gullah personal pronouns 115
6.6 Some aspectual markers in Gullah 115
6.7 Some tense/aspect markers in Hawaiian English 116
6.8 Habitual aspect in African American English 117
9.1 Southern businesses with *K(o)untry* in their names 202
11.1 Language conflict in the university classroom 251
12.1 Characters, actors, and accents portrayed in *Beauty and the Beast* (1991) and (2017) (three characters were given different names in the 2017 remake; in this table, the first name was used in the 1991 version, while the second name was used in the 2017 version) 264
14.1 Demographic makeup of the neighborhoods analyzed in Purnell et al. (1999) (based on their data in Table 2, p. 15, which comes from the 1990 US Census) 316

The International Phonetic Alphabet

THE INTERNATIONAL PHONETIC ALPHABET (revised to 2015)

CONSONANTS (PULMONIC)

	Bilabial	Labiodental	Dental	Alveolar	Postalveolar	Retroflex	Palatal	Velar	Uvular	Pharyngeal	Glottal
Plosive	p b			t d		ʈ ɖ	c ɟ	k ɡ	q ɢ		ʔ
Nasal	m	ɱ		n		ɳ	ɲ	ŋ	ɴ		
Trill	ʙ			r					ʀ		
Tap or Flap		ⱱ		ɾ		ɽ					
Fricative	ɸ β	f v	θ ð	s z	ʃ ʒ	ʂ ʐ	ç ʝ	x ɣ	χ ʁ	ħ ʕ	h ɦ
Lateral fricative				ɬ ɮ							
Approximant		ʋ		ɹ		ɻ	j	ɰ			
Lateral approximant				l		ɭ	ʎ	ʟ			

Symbols to the right in a cell are voiced, to the left are voiceless. Shaded areas denote articulations judged impossible.

CONSONANTS (NON-PULMONIC)

Clicks	Voiced implosives	Ejectives
ʘ Bilabial	ɓ Bilabial	ʼ Examples:
ǀ Dental	ɗ Dental/alveolar	pʼ Bilabial
ǃ (Post)alveolar	ʄ Palatal	tʼ Dental/alveolar
ǂ Palatoalveolar	ɠ Velar	kʼ Velar
ǁ Alveolar lateral	ʛ Uvular	sʼ Alveolar fricative

VOWELS

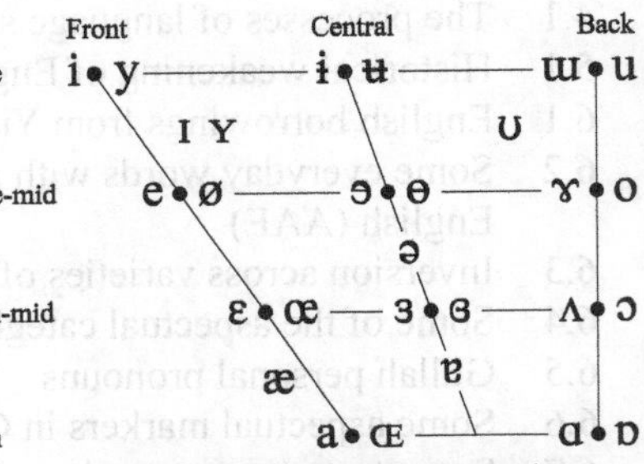

Where symbols appear in pairs, the one to the right represents a rounded vowel.

OTHER SYMBOLS

ʍ Voiceless labial-velar fricative

w Voiced labial-velar approximant

ɥ Voiced labial-palatal approximant

ʜ Voiceless epiglottal fricative

ʢ Voiced epiglottal fricative

ʡ Epiglottal plosive

ɕ ʑ Alveolo-palatal fricatives

ɺ Voiced alveolar lateral flap

ɧ Simultaneous ʃ and x

Affricates and double articulations can be represented by two symbols joined by a tie bar if necessary. t͡s k͡p

SUPRASEGMENTALS

ˈ Primary stress ˌfoʊnəˈtɪʃən

ˌ Secondary stress

ː Long eː

ˑ Half-long eˑ

˘ Extra-short ĕ

| Minor (foot) group

‖ Major (intonation) group

. Syllable break ɹi.ækt

‿ Linking (absence of a break)

DIACRITICS Some diacritics may be placed above a symbol with a descender, e.g. ŋ̊

̥ Voiceless	n̥ d̥	̤ Breathy voiced	b̤ a̤	̪ Dental	t̪ d̪
̬ Voiced	s̬ t̬	̰ Creaky voiced	b̰ a̰	̺ Apical	t̺ d̺
ʰ Aspirated	tʰ dʰ	̼ Linguolabial	t̼ d̼	̻ Laminal	t̻ d̻
̹ More rounded	ɔ̹	ʷ Labialized	tʷ dʷ	̃ Nasalized	ẽ
̜ Less rounded	ɔ̜	ʲ Palatalized	tʲ dʲ	ⁿ Nasal release	dⁿ
̟ Advanced	u̟	ˠ Velarized	tˠ dˠ	ˡ Lateral release	dˡ
̠ Retracted	e̠	ˤ Pharyngealized	tˤ dˤ	̚ No audible release	d̚
̈ Centralized	ë	̴ Velarized or pharyngealized	ɫ		
̽ Mid-centralized	e̽	̝ Raised	e̝ (ɹ̝ = voiced alveolar fricative)		
̩ Syllabic	n̩	̞ Lowered	e̞ (β̞ = voiced bilabial approximant)		
̯ Non-syllabic	e̯	̘ Advanced Tongue Root	e̘		
˞ Rhoticity	ɚ a˞	̙ Retracted Tongue Root	e̙		

TONES AND WORD ACCENTS

LEVEL		CONTOUR	
e̋ or ˥	Extra high	ě or ˩˥	Rising
é ˦	High	ê ˥˩	Falling
ē ˧	Mid	e᷄ ˦˥	High rising
è ˨	Low	e᷅ ˩˨	Low rising
ȅ ˩	Extra low	e᷈ ˧˦˧	Rising-falling
ꜜ	Downstep	↗	Global rise
ꜛ	Upstep	↘	Global fall

Typeface: Doulos SIL

Source: International Phonetic Association

Preface to the third edition

The publication of *English with an Accent* was a turning point in the field of linguistics. The book has not only influenced research that followed; it has also served as the cornerstone of a new approach to understanding the relationship between language and society. The 20+ years since Lippi-Green's text was first published has seen the emergence of new linguistic subfields like raciolinguistics – the study of how language underlies understandings of race (Alim et al. 2016). New academic journals like *The Journal of Language and Discrimination* have been introduced to handle the wave of research inspired by *English with an Accent*. Attempting to update a book that has changed the world is an incredibly daunting task. Imagine trying to "revise" Charles Darwin's *On the Origin of Species* or Rachel Carson's *Silent Spring*. We each have a deep personal connection to Lippi-Green's text. At the University of Michigan, McGowan was a student in Lippi-Green's original Language and Discrimination course, which ultimately inspired his dissertation. One of Barrett's first jobs involved teaching the same Language and Discrimination course after Lippi-Green left Michigan. The book also served as the spark that inspired Cramer's career as a perceptual dialectologist. In this edition, we have tried to capture the cornucopia of research that has been inspired by the original text. In order to reflect the current state of the field, we have made major changes to both the structure and the content of that text. The first edition of the book will always be a classic that changed the way we think about language. In this third edition, our goal has been to provide insight into the burgeoning field that has been inspired by *English with an Accent*. Although this has required major changes, we have tried our best to ensure that we present the current state of the field without losing the spirit of the original.

1 The pronunciation of difference

Reproducing inequality

An angry man yells at a restaurant employee for speaking Spanish; a white woman calls the police to report that her Black neighbor's child is using the neighborhood pool; a baseball player pulls his eyelids outward to mock an Asian player. Videos recording these sorts of racist acts have become so common that they may not even produce a reaction for many people. This genre of videos embarrassing racists suggests that racism is ubiquitous in American society, even if some seem to accept the idea that racial inequality was somehow "solved" with the Civil Rights movement of the 1950s and 1960s or with the election of Barack Obama in 2008. How is it that people can be surrounded by evidence of racism in the United States and yet maintain the belief that racism is no longer a problem?

Attention given to racists in such videos reproduces the idea that racism only persists because there are individual racists out there who simply haven't caught up with the rest of society. These sorts of videos portray racism as a series of individual acts performed by racists who deserve to be shunned and shamed for their backward views. The people in such videos are seen as individuals trapped in some sort of time warp where they maintain prejudices that "good people" rejected many years ago. According to such a view, these individual racists are the problem. This view of racism suggests that individual "racists" are becoming rarer across time, and once they are all gone, racism will cease to be a problem.

The idea that racial inequality results from the actions of a small set of individual racists is what Jane Hill (2008) called "the folk theory of racism." This folk theory suggests that once all racists have been enlightened, racism will no longer be an issue. While individual racists certainly exist, individual neo-Nazis or Klan members are not themselves responsible for economic inequality, unequal access to education and healthcare, discriminatory patterns of incarceration, or any of the other forms of social inequality related to racial difference. Indeed, the attention given to the acts of individual racists serves to pull people's attention away from the social structures responsible for racial inequality (Hodges 2016). Racism is institutional, structural, or systemic (Feagin & McKinney 2005), meaning that racial inequality is deeply embedded in social structures. This allows for a "color-blind racism" (Bonilla-Silva 2003) where racial differences are viewed as irrelevant, and racism can be denied, even though forms of social inequality clearly fall along racial lines. Language that masquerades as fighting racist ideologies may be used to maintain racism while denying its existence. This is the case with arguments claiming that affirmative action programs are somehow "racist" because they supposedly judge people based on race when a "color-blind" approach might be thought to be "fairer." Racism persists through forms of language that are not overtly recognized as "racist" but still serve to reproduce racial inequality.

DOI: 10.4324/9781003332886-1

For many, such videos are a painful reminder of similar personal experiences. For others, videos of racists provide a boost of self-esteem – "Thank goodness I'm not backward and ignorant like that." Knowing that they are "better humans" than those racists and, following from the folk theory of racism, believing that the number of such racists is continually diminishing gives those people the impression that racism is on the decline and society is continually improving. Attention to individual racists also makes people feel like they are part of the solution to the problem of racism. They can believe they are helping improve society simply by being "better" than some man they see screaming at people for speaking Spanish at a taco truck.

Of course, most people *are* probably "better people" compared to the individuals captured in the racist rants that go viral, but that doesn't prevent them from being complicit when it comes to accepting the social structures that allow for racial inequality. Sorting out exactly who is or isn't racist does nothing to change the structures and institutions that maintain forms of social inequality. Indeed, what Adam Hodges (2016) calls the "hunt for racists language game" creates a distraction that draws attention away from the broader implications of racial inequality. Language plays a central role both in this distracting hunt for racists and in the reproduction of less obvious forms of structural racism. It is through attention to language use that one can debate questions of who is or isn't "racist." However, attitudes and biases toward different varieties of language are also central in maintaining forms of structural racism. We call varieties that get the brunt of the bad attitudes *undervalued* (see Young et al. 2014); and while it is certainly true that such varieties are not undervalued by all – indeed, many people love them – it is clear that people who use undervalued varieties are marginalized in ways that deny them equal access to education, healthcare, and employment and can even threaten their personal safety. Understanding how racism persists requires paying close attention to the language used to enable, (re)produce, resist, or prevent forms of social inequality.

Consider, for example, the place of language in the events following the killing of Trayvon Martin (see Figure 1.1), one of the cases that lead to the emergence of the Black Lives Matter movement. In February 2012, George Zimmerman shot and killed Trayvon Martin, a 17-year-old African American. Martin was returning to his father's fiancée's home after walking to a nearby convenience store. He was unarmed, only carrying a pack of Skittles and a bottle of iced tea that he purchased at the store. Zimmerman (who was 28 at the time) was part of the neighborhood watch program where Trayvon Martin's father lived. In the moments leading up to the shooting, both were on the phone; Zimmerman was speaking with 911 about a "suspicious person," and Martin was talking with a good friend, Rachel Jeantel. Zimmerman claimed self-defense, arguing that Martin had attacked him so that he had no choice other than to shoot. The recording of Zimmerman's 911 call was widely discussed in search of evidence that Zimmerman was racist. At Zimmerman's trial for murder, Jeantel testified about the conversation that she and Trayvon were having in the moments before the shooting (Rickford & King 2016). A jury accepted the claim of self-defense and acquitted Zimmerman. The trial and jury decision were quite controversial, drew a great deal of attention from journalists and on social media, and sparked protests throughout the country.

The important role language plays in various aspects of the Trayvon Martin case can be seen as an example. Although Zimmerman identified as Hispanic, journalistic reports and social media discussions regularly portrayed him as a white man. The entire case was (and continues to be) portrayed as a symbol of troubled race relations between whites and African Americans. Toni Morrison (1992) describes how the language used to discuss race in the United States has a long history of presuming a binary opposition between Black people and whiteness. Often, ideas about what it means to be "American" are constructed in opposition to Blackness. In addition to its racist positioning of Black people as some sort of dangerous

Figure 1.1 A rally seeking justice for Trayvon Martin and Byron Carter (a 20-year-old African American man killed by the police), Austin, Texas, July 2013

Source: photo by Ann Harkness

Other, this opposition erases the full range of racial identifications in society. The language that people use to talk about race has been historically shaped by this binary understanding so that it often erases the experiences of Asian, Latinx, Middle Eastern, and Native Americans, as well as people who identify with more than one racial category. Within this binary discourse, Zimmerman *had* to be understood as "white" before the discussions of the racial implications of the case could begin.

The killing of Trayvon Martin is also a prime example of the "hunt for racists" phenomenon (Hodges 2016). In television reporting on the case, reporters repeatedly focused attention on a 1.6-second segment of Zimmerman's 911 call. Some listeners believed that Zimmerman uttered a racial slur in this short audio clip. Indeed, CNN spent an entire hour-long program focused entirely on what Zimmerman was or wasn't saying on the 911 call. The possibility of Zimmerman saying a racist slur became a central issue that was never resolved. If he had said it, then he was racist, and the killing of Trayvon Martin might be explained as the act of an isolated "racist" rather than part of a larger pattern of disregard for the lives of young African American men and boys. Similar attention was given to the question of what it meant for Martin to use the word "cracker" to describe Zimmerman. If "cracker" were a slur and Martin were somehow racist, then Zimmerman's story of being attacked would become more believable. Journalists focused on the words of those involved because those words held the possibility of "explaining" the killing through the folk theory of racism. While on the surface the "hunt for racists game" serves to combat racism, it often prevents people from fully recognizing the structural bases of racism in American society.

A final way in which language played a central role in the Trayvon Martin case involves the reception of testimony from Rachel Jeantel, the friend Martin was talking to on the phone in the moments before he was killed. Linguists John Rickford and Sharese King (2016) analyzed Jeantel's testimony and the responses to her testimony from journalists and jurors and on social media. Jeantel spoke a variety of English that was unfamiliar to journalists and jurors. Rickford's and King's research (discussed in more detail in Chapter 14) demonstrated that Jeantel spoke a regular, rule-based variety of English even though her speech was not the "standard" English typically expected in courtrooms. During the trial, lawyers on both sides regularly problematized Jeantel's language, claiming to not understand her and attempting to make her seem like an uncooperative and untrustworthy witness. After Zimmerman was acquitted, one juror stated that the jury ignored Jeantel's testimony entirely because they didn't trust her based on the way she spoke. The jurors rejected Rachel Jeantel's testimony not specifically because she was Black but because they reacted negatively to the way she spoke. It would be unfair to call the jurors "racist" because their decision was not based on their view of Jeantel's Blackness. Rather, they were just following their common sense expectations for how one should speak in the context of a courtroom trial. Those expectations for language use end up having consequences that reproduce stereotypical forms of racism.

This book is about the various ways in which language serves to (re)produce, negotiate, resist, and enable forms of social inequality, as in these examples from the Trayvon Martin case. From the categories used to distinguish groups of people to the ways that people listen to those different from themselves, language is a keystone that holds racial inequality in place. It is through language that the very idea of racial differences emerged, and it is through language that beliefs about race continue to be transmitted and invoked, even though most people would agree that racism is a horrible thing. Language convinces polite society to accept forms of structural racism while ostracizing those few who openly espouse racist views. Language makes it possible for racism to exist without racists.

Race in America

While the 13th Amendment abolished slavery more than 150 years ago, the legacy of this period in American history continues to impact how Americans view race relations in this country. A 2019 Pew Research Center survey revealed that 58% of all adults see race relations as generally bad, with more pessimistic views from Black respondents. Indeed, when specifically asked if Black people are treated less fairly than whites in terms of dealing with police and the criminal justice system; hiring, pay, and promotions; applying for mortgages; voting; seeking medical treatment; and conducting everyday business in stores and restaurants, Black people consistently express the view that racial discrimination is common across these domains. In contrast, white respondents were much less likely to recognize racism as a problem in these contexts.

Discourse structural racism

Without racists to blame, how do forms of structural racism persist? Many different forms of inequality interact to uphold a broader system of racism: unequal funding for education limits opportunities for students in minority communities; voter suppression ensures that minority voices will not be heard; unequal access to healthcare maintains poverty. However, the bulk of the work of maintaining structural racism is performed by what linguists refer to as *discourse*. The maintenance of racial inequality through language can be considered *discourse structural racism* – that is, cases where the patterns found in language serve to uphold systemic forms of racism. Here, *structural* refers both to "structural racism" (institutionalized and systemic patterns of inequality) and to "discourse structures" (observable patterns in language use). Through linguistic analysis of the structures found in instances of language in use, the intricate relationship between language and forms of social inequality can begin to be unraveled. First, it is important to understand what linguists mean when they study various discourse structures.

Linguists view discourse in two distinct ways, often referred to as *discourse* vs. *Discourse* or "little-d discourse" and "big-D Discourse" (Gee 1999, 2015). When linguists talk about Discourse (or "social discourse"), they are referring to broad social narratives and ways of speaking that serve to support social structures. Some analysts divide Discourse into individual "discourses" that serve to regulate the ways certain issues are discussed (such as *political discourse*, *colonial discourse*, or *racial discourse*). In contrast, discourse with a lower-case d (or "interactional discourse") refers to language in use, particularly in everyday conversations. A discussion of *The Green Book* as an example of the "white savior" genre in American culture would be a discussion about Discourse, while instances of racial microaggressions or conversations about racial conflict would be considered discourse. Of course, these two types of d/Discourse are not entirely independent from one another because everyday conversations are limited by the social assumptions found in the Discourses that circulate in society. Discourse structural racism relies on both types of d/Discourse. The ways people talk (or avoid talking) about race are influenced by Discourse representations and assumptions about race in the world around us. When one talks about race, the discourse tends to reproduce these assumptions in ways that enable racism to persist.

The different types of d/Discourse can be seen in the controversies surrounding the Trayvon Martin trial. There are several ways in which Discourse played a role in the Martin killing and its aftermath. The way in which the media categorized Zimmerman as "white" reflects the dominant racial Discourse in the United States where whiteness is understood primarily as an opposition toward Blackness. The Discourse of race in American culture made it extremely difficult to talk about the incident without placing Zimmerman in the category of white people. The killing itself and the motivations for the Black Lives Matter movement emerge from commonplace aspects of American racial Discourse. Racial Discourse repeatedly represents Blackness in terms that incite fear in many white people. The importance of Discourse is clear when people exploit Discourse to justify things like war, slavery, or genocide. However, Discourse is also at play in everyday occurrences such as racial profiling.

Black Lives Matter

Black Lives Matter or, more commonly, #BlackLivesMatter, was founded in 2013. The stated goal of the foundation is to "eradicate white supremacy and build local power to intervene in violence inflicted on Black communities by the state and vigilantes." The name is linguistically interesting because of what it implies. Societies value the lives of their citizens. It should not be necessary, therefore, in an equitable society, to point out that lives matter or that the lives of a particular subset of the population have value. This is part of why "Black Lives Matter" is so revolutionary. People saying it, writing it, or wearing it on their bodies are issuing a linguistic challenge that says: I am proclaiming this thing that should not be relevant to say; this requires you to evaluate whether you live as if it is true. When proponents speak the phrase "Black Lives Matter," they do not emphasize the word "Black." Their pronunciation implies only that someone needs to hear it. It does not imply that only Black lives matter or that Black lives matter more than other lives. It is a declaration like "Airplanes fly" or "Stars shine." Some people find this simple language threatening, and that, clearly, is the point of using it.

The seemingly unending representations of young Black men as dangerous, violent "thugs" come to be real for some people, especially for those people whose deepest experience with Black people comes from seeing them on TV. Reactions triggered by stereotypes instilled through racist representations of Black violence permeate American society. The impact of this racial Discourse is there when a salesperson follows Black people around a department store, when a white woman clutches her purse and crosses the street because a Black man is walking toward her, when a potential employer has a gut feeling that an applicant who happens to be Black might not be trustworthy, and when a parent sends their child to a charter school where they won't have to interact with minorities. And, of course, racial Discourse is at the heart of cases where white police officers shoot, choke, and kill men and boys of color.

As with the Zimmerman defense, these killings tend to be presented through a common narrative. The (white) police officer believed that the Black boy was armed with a gun. The situation caused the police officer to be so afraid that he feared for his life. In fearing for his life, his only option was to defend himself by killing the Black boy. In this narrative, the actual actions of the Black boy are irrelevant. He could be holding a bottle of tea, a toy gun, a cell phone, or nothing at all. He could be in his own yard, out jogging, or playing alone in the park. He could be a star athlete, an autistic musician, or a math prodigy. Indeed, he need not even be Black or male. The victim could just as easily be a woman or girl. The victim could be Latinx or Native American. Even as the bodies of young people of color continue to pile up, the spotlight has often focused on the white person's fear. These sorts of events play out repeatedly, and the focus is all too often on the psychological state of the person who killed the Black person. The white shooter's fear could certainly be genuine. Racial Discourse creates a mindset where a white person may genuinely believe that they are in danger simply because they are interacting with a Black person. The experience of fear follows the "common sense" assumptions found in a Discourse overflowing with representations of people of color as dangerous. Through Discourse, the focus on hypothetical white fears and insecurities comes to take precedence over the repeated killing of men and boys of color. In the face of widespread complicity in racial violence, it is no surprise that people feel that American society needs to be reminded of a fact that should be utterly uncontroversial and should go without saying – Black Lives Matter.

Little-d discourse is also central to understanding the Trayvon Martin case. Both Martin and Zimmerman were on the phone with other people right before Zimmerman killed Martin. The focus of much of the media coverage was the discourse of these conversations, particularly Zimmerman's 911 call that was central to the "hunting for racists" game. Little-d discourse was also central in the trial itself, as in interactions where lawyers framed the testimony in ways that suggested Jeantel, the friend who was on the phone with Martin when he was killed, might not be trustworthy. Because discourse refers to any linguistic interaction or text, patterns of discourse regulated the entire situation from the first call to 911 to the jury deliberations where Zimmerman was acquitted. In addition to the discourse of the original participants, there is the discourse of media coverage, texts and memes shared on social media, and conversations between friends, relatives, or co-workers.

Finally, the Trayvon Martin case illustrates the sorts of interactions that arise between Discourse and discourse. The discourse of television hosts "hunting for racists" assumes the racial Discourse associated with Hill's folk theory of racism. The Discourse portraying racism as caused by individual racists must be accepted (and go unquestioned) before the journalists can even presume that the presence or absence of a single word could explain the entire situation. The conversations where jurors decided to disregard Jeantel's testimony (discourse) similarly presumed portrayals of Black people as inarticulate, uneducated, desperate, and untrustworthy. Within Discourses that reproduce ideas about "correct" or "proper" English, forms of Black language come to be emblematic of negative traits. In conversations commenting on how "bad" Jeantel's English might be or how difficult she was to understand, the Discourse of "standard English" allows conversational discourse to discount and reject anything she had said. Here, Discourse linking Black language with negative stereotypes produces a context in which the discourse silences Rachel Jeantel so that her voice, despite testifying for nearly 6 hours, is never actually heard.

Forms of social inequality persist through Discourses that lead members of society to accept forms of injustice. Because these social Discourses come to be second nature (or "common sense"), they influence the interactional discourse of everyday conversations in ways that cannot be easily recognized. Thus, the problem of racism is not one of educating or even eliminating individual racists, but rather one of both challenging the pervasive Discourses that make unequal treatment of minorities possible *and* working to avoid invoking these Discourses in interactions with others.

Language ideologies

Up to this point, we have talked only about race and racism, but the patterns involving d/Discourse are generally the same regardless of the type of prejudice or discrimination. It is through reactions to Discourse that people navigate social differences related not only to race or ethnicity but to a wide range of social categories. These include broad general categories like gender identity, sexual orientation, religious beliefs, national origin, or age. These may also be more local or specific, such as *people from Bakersfield, alcoholics, jugglers, scrapbookers, Beyoncé fans, vegans, students in Ms. Zbornak's third period English class*, or *members of the Kilgore College Rangerettes*.

Because these various social categories are a critical part of how members of society understand the world around them, they can use the inherent variation in language to convey and interpret the various social categories at play in any given context. All human languages involve vast amounts of variation throughout their various structures. This variation is everywhere – from the tiny differences in exactly where one's tongue lands when making a particular sound to the exact space speakers feel they need to maintain between one another while talking. This rampant variation is a basic and critical part of all human languages. We use it to interpret what is happening around us. When we hear or read an instance of language in use, we rely on our understanding of how a particular instance of language compares to different types of language (variation) we recognize from prior experiences.

Consider the volume of your voice when you speak. The volume of your speech shows massive variation across contexts. Without thinking about it, you adjust the volume of your speech to fit a given context, like when you are talking near a sleeping baby, on the phone, at the library, in a crowded bar, or at a sporting event. When language is used, people use the variation that language contains to interpret what is happening around them. If we hear someone speaking extremely loudly, the volume of speech has a broad range of possible meanings. For many speakers of American English, the interpretation might be that the person is angry, distressed, or excited. They could be trying to handle some obstacle to communication such as overcoming background noise, talking at a distance, or interacting with someone who is hard of hearing. When we hear someone speaking loudly in an unexpected context, we look for other aspects of the context around us to interpret why the volume of their speech is louder than expected. If the person is standing directly in front of someone else and flailing their arms, perhaps we interpret the high volume as conveying anger. If the person is running and covered in blood, we might interpret the high volume as a marker of distress. If the person is trying to talk while wearing earbuds, it is likely we interpret the high volume as signaling a feigned attempt to overcome the noise to avoid turning off the music. If the person they are talking to is leaning out a third story window, we could assume the higher volume is meant to overcome the distance between speakers. And so on.

Modulating speech

Volume is just one of many ways we naturally and automatically modulate the way we speak. Another is speaking rate or tempo. Sometimes we speak fast, and sometimes we speak slowly. What conditions might make us speak faster? What conditions might make us speak slower? How do you know?

This practice of comparing language variation to the context where it occurs is the basic way in which people understand experiences. Making these sorts of inferences from the language-context relationship is an automatic reaction. Most people are generally unaware that they are even doing it. The range of variables that cause listeners to react is just tremendous. In addition to things like volume, there are differences in the words individuals use: Is it an *elevator* or a *lift*? Do you drink *soda*, *pop*, or *coke*? What is a *frontage road*? There are differences in how different words are pronounced: Is the stress on the first or second syllable of the word *Thanksgiving*? Does the word *schedule* begin like the word *sheep* or like the word *skunk*? There are differences in the sounds used to create words: Do *Dawn* and *Don* sound the same? Does *tired* rhyme with *hard*? Is there an 'r' in the word *party*? There are differences in how words can be combined in sentences: Does one wait *in line* or *on line*? Do you say *used to be able to* or *used to could*? Regardless of what they are saying, these forms of variation constantly emanate from the language people hear and use. The ability to recognize and process this variation in language and context is itself an amazing achievement, but each of these different forms of variation is also associated with a set of potential social meanings. Just as with volume, people have specific ideas about what it means for individuals to speak one way instead of another. Depending on individual experiences in life, everyone can have a reaction to people who think of Mountain Dew as a type of *coke*, people who say *conversate* instead of *converse*, or people who say *something* with a "t" sound rather than a "th" sound.

Language is filled with huge amounts of variation that can be used to interpret social interactions. This variation *indexes*, or points to, a set of possible social meanings. As with volume of speech, people use these social meanings to understand what is happening around them. These social meanings, or *indexical meanings*, depend on an individual's personal experiences with language. If someone has never encountered a variable before, they won't know its indexical meaning. When talking with someone whose speech contains several variables that are new to us, we may come to wonder how to interpret the variation. Because such interpretations are not always shared across individuals, language variation becomes the nexus through which we negotiate forms of social difference. The Discourses of social difference interact with people's understandings of the indexical meanings associated with language variation in ways that reproduce forms of social inequality in everyday interactions. Just like the jurors in the Trayvon Martin case, most people interpret the social meaning of language variation without recognizing the ways in which those meanings reproduce forms of inequality. Beliefs about language variation thus become the foundation for numerous types of implicit biases.

The beliefs and attitudes toward forms of language variation cluster together in *language ideologies*. Judith Irvine has defined *language ideology* as "the cultural (or subcultural) system of ideas about social and linguistic relationships, together with their loading of moral and political interests" (Irvine 1989: 255). In other words, language ideologies are the belief systems surrounding the indexical meanings associated with language variation and the forms of Discourse that connect those meanings to broader social structures. Thus, language ideologies range from broadly accepted ideas like "There is a correct way to speak English" to beliefs where the prejudice involved might be more obvious like "People who think the word *coke* includes Mountain Dew are just stupid." Indexical meanings are the core beliefs within any language ideology. Just as the individual indexical meanings that a person recognizes depends on that person's individual experiences, language ideologies vary across social groups and individuals.

As an example of the ways in which language ideologies interact with broader social structures, consider the history of beliefs about third person pronouns (it, he, she, they) in English. Throughout the first half of the 20th century, it was broadly held in the United States that "proper" grammar required that if one doesn't know the gender of the person involved, one should use *he* to refer to that person, as in example 1:

1. If a student is outside of the classroom, he must have a hall pass.

Of course, sentences like this give the impression that this might be an all-male school. However, it was argued that *he* was "generic" and could refer both to a single male or to an individual of unknown gender. This language ideology regarding *androcentric* (male-centered) *generic* is also seen in other antiquated phrases like *all men are created equal* and *we are all brothers*. The problems with such phrases are obvious, but the idea of using something inclusive like *he or she* was openly mocked as a silly idea. In 1971, the linguistics department faculty at Harvard wrote a joint letter to *The Harvard Crimson* responding to a suggestion to use more inclusive language. In their letter, the linguists wrote that the unmarked masculine seen in phrases like *Madame Chairman* was merely an issue of grammar:

> The fact that the masculine is the unmarked gender in English . . . is. . . a feature of grammar. It is unlikely to be an impediment to any change in the patterns of the sexual

> division of labor. . . . There is really no cause for anxiety or pronoun-envy on the part of those seeking such changes.
>
> (*Harvard Crimson*, November 16, 1971)

The patronizing tone of what came to be known as the "pronoun envy letter" promotes a language ideology in which the patterns of language are independent from social experiences. This language ideology is presented as if it were an obvious fact to mock and deflect the controversial (at the time) proposals of feminists.

But other linguists (Lakoff 1975) pointed out that androcentric generics allowed for sentences like the following:

2. We advise that one take vitamins during pregnancy to ensure the health of his baby.

While there are certainly trans men who experience pregnancy, sentence 2 sounds like it might be suggesting that even cisgender fathers should be taking the vitamins.

After much research, linguists and psychologists demonstrated that the use of *he* triggered associations with male referents and the use of *he or she* began to take hold, as in the following:

3. If a student is outside of the classroom, he or she must have a hall pass.

What is interesting about the use of both generic *he* and *he/she* is that both have a history of being treated as "correct" English even though colloquial English grammar also offers the option of singular *they* to refer to persons of unknown gender, as in example 4.

4. If a student is outside of the classroom, they must have a hall pass.

Grammarians often find this use singular *they* unacceptable or, at least, dispreferred. For example, the 7th (2017) edition of the *Chicago Manual of Style* advises caution when using singular *they*:

> Many people substitute the plural *they* and *their* for the singular *he* or *she*. *They* and *their* have become common in informal usage, but neither is considered fully acceptable in formal writing, though they are steadily gaining ground. For now, unless you are given guidelines to the contrary, be wary of using these forms in a singular sense.
>
> (*CMoS* 7, 5.256)

If the authors are correct that singular uses of *they* and *their* "are steadily gaining ground," singular *they* and *their* have been gaining ground for almost 500 years! The use of singular *they* has never been restricted to "informal usage" and occurs in some of the most important literature in the history of the English language. Consider the following examples, dating back to early translations of the Bible.

- Neyther Tyndale there nor thys precher . . . hath by *theyr* maner of expounyng . . . wonne *them* self mych wurshyp. (Sir Thomas More, "Apology," published in 1533)
- Then shalt thou bring forth that man, or that woman . . . unto thy gates, even that man, or that woman, and shalt stone them with stones till *they* die. (King James Bible, Deuteronomy 17:5, 1611)

- God send every one *their* heart's desire! (William Shakespeare, *Much Ado About Nothing*, 1623)
- A person can't help *their* birth. (Jane Austen, *Emma*, 1815)

Nevertheless, the *Chicago Manual of Style* and other purported language authorities continue to take the stance that singular *they* is a recent and unhappy development that should only be used in informal contexts. Apparently, these "informal usages" include reading from the King James Bible in church or performing a Shakespearean play. Of course, the idea that Shakespeare represents informal usage seems ridiculous, but language ideologies usually don't care about such facts.

The *Chicago Manual of Style* 7th Edition did, however, introduce a shift from treating singular *they* as universally wrong to providing a warning about the danger of using it. This shift, in large part, emerges from efforts to promote the use of singular *they* to refer to individuals whose gender is known but who do not align with the categories of *male* and *female*. For transgender people who identify as non-binary, singular *they* allows people to refer to them without having to assign them a gender category, as follows:

5. I talked to Maria and they said they weren't coming to the party.

In contrast to the singular *they* with an unknown referent, the 2017 edition of the *Chicago Manual of Style* accepts the use of singular *they* as in example 5, taking the view that one should respect an individual's preferred pronouns. For some speakers of English, sentences like the one in sentence 5 sound funny, wrong, or even impossible. These speakers tend to be older and unfamiliar with individuals who identify as non-binary. In their research, linguist Kirby Conrod (2020) has shown that this use of singular *they* is undergoing change. Compared to Boomers and Gen Xers, Millennials and members of Generations Z and Alpha are much more likely to accept, use, and understand sentences like sentence 5. Like this use of singular *they*, the use of Mx. (rather than Ms. or Mr.) and terms like *Latinx* serve to mark inclusion for those with non-binary gender identities. Of course, such changes are often controversial. Again there are competing language ideologies that clearly interact with broader social and political Discourses.

Gender-neutral pronoun success?

Like English, Swedish has pronouns for female and male referents (*hon* means *she*, and *han* means *he*). A gender-neutral pronoun, *hen*, was added to the Swedish dictionary in 2012. Researchers asked native Swedish speakers to use a pronoun for a non-gendered stick figure, and most chose the gender-neutral option, thus suggesting its successful integration into the language for non-binary uses. While English speakers can use singular *they* in non-binary situations, native English-speaking participants in another study indicated that they still associate singular *they* with the masculine gender.

Although the Harvard linguists once argued that gendered pronouns in English are "simply a feature of grammar," these pronouns show huge amounts of meaningful variation. The difference between *Maria lost their keys* and *Maria lost her keys* is certainly a trivial distinction in terms of grammar. There is no reason for English grammar to care about Maria's gender identity. One could easily argue that arguments about the "grammar" of gendered pronouns is not actually about grammar at all. It is doubtful that people who object to Maria choosing *they* as their preferred pronoun have based their objections solely on grammar. The "grammar" of singular *they* seems unfamiliar because the *idea* of non-binary gender is unfamiliar. Indeed, research suggests that judgments of singular *they* as "bad grammar" are dependent on an individual's (lack of) experiences with people who are non-binary (Ackerman & Wallenberg 2017). Thus, it seems like such objections are less an issue of grammar and more the result of individuals being uncomfortable with transgender people and hoping to avoid having to recognize the existence of people who might challenge their "common sense" assumptions concerning gender.

This points to another important aspect of language ideologies – they aren't actually *about* language. Rather, language ideologies reflect perspectives on sociocultural and political structures. Attitudes toward language come to "stand in" for attitudes toward groups of people, so that language ideologies serve to enact forms of discrimination. This pattern is known as *symbolic revalorization of language*, meaning that language comes to take on symbolic value that serves to enable forms of discrimination that would otherwise be socially (or legally) sanctioned (Woolard & Schieffelin 1994). For example, an employer could not openly declare that they didn't hire a particular individual because the person was African American. However, if the same employer decides against hiring the person because they pronounced the word *ask* the same as *axe*, which the employer thinks suggests that the applicant has "poor English," many people would say that the employer had made a reasonable decision. The fact that this particular pronunciation is more common among speakers who are African American comes to be incidental. Discrimination against people because of the way they talk makes discrimination based on things like gender identity or race come to seem acceptable. Similarly, a statement like "I hate Mexicans" will get one caught in the "hunt for racists" game, but one might claim that statements like "I hate people who refuse to speak English" makes no direct reference to race. Thus, language ideologies come to sanction particular forms of discrimination.

When someone hears a voice that includes variables that index negative stereotypes, they may be reacting to language, but their reaction is constrained by the Discourses that regulate their understandings of social difference. While language-based discrimination may be directed toward any group, there are two broad categories of linguistic bias common among Americans. Language ideologies may convey attitudes toward native speakers of different varieties of English or attitudes toward native speakers of other languages and their use of English as a second language. In both cases, attitudes toward language serve to trigger associations with negative stereotypes in ways that often go unrecognized.

Regardless of where language-based prejudice may be directed, it is important to recognize that language ideologies never exist in isolation. Borrowing from work in ecology, Paul Kroskrity (2018) suggests that the best way to conceptualize language ideologies is as *assemblages*. The concept of language ideological assemblages draws attention to the fact that there are always multiple language ideologies competing and interacting with one another. For example, language ideologies about "proper" English may overlap with ideologies of how language indexes social class, which, in turn, intersect with ideologies about language and gender identity. Thus, when we talk about language ideologies, it is crucial to remember that language ideologies are never universally accepted or static. They are always challenged and always changing, but they persist over long periods. The influence of language ideologies on society is ever present.

In the cases of African Americans killed by the police, centuries old language ideologies are sometimes brought to bear on the situation. These ideologies involve indexical associations linking African Americans to social traits that suggest that Black people are somehow less than human. In the following section, we will investigate the history of this dehumanization Discourse.

Red Summer

The heart of discourse structural racism is the mistaken belief that race is a biological fact. The myth of biological differences between races has been repeatedly used to justify horrific acts such as the enslavement of Black people and the genocide of Native Americans. Recognition that such acts are immoral and inhumane is usually insufficient for undermining the effects of discourse structural racism. The persistence of racist ideologies allows differential (violent, destructive) treatment of people of color. Consider, for example, the summer of 1919, 54 years after the end of slavery.

The famed poet and civil rights activist James Weldon Johnson dubbed the summer of 1919 as "Red Summer" due to the widespread violence against African Americans that occurred that year. Between May 1 and August 31 of that year, there were more than 40 cases of lynching and mass murders across the United States. White mobs incited violence against Black people in New York City, Syracuse, Philadelphia, Chicago, Omaha, and Washington, D.C. Lynchings and attempted lynchings occurred throughout the country. In several instances, the victims were veterans returning from World War I, and some lynchings were planned specifically to interrupt the welcome celebrations for Black veterans. At the end of September 1919, a large massacre occurred in the rural town of Elaine, Arkansas. Sparked by sharecroppers' efforts to unionize to gain basic workers' rights, a white mob murdered around 200 Black people over the course of two days. Although no white people were ever arrested for the destruction of Elaine, 122 Black people were arrested, some of whom were wrongly convicted of murder. Although the Red Summer was more violent than many other years, it was not at all unusual. Throughout the latter 19th and early 20th century, the murder of Black and Brown people was a common occurrence.

Racial violence in Tulsa

On Memorial Day of 1921, mobs of white people decimated Greenwood, a Black neighborhood in Tulsa, Oklahoma. Greenwood was a thriving community, and due to oil revenues it was home to many of the wealthiest African Americans at the time. Dick Rowland was 19 years old and worked in a building where Black people were only given access to one restroom on the top floor of the building. By most accounts, Rowland tripped as he stepped into the elevator and grabbed the elevator operator's arm to keep from falling. The elevator operator was a young white woman, who screamed and accused Rowland of sexual assault. Rowland was arrested and placed in jail where a mob of white people gathered hoping to lynch him. After an outbreak of gunfire at the Tulsa courthouse, the mob decided to destroy the Greenwood neighborhood, eventually murdering over 300 Black men, women, and children. The mob burned down every Black business in Greenwood, even going so far as to drop balloons full of turpentine out of planes onto the buildings to spread fire more quickly. Some 6,000 Black Tulsans were forced to move to internment camps after their homes had been destroyed. The decimation of Greenwood came after a 20-year rise in racist ideology and violence against Black and Brown people.

The period from 1900 to 1920 was marked by extreme racism. Across the United States, towns erected monuments celebrating the Confederacy at an unprecedented rate. In 1915, D. W. Griffith's film *The Birth of a Nation* was released. The film was originally titled *The Clansman*, and the "nation" born in the film is the Ku Klux Klan, who Griffith portrayed as a patriotic group of valiant heroes protecting white people. Often praised for its supposed cinematic artistry, the film is basically a montage of racist tropes. Using white actors in blackface, the film portrayed African American men as violent, untrustworthy, and unable to control their lust for white women. The intertitles in the silent film included racist quotes from then-President Woodrow Wilson and outrageous melodramatic race-baiting like "The former enemies of North and South are united again in common defense of their Aryan birthright." *The Birth of a Nation* was the first major blockbuster, and its pro-Klan message incited a new wave of violence against African Americans. The Klan had faded out of existence in the 1870s but was reorganized in 1915. The film is particularly notorious for propagating what Angela Davis (1981) called the "myth of the Black rapist," which attempts to claim that African American men are naturally violent, hypersexual, dangerous, and uncontrollably attracted to white women. This myth was used to excuse murders of African American men as necessary for the protection of white women. Similarly, the racist portrayal of African American women as licentious and hypersexual attempted to legitimize white men raping Black women. *The Birth of a Nation* did not create this myth, but the film's success was critical in getting people to believe the lie and murder on the basis of that lie.

Between 1880 and 1950, white mobs lynched over 3,000 African Americans and over 600 Mexican Americans. Lynching was not simply a matter of mob violence or murder. Particularly in the South, lynchings were major events, often planned in advance and announced in the local newspaper, where the murder of a Black person served as entertainment for a family outing. Southerners referred to lynchings as "having a barbecue" and people would bring picnic lunches to eat as they watched an innocent person being tortured and murdered solely on the basis of their skin color. The victim was usually beaten and tortured as warm-up act for the main event of murder. Death was typically by hanging, although some victims were burned alive or butchered alive before they were hung from a tree. When the victim died (and sometimes before that), their body was often cut up into pieces and distributed among the crowd as souvenirs. For male victims, this butchering usually began with castration and (regardless of the sex of the victim) it often ended with passing out bits of fingers and toes to children as souvenirs of the event. Spectators could also pose for photos with the corpse and buy postcards commemorating the special day.

In cases of violence by angry mobs genuinely seeking some twisted form of justice, members of the mob don't typically plan in advance, print open invitations in the local newspaper, or prepare picnic lunches to consume during the murder. Lynchings were not about seeking justice, even for imagined or ridiculous crimes. Rather, lynchings were intended to inflict terror upon Black and Brown communities by making minorities aware that their lives had no value, that they were entirely expendable, and that murdering them was just another reason to have a picnic. The acts of castration and the dissection of the hanging corpse reproduced the actions used in the slaughtering and butchering of animals, emphasizing the murderers' belief that their victims were less than human. But what could bring people to not simply sit by and watch a murder, but to go so far as to treat that murder like a family-friendly celebration worthy of souvenirs?

The Discourses that dehumanize minorities, like the sign in Figure 1.2, have deep histories filled with horrific violence including the genocides of Native Americans and Jewish people in Europe to the horrors of slavery and lynching to more recent police violence against people of color. Maintaining this dehumanizing Discourse requires the promotion of myths (lies) that would justify the belief that white people are somehow naturally superior to those of other races. The myth of the Black rapist is part of the dehumanizing Discourse, which repeatedly draws connections between Black people and characteristics associated with animals: low intelligence, an unwillingness to work or follow directions, and an inability to control one's supposedly primitive sexual and violent urges.

This is not unique to representations of African Americans. For example, in a study of metaphors used in representations of Latinx immigrants in the *Los Angeles Times*, Otto Santa Ana (1999) found that the most common metaphor was "immigrant as animal." Racist discourses require creating indexical links between minorities and such signs that carry dehumanizing meanings. Establishing these indexical bonds requires a steady flow of representations that reinforce the lie of white superiority in myriad ways. When racist Discourses persist over long periods of time, examples of racist indexical meanings multiply and become embedded in multiple discourses (such as legal discourse or medical discourse). Because these indexical meanings are incessant and reinforced in the texts and images that surround us, having these negative traits come to mind in encounters with those of other backgrounds can easily come to be an automatic response. It is not, however, a reaction that cannot be overcome.

Figure 1.2 "No Dogs, Negroes, Mexicans" Texas Restaurant Sign, circa 1940s

Figure 1.3 "I am a man" mural commemorating the 1968 sanitation workers protest in Memphis, designed by Marcellous Lovelace and installed by BLK75

Source: photo by Joshua J. Cohen

"I am a MAN"

Through the constant repetition of dehumanizing Discourse and terrorist acts like lynchings, discrimination and violence against African Americans came to be accepted as part of the natural order. In March of 1968, Dr. Martin Luther King, Jr. marched with striking sanitation workers in Memphis, Tennessee. The striking workers wore signs bearing the slogan, "I am a man" (see Figure 1.3). The slogan purposefully altered the opening line of Ralph Ellison's *Invisible Man* ("I am an invisible man"), taking out the "invisible" to emphasize the goal of making African American men's humanity recognized and visible. Like "Black Lives Matter," "I am a man" attempted to disrupt the dominant racial discourse that treated African American men as not being fully or equally human. Although it is obvious that the sanitation workers were "men," society had failed to recognize them as men. Shortly after this march, on April 4, 1968, Dr. King was assassinated in Memphis.

Given the constant flood of racist indexical associations throughout Discourse, it is not surprising that many white people continue to experience irrational fears when interacting with people of color. These automatic reactions can lead to unconscious irrational displays of fear, like when a white person waits for the next elevator to avoid being too close to a person of color. It also happens when a white teacher labels an African American child as "disruptive" because of the volume of the child's voice. Therefore, while it may seem "harmless" for someone to take the next elevator, when irrational fears guide how a student is treated in the educational setting, it becomes clear that the Discourse has the power to impact the lifelong trajectory of an individual.

The same discourses that foster white fears also surround people of color. Repeated imagery of Black and Brown people being killed by police reinforces an indexical association between law enforcement and violence against minorities. The constant barrage of biased representations can have detrimental effects on an individual's mental and physical health. This is what W.E.B. DuBois (1903) called *double consciousness:* the constant awareness of the ways the dominant culture sees you. Everyone has a sense of self, an understanding of who they are and how they fit into society. When surrounded by indexical signs that associate a person with negative traits that have nothing to do with reality, an individual comes to have a clear picture of how people outside of their own race think about them. In other words, a person can come to expect others to treat them based on a stereotype that treats them as less than human. This means that members of minority groups often find themselves monitoring their behavior in response to this awareness of racism. This is at the heart of "the talk" that African American parents typically have with their children about race – teaching the need to monitor one's behavior for one's own safety, particularly in interactions with police. The same is true for language, with speakers of ethnic dialects learning to monitor their speech or even undergoing speech therapy in order to avoid unfair treatment due to the way they speak.

Segregation

It is much easier to maintain the belief that some group is naturally inferior if one never has meaningful interactions with members of that group. Once you come to know another person well, it becomes impossible to see them as anything other than equally human to yourself. Therefore, countries like the United States and South Africa long enforced forms of segregation like Jim Crow laws and apartheid. Through laws or intimidation, specific neighborhoods excluded anyone who wasn't white. In the 1920s, white people in Los Angeles fought to keep Japanese immigrants from living in their neighborhoods (see Figure 1.4).

Racist discourse paralleled and justified legal forms of racism. For example, in addition to laws prohibiting interracial marriages, racist discourse promoted the idea that members of different races could not have children (or their children would be severely disabled in some way). This idea persisted despite the many counterexamples living at the time. It wasn't until 1969 that interracial marriage became legal nationwide with the Supreme Court decision in the case of *Loving v. Virginia.*

Where we are headed

Thus, discourse structural racism (like other forms of discourse-based inequality) is enacted, reproduced, resisted, negotiated, and challenged through the language ideological assemblages at play in any given sociocultural context. If people want to understand how language enacts social inequalities, they must understand some things about how language works. Thus, this book introduces concepts from linguistics, the study of how language works. Of course, linguists are not themselves immune from language ideologies. We see this in the "pronoun envy" case, where linguists fell on both sides of the language debate over generic *he*. Although linguists may disagree on some aspects of language ideology, they agree on numerous facts about language, facts that have been empirically demonstrated time and time again.

Figure 1.4 Hollywood Protective Society sign protesting the opening of a Japanese Presbyterian Church in their neighborhood

Source: *Los Angeles Examiner*, May 18, 1923

What is linguistics?

Linguistics is the study of language, and linguists study many different facets of this uniquely human phenomenon. Here are some subfields of linguistics and what they study:

- Syntax: the study of sentence structure
- Morphology: the study of word structure
- Phonetics: the study of the sounds used in language
- Phonology: the study of sound structures and combinations
- Semantics: the study of meaning without reference to linguistic context
- Pragmatics: the study of meaning as it relates to the context of language use
- Language acquisition: the study of how people acquire and learn language
- Psycholinguistics: the study of how the brain processes language
- Sociolinguistics: the study of the two-way interaction between language and society
- Historical linguistics: the study of language change over time

In addition to introducing the ways in which linguists think about language, this book aims to demonstrate the ways in which language ideologies serve to enact discourse structural racism. The first few chapters discuss patterns of language variation as they relate to social categorization and language subordination. After discussing the ways in which language serves to create distinct social categories, we look at the ways in which social stereotypes come to be linked to patterns of linguistic variation. We compare common language ideologies with the facts that linguists know about language to demonstrate how language subordination serves to enact discourse structural racism.

We then look specifically at the ways in which language ideologies influence our perceptions of different ways of communicating. These include different regional dialects of English, forms of variation that index racial or ethnic identities, attitudes toward bilingualism and speakers of other languages, and the treatment of deaf individuals who speak signed languages. In these examples, we see how language ideologies create obstacles for speakers who communicate in different ways.

The book then turns to specific language ideological assemblages. The first of these involves the assemblage of ideologies involving Southern (US) varieties of English, where ideologies portraying those with Southern accents as backward yahoos compete with ideologies that allow Southerners to express their emotional bond with the distinct ways in which they speak. We will look at the history of language ideologies involving the "r" sound ([ɹ]) in American English. Attitudes toward different productions of this sound have undergone huge shifts across time. In examining these shifts, we can gain insight into the ways that beliefs about linguistic variation interact with Discourses of social difference. We then consider the ideology of monolingualism (and monodialectalism) in American society. We can see this ideology in efforts to promote English as the official language of the United States. Language ideologies that denigrate speakers of other languages interact with ideologies that denigrate speakers of different native varieties of English to maintain a broader pattern of social inequality.

The remainder of the book examines the impact of language ideologies in different aspects of everyday experience. We explore how language ideologies enact inequalities in the realms of education, media representations, the workplace, the judicial system, access to housing, and media. The chapters in this section are intended to illustrate the far-reaching implications of language ideologies in reproducing and reinforcing forms of social inequality.

When people think of linguistics (if they ever actually *do* think about linguistics), they probably do not immediately think of the field as a site for studying patterns of social inequality and discrimination. But language is the foundation of human sociality. Language is the tool we use to relate to one another, to form social bonds, to create social divisions, and to negotiate peace. And the beliefs we hold about language have huge social implications that typically go unnoticed. Given the centrality of language in all human endeavors, linguistics is the perfect starting point for understanding how humans come to accept and reproduce forms of social injustice.

Discussion questions

1. Look at the transcript of Rachel Jeantel's testimony linked in this QR code. How many times was Jeantel asked for clarification? How many times did the transcriber of the testimony refer to her language as "mumbling" or "unintelligible"? What amount of responsibility does the listener/transcriber have in a conversation? Do you think every party involved was holding up their end of the deal?

2. In addition to broad categories, we said that social categorization can be local and specific, like *Beyoncé fans*, *vegans,* and *scrapbookers*. Think of one of the local/specific social categories that you belong to and describe what kinds of d/Discourses that circulate within that group. How do the little-d discourses operate within the confines of the big-D Discourses of the group?
3. Gender-neutral words for professions have become common (for example, *server* rather than *waiter/waitress* or *flight attendant* rather than *stewardess*). However, gender-neutral words often maintain gendered associations. This can often be seen by adding a gendered adjective before the noun. For example, the term *male nurse* sounds fine for many people, but the term *female nurse* sounds funny (without some context where gender might be relevant). This suggests that people tend to expect nurses to be female. Which of the following words do you think maintain gendered meanings: *bodybuilder*, *nanny*, *model*, *serial killer*, *wrestler*, *stripper*, *sex offender*, *truck driver*, *prostitute*? What might these gendered associations imply about dominant beliefs about gender and sexism?
4. When someone hears a voice that has linguistic features that differ from their own or the ones expected in some circumstance, people quickly jump to conclusions about *why* those differences exist. This is a key concept in this book, and a very good place to start for exploring this content is to come face to face with your own assumptions about language and social categories. What kinds of things do you think about people who sound differently than you do? What about people who use certain "informal" language forms in formal situations? Do you have any prejudices that you can identify about language? Where do they come from? Could they actually be prejudices against groups of people?

2 Language, categorization, and social identities

Fifty shades of grue

Language is the tool that humans use to convey their thoughts and experiences to one another. Although it is possible to convey the same complex ideas in any language, the specific ways that those ideas are transmitted varies from language to language. This is because different languages categorize human experience in different ways. These different categorizations mean that different languages are likely to emphasize different aspects of the human experience. A language like English tends to mark when an action occurred (past, present, future). Other languages focus on why the speaker knows the event happened (did they see it or hear about it?). Still others center on how the event occurred (was it repeated? completed? spontaneous?). An example of a language that requires speakers to state how they know an action occurred is Eastern Pomo, a Native American language spoken in northern California (McLendon 2003).

In Eastern Pomo, verbs are marked with suffixes that distinguish different reasons why the speaker knows the event happened. There are four basic suffixes of this type:

- *-ink'e* marks non-visual sensory information
- *-ine* marks a logical inference
- *-le* marks hearsay or reported information
- *-ya* marks knowledge gained from personal experience

Adding these suffixes to the same verb doesn't change the nature of the event described but the reasons the speaker knows the event occurred. Consider the event of cookies being in the oven too long and burning. In telling someone that the cookies burned, speakers of Eastern Pomo would need to also convey how they know that the cookies burned. For example, if the speaker smelled burning cookies, the verb would be marked with -ink'e (non-visual sensory information). However, if someone told the speaker that the cookies burned, the verb would be marked with -le to convey that another person reported the information. Similarly, if one walked into the kitchen and saw smoke, one might end the verb with -ine to show that the knowledge of burned cookies came from logical inference rather than from direct observation.

Of course, it is possible to convey any of these ideas about an event in languages other than Eastern Pomo. If someone wanted to emphasize how they knew an event took place, they could do that in English. One could easily say, "I know the cookies burned because I smelled burned cookies." But English doesn't *require* speakers to say that, and English doesn't give speakers an easy way to say it (like a suffix on verbs). Instead, English requires, in terms of verb suffixes, that speakers attend to whether an event occurred in the past or

DOI: 10.4324/9781003332886-2

not (indeed, English speakers often *think* the language has past, present, and future tenses, but the verb form for present and future tense is the same with future tense requiring a helping verb to get the right meaning). English speakers would normally just say, "The cookies burned" without giving information on how they know the cookies burned. English speakers are less likely to include information about how they know an event occurred because the grammar of English doesn't require such information, and there are no simple mechanisms to convey information about this kind of speaker knowledge.

The important distinction is not whether one *can* convey a particular idea in different languages, but whether a given language *requires* speakers to convey such information. While English requires speakers to pay attention to the time when an event occurred, Eastern Pomo requires speakers to pay attention to how they obtained the knowledge they are trying to convey. Given that the grammars of Eastern Pomo and English require speakers to focus on different aspects of the same event, one might expect speakers of these two languages to focus attention on the aspects of the event that their language requires them to convey.

If a language requires speakers to refer to particular categories repeatedly, speakers often naturally come to automatically think of the world in terms of those same categories. Let's consider another example. Most nouns in English may be marked for plural (*book: books*; *dog: dogs*). In contrast, Yucatec Maya (spoken in Mexico) only marks plurality on nouns that refer to living things (so that *book* would not have a plural form but *dog* would because dogs are alive). In experiments comparing reactions of speakers of English and Yucatec, John Lucy (1992) briefly showed speakers pictures with different numbers of particular objects. Speakers were then asked the number of the various objects in the picture. Lucy found that English speakers were much more likely to remember the exact number of inanimate objects compared to Yucatec speakers (whose language doesn't mark plural on these nouns). Similarly, Yucatec speakers were better at remembering the exact number of animate objects (where their language requires plural marking). Thus, English speakers were better at remembering the number of sticks or jars, while Yucatec speakers were better at remembering the number of dogs or pigs in a picture. Because speakers are required to constantly refer to the categories in their language, understanding the world in terms of those categories becomes an automatic, habitual reaction.

Structural properties of languages

English marks nouns for number. Spanish marks nouns for gender. Languages can encode a lot of information on nouns. Languages like Japanese, sometimes referred to as classifier languages, mark nouns for various taxonomic characteristics. So if you want to say "five chickens," you not only have to use the word for "five" and the word for "chicken" but also the suffix -wa, which marks the noun phrase as referring to something classified as a bird:

niwatori *go-wa*
chicken five-"bird classifier"
"five chickens"

Japanese has lots of suffixes like this that differentiate nouns based on type, size, animacy, etc. Thinking about the perception experiments discussed, how do you think this structural property of Japanese would impact Japanese speakers?

Saying that the structure of one's language creates habitual patterns of thinking certainly does not mean that one can only perceive the world in terms of their own language. It is certainly possible to think outside of the structures found in any given language. It is important to distinguish between *habitual thought*, which reflects "automatic" everyday categorizations, and *reflective thought*, which involves focusing specifically on a particular concept or category in a thoughtful way. Although people may recognize different ways of categorizing experience in reflective thought, these differences tend to be ignored in the habitual thought behind most everyday interactions. It is these patterns of habitual thought that are likely to correlate with the categories found in a particular language.

Consider the case of basic color terms (like red or yellow, not more specific colors like burgundy or maroon; see Table 2.1). The spectrum is a continuum of colors without natural divisions between categories like blue or green. Different languages divide the spectrum in different ways. Some languages mark only two distinctions ("dark" and "light") while others make five or six basic distinctions. One common pattern is for green and blue to form a single category (which linguists sometimes call *grue*). Any human who isn't visually impaired will see the same color contrasts so that speakers of languages with the color grue can still recognize the difference between blue and green. An example can be found in K'iche' Maya (spoken in Guatemala). Although speakers of K'iche' habitually refer to things as being grue (*rax* in K'iche'), in cases where a distinction between blue and green is relevant, speakers make a distinction by referring to objects as being "sky grue" or "grass grue." This is the same way that English speakers mark different colors within the same category (like lemon yellow vs. school bus yellow).

Even though human color vision doesn't vary according to language, the ways in which languages categorize those colors may influence speakers. For example, languages usually don't have separate categories for different saturations of the same hue. English usually uses "light" or "dark" to make such distinctions, although it has a specific word for lower saturations of the red category (*pink*). In contrast, Russian has distinct words for light blue (*goluboi*) and dark blue (*siniy*). Of course, Russian speakers can see the difference between red and pink, just as English speakers can see the difference between light blue and dark blue. The languages differ in terms of whether shades of blue or red count as two different colors. Given that Russian speakers must habitually distinguish shades of blue from one another, it isn't surprising that Russian speakers are faster (compared to English speakers) when determining if two colors are the same in cases where the two colors are shades of blue (Winawer et al. 2007). One would expect English speakers to have the same advantage when comparing shades of red because the language distinguishes between red and pink.

When a language marks a distinction between categories, those categories become second nature for speakers of that language. Many speakers of English come to feel that the distinction between blue and green is a natural and universal distinction, even though in actual experience they might recognize that the distinction is often fuzzy (as with teal, turquoise,

Table 2.1 Basic color terms in English, Shona (Zimbabwe), K'iche' (Guatemala), and Bassa (Liberia, Sierra Leone)

<table>
<tr><td>English</td><td>purple</td><td>blue</td><td>green</td><td>yellow</td><td>orange</td><td>red</td></tr>
<tr><td>Shona</td><td>cips^{w}uka</td><td colspan="2">citema</td><td colspan="2">cicena</td><td>cips^{w}uka</td></tr>
<tr><td>K'iche'</td><td>keq</td><td colspan="2">rax</td><td colspan="2">q'an</td><td>keq</td></tr>
<tr><td>Bassa</td><td colspan="3">hui</td><td colspan="3">ziza</td></tr>
</table>

jade, aquamarine, blue-green, sea green, etc.). The distinction between green and blue isn't a clear and natural division. Rather, it is a distinction created primarily through language. A distinction one's language regularly requires speakers to make creates categories that may seem like the only natural and reasonable ways to understand human experience. Indeed, people may come to view other ways of categorizing experience as strange, silly, or even irrational.

Languages also provide mechanisms to categorize what types of people exist in the world, which can have a huge impact on how people understand social experiences and even themselves. When one meets a new person, they often immediately and automatically begin to categorize them in various ways (gender, age, race, etc.). Many people have experiences where they have made a mistake in categorizing someone or have witnessed some other failure in the social categories available. For example, some individuals whose physical appearance isn't easily categorized as belonging to a particular racial group often have the experience of being asked offensive questions like "What are you?" by people compelled by the desire to categorize other humans. In other words, when faced with individuals whose appearance doesn't fit their assumptions about racial categories, people often question the individual rather than the categories themselves.

Even though categories of race are seen as central to understanding society, these categorizations only exist through language. They are produced through Discourse. Categories of race are not scientifically valid and vary across languages, cultures, and times. In this sense, the concept of race belongs to the set of things that people have words for, know, and recognize but that have no basis in reality (like Klingons, unicorns, and Pokémon). Even though race is imagined, it has become a basic part of how people understand the world, and it has huge consequences in society, particularly for those who are victims of institutionalized forms of racism. This chapter examines the ways that language shapes how humans categorize other humans. After discussing why racial categories are unscientific, we examine differences in categories of race across languages and the ways that the racial categories used in the United States evolved. The chapter then turns to the structure of categories themselves and the ways that categories (and stereotypes about those categories) emerge and persist.

Only skin deep

The idea that people naturally fit into distinct biological "races" reflects a basic lack of understanding of how genetics works. Alan Goodman and his colleagues (2019) showed that most of our genetic makeup is common to all humans, and the physical features associated with race (like skin color) are continuous and do not fall into distinct categories. Just as the spectrum doesn't contain natural divisions between blue, green, and yellow, skin colors don't fall into natural categories either. And just as languages have different divisions between colors, different cultures have distinct ways of dividing humans into distinct racial categories.

The idea that there are natural (biological) categories of race is a myth. Although individuals with ancestry from the same part of the world may share some physical features related to environmental adaptation (like skin color), these features do not predict other genetic traits. The important distinctions in human genetics are independent of the racial categories imposed on physical features. Consider a trait like blood type (A, B, AB, O), which is not visible and has no relationship with traits like skin color, eye color, or hair texture. If you need blood, the physical appearance of the person who donated the blood is irrelevant. It only matters that the blood types are compatible. Bothering to ask the nurse the donor's race, for example, would come across as racist. It is the same with other genetic traits. Physical appearance doesn't tell you much about a person's individual biology.

The racial categories created through language often interfere with assumptions made with respect to science. For example, many assume that particular health conditions or diseases are more common in (or even specific to) members of particular racial categories. However, in cases where conditions are more common for members of a given category, the explanation for the correlation is not due to some shared set of racially marked genes. Rather, the correlations are due to issues related to the physical and cultural environments of individuals and their ancestors. Let's consider two cases: Sickle Cell Disease (SCD) and hypertension.

Disregarding colonial patterns of migration, skin color is an adaptation to levels of ultraviolet (UV) radiation in the environment in a geographic region (Goodman et al. 2019: 106ff). Individuals from similar lines of latitudes will have similar skin tones even if they are from opposite sides of the world. This is why native peoples from India, Saudi Arabia, Thailand, Hawai'i, and Mexico all have similar skin tones. These places are all at a roughly similar lines of latitude and thus have similar levels of UV radiation. Like other genetic adaptations, skin colors emerged over many generations. High levels of UV radiation can be extremely dangerous, but some UV radiation is necessary for the body to produce vitamin D. As humans evolved in Africa, genetic responses evolved as forms of natural sunscreen. These responses include higher levels of melanin, the pigment responsible for darker shades of skin color. Because melanin deflects or absorbs UV radiation, it protects against overexposure. As humans moved out of Africa and further away from the equator, they encountered much lower levels of UV radiation. This means that it was harder to absorb the UV radiation needed to produce vitamin D. Over many generations, this environmental pressure led to a gradual loss in melanin, so that people further north came to have lighter and lighter skin over time. As people from northern Europe have moved to parts of the world with high levels of UV radiation, problems related to lower levels of melanin (like skin cancer) have risen.

While skin color is related to prehistorical adaptations to UV radiation, other genetic traits have evolved in response to other aspects of the environment and are therefore unrelated to skin color. SCD, a condition that is often presumed to be restricted to people categorized as Black or African American, is an adaptation to the prevalence of malaria in a region (see Figure 2.1). As the occurrence of malaria does not exactly align with levels of sunlight, there is not a direct relationship between skin color and the occurrence of SCD. Individuals with SCD have red blood cells that are "sickle" shaped rather than round. Because the blood cells are curved like a sickle, they can become caught on one another and create problems with blood flow. Why would such a trait evolve? The genetic trait that causes SCD is a recessive trait that helps protect against malaria. Individuals with this trait have red blood cells that are harder for malaria to infect. Protection against malaria provides a major evolutionary advantage, so the trait persisted despite causing SCD in individuals who receive the recessive trait from both of their parents. While children who receive the dominant gene from both parents will be free from SCD, they will also lack protection from malaria. The advantage of being protected from malaria was strong enough to allow for the sickle cell trait to emerge and persist even though it causes SCD in a subset of the population. Given that SCD emerged as a response to the environmental threat of malaria, the genetic trait emerged where malaria was a threat. In addition to occurring in Africa, the sickle cell trait is found in other areas where malaria occurs, including in parts of what are now India, Pakistan, Saudi Arabia, Turkey, Greece, and Italy. Thus, in addition to occurring in people of African descent, the sickle cell trait can be found in people who are European, Middle Eastern, and South Asian. SCD is therefore not a disease found

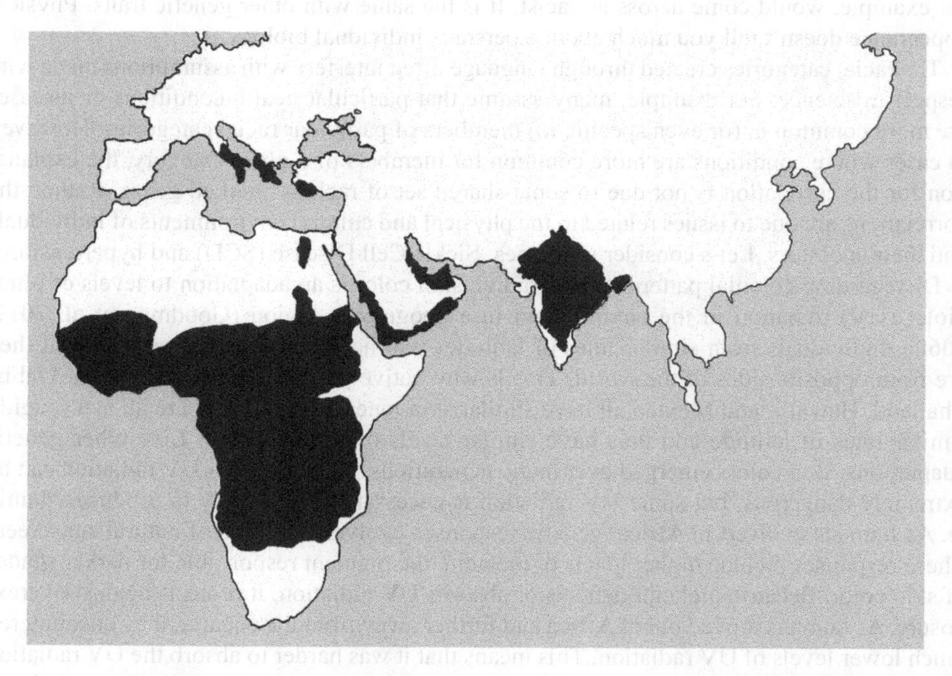

Figure 2.1 Map showing the distribution of SCD, including regions outside of Africa among populations categorized as white or Asian

Source: adapted from an image by Tony Allison

among Black people but rather among those whose ancestors lived in areas affected by malaria. The racial category is a poor fit for the actual incidence of SCD.

Another example of the problem of assuming a correlation between race and disease is the case of hypertension (Goodman et al. 2019: 216ff). One theory proposes that the higher incidence of hypertension among African Americans is due to a genetic tendency to absorb and conserve salt within one's body. The theory argues that the middle passage, when Africans were brought to the Americas as enslaved people, caused most passengers to die from infectious diseases affecting the digestive system. Presumably, the predisposition to conserve salt is a trait commonly found in western Africa. Those Africans with this trait would be more likely to survive such diseases and live through the journey to reproduce (and pass along their tendency to absorb salt).

However, it is also possible that rates of hypertension are higher because African Americans live in a society where they experience higher levels of stress combined with poorer nutrition and access to healthcare. Indeed, a comparison of hypertension in different countries suggests that higher levels of hypertension among minorities is not genetic; it is the result of racism. For example, rates of hypertension are much lower among Black Nigerians who would certainly be categorized as the same "race" as African Americans. The dominance of essentialist beliefs about the importance of racial categories is so strong that a disease that results from systemic racism comes to be blamed on the genetic makeup of the victims of racism themselves.

Given that there is no natural or biological basis for the racial categories used in society, it should not be surprising that such categories vary across cultural, linguistic, and historical contexts. Different languages categorize patterns of human variation in different ways, making it clear that the categories are not built based on any actual patterns of human genetic variation. Rather, that are built entirely through d/Discourse.

Sorting humanity

The United States and Brazil both have similar demographic characteristics due to similar histories of bringing Africans as enslaved people and decimating Indigenous populations. However, the official (government-recognized) racial categories in the two countries are quite different. While the categories in the United States are framed primarily in terms of presumed ancestry, the categories in Brazil focus more (though not entirely) on skin color. While both Brazil and the United States have long histories of racial inequalities and discrimination, racism in the two countries developed with very different ideas about racial categories and social inequalities. We can compare these systems with the system of *castas* used in Spanish colonial society (see Table 2.2 and Figure 2.2). The full set of *castas* contains many different categories, reflecting a preoccupation with ancestry. In order to fully understand these types of differences, it important to recognize the historical emergence of beliefs about racial difference in different contexts.

Although the act of categorizing humans into different groups is probably universal, the racial categories used today have their roots in the 18th century, particularly in the work of the Swedish naturalist Carolus Linnaeus. In his 1758 *Systema Naturae*, Linnaeus categorized humans into four basic categories: Africans, Asians, Europeans, and Americans. Linnaeus linked the categories to skin colors (black, yellow, white, and red) and to other characteristics related to personality and behavior. For example, Linnaeus held that (Native) Americans were "obstinate" and "merry," Africans were "crafty" but "indolent," while Asians were "haughty" and "avaricious." It isn't particularly surprising that the traits Linnaeus associated with white people were more flattering, like "inventive" or "gentle." Obviously, the traits Linnaeus links with his categories are simply racist stereotypes, but it is important to recognize that categories of race have never been independent from racism itself. That is, the very idea of "race" is founded in racist ideology, and while the categories have no basis in science, they have devastating social

Table 2.2 Different categories for race in Brazil, the United States, and early Spanish colonies

Brazilian categories	*US (2010) categories*	*Spanish colonial castas (De Mente 2011: 14)*
Indigena (Native)	Ethnicity:	Mestizo: Spanish father/Indian mother
Parda (brown)	• Hispanic	Castizo: Spanish father/Mestizo mother
Amarela (yellow)	• Non-Hispanic	Espomolo: Spanish mother/Castizo father
Preta (black)	Race:	Mulatto: Spanish and black African
Branca (white)	• White	Moor: Spanish and Mulatto
	• Black/African American	Albino: Spanish father/Moor mother
	• American Indian (or	Throwback: Spanish father/Albino mother
	Alaskan Native)	Wolf: Throwback father/Indian mother
	• Asian	Zambiago: Wolf father/Indian mother
	• Pacific Islander	Cambujo: Zambiago father/Indian mother
	• Other	Alvarazado: Cambujo father/Mulatto mother
		Borquino: Alvarazado father/Mulatto mother
		Coyote: Borquino father/Mulatto mother
		Chamizo: Coyote father/Mulatto mother

Figure 2.2 Eighteenth century painting depicting 16 different *castas*, referred to when categorizing individuals

Source: Museo Nacional del Virreinato, Tepotzotlán, Mexico

ramifications. These 18th century stereotypes about racial categories persist even though the details associated with them have changed over time. In various historical contexts, these ideas have been used to justify political domination, colonization, forced migration, slavery, and genocide.

Because of the prevalence of such ideas about race, early US law restricted the right to become naturalized citizens to "free white persons." Of course, defining who actually gets to count as a "white person" is not obvious, and American laws and court cases have long dealt with questions of whether the law applies to particular types of people. The Chinese Exclusion Act (1884) officially denied the right to naturalization (and therefore citizenship) to people of Chinese ancestry. This started a chain of court cases determining that different types of people did not really count as "white." In 1889, Chae Chan Ping lost a case challenging the Exclusion Act, and in 1922, Takao Ozawa lost a similar case arguing that citizenship should be open to people of Japanese ancestry.

Although a number of individuals fought to be considered white under the law, they were universally excluded from the category, even in cases where the science of the time supported including a group as "white." In the 1923 case *United States vs. Thind*, for example, the court determined that people from the Indian subcontinent (like Thind; see Figure 2.3) do not count as white, even though the categories at the time treated people from northern India as "Caucasians," and scholars had long recognized that Hindi and English were both part of the same (Indo-European) language family. In determining that Thind was not white, the court dismissed scientific claims to rely on everyday racism. In the majority opinion, the court wrote, "It may be true that the blond Scandinavian and the brown Hindu have a common ancestor in the dim reaches of antiquity, but the average man knows perfectly well that there are unmistakable and profound differences between them today" (Sutherland 1923). The Thind case makes it clear that categories of race are not determined by science, but rather they are determined by governmental and legal institutions that have control over the political agency of members of different possible racial categorizations.

Just as the courts were struggling to determine who exactly counts as white, the racial categories used in the US Census have changed regularly over time. These changes are due to changing beliefs about race, which are motivated by goals of political and economic control, and which reflect a history racist fears and prejudice. Such changes further demonstrate that racial categories are not based on actual genetic properties. Rather, the categories are founded in racism itself. Before the Civil War, the categories focused primarily on two issues – whether a person was enslaved or free and whether a person was Black or white. The government did not attempt to count Native Americans until 1860. From 1860 to 1890, the US Census introduced a number of new racial categories related to the rise of Social Darwinism. Social Darwinism was a dominant Discourse from the 1870s until World War II when the horrors of the Holocaust made the terrible implications of the idea quite apparent. As a theory, Social Darwinism proposed that biological evolution applies to different "races" of humans. Through the "survival of the fittest," white people supposedly evolved further than the other more "primitive" races. In contrast to actual evolution, the view from Social Darwinism applied the idea of "survival of the fittest" not only to natural ecology but also to social, political, and economic contexts. Within this racist Discourse, white people dominated not because of desires for power and wealth but because white people were thought to be genetically evolved and therefore destined to be in charge. The idea was common for many decades and persists among white supremacist groups today.

If one believes that biology alone is responsible for success in life, it isn't that big of a step to suggest that society can be improved by creating people who have genes that are supposedly advantageous. The idea of improving society by "breeding" humans (also called *eugenics*) took hold in the late 18th century. This concept took different forms in different parts of the world. In Brazil, for example, people of color were encouraged to mate with people with lighter skin so that the entire society would slowly become whiter and whiter. In contrast, the

Figure 2.3 Bhagat Singh Thind, who was denied citizenship twice by the courts, was eventually granted US citizenship in 1936 and earned a doctorate in Theology, in his uniform during World War I

United States tried to limit the potential for people of color to reproduce both by encouraging birth control and performing forced sterilization. Sterilizing Black women without their consent was seen as a positive way to improve society by helping to curb the Black population.

The racism of Social Darwinism led to new census categories attempting to determine how much Black ancestry different individuals might have. In 1860, the category of mulatto was introduced to refer to individuals with one Black and one white parent. In 1890, the US Census added the categories of quadroon (1/4 Black, 3/4 white) and octoroon (1/8 Black, 7/8 white). Given that race was assumed to be entirely about biology, the government assumed that race could be accurately determined based solely on physical appearance.

Census workers had to undergo special training to learn to determine how many Black great grandparents a person has just by looking at them. Of course, it is not possible to actually recognize such distinctions. It wasn't until 1970 that the US Census began actually asking individuals their race rather than having census workers choose a category based on physical appearance. The various racial categories used in the US Census are in Table 2.3, and a discussion of outdated and potentially offensive terms like "Colored" or "Negro" follows in the final section of this chapter.

The emphasis on physical appearance in American racial categorizations creates problems when people of shared cultural heritage don't happen to all have the same skin color. Such problems arose when the US Census began to attempt to record communities who were likely to speak Spanish. The category they created, Hispanic, was first introduced in the 1980 US Census. The new category lumped together groups who shared a common language but came from very different backgrounds. The problem was that "Hispanics" didn't fit well with the race-based categories the US Census had always used. What should they do with Black Puerto Ricans, Dominicans, and Cubans? What about Asian Latinxs? It was decided that Hispanic was different from race and should be a separate categorization of "ethnicity." The US Census then established two questions – one about "ethnicity" and the other about "race."

While race originally refers to biology, ethnicity has to do with cultural heritage, so treating Hispanic as an ethnicity seemed reasonable. Of course, treating "ethnicity" as equal to Hispanic wrongly suggests that other people don't have ethnicities. The problem for the government was that, apart from the Asian, Black, and Indigenous Latinxs, there wasn't a racial category for the majority of potential Hispanics. The government decided that most Hispanics were white. The officials charged with understanding the results, however, found a recurring problem – people who mark "Hispanic" often choose "Other" as their racial category. Of course, Latinx people often have brown skin and are subject to racial discrimination based solely on their appearance. It shouldn't be surprising, given disparate treatment, that many Latinxs don't think of themselves as white.

Starting in 2000, the US Census began to allow people to choose more than one option when checking boxes for race. The options for these questions remained roughly the same in 2010 and 2020. In 2020, question 8 first asks about ethnicity ("Is Person 1 of Hispanic, Latino, or Spanish origin?") followed by question 9 about race. The available answers for race have evolved since 2000 when they fell into four basic categories: white, Black, Asian/Pacific Islander, and Native American. There was also an option for "other." In 2020, individuals were asked to list what "type" they were within their racial category. White people, for example, have the suggested possible "types": German, Irish, English, Italian, Lebanese, Egyptian, etc. The idea that white people all have and know their ancestry reinforces the idea that racial categories are somehow real.

Table 2.3 Racial categories used in the US Census over time

Year	*Racial categories used*
1790	free white male, free white female, other free person, slave
1820	free white male, free white female, free Colored person, slave
1870	white, Black, mulatto (1/2 Black and 1/2 white), Chinese, (American) Indian
1890	white, Black, mulatto, quadroon (1/4 Black), octoroon (1/8 Black), Chinese, Japanese, Indian
1920	white, Black, mulatto, Indian, Chinese, Japanese, Filipino, Hindu, Korean, Other
1950	white, Negro, Indian, Chinese, Japanese, Filipino, Other

The distinct local histories of racial categories can lead to cultural differences in the ways that people go about assigning individuals to racial categories. In a study on the categorization of multiracial individuals, Jaqueline Chen and her associates (2018) found significant differences in the ways that Americans and Brazilians go about racial categorization. Remember that the census categories in Brazil are based primarily on skin tones with a history of government encouraging interracial families. In Brazil, the eugenics movement pushed for the "lightening" of society by pushing people with darker skin to seek lighter skinned mates. The government also tried to deny the usefulness of racial categories (expect for the category of Indigenous), framing Brazil as a country "without race." This contrasts sharply with the US history of sterilizations forced upon women of color. The "one drop rule" (from the *Plessy v. Ferguson* trial in 1896) held that anyone with a single drop of "Black blood" counts as Black. While Brazil tried to impose white domination by making more people white, the United States tried to impose white domination by limiting access to the white category and restricting the reproductive rights of minorities. While both cultures have long histories of racial domination and slavery, their historical perspectives on race are quite distinct.

When Chen and her associates asked Brazilians and Americans to categorize multiracial individuals, Brazilians focused almost exclusively on skin color while Americans focused more on facial features and hair. Given that "race" is basically equivalent to "skin color" in Brazilian history, it isn't surprising that Brazilians focused on this feature. Americans, on the other hand, have a history where legally, a person with a single Black ancestor counts as Black. Thus, light skin isn't necessarily a marker of race, as other facial features might give clues to ancestral history. Another difference occurred in how subjects categorized multiracial individuals into categories of Black and white. Brazilians divided subjects fairly evenly between Black and white, while Americans tended to place everyone who might have some Black ancestry in the Black category. Compared to Brazilians, Americans were much more likely to categorize individuals as Black. The history that shapes the categories in society influences the way members of society think about those categories. To understand how that happens, it will be useful to have a little more background on how people think about categories in general.

Categories and cognition

Two basic aspects of these reflective mental representations of categories are important for understanding racial categories. First, representations of categories are hierarchical in that they break down into smaller and smaller subsets. For example, the category of furniture includes smaller categories (e.g., chair, bed, table) that all contain their own subcategories (e.g., lawn chairs, recliners, highchairs). The second aspect of the mental representation of categories is that membership can be thought of in terms of the attributes associated with the "prototypical" members of a given category. If a category is defined by a set of attributes, the prototypical members of the category are those possessing the highest number of those attributes. Let's say that the prototypical chair is a basic dining chair made of wood with four legs, a square seat, and a straight back. Of course, many chairs don't have these attributes. Chairs that don't have these attributes (like a beanbag chair) are still chairs, they just aren't typical chairs.

The hierarchical nature of cognitive categories is central to understanding the ways people think about racial variation. The hierarchy determines how individuals are grouped together, allowing individuals to position themselves at different levels within the hierarchy. So a person might identify as white or as an Italian American or simply as Italian. A number of factors may determine where individuals decide to position themselves. White people whose families have immigrated more recently are more likely to identify with a specific European heritage as are people from communities or neighborhoods that are more homogenous in terms of lower-level identities (such as an Italian neighborhood). A history of oppression or exclusion may also influence where individuals place themselves in a hierarchy. For groups that were once excluded from the category of "white people" but are now considered white (such as Irish Americans, Italian Americans, or Polish Americans) it is more common to maintain the lower-level ethnic category (Irish or Irish American in addition to being "white").

Another factor is whether the higher-level categories reflect the actual identities communities use themselves. The US Census category of Asian, for example, covers such a wide and diverse range of peoples that the majority of individuals do not habitually refer to themselves as Asian; instead, they prefer lower-level categories like Japanese American, Filipino American, Tibetan, Sri Lankan, or Vietnamese (see Lien et al. 2003). Again, histories of oppression may influence how individuals refer to themselves. For example, according to Lien and colleagues, Japanese Americans are the most likely to use "X American" (as opposed to simply Japanese). Given the history of internment camps for Japanese Americans, the tendency to emphasize their Americanness is not particularly surprising.

As with Asian Americans, the categories of Latinx or Hispanic also join communities from disparate backgrounds. The "Hispanic" category was created by the US Census Bureau and is based on communities traditionally speaking Spanish. In contrast, the "Latino" category refers to groups originating in Latin America. This means that "Hispanic" includes people from Spain but not Brazilians, who speak Portuguese. "Latino" is reversed, including Brazil but excluding Spain. When such imposed categories do not align with the ways in which people see themselves, groups are likely to challenge higher-level categories that erase differences between the communities grouped together. In the 1960s, for example, different political problems faced different communities that were labeled as "Mexican" in the United States so that long-term residents whose families had been in the same region when it was part of Mexico needed to distinguish themselves from more recent immigrants. This led to the introduction of the term "Chicano" (based on a way of pronouncing *Mexicano*) to distinguish those whose families have always lived in what is now the United States from those (Mexicans) whose families have immigrated more recently (Comas-Diaz 2001).

The hierarchical nature of categories produces subcategories that only represent a subset of the actual members of the category. An example would be the term *Latino* in English. When first introduced, many complained that the category sounded like it only referred to men, as women would refer to themselves as *Latina* (rather than *Latino*, which implies male). This led some to use combined forms like *Latina/o* or *Latin@* to try to create a label that was inclusive of both men and women. However, breaking the category into a binary opposition between men and women excludes those individuals who identify as non-binary. In other words, having only two subcategories tied to gender excludes those with non-binary gender. To try to rectify this problem, new categories have been introduced in both English (*Latinx*) and Spanish (*latine*). Even though, in reflective thought, one can recognize that a category like Latino (or Hispanic) includes people who happened to be women or non-binary, the problem remains that, in habitual thought, the automatic categorization of individuals often leads to patterns of exclusion.

Is that a sandwich?

In the 1970s, Eleanor Rosch and her colleagues began to uncover numerous features of the ways in which humans think about categories in reflective thought. Mental representations of categories are based on the attributes of the most "prototypical" member of the category. Rather than having clear-cut categories with rigid boundaries, categories overlap and have ambiguous boundaries. Members of a category that share the fewest number of attributes with the prototypical member will lie at the periphery of the category (where they are perhaps more likely to overlap with a different category). Even simple categories have slippery definitions of their boundaries that are best understood in terms of prototypical attributes. Consider, for example, the category of sandwiches. Now that you read the word, you probably have a mental image of a prototypical sandwich right now, and it's not likely a burrito or a hot dog. But if a sandwich is defined as something like "meat (among other possibilities) between bread," such foods would fit the definition.

It turns out that defining a sandwich isn't so easy after all (Debczak 2018). In a 2006 court case in Massachusetts (*White City v. PR Restaurants*), the court was asked to decide the question of whether burritos count as sandwiches. The case involved a Panera Bread restaurant, which sells bakery breads and related items, in a shopping center that didn't allow two stores to sell the same item. When a Qdoba restaurant, which sells burritos, planned to move into the shopping center, Panera Bread sued on the grounds that the two companies sold the same product. But many people don't think of burritos as sandwiches, and the judge ruled that Qdoba could move in.

Due to such situations, a number of states have specific laws defining what "counts" as a sandwich. Trying to define sandwich in terms of "something between bread" requires more and more precision when faced with the question of whether a corn dog (or a pork bun or an Oreo cookie) counts as a sandwich. This is the same issue with court decisions regarding the definition of whiteness discussed earlier. Because the category of "white" doesn't have clear boundaries, the courts were forced to deal with case after case that dealt with whether individuals of a particular background would obtain the privileges afforded to white people.

When faced with trying to define the prototype category of sandwiches, attempts to produce a precise legal definition also fail. Laws concerning sandwiches usually end up having to list examples of things that do or do not fall into the category. This actually results in different definitions of sandwiches in different legal jurisdictions. In California, hot dogs count as sandwiches but burritos don't. In New York, both hot dogs and burritos may be counted as sandwiches. The USDA definition excludes both hot dogs and burritos, as well as any potential sandwiches that don't contain meat (like grilled cheese or peanut butter and jelly).

The problem of defining sandwiches is that individuals don't think of categories in terms of definitions but rather in terms of the attributes associated with prototypical members of the category. A hot dog isn't a prototypical sandwich because the meat isn't two-dimensional or sliced, the bread isn't square or round, and so on. In other words, people often assess membership in the sandwich category in terms of similarity (or lack thereof) with the prototypical sandwich. Of course, the prototypical sandwich isn't exactly the same for all individuals. What people think of as "typical" depends on personal experiences with sandwiches and potential sandwiches.

What counts as a sandwich?

The problem of what is a sandwich extends beyond burritos and hot dogs. Which of the following would you think belongs in the sandwich category? Which examples are prototypical? What attributes define the prototypical members of the sandwich category?

> burger, PB&J, grilled cheese, lobster roll, McGriddle©, stuffed pita, fajita taco, chicken wrap, calzone, Hot Pocket©, sausage biscuit, egg roll, sloppy joe, po'boy, quesadilla, ravioli, chicken salad on wheat, corn dog, beef Wellington, Oreo©, ice cream sandwich, club sandwich, soup in a bread bowl, Reuben, hot brown, pork bun, cheese and crackers, ham and Swiss on rye, egg salad on white, gyro, pig in a blanket

The way in which people understand prototype categories is important in understanding how gender and racial categories come to (re)produce forms of stereotypes. While in habitual thought individuals may be placed into racial categories, those categories are stored in terms of attributes marking prototypical (or stereotypical) category members. But all categories have more or less prototypical members that reflect stereotypes. Even the physical differences that supposedly define racial categories depend on stereotypes. Among Black people, for example, skin colors vary widely so that it is common to talk about light-skinned or dark-skinned individuals. But light-skinned compared to what? The comparison is being made to a mental image of the prototypical Black person who falls somewhere between light and dark in terms of skin tone. All sorts of activities and social practices are potential attributes associated with an (imagined) racial category, which ultimately results in stereotypes. To understand this, we need some background on how signs work.

Some basic semiotics

Semiotics is the study of the "signs," or the words and images used to convey meanings of all kinds. Signs fall into three classes: icons, symbols, and indexes. An *icon* is a sign that directly represents the meaning it conveys. Examples would be road signs with pictures of things like a deer or a firetruck where the image tells us to watch out for something specific. Another example of an icon would be words for sounds that "sound like" the sound they refer to (often called *onomatopoeia*), like *meow*, *boom*, or *cockle-doodle-doo*. A *symbol* is arbitrary in that it doesn't represent a specific object and is linked to a given meaning through convention. This is the case for most words in any language. The sounds in the word "dog" don't represent the meaning of the word. These words – *kinne*, *mbwa*, *tz'i'*, *galu*, *qimmeq*, *nāy*, *gihli* – probably don't mean anything to you (unless you speak Frisian, Swahili, K'iche', Chichewa, Kalaallisut, Malayalam, or Cherokee). These words all mean "dog," but because the words are arbitrary symbols, their meaning is conventionalized and unavailable to those who don't know the language.

The third type of sign is an *index*. The meaning of indexical signs depends on the context in which the signs occur. Words like *she*, *here*, and *then* refer to different things in different contexts. One can use "she" to refer to lots of different people – we can't know who "she" is without a context. As noted in Chapter 1, indexical signs are like pointers. Indeed, that's about all that words like *here* and *there* really do. Through their ability to point toward particular meanings, indexical signs are central to the construction and maintenance of social categories. The clothes people wear are a good example of an indexical sign. Some people wear uniforms that tell others their job (like police officer, nun, marine, referee, and so on). For those in uniform, clothing indexes the act of doing some type of work. But even without uniforms, clothing can index aspects of the type of person the individual wearing them wants people to recognize them as. We might wear shirts for specific sports teams, for example, because we like those teams, and we want others to know that. People also dress to index specific contexts. What do you wear to go to the grocery store? A business suit? An evening gown? Pajamas? A bathing suit? Because they can point to different contexts and social identities, indexical signs are central to understanding how language creates different expectations across categories related to gender, race, and other forms of human variation.

In order to understand how indexical signs serve in the construction of social categories, we need one last concept: *performativity* (Austin 1962). Utterances can be broken down into two basic types – those that describe the world (referential utterances) and those that change the world in some way (performative utterances). Because they have the ability to make "real-world" changes, performatives can be thought of as actions rather than statements. Referential utterances (like "It is raining," "I have the flu," and "The store is closed") are either true or false. In contrast, performative utterances (like "I now pronounce you husband and wife," "You're grounded for two weeks," and "I promise I'll pay you back") are not really true or false. Instead, performative utterances either "succeed" or "fail" to make some change in the world. For example, "I sentence you to three months in jail" would only succeed in contexts where the speaker actually had the authority to send people to jail.

There are particular conditions that must hold for a performative to be successful. First, the participants involved must have particular identities (parent and child for the act of grounding, for example). A successful performative also needs to be spoken in a recognizable context (a judge can't randomly sentence people as she walks down the street). The form of the utterance must also be recognizable in that it matches prior cases where the utterance has been successful. An employer can't say, "You're flippity-flooped" and expect an employee to know they've been fired. All of these conditions require a given performative to "match" prior instances where it was successful. In other words, performative utterances succeed because they follow a history of other successful uses of the same utterance. An utterance like "I sentence you to three months in jail" succeeds because of a history of judges sending people to jail. An utterance like "I sentence you to kneel on gravel while everyone in town takes turns saying horrible things about you over a loudspeaker" is unlikely to succeed in a US courtroom. However, in highland Guatemala, where such a punishment is a common practice with a long history, it might succeed. Thus, the success of a performative depends on a cultural history where that performative is recognized through a history of prior successes.

Indexical signs are performative rather than referential. The change that indexical signs make is to place individuals into particular social categories. Every aspect of the way a person dresses, talks, and moves through the world are all indexical signs that let others know what type of person they are. Even categories one might think of as driven by biology (like sex) are conveyed through indexical signs. The main difference between male and female vocal tracts is length. Because men tend to be taller, they tend to have longer necks resulting in voices with lower pitch. However, young boys and girls make differences in pitch long before puberty sets in and the boys' necks begin to grow. Even at a young age, the difference between sounding like a boy or a girl is performative. Similarly, the phonetic cues that distinguish "male" and "female" voices differ from language to language so that they cannot result from biological differences between men and women (Johnson 2006). Women who are taller than the average man and men who are shorter than the average woman still make differences in their speech despite having necks that don't align with assumptions about their biological sex. And there is no direct link between biology and gender identity as individuals may not identify with the sex they were assigned at birth. We can think of sex as the biological category an individual was assigned at birth (male, female, intersex) and gender as the social realization of an identity (masculine, feminine, non-binary). The difference between "male" and "female" voices is performative and is constructed through indexical signs (like the pitch of a voice, for example).

As with other performatives, the meaning of indexical signs depends on the existence of prior instances when the index successfully pointed to a given category. Because indexical signs depend on the recognition of prior uses that link the sign to social meanings, they are culturally relative. In American culture, shaving one's armpits has historically indexed femininity. This is culturally relative, and most cultures do not share this indexical relationship between armpit hair and gender identity. Shaved armpits only succeed in marking femininity in a context where people have prior experiences of gender being conveyed through the presence or absence of armpit hair. Because the sign of (un)shaved armpits points to a prototypical attribute, the connection between armpit hair and gender will not match exactly with the individuals who identify as male or female. Women, for example, may choose to not shave their armpits so that they can convey that they are not stereotypically feminine.

Times, they are a-changin'!

Interestingly, even the cultural practice of shaving in the United States seems to be shifting. A *USA Today* story suggests that millennial women are opting for unshaven underarms and legs. This shift means that while shaving one's armpits has long been an index of American femininity, not shaving them may be on its way to indexing a new kind of femininity.

It is also possible to have an unintentional performative where a sign carries an indexical meaning by coincidence of chance. A male swimmer who shaves his armpits to compete might be teased for his "girly" armpits even though his act of shaving is not meant to express femininity. Because indexical signs may point to multiple contexts, their meanings are not fixed. The specific meaning of an indexical sign can often be determined in combination with the signs that occur alongside it. A cisgender man with shaved armpits combined with a speedo and a swimming cap conveys a very different meaning than a cisgender man with shaved armpits in a sleeveless dress and heels.

The performative property of indexical signs is at the root of how people understand social experiences. Indexical meanings operate at many different levels. The act of reading this book indexes your identity as someone who knows English. It also marks you as a person with high literacy skills. It might mark you as a student in a particular class. Thus, we can think of indexical signs as operating at different "levels" ranging from how we present ourselves in an interaction (as angry, confused, embarrassed, shocked, or joyful) to very broad social categories (like "speaker of English").

Penelope Eckert (2008) developed a model that divides these indexical meanings into three basic levels. Signs may point to categories, traits, or interactional stances. Here, *category* refers not only to demographic categories like racial, class, gender, sexual, or regional identities but also to more narrow categories like emo, runner, stoner, gamer, or librarian. *Trait* refers to "types of persons," including aspects of personality and identity. This could include things like prudish, outgoing, educated, naïve, articulate, or inquisitive. The final type, *stance*, refers to momentary ways of interacting in a specific situation. This would include things like emotional states (angry, exhausted, frightened), cognitive states (certain, confused, alert), or how one orients to the interaction at hand (engaged, disinterested, confrontational).

These three types of indexical signs are not intended to capture the full complexity of the matrix of indexical meanings employed. However, they can help people think about how stereotypes about social categories come to persist. The meanings in each of these categories are related to one another so that indexing a particular stance typically triggers associations with personal traits and social categories. In many Protestant African American churches it is common for congregants to speak out individually during the sermon (with exclamations like "Amen!" or "Preach!"). This speech event could index a stance of being highly engaged in the situation at hand. But acting highly engaged also suggests a particular type of person – religious, outgoing, uninhibited, etc. Of course, the way of marking stance in this particular context also marks membership in various categories – Christian, African American, English speaker, etc. Thus, when an individual interacts with other people, that individual constantly gives off indexical meanings about themselves and how they feel about the situation around them. They can use these meanings to accept or challenge the status quo or an interactional moment. For example, one can accept the context of the church service by saying things like "Amen!" or "Preach!" But one could challenge the context by using indexical signs not typically linked to the context of church (like screaming obscenities during the sermon). Additionally, one could invoke a church-like context outside of church, say at a meeting or other live event, by saying "Amen!" when wanting to garner the status and respect associated with the church while also showcasing one's Blackness and creating an atmosphere for listeners that makes one's message positively received (Britt 2011).

Members of individual societies are also constantly interpreting the indexical meanings they perceive in the behavior of those with whom they are interacting. When they interact with others, they compare those they have met to the prototypical member of all sorts of different categories ranging from things like people who are angry to broader categories like police officer or Mexican American. It is through these indexical meanings that people come to perceive social categories related to things like racial, regional, class, gender, or sexual identities. These indexical meanings lead some people to treat different individuals in different ways, thus serving as the basis for preserving or challenging forms of discrimination.

Language and racialization

Through racial Discourse, specific characteristics come to be indexically associated with categories, producing and reproducing stereotypes about social groups. This can take a variety of forms. One way in which racism works is by reducing the definition of a category to a small set of attributes or even a single attribute like skin color or eye shape. Terms like "redskin" or "squinty eye" are offensive because they reduce individuals to a single physical property. Treating individuals as if they are no more than a particular physical trait is dehumanizing and degrading. The opposite pattern – assuming that any member of a category must share a particular attribute – is equally problematic. For example, telling an African American that they are "articulate" is offensive because it implies that articulate Black people are somehow rare and unexpected (Alim & Smitherman 2012). It is rare for white people to convey this type of "compliment" to other white people, suggesting that they assume white people are naturally "articulate."

Another way in which categories contribute to prejudice is through the aggregation of signs that index a stereotyped representation of the prototypical member of a category. Stereotypes persist even in cases where they are obviously irrational. Because indexical meanings must be repetitions of early repetitions to succeed in pointing toward a particular racial category, racist representations may persist long after their original intent has been lost. Consider, for example, the case of Native American mascots (e.g., Cleveland Indians, Washington Redskins, Atlanta Braves). On one level, such mascots were/are offensive because they erase actual Native Americans' lived experiences and reduce Native cultures to a monolithic caricature. But they also encode histories of racism and genocide in ways that may not be obvious to sports fans. The term "redskin" came into wide circulation as a tool in the genocide of Native Americans when cash rewards were given for the "red skins" (scalps) of murdered Indians. Although racist stereotypes portray scalping as a Native tradition, it was actually introduced by Europeans. In order to depopulate Native lands, white frontiersmen could receive a government-sponsored reward for bringing in the scalp of an Indian they had killed to receive government payment. The scalp was needed to prove that a Native American had actually been killed. Stores advertised that they took cash for scalps with the (still common) displays of wooden "cigar store Indians" and with images of a Native head cut off from the rest of the body (much like the images used by the sports teams like the Washington Redskins or the Chicago Blackhawks). Such Indian head mascots reproduce these histories of rewarding people who murdered Native Americans. Although this history may not be known to fans of teams with Native mascots, as a sign, the decapitated Indian head indexes numerous other traits associated with the genocide of Native peoples. Such mascots are typically linked with tomahawks, "war paint," and other imagery linked to the racist Discourse portraying Native peoples as violent, savage, and dangerous that was used to justify genocide. The racist stereotype of the dangerous Indian (rather than actual Native culture) is usually the motivation for having a Native mascot in the first place. With growing awareness of the messages conveyed by such mascots, a number of teams have dropped the use of Native mascots entirely, including the Cleveland Guardians and the Washington Commanders.

Because the indexical signs linked to a racial category are also linked to specific social contexts, the labels for the categories themselves can come to be negatively evaluated over time. Repeated use of a term in a way that is inhumane or degrading is likely to make the term eventually come across as pejorative. Sometimes a term becomes so weighed down with negative indexical meanings that people argue for it to be replaced. Older terms for the category of Black people, for example, are sometimes highly offensive today because of their association with historical eras of racism. However, institutions tend to maintain older terms in their names to continue to index the harsh conditions in which they emerged. In the early history of the United States, Black people were called "Africans," and this has been maintained by institutions like the African Methodist Episcopal Church (established in 1816). Similarly, the National Association for the Advancement of Colored People (1909) and the United Negro College Fund (1944) preserve terms that some would find offensive today. However, the terms serve a purpose in indexing the specific types of racism experienced by Black people when they were founded. Use of a word like "Negro" (perhaps especially when used by a white person) today is often considered offensive precisely because it indexes a period when segregation and other forms of legally sanctioned discrimination were common throughout the United States. In other words, it reproduces the racist ideology that prevailed when the term was commonly used. It is unlikely that such words (as well as ethnic slurs) can be used without indexing a social context of racial discrimination for some listeners.

Indexical meanings can be attached to pretty much anything: tastes, styles, imagery, activities, and so on. It is through these meanings that people both construct their own identities and interpret the identities of others. One of the main ways that language contributes to the process of racialization is through fostering indexical connections between inanimate objects and racial categories. These indexical links take on lives on their own so that the connection between some "sign" and a racial category may persist even if the indexical relationship has no connection to reality. Often indexical links are related to physical traits supposedly shared with a racial group. For example, white supremacists use the woodpecker as a symbol because the bird has a white face with red hair. Having red hair is seen as a sign of racial purity, as only white people are supposed to be redheads, which ignores the fact that there are people of other races with red hair. Similarly, white supremacists often use imagery of classical Greek and Roman statues to stand in for "white" culture largely because the statues are white in appearance. However, the classical world was ethnically quite diverse, and the statues were originally painted a wide variety of skin tones. The statues are only white because time has washed away the colors they originally contained (Talbot 2018). Even so, invoking classical society also ignores the fact that Greek and Italian immigrants in the early 20th century faced discrimination because they weren't considered white. As with the indexical associations found with Native mascots, the classical imagery used by white supremacists indexes an imagined rather than an actual history.

Another indexical sign adopted by white supremacists is the act of drinking milk (Freeman 2017; Harmon 2018). The explanation for milk as a marker of whiteness goes back to a long-held racist belief that part of the reason northern Europeans became "superior" is through the consumption of dairy products. Given the long history of dairy consumption in northern Europe, it is perhaps unsurprising that lactose intolerance is less common among white people. The white supremacist line holds that Black, Asian, Native American, and Latinx people are all lactose intolerant so that drinking large amounts of milk indexes a supposedly "white" genetic trait. As one might expect, low rates of lactose intolerance are also found in parts of the world with high dairy consumption regardless of the race of people in those areas. Thus, for example, in parts of eastern Africa where cattle-based economies are prevalent, lactose intolerance is quite rare. And milk (like washed out statues or woodpeckers) is white in color, reinforcing the indexical relationship between colors and imagined racial differences. In each of these cases, some object (or animal) is exploited as an indexical marker of "white" identity even though none of the connections are based on any science or even on actual human experience. This is an example of how racist discourses persist despite being demonstrably false.

While the cases discussed in this chapter focus primarily on the way that language participates in the racialization of society, it is also the case that grammatical patterns in various language varieties may also come to index social categories related to race, gender, age, sexuality, or any other means of categorizing individuals in society. The way an individual speaks is a basic reflection of who they are and where they come from. In this sense, treating particular ways of speaking as "wrong" is really no better than suggesting that a particular skin color is somehow "wrong."

As we have seen, the social categories that occur within a given culture are created through language. For the most part, ideas about who does or doesn't belong in each category do not reflect reality. The belief in meaningful biological differences between members of different "races" is not based on science. It is a myth. Such myths are a central part of understanding how beliefs about social difference come to reproduce forms of social inequality. In terms of myths about social differences, those related to language are some of the most widely accepted. Myths about language serve as the basis for the language ideologies that perpetuate inequality. Because of their central role in propagating discriminatory language ideologies, myths about language often have consequences that can be devastating for individuals who happen to speak varieties other than the mythological "standard" English. In the next chapter, we will lay out some of the common misunderstandings that people have about language. Understanding how language works provides important insights into how forms of prejudice and discrimination come to be perpetuated.

Discussion questions

1. What makes a question like "What are you?" offensive? Think about the exact wording here and determine why someone would react negatively to such a question. What are some ways that you could find out more information about a person without this kind of question?
2. Given the categories of the 1890 US Census (in Table 2.3), which category would you have had to select? What about the 1920 categories? How well do you think this label defines you? Would you have struggled with answering this question? Recall that until 1970 individual citizens were not actually asked the question; the census taker guessed. Do you think the census takers would have identified you in the same way that you identify yourself?
3. Let's say that you walk out of your classroom and find a note on the floor. It says, "He will be there tomorrow." What information do you know? What information is left unanswered? How so? What does this have to do with the indexical meanings of words?
4. Consider the following utterance: "You're fired." Think of all of the ways that such a performative utterance could "succeed" or "fail." What factors have to be in place for such an utterance to make a change in the world? What are some scenarios where it could be uttered but to no avail?
5. What are some other ways (linguistic or otherwise) that Americans "perform" masculinity and femininity? What are some ways that Americans contest those categories through performances?

3 Things linguists know about language

Facts about language

We have seen that language produces the social categories that are relevant in any given culture. Stereotypes develop through repeated d/Discourse representations of category members as indexical links solidify between a category and particular practices, styles, actions, and ways of being. The richest set of such indexical links within any culture is the set of indexical meanings associated with forms of language variation. Stereotyping a social group as being violent or uneducated is typically recognized as a form of prejudice. Through symbolic revalorization, however, patterns of language variation continue to be open to stereotypes and public criticism. The way people speak is often treated as if it were simply a matter of choice, as if speaking an undervalued variety of English were a conscious act of anti-social rebellion. This is because the dominant language ideology in the United States continues to promote beliefs that linguists know to be myths, ideas that have no concrete basis in reality.

What is symbolic revalorization?

Symbolic revalorization of language is a term used in linguistic anthropology to describe the process by which the attitudes one holds about language (e.g., a word, an expression, or the whole system of meaning) come to symbolically stand in for (and replace) the attitudes they hold about the group of people who use that language. Or, as Woolard and Schieffelin (1994: 92) put it, "Symbolic revalorization often makes discrimination on linguistic grounds publicly acceptable, whereas corresponding ethnic or racial discrimination is not."

Just as racial categories persist as an idea despite biological evidence to the contrary, the ideas associated with "standard" English persist despite linguistic evidence to the contrary. Discriminatory language ideologies persist through deeply embedded Discourse related to language. Society has largely stopped teaching racist beliefs about imagined biological differences, but it continues to feel normal to tell particular groups of children that the way they speak is somehow "wrong." The persistence of discriminatory language ideologies is also aided by the widespread belief that everyone "knows" about language. People often feel that they understand language because they are able to speak one. This is no different from claiming to understand how the human brain works because you have one or that you understand

DOI: 10.4324/9781003332886-3

the laws of physics because an apple fell on you. It is still common for people to not know exactly what linguistics is or why it might be important. A few basic facts about language should demonstrate why the dominant language ideologies in American society reproduce forms of social inequality. In this chapter, we outline some basic linguistic "facts of life," including the following:

- All languages (whether spoken, signed, or written) are equal in terms of linguistic potential
- Variation is intrinsic to all languages at every level; that variation carries indexical meanings that serve to reproduce social structures
- Everyone speaks a dialect; everyone has an accent
- All living languages change over time
- Children know the rules of their native language at an early age – well before they would begin school

These facts are crucial to understanding why language ideologies that promote the idea of a single variety of "standard" English are wrong and not just a question of taste or opinion. As it relates to English in the American context, we explore how:

- "Standard English" is an idealized imagined dialect
- The fact that children know the rules of English before they enter school means that teaching "standard English" can be seen as an attempt to eradicate patterns of variation that convey minority identities
- Communicative effectiveness results not from using "proper" grammar but rather from using linguistic variables with indexical meanings that align with the expectations for a given context

Linguistic potential

All over the world, right at this moment, very young children are acquiring a first (and, in the majority of the world's children, a second) language, and every one of them is going through the same stages at just about the same ages. A child in Papua New Guinea and a child in Carson City, Nevada, born on the same day will mirror one another as they go through those exact same stages, even if one of them is acquiring Kaluli and the other is acquiring American Sign Language. In Nairobi or El Paso, Okinawa or Bruges, the stages are the same. Those stages are:

1. babbling (repetitive consonant – vowel syllables such as bababa or tatata)
2. one or two syllable words in isolation (duck, car, teddy)
3. two-word strings (more juice, get down, want that)
4. the telegraphic stage, where grammatical bits are mostly left out (Elmo kiss baby doll, Where mama going? I tie it myself) (see Burkette & Kretzschmar 2018)

The regular progression of acquisition continues until a child has full knowledge of a language's grammatical elements and complex structures and knowledge of what forms of language to use in which social contexts. Children with regular exposure to more than one language will move through these stages in both languages simultaneously until they are able to speak both.

One of the most important linguistic insights of the last century was a quite simple explanation of this pattern: this species-wide, universal pattern of acquisition across languages could not be coincidental. Noam Chomsky proposed what now seems obvious:

> The fact that . . . children acquire essentially comparable grammars of great complexity with remarkable rapidity suggests that human beings are somehow specially designed to do this, with data-handling or "hypothesis-formulating" ability of unknown character and complexity.
>
> (Chomsky 1959: 62)

In other words, brains are hard-wired for language; it is part of a human's DNA. As with any biological capacity, there will be tremendous individual variation in how this capacity is expressed. Children vary in terms of exactly when they pass through each stage of acquisition, and some children may acquire language only with great difficulty or not at all. The children in this last group are described by doctors and researchers as having a language disorder (LD); LD can be associated with another medical condition (such as non-verbal autism or Down syndrome) or it can be specific to language (developmental language disorder, which has historically also been called a *specific language impairment*).

One fact that will be familiar to parents but might surprise people without experience with language acquisition is that when, or even if, human children acquire language has nothing to do with intelligence. Language acquisition in children appears to be about expressing the individual's capacity for language acquisition; no more, no less. A child has the innate capacity to acquire language, something like a blueprint in the mind, that makes it possible to recognize and absorb the structural patterns and sounds or signs of language. A child will naturally and automatically draw on their experience of the language around them to fill in and adapt those blueprints until they are completely competent in the language they are acquiring.

Given that children acquire language in the same way, it should not be surprising to find that all varieties of all human languages have the same basic structures. Each language contains a finite set of potentially meaning-bearing units. For signed languages, these units include handshapes, facial expressions, and the movement of a sign through space. For spoken languages, these units include vowels, consonants, melodies, and silences. In both cases, the set of possible units a language can use is universally constrained by the human bodies that produce and perceive them. In terms of sound, each language uses some, but not all, of the sounds that can be produced in the human vocal tract. Although the set of possible sounds a language can use is universal, languages vary widely in terms of which and how many of the sounds they use. For example, Taa (also known as !Xóõ, spoken in Botswana and Namibia) uses more than 80 different consonants while Pirahã (spoken in Brazil) uses only seven. The same is true for dialects of a single language.

The International Phonetic Alphabet (or the IPA)

Occasionally in this book we will refer to sounds using symbols from the International Phonetic Alphabet (IPA) which is included at the front of this book. The IPA is an attempt to create a (more or less) one-to-one mapping of written symbol to speech sound. The Latin alphabet, used to represent English spellings, does not have this same sound-symbol correspondence for English pronunciations. For example, the letter "c" can be "soft," and sound like the letter "s" (like in "cent"), or it can be "hard," and sound like the letter "k" (like in "cup"). Linguists don't use this hard/soft distinction; instead, when a word features the letter "c" and it sounds like an "s," they use the same phonetic symbol that they would use to represent the letter "s" when it makes that sound: [s]. Same thing if it sounds like a "k." So the words "sent" and "cent," which are homophones despite this difference in spelling, would both be presented as beginning with [s]. IPA symbols are written in these square brackets to represent speech sounds. Linguists have created this system of symbols to represent the consonants and vowels of all the world's languages!

The sounds of a language are organized into systems in which each element stands in relationship to the other elements (linguists call this *phonology*). A language's phonology includes both the inventory of sounds available and, just as importantly, the way those sounds can be combined. English, for example, uses the sound linguists call "engma" [ŋ], the sound at the end of words like "ring" or "song." However, English does not contain any words that begin with this sound; the sound must always be in the middle ("kingdom") or end ("slang") of a word. This is not a physical limitation in the way engma is produced or perceived; other languages have no problem starting words with engma. You have probably encountered Vietnamese Americans who have names that start with the sound, such as Nguyen. Because one's ability to hear sounds is constrained by the phonology of the language(s) spoken, English listeners have no trouble hearing engma in the middle or at the end of a word but often hear this name as if it were the question "when?" pronounced with great emphasis so it has two syllables "whe-en?" with no engma sound at all! Children learn to recognize and produce all and only the sounds they hear used around them. They also learn the patterns for where each sound can and can't occur.

The ability to acquire language with ease seems to atrophy in adolescence. While learning a language in childhood is effortless, trying to learn a new language as an adult takes a huge amount of effort. When it comes to adult language learners, it seems most have the same difficulty in learning a second language. Their ability to sound native-like in the new language has faded. Brains have native phonologies to lean on, so they do. The product is a variety of the learned language that has clear indicators of the speaker's native language. This is why people who have learned a second language as adults tend to have foreign-sounding accents in that second language. Such accents are distinct from a language learner's skill in actually using the target language. Speaking another language with this kind of accent has little to do with the ability to speak and understand the language across different contexts. Rather, the inability to be "accentless" in a foreign language is just a natural result of the way in which the biochemical changes of adolescence alter the way the brain works.

As noted in Chapter 2, languages are arbitrary systems of signs used to convey human experience. People generally don't say that one arbitrary system is better than another because both are thoroughly arbitrary. It is the same with languages. It is not "better" for Eastern Pomo to mark epistemic states in its verb morphology any more than it is "better" for English to avoid conveying this information. All languages are equal in their ability to convey abstract, complex thought. They simply convey that thought in different ways. Some argue that some languages are "primitive" or "unusable" because they don't have words for concepts in the modern world. This is particularly silly because languages come up with new words (neologisms) all the time. Borrowing words from other languages is a particularly common way of filling such gaps. Ultimately, coming up with words for speakers to use in a language is a trivial issue that is easily resolved. Indeed, Indigenous languages often come up with neologisms for use in educational contexts. For example, the K'iche' Maya Language Academy (in Guatemala) has come up with numerous neologisms in their language, including things like the term "metal bird" (*xik'ik'el ch'ich'*) to mean "helicopter."

Borrowings in English

English has borrowed words from a number of different languages. Can you match the English words with their original languages? Answers are below.

1. algebra	Twi
2. checkmate	Abenaki
3. tattoo	French
4. chocolate	Hindi
5. cigar	Japanese
6. skunk	Tahitian
7. okra	Maya
8. money	Farsi
9. shampoo	Arabic
10. honcho	Nahuatl (Aztec)

1. algebra, Arabic
2. checkmate, Farsi
3. tattoo, Tahitian
4. chocolate, Nahuatl
5. cigar, Maya
6. skunk, Abenaki
7. okra, Twi
8. money, French
9. shampoo, Hindi
10. honcho, Japanese

Neologisms in K'iche'

The following K'iche' neologisms are given with their literal translations in English. Can you match the neologisms with the English word with the same meaning? Answers are below.

volcano's vomit (uxa'oj ixkanul)	telescope
fingernails to eat with (ixk'eqwab'al)	passport
killer of bugs (kamsab'al chikopil)	crossword puzzle

volcano's vomit (uxa'oj ixkanul)	telescope
tool to block rain (q'atb'al jab')	magma
silver memento (pwaq natajsab'al)	umbrella
paper for crossing countries (wujq'axb'äl amaq')	fork
fire under the earth (q'aq' uxe'ulew)	remote control
tool to turn on and turn off (tzijchupub'äl)	lava
tool for seeing the face of the sky (ilb'al uwach kaj)	insecticide
lining up words (cholb'al tzij)	medal

1. lava
2. fork
3. insecticide
4. umbrella
5. medal
6. passport
7. magma
8. remote control
9. telescope
10. crossword puzzle

All languages (spoken or signed) share the same common basic structure that children automatically acquire in exactly the same way. Despite the linguistic evidence that speaking a language is an innate human ability and that all languages are equally able to convey any given idea, the dominant language ideologies in the United States continue to hold the discriminatory view that some languages (namely English) are naturally better than others. The same is true for dialects of English. All are equally valid systems for communicating human experiences, but some are treated as inherently "wrong" or "inappropriate" for use in particular contexts. The dialect that is typically deemed "correct" and "appropriate" is the dialect spoken primarily by speakers who are middle-class, cisgender, male, heterosexual, and white. Societies seem to always find a way to further marginalize the language varieties spoken by (already) marginalized people. To paraphrase George Orwell, all languages are equal, but some are more equal than others.

Variety is the spice of life!

Spoken language varies for every speaker in terms of speech sounds, sound patterns, word and sentence structure, intonation, and meaning. This is true even for those who believe themselves to speak an educated, elevated, supra-regional English. Variation is not a frivolous, sloppy, or useless feature of language. Quite the contrary, the variants available to the speaker to choose from are not neutral. The choice between these various options may not always be conscious, but it is often purposeful. The choices people make between variables, even if entirely unintentional, are reactions to their expectations regarding language use in a particular context. Although some people can recognize that others are speaking a different language or a different type of English, most linguistic variation usually fails to reach the level of consciousness. It is in the production and perception of speech sounds (functioning in relationship to one another) that there is perhaps the greatest potential for variation in language, much of which goes unnoticed.

Linguistic variables fall into two broad categories: stable variation (where variables are used in the same way over a relatively long period of time) and change in progress (variables that are undergoing a change in their patterns of usage). An example of a stable variable would be saying the -ing suffix with the back of the tongue raised against the soft palate or velum (the [ŋ] sound in the International Phonetic Alphabet) or with the front of the tongue pressed against the (alveolar) ridge right behind the teeth (the [n] sound). In orthography, this variable is often represented as "g-dropping" (e.g., *runnin'* vs. *running*), and English speakers sometimes think of the [n] variant as lazy or informal even though the [n] and [ŋ] tongue movements require the same amount of energy to accomplish (see Campbell-Kibler 2007). An example of change in progress would be the movement of the [ɑ] vowel (the vowel in "pot") forward in the mouth to sound more like the [æ] vowel (the vowel in "pat"). This is a change currently spreading across cities along the southern shores of the Great Lakes (discussed further in Chapter 5). It is this change in progress that results in an accent where the word "Wisconsin" sounds like "Wis-CAN-sin."

All languages contain both types of variation. Language change is always happening. As particular variables come to take up indexical meanings, people begin to use or avoid those variables in new ways. When a variable comes to index characteristics that people find desirable, that variable is likely to spread. As long as a language has speakers, that language will be undergoing constant change. Young people always desire to distinguish themselves from their parents' generation so they will produce patterns of variation that are different from the generation above them. Although young people are often accused of "ruining" the language with their new-fangled ways of talking, innovations spread by young people are a sign that a language is alive. Indeed, in the same way that a forest will continue to add new leaves and branches as long as it is thriving, a language only ceases to undergo change when there are no longer speakers living their lives in that language.

You from Missouruh?

The reality of language change is that it often reflects "linguistic fashion" as much as it does anything else. A wonderful example of a feature that has had its ups and downs in linguistic fashion is something linguists call "schwa raising." The schwa sound, represented as [ə] in the IPA, is a very common vowel in English, and it is the vowel sound in the second syllables of words like "soda" and "Sarah." When the pronunciation of such words ends with an "e" sound ("sody" or "Sary"), the vowel has been raised, represented by [i] in the IPA. This pronunciation is still pretty common among rural Southerners (words like "sody" as well as "Santy Claus" and "Grand Ol' Opry" are common examples), but, at some point in history, this feature, which was generally innocuous, became seen as "rustic" and therefore "not good." To "fix" their speech, some people tried to move back to the schwa pronunciation, and when they did so, they overextended the rule to include words that were pronounced with an [i] at the end but had not historically had a schwa, like "Missouri" and "Cincinnati." We write "fix" in quotes because this is what linguists call hypercorrection, a type of error caused by overgeneralizing the fix to a perceived error to words and forms where it never happened. This hypercorrection of schwa raising is why some people pronounce "Missouri" and "Cincinnati" as "Missouruh" and "Cincinnatuh" (but see Lance 2003 for more on the topic).

Are you a robot?

As patterns of language change spread in different ways, variables come to cluster together across social groups or regions forming distinctive dialects. For linguists, dialect simply refers to a set of variables that are shared across some group of speakers (defined by region or social group). So anyone who speaks a language also speaks a dialect of that language. Although non-linguists sometimes use dialect in a negative way, linguists see all varieties of any language as dialects, including even the most uppity, prestigious way of speaking you can think of.

Often when people talk about varieties of English that don't fit some idea of a "standard," they think of people who seem to have an "accent" of some sort. In so far as linguists are concerned, the term "accent," as it is used by non-linguists, has no technical or specific meaning, except, perhaps, that it is loosely connected to the pronunciation of some language variety. Although the term "accent" is widely used by non-linguists as a loose reference to a specific "way of speaking," people rarely give any official or technical specification for what this might mean in actual linguistic terms. There are two widely recognized elements to what serves to distinguish "accents" (or "ways of speaking") in the minds of speakers.

1. Prosodic features. The sound structure (phonology) of a language includes consideration of intonation or patterns of pitch contours. This includes stress patterns, both at the lexical and sentence level, but it also touches upon other factors such as rate of speech, volume, or patterns of pausing.
2. Segmental features. People acquire, as part of their first language, the sounds of the language which fall into two major categories: vowels and consonants. As children, they acquire the specific ways in which each of these sounds are produced by the speakers in their communities.

As an example of element 1, currently in American English, there is one very active point of variation having to do with stress, in a small set of words including *insurance*, *adult*, and *cement*. First syllable stress has been documented for these words in the South, while in other parts of the United States the stress is more commonly found on the second syllable: INsurance (South) vs. inSURance (elsewhere). For element 2, some speakers of US Englishes distinguish between the words *dawn* and *Don* (Southerners, Northeasterners, and some people in northern cities like Detroit and Chicago), while for others these are homophones. The same is true of words like *tent* and *tint*, which are pronounced the same way for most Southerners but tend to be pronounced differently in other parts of the country. This follows quite reasonably from the fact that there are many possible sound systems for American English. Each of these different sound systems could be considered a different "accent."

Hawgs and Dawgs and Hawt

The mascots of the University of Arkansas (razorbacks, or "hogs") and the University of Georgia (bulldogs) are often spelled as *hawg* and *dawg*. This non-standard spelling emphasizes the regional pronunciation of these words with the vowel in Dawn or taught ([ɔ]) rather than with the vowel in Don or tot ([ɑ]). In many other parts of the country people pronounce these words with the same vowel ([ɑ]) and typically can't hear a distinction between words like *taught* and *tot*. For many speakers, the "aw" ([ɔ]) pronunciation came to index being from the South.

This photo (Figure 3.1) shows a B-29 plane from World War II on display at the Imperial War Museum in Duxford, UK. Pilots often painted the sides of their planes, and this pilot (presumably from Arkansas) chose to paint a Razorback, or "Hawg." This is also an example of hypercorrection, and it showcases why some people write or hear people pronounce words like *hot,* which have traditionally had the [ɑ] (cot, tot) vowel, as "hawt" hypercorrecting to a novel [hɔt] pronunciation.

Figure 3.1 Hawg pilot from World War II
Source: photo by ducatipierre

This is exactly why linguists say that there is no such thing as an "unaccented" variety of a language. Accent simply has to do with the sounds (or signs) used in a language: which sounds occur, what handshapes are used, how those forms are distributed, and how those forms are produced. No spoken language can exist without phonology, and since "accent" refers to variations in phonology, everyone who speaks a language has an accent. Indeed, even if everyone spoke English in the same way, their language would still be "accented" because it would necessarily have sounds. The same is true of signed languages, where the organization and location of handshapes and the specific movements a speaker uses combine to result in different "accents" of a signed language. Every native speaker of American English (or any other language) has an accent, no matter how unmarked or marked the person's language may seem to be. This includes broadcast news personalities, English professors, actors, politicians, or anyone else who is generally thought to speak "properly." Accents are nothing special. Everybody has one. You've got one too.

Accent can be understood and defined in a comparative sense. You travel to a small town in Kansas, and unless you are from that area, *your* accent will likely be recognized as different, as locals tend to notice the differences between a new person's speech and the local speech. Often people assume that only those from other places ("outsiders") have accents. People often have strong, if conflicting, attitudes toward the different ways that English is pronounced in different places. For example, compare the results when the blog Gawker sponsored a competition to see which city has the "Ugliest Accent" in the United States (see Figure 3.2, left) with the results of the Big 7 travel website's annual poll of the "Sexiest American Accent" (Figure 3.2, right). The same places, representing the same accents, rank high on both lists.

The differences in speech across regions or social groups can be examined and identified so that a linguist might make a study of prosodic features and phonology to determine exactly what marks a person as from "someplace else." That "someplace else" can be another state, country, or even a different social group.

Although they are based in the regular variation in the production of the sounds of English, accents are primarily about how that variation is perceived. Sociolinguists (especially those involved in perceptual dialectology; see Chapter 9) know that the perception of accents is intimately linked to stereotypes about the social categories that are indexically

Figure 3.2 Top ten "ugliest" and "sexiest" accent rankings compared

associated with the "accented" speaker. The pronunciation of "tire" as homophonous with "tar" is likely to be perceived as indexing not only Southernness but also traits such as ignorance, racism, and barefootedness. Thus, when someone listens to another person speaking, they pay attention not only to how that person talks but to what they look like, how they dress, and so on. McGowan (2015) showed that even listeners with very little experience with Chinese-accented English who were asked to transcribe Chinese-accented speech did better when also shown a Chinese face. This finding suggests that these listeners were using both the sounds and the photograph to understand what was being said. In listening to others, people utilize the full spectrum of information about variation (in the speech stream, in image, in context, etc.) to simultaneously engage both linguistic and social categorizations. It is through such direct associations between speech and social stereotypes that language comes to reproduce forms of social inequality as individuals come to be judged in particular ways based simply on where they fall in the range of variation in the production of the sounds of English.

Gawker can create debate about which city has the "ugliest" accent because the perception of an accent as "pleasant" or "ugly" (and so on) depends on the perspective of the listener. Individuals are less likely to perceive an accent as "ugly" when that accent is similar to their own. Another important factor in the perception of accents is whether an accent occurs in a person's first language or in a language they learned later in life. In the case of first language accents, listeners tend to categorize them according to the social categories that are relevant in a given cultural context. The most common way in which first language accents are perceived is in terms of variation association with geography; in American English, that might mean an Appalachian accent, a Utah accent, a Seattle accent, or a Boston South Shore accent. In addition to variation across regions, first language dialects may refer to other social categories such as gender identity, race or ethnicity, social class, religion, or sexual orientation. These accents are invoked when listeners perceive a voice as "sounding like" the speaker is white, Jewish, gay, etc. First language accents may also index aspects of individual identity, as personality traits are often attributed to particular accents. People commonly remark on voices when they make statements like "She sounds nice" or "He sounds stupid."

Second language accents, on the other hand, occur when a native speaker of one language learns another language. When a person learns a language later in life, the phonology of their first language will usually influence how they are able to hear and produce the language they are learning. In American English, the vowel in "bait" is represented in IPA as [eɪ], which is a diphthong, or a single vowel during which the tongue moves between two places in the mouth. The production of the vowel in "bait" involves lifting the tongue as one makes the vowel so that one ends more like the vowel in "beat." Because this pronunciation of the "bait" vowel is automatic for English speakers, they typically continue to produce the vowel in this way when learning another language. A Spanish language teacher might become frustrated with their English-speaking students pronouncing this vowel "incorrectly" because the vowel is monophthongal, or with only a single configuration of the vocal tract, in Spanish. In IPA, it would be written as [e], which does not occur in English; these English-speaking students pronounce the name *Pedro* with the diphthong (['peɪ.dɹoʊ]), which sounds funny to native Spanish speakers.

When an English speaker says that a person has a Welsh accent, a Polish accent, or a Tagalog accent, then they are reacting to the ways in which their English pronunciation might be influenced by the phonology found in their first language. Spanish doesn't distinguish between the sounds at the beginning of the English words *sheep* and *cheap* ([ʃ] and [ʧ], respectively, in IPA). Because of this, a “Spanish accent” may refer (in part) to variation in which these two sounds occur in the same places (such as pronouncing “chair” as “share”). Similarly, Japanese does not distinguish between “r” and “l” sounds so that variation in the distribution of these sounds may be perceived as “sounding Japanese.”

Second language learners vary widely in the degree to which their native phonology impacts their pronunciation in a second language. In some cases, people might describe someone as having a particular second language accent simply because they know that speaker is from some other country or racial background associated with immigrant communities. Thus, native speakers of English from the Midwest who are perceived as Latinx or Asian may find themselves complimented on how amazing it is that they speak with their native central Ohio accent: “Your English is so good!”

English is spoken as a majority native language in more than 30 countries and territories and as a second (or third, fourth, eighth, etc.) language the world over, and it can be tricky to tease apart the perspectives people have about the many different kinds of English accents used. Americans tend to have positive attitudes toward the varieties of English found in the United Kingdom and in countries with high amounts of white settler colonialism. Braj Kachru (1992) refers to such countries as the “Inner Circle” countries, and this classification includes the varieties of English spoken in the United Kingdom, the United States, Canada, Australia, New Zealand, and South Africa.

On the other hand, the accents of native English speakers not descended from white colonial settlers (in Kachru’s classification system, these are called “Outer Circle” countries) are often viewed negatively. Native speakers of English from Asia and Africa are often seen as being more closely aligned with non-native English accents even though English is their first language. Indeed, varieties like Indian English are often openly mocked as part of racist caricatures, such as the character Apu on *The Simpsons*. These imagined caricatures influence the way many Americans genuinely experience interactions with speakers of Indian English working at call centers, for example.

The varieties of English spoken in communities descended from enslaved Africans also tend to have accents that may be subject to prejudice. These varieties of English are sometimes even treated as if they form some different class of languages (“Creoles”) that some have argued shouldn’t even be considered varieties of English. Thus, one could conceive of Americans’ attitudes toward English accents as reflecting the dominant language ideology in the United States. Because these attitudes are not about the actual structure of the language, the hierarchy usually aligns with other, non-linguistic forms of social prejudice. Thus, societal racism aligns with attitudes toward English accents; the varieties spoken by middle-class white people are often seen as the “best” accents while varieties spoken by immigrants and minorities are often perceived as “bad” accents.

What could be seen as troubling, from a categorization perspective, is that each of these accents can, by definition, be described as simply containing variant ways of saying the “same thing.” Thus, other accents differ from American English because they have feature X where “standard” English has feature Y and have feature A where “standard” English has feature B. For example, the consonant “d” is produced with the tongue curled back in Indian English but with the tongue pointed forward in American English. Similarly, American English uses a flap of the tongue to produce “t” or “d” between vowels in words like *water* or *flooded*, while British English may produce these words with a break in airflow (what linguists call a glottal stop, or [?] in IPA), as in “wa-uh” for *water*. There is no linguistic reason for the different pattern found in Indian English to be “bad” nor is there any reason to view the difference found in British English as “better.”

Beliefs about differences in accents are not about the accents themselves. Rather, they are about the social identities of speakers. For example, in "good" French accents, the [h] sound is never produced at the beginning of a word (as in *herbe*), but in British English, a "good" accent always pronounces [h] at the beginning of a word, such that *herb* and *Herb* are homophonous. If pronouncing word-initial [h] is "bad" for French but "good" for English, there is clearly nothing inherently "good" or "bad" about [h] itself. That is to say that attitudes toward different ways of speaking are about social, political, and historical perspectives. The actual linguistic features being discussed are secondary and may even be entirely irrelevant. Such attitudes are about the identities of those who speak "bad" English. This allows forms of discrimination to persist under the guise of "control" over a particular way of speaking. An employer can refuse to hire an African American because she pronounces words in a particular way and feel that they have not done anything that might be considered racist. Making hiring decisions based on "accent" will greatly reduce the number of immigrants and minorities in the applicant pool, thus making it much more likely for a white person to be employed. By narrowing opportunities for minority groups, language ideologies that perpetuate negative attitudes toward different English "accents" serve as a central component of discourse structural racism.

So-called Standard English

People have a natural tendency to think of "English" as a single, mostly uniform way of speaking associated with beliefs about the mythological "standard English." Milroy and Milroy suggest that standard varieties should not be understood as any specific language, but as "an idea in the mind rather than a reality – a set of abstract norms to which actual usage may conform to a greater or lesser extent" (1985: 22–23). The idea of a uniform variety of standardized English is just another myth that serves to maintain forms of social inequality. Yet people will say in all seriousness that they know people who speak "standard English," in all its supposed accentless glory. Despite all the hard evidence that all languages contain variation and undergo change, people steadfastly believe that a homogenous, standardized, one-size-fits-all language is not only desirable, but it is truly a possibility. In their efforts to promote this mythical, perfect standard variety, speakers of minority varieties of language often find themselves facing discrimination based purely on the ways in which they speak.

The language ideology promoting "standard" English openly creates fear and self-doubt when it comes to assumptions about the particular way an individual speaks. The potential consequences of not using the "appropriate" form of English serve to intimidate those who might already be concerned about the security of their position in American society. Google searches provide a sense of how large these issues loom in the minds of people more generally (see Table 3.1). Many people wanting to know more about "standard" English might search for information about "grammar," and a survey of discussions on this topic brings

Table 3.1 Number of Google hits for grammar terms

Google term search	*No. of hits January 2022*
"bad grammar"	293,000,000
"grammar advice"	256,000,000
"English grammar errors"	64,600,000

up hundreds of examples. Ultimately a large portion of the threads discovered with such a search have nothing to do with grammar, per se, but with matters of punctuation. No matter the topic, the tone can be affronted, sarcastic, condescending, servile, and, on occasion, silly to the point of absurdity.

The Discourse promoting a "standard" language is constructed and reconstructed on an ongoing basis by those who have a vested interest in the concept. People continue to accept this mythical language as not only real but somehow actually obtainable. Indeed, people are so comfortable with the idea of a standard language that they are very willing to describe and define it, much in the same way that most people could draw a unicorn, describe a being from *Star Trek*'s planet Vulcan, or explain what the Tooth Fairy does. For the most part, people will undertake describing any of these even though they know that the thing they are describing is imaginary. That is, your description of a unicorn would be a great deal like those of others familiar with the concept because the concept of a unicorn is a part of shared cultural heritage, but it is still not a creature that you have seen or ever will see. You picked up your mental image (likely a horse with a single pointed horn growing from its forehead) at some point in your life; most probably you don't remember when or where. The same is true for what has been called "standard" American English.

The language ideology promoting "standard" English is an example of prescriptive grammar. Just as a doctor prescribes a particular regimen of medication or diet, prescriptivists are people who "prescribe" the "right" grammar for a speaker's "own good." The most extreme examples of prescriptive grammar come from those who make a living promoting the concept. Writers like Edwin Newman, John Simon, and James Kilpatrick published extensively on how English "should" be spoken and written. But unlike a doctor writing a prescription, prescriptive grammarians need not have any actual training or educational preparation to become language experts. Prescriptivists do not typically address the source of their authority directly; their expertise is taken for granted. They assume you will grant them authority because they demand it and because it has always been granted. Such people have made careers for themselves as prescriptivists because they meet a demand they created themselves.

Which is "correct"?

Of the following sentences, there is only one that prescriptivists accept as "proper" English. Can you tell which one? The answer is below.

1. I gave both of the boys twenty dollars.
2. He was running like his life depended on it.
3. The women whom the senator criticized in the papers are they.
4. We are still waiting on word from the doctor.
5. Who were you talking to?
6. The express lane is for customers with ten items or less.
7. You have to really study to pass that class.
8. You better not break that vase.
9. I need a book that will teach me about linguistics.
10. My answer is different than yours.

1. both should be each 2. like should be as if 3. "correct" 4. on should be for 5. rewrite as "To whom were you talking?" or, even better, "To whom were you speaking?" 6. less should be fewer 7. remove really to avoid split infinitive 8. "You better" should be "You had better" 9. that should be which 10. than should be from

What is it about the other sentences that make them "unacceptable"? How do you know? What does this tell you about "standard" English and how certain items come to be seen as "proper"?

In contrast to prescriptive grammar, linguists are interested in descriptive grammar, or the analysis of language as it is actually used by speakers. Linguists are interested in understanding how language works as a biological fact, a cognitive system, and a sociocultural phenomenon. This requires empirical, scientific methodologies. Unlike deciding to become a prescriptivist, becoming a linguist requires serious study and specialized knowledge. Because they are self-appointed experts, prescriptivists tend to approve of the linguistic varieties that are closest to their own speech (or, at least, how they imagine their own speech). Linguists Robin Queen and Julie Boland (2015) performed a series of experiments to determine what drives people to adhere to the language ideology of prescriptive grammar and, in turn, judge people who don't follow prescriptive language ideologies. They found that personality type was the strongest predictor of who is more likely to have negative reactions to "grammatical errors" (such as harshly judging people who confuse "you're" and "your"). People who were less agreeable, less open, and more conscientious were more likely to negatively evaluate others solely on the basis of grammar. It seems, then, that the main requirement for being a prescriptivist is having a particular (rather grumpy and rigid) personality (see Figure 3.3).

Like all myths, the details of "standard" English are hard to pin down. The various definitions that prescriptivists have proposed provides a sense of why the idea of "standard" English is untenable. The hypothetical Standard American English is the language spoken and written by persons:

- with no regional accent
- who reside in the Midwest, Far West, or perhaps some parts of the Northeast (but never in the South)
- who are easily understood by all
- who pay attention to speech and are not sloppy in terms of pronunciation or grammar
- with more than average or superior education
- who are themselves educators or broadcasters
- who enter into a consensus of other individuals like themselves about what is proper in language

It makes no sense to claim that speakers of the "standard" do not have a regional accent but only come from a particular region. It seems that prescriptivists want language to be geographically neutral because they believe that this neutrality will bring with it a greater range of communication. The assumption seems to be that the Midwest is somehow neutral. In the minds of the non-linguists (see Chapter 9 on perceptual dialectology), the areas of the country in which the hypothetical Standard is not spoken (primarily the South and New

Figure 3.3 Some people just can't contain themselves when it comes to correcting other people's grammar!

Source: photo by Eli Reusch via Flickr

York City) are the logical home of accents. From this assumption it follows that everybody else speaks the hypothetical Standard and has no accent. A native of Mississippi or Brooklyn may have exactly the same educational background, intelligence, and point to make as their counterparts in Ohio and Colorado, but many believe that their accents compromise the quality of the performance.

The definition that a speaker of the standard is one who is "understood by all" is equally silly. Are there really any speakers of American English who wouldn't understand sentences like "I ain't got no chocolate!"? The thinly veiled racism of prescriptivist language ideologies is apparent in the claim that speakers of the "standard" are those who "pay attention to their speech" and "aren't sloppy." Does it seem likely that speakers of undervalued varieties are "sloppy"? Is the argument that hip hop artists fail to pay attention to language when they write lyrics in undervalued Englishes (cf. Alim 2006)? Surely Alice Walker was paying attention to language when she wrote *The Color Purple*.

One claim associated with "standard" English that feels a bit closer to the truth is that its speakers enter into a consensus of other individuals like themselves about what is proper in language. Across these definitions the cycle that allows prescriptivism to persist is clear. The speakers of the elusive "standard" are educated, but they are also educators. Those who spend the most time trying to learn the "standard" are more likely to be the same people who spend their time promoting prescriptivism. For these "educated" people, something as important as language cannot be left to itself; "normal" people are not smart enough and not aware enough to be in charge of their own language. There must be experts, mavens, lexicographers – someone in charge. Language variation needs to be controlled through structured authority.

The problem is that those who declare themselves authorities on language tend to be white, upper-class, heterosexual, cisgender men and women who evaluate all other forms of language against their own. For the men in these categories especially, this is a common pattern. If we look closely at forms of structural racism, sexism, anti-Semitism, transphobia, etc., the behavior of straight white cis men seems to serve as an unspoken norm against which all others are judged. From a legal perspective, Mari Matsuda notes the similarities between the construction of the hypothetical Standard, or English without an accent, on one hand and hidden norms codified in legal institutions on the other:

> As feminist theorists have pointed out, everyone has a gender, but the hidden norm in law is male. As critical race theorists have pointed out, everyone has a race, but the hidden norm in law is white. In any dyadic relationship, the two ends are equidistant from each other. If the parties are equal in power, we see them as equally different from each other. When the parties are in a relationship of domination and subordination we tend to say that the dominant is normal, and the subordinate is different from normal. And so it is with accent. . . . People in power are perceived as speaking normal, unaccented English. Any speech that is different from that constructed norm is called an accent.
>
> (Matsuda 1991: 805)

Thus, "standard" English serves as a means of maintaining power. The myth of standard language persists because it is carefully tended and propagated, with huge, almost universal success, so that language, the most fundamental of human socialization tools, becomes a commodity. But the commodity that is "standard" English is almost universally the native dialect of the people in power. By rejecting the dialects of outsiders as "wrong," the group in power can propagate a linguistic obstacle that is required for economic success. This "standard" dialect is a myth, and its structure is never clearly defined. This lack of definition allows individuals to wield their self-proclaimed knowledge of "correct grammar" to silence the voices of anyone they see as a threat.

It is common to hear people say that "standard" English is needed to "unite" society. But this unification can only come through assimilation to a mysterious way of speaking that can never be pinned down. It seems that "standard" English does very little to actually bring Americans together. Rather, it serves not only to keep people apart, but to keep many silent and powerless. The ideology of "standard" English is the heart of discourse structural racism.

Communicative effectiveness *depends* on variation

Linguists and non-linguists both see grammar as a set of rules which must be obeyed, but they differ on the nature and origination of those rules. When linguists talk about grammar, they are thinking about the rule-driven structure of language. On the basis of those rules, individuals generate sentences. Children have acquired a working knowledge of the grammar of their native language by the age of 4. Because the idea of "correctness" is so bound up with prescriptivist ideologies, linguists use the term *grammatical* (rather than "correct") to refer to sentences that follow the set of rules that a person learns as a child. Something is only ungrammatical if it is something no native speaker of a language would say. Linguists mark sentences that are ungrammatical with an asterisk (as in "*Boots Jorge's muddy got when walked home in the rain he did.")

Noam Chomsky (1957) famously demonstrated the nature of grammaticality with the following examples:

1. Colorless green ideas sleep furiously.
2. Furiously sleep ideas green colorless.

Neither of these sentences conveys a meaningful idea. Ideas aren't green, nothing can be both green and colorless, sleep can't be done furiously, and so on. However, a speaker of any variety of English will recognize that the first sentence follows the rules of English grammar, while the second sentence does not. "*Furiously sleep ideas green colorless" is not grammatical for any speaker of English, descriptivist or prescriptivist. No child growing up in an English-speaking community would produce this sentence because they would naturally know that it didn't follow the rules of their grammar. Just as you never have to remind a child about other aspects of language-internal, rule-governed grammar, one need not tell a child to avoid saying such sentences. Doing so would be equivalent to telling a child something like: "Stop putting your articles after your nouns!"

One methodology linguists use to determine whether a sentence is grammatical is very simple: a person is asked if a given sentence suits their personal intuitions about what is OK (grammatical) to say in their variety of English. A set of four sentences will help demonstrate how this works:

1. Sam put a red scarf on the dog.
2. George took the dog.
3. Linda asked what Sam put the red scarf on.
4. *George took the dog that Linda asked what Sam put a red scarf on.

The first three sentences are grammatical (they sound well-formed, as something you might say or hear said) for native speakers of English. The third one will make most people stop and think, but it can be unraveled. The last one cannot. All varieties of all languages have rules that make some sentences grammatical and some ungrammatical, but because languages always contain variation, individuals will have slightly different rules, resulting in different patterns of grammaticality. Thus, for example, a speaker from the upper Midwest would likely find a sentence like "I'm going to the store, do you want to come with?" to be perfectly grammatical. However, a sentence like "*I'm gonna sit in the front, do you want to sit with?" would not be grammatical. Similarly, a person from the South might regularly say sentences like "I might should go to the store," but "*I should might go to the store" would be ungrammatical. In terms of prescriptivism, many of the sentences that are recognized as grammatical will simply be "incorrect." Thus, the goal of prescriptivism is not to teach the rules of English; those are known to native speakers before they ever enter school. The goal of prescriptivism, rather, is to push for forced linguistic assimilation as a way of marginalizing entire communities of speakers and creating obstacles that help preserve forms of social inequality.

In terms of effectively communicating, there are plenty of contexts where "standard" English would be inappropriate and ineffective for addressing a particular audience. In many Southern and/or African American churches, for example, preachers regularly use varieties that are undervalued in some groups and contexts for rhetorical effect. Undervalued varieties of English can be found in literature, film, popular music, and social media. It might be strange, for example, to have a song title like "Ain't no mountain high enough" be in "standard" English (imagine, "There is no mountain that is sufficiently tall"). There are many contexts where the use of "standard" English is not an appropriate option.

Prescriptivists often confuse the acquisition of literacy skills with the process of learning a second dialect of ("standard") English. If the language in the classroom is the same as the language a child uses at home, the child is taught literacy skills in their own language. However, a student who comes to school with some other variety of English has to learn the dialect spoken in the classroom in addition to learning to read and write. This creates an additional obstacle for children who come to school with undervalued Englishes, as they are typically expected to acquire "standard" English without any explicit instruction (see Chapter 11). But expecting children to change the language they speak when they walk into school does much more than simply create one more roadblock for children who are already marginalized in the classroom. It sends a cruel and heartless message to children; it tells children that the language they use to think is simply wrong. Demanding "standard" English tells many minority, rural, and working-class children that everything they have known in their life up to this point has been wrong. It tells children that expressing their identity in public is wrong and potentially that their very existence is "inappropriate" for the school environment. If the language they speak does not belong in the classroom, it won't take long for children to assume that they don't belong in there either. At this point, prescriptivism has succeeded in segregating an otherwise integrated school (see Figure 3.4).

The failure to distinguish between learning to read/write and learning a second dialect is promoted through the idea that written language and "standard" English are somehow the same thing. Of course, any variety of English can be written. The use of undervalued Englishes is ubiquitous in American literature. If writing were truly limited to representations of "standard" English, a lot of amazing literature would be unavailable: Zora Neale Hurston's *Their Eyes Were Watching God*, Harriett Arnow's *The Dollmaker*, Blackhorse Mitchell's *Miracle Hill: The Story of a Navajo Boy*, Gloria Anzaldúa's *Borderlands/La frontera*, Angie Thomas's *The Hate U Give*, and so on. In these works, written language represents patterns of spoken linguistic variation. In addition to attempting to reflect spoken variation, there are patterns of variation specific to written language, including variant spellings (*color/colour*), abbreviations and shortened forms (*jk/lol*), different font choices (or font choices), or the use of emojis (☺). Just as with spoken language, variation in written language conveys indexical meanings. For example, going to the *theatre* is not entirely equivalent to going to the *theater*. Just as with spoken language, the exact indexical meaning of the variations (*theatre* and *theater*) may vary depending on the specifics of a given interaction. The spelling might index the location where the theater is actually located. Because *theater* is an American spelling, the use of *theatre* might index the theater as being outside of the United States. However, *theatre* could refer to a place in the United States that has been named with the less common spelling. Depending on the details of the context in which the theater is discussed, the theatre spelling could index some characteristic of the theater owners wish to convey. In such cases, the meaning of the theatre spelling would become clear when one considers the other variables that co-occur with *theatre*. It could index Britishness or some point in past time, as in *The Olde Theatre Diner* (located in Coventry, Rhode Island). It could also draw on the use of the *theatre* spelling in French to index prestige or social class, as in the *Chattanooga Theatre Centre* (located in Tennessee).

There are numerous web resources discussing "how to email your professor," and writing courses sometimes even address the "proper" way to do so. What should you call them? How

Figure 3.4 Companies like Grammarly.com depend on the fear that one's language might cause rejection by potential employers, teachers, or significant others

Source: photo by Victor D'allant

do you open the message? *Hi Professor!*; *Dear Dr. Chávez*; or simply *'Sup?* The reason there are websites giving this advice is because writing such an email can be intimidating. Before a person goes to college, they may have never written an email message to a college professor, but they will likely understand the power dynamics – they likely believe that the professor is in the power position, they are the subordinate, and choosing the appropriate form of address, tone, etc. is important. Without prior examples to compare to, however, one doesn't know what form the message should take. The fact that college is an environment associated with beliefs about "standard" English only makes the anxiety worse. This is common with prescriptivist ideals – people are expected to adhere to them even though they never know exactly what it is they are trying to adhere to. In a context that is familiar, people don't need an explanation of what language is "appropriate" – you probably wouldn't get many hits on a website explaining "how to write a text message to your best friend." If an older relative asked you how to text like "kids today," you could probably come up with a list of rules they don't know (e.g., stop using periods, writing in all caps means screaming, use the right emojis). Teaching a grandparent to text would not be particularly different from teaching a student how to email a professor for the first time. In both cases, a person doesn't know which linguistic variables to use in a novel interactional context. Effective communication requires understanding which linguistic forms are more likely to appeal to a particular audience in a particular context.

Speakers are constantly adjusting to the interactions and events happening around them. They adjust their speech so that they use the linguistic forms that seem indexically appropriate for the context. When the context is unfamiliar, it makes it more difficult to communicate effectively. In addition to not knowing the indexical meanings associated with a context, a lack of familiarity creates anxiety which can further hamper the ability to communicate. Although an understanding of audience, goals, and context are critical, the most important factor in producing effective communication is the listeners' openness to the person speaking and the interaction taking place. If the audience fails to listen or refuses to cooperate, effective communication can never occur. Prescriptive ideology actually encourages people to refuse to cooperate with others. Those who speak in ways that don't align with expectations regarding some idealized "standard" are interrupted, corrected, and told that they are wrong. This turns the attention to the language the speaker used rather than the message they were trying to convey. The message gets lost in the shuffle, effectively silencing the person whose English was judged to be unacceptable. Although people are regularly taught how they should speak and write to communicate clearly, they are usually not taught how to listen to communicate clearly. For effective communication to occur, one must first acknowledge one's own role in comprehending those who speak differently from themselves.

Discussion questions

1. There are a number of borrowings in English that convert the sounds of the borrowing's original phonology to better fit with the sound system of English. For example, both Spanish and French (and most other languages, see Chapter 10) pronounce "r" sounds (also called rhotic sounds) differently than English. What is different in how a native speaker of English and a native speaker of Spanish say the word "burrito"? What about a French speaker saying "rouge"? What are some other examples of words English has borrowed that sound very different when spoken by a native speaker of the "donating" language?
2. Why would it be offensive to someone who is Latinx or Asian American and who was born and raised in the United States to be told that their English is "good"? What assumptions underlie such a statement?
3. Myths are a big part of the everyday lives of members of a culture. Most people within any given culture already understand them. How can such myths be explained to people who are unfamiliar with them? For example, how would you describe the Tooth Fairy? How does she get in? How much money does she bring? Now apply this thinking to

the idea of "standard" English. How would you describe it? Would you be able to tell someone exactly how to speak it? Why or why not?

4. Some people say "standard" English serves to "unite" society. Can you think of examples around the world where two groups speak the same language but have no societal unity? What about cases in the past where two groups spoke the same language but could not get along? Is it possible to have groups who speak different languages but live together peacefully?

4 Language subordination

Reading a textbook: roles and responsibilities

When you read a textbook, like you're doing right now, it's very clear that we, the authors, have certain obligations to make the text understandable and believable. For one thing, we should eschew obfuscatory locution wherever possible and, instead, use words that are clear and familiar. We try to keep sentences to a single point, to organize those sentences into sensible paragraphs by topic or theme, and to further organize those paragraphs into subsections, sections, and chapters that will enhance your ability to follow the argument we are making. And we never lose sight of the fact that we are, in fact, making an argument. This means we have to say only things that are true to the best of our knowledge and to provide evidence when claims are likely to seem outlandish to you, the reader.

Every step of what we have just described requires accommodation on our part: word selection, sentence design, and understanding which topics are likely to be unfamiliar so that they require more careful explanation and which topics are likely to seem outlandish or exciting so that they require a higher degree of evidence. Every step of this process requires us, the authors, to imagine you, the reader. We must consider what you are likely to know already and, much more importantly, what you do not yet know that seems obvious or second nature to us. These are the topics where we must be especially careful not to make any assumptions, to step back and to remember what it felt like to discover these things for the first time, and to try to give you the clearest, fairest presentation of the ideas our expertise and writing ability allow. If we do any of these steps poorly – if we guess incorrectly about who you are and what you believe, if we forget to lay out crucial ideas clearly, if we fail to provide evidence you find compelling – then our book becomes difficult to read, confusing, or, worst of all, unconvincing. If, on the other hand, we do our jobs well and you find yourself thinking "but what about X?" or "I don't think I agree with Y" just before we tackle the question you thought of or address the concern you're having, then we've created an artifact that will help us and other linguists teach you things we believe will be valuable to you and to society more generally.

So those are the obligations of the authors. But what are the obligations of the reader? What is your role in making this book readable, understandable, and thought provoking? Well, first you should be prepared to read critically. This is not the same style of reading you probably use to take a quiz on Buzzfeed or to read a book like *The Hunger Games* (but it is pretty close to the style of reading you might use to read a poem or a religious text). Although we do hope this book is at least somewhat enjoyable to read, you'll notice that "writing a story for you to enjoy" was not listed among what we feel to be our obligations in writing this book. This book presents ideas and challenges you to engage with them. This means you need to read actively.

DOI: 10.4324/9781003332886-4

You should be reading the words in this book for understanding, not merely recognition. It isn't enough to get to the end of a paragraph and make certain that you know what we said in case it is on a quiz or a test. You should get to the end of a paragraph and wonder why we've bothered to include that paragraph in a book that gives us only limited space to convey many difficult ideas. Why are we making a particular point? Why are we including a particular piece of evidence? Why might we be excluding other types of evidence? Reading this book properly does not mean coming away from it agreeing with everything we've said (not at all!). But reading this book properly does require you to try the ideas out, imagine what the world would be like if they were true, and try to imagine how your instinctive, habitual reactions to the ideas presented here might be shaped by the experiences, difficulties, and privileges you have had in life.

In other words, this book is an act of communication, and, like *any* act of communication, both the writer and the reader (or the speaker and the listener) have a role in achieving understanding. We've described ways in which we might fail, as authors, to hold up our end of the bargain. What are some ways that you might fail, as readers, to hold up your end? We can think of this mutual responsibility as a shared burden we are carrying together; it is *our* communicative burden. If you approach a book like this while distracted by your phone or while watching a movie in the background, then you have not upheld your part of the communicative burden, and the book is exceedingly unlikely to be readable, understandable, or thought provoking. Similarly, if you arrive at this book already certain that you know that our claims are wrong or not worth engaging with, then you have failed your end of the communicative burden.

So what? The thing about communicative burden is that there are consequences for both people involved when communication fails. In the case of a textbook, our peers may decide not to assign our textbook if we do a poor job of upholding our end of the communicative burden, and we will suffer public embarrassment and the loss of professional respect. Failure to uphold your end of the burden, for this or any other course material, can mean reduced understanding, a missed opportunity to think in new and expansive ways, lower grades, etc. These things are serious business. If a book is boring, or if you find a topic particularly challenging, you can adjust the amount of effort you put into reading it. In the same way that an author will adjust the amount of time, energy, and care devoted to writing about a particularly complicated idea, the reader can adjust the amount of time, attention, and care to take up more of the burden of understanding and, in doing so, help ensure communicative success. When communication fails in daily life, though, the consequences can be even more serious; failure of communication in a hospital, courtroom, squad car, or classroom can literally be a question of life or death.

Rejecting the gift: the individual's role in the communicative process

The most common rationalizations for discrimination against stigmatized accents and languages have to do with communication. "I've got nothing against [Taiwanese, Appalachians, Black people, female politicians]," the argument will go; "I just can't understand the way they talk." It is not hard to find people who won't hesitate to publicly reject, denigrate, and mock varieties of English other than their own. People also have no problem silencing voices that aren't in the imagined "standard" variety. Rather than try to understand and interact with someone, standard language ideology provides the additional option of rejecting everything a person says because of the way they say it with the added benefit of placing blame for the communication failure on the other person.

Communication seems to be a simple thing: one person talks and another listens; then they change roles. But the social space between two speakers is rarely neutral. Think of the people you have talked to today. Each time you begin an exchange, a complex series of calculations begins: Do I need to be formal with this person? Do I owe her respect? Does he owe me deference? Will she take me seriously or reject me out of hand? What do I want from them, or them from me? Those calculations are more conscious in unusual encounters; for example, if you suddenly were introduced to the Queen of England, without preparation, would you be comfortable talking to her? For people and social groups that you interact with every day, the calculations are fast and typically well below the level of consciousness. When people are confronted with a new person they want to, or must, talk to, an individual makes a quick series of social evaluations based on many cues: hair, clothing, skin tone, body language, affect, gender, body type, and attractiveness along with language and accent. On the phone, of course, nearly the only cues one gets are from the talker's voice.

In any situation, a person can simply refuse to communicate. In an adversarial position, one may understand perfectly what their partners, parents, and friends say to us but still respond with "I cannot understand you." One can also say "You just don't understand" when in fact the issue is not comprehension but difference of perspective. Lindemann (2003) explored interactions between "standard" English speakers and non-native English-speaking Korean students to look for a connection between negative attitudes and poor comprehension. In all cases where the native English speaker held neutral or positive attitudes about the Korean-accented English speaker, communication was successful and described as successful by the participants. In cases where the native English speaker held negative views, though, one-third of communication attempts failed, and, regardless of success or failure, all participants rated their communication as unsuccessful. Simply believing that someone will be difficult to understand impedes communication and constrains a person's ability to notice when communication is successful. When a person rejects another's message in this way, they are refusing to accept responsibility in the communicative act, and the full burden of ensuring that communication is successful is put directly on the other. "I can't understand you" may mean, in reality: "You can't make me understand you."

Any communicative act is based on a principle of mutual responsibility, in which participants in a conversation collaborate and cooperate in the transfer of information. This involves complicated processes of repair, expansion, and replacement that are repeated until both speakers feel the information at hand has been conveyed. When a person is confronted with a voice they perceive as somehow "incorrect" or "improper," the first decision they must make, consciously or not, is whether to participate in the interaction at all. What happens again and again in cases of language-based discrimination is that members of the more dominant language group in a particular interaction feel perfectly empowered to reject their communicative responsibility and to demand that the subordinate person carry the majority of the burden in the communicative act. Conversely, when both speakers have approximately the same level of social status, the first response is not to reject the communicative burden but to take other factors into consideration and to work harder at achieving understanding, even when one's conversation partner is legitimately difficult to understand.

Based on personal histories, backgrounds, and social selves, which together comprise a set of filters through which an individual hears the people they talk to, that person will take a communicative stance. Most of the time, people will agree to carry their share of the burden. Sometimes, if they are especially positive about the configuration of social characteristics of the person or if the purposes of communication are especially important to us, one may even accept a disproportionate amount of the burden. Figure 4.1 presents the concept of

Figure 4.1 The balancing act of the communicative burden

communicative burden as a balance. Carrying around negative opinions of one's communication partner increases the amount of effort the partner must exert (if they can!) to restore balance to the conversation. Accepting or rejecting the communicative burden shifts the load one's conversation partner must bear.

Speakers of varieties recognized as "standard" typically don't even realize that they are refusing to do their part to produce effective communication. After all, they are the one who is speaking "correctly." The fact that speakers of other varieties must struggle to be heard typically goes unnoticed. This affords speakers of the "standard" the privilege of deciding whether to listen. This an example of what Robin Queen (2019) calls "standard" *English privilege*, the set of social assumptions that afford additional opportunities and allowances that are unavailable to speakers of undervalued varieties of English. Those raised in communities where some variety of the "standard" was spoken have automatic social and economic advantages simply because of the language they were exposed to as a child.

Hesitance and uncertainty?

The truth is that employers, teachers, police officers, and really anyone who holds some kind of powerful position feels it is their right and their duty to hold those in lower positions to some kind of standard. The manager at McDonald's knows they must make sure their employees properly clean the ice cream machine. A sergeant must ensure that the soldiers beneath them adhere to the proper standards of behavior and dress. Language is no different. Speakers who believe themselves to be speakers of "standard" English feel it is their right and duty to ensure that others know and use "proper" grammar. But the judgment of another's grammar or accent has nothing to do with race, regional, or ethnic stereotypes occurs in the evaluation of female speech. Women (even those with "no regional accent," from the Midwest, with average or above average education, and so on) experience the power of language ideologies every time they open their mouths. Even in the cases where what comes out of their mouths is *exactly* like the speech of their male counterparts.

One example is the use of apologies. When men make apologies in the workplace, they typically go unnoticed, but an apology from a woman is likely to be seen as a sign of insecurity and a lack of assertiveness. Another important example is *creaky voice* (see Figure 4.2). This phenomenon, also called *laryngealization* or, derisively, "vocal fry," is a type of vocal production in which the cartilages that control the vocal folds are held tightly so that part of each vocal fold can vibrate freely while another part is restricted in its movement. In Figure 4.2 one can literally see the result of these tight vocal folds as vertical white lines in the spectrogram on the right. These are instances of air escaping through the glottis without vibrating the vocal folds. Compare this with the spectrogram on the left showing a non-creaky pronunciation of "eye." For the listener, the perception of the irregularity visible in the creaky spectrogram has been described as a rough popping or rattling sound. There is nothing dangerous, harmful, or even strange about this type of phonation. It is used stylistically in English, but the modal/creaky distinction also serves to distinguish different words from one another in languages all over the world like Mandarin Chinese, Hausa, Jalapa Mazatec, Montana Salish, and many others. It is a natural component of language. In American English, creaky voice is used approximately equally by men and women and can often be heard when someone is speaking in a low pitch, when they need to sound authoritative, and at the ends of phrases.

Despite being a natural part of the speech of both men and women, it is only women who receive scorn for it. The internet is filled with numerous attacks on only women for their use of this production type. The ironic fact is that creaky voice is very frequently used by young women to convey a kind of confidence or authority in what they are saying. Linguistic research on the feature (e.g., Pittam 1987; Henton & Bladon 1988; Gobl & Ní Chasaide 2003) has connected its use to masculinity, aggression, and authority. Podesva and Callier (2015) describe the association between masculinity and creaky voice as "iconic." Women's use, therefore, can be understood as an attempt to sound more authoritative (Dilley et al. 1996). For women, creaky voice offers the possibility of conveying assertiveness

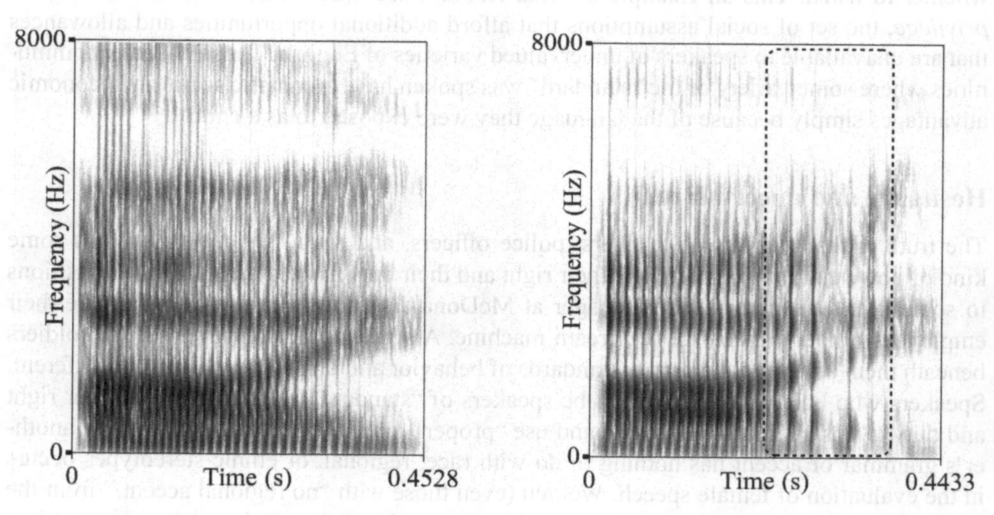

Figure 4.2 Spectrogram of the English word "eye" spoken in modal voicing (left) and creaky voicing (right)

and authority (the indexical meanings creaky voice carries when men use it) while avoiding more conventional ways of showing authority (ways that women know will be judged negatively).

Ultimately, such attempts at indexing authority tend to fail. Yuasa (2010: 316) found that while listeners' ratings of American women's creaky voice were basically positive in 2010, creak already sounded more "hesitant" and "informal" than non-creaky modal voice. During the early part of the 2010s, however, the positive associations appear to have faded. Lee (2016) asked listeners to rate both male and female speakers' modal and creaky speech. She found that while listeners rated both male and female speakers as more "masculine" they were also heard to be more "hesitant" and less "feminine," "educated," "confident," and "intelligent" when speaking in creaky voice, and these judgments were consistently harsher for the female speaker. The iconic masculinity that Podesva and Callier (2015) ascribe to creak simply does not appear to be compatible with contemporary American conceptualizations of female voice. The use of creaky voice among women, particularly young women, has become entangled with what Slobe (2018) has described as "pervasive anxieties surrounding girls' linguistic and social practice" rising, in the 2010s, to the level of a "moral panic."

Deficit vs. disorder

Creaky voice is one of the more recent phonation types to spark the ire of media and language mavens alike. They love to claim that using this vocal style is "bad for your voice" (even though no research confirms this). While there are certain pathological reasons that a speaker might need treatment (e.g., vocal-fold lesions, respiratory or neurological issues) with respect to this phonation type, speech pathologists (and their American professional organization, the American Speech and Hearing Association, or ASHA) recognize the difference between a speech deficit caused by a pathology and a speech difference such as the stylistic use of creaky phonation in American English. See Blum (2016) for a more intense discussion of this debate.

As discussed in Chapter 3, the issue of perceptions returns. The exact same linguistic feature is found in the speech of women and men but elicits wildly conflicting reactions. The same thing happens with other features, too: apologies, conversational interruptions, "uptalk," overlaps, and the use of obscenities. These are all features shared by both women and men. When men use them, these features usually go unnoticed. However, when women use the same features, the features are not only noticed but judged to reflect some negative attribute that women supposedly possess. In such cases, the indexical meanings available to men (to convey authority, assertiveness, etc.) are not acknowledged when women employ the same indexical signs. This is the typical double bind of sexism – women are ignored unless they speak like men, but if they speak like men, they are perceived negatively (as a "bitch" and so on). Again, negative evaluations of language often have nothing to do with language itself and *everything* to do with the identities of speakers. When a *he* uses creaky voice, it is "professional" and "authoritative," but when a *she* uses it, it suddenly suggests that she is "hesitant" or "untrustworthy."

Just women?

Listen to the episode of the radio show *This American Life* linked on the website for this book both to hear the complaints listeners feel comfortable associating with creaky voice but also to see if you can hear how much more creaky voice the show's male host, Ira Glass, actually uses than any of the female reporters. As they discuss themselves, the show receives a seemingly constant stream of complaints about creaky-voiced women and no commentary at all about the men. These complaints about creaky-voiced women are relatively new, but the stream of complaints, unfortunately, is not. Before listeners inundated podcasts with complaints about women creaking, they used to inundate radio stations with complaints about women using rising intonation – so-called "uptalk." In "uptalk," or more formally, high rising terminal (HRT) intonation, speakers use a rising pitch curve in a semantically declarative sentence. As with creaky voice today, in the heyday of uptalk complaints, most of the complaints were directed toward young women.

This is the real power of myths and ideologies. The relationship between language ideologies and social power is most clear in cases like these, where the features themselves are constant. Power is the only difference. Unfortunately, members of groups who look down on or feel superior to young women latch onto creaky voice and other linguistic features as the target of their ire. Today they dismiss the young woman for her creaky voice, but they also used to do this for uptalk, and in the future they will do it for some new imagined linguistic slight that becomes indexically linked to young women. On this basis, they reject the communicative burden and place the work of understanding and being understood entirely on the shoulders of the female speaker.

Standard language ideology

Standard language ideology is used to justify the subordination of anything other than "standard" English. The argument is that children must be able to read, speak, and understand "standard" English so that they will be productive members of society. This position is belied by studies demonstrating that identical coursework will receive lower grades and harsher teacher commentary when the purported name attached to the work suggests that the child is not from the dominant group (Harari & McDavid 1973; Anderson-Clark et al. 2008; Kaiser et al. 2009). Because the actual structure of a uniform "standard" is left vague and unspecified, whether something is "correct" comes to be subjective. The indexical associations of the name at the top of a paper can predict which papers will have the worst grammar. Regardless of the grammar they ultimately use, minority children are typically assumed to speak "bad" or "broken" English. This "bad" English serves as the basis for discrimination, even though the motivation for deciding their English is "bad" is founded in racism. Claims that the pressure to assimilate to "standard" English is fundamentally about communication, positive, and in the best interest of the child are difficult to sustain considering this deep-seated bias.

One of the ways that systemic racism persists is by creating obstacles that make it more difficult for minorities to gain access to the institutions that might allow one to change the system itself. Language becomes one of these obstacles. But overcoming the obstacle is tricky because the goal is a moving target; what "counts" as proper language remains vague and imprecise and regardless of how you say something, it will never be "heard" as being quite proper enough. Toni Morrison (1975) suggests that distractions such as "proper" English is perhaps the main ways in which racism persists:

> The function, the very serious function of racism is distraction. It keeps you from doing your work. It keeps you explaining, over and over again, your reason for being. Somebody says you have no language and you spend twenty years proving that you do. Somebody says your head isn't shaped properly so you have scientists working on the fact that it is. Somebody says you have no art, so you dredge that up. Somebody says you have no kingdoms, so you dredge that up. None of this is necessary. There will always be one more thing.

Saying that someone doesn't have language or can't learn grammar is no more reasonable than telling someone their head has the wrong shape or that they don't walk properly. The ubiquity of Standard Language Ideology results in a day-by-day, persistent devaluation of the social self, be it through résumé whitening that denies one's own name and unique experiences or by attempting to change one's voice to avoid being mocked. Because everyone has individual experiences of the language around them, each person recognizes a unique collection of potential indexical meanings. Language ideologies are therefore not always uniform across individuals or communities. Within any given society one can find assemblages of different language ideologies that reflect the diversity of experience and perspectives within that society. Such assemblages of language ideologies are a natural result of language being used across multiple contexts and communities. So, for example, the same linguistic variable may index different meanings for different participants in the same interaction. Your attempt to convey a polite and proper social persona may come across as stiff and boring to someone else. Awareness of the indexical meanings others probably link to you is the heart of DuBois's *double consciousness* (see Chapter 1). It is rarely a concern that native speakers of privileged varieties (i.e., close to the idealized "standard") face.

Society has begun to recognize the value of having multiple perspectives provided by a diverse set of voices with distinct cultural backgrounds. However, when it comes to language, most will happily insist that people conform to a single language ideology: one in which the language of some people is treated as if it were inherently better than the language of others. A claim that white people are inherently superior to others is rightly recognized as an obviously racist statement that many would deem unacceptable in public discourse. Yet the claim that the language (many) white people speak is inherently superior to the language of others is ubiquitous and inescapable. *Standard Language Ideology*, or the belief that there is a single "correct" way to speak English, silences the voices of those who do not speak the "standard." Of all the various language ideologies in American culture, Standard Language Ideology is not only the most powerful and the most widely accepted but also the one that causes the most damage. In this section, we outline the ways in which standard language ideology comes to enforce acts of language subordination.

A particular class of beliefs and expectations about language emerge from and create the notion that one particular variety of a spoken language is the "standard" variety. This ideology proposes that an idealized nation state has one perfect, homogenous language. That hypothetical, idealized language is how 1) d/Discourse is seized and 2) rationalizations for that seizure are constructed. It is also a fragile construct and one that needs constant and vigilant protection. This constant protection is perhaps most visible in online responses such as YouTube comments, Twitter, and the default Reddit subreddits. In these places, any deviation from the fragile standard, no matter how small, will be latched onto and attacked, sometimes by hordes of users all saying exactly the same thing about "they're vs. their vs. there" or "don't vs. doesn't." Notice that these threads typically pay so little attention to the actual content of the material being commented on that you can freely move them to any other video, article, or tweet with no apparent loss of coherence. Such comments are not about communication or comprehension, as the "correct" forms do nothing to improve understanding. Compare, for example, spoken English where listeners have no problem understanding which *there/their/they're* a speaker intends even though the orthographic differences are unmarked.

It might be argued that in American culture, which obliges everyone to participate in the educational system, everyone has access to public d/Discourse and the opportunity to learn "proper" English. But the educational system is the heart of the standardization process. Children who do not approximate the school's idea of "standard" English will not find acceptance and validation in the schools and to suggest otherwise is, in a word, ludicrous. A child who tells their stories in stigmatized varieties of English is quickly corrected. They must assimilate or fall silent. These children are rarely given an explanation of why something they said was "wrong." They are left to sort through the maze of red ink, hoping to understand exactly why the language they use is wrong. Sledd (1988) sees this as an institutionalized policy to formally initiate children into the linguistic prejudices (and hence, Standard Language Ideology) of the middle classes. The imposition of Standard Language Ideology may also lead minority children to feel that school is an unwelcoming environment, a place where every time you open your mouth you are silenced and told that you are wrong. The well-intended goal of teaching "standard" English results in teaching some children that they do not belong and that their very identity is unacceptable. Speakers of undervalued varieties of English learn early in life that their language is going to hold them back.

Fighting back!

In 2014, Oak Ridge National Laboratory in Tennessee announced a short course on "Southern Accent Reduction" to be offered to employees wanting to get rid of their Southern drawls. They had hired a professional accent reduction trainer to help employees "[f]eel confident in a meeting when you need to speak with a more neutral American accent, and be remembered for what you say and not how you say it." While the origination of the request for such an offering came directly from one employee, the introduction of this new "opportunity" sparked outrage among many employees who objected to the course and felt offended that the company would even suggest it. The lab canceled the course.

Standard language ideology reproduces forms of everyday prejudice and makes them palatable because they are "about" language (rather than gender, race, age, etc.). Communication between speakers of different varieties of English may indeed be difficult or fail entirely. In many cases though, possibly even most cases, breakdown of communication is due not to a speaker's accent or linguistic difficulty but to negative social evaluations of the speaker or listener in question and a rejection, typically because of Standard Language Ideology, of one participant's part of the communicative burden. In effect, this ideology makes it acceptable to ignore the voices of certain groups and to block them from public discourse. Standard Language Ideology does not ensure that communication in American society flows more easily. On the contrary, it is a tool used to silence minority voices and to maintain control over public discourse. As we have seen, racism is maintained through Discourses that encode stereotypes in ways that some people might find difficult to recognize.

Table 4.1 presents a model of the process of language subordination. The first stage of the model is the formation of social categorizations (discussed in Chapter 2). Racial categories differ from culture to culture, and the racial categories active in a society have no biological basis; they are created and maintained through language. In the next stage of the model, these social categories become entrenched through repeated use of *indexicality* linking signs (including, but not limited to, language) with a range of possible indexical meanings that may mark various aspects of an interaction (including, for example, the race of speakers). Over time these indexical meanings come to form sets that work together to create stereotypes characterizing various social groups.

This ideological relationship is like the definition of *indexicality* given earlier which produces links between signs and attributes of social structures. These signs do not have to be specific to language. For example, an indexical relationship could produce links connecting things like an inability to dance or love of mayonnaise with whiteness. This pattern serves as the basis for racial stereotyping and, in turn, patterns of discrimination.

Table 4.1 The processes of language subordination

Social categorization is constructed.
There are differences such as race, gender, age, ethnicity, and regional or national origin that exist and define who you are and what you are capable of. It is right to rise above your social categorization and conform to the standard.

Social groups are linked to ways of speaking.
Due to the linking of particular indexical meanings to ways of speaking, the way you talk is reflective of the social groups to which you belong.

Language is mystified.
You can never hope to comprehend the difficulties and complexities of your mother tongue without expert guidance.

Authority is claimed.
We are the experts. Talk like me/us. We know what we are doing because we have studied language, because we write well.

Misinformation is generated.
Your usage is inaccurate. The variant I prefer is superior on historical, aesthetic, or logical grounds.

Targeted languages are trivialized.
Look how cute, how homey, how funny.

Conformers are held up as positive examples.
See what you can accomplish if you only try, how far you can get if you see the light.

Non-conformers are vilified or marginalized.
See how willfully stupid, arrogant, unknowing, uninformed, and/or deviant these speakers are.

Explicit promises are made.
Employers will take you seriously; doors will open.

Threats are made.
No one important will take you seriously; doors will close.

As these indexical signs come to form a system of relationships that link various attributes with members of different social categories, one can think of ideologies as the matrix of indexical signs (and the relationships between them) that construct social reality and define perceptions of oneself and of others. As we saw in the discussion of categorizations, categories are built upon the attributes of a prototypical member. When this cognitive process is applied to racial categories, the imagined "prototypical" member becomes the type of person who fits all the (often racist) stereotypes associated with a category. These connections become solidified through discourses that present incessant instances of these indexical relationships.

Ultimately, people have typically seen various indexical relationships play out so many times that they may automatically come to mind when they interact with individuals from social groups that they may not be familiar with. Because these indexical relationships are so pervasive in Discourse, they may result in forms of discrimination that go unquestioned or even unrecognized. The repeated reproduction of these indexical relationships means that they become part of one's habitual thought processes, even if unconsciously. Even if people are careful to avoid using particular racist words or ideas, the traces of racial ideologies may surface in other ways, such as through microaggressions or "dog whistles." Indexical signs have *potential* meanings that may resonate in different ways across different contexts. It is this slippery nature of indexical possibility that allows forms of discrimination to persist despite laws enacted in the hope of bending the arc of the moral universe toward justice.

The process of language subordination requires that language be mystified as speakers are told that they don't understand the structure of their language enough to know when they are wrong. The fact is that people do communicate with each other effectively in vernacular varieties, and they do so daily with no need for specialized or explicit knowledge of language. The claim that spoken language is so complex that mere native speakers can never sort things out for themselves is countered by the evidence of common experience, but the mystification message is so strong that many people believe they don't speak their own language well.

This lack of knowledge means that one must rely on experts to let them know that they are wrong and that effective communication is only available to those who follow their guidance. Such experts are usually self-appointed. This knowledge of "right" and "wrong" is not based on any linguistic facts. Instead, the way that an "expert" typically speaks serves as the basis for their judgments of what is "(in)correct." They claim authority because they are confident that their speech is superior to other varieties. As this authority is not based on actual knowledge of linguistics, it requires the sustained production of false information about language. Misinformation about language becomes so common that most people find it acceptable to have negative (prejudicial) evaluations of the ways of speaking that have been mislabeled as "bad" or "broken" English.

Once the purported inferiority of certain varieties of English is widely accepted, ostracizing speakers who use those varieties becomes socially acceptable. These undervalued varieties of English come to be trivialized. Speakers of these varieties deserve to be mocked and ridiculed for the way that they speak. Representations of speakers of different varieties typically treat speakers of more "standard" varieties as role models for others to follow – *He's so articulate* or *Her English is so good.* Of course, such praise for those who command "standard" English is accompanied by the vilification of speakers who do not conform to ideologies of "proper" English. The denigration of non-native speakers and speakers of non-standard varieties allows others to drop their share of the communicative burden if their interlocutor speaks "bad" English.

People resist standard language ideology in a variety of ways. Art, literature, and music that celebrate undervalued Englishes are forms of resistance against the idea that only one "standard" language variety can be "beautiful" or "poetic." But standard language ideology is so pervasive that there are contexts where resistance is not an option. Imagine trying to explain to a potential employer that your language is acceptable even though it is not "proper." For speakers of undervalued Englishes, language subordination is inevitable. Speakers of stigmatized Englishes are promised large returns if they will just adopt "standard" English. They may be told that if they hope to have any success in life, they must first change the way they speak. In contrast, those who persist in their allegiance to undervalued varieties of English are threatened. They are told that without "better" English they will be cut off from the everyday privileges and rights of citizenship at every turn, regardless of inherent talent or intelligence. Of course, even if one does work to learn the "standard," their speech may be perceived as unacceptable not because of its structure but because of the speaker's assumed social categorization.

Confronting ideologies

Adherents of "standard" English typically have strong negative reactions to any attempt to cast a stigmatized variety in a positive or legitimate light. Dominant institutions lead the charge in cases like these, and the results are loud and shrill. More than 50 years of empirical work in sociolinguistics has established that language variation is neither an exotic feature of obscure dialects nor the result of "lazy" or "uneducated" speakers. Language variation is a core feature of how every living language works. This variation is central; it marks a language as robust and alive, and the variation itself carries meaning. Things like speech sounds, words, and sentence structures mark social attributes in meaningful ways. Whether people are aware of it, they use variation in language to construct themselves as social beings, to signal not only who they are but who they are not, who they want to be and who they do not want to be. Speakers choose among the available constructions, words, and sounds to create, in the minds of their listeners and for themselves, the identity they wish to convey. The choice may be to use a form or to strictly avoid a form that might send the wrong signal about the speaker. Both are meaningful choices. The choice itself can be conscious, although it is more likely to happen entirely below the level of conscious awareness. Either way, these choices group together into styles which are usually recognizable and interpretable to other speakers in the community. This process is a functional and necessary part of the way people live and interact. It is an essential feature of spoken language and of meaning more generally – not an optional one.

When a person is asked to reject their own language, they are being asked to drop allegiances to the people and places that define them as an individual. One doesn't – and cannot – ask a person to change the color of their skin, their religion, or their physical abilities. It is controversial when laws require people to use a bathroom that does not match their gender, but people routinely demand that others suppress or deny their native accent: the most effective way humans have of situating themselves socially in the world. Consider these possible utterances and ask yourself what each one is really communicating:

1. I don't care about the color of your skin but go talk like that someplace where it won't insult my ears.
2. You were a successful engineer in Ukraine, sure, but why can't you speak real English?
3. If you just didn't sound so cornpone, people would take you seriously.

4. Please take this woman off the radio, it sounds like she's gargling gravel when she talks.
5. You're the best salesperson we've got, but do you have to sound so gay?

What can utterances like these really tell us about the ideologies of the person speaking them? Take the first one, for example. Regardless of your own race and social background, chances are you have heard or even said something like this at some point. Given the history and culture of the United States, can the first part of this utterance really be true? Particularly when followed by the second half of the utterance, revealing negative language ideologies, but also just as a general statement. Is it likely that someone who feels comfortable saying such things actually "don't care about the color of your skin"?

I'm not racist, but . . .

Sociologist Eduardo Bonilla-Silva (2003) has studied the discourse associated with *color-blind racism*, or uses of language that attempt to deny the potentially racist indexical associations they convey. Phrases like *I'm not racist, but . . .* attempt to preempt the interpretation of one's words as indicating that one is, indeed, racist. This particular example has become so common that it is readily recognized as insincere. One user on urbandictionary.com defines *I'm not racist, but* as "Something an idiot says just before making a comment that proves the idiot is, in fact, a racist." Even so, there are many people who claim to "not see color." Even if it could be true, proclaiming that one is entirely "color-blind" does nothing to reduce or prevent racism. It simply claims to ignore the racist indexical meanings that occur throughout public discourse, which is no better than denying racism as a social problem.

When you look closely at language-focused discrimination like the list of examples earlier, you will, of course, recognize that it is not language per se that is the target of complaint; instead, it is the speaker's statements and beliefs about *language* that reflect their implicit and explicit beliefs, their ideologies, about *people* and the culture they are a part of. These sets of ideologies not only shape the way speakers and listeners talk to or about one another but may also influence the success or failure of any attempt to communicate.

None of this is to say that there are no rules to language use or that people are free to communicate with whatever forms or usages strike their fancy in the moment. Rather, choice among linguistic variants is always constrained by who the speaker is, how they hope others see them, and the context within which they are communicating. This is not just true of "standard" English; this is true of all language varieties. At the end of the previous paragraph that contains the list of utterances, we used *don't* in a context where "standard" English would require *doesn't*. Did you notice it? If you didn't notice it, why do you think that is? If you did notice it, how did it make you feel? We were careful to do this in a way that was clearly and unavoidably an error (incorporating quoted material in a way that violates the syntax of the sentence). Throwing in a single form that is incongruent with established expectations is a stylistic choice one might make, in speaking or writing, but it is always meaningful. If the use of *don't* above upset you, you might should ask yourself how come do you care so much what sort of English people use if you can understand what they mean?

Dominant institutions promote the notion of an overarching, homogenous standard language based primarily on (the imagined speech of) white, upper middle-class, straight, cisgender males and derived from an imagined middle-America devoid of people of color, immigrants, women, or LGBTQ+ people. Whether the issues at hand are large-scale and sociopolitical in nature or more subtle, whether the approach is coercion or consent, there are two sides to this process: first, devaluation of all that is not (or does not seek to be) politically, culturally, or socially marked as belonging to the privileged class, and second, validation of the social (and linguistic) values of the dominant institutions.

The process of linguistic assimilation to an abstracted standard is portrayed as natural, necessary, and even positive for the greater social good. In addition to its power to deny access and create obstacles for specific groups of speakers, Standard Language Ideology licenses the practice of ignoring or rejecting speakers who use a stigmatized language variety. Listeners may "shut down" and refuse to interact with someone based on that person's variety of English. It provides speakers of the "standard" with the privilege of deciding when they want to interact with people different from themselves.

What we have attempted to demonstrate is that suppression of socially meaningful linguistic variation – everything from seemingly benign commentary to physical violence – in favor of a mythical standard variety is unavoidably about suppressing the kinds of people who (are presumed to) speak in ways that are widely denigrated. Precisely *because* choice of linguistic variants is constrained by who we are, the life we have experienced, and the context within which we are communicating, subordinating particular linguistic variants, barring them from use in everyday contexts, is using language ideology to subordinate people.

Discussion questions

1. As we'll continue to see in later chapters, people are pretty good at discerning certain information about other speakers, even given very little linguistic information to go on. Is it problematic in and of itself to be able to know someone's race, ethnicity, etc. from hearing them talk? When does being able to notice such information become discriminatory?
2. We have seen several distinct slogans created by civil rights activists: "Black Lives Matter," "I AM a man," "A man was lynched yesterday," "Say their names," etc. What aspects of dominant racial discourse do these slogans challenge? What sort of patterns within discourse structural racism do they attempt to undermine?
3. Children come to school speaking whatever language varieties they hear at home and in their communities. This is true for all language varieties: Italian, Japanese, Cherokee, American Sign Language, Appalachian English, Jewish American English, etc. In what ways could we consider undervalued Englishes spoken at school as similar to languages other than English spoken in American schools? In what ways are these scenarios different? Why?
4. When interacting with someone for the first time, how do you know what term of address to use? Should you use titles like Mrs., Dr., or Rev.? Should you use their first name? Should you use a nickname or a shortened version of their name? What would you do if someone used the "wrong" address form for you? What would you do if someone corrected your choice of address term?
5. Most people who complain about creaky voice and uptalk in the voices of female broadcasters will vehemently disagree with the idea that they are actually complaining about

the gender of the speaker rather than the linguistic facts of the situation. From the *This American Life* story linked on the website for this book, what evidence can you find to support or refute this claim? While thinking about uptalk, notice that most questions in English *do not*, in fact, rise at the end. Compare "When was George Washington president?" or "Who is buried in Grant's tomb?" to "Do you understand what I'm saying?" or "Can you hear me?"

5 Place-based variation in the American context

The social meaning of place

There is a common belief that regional differences in American English are eroding, and that, as time passes, people will all sound more and more alike. Broadcast, print, and social media outlets are believed to be the power that fuels this march toward homogeneity, and remarks on this topic show up in letters to the editor, on discussion forums, in human interest news stories, and on blogs. Though many linguists would call such a belief one of the more pervasive of the language myths (e.g., Chambers & Trudgill 1998), the full impact of such media on language is understudied in sociolinguistics (e.g., Stuart-Smith 2007; see Chapter 12 for more on language and media).

It is unclear who originated the idea that media destroys regional variation, but one can say with certainty that regional varieties of English are *not* becoming more alike over time, despite mass communication. It seems so intuitive that media would erode regional differences, but intuition is a terrible way to do science. Hard evidence makes it clear that just the opposite is true. Regional varieties of American English are changing, and many of the changes in progress are causing differences to intensify rather than diminish. Of course, regional dialects show internal variation with individual speakers adopting or rejecting innovations to convey a unique social persona. Regional dialects also interact with other types of variation in different ways. As with much social science research, discussions of regional variation have a history of being based on a limited population of (usually white) speakers. As you read through these descriptions of regional varieties, remember that regional dialects contain internal variation that may index social factors beyond region. Because of interactions between varieties and distinct histories, patterns of regional variation may differ for speakers of different genders, classes, or ethnicities. For example, many features categorized as "Southern" are maintained by African Americans outside of the South.

NORMs

Early work in American regional dialects sought out what they called NORMs as research participants – **n**ative (to the region), **o**ld, **r**ural **m**en – because they were thought to have the speech variety that was the most conservative (which is to suggest "unchanging" and therefore close to the "real" dialect of the area). The choice of name, therefore, is not coincidental; these early researchers saw the speech of NORMs as the "norm" against which all other varieties (for example, those of newcomers, young

DOI: 10.4324/9781003332886-5

people, urban people, and women) would be compared. As might be expected, these participants were also usually white. Later work, especially that conducted within the Linguistic Atlas Project, sought to broaden the subject pool so as to represent more of the voices that make up American Englishes.

There have been several research projects focusing on regional variation in American English. The largest of these is the Linguistic Atlas Project, which has been conducting dialect surveys for almost 100 years. Another is the Dictionary of American Regional English (DARE) project, which works to compile and update a comprehensive dictionary of regionalisms. *The Atlas of North American English* (Labov et al. 2006) provides a snapshot of regional dialect variation in the urban areas of the United States and Canada based primarily on phone interviews collected between 1992 and 1999. The results of this project are shown in the map in Figure 5.1. The linguists who contributed to the identification of dialect areas do so on the basis of the boundaries of bundles of linguistic features (or *isoglosses*) that constitute a kind of fluid linguistic border. Some of the changes in progress discussed in this chapter may seem unlikely to you, but upon closer examination you will probably recognize most of them from your own experiences.

Because these various types of variation typically cluster together across communities of speakers, variables come to cluster together as well, producing a distinct variety of English – what linguists call a *dialect*. A dialect is a particular variety of a language that varies by any number of social features (like region, age, race, etc.), and like other linguistic varieties, dialects are complex, subtle, rich, powerful, and completely adequate for meeting the communicative needs of their speakers. Variation is intrinsic to all spoken language at every level, and virtually all forms of variation index some form of social meaning.

As shown in Chapter 4, language variation is a fact of life. All language varieties are equally systematic, which means they are all rule-based. There are no grammarless languages. The same is true for dialects. Every facet of a dialect can vary. The words we choose, the sounds we use, the meanings we make – from region to region you can find a wide range of different linguistic phenomena, and it is most likely that, as a native speaker of that language, you'll still have no trouble understanding. Some of this variation is stable, like, for example, the pronunciation of a word like *walking* as *walkin'* (with an alveolar [n] rather than the velar [ŋ]). Its pattern of usage in countless dialects (and across various speech situations) is predictable. In an utterance like *They hit my friggin' car!*, for example, one might be surprised to hear a speaker use the -ing [ŋ] variant. Other linguistic variables are in flux, undergoing a change in progress. Examples of this type can be seen in some of the characteristics of the Southern Vowel Shift (described further in this chapter).

The study of dialects and dialectal variation is important for a number of reasons. Like all of linguistics, dialectology helps linguists determine what is possible in human language and adds to the body of knowledge concerning both linguistic description and human cognition. And if every dialectologist were to be honest, you would find that many of them, like many others, are simply fascinated by dialects. But their fascination goes beyond that of the hobbyist; as experts in the field of study, dialectologists are charged with holding steadfast to the idea that all languages vary, all languages are structured, and all languages are equal in their ability to convey human experience and thought. It is crucial for the dialectologist to

Figure 5.1 Dialect regions as defined by *The Atlas of North American English*

Source: adapted from Labov et al. (2006: 148)

separate fact from fiction, keeping personal biases (everyone has them) out of the research picture. If they are successful, the research conducted by dialectologists can have important implications in many areas. In particular, dialectal research is important in correcting bias in education, particularly in testing and assessing language education, literacy skills, speech disorders, and so on. So when dialectologists study language variation, they are looking at more than just whether you say *coke*, *soda*, or *pop*. While lexical variation is one of the more common features people think of when they think of dialects, as we will see, the variation apparent in American English includes not only differences in word choice, but also differences in phonetics, phonology, syntax, word structure, and every other aspect of language.

Regional varieties of American English

All languages with living speakers constantly undergo change. Changes spread unevenly across speakers and geographic areas so that clusters of variables tend to develop among groups of people who interact with one another regularly. Because geography is a strong determiner of who individuals see and interact with, dialects tend to develop in specific regions. There is a strong analogy to be made to Charles Darwin's observation of more than a dozen distinct species of finches in and around the Galápagos. When geography divides and redivides members of a single species of birds, there is a proliferation of new species that evolves. The same is true in language: a distinctive dialect of a language may emerge due not only to physical barriers but also social and ideological ones. In the specific case of American regional variation, historical factors like settlement and migration patterns across the country, geographic factors like the presence of rivers and mountains, and social factors like the use of another language nearby have all had some impact on the Englishes spoken in the United States today. And despite the fact that the advent of the internet and other mass communications technologies have made it easier to communicate over longer distances, dialects do not appear to be on the decline. If anything, one might say dialects are actually becoming more distinct, not less (Ho 2011). One shining example of this kind of variation can be found in the American South (see Figure 5.2), the region that has been given the most attention by American dialectologists.

There are a few features that almost all the Southern varieties of American English have in common and that are salient and distinct markers of the South. These are three of many features that outsiders will try to use when imitating someone from the South. That is, this is what most Northerners expect to hear when venturing South of the Mason-Dixon line:

1. The "pen/pin merger" where the /ɛ/ vowel (in *pet*) merges with the /ɪ/ vowel (in *pit*) when it occurs before a nasal consonant (such as [m], [n], or [ŋ]). This means that *pen* sounds the like *pin* ([pɪn]), and *hem* sounds like *him* ([hɪm]).
2. The monophthongization of /ai/ to /a:/ as in the words *tie* [tai] and *dime* [daim], which will sound something like "tah" ([ta:]) and "dahm" ([da:m]).
3. *You all* or *y'all* (rather than *you*) for the second person plural pronoun.

Although there are other features that occur within the South, these variables seem to be most associated with the region, at least for outsiders. The correlation between the pen/pin merger and the South, for example, is shown in Figure 5.3.

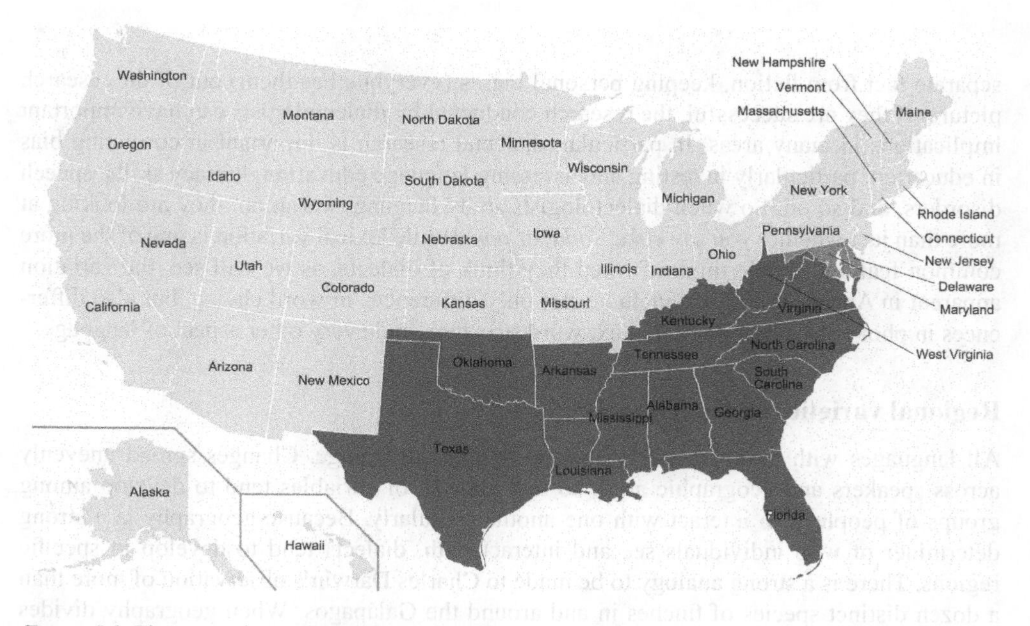

Figure 5.2 The states that make up the American South

Source: adapted from an image by Gigillo83

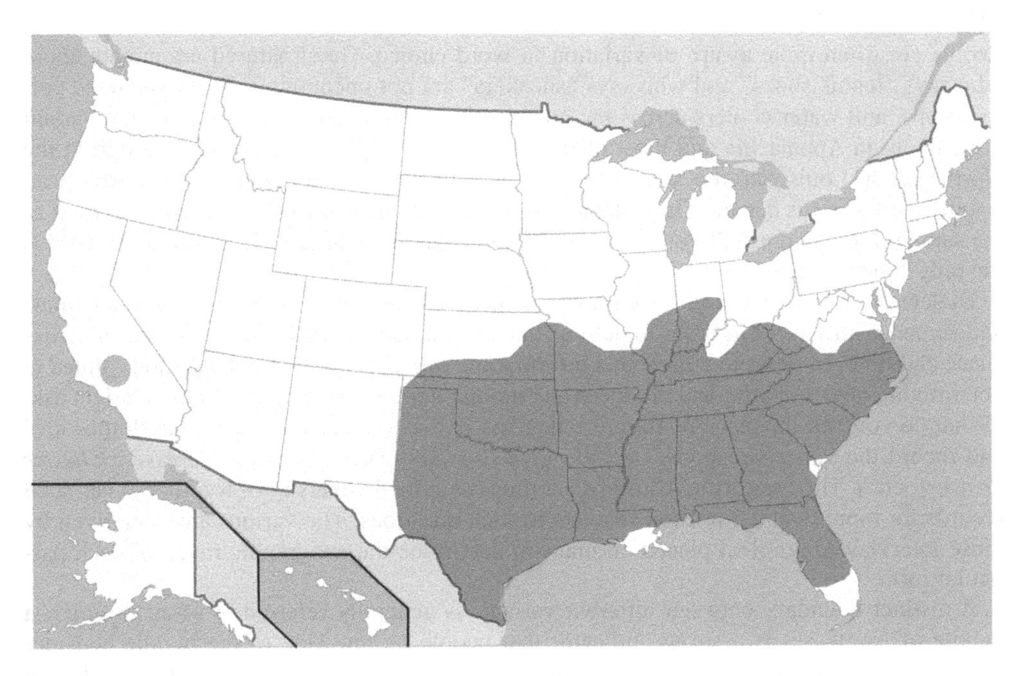

Figure 5.3 Geographic distribution of the pen/pin merger

Source: adapted from an image by Ras67

There are, of course, other variables that index social identities within the South and other variables that convey Southernness. This doesn't mean that everyone in the South will speak with these variables. Many Southerners who do use these variables don't use all of them all of the time. The relationship is indexical so that these variables may mean different things across different contexts. This is because, as we've discussed, all dialects contain variation and linguistic forms that index regional identities interact with forms that index other aspects of identity, such as ethnicity or gender.

In addition to geographic factors, regional dialects may be shaped by historical and political forces as well. For example, a number of features traditionally described as Southern also occur in African American communities outside the South. Thus, while the greatest dialectal division for white speakers is between Northern and Southern varieties, patterns of regional variation in African American communities follow historical patterns of movement during the Great Migration of African Americans moving out of the South in the first half of the 20th century. Because of different migration patterns, regional differences across African American communities show greater differences between the Eastern and Central regions of the country. Thus, the forms found in Mississippi extend north to St. Louis, Chicago, and Detroit. In contrast, the forms found in Georgia typically extend north to Philadelphia and New York (Jones 2015).

In what follows, we outline some of the regional linguistic features of several dialects of American English with which readers might be familiar, as well as some that usually hide from non-linguists' conscious awareness. It is our hope that this discussion will reveal the systematicity of dialectal variation, casting aside the notion that variation from a standard entails a lack of a grammar. As we have seen, all language varieties have grammar.

Spread the word

People are often quite aware of variation in word choice. Good-natured arguments about who says "tennis shoes" and who says "sneakers" are not uncommon. At universities, coffee shops, and water coolers across the country, discussions on the use of *pop* (the variant most likely in Appalachia and most of the Midwest) versus *soda* (the variant found in the Northeast, St. Louis, and the Southwest) versus *coke* (the variant common in the American South) spark serious debate. These debates center on people using different words to refer to the same thing – and usually on the idea that someone in the argument is sure their word is the only "correct" one.

Dialectologists map out the geographic distribution of different words, pronunciations, and sentence structures in order to help us understand patterns of language variation across space and time. In order to collect this information, linguists ask pointed questions aimed at determining how an individual produces a particular item. For example, a linguist might ask, "What do you call the piece of furniture that has drawers for you to keep your clothes in?" and record the various responses people give (*bureau*, *chest of drawers*, *dresser*, *Chester drawers*, etc.). The Linguistic Atlas Project (housed at the University of Kentucky) has such records for more than 2.5 million answers to such questions. The various answers given by those interviewed are then placed on maps to determine the geographic range of each particular form.

A distinct boundary between different variants is generally referred to as an *isogloss*; a bundle of isoglosses is a strong indicator that people on one side of the bundle consider themselves different (at least linguistically) from people on the other side of the bundle. On maps with isoglosses, each line represents a border between linguistic variables. Those on one side say X while those on the other side say Y. So you could have an isogloss for where people say *coke* vs. *pop*, indicating the general regional distribution of such terms. Isoglosses marking these different boundaries bundle together following a general pattern that allows us to see certain language practices to be shared within a similar geographic space.

Figure 5.4 Taste of Dahntahn, a restaurant in Pittsburgh

Source: photo by Doug Kerr

Of course, one way in which lexical variation has been studied is to see how use of regionally-marked lexical items like these may contribute to the construction of a local identity associated with a specific place. For example, the regional dialect of the Pittsburgh, PA, area is known for regional words (like *gumband* and *slippy*) and specific pronunciations, such as the change of the diphthong vowel [aʊ] (as in "town") becoming a monophthong [a:] (similar to what happens to [aɪ] in the South; see Figure 5.4). Speakers use these words and pronunciations to differentiate "Pittsburghese" from other varieties of English (Johnstone 2006, 2013).

Do you speak Pittsburghese?

The following words typically occur on t-shirts, posters, and mugs depicting the local dialect. How much Pittsburghese do you know? (Answers appear below.)

1. babushka
2. flanken
3. gutchies
4. gumband
5. slippy
6. yinz
7. worsh
8. stillers
9. nebby
10. jagoff
11. jaggers
12. sammitch
13. dahntahn
14. redd up

Answers:

1. a head scarf
2. a type of steak
3. underwear
4. rubber band
5. slippery
6. y'all
7. wash
8. Steelers
9. nosy
10. a jerk
11. thorns
12. sandwich
13. downtown
14. clean up

Researchers at the University of Pittsburgh have put together an online dictionary of items of speech, including additional resources like a discussion of the history of language in the area, podcasts about the variation present, and much more.

Although such popular depictions of local dialect are usually presented as lists of words, dialects are much more than words. There are pronunciation, syntactic, and other features that go along with Pittsburghese. On t-shirts, posters, and other public depictions of Pittsburghese, for example, phonetic variation is often presented as if it were actually lexical variation. The "word" *dahntahn* is simply the word *downtown* written to reflect the monophthongization of [aʊ]. Similarly, *worsh* is the local form for *wash*, and *stillers* is simply the local pronunciation of *Steelers* (a vowel merger also found in the pronunciation of pairs like *deal* and *dill*).

The treatment of phonological variation as differences in vocabulary reflects the fact that many people tend to think of dialects as different "words" rather than recognizing the full range of phonological and syntactic variation that distinguishes dialects. However, even just considering the words of Pittsburghese, one can see elements of the city's history through the dialect's borrowings from other languages and dialects. For example, borrowings that index a Pittsburgh identity highlight the influence of immigrants from Eastern Europe, particularly Jewish immigrants fleeing oppressive governments. Thus, words that have likely been borrowed from languages like Yiddish and Ukrainian are apparent. Examples include *babushka* (from the word for grandmother in Russian), *flanken* (likely borrowed from Yiddish), and *gutchies* (likely borrowed from Ukrainian). Other common sources for forms that came to be associated with Pittsburgh are Irish and Scottish dialects of English. Examples include *slippy*, *redd up*, and *yinz* (from "you-inz," itself a condensing of "you ones," both serving as a second person plural pronoun). The use of some version of "you-inz" for the second person plural is not unique to Pittsburgh, and it can be found in other parts of Appalachia (sometimes as "you'uns"). This overlap results both from early settlement in western Pennsylvania and Central Appalachia and from migration to Pittsburgh from areas to the southeast, like Kentucky and West Virginia. Thus, words like *you-inz* or *buggy* (shopping cart) can be found well beyond Pittsburgh, often by people with relatives who moved to Pittsburgh many years ago. This migration from Appalachia is the source for the pejorative term for southwestern Pennsylvania as "Pennsytucky."

Same or different?

Some varieties feature a distinction between [ɔ] and [ɑ] while others do not. Say these pairs of words out loud. Do these pairs sound the same or different to you?

[ɔ]	[ɑ]
taught	tot
dawn	Don
sawed	sod
caught	cot
bought	(ro)bot
wrought	rot
hawk	hock
law	la

As the idea of Pittsburghese as a unique dialect has gained in popularity, beliefs about what "counts" as part of that dialect have solidified (Johnstone 2013). Forms of variation come to indexically mark local identity, clustering together to form a stereotype of the language associated with the social category of Pittsburgher (see Chapter 2). Thus, Pittsburghers have appropriated items not unique to the city to mean "Pittsburghness," and they wear that badge proudly. This, of course, further solidifies the local dialect as people come to use forms of variation they come to associated with local identity. This is part of the regular cycle of language change found in all varieties of all languages. The distinctive regional varieties of American English differ in terms of changes that took place across certain regions, as well as changes that are currently spreading across different parts of the country.

Vowels on the move

Words are just one way that languages vary. The most common comments made about someone's dialect usually have to do with their accent, or the way they sound. And those comments are often specifically directed at a person's vowels. The vowels are said to be the patterns that "differentiate regional dialects of English on this continent" (Labov et al. 2006: 4). And in those regional dialects, the vowels are on the move. In order to understand the ways in which vowels are moving, we need to explain a bit about how the articulation of vowels occurs within the mouth. Figure 5.5 is an abstraction of the shape of the human mouth that indicates the point of articulation for individual vowels. Any vowel can be described by its place of articulation (although a close transcription requires additional features be identified). To the right of the vowel chart is a list of example words featuring each sound.

While the vowel chart presents a static, clean picture of vowel behavior, what we know is that most American varieties exhibit shifting or shifted vowels, so that most speakers speak with vowels that do not pattern in the same way as depicted in Figure 5.5. Often, when people say that someone has an "accent," they are reacting to these different patterns of vowel articulation. For many speakers of English, the [ɔ] vowel (as in *caught*) has merged with the [ɑ] vowel (as in *cot*). Linguists often call this the caught/cot merger. If the names *Don* and *Dawn* sound the same to you, then these vowels are merged in your variety of English.

Speakers with merged vowels have difficulty hearing the difference other speakers make between pairs like *sawed* and *sod*, and actually producing the difference may seem like an impossible task. Many people pass through life without noticing whether the people they are talking to distinguish between these two vowels. They understand what people are saying without even noticing if they have one vowel or two. This is just part of the natural variation

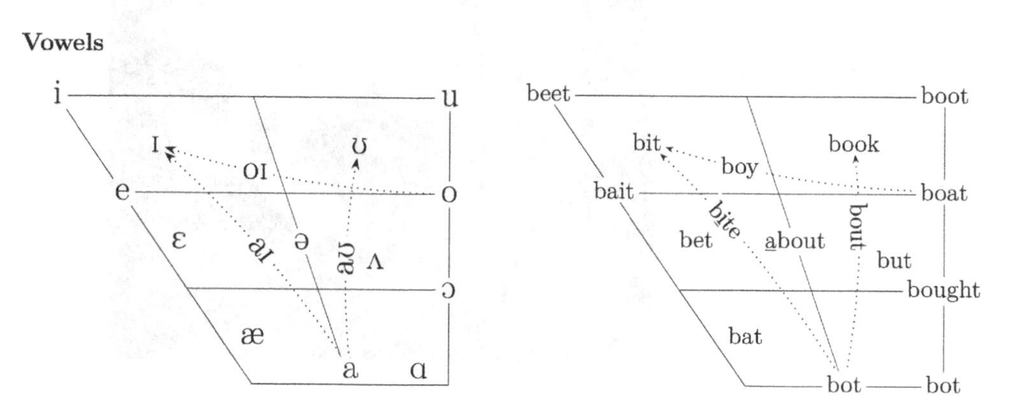

Figure 5.5 English vowels and sample words

found in all languages. For speakers who have the caught/cot merger, the change has occurred in every word in the language. That is, speakers don't have [ɔ] in some words, but [ɑ] in others; they have [ɑ] in all the words where other speakers might have [ɔ]. Other changes in vowels may be constrained by the consonants nearby. For example, the pen/pin merger (described earlier) only occurs before the nasal consonants [m, n, ŋ]. Other mergers include [æ] merging with [ɛ] before /ɹ/ (so that *Aaron* sounds the same as *Erin*) and the merger of [i] and [ɪ] before /l/ (so that, as in Pittsburgh, *deal* sounds the same as *dill*, as in Figure 5.6).

The distribution of the caught/cot merger cuts across the middle of the eastern United States (starting in western Pennsylvania) but covers almost all of the western part of the country (except for parts of San Francisco). The regions above and below the caught/cot region in the East are marked by two distinctive vowel shifts. Dialectologists refer to these vowel changes as the Northern Cities Shift (NCS) and the Southern Vowel Shift (SVS). In the NCS, six vowels have been shifting (Figure 5.7) in a kind of domino effect in a large part of the Midwest, as seen in Figure 5.8 (Gordon 2001).

Figure 5.6 "I'm kind of a big dill" shirt

Source: image courtesy of Jennifer Cramer

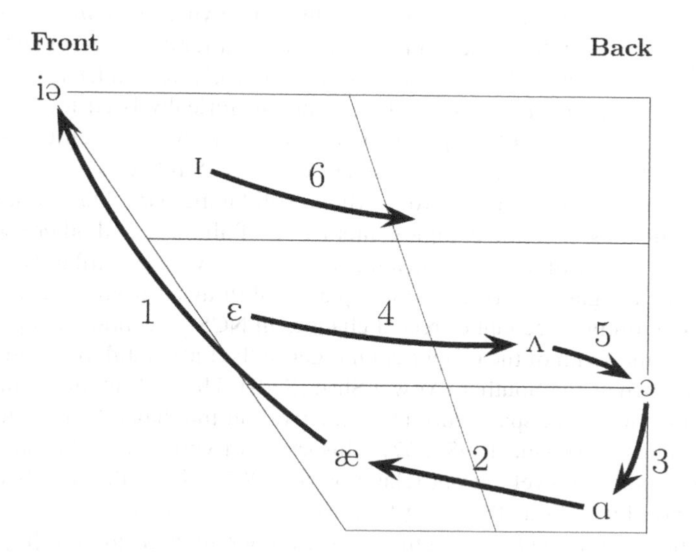

Figure 5.7 Patterns of the Northern Cities Shift

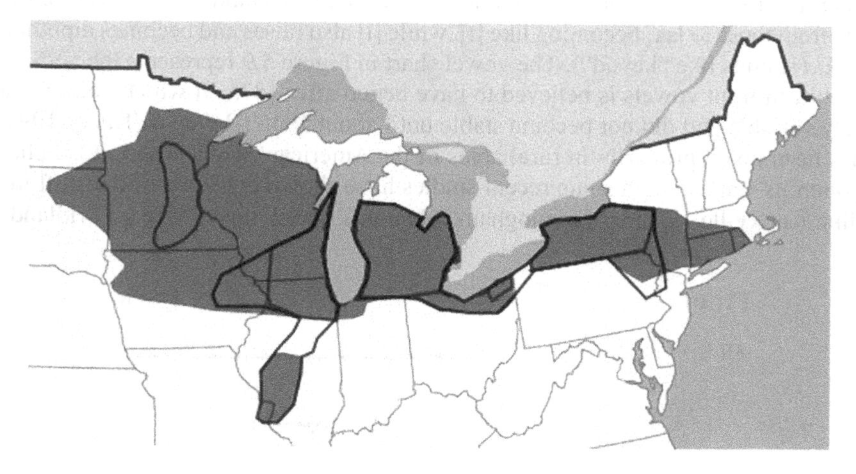

Figure 5.8 Geographic distribution of Northern Cities Shift

Source: adapted from an image by Angr

Research on the NCS suggests that the first stage of this series of shifts began sometime in the mid-20th century, most likely with the raising, tensing, and diphthongization of /æ/ (as in *bad*) moving toward the diphthong /ɪə/. If you say *be* + *at* together quickly, you'll end up with something close to the shifted version of *bat* (bæt > bɪət). Another example: the woman's name *Ann* is pronounced like the man's name *Ian* where the NCS has taken place. As the first stage of the change goes forward and /æ/ moves out and into the diphthong system, the empty spot begins to be filled with the second stage shift, /ɑ/ > /æ/ (*sock* sounds like *sack*) and so on.

A series of related phonological changes like this is known as a *chain shift*. Although this might sound as if vowels fall in a neat line, one changing after the other, in fact, it's a messy, drawn-out business that can only really be examined once it's well underway. While the NCS is currently receding in most locations where it had historically been found (at one point, about 34 million people were taking part across many Midwestern cities), sociolinguists have been especially interested in how the stages of the NCS relate to each other and why it is receding. Is there a specific social group who is still taking part? Does it have to do with age, gender, economics, or some complex interaction of all these and other social markers? Are speakers more aware of the social meanings associated with the shift today? Those social meanings are often negative, which might explain a shift away from their use (see Nesbitt 2021 for a more thorough account of recent changes in NCS perception and production).

In the states to the south of the caught/cot merger in the East, a different pattern of vowels has emerged, known as the Southern Vowel Shift (SVS). The SVS involves an "interrelated series of rotations in vowel space currently underway in the dialects of Southern speakers in the United States" (Fridland 1998: 267). This series of vowel shifts began with the most quintessential Southern vowel variant (Baranowski 2007: 149) – the one that's commonly referred to by non-linguists as the "long I," in which words like *tie* sound more like "tah." This phenomenon is referred to by linguists as the monophthongization of [aɪ] to [aː]. In the second and third stages of the shift, the front tense and lax vowels are switching places in the vowel space. This involves the inversion of [i] and [ɪ] and [e] and [ɛ]. The movement of [e] prompts [ɛ] to raise and become diphthongized (so that *bed* sounds like "bayud"). Like [e], [i] shifts from tense to lax, becoming like [ɪ], while [ɪ] also raises and becomes diphthongized (so that *kid* sounds like "keyud"). The vowel chart in Figure 5.9 represents the SVS.

This shift in front vowels is believed to have begun after 1875, at which point it was still relatively variable and did not become stable until about 1945 (Bailey & Tillery 1996). The SVS has been noted primarily in rural areas of the American South, where it is believed to have gotten its start, though some recent studies have shown evidence of the shift in larger cities like Knoxville, Atlanta, Birmingham, Memphis, and Louisville (e.g., Fridland 2001;

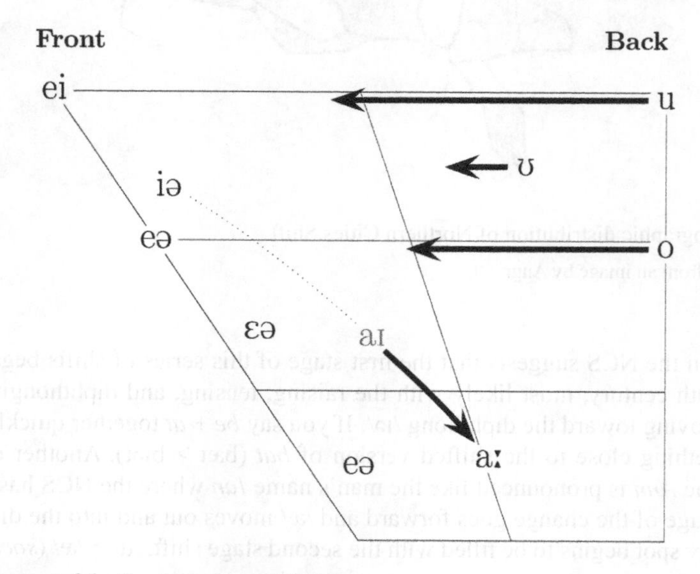

Figure 5.9 Patterns of the Southern Vowel Shift

Feagin 2003; Labov et al. 2006; Cramer 2016), likely caused by massive migration out of rural areas due to decreasing agricultural needs (Feagin 1986). The shift is most complete in Appalachia, southern Georgia, and a large part of Texas (Labov et al. 2006).

Far from finalized, the SVS continues to change. For many Southerners, the change that led the shift, monophthongization of [aɪ] to [a:], has become so common as a stereotyped feature of Southernness that some speakers are beginning to move away from it to avoid the negative stereotypes associated with Southern speech. Like the SVS itself, the distribution of this shift away from the older form [a:] to [aɪ] also shows distinct patterns. In Charleston, SC, for example, Baranowski (2007: 154) found that the wealthiest are more likely to use the newer variant [aɪ], while the lower economic classes are more persistent in the use of the more traditional [a:] before particular consonants and at the end of words.

A more recent series of changes is the California Vowel Shift (CVS), as seen in Figure 5.10. This shift, which has been primarily documented in northern California (though research suggests it is also found in other communities in the western United States and Canada), involves some simple movements and some more complex ones. The CVS exhibits unconditioned vowel changes (ones that occur everywhere) as well as conditioned changes (which only occur when they occur near specific sounds or at the end of words). Unconditioned changes include the fronting of the vowels /u/, /ʌ/, and /o/; fronting and lowering of /ʊ/ (so *look* sounds like "luck"); and lowering of /ɛ/ (so *bed* sounds like "bad"). Other vowel movements are conditioned: the raising of /ɪ/ occurs before /ŋ/ (so *king* sounds like "keeng"), though the lowering of the same vowel occurs before other consonants (so *bid* sounds like "bed"). Similarly, the /æ/ vowel becomes like a raised diphthong before nasal consonants (so *man* sounds like "mee-an") but shifts down and back in other environments (so *back* sounds like "bock"). Additionally, the distinction between /ɑ/ and /ɔ/ has been lost so that the two vowels are merged (in which case, *cot* and *caught* are homophones).

Although we have focused on patterns involving vowels, the changes that lead to distinct dialects may also involve consonants. Examples include the presence/absence of [ɹ] before

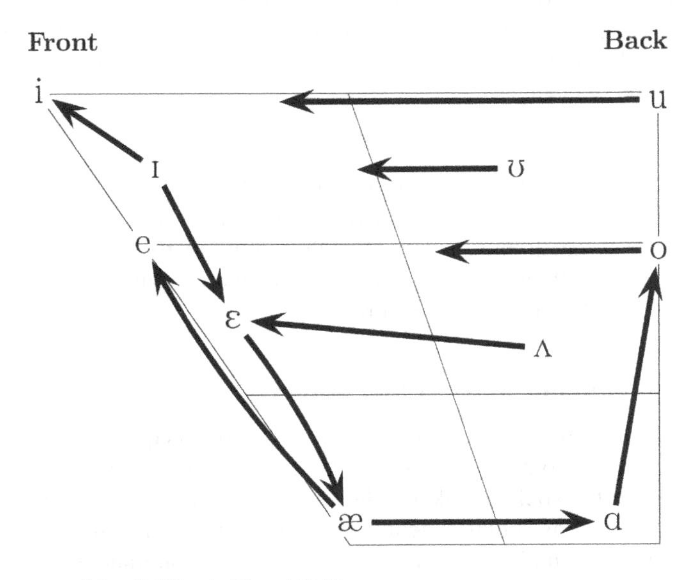

Figure 5.10 Patterns of the California Vowel Shift

consonants and at the end of words (see Chapter 10) and similar/different pronunciations of word-initial /l/ (as in *loop*) and word-final /l/ (as in *pool*). Another common pattern of variation is consonant cluster reduction, which occurs to some degree in almost all varieties of US English. In the Midwest, a nasal ([n] or [m]) followed by a stop ([b] [p] [t] [d]) will usually reduce to a nasal alone, as in the word *hunter* which is pronounced like "hunner." In other regions, consonant cluster reduction may apply word-finally, so that *stand* comes to sound like *stan*. Although vowel patterns alone can be used to distinguish dialects, they are just one part of the complex set of phonological patterns actually involved in the differentiation of regional varieties of English.

In all of these examples of language change, there is variation in terms of who does and who does not participate in the change in progress. This is because these variable vowel patterns do not simply index identity as a person from a given place; they also index personal traits that are associated with those speakers who are participating in the shift. As a vowel shift spreads through a community, these indexical meanings can change, further changing patterns of which people within a region are participating in the shift. For example, Carmen Fought (2002) found that whether a Chicano gang member has the CVS pattern can index which type of gang he belongs to. Rob Podesva (2011) has argued that heavy use of the CVS indexes notions like "laid back" and "fun," which has been used by gay men in northern California when adopting a "partier" persona.

It's important to remember that vowel shifts like these emerge and begin to spread well below the level of consciousness. Apart from actors trying to mimic a particular dialect, most people do not make a conscious decision to participate in a linguistic change in progress. Of course, changes (in whole or part) can be resisted, but these are usually features that are wholly rejected by certain groups or those that reach the level of stereotype (like [aɪ] monophthongization in the South). For example, earlier research showed that race and ethnicity had something to do with whether an individual participates in the NCS, as Gordon (2000a) established in a study of speakers in northwest Indiana. He found evidence that

> the pronunciations associated with the NCS are overwhelmingly more prevalent among white speakers. Some of the speakers of mixed ethnicity show signs of adopting the NCS variants, but the Mexicans and African Americans were not generally found to participate in these changes.
>
> (Gordon 2000b: 122)

Later work in Lansing, Michigan, showed more participation among African Americans (Jones 2003) and Mexican American women (Roeder 2006). The patterns of regional dialects, then, can convey much more information than simply letting us know where a person is from. These vowel shifts involve hugely complex sets of changes distributed over time, space, and dozens of different social categories.

Regional variation in morphology and syntax

Unlike lexical variation, which often elicits comments about its quaintness, or phonetic variation, which often elicits comments about "bad accents," morphosyntactic variation usually gets the worst end of the stick. Speakers who use these non-standard grammatical features are often quickly cast off as "unintelligent" or "without grammar." But speakers using non-standard forms are not simply "messing up" the rules of grammar; they are following a different set of rules – rules that are part of a natural, native, and systematic grammar. These rules include those related to variation in particular forms of words (morphology) and sentence structure (syntax). Examples of morphological variation include having different forms for a given word (*converse* vs. *conversate*), distinct patterns of subject-verb agreement (*She walks home* vs. *She walk home*), and variation in related forms of a word (*My phone is broke* vs. *My phone is broken*). Syntactic variation involves having different rules for putting sentences together. Because speakers have different rules, they do not have the same intuitions about which types of sentences are grammatical or ungrammatical.

In some cases there is a recognizable corresponding rule that people imagine to be part of "standard" English. For example, *I ain't got no umbrella* corresponds (or "translates") to *I do not have an umbrella*. Although the sentences have the same referential meaning, they carry very different indexical meanings. This is the pattern for most forms of variation, but there are also cases where non-standard varieties contain grammatical distinctions unavailable in "standard" English. Because these distinctions convey meanings in ways that don't exist in the "standard," it can be difficult to determine what the "standard" rule might be. For example, in parts of Appalachia and the Ozarks, there is a distinction between sentences like those that follow (Barrett 2008):

1. I don't know <u>who she is dating</u>.
2. I don't know <u>who is she dating</u>.

The first sentence (. . . *who she is dating*) means "I know she is dating someone, but I don't know who it is," while the second sentence (. . . *who is she dating*) means *both* "I don't know if she is dating someone" and "if she is dating someone, I don't know who they might be." A prescriptivist faced with a sentence like *I don't know who is she dating* would likely "correct" the sentence by moving the auxiliary *is* to give *I don't know who she is dating*. Of course, this simply turns sentence 2 into sentence 1, losing the distinction in meaning. Thus, there is no easy way to convey the information in sentence 2 in anything like "standard" English. We would be left with something like *I know neither whether she is dating someone nor who it might be that she is dating if she is indeed dating someone*. Thus, it doesn't make sense to say that a sentence like *I don't know who is she dating* "violates" the rules of "standard" English. It would be more accurate to say that "standard" English lacks grammatical rules that provide an easy way to express the distinction in meaning between sentences 1 and 2. We will discuss this pattern in more detail in Chapter 6.

The same is true for morphological variation. The various regional forms of the second person plural (*you guys*, *youse guys*, *you-ins*, *yinz*, *y'all*) are not "mistakes" in grammar. They actually fill a gap in the pronouns associated with "standard" English. The ideology of "proper" grammar dictates that *you* can be both singular and plural, a fact that creates ambiguity when addressing more than one person. When talking to a group of three people, the question *Are you coming to the party?* could be directed at all of the listeners, two of the three listeners, or just one of the listeners. The options for dealing with this ambiguity in "standard" English are cumbersome and unnatural for many (*Are both of you coming to the party? Are the three of you coming to the party?*). The diversity of "non-standard" regional forms for the second person plural pronoun suggests that the intuitive sense that English needs such a pronoun is fairly widespread. Thus, rather than saying that *youse guys* is "wrong," it makes more sense to say that "standard" English has a gap that *youse guys* (and *y'all*, *yinz*, etc.) is able to fill.

L'imparfait

Anyone who has ever studied a language other than English can likely understand the problem of not having a one-to-one matchup in verb forms. There are often times in language classes where verb conjugations and sentence structures are presented to students that have no exact match in English. For example, Romance languages like French and Spanish have an imperfect past tense that has no exact mapping in "standard" English verb conjugations. The imperfect, which is actually something called verbal aspect, a verbal feature that tells how an action takes place over time, expresses that something continues over time. In French, you might say "Phillipe portait un chapeau blu," which means something like "Phillipe wore a blue hat," but it also indicates that this was a typical state of affairs for Phillipe. It is not to say that English cannot do this; it just requires more than a verb conjugation. You would have to add the word "always" to get this understanding in English.

Pronominal forms can also convey even more subtle distinctions, such as the distributive versus the collective possessive plural. In parts of the South, speakers distinguish between *y'alls'* [jɑlz] and *y'alls's* [jɑlzɪz] so that the first refers to a set of objects collectively owned by *y'all* while the second refers to a set of objects individually owned by each person included in *y'all*. Thus, *y'alls'* [jɑlz] *books* would convey shared ownership of the books (the books belong to all y'all), while *y'alls's books* [jɑlzɪz] would indicate that each individual owned one of the books involved (each book belongs to one of y'all). This is, of course, a distinction that is difficult to convey in "standard" English. Even though they mark a nuanced distinction unavailable in the "standard," these forms are stigmatized as "wrong," "uneducated," or "hillbilly" ways of speaking. Rather than recognizing the subtleties available in undervalued Englishes, they are simply considered to be "wrong." Here again, prescriptivist ideologies aren't actually about the grammar of undervalued varieties, but they instead reflect broader forms of social prejudice toward the people who speak those varieties, even in cases where people do not realize it. An undervalued English may offer expressive possibilities unavailable in the standard but which are rejected as "incorrect" based primarily on the identities of speakers.

One form of morphological variation that is seen in a number of dialects involves different forms of particular verb. Most English verbs fall into one of two groups: strong or weak. Weak verbs (also called regular verbs) form the past tense and the past participle by the simple addition of a suffix (for example, -ed, as in *talked*, *climbed*, and *cleaned*). Strong (or irregular) verbs are much harder to predict because the past forms are generated by a change to the vowel in the root syllable and sometimes to consonants as well, for example, *shrink*, *shrank*, *shrunk*. Bybee and Slobin (1982) summarize the history and relationship between weak and strong verbs and establish that while there are thousands of verbs that fall into the weak (-ed) class, only 200 or so can be identified as strong. On the other hand, "of the 30 most frequent past-tense forms, 22 are irregular [strong]" (1982: 265). Since the Old English period, hundreds of strong verbs have weakened, for example, see Table 5.1.

In this example, the Old English verb for "shove" distinguished the past from the present by changing the vowel (like *sing* vs. *sang*). You might hypothesize that this movement from strong to weak verbs would be over and done with so many hundreds of years after it began,

Table 5.1 Historical weakening of English strong verbs

Old English (strong)	scūfe	scēaf	Scofen
	↓	↓	↓
Modern English (weak)	(I) shove	(I) shoved	(I had) shoved

but, in fact, it is still moving forward – and backward. Weak verbs have been metamorphizing into strong verb forms for a very long time, but sometimes a strong rule pattern will stick to a weak verb. For example, there are areas in Great Britain and the United States where *sneaked* has become *snuck*, *dived* is now *dove*, and *dragged* is *drug*, much to the horror of many prescriptivists. This variation is active and vigorous, and it has been widely documented. A Google search of "dragged or drug?" brings up more than 23 million hits, which indicates real confusion among English speakers. Speakers often show this kind of confusion and breakdown of contrasts when changes in progress are solidifying. The confusion is not caused by the change in progress but by the Standard Language Ideology which forces speakers to choose between *dragged* or *drug* even though readers or listeners will typically understand either one with no trouble at all.

Another change in the *shove* example involves the past participle, which, in Old English, ended with the suffix -en (as in *take/taken* or *fall/fallen*). This is another way that *shove* has changed to become more regular. The Old English form would predict that the Modern English would be *She was shoven* rather than *She was shoved.* There was, in fact, a period when *shoven* was the form in use, but it gave way to the more regular *shoved.* This is one area of grammar where changes in different verbs resulted in differences across dialects. The forms of strong/irregular verbs have long been in flux, so which verbs fall into which categories is variable. Even so, some patterns of conjugation are seen as "wrong" while others are "right." It is arbitrary that *She has never drank alcohol* is "correct," but *She has never drunk alcohol* is "incorrect." Similarly, *That vase is broken* is "right," but *That vase is broke* is "wrong." Perhaps that vase is broke because someone had shoven it off the table. Whichever form one happens to use doesn't prevent an individual from being able to convey the same ideas.

One of the most commonly "corrected" forms of syntactic variation is "double negatives" (or "negative concord") in which a verb is negated not with one negation marker but with (at least) two, as in *We ain't got no sugar.* This feature is found in countless varieties of American English (like those spoken in the South and Appalachia or like those associated with African American and Latinx communities) and in other Englishes around the world. However, it is often described as illogical by prescriptivists. The annoyed grammar nitpicker will proclaim, "Two negatives make a positive, so that sentence means that 'we' do, in fact, have sugar." So if someone says *We ain't got no sugar*, would it be logical to ask them to go ahead and add it to the Kool-Aid?

A rule like "two negatives makes a positive" works nicely in math but not in language. Many of the world's languages (French, for one) actually *require* two negative components to "correctly" produce a negative. The standard French way to say the English sentence in the previous paragraph would be "Je n'ai pas de sucre," where both the *n'* and the *pas* are required negative components. Interestingly, non-standard varieties of French eschew one of the pieces, making French "single negation" the bane of the French grammar police. Here again, the same form can be "correct" in one "standard" variety and "incorrect" in another. The prescriptivist view of English negation would clearly be considered "wrong" by French prescriptivists.

Old English y'all

Older versions of English actually had a distinct second person plural personal pronoun. In Old English, *þū*, pronounced [θu:], was used to address one person, *ġit*, pronounced [jɪt], was used to address two people, and *ġē*, pronounced [je:], was used to address more than two people. In Middle English, second person singular had a subject form of *thou* and an object form of *thee*; second person plural had *ye* in the subject position and *eow* in the object position. By Early Modern English, *you* only served as the second person plural in the object position, with *thou*, *thee*, and *ye* maintaining the other distinctions of Middle English. The loss of the distinction only occurred after the 17th century.

There are a number of other syntactic patterns that vary across regional dialects of American English. One change that seems to be spreading is a construction linguists refer to as the "needs washed" construction. This non-standard verbal construction is approximately equivalent to the "standard" English "needs washing" or "needs to be washed." This variable form seems to have emerged in western Pennsylvania and Ohio and is spreading to other regions. Because the change is currently spreading, individuals may find the construction grammatical for some verbs and ungrammatical for others. For example, people in many parts of the country accept sentences like *My car needs washed* but using the same construction with other verbs is much less common outside of the region where the change initiated. So while *My car needs washed* is likely to be accepted by speakers in many different parts of the country, a sentence like *That dog likes petted* is likely to be ungrammatical for many of those same speakers.

There are a number of specific syntactic patterns that are found in Southern dialects. One involves whether "stative verbs" (*know*, *be*, *seem*, etc.) are grammatical when used as progressives (*is/was X-ing*). Thus, for some Southern speakers, forms like *It hasn't been being cold lately* or *I've been knowing her my whole life* are perfectly grammatical. Another example is known as the "Southern dative" found in sentences like *I'm going to eat me some sushi*. In these cases, use of the additional dative (*me*) indexes that the action is deliberate, emphatic, or pleasurable. So *eating me some sushi* is a much more enjoyable and purposeful action than simply *eating some sushi*. Another Southern feature, known as "double modals," involves connecting two modal verbs, a pattern which is ungrammatical in other dialects of English. Examples include *might should*, *might could*, *might ought to*, and *used to could*. Of course, these modals are also subject to rules so that some combinations are ungrammatical for speakers of varieties that contain them. Thus, *I might could help you* is fine, but **I could might help you* is not. The difference between these Southern modals and the "single modals" in other varieties is not simply a question of word choice or sentence structure. When a Southerner chooses the double modal construction, that speaker is lessening the force of the utterance; the issue comes down to politeness. In the utterance earlier, the speaker may be able to do the task at hand, but they may not have the desire to do so. In such a situation, an outright rejection of the request would be rude. So the speaker uses this device to save face in the situation. Linguists refer to such variation based on speaker beliefs and intentions as *pragmatic variation*.

OMG! There's, like, so much more variation!

As indicated previously, everything in a language system can vary. In discussions of dialects, people often think only about the words, sounds, and sentence structures that people use differently, but the linguistic system includes other components that might vary by place. The structure of discourse can also vary. In some cases, regional varieties may have particular expectations for how certain interactional "routines" ought to occur. In some regions, for example, requests must be preceded by greetings and small talk so that making a direct request without chatting a bit first is considered rude. In parts of the South, it is considered rude to accept an offer too quickly so one typically says "no" to an offer the first time (and expects there to be a second offer, at which point it's OK to say "yes" without sounding rude).

There are also differences in the use of lexical items which function as discourse markers. Discourse markers are words used to organize pieces of conversation into smaller chunks, such as *so, well, um, but, like*, or *you know*. For example, if someone invites a person to dinner and that person begins their response with *well*, the inviter will likely know that the invitee is going to decline the invitation before they even finish the sentence.

You have perhaps never thought of *um* as being part of "grammar," but there are very specific patterns in terms of how it is used in actual speech (see Erard 2007). There is even a regional divide on the use of *um* or *uh* as the preferred discourse marker in tweets, as in Figure 5.11 (drawn from data and methods in Wieling et al. 2016; Grieve et al. 2018; Grieve 2019). The patterns of discourse markers are extremely complex in structural, social, and stylistic terms, so linguists spend a lot of time studying them (Barbieri 2009; Dailey-O'Cain 2000; Rickford et al. 2007; Tagliamonte and D'Arcy 2004).

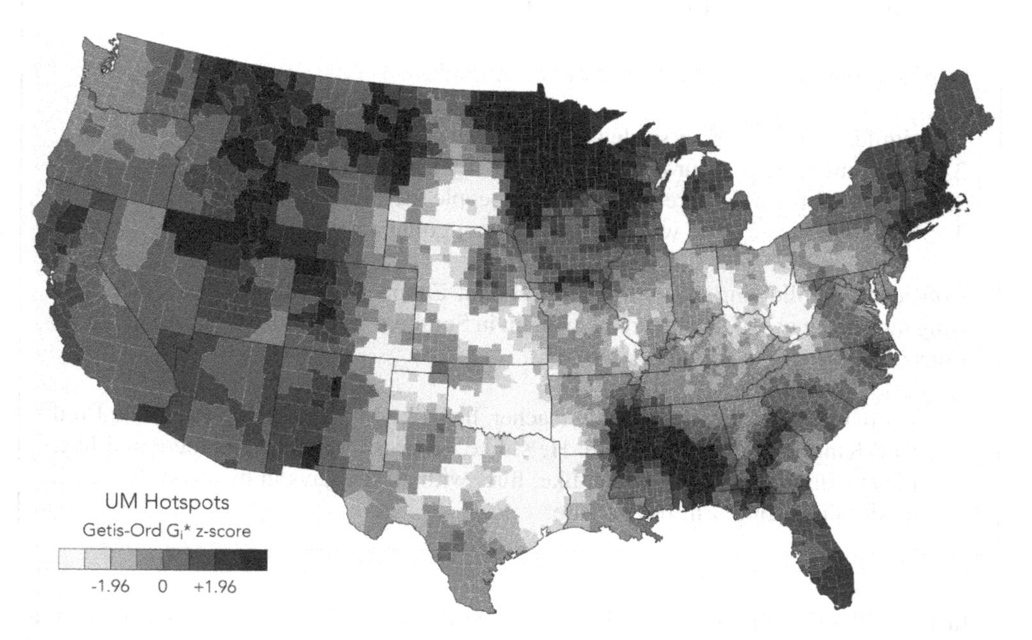

Figure 5.11 Geographic distribution of *um* and *uh* based on geolocated American Twitter data from October 2013–November 2014 (hotspot map produced with local spatial autocorrelation, using getis-ord gi*, 25 nearest neighbor binary spiral weights matrix)

Source: courtesy of Jack Grieve

Often, prescriptivists show concern about using particular discourse markers, especially when the discourse markers are indexically associated with younger speakers who identify as female. An example is the use of *like* as a discourse marker, discussed briefly in Chapter 4. For decades, prescriptivists have complained about women's use of *like*. This criticism, however, typically shows little understanding of the different functions *like* (or, more accurately, the various *likes*) actually do in discourse. There are at least four distinct uses of *like* in contemporary English (beyond the verb *to like*). There is, of course, the traditional *simile* use of *like* (as in *sweet like sugar*). Nobody seems to get upset about this use of *like*. Another pattern is to use *like* to mark focus on a particular phrase or utterance. This use of *like* often opens a clause, as in *like, there are so many people here*, but it may also place focus on a part of a larger sentence, as in, *could you, like, be quiet for a minute*. In both cases, the presence of *like* lets the listener know that what follows is important to the speaker. A third use of *like* is to mark an estimation of a lack of precision. This *like* operates as if it were the opposite of *exactly* (Siegel 2002). For example, if one said *there were exactly five people in the room* the sentence would not be true if there were four or six people in the room. However, if *like* is substituted (*there were like five people in the room*), the statement becomes true for a range of possibilities (so that, the statement is still true if there are four or six people in the room). The final type of *like* is the quotative like, which is a synonym for *say*. An example would be *I asked her, and she was like "OK."* Of these four *likes*, the last three are often proposed as examples of "bad grammar," particularly among young women, who are most likely to be criticized for "saying *like* too much."

Four different uses of *like* in English

Here are some examples of the use of *like* in English.

1.	simile	Your smile is *like* a breath of fresh air
2.	focus-marking	Your brother is *like* totally annoying me
3.	imprecision	There were *like* four people there
4.	quotative	She was all *like*, "I'm not going anywhere"

Consider the following lyrics from Moon Unit Zappa's 1982 hit "Valley Girl." The song mocks the use of *like* by young women in Southern California. What are the functions of Moon Unit's various uses of *like*?

> It's really sad. Like, my English teacher, he's like Mr. Bu-Fu. We're talking Lord God King Bu-Fu. I am so sure. He's, like, so gross. Like, he sits there and like, plays with all his rings and he, like, flirts with all the guys in the class. It's, like, totally disgusting. I'm like so sure.

Just as with other forms of variation, these "new" uses of *like* (as a discourse marker, as a quotative, or to mark approximation) are part of language change in progress. Although prescriptivists regularly complain about innovative forms, they are a basic part of language variation and change. As such, it is hard to maintain negative attitudes toward forms that are becoming more and more common. For example, Dailey-O'Cain (2000) found that people

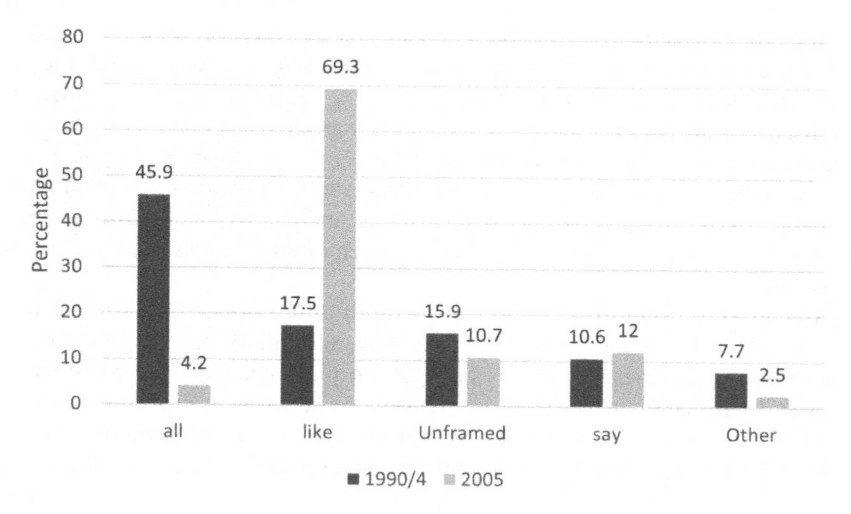

Figure 5.12 The use of quotative discourse markers over time in California

Source: adapted from Rickford et al. (2007)

talked one way about the quotative use of *like* ("bad grammar") but did not necessarily evaluate speakers who used it negatively. Age always played an important role in both the use and perception of quotative *like*. This is because innovations in language are always more familiar to younger speakers. The patterns of quotatives have been undergoing change for some time. John Rickford and colleagues (2007) found distinct changes over time for quotatives in both speech and popular media (chat, blogs, discussion boards) in California (Figure 5.12).

Thus, while a quotative like *say* seems to be staying fairly constant, other quotatives become more or less popular over time. For example, in the late 1980s, *all* emerged as a common quotative (as in *He was all, "Leave me alone"*) and gave *like* some competition. However, by the early 21st century, *all* fell out of favor, and *like* became the most common quotative. Following patterns of language change can tell us a lot about what is happening in society. Sometimes a particular use of language may seem to be unimportant or even trivial; certainly, in this case, innovative quotatives often invite mocking and humor. However, a close study of this kind of subtle marker can reveal a great deal about the community of speakers who use it. It seems even the tiniest pieces of language play a central role in defining who we are, where we came from, and how we understand our relationships to others.

Structured variation: the hidden life of language

Variation across regions is a central feature of all language communities. Just as English shows regional variation, other languages spoken in the United States have regional varieties. As we shall see in more detail in Chapter 7, the Spanish spoken in Texas, for example, differs from the Spanish found in New Mexico, California, Florida, or New York. Native American languages also display regional variation often tied to movement caused by the forced removal of tribes, such as the Trail of Tears. Thus, the varieties of Cherokee, Choctaw, and Cheyenne spoken in Oklahoma differ from the varieties spoken in North Carolina, Mississippi, and Montana, respectively.

The forms of variation that are found across different regions can be quite complex in terms of the range of variables available, the contexts in which variable forms may occur, and the frequency with which different speakers use variable forms. Indeed, the study of sociolinguistic variation can be exceedingly complex, requiring advanced statistical techniques to tease out the patterns involved. Human beings choose among thousands of points of variation available to them not because the human mind is sloppy or language is imprecise: just the opposite. Individuals exploit linguistic variation available to them in order to send a complex series of messages about themselves and the way they position themselves in the world. And they perceive variation in the speech of others and use it to structure their knowledge about that person.

The parameters of linguistic variation are multidimensional. In large-scale terms, these are social, stylistic, geographic, or temporal, and in any one case of active variation, more than one of these factors is probably at play. Different factors interact with each other and with language-internal influences; the result is the variation you hear (or don't hear, but still perceive). When people choose among variants available to them – a process which happens well below the level of consciousness – they use those variables that will index them as belonging to specific social groupings and being different from members of some other groups. The variants people use let a listener know if the speaker is happy, angry, or depressed. People use this variation even when they are trying not to. It is inescapable because it is a central component of how individuals understand and navigate their social worlds. Language variation can be emblematic for dozens of different kinds of social allegiances: national origin, socioeconomic class, ethnicity, occupation, religion, kinship, etc.

Sociolinguists have demonstrated beyond a doubt that variation is an intrinsic and functional feature of language. So then, what do people really mean when they talk about "nonstandard" or "incorrect grammar"? How do these labels get attached to specific points of variation and to what end? More often than not, these labels become linked to the dialectal variation of social groups that are already marginalized in some way. In the chapter that follows, we will look at the ways in which language variation serves to reproduce and propagate beliefs about race and ethnicity.

Discussion questions

1. In this chapter, we have seen that there are similarities between varieties, such as the common features shared by white Southerners and many African Americans across the country or the overlap between Pittsburgh English and Appalachian varieties. What do these patterns of overlap tell us about how language changes spread?
2. Before reading this chapter, what regional varieties of American English were you familiar with? What kinds of linguistic features did you associate with them? Did you recognize the potential for internal variability in those regions? Did you think of those regions as monolithic in terms of not only language but person-type (i.e., made assumptions about race, ethnicity, gender, etc. of "typical" members of that region)?
3. While language mavens focus on the idea of correctness, regular people use language for purposes besides "speaking correctly." For example, we said that double modals like "might could" can serve a politeness and face-saving function for Southerners. Can you think of any linguistic things you do in your variety of American English that serves

some role other than being "grammatical" or "proper"? Is it "non-standard"? Why do you do that?

4. Grab a notebook and start taking notes on how many times you, your friends, and your family members use *like* (as a discourse marker) on one specific day. Keep track of how many times per sentence it is used, who used it, and what function it serves. Who uses it the most in which function? Are there certain topics that seem to make people say *like* more?

6 Language, racialization, and racism

No MSG

In 1968, Dr. Robert Ho Man Kwok wrote a letter to the prestigious *New England Journal of Medicine* to describe what he believed to be a new illness he dubbed *Chinese restaurant syndrome* (Kwok 1968). He reported that, unlike food he had eaten in China, the food at American Chinese restaurants made his neck go numb and caused heart palpitations. The journal soon began receiving more reports from individuals reporting their own experiences of a variety of symptoms that were attributed to Chinese restaurant syndrome. Although the disorder was first described by a Chinese immigrant, the overwhelming majority of those who suffered from Chinese restaurant syndrome were white. A study the following year in *Science* purported to have found the cause of this illness – monosodium L-glutamate, or MSG (Olney 1969). Soon people were avoiding Chinese food or demanding that restaurants prepare their food without MSG, and restaurants began to advertise as "No MSG" establishments. The idea that MSG was a dangerous chemical that could make one sick soon became widely accepted. But there were several problems with this idea.

The human tongue is sensitive to five distinct tastes: sweet, salty, sour, bitter, and umami (which is roughly similar to *savory* in English and might best describe something like cheese). Unlike "salty" or "sour," however, the majority of people who were not Asian were unfamiliar with the notion of umami and thus did not understand the purpose of MSG. Because of its ability to enhance taste, MSG is widely used in many commonplace processed foods like crackers, potato chips, and corn chips. However, nobody ever complained of experiencing "post-Doritos syndrome." Somehow, MSG only made people sick when used in Chinese cuisine.

In the half century since Chinese restaurant syndrome was first "described," there have been many scientific studies of the illness, yet there is still no conclusive evidence that MSG causes any of the symptoms commonly associated with the illness (Freeman 2006; Tracy 2016). It turns out that MSG is no more harmful than salt, and the symptoms associated with Chinese restaurant syndrome are entirely psychosomatic. Chinese restaurant syndrome is not a medical condition but rather a psychological expectation based within a history of racist stereotyping. So the cause of Chinese restaurant syndrome is not MSG but racist stereotypes of Chinese people as being dirty and having poor hygiene that leads to the spread of disease. The source of Chinese restaurant syndrome is the fear that one's food was prepared by Asians with poor hygiene and dirty kitchens. Racism can make you physically ill.

Compare sodium chloride (or salt) to monosodium L-glutamate (MSG). Salt has a long history of associations in European culture, and English contains many expressions that

DOI: 10.4324/9781003332886-6

Figure 6.1 Chinese restaurants still promote "No MSG" food

Source: photo by Richard Masoner

convey indexical associations to salt (*salt of the earth, salt in the wound, take it with a grain of salt, salt and pepper hair*). One can think of MSG in the 1960s as a sign that is relatively "empty" of indexical associations, especially for those unfamiliar with Asian cuisine or umami. When faced with a new concept, individuals seek to fill in indexical associations in order to understand that concept. Without experiences to draw on, people tend to fill in missing indexical meanings using stereotypes that are already familiar to them. In American society, the most familiar social stereotypes tend to be those that have histories rooted in racism. In the case of MSG, people unfamiliar with the seasoning interpreted MSG in terms of racist stereotypes of Chinese Americans as unclean, living in crowded spaces, and likely to spread disease.

Contradictions in stereotypes

The use of blatant racist stereotypes of Asians, Native Americans, and African Americans to market soap often relied on contradictory stereotypes of minorities as "dirty" yet also particularly skilled at jobs cleaning for other people. This contradictory racism is also present in contemporary representations of Latinxs. In the late 1800s, the idea of the "Chinese laundry" was widespread, and Chinese Americans were seen as being especially skilled at cleaning clothing and linens. Ads for laundry soap often portrayed

Figure 6.2 Magic Washer advertisement

Source: archived by the Library of Congress

Asians as preferring a particular brand to suggest that the brand is the choice of professionals. However, Asians were simultaneously portrayed as "dirty." Representations of African Americans were similar with dish soap advertisements using recommendations from Black housekeepers, while bath soap was marketed as somehow unfamiliar to Black people. These contradictory stereotypes are apparent in the Magic Washer ad in Figure 6.2.

The ad appeared shortly after the Chinese Exclusion Act was passed in 1882. The proclamation Uncle Sam is holding reads "under penalty for being dirty," implying that the Chinese were being kicked out of the country because they are "dirty." However, the caption reads, "we have no use for them now that we got this wonderful washer," implying that Magic Washer gets your clothes as clean as the local Chinese-run laundry, so Uncle Sam can kick Chinese immigrants out of the country. In discourse structural racism, such illogical contradictions can easily co-exist because racism, like most forms of hatred, depends on creating visceral responses that defy logic.

Of course, people who believed they had suffered from Chinese restaurant syndrome were not necessarily racists, and most probably never made a conscious connection between their experiences with MSG and racist stereotypes concerning Asians. Often, discourses that reproduce racist stereotypes are so pervasive that people might not even be aware when they evoke them. Saying that Chinese food tends to make you sick is not typically interpreted as a racist statement even though it evokes (and buttresses) centuries of negative representations of Asians. Such racist representations have been repeated often enough that they become second nature. Discourse structural racism often displaces racist tropes so that they come to be linked to issues unrelated to race (e.g., health, hygiene, politeness norms, grammar). Chinese restaurant syndrome typically went unrecognized as a form of racism because it is "about" MSG, not "about" race itself. Yet with the spread of Chinese restaurant syndrome, MSG entered into the broader discourse promoting racism toward Asians.

One can say that MSG has undergone *racialization*, the process by which objects, ideas, individuals, or social practices come to be drawn into racial discourses. In other words, an inanimate object (MSG) marked a point of presumed difference between the cooking practices of two cultures, and the actual reasons for that difference were largely unknown. This made it fairly easy for MSG to become indexically linked to pre-existing racist stereotypes associated with food, health, and hygiene. Through the repetition of indexical links between Chinese cuisine and illness, MSG and Chinese restaurant syndrome become part of discourse structural racism, the broad set of social Discourses that uphold racial division and social inequality.

Patterns of language variation often undergo this process of racialization. We have already seen that variation and change are intrinsic and functional aspects of language. Just as patterns of variation may cluster in particular regions, they may also cluster within communities that share other aspects of identity, including ethnicity, gender, sexuality, religion, class, and so on. Consider the distinction between *she working* and *she be working* in the Englishes of many African American communities. Prescriptivist criticisms of African American speech

"~~Corona~~ Chinese Virus"

In times of crisis, it is common for marginalized groups to become scapegoats, where they are wrongly blamed for acts of nature. For example, the 1918 "Spanish Influenza" epidemic was blamed on Spaniards even though the disease first emerged in Kansas. The onset of the COVID-19 pandemic in late 2019 saw a rise in racial harassment and hate crimes against Asian Americans. Obviously, Asian Americans were no more connected to the virus than any other groups of Americans. However, the rise in racism was linked to the fact that the virus first emerged in China. As with MSG, the racism associated with COVID-19 drew upon long-standing stereotypes of Asians as living in unsanitary conditions and eating bizarre foods. Rather than discussing the fact that viruses can mutate and move from species to species, popular discourse about COVID-19 often attempted to explain the virus through racist portrayals of Chinese people in crowded dirty markets eating bats, snakes, or pangolins.

In March of 2020, the President of the United States gave a speech in which the phrase "corona virus" had been marked out and replaced with "Chinese virus." When critics suggested that using the phrase "Chinese virus" was racist, the President said he was simply referring to the place where the virus originated. This was also his explanation for using the term kung flu, which many found even more insulting.

rarely recognize the meaning and purpose of this distinction (marking progressive vs. habitual aspect) and simply interpret both forms as "bad English." For many white people, such variations in grammar are understood largely in terms of racial bias. Rather than indicating aspectual meanings unavailable in "standard" English (like *be working*), such forms are simply described as "wrong" – they are examples of "bad English." Understandings of what "bad English" might imply simply repeat long-standing racist stereotypes; it is the language of the poor, inner city, uneducated, and so on. Basic patterns of linguistic variation get swept up into the storm of pre-existing Discourses of race. However, just as Chinese restaurant syndrome is supposedly "about" MSG (and not race), the racism of prescriptive grammar is typically viewed as being "about" language (and not race). Here, language ideologies not only help racist ideas propagate; they also serve as racist gatekeepers restricting access to employment and education for speakers of undervalued Englishes.

As we saw in Chapter 2, race is a belief system rather than a biological reality. Because of this, the idea of racial differences survives through Discourse. Language is therefore central to the process of racialization. In addition to the formation and persistence of social categories (as also discussed in Chapter 2), racialization refers to the process by which different ways of speaking and interacting come to be linked to racial categories and to serve as indexical markers of racial and ethnic identities. Next, we will look at the linguistic variation associated with different racial/ethnic groups and consider how that variation comes to index aspects of racial stereotypes. We will then examine the role of this variation in upholding discourse structural racism, including how beliefs about variation reproduce racial differences and support forms of social inequality.

Race, ethnicity, and linguistic variation

In Chapter 2 we saw how social categorizations are constructed through language. Although the concept has no biological basis, *race* is typically presumed to be an innate set of physical traits. In contrast, ethnicity refers to a person's cultural heritage without implying some connection to the imagined biological similarity between members of a given group. Members of the same "race" may have different "ethnicities," so that the terms are sometimes used in a hierarchical fashion with "ethnicities" (Jamaican American, Irish American) being subsets of "races" (Black, white, etc.). Such hierarchies contribute to Discourse structural racism by reinforcing the categorization of individuals on the basis of physical attributes like skin color. In this chapter, our usage attempts to reflect current social norms for treating particular categories as "races" or "ethnicities" but is sometimes left ambiguous to highlight the fact that such distinctions are linguistic (and not biological) constructions.

People who see themselves as belonging to a shared social identity typically come to share rules of grammar, ways of interacting in conversations, and ways of telling stories or jokes. Just as variation clusters into regional dialects (see Chapter 5), forms of variation may cluster within ethnic groups, particularly when members of the groups are in close, regular contact with one another. Because language is always changing, there are always changes that come to index different social groups. Forms of racial segregation and integration can contribute to the emergence of racial/ethnic varieties. An example is American Sign Language (ASL) in the South, where schools for the deaf were segregated by race. A distinct dialect known as Black American Sign Language developed during this time. Now that education for the deaf is no longer racially segregated, the use of Black ASL has declined (McCaskill et al. 2011). A very similar pattern occurred in Ireland where a unique dialect spoken by women emerged in schools that were segregated according to gender. Just as with Black ASL, the use of Women's Irish Sign Language declined after the schools became gender integrated (LeMaster 2006). Such patterns of integration and segregation influence the development and persistence of variation that indexes racial and ethnic identities.

One common pattern in the United States is for variation associated with ethnic identities to develop from contact between English and other languages. It is common for immigrant communities to shift to English across generations. The first generation of immigrants may not be fluent in English, but their children are typically bilingual, speaking both English and their parents' language. The third generation (the grandchildren of the original immigrants) is typically monolingual in English, but they may retain some forms from their grandparents' language. For this third generation, there may only be a few words that index ethnic identity. So, for example, an Italian American might call a colander a *scolapasta* or a Filipino American might know a good recipe for *lumpia*, but knowledge of a few words in your grandparents' language is quite different from speaking a unique ethnic dialect.

Of course, there are also many communities who maintain a language other than English over long periods and multiple generations. Examples include many Native American languages, Spanish, and Yiddish. In such communities with long histories of bilingualism, there are often unique ethnic varieties of English resulting from contact between English and the other language. In such cases of sustained bilingualism, ethnic dialects of English are likely to contain more borrowings from the other language. Sustained bilingualism also increases the likelihood that elements of grammar will reflect a history of language contact. For example, the English of Jewish Americans may include borrowings from Yiddish, like *yutz* (clueless person), while monolingual Latinx speakers of English may regularly use words that originated in Spanish, such as *chancla* (flip-flop), *to pica* (to be spicy, to prick, or to sting), or *pedo* (fart). But the varieties of English in Latinx communities may also show patterns of grammar that overlap with patterns found in Spanish. An example would be the following sentence from Chicanx English in Texas:

1.

Chicanx English (Texas)	**Spanish**
He's not doing you nothing.	Él no te hace nada.
	(literally) He not you doing nothing.

This example demonstrates two grammatical patterns that overlap between Chicanx English and Spanish. The first pattern is multiple negation (also called negative concord), a pattern in many languages in which negation can be marked in multiple places in a sentence. As noted in Chapter 5, the presence of negative concord is common in many undervalued Englishes (e.g., *I don't want no help*, *He don't like nobody*, *She didn't say nothing*). The other pattern involves the placement of the indirect object *you.* In both English and Spanish, indirect objects may appear next to the main verb or in a prepositional phrase following the verb:

2.

"standard" English	**Spanish**
a. She didn't give me anything.	Ella no me dio nada.
	(literally) She no me gave nothing.
b. She didn't give anything to me.	Ella no dio nada a mí.
	(literally) She no gave nothing to me.

In both languages, some verbs allow both patterns, and other verbs only allow one or the other. For example, in many varieties of English, the verb *to say* is only grammatical when the indirect object is in a prepositional phrase: *He didn't say anything to me* vs. **He didn't say me anything*. In example 1, the verb *to do* allows both types of indirect object (where "standard" English would require a prepositional phrase – *do anything to me*).

Although these two features of Chicanx English overlap with Spanish, they also reflect common patterns of language change. As noted in Chapter 5, negative concord is one of the most common features across undervalued Englishes. The other pattern (using the dative indirect object with a verb like *to do*) is an example of regularizing a pattern that differs across verbs. This is similar to the merger between past tense forms and past participles also discussed in Chapter 5, such as in *(has) broken* > *(has) broke*. Whether they emerge from contact or due to regular patterns of language change, it is important to recognize that patterns of linguistic variation have unique histories and follow regular rules of grammar.

Linguists often talk about ethnic/racial dialects as if they were distinct entities like African American English, Chicanx English, or Jewish English. Of course, there is no direct correlation between linguistic structures and race or ethnicity. There are white speakers of African American English, just as there are many African Americans who do not speak the variety. In this book, terms like "African American English" refer to a set of linguistic forms that have the *potential* to index aspects of African American identity. For example, Navajo English is not a label that describes how *all* Navajo speak English. Rather, it is a set of grammatical forms that potentially index Navajo identity. Because ethnicity may be foregrounded in certain situations, individual speakers may utilize such features to very different degrees across contexts. Some speakers may use an ethnic variety across all contexts while others may show variation depending on factors such as who one is talking to or what one is talking about.

One way of thinking about variation across contexts is to view speakers as having a "repertoire" of ethnic-associated forms that may be used to convey ethnicity in different situations. Sarah Benor (2010) uses this model to discuss the ways that Jewish Americans use language variation across situations. For example, Jewish English has numerous borrowings from Yiddish that may not be familiar to gentiles. In situations where Jewish identity is highlighted, speakers are likely to use Yiddish borrowings at a higher frequency. White suburban teenage boys may use elements of African American English in an attempt to index aspects of their masculinity. However, they typically have a much narrower repertoire of African American English forms compared to speakers who are actually from African American communities.

As we'll see, the types of linguistic variation that index ethnic identities, as is the case with regional dialects, occur at all levels of grammar, including what words one uses, how particular words are pronounced, how words and sentences are put together, and ways to convey subtle distinctions in meaning.

Ethnicity-indexing variation: words and sounds

Like all languages, ethnic varieties have sets of words (lexicons) and regular, rule-governed grammars. In ethnic dialects, distinct words may involve things borrowed from another language, such as the presence of Spanish borrowings in varieties of Latinx Englishes or Hebrew and Yiddish borrowings in Jewish English. These borrowings are words used by monolingual speakers of English and sometimes spread beyond their usage as markers of ethnicity. For example, there are large Yiddish-speaking Orthodox Jewish communities in Brooklyn. In these communities, Yiddish is used for religious (Talmudic) study so that speaking Yiddish may index being especially religious (Fader 2009). Given the strong indexical link between Yiddish and Jewish identity, English speakers who do not speak Yiddish may still use borrowings from the language to index Jewish identity. However, because of the large concentration of Yiddish speakers in New York City, some speakers who are not Jewish appropriate those Yiddish borrowings to index regional identity as a New Yorker. When a word comes to be used to index New Yorker rather than Jewish, the original indexical meaning begins to be lost. A number of Yiddish words have traveled this path on the way to becoming part of mainstream varieties of English with no connection to New York or Jewish identity. When an ethnic-indexing form falls into widespread use among outsiders, it will naturally begin to lose its original indexical meaning. When the association between a form and indexical meaning become weaker, linguists say that the form has undergone *indexical bleaching* (Squires 2014). Indexical bleaching is not restricted to forms appropriated from ethnic dialects. Any form that expands from being restricted to specific local contexts to occurring in widespread usage will undergo indexical bleaching as it loses associations with its original local context.

Table 6.1 shows some borrowings from Yiddish that have undergone different amounts of indexical bleaching. Different words have different histories, so the potential for different words to index Jewish (or New York) identity will vary widely. Some words (like *bubbe* for "grandmother") may maintain a strong connection to Jewishness, while others (like *schlep*) may come to index New Yorkness, and still others (like *glitch*) may have been completely bleached so that it has lost all indexical associations.

Another pattern is for English words to take on new and distinct meanings in ethnic varieties of the language. This is particularly common in African American English where several everyday words have unique meanings not generally found in "standard" English. An example would be the word *to stay*, which means "to reside (permanently)" in African American

Table 6.1 English borrowings from Yiddish

bubbe – grandma	nosh – to snack
chutzpah – confidence, nerve	putz – a fool
klutz – clumsy person	schmooze – to make small talk
kvetch – to complain, to whine	tchotchke – knick-knack
shmuck – a stupid or obnoxious, annoying person	tuchus – (also tush/tushy) rear end
schlepp – to haul or drag something (a long distance)	glitch – minor malfunction

Table 6.2 Some everyday words with additional meanings in African American English (AAE) (Smitherman 1994)

	Common meaning	*Additional AAE meaning*
ash	the remains of a burned substance	dry skin (especially *ashy*)
crib	special bed/cage for a baby	home
front	part of an object forward facing	(verb), to put on a false persona, especially in order to scam or trick people
kitchen	room where one cooks	lowest hair on the nape of one's neck
relax	to become less tense or anxious	to chemically straighten one's hair
word	lexical item	true, real, sign of agreement

English (e.g., *She stay in that big house on the corner of Oak Street*) but means "to reside (temporarily)" in "standard" English (*When she's in town, she stays with her sister*). In addition, there are many words in "standard" English that also have additional meanings in African American English. Some examples are in Table 6.2.

Ethnic variation in pronunciation follows regular patterns of language contact and language change. Sound patterns emerging from language contact often involve the introduction of patterns and distinctions from another language into English. For example, in Yiddish, the consonants /b, d, g/ become /p, t, k/ (respectively) at the end of words. Some monolingual speakers of Jewish speakers of English show this pattern in their English, like *wrong* pronounced as "wronk" [ɹɔnk] or *beard* pronounced like "beart" [bɪəɹt] (Benor 2009).

Ethnic-indexing variation in pronunciation may also result from regular sound change. One regular pattern involves changes in what counts as a possible syllable. English tends to allow complex strings of consonants at the end of syllables (e.g., *sixths* [siksθs]). Numerous dialects of English have restrictions on what can occur in this context. For example, African American and Native American Englishes may prohibit longer strings of consonants at the end of a word so that final /t/s and /d/s may not occur. There are also varieties that don't allow /r/ to end a syllable, a pattern sometimes found in African American English, Italian American English, and Jewish English, in addition to some regional varieties (see Chapter 10). Another common form of variation involves the interdental "th" sounds: [ð] as in *breathe* and [θ] as in *breath*. These sounds are relatively uncommon across the world's languages, so it is not particularly surprising to find dialects that replace them with other sounds. For example, in Latinx Englishes the [θ] sound may be replaced with [t], especially in words like *something*, *nothing*, or *anything*. In African American English, this same [θ] sound occurs at the beginning of words but alternates with [t] between vowels and is often realized as [f] word-finally. Similarly, in a number of ethnic dialects the [ð] sound alternates with [d] (as in *dis* and *dat* for *this* and *that*).

Some of the patterns of variation in ethnic varieties overlap with those found in regional varieties. Thus, for example, the absence of /r/ at the end of a syllable also indexes local regional identity in parts of New York and New England. Because of the influx of Southern African Americans to the North during the Great Migration, there is overlap between general Southern speech (among all ethnicities) and the speech of African Americans in the North. This overlap includes the pin/pen merger and monophthongization of the /ai/ diphthong (both discussed in Chapter 5).

Because indexical meanings depend on context, a pattern like the pin/pen merger may serve to evoke Southernness, Blackness, or both. Ethnic-indexing variation may also emerge through the ways in which minority groups orient toward sound changes associated primarily with white speakers. For example, among Arab American youth in Dearborn, Michigan, adoption of the pronunciations associated with the Northern Cities Shift (see Chapter 5) index distinctions within the local community, such as whether a person is Lebanese (Samant 2010). In comparing the vowel patterns of Chinese Americans in San Francisco and New York, Amy Wong and Lauren Hall-Lew (2014) found that speakers in both cities used patterns that were locally distinctive, but speakers in the two cities had much more in common with their local non-Chinese counterparts than with each other. Thus, it is important to bear in mind that ethnic dialects also show other forms of variation, including variation that indexes region, gender, social class, sexual orientation, and so on.

Ethnicity-indexing variation: sentences and meanings

In addition to their lexicons and sound systems, racial/ethnic dialects show variation both in terms of how words and sentences are put together and in the specific meanings of different verbal constructions. In terms of putting words together, variation often involves regularizing paradigms. One common pattern is the loss of the /+z/ with third person singular present tense verbs (*She digs* > *She dig*), a change found in numerous regional and ethnic dialects of English. Plural marking shows similar variation. In African American English, plural marking is optional when numbers make marking the plural redundant (e.g., *It was five book on the table*). It is also common for irregular plurals to be "fixed" to align with the regular pattern (e.g., *sheeps* in Navajo English). The possessive /+z/ suffix is also optional for some speakers of African American English (*Mary house* ~ *Mary's house*).

As with sound patterns, sentence structures may result from combinations of language contact and regular language change. Patterns of inversion in questions and subordinate clauses exhibit this. The standard patterns of inversion involve switching the subject and auxiliary in yes/no questions and wh-questions (who, what, where, when, why, and how). However, "standard" English generally prohibits this inversion in embedded clauses, as in the following example 3.

3. "<u>She is</u> going to the store"
   a. yes/no question: <u>Is she</u> going to the store?
   b. wh-question: Where <u>is she</u> going?
   c. embedded clause: I wonder where <u>she is</u> going.

This set of alternations shows very different patterns in some undervalued Englishes. In most varieties of English it is acceptable to produce a yes/no question without inversion (e.g., "You bought milk?"). For some speakers of Indian English (both in India and the United

States), all three forms can invert the subject and auxiliary or simply leave them alone with the auxiliary preceding the subject. Thus, a sentence like "Where she is going?" would be considered grammatical. In Chicanx English, inversion always occurs with wh-questions, but it also often occurs with embedded clauses. This is not surprising since Spanish allows inversion in embedded clauses. Some cases of variation in inversion originated with contact between the Irish language and English. In Irish, the word order of direct questions (such as in 4a) is the same as in indirect questions (such as 4b).

4. Irish question word order

a. *An* *raib* *tú* *sásta?*
Question Particle be-**Past** you-**SG** content?
"Were you content?" (O'Siadhail 1989: 321; cited in Filppula 2000: 448)

b. *Chuir* *se* *ceist* *ort* *an* *raibh* *tú* *sásta.*
Put he question on-you **Question Particle** be-**Past** you-**SG** content.
"He asked were you content."

In Irish English, alternation between inversion and non-inversion came to mark a distinction in meaning in embedded clauses. Cases where the embedded clause is inverted, as in Irish, indicate that the speaker is uncertain about whether the embedded clause might be true. Cases without inversion indicate that the speaker believes the embedded clause to be true. This pattern survives in Appalachian and Ozark regional varieties as well as in African American English (Barrett 2008). This pattern is demonstrated in example 5.

5. Examples from Ozark English (Barrett 2008)

a. I wonder where she is working.
"She definitely has a job, I just don't know where it is."
b. I wonder where is she working.
"I don't know if she has a job, but if she does I also don't know where it is."
c. I don't know where she goes to church.
"She goes to church, I just don't know where."
d. I don't know where does she go to church.
"I don't know if she goes to church, and if she does, I don't know where."

Irish and Scottish immigrants made up a large portion in the mountainous regions of central Appalachia (and subsequently the Ozarks), so it is not surprising that this distinction still occurs in these regions. This pattern from Irish American English also became a feature of African American English very early in the colonization of the future United States. The earliest enslaved people taken from Africa tended to work alongside indentured servants from Ireland, and today's African American English maintains several features that originated with Irish English. However, in many varieties of African American English, this distinction in meaning has been extended to cases of inversion in wh-questions. So a question like "Where your car is?" indicates that the speaker knows that the addressee has a car. Here, inversion ("Where is your car?") would indicate that the speaker did not know if the addressee actually has a car. Because of this distinction in meaning, some wh-questions usually occur without inversion. For example, "What your name is?" makes more sense than "What is your name?" because the latter implies that the addressee might not have a name, and the odds of someone not having a name are pretty low.

These various patterns of inversion are outlined in Table 6.3. Regional and ethnic dialects may interact in complicated and interesting ways. Here, dialects differ both in terms of whether inversion is required/allowed in different contexts and in terms of whether inversion indicates a difference in meaning. This type of distinctive local meaning may go unrecognized by outsiders.

Some ethnic dialects, like Navajo English and African American English, have distinctive ways of expressing exactly how an action plays out across time. Grammars may convey the temporal aspects of an utterance as *tense* or *aspect*. Tense refers to the time when an action occurred (past, present, future), while aspect marks a relationship between an action and time. Aspect includes things like whether an action continued across time or happened quickly, whether an action occurs once or happens repeatedly, whether an action is starting or ending, and so on. In "standard" English, aspectual markers include past perfective (indicating that an action has ended, e.g., *She had run*) and imperfective (indicating that the action continued for some time, e.g., *She was running*). Ethnic varieties of English may mark forms of aspect (such as marking habitual or repeated actions) that aren't found in other dialects of English.

In Navajo, verbs mark aspectual meanings that are quite different from those found in European languages like English. A few of the many possible aspectual meanings include those in Table 6.4.

Compared to English verbs, Navajo verbs convey a wider range of aspectual meanings. One might say that English is more concerned with *when* an action occurred, and Navajo is more concerned with *how* an action takes place. Given that English doesn't have an easy way to convey the range of aspectual distinctions found in Navajo, it is not particularly surprising that Navajo speakers have ways of indicating these distinctions in English. For example, the Navajo usitative aspect indicates that an action was habitual. The usitative

Table 6.3 Inversion across varieties of English (after Young et al. 2014)

Variety	*Inversion in yes/no questions*	*Inversion in wh-questions*	*Inversion in embedded clauses*	*Inversion caries meaning?*
Indian American English	optional	optional	optional	no
African American English	optional	optional	optional	yes
Chicanx English	optional	required	optional	no
Appalachian/Ozark English	optional	required	optional	yes
Irish American English	optional	required	optional	yes
"Standard" English	optional	required	prohibited	no

Table 6.4 Some of the aspectual categories in Navajo (see Young and Morgan [1987])

iterative – an action that occurred repeatedly
usitative – an action that usually occurs (habitual)
momentaneous – an action that begins or ends in an instant
semelfactive – an action that occurs only once and isn't continued or repeated
durative – an action that occurs across an extended period

marks regularly occurring events – things that "usually" happen. Speakers of Navajo English may express this distinction by using present tense verbal forms to mark past events. This is a regular pattern in Navajo English and is not limited to native speakers of Navajo, but also occurs in the speech of (especially older) Navajos who are monolingual speakers of English. Consider the examples in 6, taken from student essays (Bartelt 1980):

6. Aspectual marking in Navajo English

   a. I was working in the store this summer . . . always I have to put in gas for the people; also I have to stack things on the shelf. Every after work I have to sweep the floor and clean the counter.
   b. I worked at Kaibito School. My position was clerical typist. I used to go to work 8 am to 12:00 and 1:00 to 5:00. also I worked overtime sometime, and my duties is to do typing and doing some secretary work.

In both examples, the authors are describing past events. However, when discussing the habitual actions that were part of their regular job duties, both authors switch to present tense verbs (*have* and *is*). Here, Navajo English has created a way to use English tense markers to indicate the usitative that occurs in Navajo.

Gullah English is another variety with distinct ways of marking habitual events. Gullah (also known as Geechee) is a variety of English spoken primarily along the coast of Georgia and South Carolina. Although most Gullah speakers are African American, Gullah is quite distinct from other varieties of African American English. Gullah and "standard" English are different enough that some linguists treat Gullah as a separate language from English (Schulz 2020).

"Kumbayah"/"Come by Here"

One example of Gullah that might be familiar is the Christian song "Come by Here," which is often known as "Kumbayah" (especially in white-majority churches). The "Kumbayah" version is meant to represent the phrase "come by here" in Gullah. So *kum* is just *come*, and *ba* is the word *by* with the monophthongization found in the South ([baɪ] < [ba:]). Finally, *here* is produced without a final /r/ as [hijə] which is then shortened to [ja:]. So the "Kumbayah" version is based on (racist) stereotypes of Gullah speakers. This may be why most Black churches sing the original "Come by Here" instead of "Kumbayah."

Gullah has many borrowings from African languages and distinct grammatical patterns. For example, Gullah uses a distinctive set of personal pronouns, as seen in Table 6.5. Most of the pronouns are based on English forms, except for *una* (sometimes spelled "oona"), which is African in origin (and is also used in Jamaican English/Patwa).

Aspectual marking is one of the distinct patterns found in Gullah English (see Table 6.6). For example, Gullah marks habitual actions with the auxiliary *da* (< English *do*). Past tense is marked with the auxiliary *been*, which can be combined with *da* (to *beena*) to mark habitual actions in the past tense.

Table 6.5 Gullah personal pronouns (see Mufwene 2004)

Person	*Gullah form*	*Examples*
1st singular: I, me, my	mi	Mi go ta town. (I go to town.) Dey mi dog. (Those are my dogs.)
2nd singular: you, your	una (oona)	Una go ta town. (You go to town.) Dey una dog. (Those are your dogs.)
3rd singular subject, possessive he/she/it/singular they	e (IPA [i])	E go ta town. (She/he/they goes to town.) Dey e dog. (Those are his/her/their dogs.)
3rd singular object him/her/it/ singular them	im (IPA [ɪm])	Mi done help im. (I had helped him.)
1st plural (we/us/our)	wi (IPA [wi])	Wi go ta town. (We go to town.) E done help wi. (He helped us.)
2nd plural (y'all)	una (or oona)	Una go ta town. (Y'all go to town.) Dey una dog. (They are y'all's dogs.)
3rd plural subject, possessive (they/their)	dey	Dey done help mi. (They helped me.) Mi dey breda. (I am their brother.)
3rd plural object (them)	dem	Mi done help dem. (I helped them.) Mi see dem. (I see them.)

Table 6.6 Some aspectual markers in Gullah (see Mufwene 2004)

ø (no auxiliary) – present tense	E wok. (She/He/They are working.)
da – habitual aspect	E da wok. (She/He/They usually work.)
done – completive aspect	E done work. (She/He/They has finished working.)
been – past tense	E been wok. (He worked.)
gwine – potential/future	E gwine wok. (He will work.)
beena – past habitual	E beena wok. (She/He/They used to work.)

The emergence of Gullah involved contact between a number of different languages and dialects. Languages that emerge from contact across languages in this way are often referred to as Creole languages. Although the term Creole captures the multilingual origins of languages labeled as such, recent research suggests that Creoles do not share any common set of grammatical features. Thus, Creoles are better considered varieties of their lexifier languages (the ones that contribute the most words) rather than being part of some distinct group of contact languages (e.g., DeGraff 2005; Blasi et al. 2017).

The Gullah version of the New Testament

Gullah combines elements of African languages with elements of English to create new grammatical structures. Because Gullah is primarily spoken (and usually not written), spellings for Gullah vary widely. In the Gullah translation of the Bible, for instance, some words are spelled to reflect Gullah pronunciation, while other words (like *gwine* for "going") are spelled in ways similar to literary representations of African American language (like Mark Twain or Joseph Chander). It is important to remember that it is a regular language with its own grammatical rules that are distinct from other varieties of English. The following is the story of the birth of Christ from the Gullah New Testament, (Luke 2: 8–12). The first two sentences are the Gullah translation of "And in that region there were shepherds out in the field, keeping watch over their flock by night." Can you figure out the other sentences?

> Now some shephud been dey een de fiel dat night. Dey beena stay dey, da mind dey sheep. Den one angel ob de Lawd appeah ta um. De night time done lightnin op jes like day clean broad. Cause ob dat, de shephud mos scaid ta det. Bot de angel tell um say, "Mus dohn feah! A hab good nyews wa gwine mek ebrybody rejaice. Cause A come fa tell oona, 'Right now, dis day, a Sabior done bon fa oona. E Christ de Lawd. An e bon een David town!' A gwine tell oona wa oona gwine see dey. Cause ob dat, oona gwine know A done tell oona de trute. Oona gwine find de chile wrop op een closs wa been teah eenta scrip, an e been led down een a trough."
>
> (American Bible Society 2005)

Another variety typically labeled as a Creole is Hawaiian (Creole) English, often called *Pidgin* by Hawaiians. Hawaiian English emerged in the later part of the 19th century on plantations where speakers of many different languages worked. The languages that have contributed to the emergence of Hawaiian English include Portuguese, Japanese, Hawaiian, Cantonese, and Tagalog. Similar to the verbal system of Gullah, Hawaiian English has a unique system for indicating tense and aspect, as shown in Table 6.7.

African American English is another variety that marks aspectual distinctions aside from those available in "standard" English. We have already seen how African American varieties of English may mark habitual actions with the auxiliary *be*. Some examples of this kind of habitual marking can be seen in Table 6.8.

The history of habitual marking in African American English is a highly debated issue among linguists. Some believe that habitual marking is due to the influence of Irish English

Table 6.7 Some tense/aspect markers in Hawaiian English (see Sakoda & Siegel 2003)

Form	*Meaning*
gon	future tense (> "going") e.g., Jawn gon bai buk. (John is going to buy a book.)
wen	past tense (> "went") e.g., Ai wen si om. (I saw him.)
yustu	habitual past (> "used to") e.g., Ai yustu plei futbawl. (I used to play football.)
pau	completive (> *pau*, "to finish" in Hawaiian) e.g., Hi wen pau work. (He has finished working.)
ste	progressive (ongoing action) e.g., Where yu ste go? (Where are you going?)
stat	inchoative (beginning of an action, > "start") e.g., Ai stat working. (I began working.)

Table 6.8 Habitual aspect in African American English (see Rickford and Rickford [2000])

She working.	"She is working right now."
She be working.	"She usually works."
She happy.	"She is happy right now."
She be happy.	"She is usually happy." (~ "She is a cheerful person.")

in the early colonial period, as the Irish habitual-marked expression *bíonn mé* occurs in Irish English as "does be" and similar forms. Newfoundland English, with its clearly documented influence from Irish English, for example, has habitual marking. Other linguists believe that habitual aspect emerged in African American English independently in the 20th century, while still others hold that the habitual/non-habitual distinction is retained from African languages. A number of languages from West Africa mark habitual aspect; the distinction is also found in most of the varieties of English and French spoken by African diasporic populations throughout the Caribbean (for a fuller discussion, see Rickford & Rickford 2000; Wolfram & Thomas 2008).

In addition to marking habitual aspect, African American English verbs convey additional aspectual distinctions. For example, the stressed auxiliary been (as in *I BEEN hungry*, in which case the capital letters here indicate that the main stress in the sentence goes on that word) marks an event that began a long time ago and continues up to the present. Thus, "He BEEN married" would mean that he has been married for a long time (and still is). The unstressed counterpart operates similarly to *been* in other varieties of English (He been married ~ He has been married). African American English also marks the aspect linguists call *inchoative*, which indicates that an action is just beginning or is about to begin. In African American English, this aspect is marked with *finna* or *fi'na* ([fɪʔnə]), a form also found (often as "fixin to") among white and Latinx speakers in the Southern United States.

No MSG, no lazy grammar

This discussion of the structure of ethnic varieties demonstrates the range of diversity found across varieties of English. All forms of ethnicity-indexing variation follow regular, logical rules of grammar. However, many people treat this variation as simply "bad" or "wrong" English. Negative evaluations of ethnic variation are often patronizing, showing pity or concern for the poor children who have been "deprived" of proper grammar. Thus, rather than teach white children to understand other varieties of English, American culture expects all children to adopt a uniform way of speaking (that could be considered similar, in some respects, to how most white people speak). This "standard language privilege" (Queen 2019) operates in the same way as "white privilege." Like whiteness, "standard" English is considered unmarked (that is, it is assumed to be the norm) so that people who present themselves as monodialectal speakers of some kind of "standard" English are not thought of as indexing whiteness but rather simply as speaking "English."

In the case of Chinese restaurant syndrome, people (who didn't really know what MSG was) used MSG to index a wide range of racist stereotypes against Asians (as dirty and likely to spread illness). People who suffered from Chinese restaurant syndrome felt severe pain, even though there was no medical basis for their symptoms. This demonstrates how deeply rooted discourse structural racism in American culture. When people don't understand something, they often fall back on stereotypes.

To make matters worse, the same racist stereotypes get applied to almost any aspects of life, including things like clothing choices, musical preferences, and ways of speaking. Often, if some sort of social practice is common among members of some minority group, that practice will also come to index pre-existing racist stereotypes. We have talked about this process of *symbolic revalorization* in which some social practice (like language) comes to stand in for more conventional (and obvious) forms of racism.

Examples of racist stereotypes being connected to social practices which results in real-world implications for those involved can frequently be seen in the news. In 2014, a white Florida man fired multiple shots into a car of young African American men, killing 17-year-old Jordan Davis, who was riding in the back seat. The man's explanation for murder was that the young men in the car had been playing loud "thug music" (Grimes 2019). The actual type of music itself doesn't matter; the motive was the race of the men listening to it. If young Black men only listened to 18th-century opera music then opera would likely be categorized as "thug music."

Clothing styles are another place where symbolic revalorization often occurs. In cases where police murder young Black men, it is common to see references to the fact that the victim was wearing a hoodie (see Figure 6.3). Of course, nothing about a hoodie alone ought to be relevant to a murder case. Giving attention to the clothing a murder victim was wearing only comes to make sense once that clothing has come to index racist stereotypes of those who choose to wear it. In other words, hoodies come to index "dangerous" or "violent" behavior through an illogical and warped analogy: young Black men like to wear hoodies, and young Black men are dangerous, therefore, a person wearing a hoodie is dangerous.

Symbolic revalorization of clothing is nothing new. In the 1940s, the indexical meanings associated with hoodies today were applied to zoot suits, a style of men's suit with a long (just above the knee) jacket and extremely baggy pants. The zoot suit style was especially popular among young Black, Chicano, and Filipino men. In California, the zoot suit came to index stereotypes of young Filipino and Chicano men as dangerous gang members. In addition, the baggy style of the suit was seen as "unpatriotic" because it used extra fabric during World War II, when people were rationing things like fabric to aid in the war effort. In Los Angeles in June 1943, there was an altercation between a group of white sailors and a group of Chicano men in zoot suits that sparked a series of riots. For five days, gangs of white men attacked young Chicanos (as well as some Filipino and African American young men) who happened to be wearing zoot suits. In many cases, the rioters attacked the suits themselves, destroying the clothes, and, in some cases, leaving victims nearly naked in the street. The majority of people arrested (see Figure 6.4) during the violence were young Chicano men. The Los Angeles City Council eventually passed a resolution making it illegal to wear a zoot suit because the suits were seen as a marker of being a "hoodlum" (Bruns 2014). Of course, the clothes themselves weren't the problem. The problem was the race of the people who wore them.

This same process of symbolic revalorization is evident in the reception of ethnic varieties of English. Ethnic variation is an important sociolinguistic resource. It allows people to convey their personal history and heritage through the language they speak. Ethnic varieties may also convey distinctions in meaning that do not align with those of "standard" English. When faced with subtle semantic distinctions that they do not recognize (like the use of habitual aspect), prescriptivists remain proudly ignorant of the meaning involved and reject the utterance entirely as "bad" grammar. Indeed, prescriptivist ideologies could be viewed

Figure 6.3 The hoodie has come to index racist stereotypes of young Black men as dangerous

Source: photo by Philipp Lansing

Figure 6.4 Young men arrested during the zoot suit riots in Los Angeles, 1943
Source: UCLA Charles E. Young Research Library Department of Special Collections

as part of a larger system of discourses that maintain white control over public spaces (Hill 1998). Through symbolic revalorization, language ideologies that denigrate ethnic dialects substantially contribute to structural racism in American culture.

Language, interaction, and ethnic inequality

In addition to differences in patterns of grammatical variation, communities have specific interactional norms, or what linguist Deborah Tannen calls "interactional styles." Interactional styles include things like how loudly people speak, the distance maintained between speakers, the amount of overlapping speech in a conversation, and the ways in which conversations are expected to proceed. For example, compared to most white communities, the volume of speech may be higher among African Americans, Latinx Americans, Jewish Americans, Italian Americans, and South Asian Americans. For people unfamiliar with this cultural difference, this louder volume may be an "empty" indexical that gets "filled in" with stereotypes. Of course, since stereotypes of different ethnic groups differ, the indexical meanings associated with the same sign, e.g., louder volume, creaky voice (see Chapter 4), etc., will vary across contexts. For Italian Americans, this louder volume may be interpreted as reflecting a passionate and emotional personality, while for African Americans and Latinx Americans, it might be interpreted as indexing a violent, threatening personality. As these sorts of indexical associations become entrenched, language ideologies come to mirror ideologies of race (or gender, or class, or sexuality, etc.).

Differences in interactional styles may also refer to the linguistic norms about when it is appropriate to speak and when it is best to remain silent. For example, the Western Apache avoid speaking in certain culturally specific contexts (Basso 1970). For example, people who meet for the first time remain silent for some time, waiting to speak until they have reached a point where they feel like they know each other. Similarly, when two people begin a romantic relationship, they also maintain silence until they become more acquainted with each other. When a child comes home from college, for example, parents and siblings would maintain silence until it was clear that the returning child had not changed while away. People also maintain silence around those who are depressed, angry, drunk, or suffering from mental illness. Those in these states are understood as not fully present in an interaction, such that interacting with them is seen as pointless. Of course, white American English speakers often find silence uncomfortable and feel the need to speak in order to avoid silent moments. For the Apache, an unfamiliar person who speaks excessively is seen as nervous and anxious. Too much talking is interpreted as a sign that a person is about to ask for some sort of favor. In turn, white people have often interpreted Apache silence as resulting from some negative stereotypes of Native Americans like "their primitive language makes it difficult for them to speak a complex language like English" or "their people are naturally cold and emotionally distant." We could just chalk this up to misunderstandings – one group views silence one way and another group views silence differently. And if that were the case and people could talk out the misunderstanding, there would be no concern. Yet because the silence is thought to be meaningful, each group fills in the indexical association with their own stereotypes of the other.

Although people reading this book understand that race has no biological foundation, scientists and physicians continue to consider race as a relevant factor in medicine. Some apps to help in diagnoses continue to use algorithms that punish patients who aren't white. The study of physical pain is a good example. Discourse structural racism has long promoted the myth that Black people feel pain at lower levels compared to white people. This bad idea probably emerged long ago, likely as an excuse for the brutal history of whippings, brandings, and other forms of pain inflicted on enslaved people. Scientists have attempted to determine if there were racial differences in experiencing pain (Woodrow et al. 1972), and, when combined with the discursive stereotype of Black people as less sensitive to pain, results of such studies lead white physicians to believe that when Black people complain about pain they are somehow exaggerating the extent of their suffering. In expressions of pain, racist stereotypes may override more conventional indexical meanings, so that saying "ouch" fails to successfully convey its usual association with pain. Because of the myth that Black people exaggerate expressions of pain, it is still the case that while white patients are often given pain relievers immediately upon complaining about their pain, Black patients must ask repeatedly before their pain is treated. More recent research using brain scans to study the issue suggests that, in African American patients, pain corresponds to brain activity associated with chronic pain, particularly the type of chronic pain found in individuals who have suffered extreme stress or trauma, particularly for long periods (Losin et al. 2020). Thus, while norms for interaction might explain part of the ethnic differences in experiencing pain, it may well be that the unavoidable stress and trauma caused by constant experiences of racial discrimination may cause the brain to adapt in ways that increase experiences of pain.

Serena Williams and the (dis)belief in Black pain

On September 1, 2017, in West Palm Beach, Florida, tennis superstar Serena Williams gave birth to her daughter, Alexis. Years before, in March of 2011, Williams had undergone emergency treatment for a pulmonary embolism, a blood clot in the lungs. These clots form elsewhere in the body and ultimately lodge themselves in the lungs causing shortness of breath, severe pain like that of a heart attack, and coughing (often with blood). When Williams began experiencing these symptoms the day after Alexis was born via Cesarean section she quickly alerted a nurse.

While gasping for air, she explained to the nearest nurse what she was experiencing and requested "a CT scan and intravenous heparin (a blood thinner) right away." The nurse thought perhaps Williams was simply confused because of the pain medication she was already receiving, but Williams was insistent. After a series of missteps, which included an ultrasound of Williams' legs, the hospital did eventually order a CT scan of her lungs which revealed several small clots that had settled in her lungs. Having previously had an embolism, pregnancy, surgery, and bed rest are all risk factors for a pulmonic embolism. Williams had experienced these symptoms before and knew not only the test but also the treatment that could save her life and mitigate her pain. Instead, the medical staff disregarded her words and treated her diagnosis as if beginning from scratch. The following day, although the embolism itself had been treated, Williams' coughing was so forceful that the sutures from her Cesarean section ruptured and had to be reclosed.

According to the CDC, 700 women die from pregnancy or childbirth related issues every year in the United States (19 in 100,000 pregnant women; giving the United States a ranking of 56th in the world in terms of maternal mortality, tied with Romania, Oman, Moldova, Latvia, and Ukraine). The CDC also conservatively estimates that 50,000 American women deal with dangerous or life-threatening pregnancy-related complications every year. Even within this group, Black women are three to four times more likely than white women to die from these same complications (Hoyert 2021).

These sorts of disparate treatment relate to failures for indexical meanings to be successfully understood. Children who speak ethnic dialects may be sent to speech therapy to "correct" their "deficient" English, employees are told to adjust their speech to mirror a white norm, and young men are murdered because their linguistic behavior is misunderstood as posing some sort of threat. Just as other kinds of misunderstandings have real consequences for real people, one must understand that these racially and ethnically-derived misunderstandings go beyond simple errors. They result in pain and death.

The linguistic variation associated with ethnic dialects is perhaps the most straightforward way of expressing one's ethnic identity. Correcting or attempting to change such speech only serves to deny, dismiss, and disrespect the identity of the speaker. Racist discourse may influence how indexical signs are interpreted. Because indexical meanings are always potential meanings, their interpretation can never be entirely controlled. As it is, patterns of social discourse and language appropriation serve to impose negative indexical meanings onto forms of ethnic variation.

Language, race, appropriation, and whiteness

The treatment of ethnic varieties of English as simply "bad" English has a number of effects that directly contribute to discourse structural racism. Because language variation is how individuals express their identities, the enforcement of prescriptivism attempts to create public spaces and discourses reserved for white people (Hill 1998). Language variables indexically linked to ethnic identities are corrected, criticized, derided, and mocked across endless contexts. School children, college students, and employees are repeatedly told that their language (and, in turn, their identity) is "wrong." Because of different interactional styles, failing to interact according to an unmarked, unspoken, and largely undefined white norm can be deadly. This is especially true for those with conditions that make social interactions difficult, such as autism. Given that these norms for interaction are almost never discussed, people of color are constantly at risk of violating some interactional expectation and unknowingly indexing racist stereotypes. This risk helps public discourses focus on white people while marginalizing or erasing the experiences of people of color.

Same slur, different century

The cartoon in Figure 6.5 appeared in *Life* magazine in 1911. Within the racial ideology of the time, the category of "white people" was imagined as excluding all immigrants who weren't from Northern Europe, European immigrants who were Catholic or Jewish, and immigrants who were from Ireland or countries in southern, central, and eastern Europe (like Italy, Greece, Spain, Russia, Poland, Hungary, etc.). Although the racial ideologies have changed (so that Irish Americans and Italian Americans are now "white"), the racist discourse used to marginalize immigrants has remained fairly constant. The cartoon portrays an Italian American immigrant with the slur *wop*, a racist term to describe Italian immigrants that was shorthand for "without papers." This is basically the same slur found in terms like *illegal alien* or *wetback* (a racist slur for Mexican Americans, implying that they arrived without documentation by crossing the Rio Grande). The poem below the cartoon is written in Mock Italian American, with features like -a added to the ends of words that end in consonants. The text reproduces numerous prejudicial stereotypes of Italian Americans at the time: smelling of garlic, eating spaghetti, carrying a stiletto knife, and being skilled at being a bootblack (polishing shoes). Although the usual targets have changed over time, mocking of ethnic dialects or non-native accents continues to be a basic feature of racist discourse.

Racist language ideologies are also disseminated through forms that mock the language of communities of color. Humor "about" non-native accents or Black language (sometimes called Ebonics or Jive) often simply repeat racists jokes under the guise of laughing about language (Rickford & Rickford 2000). In some cases, old racist jokes are simply relabeled as "Ebonics jokes." This mocking use of Black language links stereotypes about Black

Figure 6.5 Anti-Italian cartoon from *Life* magazine

language with racist stereotypes of Black people. The grammar of mocking does not utilize the complex grammar of African American English and often includes ungrammatical forms. Rickford and Rickford (2000) give an example of one such joke, as seen in example 7.

7. Why were there only 49 contestants in the Miss Ebonics pageant?

   Nobody wanted to be Miss Idaho.

Here, the punch line ("Idaho" and "I da ho") is ungrammatical in African American English, where the first-person pronoun "I" always requires a form of the verb to be ("am"). By using the term "ho," the joke reproduces racist stereotypes about Black women despite the fact that the joke is "about" language. Similarly, websites that offer joke automated "translation" into ethnic dialects (like "Jive") regularly produce forms that are ungrammatical for actual speakers of African American English. In particular, the racist bots repeatedly violate the rules for marking aspect in African American English (such as using habitual *be* to mark the simple present). The mocking demonstrates that prescriptivist ideologies are about something other than grammar.

Aunt Jemima

Indexical bleaching is common when the racist origins of popular texts and marketing campaigns come to be obscured over time. In the late 19th century, many products were marketed using representations drawn from the blackface minstrel shows that were popular at the time. The use of Minstrelese (the ancestor of Mock Ebonics) in advertising was quite popular for many years. For example, Uncle Remus Syrup brand syrup debuted in the 1920s with the ludicrous slogan, *Dis sho am good!* Over time, the indexical associations of many surviving minstrel tropes have been bleached.

An example can be found with the use of the Aunt Jemima character, as in Figure 6.6 (Manring 1998). In 2020, the brand decided to drop the Aunt Jemima character even though she had been redrawn several times over the years to make her less and less of a caricature and more like an actual woman. The character of Aunt Jemima originated in minstrel shows played by a white man in blackface and drag. Early advertisements for Aunt Jemima brand depicted this character and included the Mock Ebonics phrase *I'se in town, honey*. A woman named Nancy Green was hired to travel the country portraying Aunt Jemima (announcing her shows with billboards reading *I'se in town, honey*). Over time, the company has attempted to bleach the indexical associations of the racist context in which Aunt Jemima products emerged, but these racist associations with the original character could not be entirely erased.

Given the language ideological pressure to banish Blackness from public discourse, one might assume that white people entirely avoid forms that might index other ethnic identities. But the truth is that white people use Black language all the time. The strong indexical link between Black language and the racist "gangsta/thug" stereotype means that, for many white people, Black speech indexes toughness and masculinity. The ability of Black language to index masculine identities is the basis for the use of Black speech among cis hetero white men and boys (see, for example, Bucholtz & Lopez 2011). The use of Black speech by white teenage boys is largely an attempt to establish a masculine persona. Hence, there are some white teenage boys who exhibit a desperate desire to say the n-word, perhaps the strongest indexical marker of masculinity in Black speech. However, even grown white men commonly use language and gestures that index Black masculinity (such as the fist bump).

While white people often view the speech of African American men as threatening and dangerous, the speech of African American women is typically understood as indexing a sassy, "in your face" attitude. In some cases, white gay men may exploit this indexical link by appropriating the speech of Black gay men and women (e.g., Miss Thang, shade, reading, work it, hunty, etc.). Memes and catchphrases disseminate racial stereotypes alongside language forms that mock African American speech (e.g., *Ain't nobody got time for that!*).

Figure 6.6 1894 advertisement for Aunt Jemima pancake flour

Racism in child's play

Despite attempts to retire racist marketing techniques, an astounding number of elements from blackface minstrel shows have undergone enough indexically bleaching that their racist origins generally go unnoticed. Mickey Mouse was originally drawn to look like a minstrel character (with big eyes and an oversized mouth to create a mouse in blackface). Many common children's songs are bleached versions of songs originally used in blackface minstrel shows; "Oh, Susanna!," "Jimmy Crack Corn," and "Camptown Races" were all originally written for minstrel shows. Indexical bleaching allows for racialized forms of language to persist well past the racist context in which they emerged. Many of these songs were originally composed with forms of Mock Ebonics, as in this verse from "The Levee Song" (commonly known as "I've Been Working on the Railroad") written for minstrel shows performed at Princeton University in 1894.

> I been wukkin' on de railroad
> All de live-long day:
> I been wukkin' on de railroad
> Ter pass de time away.
> Doan' yuh hyah de wistle blowin'?
> Rise up so uhly in de mawn;
> Doan' yuh hyah de capn' shoutn',
> "Dina blow yo' hawn?" (Pyne et al. 1894)

The use of language that indexes a social group one doesn't belong to is a phenomenon linguists call "crossing" (Rampton 1995). When speakers use the language of another group to index stereotypes associated with that group, it is a form of *cultural appropriation*. In appropriation, speakers take language (and other elements of culture) from other groups in constructing a social persona. Appropriation may reproduce stereotypes by reducing another group to some stereotype (as in the use of Blackness to index white masculinity). Appropriation contributes to indexical bleaching by using a form in new contexts (that do not index Blackness, for example). The appropriation of linguistic forms that index minority identities is a basic way in which white Americans convey their social identities.

White people use occasional Spanish words or forms of Black language as a way of indexing the identity of a person familiar with the world beyond the white norm, as a person who is cosmopolitan and aware of current cultural and social trends. In a study of language use among self-identified white "nerd" girls, Mary Bucholtz (1999) found that "nerd" identity is indexed through a "superstandard" way of speaking that (among other things) avoids the borrowings from ethnic dialects used by their non-nerd white counterparts. Bucholtz concludes that mocking of "nerds" as social misfits is based on their failure to appropriate, making their speech "too white." In other words, white people who don't incorporate appropriated forms into their speech index a persona that is out of touch with current cultural trends, a person that is boring and worthy of disdain.

However, when ethnic-indexing forms undergo indexical bleaching, the process contributes to the maintenance of white public space. The appropriation of a form from communities of color causes indexical bleaching because the contexts in which that form is used has been overrun with usage by white people. Once a form has lost its ability to index the identities of the form's original users, communities of color must develop new ways of saying the same thing to maintain the indexical association between language and ethnicity. In her study of language ideology and hip hop identity, Marcyliena Morgan (2001: 194) refers to this process of constantly inventing new ways of speaking as creating *lexical havoc*. This is particularly common in hip hop where artists try to ensure that they use new and innovative forms because the indexical associations of new words can quickly turn. As Morgan (198) notes, "the value of lexical items rises and falls for reasons that range from poor artistic and musical expression to uncritical appropriation by suburban youth."

African Americans (especially men and boys) must repeatedly invent new slang to keep ahead of the white people (especially white men and boys) who appropriate. Of course, the new words will be appropriated by white people again, creating the need for newer words, which will eventually also be appropriated. This creates a repetitive cycle of invention and appropriation in which common slang terms constantly change.

Another example of indexical bleaching is the refusal to attempt to pronounce names with origins in languages other than English. Those with names that are unfamiliar to white people have likely experienced someone refusing to say their name: "I don't think I can say that, let's just call you Cindy." In June 2020, for example, a math professor in California was placed on leave after refusing to say the name of one of his students, Phuc Bui Diem Nguyen. The professor claimed that Phuc Bui's name, which rhymes with "hook bouy" [fʊk bui], sounded too obscene in English and asked her to pick a different name. When she was offended, he told her that if his name happened to mean "eat a dick" in Vietnamese, he wouldn't use the name in Vietnam (Taylor & Morales 2020). These language ideologies serve to enforce what Jane Hill (1998) has called "white public space," the control of public spaces (both physical and discursive). Such language ideologies are strong enough to lead some to be complicit in the public humiliation of those with "foreign-sounding" names. The forced indexical bleaching of names is an old American tradition. Immigrants arriving at Ellis Island in the first half of the 20th century were regularly forced to change their names because they sounded "too Italian, too Jewish, or too Irish." One's name, of course, is the strongest indexical marker of a person's individual identity so that having one's name "bleached" is one of the most painful results of language ideologies.

Language is love

The linguistic varieties of English that index ethnic identities show regular and typical grammatical patterns. Although they may have regular differences from "standard" English, ethnic dialects are no different from any other of the world's languages. And just like any variety, ethnic dialects can index the unique cultural experiences and intimate contexts of interaction for their speakers. Speakers of ethnic varieties (and many other undervalued varieties) often have strong emotional and intimate attachments to the non-standard forms in their variety of English. This deep love for the language of one's own community often emerges as a reflection of deep emotions, such as in the creation of verbal art like poetry or song lyrics. For example, the use of Navajo English is common in poetry and fiction by Navajo authors such as Laura Tohe or Blackhorse Mitchell (see Webster 2012). Many of America's greatest authors have written works in undervalued Englishes of one type or another. What is sometimes referred to as "dialect literature" is often a means of celebrating the natural expressiveness and beauty of undervalued varieties of English. Ethnic varieties of English are thus deeply personal and treasured by speakers. This emotional attachment makes attempts to erase or appropriate forms of ethnic grammar particularly harsh.

James Baldwin wrote (1979), "It is not the Black child's . . . language that is despised; It is [their] experience." In other words, the issue that some people have with ethnic varieties of English has nothing to do with the grammatical forms actually found in those varieties. The actual forms of variation could be entirely different, and they would still index the same meanings drawn from racial discourse. The "problem" is that those forms of grammar index ethnic identities, and these identities are seen as unwelcome in spaces that public discourse presumes should be under the control of white people. Thus, prescriptive prohibitions against racial and ethnic variation are tools of racial and ethnic domination.

Discussion questions

1. Linguists are not infallible, even when it comes to discussing linguistic topics. For example, the labels used to define African American English have changed over time, sometimes according to trends in naming (choosing "African American" over "Black") but sometimes because of something underlyingly bad (calling such varieties "substandard," for example). Why is it important to think about the appropriate name for a language variety? Whose opinion on the name and description of the variety matters most – a linguist or a speaker? How so?
2. If racial and ethnic varieties of language are not inextricably linked to race and ethnicity, why do linguists use labels like "African American English" that are connected to race and ethnicity to discuss them, even though there is no biological basis for racial categories?
3. We said the African American English form *finna* is related to the Southern American English expression *fixing to*. What do these expressions mean? Why might they be related? Assuming *fixing to* was the original form, what sound changes had to happen to arrive at *finna*? Note: the differences in these forms, like in all languages, is the result of systematic, not random or lazy, variation.
4. If one doesn't already exist, imagine what it would be like to have a dialect generator that generated versions of your own variety AND always made examples that connected such language use to being ugly, violent, or incestuous. How would it make you feel? If you have encountered one that purports to represent speech with which you identify, how did it impact your understanding of your own language? Why do such dialect generators exist?
5. Names are very important parts of people's identities. How would it feel to have your name mispronounced or ignored altogether? How can people change how they think about pronouncing unfamiliar names? What approaches might be useful?
6. Go back to Table 6.1. Of the words listed there, how many do you recognize, and what are their indexical associations? Are there other borrowings into English from Yiddish that you are aware of? What do they index?
7. Why might it be racist to repeatedly use phrases like *Chinese virus*, *kung flu*, or *Wuhan virus*, especially in light of the fact that other names like *coronavirus* and *COVID-19* were already in wide circulation at the time?
8. Thinking of Baldwin's quote in the last paragraph, what would it mean if the opposite were really true: that the Black child's language is despised and not their experience? Would this predict that Black children whose language was highly similar to standard ideals would not experience racism?

7 Language diversity in the United States

Estados Unidos no tiene un idioma oficial

In 2019, during one of the early debates among those seeking the Democratic nomination for president, candidate Beto O'Rourke switched from English to Spanish as he answered a question about immigration. This prompted additional use of Spanish during the debate by Senator Cory Booker and former Secretary of Housing and Urban Development, Julián Castro (the only Latinx candidate in the race). In discussing this unprecedented use of a "foreign" language in a presidential debate, many commenters and journalists saw the use of Spanish by candidates who are not Latinx as the worst kind of political pandering. To monolingual English speakers, O'Rourke and Booker (as well as Pete Buttigieg, who also often spoke Spanish during the campaign) seemed to be showing off their language skills to win points with Latinx candidates. The response from the Latinx journalists, however, was less critical, arguing that while speaking Spanish wasn't enough to win over Latinx voters, it was a positive step. For example, acclaimed journalist María Elena Salinas tweeted:

> Estados Unidos no tiene un idioma "oficial." El intentar hablar español aunque no es suficiente para ganar el voto latino, es una muestra de respeto a nuestra cultura. Obvio los votantes hablan inglés, son ciudadanos.
>
> [The United States doesn't have an "official" language. Although trying to speak Spanish isn't enough to win the Latinx vote, it is a sign of respect for our culture. The voters obviously speak English, they are citizens.]

These variations in viewpoints represent tensions between the potential indexical meanings one might link to the use of Spanish in a major national political debate. Because indexical signs convey *potential* meanings (as discussed in Chapter 1), the same sign may have different, even conflicting, interpretations. Some indexical meanings mark public uses of Spanish negatively. These meanings contribute to the language ideology that upholds the preservation of white public space by ensuring that critical public contexts are restricted to English.

While Booker and O'Rourke were seen as show-offs for demonstrating their Spanish competence, journalists treated Julián Castro's Spanish quite differently. Many reports of the debate noted that Castro had "admitted" that he was not fluent in Spanish, and some openly said that Booker, O'Rourke, and Buttigieg all spoke "better" Spanish compared to Castro. For US Latinxs, being told how "bad" your Spanish is a sadly familiar experience. The negative assessment of Castro's Spanish is founded in language ideologies about bilingualism in general, and US Spanishes in particular.

The Standard Language Ideology discussed in previous chapters has, as its foundation, the assumption that there is one true and correct way of speaking. In the United States, this

DOI: 10.4324/9781003332886-7

"true" and "correct" language is English, and it is the imagined standard variety of this one language that is presumed to be the only appropriate language for public communication. The use of Spanish in a presidential debate is a major challenge to that ideology. A dominant American language ideology presumes that being monolingual is natural and preferable. Even though most of the world is multilingual, some people who grow up in bilingual communities in the United States (and many other Anglophone countries) are therefore presumed to be not fully capable speakers of two languages, but monolingual speakers of some language other than English.

Asian, Middle Eastern, and Latinx Americans are also familiar with being told how good their English is, as if native English speakers only come in Black and white. Castro graduated from Stanford and Harvard Law and served as Secretary of Housing and Urban Development. Obviously, his English is better than "good." Since people often wrongly presume that people normally speak a single language, Castro's "lack" of Spanish serves to legitimize his "good" English. Of course, many Latinxs in the United States do not speak Spanish at all. Like Castro, they are often faced with being treated as somehow "inauthentic" Latinxs because they don't fit the stereotyped view of Latinx language use. Indeed, one congressional representative went so far as to say that Julián and his twin brother Joaquin studied Spanish as adults to become "retroactive Hispanics." Such use of linguistic competence to draw boundaries is a common way to enforce the assumptions within discourse structural racism. People of color who are perceived (usually by white Americans) as "articulate" in "standard" English are seen as somehow suspect, as if they then can't be legitimate members of their own ethnic group.

It is helpful, at this early stage of the discussion, to distinguish between foreign-accented (or L2) speech as discussed in Chapter 4 and bilingualism as we are discussing it here. The question of what it means to be a native speaker of a particular language is surprisingly complicated and deeply entwined both with the issues of language ideology discussed in this book and with questions of thoroughness or completeness of cultural and linguistic competence. Let us assume, for the purposes of our discussion, an overly simplistic definition of "native" which means something like "acquired the language as a child." This is often what linguists mean by the term, but it is wise to proceed with great caution since this definition of "native" excludes, among others, adults who learn to speak a truly foreign language in college or later, heritage language speakers who grow up with personal access to a second language through the voices of their parents, grandparents, or tribe, and members of the deaf community who, for whatever reason, acquire a signed language after childhood.

When we use the word bilingual (or trilingual, etc.), linguists typically mean people who have native competency in more than one language. Someone who is an English/Hindi bilingual has native speaker judgments, productions, and perceptions in both of these languages. This person may *sound* to an uninformed listener as if they have a foreign accent and therefore lack native speaker judgments about English. Or this person may sound as if they have "no accent" in both their English and their Hindi. The bottom line is that children born in the United States who grow up speaking both English and another language are still native speakers of American English just as they are native speakers of their second language. The reason this is important will become clear as we tease apart and investigate the various language ideologies monolingual Americans hold about the linguistic competence, authenticity, and, indeed, foreignness of people who speak languages other than, and in addition to, English.

It is also important to be careful with the use of the word "foreign." A bilingual speaker of English and Navajo cannot, in any sense, be said to be a speaker of a "foreign" language. ASL is not a foreign language. Hawaiian is not a foreign language. Arabic, Cantonese,

French, German, Hokkien, Mandarin, Swahili, Yoruba, and hundreds of other non-English languages are all learned by American children from American parents in the United States every day. As we will see, these children are almost always bilingual in English too but to call them or their non-English languages 'foreign' is really a comment on the acceptability or American authenticity of the person and not a statement of linguistic fact.

Spanish has been spoken in (what is now) the United States longer than English has, so it is not at all surprising that distinctive dialects of Spanish have emerged over time. Many parts of the future United States were colonized by Spain (rather than England) and, consequently, these regions have had Spanish speakers for centuries. For example, much of the southwestern United States belonged to Mexico before the Mexican American war (see Figure 7.1). Before the 1830s, Mexico controlled all of Texas, California, New Mexico, Arizona, Nevada, and Utah, as well as parts of Colorado.

In 1836, the Texas Revolution resulted in Texas leaving Mexico and becoming an independent nation. Mexico did not recognize Texas independence, so when Texas joined the United States in 1845, a war between Mexico and the United States ensued. The Treaty of Guadalupe Hidalgo (1848) ended the war with Mexico ceding what is now the southwestern

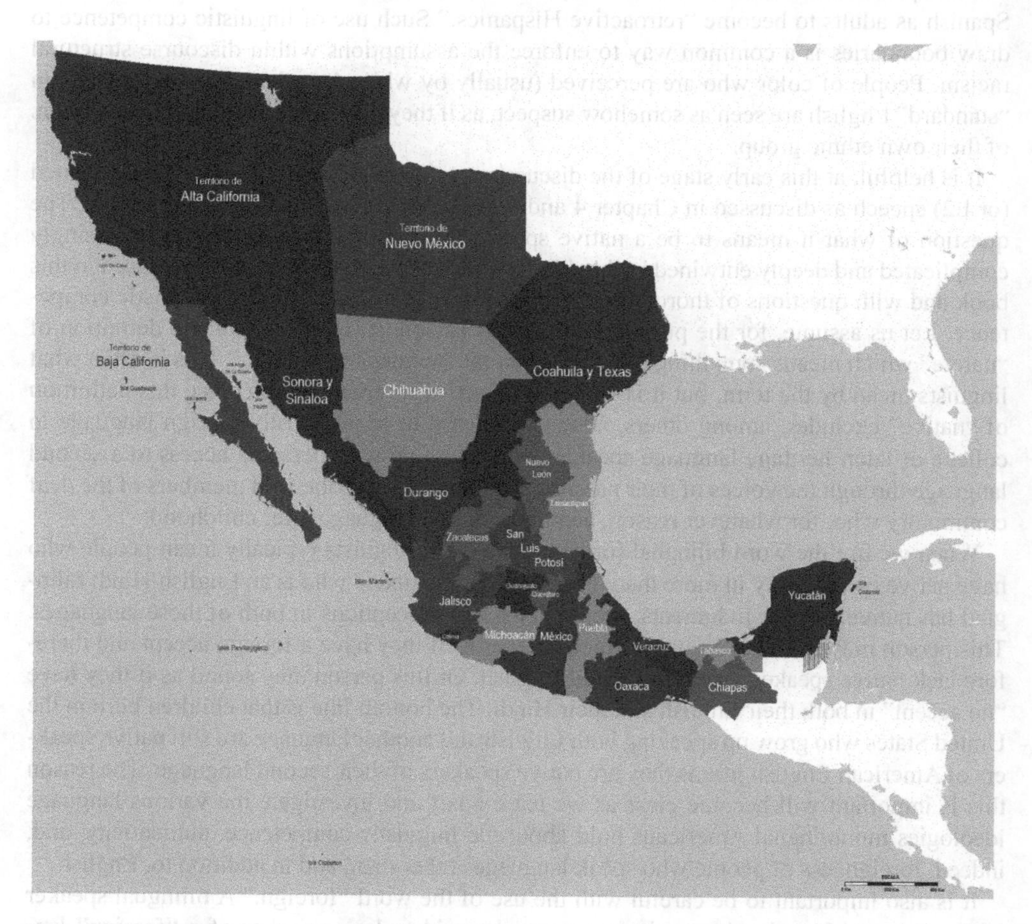

Figure 7.1 A map of the states of Mexico before the Texas Revolution (1835–1836)

part of the United States. Of course, many of the people living in or west of Texas were Spanish speakers, and many of their descendants continue to use Spanish today. The term *Chicanx* refers to these Spanish-speaking communities (and today the term is sometimes used to refer to all Mexican Americans who were born in the United States). While Chicanx Spanish is the main variety in the Southwest, the Spanish spoken on the East Coast shows more variation with numerous speakers of Caribbean Spanishes, like Cuban, Dominican, and Puerto Rican Spanish.

As with ethnic varieties of English, the Spanishes of US Puerto Ricans, Dominicans, Cubans, and Chicanxs are often regarded as "incorrect" compared to the "standard" Spanishes of Spain or Mexico. We have seen how language ideologies about American English end up reproducing racist stereotypes. Ideologies of Spanish show the same pattern. Language ideologies in the Spanish-speaking Americas typically view Chicanx and Caribbean American varieties of Spanish negatively. This is not particularly surprising as these are the varieties with a history of Native American (Chicanx) and/or Black (Caribbean) speakers. Indeed, the most denigrated variety of Spanish is probably Dominican Spanish, the dialect with the highest percentage of Black speakers. Chicanx Spanish (sometimes called *Caló* or *Pachuco Spanish*) is also highly denigrated throughout Mexico and Central America, with representations constantly linking Chicanx Spanish to racist stereotypes of "cholo" gang members. Even if Julián Castro had grown up speaking both Spanish and English, he could not use San Antonio (Chicanx) Spanish in a formal context without invoking these racist stereotypes and sounding especially "unpresidential."

These language ideologies reproduce the "double bind" seen with ideologies regarding ethnic dialects. Either one somehow merits discrimination because they are unable to speak "standard" English or they can't be a "real" member of their ethnic group precisely because they *are* able to speak "standard" English. The result is a "damned if you do, damned if you don't" approach to both languages other than English and Englishes other than the standard. The ultimate effect of this ideology is the erasure of ethnic varieties from public discourse which, again, serves to preserve white public space.

An old joke

Question: What do you call a person who speaks two languages?
Answer: Bilingual
Question: What do you call a person who speaks one language?
Answer: American
Sometimes the same joke is made about Brits. Though the focus is on the European context, you can read the perspective linked in this QR code to understand why this joke reflects a broad understanding of people who only speak English.

Language abundance

The idea that the use of Spanish in a presidential debate is surprising or somehow inappropriate demonstrates the strength of language ideologies that view the United States as a nation of monolingual English speakers. The United States has more Spanish speakers than Spain or any other country except Mexico (Instituto Cervantes 2019). Given the number of speakers of Spanish in the United States, it is rather astounding how *little* Spanish one finds in public discourse. Of course, Spanish is one of many languages spoken in the United States. There are also more than a million speakers (each) of French, German, Khmer, Vietnamese, Tagalog, Korean, and varieties of Chinese as well as hundreds of other languages with fewer speakers. The majority of these individuals also speak English, and, of course, many speak more than two languages.

There is also variation within languages other than English in the United States. Different Chinese languages occur throughout the United States with different languages dominant in different geographic areas, such as the predominance of Cantonese in New York's Chinatown neighborhood. Variation within global languages used in the States may also index specific ethnic/national identities, such as the numerous differences between Caribbean and Latin American varieties of Spanish.

The US Census asks those who speak another language at home to assess their own ability to speak English across four categories: *very well*, *well*, *not well*, and *not at all* (see Figure 7.2). Having been repeatedly told that their English is "bad," bilinguals often under evaluate their own speaking abilities. Even so, most census data tends to focus on those who say that they speak English "very well," as if those who rate themselves as *well* don't count as English speakers. Despite the possibility for underestimating English speakers, the census data show that the majority of those who use a language other than English at home are bilingual in English.

The breadth of linguistic diversity in the United States is a tremendous resource that, for the most part, remains underutilized. Indeed, in census data and educational materials, children who speak languages other than English are often categorized as "linguistically isolated" or having a "language deficit" simply because they have been exposed to a language besides English. Rather than suffering from a language deficit, it would make more sense to see people able to speak other languages as enjoying a language *abundance*. In today's globally connected society, it would make more sense to view those able to speak only one language as the ones who are somehow "deficient."

In the ideology which views native bilingualism as "wrong," one can see the interaction of language ideology with ideologies of race. People who are not easily categorized as white or Black are presumed to be foreigners or immigrants.

> Underlying the intersection of language and race is a language ideology that we call the ideology of nativeness, an Us-versus-Them division of the linguistic world in which native and nonnative speakers of a language are thought to be mutually exclusive, uncontested, identifiable groups. . . . At the core of this ideological model is a view of the world's speech communities as naturally monolingual and monocultural, whereby one language is semiotically associated with one nation.
>
> (Shuck 2006: 260)

For those who do not easily fit into the categories of Black and white, this ideology results in what is sometimes called the *perpetual foreigner syndrome* – a form of discrimination in

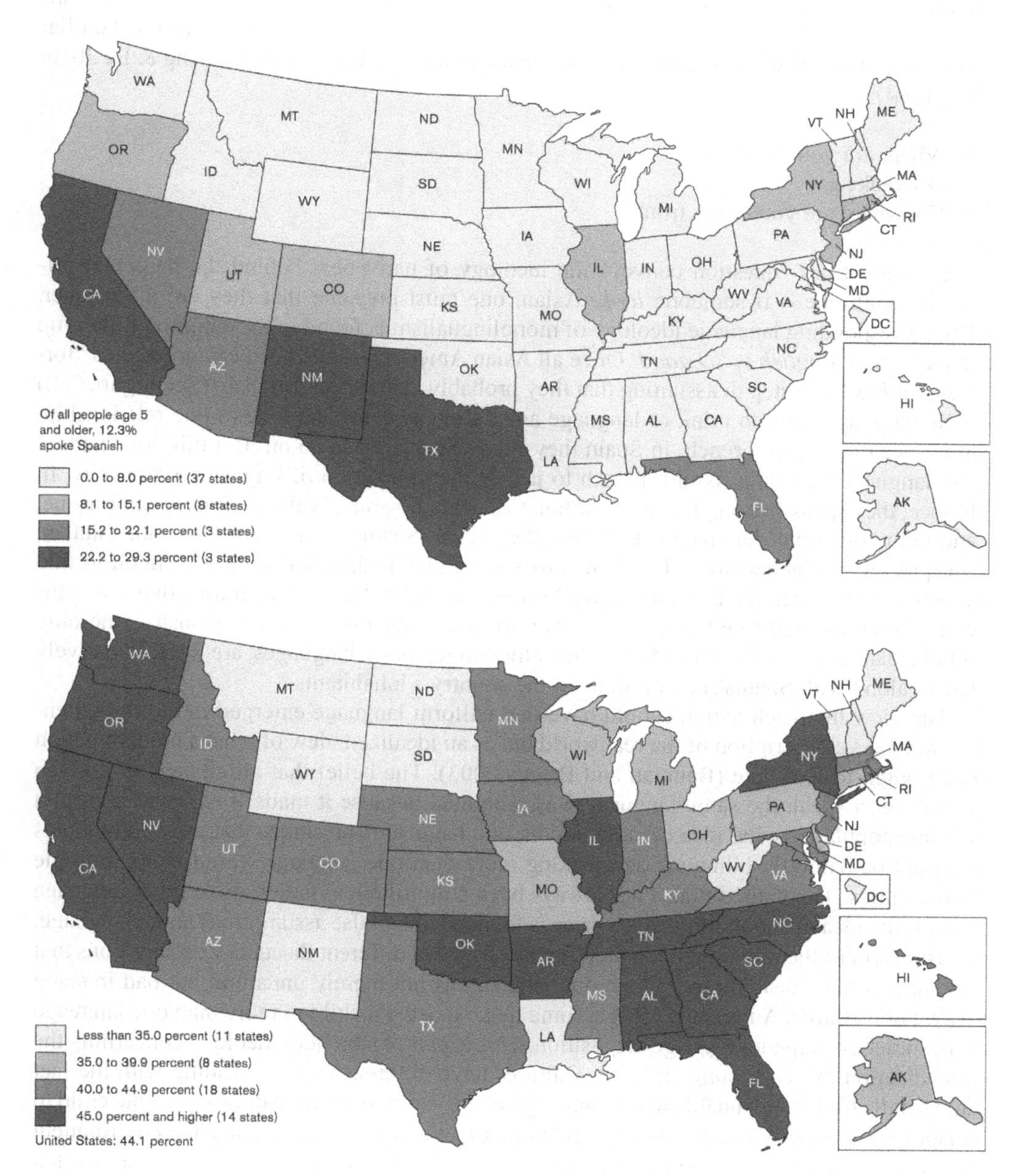

Figure 7.2 For population 5 years and older: a) Language other than English spoken at home; b) Percent of the population speaking a language other than English at home who spoke English less than "very well"

Source: U.S. Census Bureau 2007, American Community Survey

which Asian Americans, Latinxs, Middle Eastern Americans, Pacific Islanders, and others are treated as if they somehow can't "really" be American. Indeed, many Asian Americans have experienced having a stranger challenge their "Americanness" in an all too familiar routine (Cargile et al. 2010; Cheryan & Bodenhausen 2000; Kawai 2005; Chang & Le 2010; Lee 1994):

A: Where are you from?
B: Milwaukee.
A: No, where are you *really* from?

The "really from" question conveys the ideology of nativeness behind the perpetual foreigner syndrome – if someone *looks* Asian, one must presume that they are a foreigner. The corresponding language ideology of monolingualism is found in the common follow-up remark: *Your English is SO good!* Once all Asian Americans have been categorized as "foreign," it is a short step to assuming that they probably can't speak English. (See Figure 7.3.)

Some people tend to think of language and nation as being in a one-to-one relationship: in France they speak French, in Spain they speak Spanish, and so on. But this "one nation, one language" ideology is just a myth to justify the imposition of linguistic uniformity. In France, they speak French, Breton, Occitan, Corsican, Alsatian, Walloon, Provençal, Basque, and numerous other languages. In Spain, they speak Spanish, Asturian, Galician, Catalan, Basque, etc. Bilingualism is the norm across the globe, and, actually, "it is difficult to find a society that is genuinely monolingual" (Grosjean 1982: 1). Even countries that are "officially" monolingual (the United States is not), like Guatemala, where Spanish is the only official language, numerous Mayan and other Indigenous languages are spoken natively (often along with Spanish) by millions of the country's inhabitants.

The view that each nation should have one uniform language emerged in the Enlightenment, not as a description of the real world but as an idealized view of what a modern nation state ought to look like (Bauman and Briggs 2003). The belief that all citizens of a given nation must speak the same language was promoted because it made it easier to control a diverse population. The idea of "one nation, one language" presumes that most individuals will not be naturally bilingual, as speaking more than one language would index multiple nationalities. The United States has always been a multilingual nation. Like other language myths, the idea of a monolingual America is founded upon false assumptions about language.

The myth of the monolingual nation involves several different discursive assumptions that all suggest that speaking more than one language is not merely unnatural but bad in some way. For example, Americans often assume that exposing a child to more than one language will somehow impede language acquisition. This is part of a broader ideology concerning the socialization of very young children. Cultures have different ways of dealing with the fact that small children are unable to use language in the ways adults do. Some expect the child to adapt to their environment naturally while other cultures attempt to change the environment to adapt to the child. The American approach is of the latter type. Expecting parents often feel the need to "childproof" their homes before the child arrives, blocking electric outlets and placing locks on cabinet doors. The same approach is taken with language. American parents often use *baby talk* (also called Motherese or Parentese) to make their speech easier for the baby to understand. The research on baby talk is sometimes conflicting. A recent study (Ramírez et al. 2020) shows that some components of what people generally think of as baby talk (in this case, higher pitch, slower tempo, and a wider intonation range) do have the potential to enhance language acquisition.

Figure 7.3 Overt housing and zoning discrimination and language ideologies limit access for those who do not speak English, pushing languages into "ethnic enclaves" like New York's Chinatown

Attempting to adjust one's speech to compensate for a baby's inability to talk, however, is not a universal pattern. In some cultures (like the Kaluli; see Ochs & Schieffelin 1984), the idea of interacting and translating for babies is just silly. Why would you try to hold a conversation with a baby who is unable to speak? It just makes more sense to wait until the baby can reply before trying to hold a conversation. The acquisition of language is not affected by such an absence of baby talk or by lower levels of interaction with parents. Children learn language at roughly the same rate regardless of the specific types of language input they receive.

The assumption that the linguistic environment must be adapted to account for a baby extends to attitudes toward exposing children to more than one language. Children acquire whatever language surrounds them, and if two languages regularly surround them, a child will learn both and grow up to be bilingual. Making the child's environment monolingual does not help them acquire language. Being raised in a monolingual world offers no advantages for the child.

Holding babies

Cultures have different views of how adults ought to interact with infants who cannot yet speak the language of adults. Some cultures attempt to adapt the environment to the child more than others do. American parents typically adjust their speech and "translate" for children to overcome the infant's lack of language. Other cultures accept that infants are unable to talk, and adults do not usually attempt to interact directly with infants. Children will acquire language normally either way. We can see this difference in the way that people hold babies in different cultures. While Americans tend to hold babies close and face to face (Figure 7.4, left), in many parts of the world babies spend much of their time on their mothers' backs (Figure 7.4, right).

Figure 7.4 American girl holding a doll (left), Ghanaian girls holding dolls (right)

One correlate of the belief that a bilingual environment is somehow too difficult for children is the idea that people who are naturally bilingual can't really speak both languages. Within this ideology, people who grow up bilingual are viewed with a certain degree of suspicion, as if their linguistic abilities are somehow exaggerated or entirely false. This may surface about either language, including English. For example, we saw this myth in the discussions of Julián Castro's Spanish. Castro's Spanish was scrutinized in ways that just did not apply to other candidates who used Spanish in public. The myth of the suspect bilingual is also responsible for the tendency for English-speaking children with Asian or Latinx surnames to be incorrectly enrolled in classes for children who know no English at all.

The suspect bilingual myth also contributes to the denigration of US varieties of global languages. Special courses for "heritage" learners are offered for students who speak languages like Chinese or Spanish at home. Often, these courses involve high levels of criticism directed toward the language variety spoken by these "heritage" speakers. For example, some Chinese students are often criticized for their inability to read and write Chinese characters even though literacy and linguistic competence are separate issues. Spanish speakers are told that their language is "wrong" for not using the subjunctive voice (absence of the subjunctive voice is a basic feature of many US Spanishes). Thus, Latinx students, in this case, face criticism of their Spanish as "bad" or "wrong" in addition to criticism of their English as somehow deficient. This can ultimately mean that Latinx students are treated as if they have no language at all (Rosa 2016). And, of course, assuming that someone does not have the capacity for language can be particularly dehumanizing.

The assumption that natural bilingualism is not normal also surfaces in the view that bilinguals don't really speak either language but somehow communicate by putting together pieces of the two languages. This is usually conveyed by treating the two languages as a single entity, as in Spanglish, Chinglish, Konglish, Korenglish, or Navlish, among others. Terms like Navlish technically refer to using two languages (Navajo and English) in a single context. These terms tend to reproduce the negative evaluations of bilinguals' language use by placing speakers "in between" languages when the speakers are using both languages regularly. Ideas like "We don't really speak English, we speak Spanglish" simply reproduces the view that Latinx language is deficient in both English and Spanish. Here again, the reality is that bilinguals have language abundance rather than a language deficit. It is not that speakers alternate between languages because they can't speak either. Quite the opposite – people alternate languages precisely because they *can* speak them both. This process of moving back and forth between languages is what linguists call *code-switching*.

Code-switching may occur in several different ways. One distinction is whether the switch occurs between sentences (intersentential) or within the same sentence (intrasentential). Intersentential code-switching often marks some sort of shift in an interaction. For example, if you are waiting in line for a movie and speaking Vietnamese with your friend, an intersentential switch is likely to occur when you reach the beginning of the line and begin the interaction to purchase tickets. If you are speaking Spanish in a group and a monolingual English-speaking friend walks up, there will likely be an intersentential switch into English so that the friend can understand what is being said. Of course, code-switching within languages can also occur during an interaction without any obvious type of change. In some families, for example, a child may reply to their Korean-speaking parents in English so that every change in speaker is also a change in language.

Intrasentential code-switching is particularly interesting to linguists because it provides insight into the ways in which two (or more) grammars can be combined. Muysken (1997) categorizes intrasentential switches into three distinct types: alternation, insertion, and congruent lexicalization. Alternation occurs when a sentence begins in one language and switches to end the sentence in another language (example 1a). Insertion occurs when a grammatical unit from one language occurs in the middle of a sentence that is otherwise in the other language (example 1b). Congruent lexicalization occurs when the two languages are merged to such a degree that it becomes difficult to tell which language the sentence might be in (see example 1c).

1. Types of code-switching (examples from Pfaff 1979)
   a. Alternation:

      Yo se, porque *I went to the hospital to find out where he was.*
      I know, because *I went to the hospital to find out where he was.*
   b. Insertion:

      Estaba muy *fancy* y todo.
      It was really *fancy* and everything.
   c. Congruent lexicalization:

      Anda *feeling* medio *nice* y *start blowing again.*
      He goes along feeling rather (literally: medium) nice and he starts blowing again.

The types of code-switching found in each context depends on the specific indexical meanings associated with each language. In contexts where the two languages have opposing indexical meanings, switches between languages are less common. Because of the political history of animosity between French and English speakers in Canada, for example, bilinguals in western Quebec typically have clear distinctions between when English is used and when French is used (Bourhis et al. 2007). For many francophone Quebecois, French indexes "our identity" and English indexes "outsiders." Thus, intrasentential code-switching is less common than intersentential code-switching, and patterns like congruent lexicalization are extremely rare. In contrast, for US Latinxs, Spanish and English both index Latinx identity, so the two languages are used together in more contexts and code-switching involves higher amounts of insertion and lexical congruence.

Code-switching between languages

Here are some examples of mixing English with different languages.

Cajun French-English

Je	pensais	le	*phone*	devait	pas	être	*out*	*of*	*order*	quand	il	sonnait
I	thought	the	*phone*	must	not	be	*out*	*of*	*order*	when	it	rang

"I thought the *phone* must (not) be *out of order* when it rang."

(Brown 1986: 400)

Arabic-English

Enta	arif	enn-aha	jab-at	nafs	al-soa'al	*like*	*three*	*times*
You (masc)	know (masc)	that-fem	brought-fem	same	the-question	*like*	*three*	*times*

"You know she brought the same question *like three times?*"

(al-Rowais 2012: 33)

Choctaw-English

imaama	ikpisokma	*ipampers*	shofficha
i-maama	i-k-pis-o-k-ma	i-*pampers*	ø-shoffi-(hi)cha
3sPOS-mother	3pSUBJ-Neg-see-Neg-CONJ-SR	3sPOS-*pampers*	3sAGT-take off-and

"When her mother isn't looking, she takes her *pampers* off."

(Kwachka 1991: 175)

Mandarin Chinese-English

這	是	個	*good*	*question*	但是	我	没	有	*answer*
Zhè	shì	ge	*good*	*question*	dànshì	wǒ	meí	yǒu	*answer*
This	is	(a)	*good*	*question*	but	I	not	have	*answer*

"That's a *good question,* but I don't have (an) *answer.*"

(Chen 2013: 5)

Spanish-English

Bueno,	*in other words*	el	*flight*	que	sale	de	Chicago *around 3 o'clock*
Well,	*in other words*	the	*flight*	that	leaves	from	Chicago *around 3 o'clock*

"Well, *in other words,* the *flight* that leaves from *Chicago around 3 o'clock.*"

(Pfaff 1979: 300)

Vietnamese-English

(Name)	cũng	đang	*celebrate*	cái	sinh nhật
(Name)	also	(progressive)		(classifier)	birthday

"(Name) is also *celebrat*ing a birthday."

(Nguyen 2012: 44)

Intrasentential code-switching is an entirely normal linguistic phenomenon that occurs all over the world. Like all patterns in language, movement back and forth between languages is not random but is governed by rules. For example, switches from one language to another are much more likely in instances where the grammars of the two languages align. Consider the case of noun phrases in Spanish-English code-switching. In both languages, articles (like *the*) occur at the beginning of a noun phrase. But Spanish and English differ in the order of adjectives and nouns. In Spanish, most adjectives follow nouns (where English adjectives precede nouns).

2.	Spanish	la	casa	azul
		article	noun	adjective
	English	the	blue	house
		article	adjective	noun

For Spanish-English bilinguals, it sounds much better to switch languages after the article (where the grammars of the two languages align, like in 3a) than to switch between the noun and the adjective (where the grammars do not align, like in 3b).

3. a. She lives in the *casa azul.*
   Ella vive en la blue house.
   b. ? She lives in the *azul* house.
   ? She lives in the house *azul.*
   ? *Ella vive en la casa* blue.
   ? *Ella vive en la* blue *casa.*

Thus, for the examples in 3, the sentences in the first set sound fine, but those in the second set are likely to sound awkward and unnatural to native bilinguals. In Spanish-English bilingual communities, speakers (unconsciously) know these sorts of rules about possible ways to combine the two languages. So in addition to knowing the grammar of Spanish and the grammar of English, bilinguals also know the grammar of how English and Spanish can be combined. Indeed, one could argue that Spanish-English bilinguals use three times the amount of linguistic knowledge compared to English monolinguals. This is not, of course, to say that there is anything inherently wrong with being monolingual; indeed, the issue is that what could be seen as an abundance of linguistic knowledge (use of more than one language) is often represented as deficit (because it is interpreted as an inability to stay in one language due to a lack of fluency).

Like other forms of language variation, patterns of code-switching come to carry distinct indexical meanings. The contextual associations with using two (or more) languages are different from the associations afforded by each language independently. For example, speaking only Korean might be associated with formal contexts like conversations with elders or church events while English is associated with other formal contexts like school or interactions with strangers. But the combination of Korean and English might index more intimate contexts with close friends and peers who are also bilingual; speakers may develop close emotional ties to the ways in which languages may be combined. For example, Webster (2015) describes the affection many Navajos have for combining English and Navajo (described as "Navlish"), such as the combination of a Navajo possessive prefix (such as *shi-* "my") with an English noun, as in *shi*buddy ("my buddy") or *shi*heart ("my heart").

Because languages and combinations of languages carry distinct indexical meanings, norms emerge for different patterns of language use in different contexts (for example,

Spanish at church, English at school, and both at home). Of course, the most important factor in determining what language to use is the language(s) known by the person listening to you. Switching into Spanish while speaking to someone who is monolingual in English would only produce confusion. Of course, switching languages may occur without a shift in context. Because language choices carry indexical meanings, the use of one language or the other (or both) may be associated to the topic at hand. It might just seem natural to switch into Tagalog (for example) when talking about aspects of Filipino culture or when discussing highly personal or potentially embarrassing topics.

They aren't talking about you

When hearing someone speak a language that you do not know, it is common to suspect that they are somehow talking about you. But this really doesn't make sense. Have you ever traveled to a place where you do not speak the local language? If so, it is likely that you were speaking your own native language to your travel companions for all sorts of reasons: trying to find your way, deciding what to have for lunch, looking for specific landmarks, and so on. Even in monolingual contexts, you might use some form of secrecy (code words, for example) to conceal the discussion from overhearers, especially if the context is particularly sensitive.

If a person is speaking a language that you do not understand, it is usually an indication that they aren't talking to you and what they are saying is probably of no concern to you. Often, people switch into a language other than English when they are discussing something sensitive or embarrassing. So there's no need to feel suspicious when someone next to you at the grocery store switches into Vietnamese. It might just be that they really need to pee and don't want to announce it to everyone in the store!

Over and over, one can see ways in which popular discourse denigrates bilingualism through representations that suggest that bilingual speech is somehow abnormal and reflects some type of language deficit. This is another example of discourse racializing language use. A monolingual English-speaking white person who learns to speak another language fluently is often revered as having a powerful intellect. They have achieved a great feat in acquiring a second language. A monolingual English speaker who is Asian or Latinx who learns to speak their "heritage" language is not regarded in the same way (despite having achieved the exact same skill as the white person). A Korean American who grew up speaking only English who decides to study Korean is likely to be regarded as some sort of "failed" Korean trying to acquire a "retroactive" identity. An English-monolingual who decides to study Italian after discovering she is Italian American (say, from ancestry.com) is likely to be regarded positively as someone who is putting in great work to understand their ethnic heritage (the exact same thing the Korean American is doing). Bilingualism cannot be an achievement for some and a deficit for others. The view of bilingualism as some sort of deficiency is founded in racism rather than in linguistic fact.

Some argue that bilingualism is socially divisive. If people don't all speak the same language, the argument goes, then they will start to fight with one another. This is, after all, the basis of the biblical Tower of Babel story. People point to Quebec as an example of multilingualism creating social division. The world is full of people who speak different languages and have no problem with people who speak other languages. Most of the world's countries are multilingual and see no sort of social discord between speakers of different languages. One could easily use Switzerland, for example, as the counterexample to Quebec.

And, of course, social division and discord need not be based on speaking different languages. Most civil wars are not fought between speakers of different languages. Social discord among speakers of the same language is much more common. It is, for example, the reason that Bosnian-Croatian-Serbian has three different names despite being almost identical in terms of grammar. Indeed, the promotion of monolingualism can also produce serious social discord, particularly in cases where people try to forbid the use of other languages.

Yiddish in New York City

The United States has always been a multilingual nation. Although many immigrant communities switch to speaking only English rather quickly, other communities may continue using their language over long periods of time, especially in large cities with ethnic neighborhoods that allow for the language to be used in everyday life. A good example is Yiddish in Orthodox communities in New York City. A century ago, New York was a multilingual city, just as it is today. One advertisement for a play and ball being held in Manhattan in

Figure 7.5 Hatzalah ambulance in Brooklyn
Source: photo courtesy of Tariqabjotu

1912 mixes English, Russian, and Yiddish, reflecting the language diversity of the Lower East Side where the play was performed. Today, both Russian and Yiddish continue to be spoken in New York, particularly in neighborhoods in Brooklyn. Yiddish is used widely in education, religious, and daily life in Hassidic Jewish communities. There are volunteer Yiddish-speaking ambulance services (see Figure 7.5). Yiddish is used to ensure both that patients can communicate and that they are not subjected to medical procedures that violate religious laws.

The National Geographic Society regularly conducts surveys to determine the geographic knowledge of young people. One of the questions they typically ask is "Which language is spoken by the most people in the world as their primary language?" In a 2016 version of the survey (National Geographic Society 2016) given just to college students, 44% of respondents answered "English" (the correct answer is Mandarin Chinese). The language ideology of monolingualism is so deeply entrenched that the assumption most everyone in the world speaks English seems reasonable for many people. Despite the high level of confidence wielded by those willing to say, "You're in America – we speak English here!", the United States has no official language. It never has.

What the Constitution does have is the Tenth Amendment, which says, "Each state retains its sovereignty, freedom, and independence, and every power, jurisdiction, and right, which is not by this Confederation expressly delegated to the United States, in Congress assembled." This amendment gives individual states the right to make their own laws regarding anything not expressly covered or prohibited by the rest of the Constitution. So since no official language is declared in the Constitution (and it does not prohibit the establishment of an official language), states have every right to declare one themselves. And some have. Figure 7.6 shows the states (in black) that have made English the official language of that

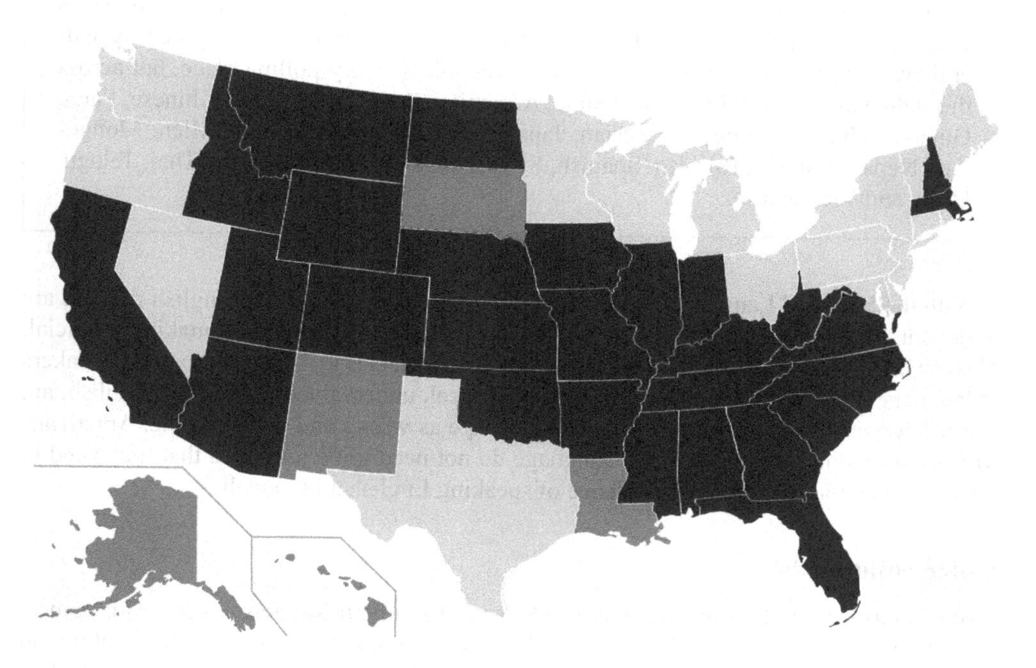

Figure 7.6 States with laws making English their official language (in black) and states that are officially multilingual to some degree (in dark gray)

state. Despite stereotypes that link English-only policies to conservatism and the South, most official English states are not in the South. The states in dark gray are those that have official bilingual policies or have given special status to some language(s) other than English. New Mexico and Louisiana have given special status to Spanish and French, respectively. Hawaii, Alaska, and South Dakota have added Native American/Indigenous languages to their policies, making them officially multilingual.

Of course, a state declaring English to be the official language is still subject to federal laws and regulations regarding the use of languages other than English. For example, the (1975 expansion of the 1965) Voting Rights Act requires ballots in other languages whenever the population speaking those languages is over 10,000 people or makes up more than 5% of the election district (the law technically combines voting districts and reservations). In 2000, President Clinton issued an executive order (#13166) requiring all federal agencies to provide adequate services to those with limited proficiency in English. This meant that any organization receiving federal funds must provide interpreters for all clients, a requirement that greatly increased access to medical, social, and legal services. For example, states that do not provide driver's license exams in languages other than English would risk losing federal highway funds. Even so, political candidates will still promise to stop offering the tests in other languages. Of course, state politicians can't change federal law, so such promises are empty appeals to xenophobia.

Voting rights

Some states may have laws with lower thresholds for determining which languages require ballots. For example, in California, state law requires ballots in languages when speakers make up 3% of the population (rather than the 5% required by federal law). Ballots in all languages are not available at every polling place, but across the state, ballots were offered in Arabic, Armenian, Bengali, Burmese, Chinese, Farsi, Gujarati, Hindi, Hmong, Indonesian, Japanese, Khmer, Korean, Lao, Mien, Mongolian, Nepali, Punjabi, Russian, Spanish, Syriac, Tagalog/Filipino, Tamil, Thai, Telugu, Urdu, and Vietnamese.

With the Standard Language Ideology operating at full force, official English policies are irrelevant. English is the language of the United States even without a law making it official. Those who do not speak English still face numerous obstacles in American society. Speakers of languages other than English, like those who speak undervalued varieties of English, are constantly reminded that many view their language as wrong and unacceptable. Americans who are monolingual in some other language do not need to be reminded that they need to learn English; they know the importance of speaking English all too well.

Stolen childhoods

Cirila Baltazar Cruz is from the state of Oaxaca in southern Mexico, a state with numerous linguistically and culturally diverse Indigenous communities. Cruz speaks Chatino, an Indigenous language in the Oto-Manguean family. Chatino is no more like Spanish than Cherokee, Chickasaw, or Navajo are like English.

Figure 7.7 Polling place in New York City

Because of racial discrimination and systemic poverty in rural Oaxaca, Cruz was forced to come to the United States to find work that would allow her to care for her family. She arrived in the United States in 2006 and took a job at a Chinese restaurant in Pascagoula, Mississippi. In November of 2008, Cruz went to the Singing River Hospital and gave birth to a healthy daughter, Rubí. Rather than call in a Chatino translator, Cirlia was provided with an interpreter who spoke Puerto Rican Spanish, and the two could not understand one another (Cruz 2010). The social services representatives in the hospital constructed a set of reasons to remove the child from her mother's custody, claiming that not speaking English amounted to endangering the welfare of her newborn daughter (Byrd 2010).

A judge declared Cruz to be an unfit mother because she could not speak English, and her daughter Rubí was taken away from her. Ultimately, it was discovered that the couple who received the baby were friends of the judge (and who had not gone through the proper legal channels for adoption). With the help of the Southern Poverty Law Center and a Chatino interpreter, Cruz was eventually able to regain custody of her daughter, but it took an entire year. Cirila Cruz was not the first woman to have her child taken from her simply because she spoke an Indigenous language and could not communicate in Spanish or English. It is quite common for speakers of Indigenous languages from Mexico and Central America to be given Spanish interpreters in medical and legal contexts (see Haviland 2003; Barrett et al. 2016). In these situations, Indigenous immigrants are harmed (e.g., refused treatment, jailed, or otherwise punished) based solely on their inability to communicate with an interpreter who doesn't even speak their language.

When the family separation policy for immigrants from Latin America was introduced in the spring of 2018, hundreds of children, many who spoke only Indigenous languages, were taken from their parents and placed in detention centers specifically for children. Although this policy of child separation was met with outrage as not reflecting American values, it is part of a long history of children being taken from speakers of minority languages, including both immigrants and Native Americans. Cirila and Rubí Cruz are part of a centuries-long tradition of taking Native children away from their families so that they could be "civilized," primarily through speaking English. In the early colonial period, children who were Wampanoag (the tribe in the Thanksgiving story) were regularly taken by British parents. Although the goal was to raise Indian children to be "civilized" though English, the children were often treated as servants rather than family (Silverman 2005).

In the 1880s, the federal government began forcing Native American children to attend boarding schools where they were separated from their families and communities. The main goal of these boarding schools was to eradicate the children's knowledge of their Native cultures, including their languages. Children from the same family were sometimes separated from one another so that it would be easier for them to lose knowledge of their languages. Children were regularly punished for speaking their language, even if it was the only language they knew. Richard Pratt, the founder of one of the largest boarding schools (Carlisle Indian Industrial School) described his motivation in this way:

> A great general has said that the only good Indian is a dead one, and that high sanction of his destruction has been an enormous factor in promoting Indian massacres. In a sense, I agree with the sentiment, but only in this: that all the Indian there is in the race should be dead. Kill the Indian in him, and save the man.
>
> (Pratt 1892)

Pratt was a strong believer in white supremacy, even going so far as to say that slavery was a "great gift" because it served to "civilize" Africans. Pratt's catchphrase, "Kill the Indian, save the man," became a popular means of justifying taking children away from their families.

Boarding schools for Native Americans often used "before and after" photographs (as in Figure 7.8) to demonstrate their success in "civilizing" Native children. This picture shows Hastiin To'Haali in 1882, when he first arrived at the Carlisle Indian Industrial School where he was renamed "Tom Torlino." The picture on the right shows Mr. To'Haali after being "discharged" four years later. Notice that the "after" photo was taken using a filter that makes the subject's skin appear to be lighter.

In some cases, when children returned to their communities, they were no longer able speak their native language, finding it impossible to communicate with their own parents. Boarding school graduates who could still speak their native language often refused to use

Figure 7.8 "Tom Torlino, Navajo, before and after," black and white photographic portrait of a Navajo by J. N. Choate,

Source: image courtesy of the Richard Henry Pratt Papers, Beinecke Rare Book & Manuscript Library

it with their own children to ensure that their children would never suffer the punishments that they endured for not speaking English. The boarding schools are one reason that many Native American languages have very few remaining speakers.

Native American languages today

According to the US Census Bureau, the Native American languages with the most current speakers are as follows:

Language estimated number of speakers (2010)

Language	*Estimated number of speakers (2010)*
Navajo	169,471
Yupik	18,950
Dakota	18,616
Apache	13,063
Keres	12,945
Cherokee	11,610
Choctaw	10,343

(*Continued*)

(Continued)

Language	*Estimated number of speakers (2010)*
Zuni	9,686
Ojibwa	8,371
Pima	7,270
Inupik	7,203
Hopi	6,634
Tewa	5,176
Muskogee/Creek	5,064
Crow	3,705

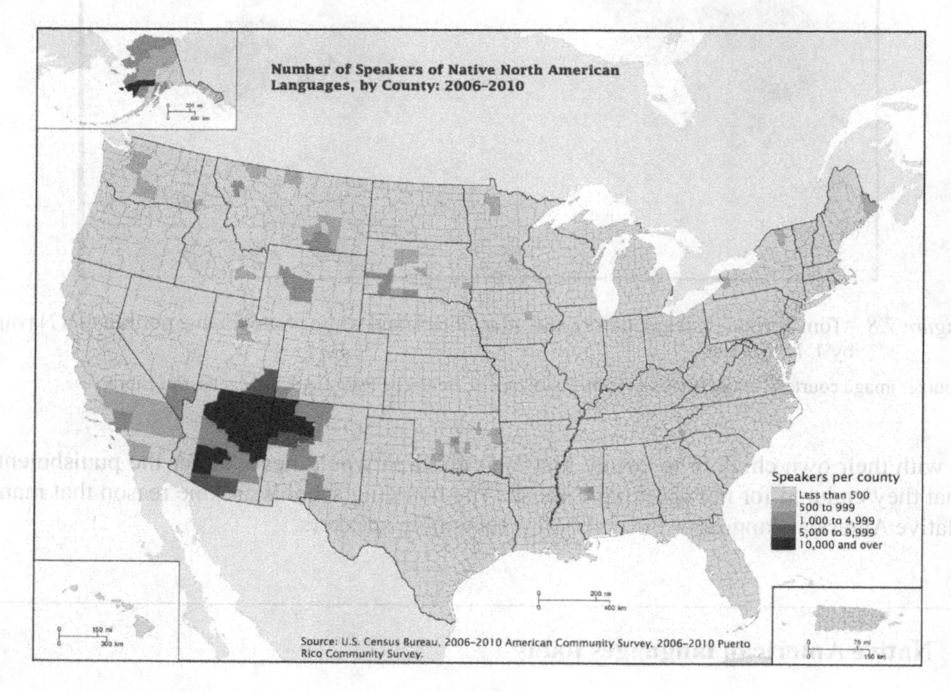

Figure 7.9 Speakers of Native American languages in 2010

Source: U.S. Census Bureau 2010

Many Native American communities have now begun efforts to conserve and revitalize their languages. Different communities have taken different approaches to the problem, depending on their unique situations. Communities with no living speakers, or "sleeping languages" (Leonard 2008), typically begin by working through archival materials documenting the language as it was spoken. These communities use grammars and texts to develop materials for learning their community's traditional language. This also requires developing new vocabulary for the language because there may be gaps in the materials or because the language has no words for things that didn't exist when there were speakers. Developing new words (or *neologisms*) typically requires research on other, related languages that may already have words for the object in question. Efforts to begin using the language again typically focus on teaching the language to children. Because children pick up language naturally, they will end up with a regular, rule-governed language even if their parents learned the language from materials collected by a linguist years ago. Several language communities have taken this approach, including the Myaamia (Miami), Wampanoag, and Tunica.

In communities where there are a handful of elder speakers, communities may adopt a *master-apprentice* language program (Hinton 2001). In this model, a single speaker works one-on-one with a single younger speaker to teach the younger speaker to use the language across numerous contexts. In communities with few speakers, this program ensures that the language is passed down to the next generation. Working with a single apprentice makes it possible to put in the great amount of effort required to learn a new language. Once the apprentice learns the language, they can begin to use the language with their immediate family and begin to increase the number of speakers. The master-apprentice model was developed in the 1990s for use by Native American communities in California where many languages had only one or two living speakers. The main goal is to ensure that the master and the apprentice have sufficient time alone together to ensure that the apprentice learns to speak the language. Usually, the master and apprentice spend entire days together participating in real life activities like making crafts, cooking meals, or walking through nature. To facilitate learning, the two are not allowed to speak English. Doing activities together makes it easier to communicate without words, making it easier to avoid speaking English. The apprentice must be an active participant in the process, deciding what activities to perform and what topics the pair should focus on. Teaching is entirely oral (rather than written) to make sure that the interaction flows naturally and without pauses. Although the master-apprentice program was designed for the specific needs of communities in California, it has since been widely adopted both in the United States and in other countries like Canada and Australia (Grenoble & Whaley 2005).

Language in the Navajo Nation presidential election

The 2014 election for President of the Navajo Nation was disrupted over issues of language fluency. According to Navajo law, candidates for president and vice president must swear to fluently speak and understand Navajo. After the primary elections, one of the two candidates remaining, Chris Deschene, was accused of not being sufficiently fluent in the language (despite having campaigned in Navajo for several months). Deschene was subjected to a public "fluency" test before Navajo educators and government officials. Deschene refused to participate, responding to all questions with answers like, *nashintaa doo akot'ée da* (you are testing me and that is not right). It was decided that his refusal to participate in the fluency test disqualified him from being president. The decision was extremely controversial and resulted in the postponement of the election for another year. Voters later passed a resolution declaring that "fluency" would be determined by individual voters and not by a group of experts (Jacobsen & Thompson 2020).

In communities where there are more elder speakers, a different type of program known as *language nests* may be adopted. In a language nest program, individual elders are assigned a "nest" of young children. Typically, the nest meets together for at least part of the day at nursery schools. The elder spends time playing and interacting with the children in their nest while only speaking in the target language. Because young children acquire language with little effort, the children in the nest will naturally begin speaking the language. The knowledge they gain in the nests is then reinforced through more formal language teaching in elementary school. The children's ability to speak their heritage language often inspires their parents to learn the language themselves. The stress of having your children speak to each other in a language you don't understand is enough to ignite interest in learning that language. The language nest program was developed among speakers of Māori, the Indigenous (Polynesian) language of New Zealand. Native Hawaiians were the first to introduce language nests in the United States, but these programs have been quite successful in other communities (Grenoble & Whaley 2005), particularly among members of the Haudenosaunee (Iroquois) Confederacy, including Seneca and Kanien'kehá:ka (Mohawk).

Many communities have combined these different approaches with other initiatives to encourage wider use of their language across social contexts. This includes the production of pedagogical materials for both children and adults and the development of classes for adults in addition to children. Companies like Rosetta Stone and Duolingo have developed teaching materials specific to several Native American languages (and continue to expand their offerings). Many communities have created online dictionaries and language lessons, including videos produced specifically for children. There are efforts to use Native American languages in social media, and more and more musicians, like Supaman (Lakota), are incorporating Native languages into their music. Several films and shows have been dubbed into Native languages, including *Star Wars* in Navajo, *Bambi* in Arapaho, and *The Berenstain Bears* in Lakota. Finally, there is a growing number of poets who write in Native languages or incorporate Native languages into their work, including Ofelia Zepeda (Tohono O'odham), Natalie Diaz (Mojave), and numerous Navajo poets like Rex Lee Jim, Laura Tohe, and Luci Tapahonso.

Language ideologies and English public space

Attempts to clear public discourse of other languages were not limited to Native American languages, as there have been repeated efforts to sanction speakers of other languages. One way that public discourse was/is kept clear of speakers of other languages is to enact laws preventing immigration from specific countries, such as the Chinese Exclusion Act of 1882. In the 1930s, over a million Latinxs who were US citizens were deported to Mexico to give their jobs to white people. During World War II, Japanese speakers were sent to internment camps to ensure that they couldn't communicate with the enemy. There have been laws banning other languages, particularly German. In 1923, Robert Meyer, a Nebraska schoolteacher was arrested for teaching a student to read the Bible in German. Meyer had broken a law that prohibited teaching children foreign languages before the eighth grade (based on the mistaken assumption that it would somehow interfere with children's acquisition of proper English). The case reached the Supreme Court where it was decided that the prohibiting the use of languages other than English was a violation of the First Amendment. Nevertheless, communities continue to attempt to find ways to restrict public discourse to English.

English dominance is ultimately achieved through discourse that promotes a monolingual language ideology. Denigrating ideologies that treat US bilinguals as if their language were deficient serve to silence speakers of languages other than English, often through self-censorship. Self-censorship is encouraged through repeated experiences of people being harassed for speaking a language other than English in public. The public use of other languages is often met with suspicion, particularly from people who are concerned that someone might be talking about them behind their back. Representations of bilinguals as secretive and untrustworthy help instill the tendency to be suspicious or anxious upon hearing an unfamiliar language. This paranoia ultimately serves to discourage the use of languages other than English in public spaces.

In looking at ethnic dialects in Chapter 6, there are times when white people might mock or appropriate ethnic-indexing variation in ways that unintentionally reproduce the language ideologies that preserve white public spaces. In addition to discourses that denigrate bilinguals, these same processes of mocking and appropriation can be seen contributing to discourse structural racism by presuming that public discourse ought to be in English. Mock representations of other languages often portray other languages as gibberish in that the sounds produced have no meaning in the target language. For example, in the film *Friday*, Smokey (played by Chris Tucker) addresses a Latino acquaintance with a series of nonsensical syllables intended to sound like spoken Spanish (*poquite*, *moroso*, *marese*, etc.). With a few recent exceptions, Hollywood representations of Native American languages follow this gibberish pattern with "languages" made up on the spot by white actors (Meek 2006).

One of the most common forms of mocking can be seen in what Elaine Chun calls *Mock Asian* (Chun 2004). Unlike mock forms targeting a specific language (like Spanish), Mock Asian targets East Asians as a monolithic group, demonstrating that the target is an imagined race rather than about any specific language or culture. It completely fails to acknowledge, for example, that Asia, as the largest continent, is home to a rather varied set of cultures and languages (including Chinese, which, despite often being referred to as one language composed of many dialects, is really many different and not mutually intelligible languages).

Features of Mock Asian include using forms that index non-native English, such as replacing /ɹ/ with /w/ ("wrong" as "wong"), switching /ɹ/ and /l/ ("flied lice" for "fried rice"), adding a final [i] vowel to words ("you breakee, you buyee"), and the use of stereotyped stock phrases like "Ah so." One of the most notorious uses of Mock Asian is Mickey Rooney's portrayal of Mr. Yunioshi in the 1961 film *Breakfast at Tiffany's*. As if to emphasize racist intent, Rooney's Mock Asian character is even given pulled-back eyes and fake buck teeth to make him even more of a caricature (Rooney was a white New Yorker). Perhaps the most common form of Mock Asian is the production of nonsense syllables meant to imitate Mandarin Chinese, especially the phrase *ching-chong* (Chun 2016). This phrase is meant as a form of pseudo-Asian mockery that indexes perceptions of Asian American language as both unintelligible and trivial because of its connection to sing-song English utterances (like *ding dong* or *ping pong*).

The use of this type of Mock Asian is ubiquitous. In 2002, for example, Shaquille O'Neal directed the form at fellow basketball player Yao Ming, saying "Tell Yao Ming, ching-chong-yang-wah-ah-soh." The use of nonsense syllables to represent the language of an ethnic group reduces their language to gibberish, indexing a lack of meaningful language (which, in turn, indexes a failure to be fully human). This mocking of the sounds of other languages also serves to push other languages out of public space – if your language carries no meaning, I can refuse to bother speaking to you at all.

Chun (2016) suggests that one of the best ways to challenge the racism of Mock Asian is through humorous responses like "You failed Chinese class, huh?" Chun discusses Jimmy Wong's "Ching Chong: Asians in the Library Song." Wong wrote the song in response to a rant against Asians posted by a white student at UCLA. In the rant, the white student complains about Asians speaking languages other than English in the library (among other things). She claims that whenever she is studying in the library, she hears Asians on their telephones saying, "Ching-chong, ling-long, ting-tong." In his musical response, Wong satirically sings about being attracted to the racist white woman, claiming that the phrase she hears ("ching-chong") actually means "I love you" in Chinese.

Wong's performance uses humor to challenge many of the racist stereotypes that underlie Mock Asian forms like *ching-chong*. Imagining himself as a charming womanizer, Wong undermines not only the portrayal of the annoying Asian on the phone in the original rant but also undermines racist stereotypes that depict Asian men as lacking masculinity. By filling in the meaning of *ching-chong* (as "I love you"), Wong challenges the use of gibberish to represent the linguistic competence of Asian Americans. The power of *ching-chong* to dehumanize depends on the word having no actual meaning. By giving *ching-chong* meaning, Wong undermines the view of Chinese as nonsense with no communicative function. Giving *ching-chong* a meaning that refers directly to the racist herself also plays on white fears that people using a language other than English are talking about them.

Mock phrases like *ching-chong* reproduce the myth that bilinguals are unable to communicate in any language. Just as complimenting African Americans for being "articulate," Asian, Latinx, and Middle Eastern Americans may find themselves being "complimented" on how well they speak English. Telling a native speaker how good their English is isn't really complimenting them at all. It simply lets them know that you assumed they were unable to speak English based on solely on their physical appearance. In addition to people told *ching-chong* by random strangers, Asian Americans may also be taunted with Mock Asian English phrases like *flied lice*, popularized in media depictions like the one in the 1998 *Lethal Weapon 4*. Forms of mocking may also be intersectional with forms often combining racism with sexism, homophobia, or transphobia. The Mock Asian catchphrases "me so horny" and "me love you long time" combine racism and sexism to harass Asian American women specifically. As with these catch phrases, mock varieties circulate widely enough to become somewhat standardized in that they have the same form across numerous contexts. Mock varieties may have no real connection to the speech of members of the mocked community.

A good example of this is what Meek (2006) calls *Hollywood Injun English*, the imagined variety of English used in media representations of Native Americans. For example, Native Americans in film have often been portrayed as greeting others by raising their right hand and saying "How." Of course, this only occurs in literary representations and Hollywood films and has nothing to do with how Native peoples greet one another in real life. Hollywood Injun English combines bits and pieces of various historical representations of Native American speech, and some forms that emerged were only through the imagination of white writers. Hollywood Injun English is easily recognized as indexing Native American identity (despite never being used by actual Native Americans). Hollywood Injun English is widely recognized and occurs in numerous films, particularly in Westerns and films marketed to children, like *Peter Pan* or *Pocahontas*.

There are a number of stereotypical features of Hollywood Injun English, including unique lexical items (*heap* to mean "very," *many moons* to mean "a long time"), the absence of a copula (e.g., "He not back by sunset," "squaw no leave"), irregular verbal agreement (*it say* rather than *says*), and the use of the nonsensical verbal suffix *-um* (*gettum, burnum*). Here, racist terms like *Injun* or *squaw* (a racist/sexist term denigrating Native American women) typically occur alongside forms of Hollywood Injun English, linking the linguistic forms of Hollywood Injun English with more overt expressions of racism. It is common for mock varieties to co-occur with other forms of racist discourse.

For many Americans who are not Native, Hollywood Injun English is much more familiar than any varieties of actual Native American English. The fact that white caricatures of

Natives are more familiar that actual Natives demonstrates how linguistic representations authorize white control over public space. Not only are Native voices silenced; they are replaced with highly inaccurate mocking forms of Native voices imagined by white people.

In the case of African American English, we explored how the appropriation of African American slang by white people produces indexical bleaching, breaking the indexical link between slang terms and ethnic identity. There is a somewhat similar pattern with the appropriation of Spanish by white speakers. This use of (Mock) Spanish often co-occurs with racist tropes, such as the brownface use of sombreros and paper cut-out moustaches on Cinco de Mayo (see Figure 7.10). Jane Hill (1993, 1998) first described this particular type of Mock Spanish in which speakers who are not Latinx insert (real and imagined) Spanish words and phrases into their English (like Bart Simpson saying "Ay, caramba!" in *The Simpsons*). For the speakers who use these forms, the Spanish carries indexical meanings associated with being witty and cosmopolitan – a social persona who is familiar with other cultures and languages and uses that knowledge in humorous ways. For monolingual English speakers, a phrase like "Hey, chica!" is light-hearted and friendly. Hill found, however, that often these uses of Spanish unintentionally end up simultaneously indexing negative stereotypes about Latinxs. This occurs through linking negative connotations to Spanish words and showing a total disregard for the grammar of Spanish. This disregard for the structure of actual Spanish reinforces ideologies of bilingual language as disordered and naturally inferior to English (in other words, the same ideologies can be found associated with Mock Asian).

Hill lays out four basic types of Mock Spanish that all serve to denigrate Latinxs in some way: semantic derogation, euphemism, hyperanglicization, and the (mis)use of elements of Spanish grammar. Semantic derogation refers to the process where words take on new, negative meanings. There are numerous historical cases of gendered pairs of words where the female member of the pair undergoes semantic derogation. Examples include

Figure 7.10 The sombrero and fake moustache is the ("brownface") fashion equivalent to Mock Spanish; here, the former president of the University of Louisville (while still president) poses with his staff

Source: courtesy of the *Louisville Courier-Journal*

master/mistress (where *master* retains the original meaning but *mistress* comes to refer to a woman in a relationship with a married man) or *bachelor/spinster* (where *spinster* took on negative connotations associated with an "old maid" rather than a young single woman). Another example is the use of "gay" to mean bad, tacky, or stupid (as in "That is so *gay*").

In Mock Spanish, the process of derogation occurs with a number of Spanish words. An example is Spanish ways of saying "goodbye," including *adios* ("goodbye") and *hasta la vista* ("see you later"). In Mock Spanish usage, these phrases are often used to mean something more like "get the hell out of here" or "good riddance" rather than the innocent "goodbye" they convey in Spanish. Hill gives the example of Arnold Schwarzenegger's use of *Hasta la vista, baby* before killing his enemy in the 1984 film *The Terminator*. Here, the Spanish "see you later" comes across more like "see you in hell." Similarly, *adios* is often used to mean "get out" rather than "goodbye." Hill's examples include an (otherwise English) ad for a pest control that says "Adios, cucarachas" (*cucaracha* is the Spanish word for cockroach) and a greeting card that says "Adios" on the front with the inside text reading, "That's Spanish for 'sure, go ahead and leave your friends, the only people who really care about you, the ones who would loan you their last thin dime. . . .'" There are also instances of *Adios* being used this way toward Latinxs, as in using "Adios amigo" to let a Latino know he is not welcome. Other examples of semantic derogation include the use of *nada* ("nothing") and *pesos*. The use of *pesos* often indexes the idea of something being cheap, inexpensive, or low quality, as in advertisements saying, "Get it for pesos!" When English speakers use *nada*, they typically mean "absolutely nothing" as if Spanish *nada* is somehow less than English *nothing*. For example, when people repeat ways of saying *nothing*, it is usually the case that *nada* comes last (as in "Nothing. Zilch. Zero. Nada").

Hill's description of *euphemism* examines the ways in which Mock Spanish forms often substitute Spanish words for English obscenities, as with words like *caca* ("shit") or *cojones* ("balls"). Repeatedly using Spanish words to replace obscene, embarrassing, or disgusting forms of English only serves to strengthen the link between Spanish speakers and negative stereotypes of Latinxs as dirty or Latino men being hypermasculine.

The process of *hyperanglicization* refers to showing a disregard for Spanish grammar or pronouncing Spanish words in an exaggerated English accent. An example is the use of *Lava sus manos* for *Lávase las manos* ("Wash your hands") on signs in restrooms. In Spanish, one says "the hands" rather than "your hands" (a common pattern in many languages where parts of your own body are not possessed) so that *lava sus manos* uses English grammar with Spanish words. Another example is the restaurant *Dos Loco Gringos* in Hope, Arkansas. Actual Spanish would be *dos gringos locos* with the adjective following the noun and a plural-marking /s/ on the adjective *loco* ("crazy"). The grammar here is entirely English even though all of the words are taken from Spanish. Exaggerated mispronunciations are particular common in place names, like the California cities of San Pedro (pronounced PEE-drow), Palo Alto (with both "a" vowels produced with [æ], the vowel in *cat*), or Los Gatos (with the word for "cats" produced as "gattis" [gærəs]). Hyperanglicization is also common in the media, such as when Napoleon Dynamite's grandmother tells him, "Go make yourself a dang quesadilla" and pronounces *quesadilla* with an alveolar [l] (so that it rhymes with "vanilla"). Although cases of hyperanglicization are usually intended to be humorous, they reproduce a view of Latinx language practices as disordered while also imposing white control over the use of Spanish.

The appropriation of elements of Spanish grammar reproduces the same ideology of Spanish as disordered. One of the most common examples is to place an /o/ vowel at the end of English words (often preceded by the article *el*), as in *el cheapo*. In particular, the -o suffix is imagined as a basic way of forming Spanish words, as in the phrase *no problemo*, where English *problem* is made "Spanish" by adding -o. The Spanish word for problem is *problema* with a final /a/ so that the Mock Spanish form uses the Anglo-imagined *-o* suffix rather than using the actual Spanish word. Another example is the suffix *-amundo* as in *exactamundo* or *correctamundo*. There is no such suffix in Spanish. These bits of imagined Spanish grammar serve to keep public representations of Spanish under the control of English speakers.

Many uses of Mock Spanish involve more than one of these strategies. For example, the phrase *Adios bitchachos* uses the "get out" meaning of *adios* in addition to *-acho*, a variant of the Mock Spanish *-o* suffix. Sometimes this phrase even occurs with an accent on the <o> in *adios* (*adiós*). This accent doesn't occur in actual Spanish, but it does seem to represent the hyperanglicized version of the word with three syllables (a-dee-yos) rather than the two syllable Spanish word (a-dyos). Although Mock Spanish seems like an innocent form of speech play, it typically indexes negative stereotypes of Latinxs and represents Latinx speech as highly disordered. It is common to find Mock Spanish embedded into anti-Latinx racist discourse, as with Donald Trump's use of "bad *hombres*" when invoking the racist stereotype of Mexican American men as dangerous gang members.

In addition to indirectly evoking racist stereotypes, the widespread use of Mock Spanish among English monolinguals leads to the use of Mock Spanish in white interactions with Latinxs. An example is the Mock Spanish phrase *no bueno* ("no good," cf. Spanish *no es bueno*), which is used by white people in some interactions with Latinxs, particularly Latinx employees. Mock Spanish often involves the code-switching pattern of insertion as in Donald Trump's 2018 statement, "The Fed is going *loco* and there's no reason for them to do it." The frequency of this pattern licenses the practice of addressing monolingual Spanish speakers with Mock Spanish. In a study of language use in an Anglo-owned Mexican restaurant (Barrett 2006), directives to Spanish-speaking employees were often in Mock Spanish, as in example 6.

6. Manager directives to Spanish-speaking restaurant employees:

   Thank you for trabajo-ing. (trabajo = "work," 1st person singular or noun)
   Did you put bolsas in your basura cans? (*bolsas* = "bags," *basura* = "garbage;" compare to Spanish *botes de basura* "garbage bags")
   You have to finish *todo eso, porque* I have other things to do. (*todo eso* = "all this," *porque* = "because")

In the last example, the only Spanish words spoken to the monolingual employee were "all this, because." The manager later chastised the employee for not finishing the work in question. When it was suggested that perhaps the employee didn't understand her directive, the manager replied that she knew he understood, but he was "just lazy." This was a common response when employees failed to understand forms of Mock Spanish. The problem was never recognized as resulting from the English speaker's failure to adequately convey a directive in Spanish. Rather, communicative failure was regularly blamed on the Spanish-speaking employee, usually drawing on racist stereotypes (of Latinxs as lazy, evasive, and dishonest). Here, the use of Mock Spanish ultimately leads directly to discriminatory treatment of Spanish speakers.

Language varieties like Mock Asian, Hollywood Injun English, and Mock Spanish all serve both to denigrate specific ethnic groups and to establish public space as English-speaking. They commonly co-occur with other forms of racist discourse. They also sanction the use of disordered language in interactions with individuals with different ethnic backgrounds. In addition to creating unwelcoming spaces through mocking, these mock varieties can result in discriminatory treatment toward ethnic minorities. Mock varieties place control over other languages in the hands of English speakers and reproduce language ideologies that serve as the basis for various forms of discrimination.

Embracing bilingualism

The indexical meanings associated with languages other than English in the United States simultaneously marginalize speakers of other languages and clear public space for discourse in English. Yet these associations are ubiquitous and impossible to avoid. A study of listener perceptions found that stereotypes of Latinxs could be triggered simply by changing the pronunciation of a single word borrowed from Spanish (Baird et al. 2018). Listeners heard English sentences containing Spanish borrowings (*taco*, *tortilla*, and *salsa*) that were produced using either English or Spanish phonology (e.g., English [ˈtʰɑkʰoʊz] vs. Spanish [ˈtakos]). When listening to a male speaker produce a single word in Spanish phonology, listeners were significantly more likely to judge the speaker as more easy-going and more masculine. When asked open-ended questions about the speakers, voices producing a word with Spanish phonology were described according to stereotypes of Latinxs. For example, when asked what sports the speaker enjoyed, listeners gave a wide range of answers for the "all English" voice, but they overwhelmingly said "soccer" as the answer when the speaker produced a single word with Spanish phonology. People are surrounded by language ideologies that forge indexical links between specific languages and racial stereotypes so that they become automatic responses that can easily be triggered with subtle forms of language variation.

The United States (and the entirety of North America, with its long-inhabited history) has always been a multilingual nation, despite efforts to ban or eradicate other languages. Although courts have repeatedly found that language choice is a matter of freedom of speech, public discourse remains English-dominated through language ideologies that denigrate other languages and their speakers. These ideologies include the belief that bilinguals are somehow language deficient despite speaking two languages, the idea that English is naturally superior to other languages, the belief that bilingualism is abnormal, and so on. It should be obvious that knowledge of more than one language is a valuable asset, yet monolingual language ideologies only recognize this value when monolingual English speakers learn another language as adults. This can be seen in the way that journalists felt the need to criticize Julián Castro's Spanish but felt no need to do the same to Beto O'Rourke, Cory Booker, or Pete Buttigieg. The ultimate result of this language ideology is the loss of the huge economic and political resources that bilinguals can offer.

The idea that everyone in America needs to speak only English is not only unrealistic but also ties directly to openly xenophobic ideas and is a form of discourse structural racism meant to denigrate Latinxs, Asian Americans, Native Americans, Middle Eastern Americans, and so on. These discourses do much more than prevent Americans from reaching their national potential in a global world; they also serve as the basis for denying basic social services and equal justice to communities where languages other than English are used. As is usually the case, racist ideologies stand in the way of progress, harming many more than those Americans who happen to be bilingual.

Discussion questions

1. Check out the census data linked in the QR code. It shows changes in the use of different languages between 1980 and 2010. What sort of trends do you notice in the chart? Which languages have seen the greatest changes across time?

2. Check out the census data linked in the QR code. What parts of the country have higher rates of people who speak English less than "very well"? What factors might contribute to these patterns? What do you think the difference might be between "well" and "very well"?

3. Have you ever studied another language? Was it difficult for you? If so, what struggles did you encounter? How do you think it would have been different if you had learned that other language as a child? If you are monolingual, how might you benefit from learning another language?
4. Read the full text of Pratt's statement linked in the QR code. What parts of this are surprising to you? Which components echo racist stereotypes about Native Americans that continue to circulate in wider discourse? Which components index stereotypes that have been overcome (in that they are no longer used in wider discourse)?

5. Think of the kinds of media you take in daily. What are some other examples of Mock Asian, Hollywood Injun English, and Mock Spanish? What are your perceptions of the characters who exhibit these mock varieties? Why do you think the creators chose to use this language?
6. Examine the code-switching examples in the text box earlier in the chapter. What type is each example (alternation, insertion, or congruent lexicalization)?

8 American Sign Language and deaf culture

How people communicate

Most people communicate with the world through sound: listening to a friend talk, watching a movie without subtitles, or knowing not to step off the curb because they hear a truck coming. This state of interacting with the world is so natural for most humans that people forget the complexity of hearing and don't typically even give a name to the group of people who live this way. When this group *is* given a name, they are called *hearing* in contrast with a much smaller segment of the population who do not communicate naturally with the world through sound, for whom we will use the familiar, but complicated, name, *deaf*.

The hearing often think of deafness as a tragic lack of hearing – as purely a deficiency to be overcome. Defining deafness as a lack of hearing is an oversimplification in at least two crucial ways. First, it essentializes complex, multi-faceted people in terms of the one ability they are sure to find difficult or impossible. As noted in Chapter 2, defining a category of people in terms of a single attribute is common in the reproduction of stereotypes. In this chapter, we will see how an ideology that reduces deaf identity to simply the inability to hear severely limits the agency of deaf people, manufacturing disability out of difference. Second, more subtly, construing deafness as merely a lack of hearing greatly constrains the ability of the hearing to see their deaf friends, neighbors, children, and fellow citizens as fully human.

When the hearing mention language, they are almost always referencing spoken (or written) language. Whether it is to complain about someone's accent or to criticize word choice, most of the hearing rarely think about sign languages or the variation that might exist within them. The experience of the deaf in a hearing world is all but erased in their minds. This erasure, however, is about more than lack of experience with people who are deaf. It is about the primary ideology hearing people have about deaf people: the belief that deafness is a deficit, not just a difference, and believing the deaf to somehow be helpless and pitiful.

Deafness is typically acquired through some sort of environmental event such as loud noise or childhood illness but can also, less commonly, be inherited. According to the US National Institutes of Health, an estimated 10% of deaf babies are born to deaf parents (known as "deaf of deaf"), but the other 90% of the time a deaf child will be born to hearing parents either due to an inherited trait for deafness or through illness during pregnancy. In the 1960s, for example, there was a pandemic of the disease rubella (aka German measles) which led to the "rubella bulge" of some additional 8,000 babies born deaf in North America during the years 1962 to 1965. This bulge is associated with dramatic and far-reaching changes to deaf education and culture which will be discussed later in this chapter. Even if not present at birth, deafness can come to literally anyone at any time through, for example, chicken pox, mumps, diabetes, prolonged exposure to loud noises, momentary exposure to extremely loud noises, etc.

DOI: 10.4324/9781003332886-8

Figure 8.1 Sign language depicted on the wall of the Washington School for the Deaf in Vancouver, WA

The view of deafness as a deficit is often framed as a lack of language and an inability to communicate. This belief reflects a discriminatory language ideology that does not recognize the fact that *sign languages* (like American Sign Language; see Figure 8.1) are basically the same as spoken languages except for a difference in modality (vision vs. sound). There are sign languages all around the world, each with its own complex grammar and each serving as the foundation for a distinct community and culture. The hearing are so accustomed to understanding the world through sound, it may be difficult for them to imagine a society that isn't entirely dependent on sound. Perhaps counterintuitively, then, we will begin this chapter on American Sign Language and deaf culture with a brief description of what sound is, precisely, and what it means to be hearing. This will allow us to address the question of what it means to be deaf without the usual assumptions and simplifications.

What it means to be hearing

Sound is movement. If a tree falls in the woods, it unquestionably makes a sound – regardless of the presence or absence of hearing human ears. Actually, it makes quite a range of sounds, from the high-pitched whistling of twigs through the air to the aperiodic crackle of crushing leaves to the deep boom of the massive trunk impacting the earth. These movements produce vibrations that emanate from their source in a sphere of waves through the air, through the ground, and through any ears that happen to be present. Low sounds, like the booming trunk, produce long, slowly undulating waves while high sounds, like the whipping twigs, produce short, quickly undulating waves. The human ear (see diagram in Figure 8.2) is part of a delicate system for transducing these waves into patterns of neural stimulation in the brain. Vibrations in the air are shaped and filtered

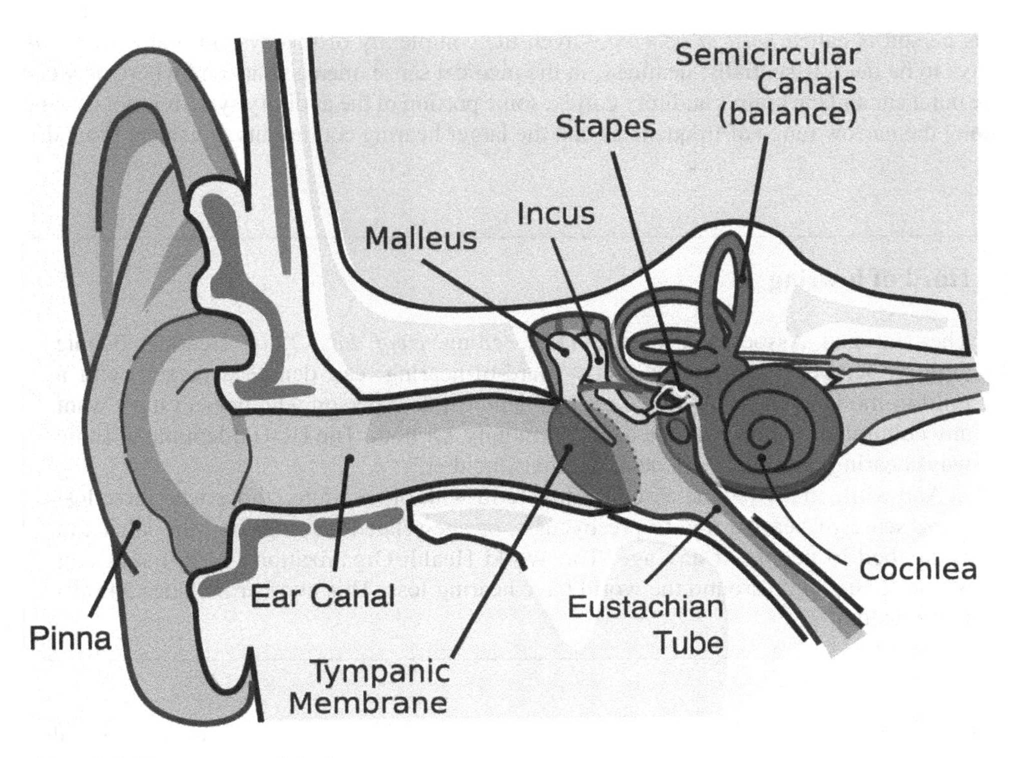

Figure 8.2 The anatomy of the human ear

by the pinna or outer ear; they are channeled through the ear canal to the tympanic membrane (aka ear drum) where this thin membrane vibrates in sympathy with the air. These vibrations are amplified by the three smallest bones in the body, the malleus, incus, and stapes, so they can be transferred from air to the salty liquid inside the cochlea. The human cochlea, as in all mammals, is a coiled tube lined with fine hairs. Different parts of this lining respond to different frequencies, triggering neurons to send a pattern of electrical signals to the brain. The louder a sound is, the greater the movement of these hairs; so that the barely audible noise of leaves landing may cause very little movement, a tree falling causes more movement, and an extremely loud sound such as a bomb or a canon being fired can cause instantaneous, permanent damage in even the youngest and healthiest of ears.

Even younger hearing people with *ideally* functioning ears can only hear waves that vibrate between 20 Hz and 20,000 Hz (vibrations per second). Pigeons, with some of the best low frequency hearing in the animal kingdom, can hear sounds as low as 0.5 Hz while some moths can hear sounds as high as 300,000 Hz (fifteen times the human range). More than this, hearing human ears are especially sensitive to sounds that vibrate between 1,000 Hz and 4,000 Hz while the lower and higher frequency sounds than this narrow window must be increasingly loud just to be detectable. In other words, even a perfectly functioning human ear is limited in terms of the frequencies and loudnesses it can turn into data for the brain to interpret as information.

If any portion of this delicate chain of hearing does not conduct, amplify, transduce, or transmit sound in a way that allows the person to make informative use of the patterns of vibrations in the air, this person is called *deaf.* If any portion in this delicate chain requires increased energy (associated with louder sounds) to make use of these patterns of vibration, this person is called *hard of hearing*. Given the complexity of this system, there are many ways to be deaf. Essentially, deafness, in the medical sense, means that somewhere between the outer ear and the brain's auditory cortex, some portion of the auditory system is not passing along the narrow range of frequencies that the larger hearing community considers "sound."

Hard of hearing

The National Association of the Deaf, citing *Deaf Life*, "For Hearing People Only" (October 1997), states that " 'Hard-of-hearing' can denote a person with a mild-to-moderate hearing loss. Or it can denote a deaf person who doesn't have/want any cultural affiliation with the deaf community. Or both. The HOH dilemma: in some ways hearing, in some ways deaf, in others, neither."

And while many people associate this term with older adults, those who have lost some sense of hearing due to presbycusis, or age-related hearing loss, the label can be applied to people of any age. The World Health Organization (WHO) says that 466 million people around the world have hearing loss. This number includes 34 million children.

Even if the auditory cortex in the brain doesn't receive information associated with a sound wave, the rest of the deaf body can still sense the vibrations of the wave. The rumble of thunder, the whispery feeling of a breeze across one's face, or the contented purr of a cat still convey their information into feet, skin, or lap and will still elicit the same trepidation, calm, or comfort they might produce in a hearing body. Finally, it must be stressed again that not all people who are functionally deaf are without hearing altogether. All deaf people still have a relationship with sound regardless of how useful it is to them in daily life; deaf bodies, like hearing bodies, create vibrations as they move through the world, but for the deaf, this can often mean feeling uncomfortable and constrained by a hearing world that judges and scolds them for the difficulty of controlling the loudness and timing of their own voices – phenomena they cannot themselves perceive.

Deaf culture

A hearing attendee at a deaf dance party would likely be surprised by how incredibly loud such parties can be. The urge to jump around rhythmically in the company of one's friends and potential love interests is not the exclusive possession of the hearing, and, indeed, deaf dance parties need to be loud so that the music will vibrate through the floor and into the feet of the dancers. Often, the hearing cannot comfortably attend such parties, even with high quality ear plugs. Not only does the physical nature of sound make dancing accessible to deaf partygoers, but there are professional deaf dancers in every genre. On the other side of the dance floor, there are many successful deaf musicians, like percussionist Dame Evelyn Glennie, rapper Sean Forbes, singer Mandy Harvey, and many others.

In addition to deaf dance and music, there is an entire genre of poetry that is simultaneously language and the performance of that language. Deaf poets who use sign languages (described in text box 2) use handshape rhyme and iconic movements in much the way that spoken poetry might use rhyming words and iconic sounds (e.g., repeated [z] sounds in a poem about bees). But beyond this, sign language poets can bring an entire world of movement and facial expression to their poems that even non-signers can understand and be moved by. The body movements between signs take on new, expressive emotional meanings of their own while variations in the way the signs themselves are created can evoke imagery simultaneously with meaning. Sign language poets can also employ simultaneous signs (e.g., signing *crying* with the left hand while sharing a story of loss with the right) to set a kind of linguistic back beat to the rhythm of their own verse.

Deaf poetry

You can find all sorts of deaf poets on the internet! Check out these artists:

Mari Klassen

Canadian-born poet and ASL program developer for British Columbia's provincial outreach program for the deaf and hard of hearing, Mari Klassen, has been a poet since childhood. In the video linked in the QR code, she interprets an example of counter poetry. In counter poetry, the first half of the poem has one meaning, and the second half of the poem is the same series of signs in reverse for a completely different meaning.

Douglas Ridloff

Poet, artist, and performer Douglas Ridloff is a sign language poet and director of ASL SLAM. ASL Slam was founded in New York City in 2005 by Bob Arnold and Jason Norman as an open mic event for deaf poets and artists to showcase their sign writings. Ridloff took the event over shortly thereafter and has brought ASL Slam on world tours and established events in Boston and Chicago. In the video linked in the QR code, you can watch Ridloff perform his poem "Symbiosis."

Another surprise awaiting a hearing attendee at a deaf dance party is that many of the revelers at such an event do not consider themselves disabled and, indeed, would not choose to become hearing even if a magic potion existed that could make them so. Of course, no such potion exists. There are assistive devices, hearing aids, and cochlear implants (see later in this chapter) that can provide some access to the hearing world for deaf people, and many deaf people use and benefit from these devices, but they are not without their shortcomings and controversy.

Just as there are many physical ways in which deafness can occur, there are many responses to being deaf. The physical state in which the brain receives information regarding sound through the ear is not the same as participating in deaf culture in the United States and anglophone Canada, and participating in activities like deaf dance parties. Participation in deaf culture typically requires knowledge of American Sign Language. *Sign languages* have naturally emerged in communities of deaf individuals all over the world. People tend to expect speakers of different languages to also have distinct cultures, and sign languages are no different. The distinctiveness of deaf culture in the United States is not due to shared deafness but instead emerges from the use of a language that is entirely distinct from English, namely *American Sign Language* (or ASL). To understand deaf culture, it will be necessary to have some additional background on sign languages.

Sign languages and American Sign Language

The first thing to understand about sign languages is that they are, in every imaginable sense, languages. This observation may seem like mere tautology, but it has had a profound impact on the way linguists think about what it is they study. Humans have an innate need to engage in language. This engagement is both mental and physical; sign languages teach us that language's physical expression can take place just as naturally and effectively through visual signs as through sounds. Although these two modalities offer different affordances and constraints, they have equal communicative capacity. Any message – whether it is communicating the weather, singing the National Anthem (see Figure 8.3), or telling one's deepest

Figure 8.3 Children at St. Rita's School in Cincinnati, OH, sign the National Anthem in 1918

secrets – can be relayed in any language of any type. And while sound is the most natural way of communicating for hearing people, sign language is the most natural means of communication for those who are deaf.

Things to know about ASL

NPR published a detailed but compact account of what ASL is and how it works, featuring the experiences of ASL users from Gallaudet University describing, in sign, the structure of their language. These students wish hearing people knew simple things like the signs for "please," "thank you," "I'm sorry," and "how was your day?" They would like hearing people to know that not all sign languages are the same, that there are accents, slang, and baby talk in ASL, just as there are in any other human language. In short, the students in this video would like the hearing world to know that ASL is a full and beautiful natural language. The chapter you are reading was written by hearing authors who benefited from the work of deaf scholars and ASL researchers and from the inspiration of these students. In the video linked in the QR code, you can watch the original NPR video that inspired this chapter.

The second critical thing to understand about sign languages is that they, like any other human language, are social constructs emerging from and, in turn, strengthening the communities that use them. Sign languages are not exclusively used by people who are themselves deaf, but it is certainly the case that these languages tend to evolve among communities of deaf or hard of hearing children. Particularly since the 1960s, many people in these communities of sign language users have come to see themselves as members of a linguistic and cultural minority group who are proud to be deaf – many of whom see themselves not as lacking hearing but as having gained deafness.

The dominant sign language in North America today is ASL (see Figure 8.4 for ASL's system of alphabetic and numeric hand shapes). Padden (2010) puts the number of native ASL users in the United States and Canada at roughly 250,000 signers and at least that many second language ASL signers. ASL, like any human language, has its own phonology, morphology, syntax, and semantics, and it is *not* merely English performed with the hands, arms, and facial expressions. Although such a system of *signed English*, with signs used to express English words in English-like sentences, does exist and is often used between hearing and deaf speakers to facilitate communication, it is slow and cumbersome compared with actual ASL (Stokoe 2002).

How can we know for ourselves whether ASL signs are analogous to English words? Linguist David M. Perlmutter suggests the following simple test: If ASL signs stood for English words, one would expect to be able to find a sign for each English word. If a single English

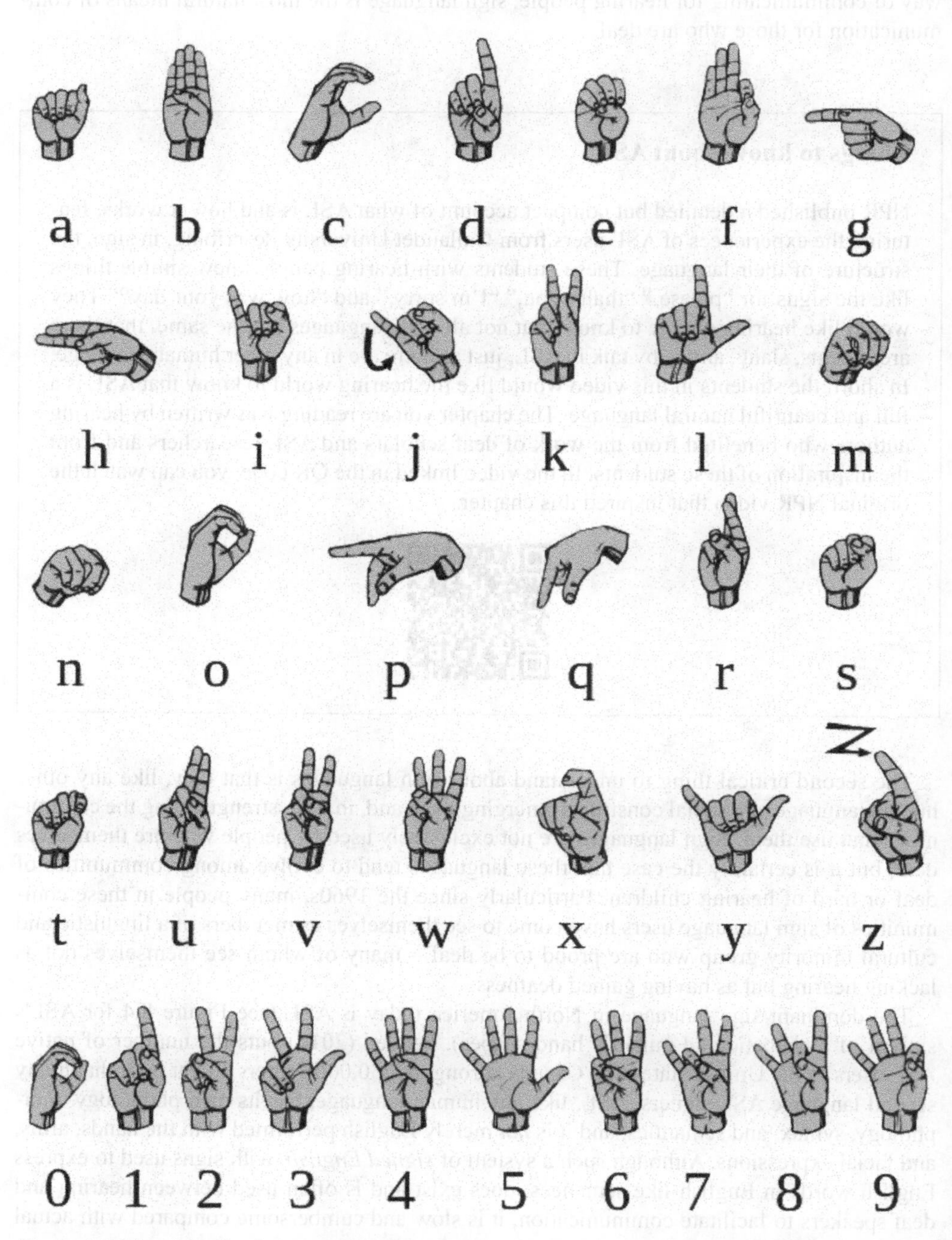

Figure 8.4 The signs for letters of the English alphabet used to spell out English words in signed English and ASL

word has multiple meanings, like the word *right* which can mean "correct," "the opposite of left," "a legal entitlement," "morally good," etc., then one can expect to be able to find a single ASL sign with all these meanings. However, ASL signs express their meaning directly; they are not mediated through English words, so these many meanings are expressed by an equal number of unrelated signs, just as they are expressed by multiple different words in French, Spanish, Russian, Japanese, and most other languages.

Truly revolutionary linguistic work by William Stokoe (1960) and his graduate students demonstrated to a skeptical world in the early 1960s that the "natural" sign language in use by their students at Gallaudet University (a university established specifically for deaf students; see discussion later in this chapter) was as robust and efficient as any other human language. Linguists have since provided abundant evidence for the rich patterns of structure at every level of sign languages. That is, the same kinds of variation in sounds, words, grammar, etc. that can be found in spoken languages can also be found in sign languages.

One can compare how these structures are exhibited in both spoken and signed languages. Spoken languages have speech sounds organized into grammars of minimally contrastive sound units composed of resonance, noise, silence, and pitch. By minimally contrastive, we mean that a word like *fan* can become the word *van* simply by vibrating one's vocal cords during the first speech sound (the [f] becomes a [v]). This makes [f] and [v] minimally contrastive sounds, and it means that *fan/van* form what linguists call a minimal pair. Sign languages have gestures organized into phonological grammars of minimally contrastive units composed of handshape, movement, location, orientation, and non-manual markers (e.g., facial expression). The words for *onion* and *apple* in ASL share handshape, movement, orientation, and non-manual markers but differ in terms of the location parameter. *Onion*, shown on the left of Figure 8.5, is produced with right hand in the "X" handshape (see X in Figure 8.4) with the knuckle of the index finger placed near the temple or high on the cheek (near the eye) and rotated twice in a clockwise direction. *Apple* is identical but performed with the hand against the cheek, shown on the right in Figure 8.5. Thus, just as the English

Figure 8.5 The ASL signs for *onion* (left) and *apple* (right) represent a minimal pair, contrasting only in terms of location of the sign

Source: images courtesy of Nóra McGowan

words *fan* and *van* display a minimal contrast between vibrating or not vibrating one's vocal cords, the ASL words for *apple* and *onion* show minimal contrast in terms of location.

Because only about 10% of deaf babies have parents who are themselves deaf, the usual mode of effortless transmission of language(s) from parent to child is typically absent because the deaf baby's parents do not (usually) know American Sign Language. Some hearing parents even resist the use of sign languages with their children, hoping instead to teach the child to read lips and to produce speech by imitating the mouth movements of hearing speakers. As we will see, gestural imitation is necessary if deaf children are to perform spoken language. Hearing children receive highly informative auditory feedback about their voices when producing speech sounds both through their own ears and through their own bones. Without this feedback, it can be extraordinarily difficult for a deaf or hard of hearing child to learn the precise movements and timing needed to make the sounds of English in a way that is intelligible to even the most caring listeners committed to upholding their end of the communicative burden.

We have learned (e.g., in Chapter 5 and Chapter 6) some of the ways that speech sounds can come to index social meanings so that the resonances of one's vowels can reveal a childhood spent in Michigan or Alabama, and the use of, for example, different patterns of intonation can communicate an African American or a Jewish American identity (e.g., Burdin et al. 2018). This same phenomenon occurs in sign languages as well, so that people from different parts of the country sign with different regional varieties. Just as with spoken languages, variable uses of signs and different manners of signing carry indexical meanings that may be used to distinguish between white and African American signers, signers who identify as male and female, young and old signers, and so on. These processes of variation and change are the soul of human language. It is through these processes that "languages" as recognizable, nameable social constructs come to exist in the first place. And just as American English is a cluster of dialects that have separated from the cluster of dialects one might call British English, ASL is best understood as a cluster of dialects that share many words, parts of words, and ways of connecting words together. And just as being a native speaker of a particular dialect of American English comes with social consequences, so does being a native speaker of a particular dialect of ASL.

Martha's Vineyard Sign Language

One consequence of American Sign Language being an entirely separate language from American English is that ASL is *not* mutually intelligible with British Sign Language (BSL). They are distinct systems with different words, different ways of connecting subjects and verbs to objects, different ways of including information about what a verb is even doing in the sentence. A native signer of ASL wishing to visit London and communicate with signers there would need to study BSL as a second language just as a hearing traveler might need to study Russian to visit Moscow or Thai to visit Bangkok. This may come as a surprise to the hearing reader, but perhaps even more surprising is the fact that a signer of ASL can travel to such places as France, Bolivia, or Russia and communicate much more easily than they could in Great Britain or Ireland because ASL is a relative to the sign languages spoken in those places. This is, again, because American English and American Sign Language have entirely distinct histories and unique relationships with other languages. For example, Figure 8.6 is a chart showing the BSL representation of the letters of the Latin alphabet, which can be compared to the characters in Figure 8.4.

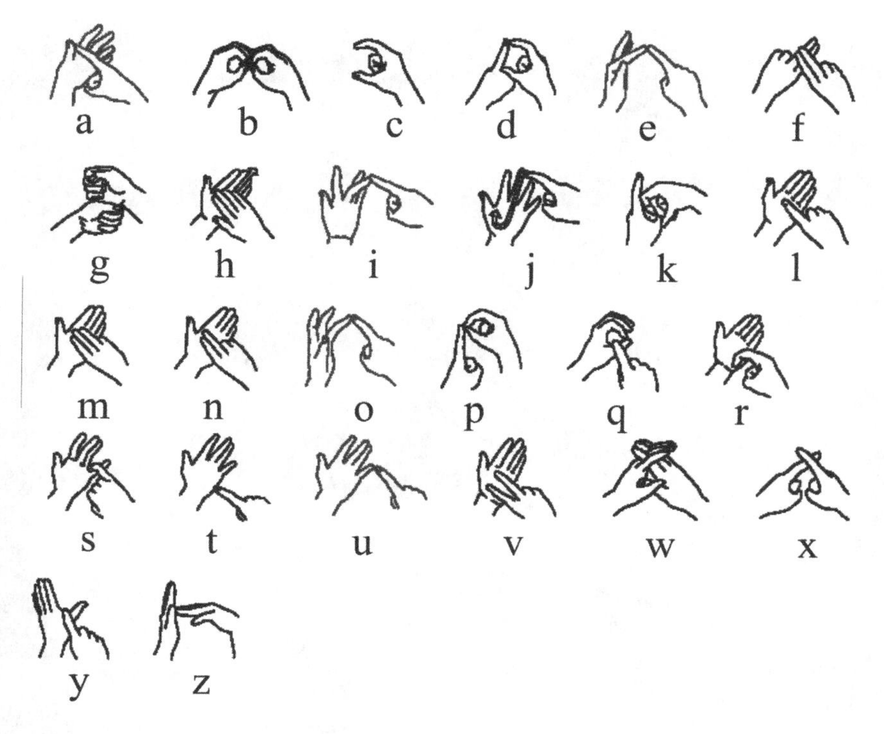

Figure 8.6 The Latin alphabet in British Sign Language

Speech does not leave fossils, so there are no records of the first time a group of hearing human beings expressed their innate need to communicate with one another. One can deduce, however, from the fact that every human community ever encountered has at least one spoken language, that such a system will arise whenever a group of hearing humans is brought together. Unlike with spoken language, there are multiple documented events of precisely this kind of spontaneous generation of a language happening with sign languages. Where there is a population of deaf people, if no one prevents them (and, as we'll see in the history of deaf education in America, even if people *do* try to prevent them), a sign language will emerge. Often this new language will show no obvious influence either from other sign languages or from spoken language(s) – truly the genesis of a new human language.

Importantly for the history of sign language in America (although not necessarily for the history of ASL, see later), one such system emerged on Martha's Vineyard (see Figure 8.7) in the 18th century. Martha's Vineyard Sign Language (MVSL) thrived throughout the 19th century but use of the language declined, and the last native signer passed away in 1952. Martha's Vineyard is a small island off the southern coast of Cape Cod in Massachusetts.

The island was originally inhabited by the Wampanoag (discussed in Chapter 7), who called it *Noepe*. The Europeans who lived on the island in the early 18th century shared it with the Wampanoag who lived on three separate reservations: Chappaquiddick, Aquinnah (aka Gay Head), and Christiantown. The population of Europeans included sheep farmers, whalers, and fishers who formed a small and close-knit community that included in its

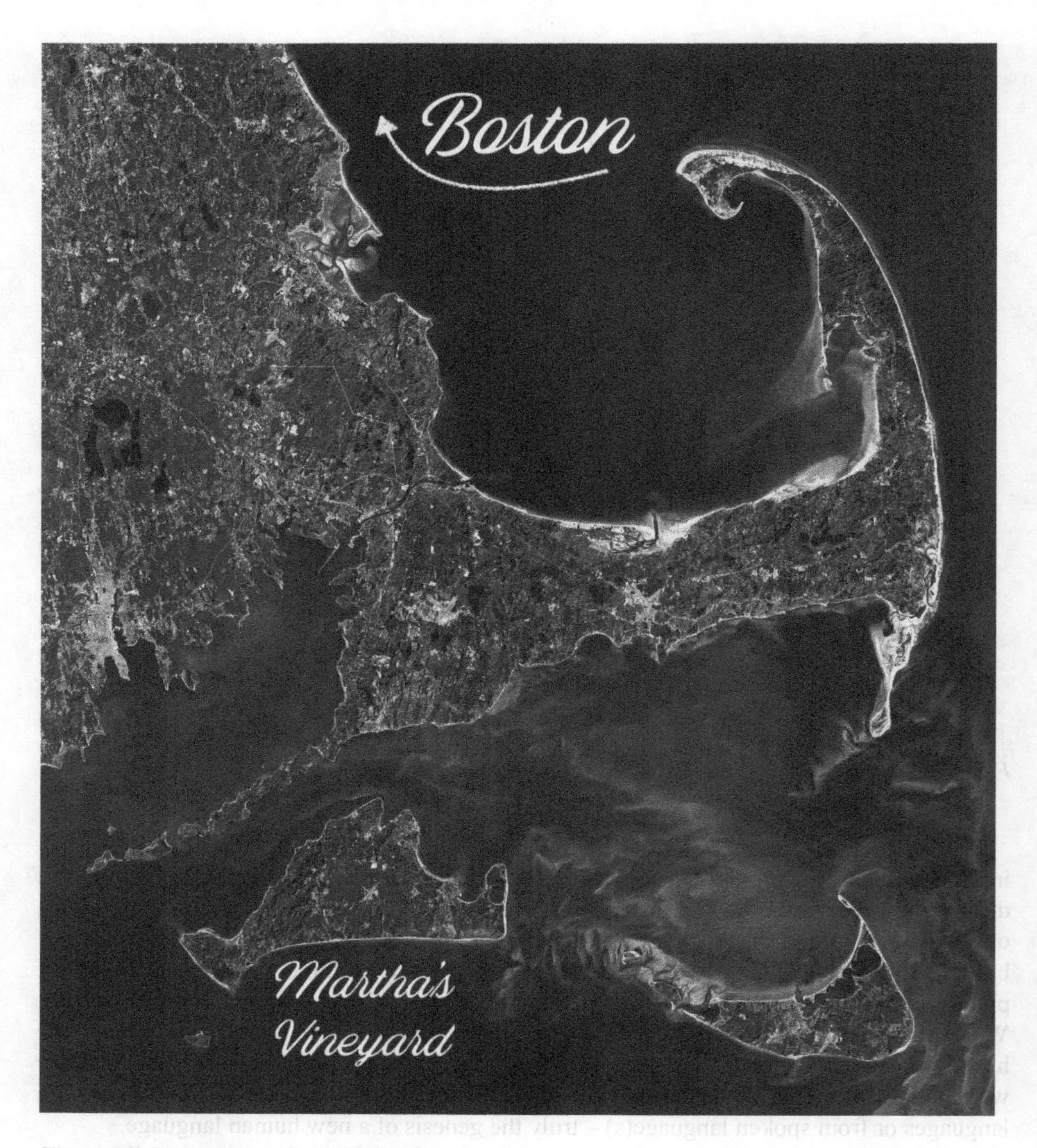

Figure 8.7 Map of Cape Cod and vicinity

genetic makeup a recessive trait for heritable deafness. There were deaf members of the European community on the island as early as 1714 (Groce 1985). Through a founder effect, whereby a population descended from a relatively small group of colonizing ancestors has reduced genetic diversity, the island soon boasted a higher-than-average rate of deafness among its residents. By one account, 45 of the island's roughly 350 residents were deaf at a time when the rate for the rest of the nation was closer to 1 in 5,700. In this small community with a high incidence of deafness, MVSL emerged naturally as a means of communication on the island.

When all the families in the area are interrelated and congenital deafness is commonplace (as it was on Martha's Vineyard at this time), it is reasonable to assume that everyone knew at least a few deaf people, and most people, deaf and hearing, had deaf relatives, friends, and neighbors. This is precisely the kind of social situation in which bilingualism thrives. Children will be born into families already fluent in a robust and evolving system of signs and, even more importantly, they will be comfortable interacting with deaf people. Ideologies about what counts as effective communication and what can be expected as reasonable accommodation among neighbors come to include sign and speech as equally valid, equally viable codes. MVSL came into common use among hearing and deaf neighbors alike such that deafness, precisely because it was widely accepted as normal, essentially disappeared as a source of social differentiation.

Being neighborly

Of course, any community can show the kind of welcoming and inclusive environment found on Martha's Vineyard. Indeed, in a neighborhood in Newtown, Massachusetts, in 2019, a group of more than 20 neighbors learned ASL to communicate with their new neighbor, Samantha, a 3-year-old girl who was born deaf. People signed up for an ASL class and learned the language to help this girl and her family feel at home. In describing this phenomenal level of support, the neighborhood's ASL teacher, who acknowledged the importance of children having full access to language, said, "What this community is doing to support Sam shows the power people have to really change one person or one family's life" (ABC7.com 2019).

In this bilingual English/MVSL community, both languages were learned in the home or in early childhood. Groce (1985) cites many reminiscences from islanders discussing the use of MVSL among hearing residents. One resident recounted that one could go to the dual-purpose general store/post office in the early 20th century, where:

> You'd go along and get your mail, or you'd buy half a pound of salt pork. . . . They'd gather every night. There'd be conversations going on between these deaf people, some of them are talking, making sign language, some of them are talking to hearing people, back and forth, and it was give and take. You never thought anything about it. And even these little kids . . . knew the sign language. And these older men would stop and talk to them kids, make signs back and forth, laugh and chuckle.
>
> (Groce 1985: 60)

Notice this informant's use of "talking" to refer to both sign and speech inclusively; her language ideologies clearly include a belief that using sign for everyday communication is unexceptional and an understanding that deafness is a normal and unremarkable human characteristic.

This knowledge of sign and general comfort with deafness had powerful social consequences for what it meant to be a deaf person on Martha's Vineyard. Deaf people on Martha's Vineyard then were run-of-the-mill members of the broader community. Many deaf people in other places at this time were limited by a worldview that excluded them, shunned them, or simply expected them to lack ability. Deaf people on Martha's Vineyard were expected to participate in religious services.

> They would come to prayer meetings; most all of them were regular church people, you know. They would come when people offered testimonials, and they would get up in front of the audience and stand there and give a whole lecture in sign. No one translated it to the audience because everyone knew what they were saying. And if there was anyone who missed something, somewhere, somebody sitting near them would be able to tell them about it.
>
> (Groce 1985: 62)

And deaf men and women were expected to work the same jobs, participate in the social life of the island, and generally just be Vineyarders.

> We would sit around and wait for the mail to come in and just talk. And the deaf would be there, everyone would be there. And they were part of the crowd, and they were accepted. They were fishermen and farmers and everything else. And they wanted to find out the news just as much as the rest of us. And oftentimes people would tell stories and make signs at the same time so everyone could follow him together. Of course, sometimes, if there were more deaf than hearing there, everyone would speak sign language – just to be polite, you know.
>
> (Groce 1985: 60)

This demonstrates that many of the disabling effects people associate with an inability to hear are not about hearing at all but rather emerge from the limitations placed on the deaf by the language ideologies and social expectations of the hearing. Deaf members of a society in which the prevailing language ideologies devalue the role of signed communications will suffer because of those ideologies – either finding themselves transformed into a minority group essentialized by their disability or required to participate in spoken communication that crucially depends on the only ability they are sure not to have. We will return to this theme of inclusion and exclusion again in the discussion of deaf culture.

Oralism vs. manualism

Outside of special situations like Martha's Vineyard, in places where the percentage of deaf people in the population is typically small and language ideologies valorize speech and hearing over signed communication, living in a deaf body is made considerably more restricting. While MVSL and its signers were thriving on Martha's Vineyard, educational leaders and advocates for the deaf in much of Europe and North America sought to extinguish the use of sign languages among deaf children and adults. Proponents of *oralism* argued that deaf and hard of hearing children should be taught to read lips and to speak by imitating the speech gestures of the hearing. These scholars, teachers, and advocates saw that communicating and learning in sign language, or *manualism*, tends to create tight-knit communities among the people who share a sign language. Some hearing people openly feared that the tight-knit communities formed by a shared language would encourage intermarriage between the deaf and, therefore, tend to increase the number of deaf babies in the world. Others merely saw these communities of deaf people as isolating themselves from and limiting access to the hearing, or "normal," world. For oralists, then, the goal of education was to eradicate sign language and push deaf individuals to try to learn spoken English:

> There is no problem which more nearly concerns every teacher in a school for the deaf than that of securing and maintaining speech intelligibility. Normal speech possesses a rhythm, a sing-song, of a natural kind, which, to the accustomed listener, is an aid to intelligibility, and often triumphs over gross phonetic faults. The speech of a deaf child lacks this natural rhythm, which can only be acquired through hearing.
>
> (W. Carey Roe, Oralist, Principal at Royal Institution for the Deaf, July 1933, in Haycock 1933: 251)

Even with modern assistive devices like hearing aids and cochlear implants, learning to read lips and produce spoken language is a very different (and much more difficult) task for deaf people compared to the acquisition of spoken languages by hearing children. This is not to say that oralism's goals are completely impossible. With sufficient time, energy, and struggle, it is possible for even a child who has been born profoundly deaf to acquire some speaking and lip-reading abilities. Lip-reading (or speech-reading as it is sometimes known among practitioners) takes advantage of a skill that all sighted listeners have to supplement (and even, under some conditions, override) the auditory speech signal with information from lip movements, jaw movements, tongue position (when visible), and facial expressions. Typically, without being consciously aware of it, hearing sighted people take in these visual cues and use them to disambiguate aspects of an utterance that might otherwise be unclear. People often become more aware of the usefulness of the visual components of the speech signal later in life when typical aging of the ear can make tasks like understanding someone in a crowded room more difficult. Lip-reading is most beneficial, therefore, to the hard of hearing – where partial hearing is present and the visual and acoustic signals can be used together or the acoustic signal can be boosted by means of an assistive device.

McGurk Effect

The way hearing people unconsciously depend on visual cues during speech perception was dramatically demonstrated by McGurk and MacDonald (1976). They combined auditory and visual stimuli in an experiment that asked listeners to identify, on an answer sheet, what syllable they heard. In a control condition, for example, participants might have heard the syllable *ga* while watching video of a person saying *ga*. The more exciting trials happens when McGurk and MacDonald presented non-matching video and audio. The vast majority (98% of adults) of listeners hearing a voice say *ba* and seeing a carefully synchronized video of a person pronouncing *ga* would report hearing *da*. A similar, albeit weaker, result was obtained by combining a voice saying *pa* with video of a face pronouncing *ka* which would reliably cause the fused perception of *ta*. McGurk and MacDonald replicated this result with children as young as 3 years old as the listeners. Even when the audio is presented clearly, via headphones, under laboratory conditions to participants with typical hearing, participants cannot resist what has come to be known as the McGurk Effect. Indeed, one of the most remarkable facts about this study is that even when listeners have the experiment explained to them and are instructed to hear *ba* instead of *da*, most participants will still report hearing *da*. Visual cues, even for hearing listeners, are simply part of the speech signal.

In the absence of any acoustic signal, or in cases where the acoustic signal is extremely attenuated, the information provided by lip-reading is of limited value. The speech sounds made with the lips ([p], [b], and [m] in English) are clearly visible but cannot be differentiated from one another by sight alone, so *pit*, *bit*, and *mitt* are impossible to distinguish except through context. Sounds using the lips and teeth together ([f] and [v] in English) or the teeth and tongue (the two sounds in English at the beginning of *thin* and *this*) can, again, be easily differentiated from other speech sounds but not from one another. Consonants at the back of the mouth ([k], [g], and [ŋ], the sound at the end of *wing* in English) can, depending on the neighboring vowel(s), provide some visual information that allows them to be differentiated from consonants produced further forward in the mouth. Beyond this, however, the remaining consonants and all vowels are all but impossible to distinguish visually with any accuracy.

Also missing in lip-reading are almost all of the prosodic cues (pitch, loudness, and duration) that hearing interlocutors use to help distinguish syllables, words, phrases, and sentences. Without either some auditory information or an unusually strong expectation of what a speaker is trying to say, even the most accomplished lip-reading by a deaf listener will contain many errors. In the absence of other forms of feedback that could highlight these errors to the speaker or lip-reader, these errors are likely to go undetected and could, in the worst case, leave the speaker with a strong sense that they have been well understood by a listener who is utterly confused and discouraged.

Compared to lip-reading, the production by spoken language by a deaf individual is more likely to succeed. Here, at least, the hearing interlocutor will typically know if they cannot understand what is being said, so opportunities for stealth miscommunication are rarer. Again, with sufficient time, energy, and struggle on the part of the deaf child, and with clear, accurate instruction from dedicated teachers, it is possible for a deaf speaker to learn to imitate most physical movements required to produce spoken language. This includes learning precise ways to move the lips, tongue, jaw, vocal cords, diaphragm, and even the velum (the port high at the back of the mouth that divides the nasal passages from the rest of the vocal tract and permits consonants like [m] and [n]). Methods vary for this instruction, but generally the student must rely heavily on the sense of touch to learn to feel the tongue gently and fleetingly touching the roof of the mouth and different teeth in carefully coordinated succession. The hands can be used to feel whether the vocal cords are vibrating and whether the nasal passages have been made to vibrate.

Understanding the speech mechanism

To understand how speech articulation works, try this: Say (in prolonged form) the sounds [f] and [v] while gently touching the front of your throat. The buzzing you feel when you say [v] is the vibration of your vocal folds (a feature linguists refer to as "voicing"), and it is the only thing that differentiates these two sounds. Or try this: Place your fingers on your cheekbones and say [aba]. Do the same thing with [ama]. The buzzing you feel is your nasal cavity vibrating, which is how you can make a distinction between [m], a nasal sound, and [b], a non-nasal or oral sound.

As indicated by the quote from Roe earlier in this section, the process of learning under oralism can be all-consuming. "Securing and maintaining speech intelligibility" becomes the primary focus of teacher and student so much so that educational content like science, mathematics, literature, and history are lost in the effort to approximate, but never match, the speech and hearing abilities that come naturally and effortlessly to the hearing. Still, oralism, as an educational philosophy, was the dominant paradigm in the United States, Great Britain, and numerous other countries from the mid-19th century through, in many places, the 1970s. In 1880, the so-called Second International Congress on the Education of the Deaf ("so-called" because, oddly, there had been no first conference) in Milan brought together delegates from Italy, Great Britain, France, the United States, Sweden, Belgium, and Germany. Of the 164 delegates in attendance, only one was deaf. The Milan conference issued eight resolutions urging governments to take the necessary steps to ensure that all deaf children receive an education but that the modality and content of that education should ban the use of sign languages in favor of an oralist methodology. Consequences of this meeting included the banning of sign language instruction, the firing of teachers of the deaf who were themselves deaf, and a wholesale switch to oralist teaching methods that lasted for generations.

One outspoken and influential proponent of oralism in America was Alexander Graham Bell. In addition to being credited with inventing the telephone, Bell was a eugenicist and Social Darwinist who feared the creation of a "deaf race" that would be deleterious to the purity of the human race (Bell 1884). Bell warned that a number of factors could result in such a scenario: the creation of residential schools for the deaf, the instruction of deaf children by deaf teachers, and the possibility of two deaf parents having deaf children. Of particular concern for Bell was the use of sign languages by the deaf, writing:

> As there are 1,500 hearing persons for every one deaf-mute, it seems difficult to formulate any plan which would restrict their choice of partners in life to deaf-mutes alone or to the hearing members of deaf-mute families. . ..
>
> What more powerful or efficient means could be found than to teach the deaf-mutes to think in a different language from that of the people at large? This is what we do. In the majority of our institutions for the deaf . . . a special language is used as the vehicle of thought, a language as different from English as French or German or Russian.
>
> (Bell 1884: 42)

Bell's recommended solution, which he personally put into action with generally poor outcomes in Scotland, Wisconsin, and Washington D.C., was to shut down residential schools for the deaf where a mixture of hearing and deaf teachers would instruct a population of deaf students using sign language in favor of day schools where hearing teachers would instruct pupils in lip-reading and speech by means of imitation.

In his time, Bell was considered a lifelong advocate for the deaf and for deaf education. His mother, Eliza Grace Bell (née Symonds), was hard of hearing and could make out some sounds by means of a speaking tube. She was a musician and young Alexander's primary teacher. Bell's wife, Mabel Bell (née Hubbard), became profoundly deaf after surviving scarlet fever at the age of 5 and was a student of Bell's oralist methods prior to their marriage. Bell's father, Alexander Melville Bell, was an oralist teacher who developed a system of writing, called Visible Speech, intended to present deaf students with an articulatory description of speech movements in the hope that it would enable them to produce more natural-sounding speech in the absence of feedback from their ears. Even so, Bell's efforts to wipe out sign language and to require that all deaf children be instructed via oralist methods have tarnished his reputation in the deaf community and left him a deeply unpopular figure to this day.

A contemporary of Bell's who espoused the opposing manualist view for deaf education was Thomas Hopkins Gallaudet. Gallaudet was tasked with founding the first school for the deaf in the United States. He was already familiar with the manualist efforts of Abbé de l'Épee and his successor, Abbé Sicard, who had repurposed the sign language of Paris for use as the most natural mode of instruction in schools for the deaf in France. L'Épee saw the use of visual sign language for deaf students as bringing students in through the window when the door was barred. In other words, l'Épee espoused using the most comfortable and natural form of communication available for the student to allow a focus on education rather than focusing on eradicating that form of communication. However, it was not to France, but to oralist England, that Gallaudet initially went seeking instruction in how to teach deaf students. There he found himself denied access to the methods of the monopolistic Braidwood Academies and feared he might be forced to return to America empty handed. As fate would have it, though, Gallaudet was in England at the same time as the Abbé Sicard and two of his assistants: Jean Mássieu and his student Laurent Clerc. These French manualists eagerly welcomed Gallaudet and instructed him in their methods. Gallaudet was even able to convince Laurent Clerc to accompany him back to the United States where they founded what is now the American School for the Deaf in Hartford, CT, on April 15, 1815. The school opened and began serving students in 1817.

American Sign Language as it is used today can trace its roots directly to the founding of this school. Most of the students at the school in the early years came from Martha's Vineyard, but significant groups also came from Henniker, New Hampshire and southeastern Maine. These groups would have brought knowledge of their own community sign languages and home signs. Clerc brought his native command of French Sign Language (or *langue des signes française*, shortened as LSF). What emerged within the Hartford school, and later at a new school in Philadelphia that Clerc was also central in establishing, was a new language: ASL.

It is tempting, given the large number of MVSL signers present at this early school, to speculate that ASL is, at its core, MVSL. Alternatively, it is tempting to speculate, given that Clerc's LSF formed the basis for the language of instruction and that modern ASL shares so many words with modern LSF, that ASL is merely a dialect of French Sign Language. Neither of these extremes is supported by the available evidence, however. Groce's interviews provide evidence that children at the Hartford school returned to Martha's Vineyard using an unfamiliar sign language that was no longer MVSL. Clerc's own journals report that the language in use among the students was not his own LSF but reflected many words and constructions brought by the students themselves, rather than the faculty (Padden 2010). About 60% of the vocabulary of ASL comes from LSF with the other words coming from

MVSL and still others emerging on their own in the context of the school. Unlike languages imported from Europe (like English or Spanish), ASL is truly an American language.

In April of 1864, at the same historic moment that the US Congress was approving the 13th Amendment, which abolished slavery, they also approved the charter for the Columbia Institution for the Instruction of the Deaf, Dumb, and Blind. Edward Miner Gallaudet, Thomas Hopkins Gallaudet's son, was the Institution's first superintendent, and the school, now Gallaudet University, bears his father's name. The ASL sign for the elder Gallaudet is made by indicating the temple of his eyeglasses, and this is also the first half of the name sign for Gallaudet University. It is difficult to overstate the significance of Gallaudet University to the deaf community over the past 150 years. It is the only liberal arts college in the world designed to foster barrier free communication for deaf and hard of hearing students. And since its inception, Gallaudet has always incorporated sign as a mode of instruction, even during the long period when sign languages were banned at all residential schools in the United States.

Name signs

Many readers might be familiar enough with ASL to know how to spell their name in finger spelling (if not, try it by using Figure 8.4). Readers may not be familiar with the idea that ASL users do not simply spell all people's names every time. Instead, name signs are developed; these are signs for individuals that are given by culturally deaf people. They create unique signs that follow the structural rules for this naming practice in accordance with the local and culturally acceptable ways of naming within the community. They are also typically reflective of the personality of the recipient.

When William Stokoe arrived at Gallaudet to teach English in 1955, he was a specialist in Middle English (especially Chaucer) with no training in either sign languages or linguistics. He and the many other hearing professors were instructed to speak normally, so that the students could lip-read, while presenting some of the words in signed English (substituting signs for English words and using English grammar rather than the grammar and lexicon of ASL) and fingerspelling any words he did not know how to sign. The prevailing, published academic wisdom of the time was that the deaf had, at best, "broken language." Even within Gallaudet in 1955, Stokoe was told by older colleagues that his deaf students would understand only the simplest language and therefore "could not achieve full mental development." Stokoe even reports one colleague who used overtly racist language and compared their eager students to dogs to reassure him that he would still enjoy teaching the deaf because they tried so hard to please (Stokoe 2002: 3).

It was in this extremely prejudicial educational environment that Stokoe recognized that the system of signs his students and deaf colleagues used to communicate with one another was far more complex and expressive than the awkward signed version of English he used in his own teaching. In 1960, he documented this robust language in the paper *Sign language structure*, which provides a scientific analysis as evidence of the status of sign language as true human language. He provides a detailed analysis of the many parallels he observed between sign language and the organization and structure of sounds in spoken languages. He proposes a nascent system for capturing sign language in writing, briefly discusses the existence of sign language dialects, and describes ongoing efforts to understand the morphology and syntax of the language in use at Gallaudet among the deaf. This groundbreaking research became the first serious study of what is now known as ASL.

Stokoe did not invent ASL nor did he discover ASL (in the same way that Newton did not "invent" gravity and Columbus did not "discover" America). Stokoe's real, significant, and far-reaching contribution to deaf culture was to describe ASL in a way that forced even ardent skeptics to recognize that, in fact, ASL is a regular human language like any spoken language. By bringing this kind of credibility to ASL, Stokoe showed that the deaf were not only able to produce language but were capable of much, much more than people had previously assumed. Stokoe's students, of course, already understood that the signing they used to interact with their community was a language, but Stokoe deserves credit for being able to see past the prevailing language ideologies of his day. Hearing teacher after hearing teacher, for generation after generation, failed to effectively reach deaf students by speaking at them in a language that they could not hear. Stokoe recognized the possibility that when there were clear communication breakdowns between himself and his students that perhaps the failing was not in the generations of ill-served deaf students but in the mode of communication teachers had attempted to use. Stokoe was not the first to see this, of course. L'Épee had seen it. Sicard, Massieu, Clerc, and the Gallaudets had seen it. Thinkers as far back in recorded history as Socrates seem to have seen it as well. But William Stokoe taught himself and then used the scientific tools of linguistics to enable others to see it too.

Recent evidence from functional Magnetic Resonance Imaging (fMRI) suggests that signing depends on the same areas of the brain that support speech in the hearing and, crucially, does not depend upon the areas of the brain activated for non-linguistic gestures (Tabak 2006: 129–131). Related to this, there is convincing evidence that a foundation in sign language is the best way to foster later development of proficiency in a second language – be that second language accessed through speech/lip-reading or reading and writing (Lillo-Martin et al. 2016). Yet there is still much that is not understood about sign languages and how they work. We cannot yet answer simple questions like how many sign languages exist in the world right now or how they all historically relate to one another. Unlike with spoken languages, we cannot reconstruct older forms of sign languages to understand how, and at what rate, these languages change. Finally, we do not yet fully understand the interaction between sign language acquisition and the use of cochlear implants. Cochlear implants are assistive devices that can bring sound sensing abilities to people with either congenital or acquired deafness. There is some research suggesting that the bilingualism granted to cochlear implant recipients by a firm foundation in sign language can improve, or at least does no harm to, their later acquisition of speech (Quadros et al. 2016).

Language ideology and deaf culture

Language ideologies like monolingualism constrain and shape what a deaf person is allowed to achieve. These ideologies shape everything from the intimate moment of how a hearing parent feels about having a deaf baby to the very public architectural decisions made by and for the hearing (from the placement of walls to the arrangement of chairs in a classroom to the presence of a vibrating air conditioner) that can be inconvenient or even painful to the deaf who must also inhabit these spaces. The deaf represent a minority group, and ASL and other sign languages are minority languages in minority/majority relationships with their ambient spoken languages.

It is difficult to reconcile the low success rates of oralist teaching with the apparently sincere belief among so many of its proponents, like Bell, that their work was in the best interest of the deaf people whose lives they so profoundly diminished. Markowicz (1972), writing at a time when oralism was still the dominant, standard form of deaf education in the United States, reports the results of a study finding that, at 88 oralist schools surveyed, only 5% of deaf children 16 or older had achieved the 10th grade – which their hearing peers typically reach when aged 15 or 16. In a separate study, only 12% of deaf children in these schools had achieved competence in reading English. Still, these oralist methods persisted into the 1980s, and the resolutions of the 1880 Milan conference were not formally rescinded until 2010 when the 21st International Congress on the Education of the Deaf released a formal declaration acknowledging the damage caused by the 1880 ban on sign language in deaf education.

How is it possible for well-meaning (hearing) teachers and academics to cling for so long to such a destructive approach to deaf education? The answer lies in some of the advice William Stokoe reports being given when he first arrived at Gallaudet. Even within the comparative safety of that bastion of sign language and deaf culture, many of Stokoe's colleagues conceived of the deaf as essentially and fundamentally incapable. They, like Bell, the Milan conference, and literally generations of oralist advocates and teachers, unquestioningly and uncritically accepted language ideologies that disabled their own ability to recognize the deaf as full human beings; these ideologies constrained the hearing's willingness to see the deaf as fully human and thereby diminished their own humanity.

If one begins with the presumption that deafness is primarily a medical disability and inability – no matter how noble one's motives might be – then the failure of an oralist mode of education will seem to be a failure of the "disabled" students rather than resulting from the modality of instruction. As with any unquestioned belief, it is exceedingly difficult to see through one's own ideologies and the prevailing ideologies of one's community and to consider the possibility that it is the mode of instruction that is to blame. Successfully seeing through these ideologies requires radical thinking and empathy, but it is not necessary to wait for exceptional individuals like Gallaudet and Stokoe to act as Prometheus and bring this insight to the world. This kind of self-critical thought is well within the ability of anyone willing to invest the effort and ask difficult questions.

One can begin to unpack the way these ideologies shape the deaf experience by analyzing *audism*. At its core, audism is the belief that one who can hear the typical range of frequencies at the typical volume is superior to someone who cannot. This ideology makes it feel natural or "common sense" to view sign languages as inferior to spoken languages (or, worse, to view them as not being languages at all) and to view anyone who cannot live as the hearing do (particularly anyone for whom sign language is the most natural means of communication) as inferior. The ideology of audism constructs the deaf and other sign language users as disabled, leaving the hearing person infected with this negative stereotype susceptible to truly appalling ideas like eugenics or comparing deaf students to dogs, as Stokoe's colleague did. Audism is merely an ideology and not a fact about the universe; in the natural experiments in history where this ideology has not been dominant, the deaf have prospered.

The situation Groce describes on Martha's Vineyard in the 18th and 19th centuries is one such natural experiment. As we have seen in the words of the Vineyarders themselves, the deaf were fully capable members of the community: they were fishers, shopkeepers, parents, and worshippers alongside their hearing neighbors. Every role that was available to hearing residents of the island was available to deaf residents. They were just normal people unhindered by discriminatory language ideology and its unquestioned dismissal of the deaf as fully human.

A strikingly different social situation has occurred within Gallaudet University since the 1960s. In 1988, Gallaudet was in the process of hiring its seventh president. There were three final candidates for the position, two deaf and one hearing. Students rallied to have one of the (fully qualified) deaf candidates selected – even holding a candlelight vigil the night before the selection was to be made. Students were unhappy when the board selected the only hearing candidate but were enraged when the chair of Gallaudet University's governing board, Jane Bassett Spilman, was reported to have said, "the deaf are not yet ready to function in the hearing world." Rallies quickly turned to protests (see Figure 8.8) as the Deaf President Now (DPN) movement marched thousands of students to the White House and Capitol building and then, on March 8, 1988, used bike locks to close administration buildings and barricaded the campus with their cars. Their unrest forced Spilman to resign, and the new board immediately replaced the seventh president with I. King Jordan, Gallaudet's eighth president and, after 122 years of operation, its first deaf president. Jordan served until 2006.

Figure 8.8 Deaf President Now students protest the selection of another hearing president at Gallaudet University

The selection of I. King Jordan through pressure from the DPN movement marks an unusual inflection point in the acceptability of a language ideology. It also demonstrates that audism, as an ideology, and oralism, as a teaching methodology, are separable. The vast majority of oralists have consciously or unconsciously accepted the superiority of hearing. The necessity of DPN demonstrates that even among those who espouse a manualist philosophy and advocate for the incorporation of sign language as a mode of instruction have also, again, consciously or unconsciously, accepted an audist ideology. After the success of the DPN movement and during the subsequent presidency of I. King Jordan, audism has come to be recognized as an unacceptable and discriminatory belief at Gallaudet. The ideologies surrounding the capabilities of deaf people have shifted so much that now Fred Weiner, a graduate of Gallaudet who was active in the DPN movement and is now an administrator at the university, describes a change in the culture whereby "being a deaf person at Gallaudet [is] considered a typical experience" and the university is "operating as a typical university who happens to have deaf people attending" (Goldgeier & Mcleskey 2018).

The final ideology we will consider here is one we have really been pursuing all along: the view of deafness as purely a medical deficit, or the *medical model* of deafness. At the beginning of the chapter, we indicated that most people communicate with the world through sound. Hearing people outnumber deaf people by a large percentage and not all deaf people sign. And it really is the case that many forms of deafness, either from birth or gained later in life, *are* the result of medical conditions. The development and distribution of a safe and effective vaccine to fight rubella, for example, is correlated with a measurable decrease in the number of deaf children entering American schools. This relationship leads many to view deafness itself as a medical condition that can only have negative impacts on the sufferers' lives. But what we have shown through the cases of Martha's Vineyard, ASL, Gallaudet University, and other examples is that the medical deficit ideology really is just an ideology. It is countered by the *cultural model* of deafness which views it as fundamentally positive. Under this model, deaf people are a linguistic and cultural minority organized around a visual and manual mode of communication with their own accents, art, poetry, dance, architecture, and more. To the extent that deafness is a struggle in a hearing-dominated society, that struggle is created by the medical deficit ideology and not by the deafness itself. While the origins of deafness might, indeed, be medical, the resulting deaf baby, child, or adult is simply a human being with dreams, ambitions, rights, and language attitudes.

The beauty of community

Actor, model, and dancer Nyle DiMarco's first language is ASL. He grew up in Frederick, MD, where he attended the ASL/English bilingual Maryland School for the Deaf. He attended Gallaudet University in nearby Washington, D.C., where he earned a bachelor's degree in mathematics. DiMarco rose to fame soon after graduation by being named the 2015 winner of the reality television show *America's Next Top Model*. He was also the winner, with dancing partner Peta Murgatroyd, of the ABC television show *Dancing with the Stars* in 2016. DiMarco is a deaf activist and has a moving way of describing deaf life: "We have our own culture, our own community. A lot of people don't realize that. They just assume that deaf people are very unfortunate, very disabled, but no. I think the biggest misconception is that people think deaf people are not able to do things."

Ideologies within the deaf community

Just as there are many ways to be deaf, there are many ways to live as a deaf person. Within the American deaf community itself, ASL is a marker of social identity (Hill 2015). The term *deaf* is one end of a spectrum. One can also be *hard of hearing* which describes someone with some hearing ability who may also use ASL and other sign languages. Someone who is *oral deaf* has no or little hearing but does not embrace deaf culture and prefers oral communication to sign languages. People who are *late-deafened* may have little or no hearing ability due to some injury or illness and may prefer signed or oral communication. Finally, one can also be *hearing*, although this term does not necessarily imply that one rejects deaf culture or preclude one from being an ally of the deaf community; these meanings are often intertwined.

Within the deaf community, assistive devices are highly controversial and can serve to further demarcate one's social identity. Some deaf people consider assistive devices anathema to deaf culture while others happily use and support the use of hearing aids and cochlear implants. The situation is contentious and highly personal. Hearing aids are essentially just personal amplifiers, worn discretely near the ear, with microphones that pick up the most important frequencies for speech and relay them, via a small earbud, into the ear. A cochlear implant, by contrast, is a medical implant that is inserted into the cochlea (the coiled tube lined with fine, delicate hair cells) to turn microphone signals into direct electrical stimulation of the auditory nerve cells (Copeland & Pillsbury 2004).

Cochlear implant hearing is not at all like natural human hearing, and not all who receive a cochlear implant will then acquire spoken language. As a further complication, the likelihood that a cochlear implant user *will* acquire spoken language decreases as the child grows older. The highest success rates are seen when deaf babies receive cochlear implants when they are very small to maximize their exposure to the normal period of first language acquisition. One common trope on the internet is the video of a deaf baby hearing their mother's voice for the first time. These beautiful moments sometimes go viral but there are no viral videos of the long and sometimes unsuccessful process of learning to translate those first aural sensations to speech perception. But for those for whom the technology works, the effect can seem very like the magic potion described earlier in the chapter. Babies who are born deaf to hearing parents (90% of deaf babies) could grow up to have hearing-like communication abilities. Here, as might be imagined, the language ideologies of monolingualism, audism, and medical deficit have profound impacts, and the discussions often become heated.

Ultimately the decisions one makes about deafness – for oneself or on behalf of a child – are highly personal. What an understanding of language variation and language ideology can teach people, definitively, is that the decision is not between a life filled with language and culture and a life of silence with neither. American Sign Language, like all sign languages, is a fully expressive, fully communicative human language. It is part of a robust culture of deaf, hard of hearing, and hearing signers who have access to art, culture, education, and careers built around the use of ASL. Fears of communicative deficit through deafness are arbitrary social constructs. These arbitrary social constructs have very real consequences for the lives of deaf and hard of hearing people, but these consequences come from the limitations imagined upon the deaf by the hearing rather than the deafness itself.

Discussion questions

1. How are sign language and spoken languages similar? How are they different? How do these two modes compare to writing? Think about these three modes of communication and write a list of similarities and differences.
2. American Sign Language, which shares some of its history with French Sign Language, looks very different than British Sign Language (BSL). See the BSL fingerspelling chart in Figure 8.6 in the chapter and describe how the letters in BSL differ from those in ASL (found in Figure 8.4 in the chapter).
3. Why do you think it was important to the students at Gallaudet University to have a deaf president? What did it represent for them? How did it transform the community?

9 Putting language on the map

How we see the language around us

Every day, in social media posts or the comments section on the website for a local news channel, one can find very specific ideas about how regular people (that is, non-linguists) think language *should* be. We often call such language mavens *prescriptivists* because they prescribe the kind of language that they think is best. Sometimes this means "correcting" what kinds of English they see and hear in use. And these language commenters rarely hold back; the following is an example of prescriptive zeal, as produced in blogger Gin Kelsey's (2011) "Open letter to *Kuntry Kitchen*":

> You, good sir, by misspelling the word country, are inferring that people who live in the country can only spell phonetically and thus would not be able to understand the word if it were spelled correctly. As someone who was raised in the country, this offends me. I am offended on behalf of my family in the country, who don't need to spell anything phonetically before they grace your establishment with their presence.

Yet the very subject of this book – how people think about and experience language, how and why they try to control it, to what ends, and with what social repercussions – has only recently received attention by linguists. Traditionally, linguists draw a strict line in the sand. They stand on one side with what they hope is their own objective, analytic approach to the study of language; on the other side they see prescriptivists who have a shallow understanding of human language and whose primary purpose is to exert an authority that they have not earned.

More recently, however, linguists have been putting aside this strict division between what linguists think and what non-linguists think in recognition of the fact that how people think about language – no matter how ill-founded their beliefs might be – is in fact important for understanding language as a social construct. Dennis Preston and many others have produced a large body of work in the field of *perceptual dialectology* that focuses on the way attitudes toward language are relevant to the study of variation and change. Preston sees the juxtaposition as a matter of focus: is the study oriented toward the participants (speakers), or is the approach analyst-centric? Research in perceptual dialectology provides us with information about how individuals make sense of the linguistic variation that surrounds them and how the indexical meanings associated with linguistic variables help construct "mental maps," or cognitive representations of the physical world (see Preston 1989a, 1989b, 1993, 1996, 1999).

However, neither traditional dialectology, with its focus on production, nor perceptual dialectology, with its focus on perception, can fully capture the lived experience of language

DOI: 10.4324/9781003332886-9

in people's everyday lives. Language mavens do not stop at what kinds of English they deem appropriate; they often also insist that, at least in the American context, English is the *only* acceptable language, no matter its form. Such an approach is entangled with the monolingual myth discussed in Chapter 7. Here, though, we turn to how that myth is realized in the world by exploring how language truly lives in various communities by examining the real-world *linguistic landscapes* in which people live: "The language of public road signs, advertising billboards, street names, place names, commercial shop signs, and public signs on government buildings combines to form the linguistic landscape of a given territory, region, or urban agglomeration" (Landry & Bourhis 1997: 25).

The linguistic variation people *see* around them influences their understanding of the society where they work, play, eat, and so on. The language varieties visible in the physical space around us conditions the way people see that space. And, of course, just like individual perception and production of language, the linguistic landscape people see around them is shaped by language ideologies. Thus, the true multilingual nature of the American linguistic landscape is explored here to further exhibit the true power of the beliefs about language held by non-linguists.

This chapter considers the ways in which language ideologies shape the way people see and understand geography. To explore the ideas of perceptual dialectology and linguistic landscapes, we will consider the case of the American South. Although we focus on white Southerners, we recognize that the lived experiences of language variation could be different for people of various races, ethnicities, etc. And while the *perception* of a lack of linguistic diversity is one focus in this chapter, it is important to explore, for example, the relationship between the speech of rural white Southerners and that of their African American neighbors (Wolfram 2002), what the use of Native American languages means in communities in the South and how they become entangled with English (e.g., Wolfram et al. 2014; Scancarelli & Hardy 2005), and what role is played by Louisiana French, Texas German, Spanish, and Gullah, among other types of variation present in broad interpretations of the South. Indeed, linguists in and of the South have been specifically called (Charity Hudley et al. 2018) to make explicit their own responsibility in diversifying the linguistic canon to include more Black, Latinx, Native American, and Asian voices in both the researcher and the researched voices.

As Cramer and Preston (2018: 337) note, "Southernness is something everyone knows something, everything, and nothing about." The media, politicians, teachers, internet trolls, and entertainers all portray very specific understandings of the South, based somewhat in fact but largely in fiction. As such, the power of linguistic ideologies and language subordination is ever-present in many people's understandings of what it means to be "Southern" in the United States.

Which states are Southern?

The dividing line of the American South is highly contested. Countless blogs, news articles, books, and other media have taken up the debate. Often ideas about what is "Southern" depend on where one is from. Does Kentucky count? What about Florida? Is it about where you can find Waffle House restaurants or which states belonged to the Confederacy? Which states do you think are Southern?

Perceptual dialectology

Drawing a map of any kind is not a neutral exercise. Crampton (2011: 12) calls mapping "a human activity that seeks to make sense of the geographic world, it is a way in which we 'find our way in the world.'" Every mapmaker brings a set of goals, presumptions, and generalizations to the task. Maps produce knowledge in specific ways, with specific categories, which in turn have specific effects. As maps become more and more embedded in people's day-to-day lives, in the form of GPS-enabled phones, for example, it becomes critically important examine and challenge the rationale behind the map.

Lying with maps

It is important to recognize that mapmakers must make decisions in presenting data on maps. One might even say that the point of maps is to tell a story, and you might want the story to say something different than the raw data says. Monmonier (1991: 1) said, "Not only is it easy to lie with maps, it's essential. To portray meaningful relationships . . . a map must distort reality." Thus, you could see maps like the following (adapted from Monmonier 1991: 41), which present the same raw data in two different ways:

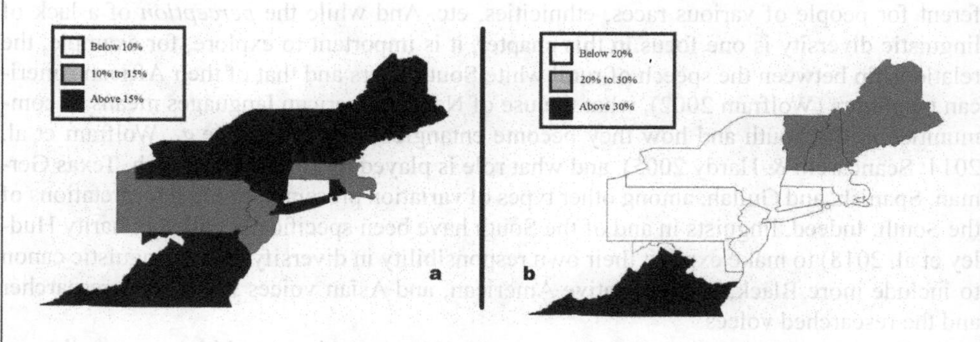

Figure 9.1 Two maps: occupied housing units in the Northeast lacking a telephone in 1960

How do these differ? Why would you want to show one over the other? What is the difference in the story?

Dialectologists and sociolinguists who draw dialect maps, with the goal of defining dialect boundaries in some territory, begin with several assumptions: that variation exists in that territory, that this variation can be grouped together into dialects, and that those dialects have geographic boundaries. The maps they draw represent generalizations of the data they have sampled and do not actually reflect the full range of variation found in each region. For example, many of the maps of regional variation in the United States (like those in Chapter 5) only represent the voices present in the data; early dialect maps, with their focus on white NORMs (native, old, rural, men), would have represented some generalization that suggested everyone in that region sound like those participants, thus silencing the voices of women, young people, city folks, recent immigrants, and people of any number of races and ethnicities.

But mapmakers are not the only ones with ideas about what constitutes a territory. Most people have a sense of the physical world around them and how they believe it is divided into different regions inhabited by different types of people. An individual's understanding of the boundaries that exist around them is a central interest of geographers who study mental maps. Work in cultural geography, like that of Gould and White (1992), uses respondent-generated maps of a given territory (see Figure 9.2) to gain insight into how everyday people see their worlds. Rather than showing physical or geographic boundaries, mental maps reveal the role that the perception of geography plays in actual human experience. The choices people make when drawing a map provides insights into what aspects of their surroundings they pay attention to and how they understand social differences across space.

Following in this tradition, Dennis Preston started asking non-linguists to map their dialect landscapes. Preston and the linguists who have followed in his footsteps have compiled a body of empirical studies that quantify and summarize non-linguists' beliefs about the geographic and social distribution of both standard and non-standard varieties of language. In asking non-linguists to draw a map showing where they believe people talk in a certain way, perceptual dialectologists have ascertained a wealth of information about the beliefs people hold about language, dialects, and linguistic variation. These maps (like the one in Figure 9.3) provide glimpses into how people label different linguistic varieties, where they

Figure 9.2 Mental map of the campus of the University of Michigan

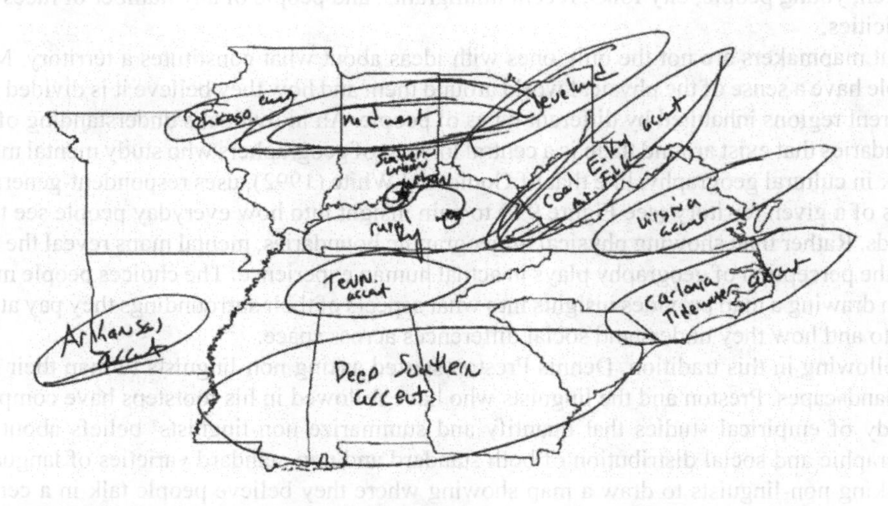

Figure 9.3 Dialect mental map drawn by a resident of Louisville, Kentucky

Source: Cramer (2016)

believe such varieties to exist, and how those varieties relate to the geographic spaces that the respondents themselves occupy. Figure 9.3 is a map drawn by a woman from Louisville, Kentucky. She divides her state into at least three dialects: the coal and mountain-associated variety in eastern Kentucky, the urban varieties of Louisville and Lexington, and the generic "rural" variety that dominates the rest of the state. There is also a "Deep Southern accent" represented on this map, which, after one's home region, is the most common dialect region to appear on mental maps drawn by Americans in perceptual dialectology research projects. As we will see, most Americans have a lot to say about Southern dialects.

It is true, though, that most work in perceptual dialectology examining variation in the United States has focused on the perceptions of white Americans (or the ethnicity of respondents has not played a role in the analyses presented). Recent work by Alfaraz and Mason (2019) is specifically focused on perceptions of the American South by non-Southern Latinx respondents and how their perceptions compare to their European American counterparts. Interestingly, Latinxs only draw and label an American South region on their mental maps 59% of the time (compared to 99% for white respondents), but when they do mark the South, they are more likely to use stereotypes of Southerners, like "racist" and "hillbilly," in their labels than European American participants. This important work highlights the impact of culture and experience in the awareness of different groups with respect to regional variation. For these Latinx participants from the North, "The social and spatial marginalization of ethnic groups means that they do not always have access to the ideologies of the majority group" (Alfaraz & Mason 2019: 376). And when looking within the South, a land with a long and robust history of ethnic diversity, it is important to "ask how traditional and emerging ethnolinguistic situations are now being altered and reconfigured" (Wolfram 2018: 345).

In addition to mapping tasks, perceptual dialectologists often ask people to rank the varieties that exist in an area. In a study focusing on where people "speak correct English,"

Preston (1996) asked 76 young white people from southern Indiana to rank all 50 states as well as New York City and Washington, D.C. The best English was 1, and the worst was 52. Figure 9.4 provides Preston's visual representation of the means for the respondents' rankings. Clearly these respondents do not value the speech of people in the southeastern United States, with a small exception for Florida.

If a high level of education is one of the primary characteristics of the hypothetical "standard" English in the United States (as explored in Chapter 3), then the opinions of these college students from Indiana would seem to provide relevant information about just where that language is spoken. Preston's analysis indicates that these informants found the most correct English in five areas: North Central (including their own speech); Mid-Atlantic (excluding New York City); New England; Colorado; and the West Coast. Standard deviations indicated that the students are most consistent in their positive evaluation in the cases of Michigan, Minnesota, and Wisconsin, with their agreement decreasing as they move eastward through Ohio, Pennsylvania, Maryland, Delaware, and finally Washington, D.C. (which showed little consistency in ranking with a standard deviation of 15.67). The largest standard deviation in the study, which presents a case where there is the least agreement among participants about the appropriate ranking, is for New York City. Preston hypothesizes this has to do with conflicting stereotypes about the city: from the center of culture to the center of crime.

Most interesting, perhaps, is the incredibly high level of consistency in the way his subjects indicated the absence of "correct" English in the South. Mississippi ranked last in terms of correct English and was also the most consistently ranked state. Preston takes the scores for the Southern states as "further proof of the salience of areas seen as nonstandard" (1989b: 56). This salience goes beyond language. Thus, in language and elsewhere, the stereotypes of the American South as painted by non-Southerners are beyond bleak; the South often serves as the scapegoat for all that is perceived as "bad" in the United States.

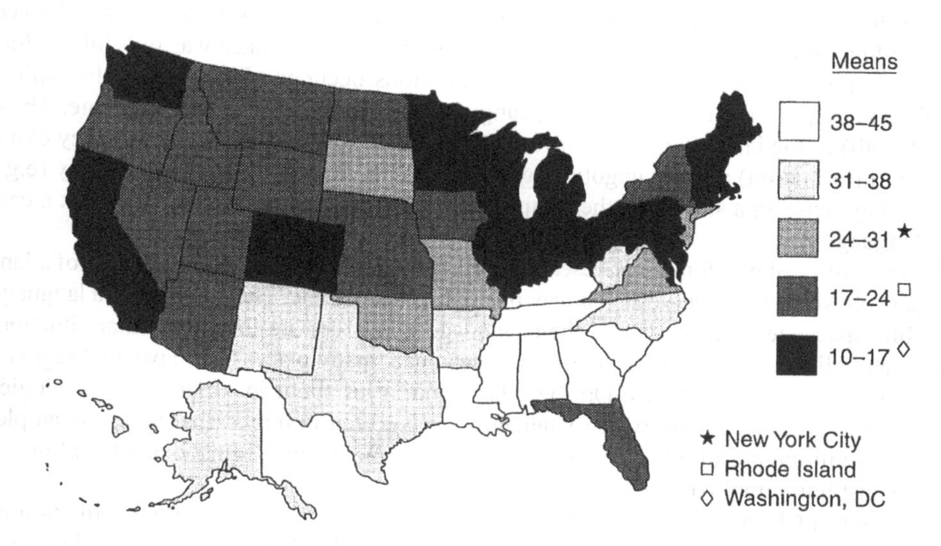

Figure 9.4 Scores for "correctness" of English spoken in different areas
Source: Preston (1996)

Linguistic landscapes

The perceptions of dialects in the United States are tied up with larger language ideologies about what counts as "appropriate" speech. One primary ideology about language held by many Americans is that English is *the* language of the United States. While this notion may be the lived experience for many Americans, it is not, for the most part, the case (see Chapter 7). It is common to see videos posted to social media showing individuals berating and harassing people who happen to be speaking in languages other than English. People recorded while yelling at restaurant workers for speaking Spanish are typically subjected to public shaming, but the (racist) idea that anyone in the United States *must* speak always English is pervasive enough that such incidents persist on a regular basis.

If English is not the official language of this country (and it isn't), where would anyone get the idea that English is the only appropriate or acceptable language one should use in the United States? One idea is that because of its *de facto* status as the "official" language, English is the primary language that exists in the linguistic landscape of most Americans. That is, when people see signs, hear radio commercials, or click through local government websites for information, those people typically hear and see English.

The field of linguistic landscapes (hereafter, LL) takes as its primary focus the "visibility and salience of languages on public and commercial signs in a given territory or region" (Landry & Bourhis 1997: 23). Centering on the presence of certain languages and the lack of others in the everyday worlds of multilingual contexts, researchers initially studied LL to understand the vitality of different languages in various communities (Giles et al. 1977). The study of LL has since grown into a methodology aimed at capturing the ways in which language can be seen as "marking the boundaries of linguistic territories through the regulation of language use on public signs including billboards, street signs, and commercial signs" (Landry & Bourhis 1997: 24).

Essentially, to explore these questions of visibility, researchers in LL simply capture (via pictures) which languages appear in each physical space and in what ways they appear. In some of the foundational work in the field, Landry and Bourhis (1997) showed that the functions of multilingual representation in the physical space was two-fold: informational and symbolic. Informational representations occur in places where the typical inhabitants require the use the multiple languages that are found in local signage. Thus, both (or all) of the languages are required for navigating the world (e.g., emergency exits, medical information) and for negotiating goods and services within the community (e.g., how to buy items in a store, whether employees in a store can be expected to speak a certain language).

In terms of symbolic functions, research in LL has shown that the mere presence of a language in physical spaces serves to convey prestige to that variety. The presence of a language in public spaces tells speakers that their language is appropriate for a particular situation. Because public use of a language conveys acceptance, many places have laws that regulate language use in public spheres. On the other hand, a lot about local language ideologies can be understood by seeing which languages are *not* seen in public spaces. For example, efforts to limit the use of other languages in public demonstrate linguistic and racial prejudice against immigrant communities.

As noted in Chapter 7, the ideology of monolingualism contributes to the formation of ethnic enclaves, where immigrants who speak languages other than English live and congregate. Some people tend to take the presence of English for granted even though it is everywhere in the United States. In ethnic neighborhoods, like the ones referred to as "Chinatown" or "Koreatown," the presence of languages other than English serves to mark boundaries between neighborhoods. Public signs in other languages marks an area as being ethnically distinctive and outside the limits of the dominant language ideology. The fact that other languages are restricted to specific neighborhoods serves to reproduce the idea that speaking anything but English is abnormal or unexpected.

Multilingual signs

The languages found on public signage typically reflect the geography of ethnic communities. In some Houston, TX, neighborhoods, for example, one would find similar clusters of signs in Spanish, Vietnamese, and other languages. However, such signs are typically English combined with a single other language.

Having more than two languages appear on the same sign is common in areas where speakers of numerous languages interact, such as in city centers. Figure 9.5, for example, shows a multilingual trash can from Seattle.

Figure 9.5 Trash can in Seattle, Washington, labeled in English, Chinese, Vietnamese, and Spanish [Note: The accent on the Vietnamese is backward.]

The distinction between informational and symbolic functions of public language is important in determining the appropriate language policies for a community. For example, Cenoz and Gorter (2006) focused on the use of two minority languages in two different contexts: Basque in Spain and Frisian in the Netherlands. Both Basque and Frisian have official legal status in their respective countries. In their research, Cenoz and Gorter showed that the non-majority status of these languages is evident in the fact that all signs containing Basque or Frisian were bilingual, including the majority language (Castilian Spanish or Dutch, respectively) alongside the minority language. In contrast, monolingual signs in Spanish and Dutch were common. Thus, for Basque and Frisian, the informational function was lacking, so that the minority languages seem to only serve a symbolic function. Shulist (2018) explored the ways in which official language policy impacted the LL in São Gabriel, Brazil. Shulist discovered that public use of minority and Indigenous languages remained limited, despite sharing "co-official" legal status with Portuguese. These types of studies allow for a more nuanced understanding of how language policies relate to lived experience. Are minority languages only given symbolic nods in the laws? What changes might be successful in promoting various languages? The study of LL provides one way of grasping how language circulates on the ground in a community.

The United States, even with its essentially monolingual landscape, can tell us a bit about the functions other languages have in an LL. Despite the *de facto* dominance of English, many spaces in this country are multilingual. Hult (2014: 507–508) used San Antonio, Texas, as an example to showcase the "centrality of visual environments in the discursive construction of multilingual settings." Hult's research showed that despite a large population of Spanish speakers (44% of the city's population, according to the study), English still stands as the dominant language in most public domains, with Spanish serving primarily in the domains of migration and family/community. The proportion of English monolingual signs along the highway system in the city is much greater than the proportion of Spanish-only and bilingual signs combined (92.8% compared to 7.2%), which indicates, especially to Spanish speakers, that their community places little value on their language. Indeed, throughout the United States, public Spanish-English bilingual signage often involves forms of "Mock Spanish" (discussed in Chapter 7) so that the text is entirely accessible to monolingual speakers of English but is less likely to be fully understood by monolingual speakers of Spanish (such as "Half price special on *cervezas*").

What does the distribution of languages in public space tell us about how Americans perceive and understand the multilingualism that surrounds them? According to the American Community Survey (US Census Bureau 2016) using data from 2009 to 2013, more than 60 million people in the United State speak a language other than English at home. Yet these languages remain largely invisible in (white) public spaces. When they do surface, they may still reproduce the stereotypes associated with speakers of other languages. This can occur through limiting the use of the minority language to contexts that index negative stereotypes (such as warnings about loitering or drug use). Signs in languages other than English may also simply reproduce stereotypes directly. For example, in 2020, the Ventura County, Cali fornia health departments released posters about social distancing during the COVID-19 pandemic. The English language sign described the distance of 6 feet as the length of a ski, while the Spanish language sign described 6 feet as the length of three produce crates (used by farm workers in the area). So while English speakers typically go skiing, Spanish speakers work picking grapes and strawberries.

The use of languages other than English in public signs may mark a community as being "outside" of the English-dominant society. In the case of ethnic enclaves, languages reflect

Figure 9.6 Signs in English and Native American languages – a) Osage/English bilingual stop sign, Pawhuska, OK, 2018; b) Women's restroom in English and Chickasaw, Sulphur, OK, 2011; c) Cherokee-English street sign, Tahlequah, OK, 2010; d) Family restroom sign in Lushootseed and English at the wəɬəbʔaltxʷ/Intellectual House at the University of Washington, Seattle, 2018

Source: photos by Jenny L. Davis

the ways in which immigrant communities use language to index inclusivity, not only for those who don't speak English, but also for monolingual English speakers who know that they will be free from discrimination in a place that speaks their heritage language. The ability of languages to index inclusivity may also serve to challenge English dominance, particularly in Native American communities working to preserve and promote the use of their languages. For such communities, the use of Native American languages pushes back against language ideologies that have long worked to eliminate Native Americans and their languages. As movements to revitalize native languages gain momentum, public uses of Native Americans are increasing, as in the images portrayed in Figure 9.6.

The linguistic perception of the American South

In the remainder of this chapter, we consider the ways in which the methods of perceptual dialectology and linguistic landscapes can be used to examine the negotiation of language ideologies in the American South. Why the South? As an entity, it appears as misunderstood linguistically as the multilingual landscapes present across the United States, and, as Edward L. Ayers and his colleagues have argued,

> The South eagerly defines itself against the North, advertising itself as more earthy, more devoted to family values, more spiritual, and then is furious to have things turned around, to hear itself called hick, phony, and superstitious. The South feeds the sense of difference and then resists the consequences.
>
> (Ayers 1996: 63–64)

Of course, proudly seeing your local culture as distinctive should not open you up to prejudicial stereotypes, but the fact that Southerners see themselves as different from other Americans makes the South stand out as an easily definable cultural region to those outside of the South. Ayers' research confirms that non-Southerners have a consistent sense of a Southern "core," which is referred to as the Deep South or the *Southern Trough*.

> [This] cuts across Mississippi and Alabama, embracing parts of Arkansas, Louisiana, and Georgia at the edges. This trough appears to most Americans as the least desirable place in the United States to live. . . . The whole South appears to be a vast saucer of unpleasant associations.
>
> (Ayers 1996: 69)

Preston (1989a, 1989b, 1993, 1996) has found that, in linguistic terms, non-Southerners also tend to perceive rough distinctions between the dialect landscape of the Southern Trough and the rest of the South. In the minds of most Northerners, Tennessee and Kentucky are perceived as the "Outer South," Texas is its own kind of South, and Florida isn't really South at all. Despite these perceived differences, Northerners remain generally unaware of what distinguishes one Southern variety of English from another. Thus, Northerners often produce a "one-size-fits-all accent" when attempting to "sound Southern."

Ethnolinguistic diversity in the South

It is patently absurd to suggest that the "real" South is or ever was monolithically white. In addition to the obvious fact that Europeans "settled" a land that was already inhabited by numerous native groups, migration to the South, both from other countries and non-white races and ethnic groups from across the United States, has a rather long history. Wolfram (2018: 344) put it like this:

> From the multiple, prehistoric Native American Indian language families dispersed throughout the region to the contemporary emergence of disparate immigrant settlement communities, the South has experienced a robust history of ethnolinguistic diversity. At the same time, the region seems to have undergone unprecedented transformation during the last half century. . . . Demographically, it is the fastest-growing area in the United States, growing by 14.3% from 2000 to 2010, and is now the home to more than 114 million people.

Included in this growth are large numbers of Latinx, Chinese, Indian, Vietnamese, Lebanese, Saudi Arabians, and people from across Southern and Eastern Europe. Thus, any myth about the monolithically white South is rooted in neither historical nor modern fact.

The English one expects to hear depends on what one expects to experience in an interaction. Many non-Southerners have never spoken face to face with anyone with a Southern accent. Often, everything they know about the South comes from media and literary portrayals of the South. The South thus becomes a bizarre mix of representations from contradictory sources like *Duck Dynasty*, *To Kill a Mockingbird*, Maya Angelou, *The Dukes of Hazzard*, William Faulkner, *Sweet Home Alabama*, *The Real Housewives of Atlanta*, *Forrest Gump*, Tennessee Williams, *Queen Sugar*, Jeff Foxworthy, *Gone with the Wind*, Zora Neale Hurston, *Deliverance*, and *Madea Goes to Jail*. This means that, for many, a Southern accent symbolizes a very limited and peculiar set of potential identities, and the notion of the South as a large and complex place seems highly implausible.

The *Encyclopedia of Southern Culture* lists a range of stereotyped Southern identities, including sadistic overseers, chivalrous men, good old boys, cheerleaders, beauty pageant mothers, Pentecostals, poor white trash, and drunken backwoods predators (Wilson & Ferris 1989). In this artificial view of the South, English has an indiscriminate "twang" or a "drawl" (labels commonly used to describe the South in perceptual dialectology studies) and is peppered with funny and clever idioms like *knee high to a grasshopper* or *God willing and the creek don't rise*. This might be considered a North-South mental divide, a binary opposition that renders the actual details of linguistic variation unimportant. It is certainly true that, by and large, outsiders cannot distinguish an Appalachian accent from a Mississippi Delta accent or a Texas accent from one from Virginia. Of course, the reverse is also true: for the most part, Southerners are unable to tell one Northern accent from another.

Aside from acknowledging pockets of Spanish speakers in Florida and Texas, some Cherokee speakers in North Carolina, a few Choctaw speakers in Mississippi, and French Creole and Cajun French speakers in Louisiana, many non-Southerners view Southern speech as a single monolithic, monolingual drawl. Even (potential) Southerners themselves are prone to ignoring variation within the South, with some drawing large, indiscriminate regions like the one in Figure 9.7 (Cramer 2016: 48). And even when they want to acknowledge some kinds of variation, ethnic and racial variation is seen as an afterthought, with no real geographic representation, like in the map in Figure 9.8 (Cramer 2016: 49).

What is more, non-Southerners rarely have reason to examine or reconsider their preconceived stereotypes of the South. If they encounter a Southerner who does not fit their stereotype, they will likely assume that person to be an anomaly (e.g., Bounds et al. 2020). In contrast to outsider stereotypes of Southern accents as indexing a lack of education, intelligence, or sophistication, Southerners often see their own language varieties as a proud marker of authenticity and an index of positively valued traits like being friendly, easy-going, and polite.

Kountry Livin'

In the South, one finds a linguistic landscape that highlights the diversity of voices found there with English still winning out as the dominant language found in public space. Within

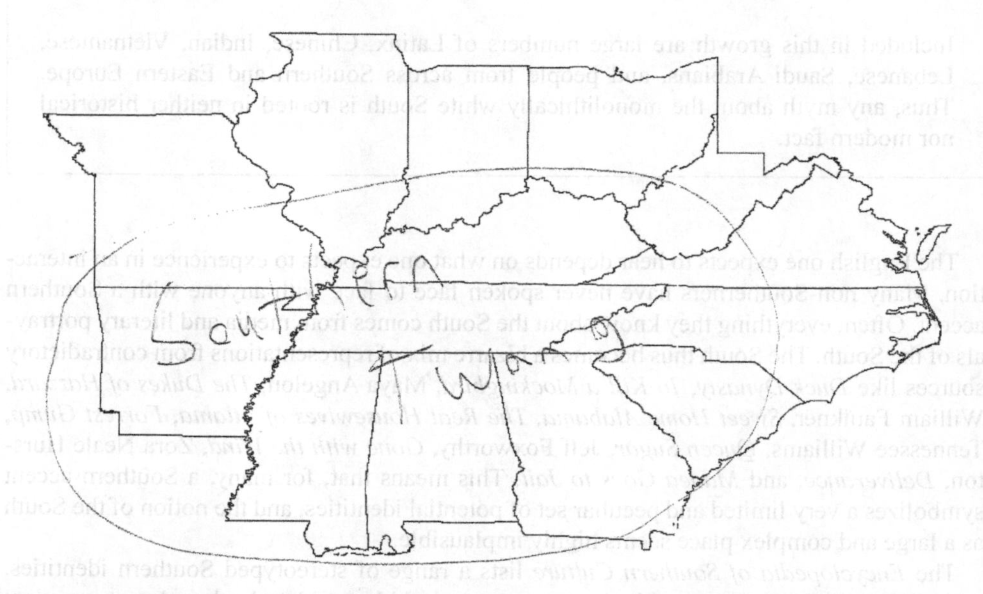

Figure 9.7 Dialect map from a resident of Louisville, Kentucky in which only one large "Southern Twang" region is included

Source: Cramer (2016)

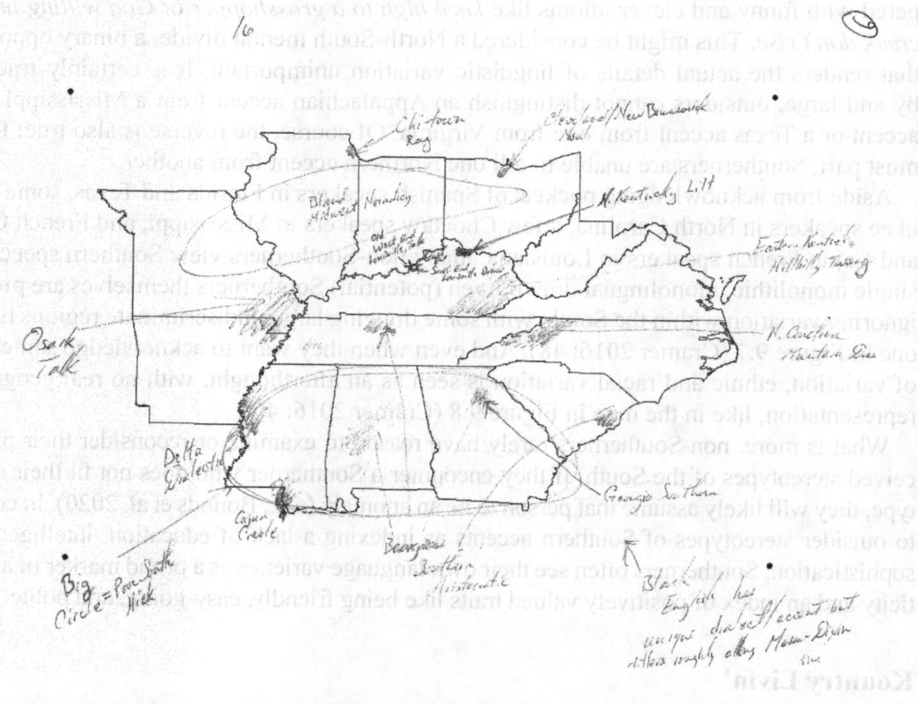

Figure 9.8 Dialect map from a resident of Louisville, Kentucky in which numerous dialect regions are included but "Black English" is written as an afterthought off the map in the bottom righthand corner

Source: Cramer (2016)

this linguistic landscape, written representations of Southern ways of speaking are also common. Figure 9.9, for example, advertises *maters*, which could be seen as confirming (or perhaps embracing) the stereotype of the semi-literate, backwater Southerner. However, the linguistic rules that govern this pronunciation (reduction of non-stressed initial syllables, like the *to* in *tomato*, and the inclusion of an 'r' sound in words that end with an "o" sound, like *fellow* as *feller* or *hollow* as *holler*) are regular and systematic, and the thought that such a pronunciation is equivalent to being uneducated is exactly the kind of negative linguistic ideology we have been talking about.

Also note that, in addition to selling *maters*, this restaurant is celebrating *Corn Daze*. Like using the word *maters*, the use of *daze* rather than *days* indexes the stereotype of the semi-literate Southerner. Unlike *maters*, however, *daze* does not reflect anything specific to Southern varieties of English. The consonant at the end of the word *days* is a [z] sound in almost all dialects of American English. If the Southern pronunciation of *daze* is not unique, what indexical meaning is this spelling meant to convey?

The example of *daze* is what linguists call "eye dialect," or the use of an alternate spelling to mark speech as different from (and inferior to) "standard" English. Forms of eye dialect (like *wuz* for *was* or *yer* for *your*) are common in stereotyped portrayals of Southern speech like that found in comic strips like *Lil'Abner*, *Kudzu*, or *Snuffy Smith*. Forms of eye dialect

Figure 9.9 Ramsey's Restaurant celebrating *Corn Daze and 'maters*

Source: photo by Whitney Scheibel of Lexington, Kentucky, creator of "Fabulous In Fayette," a local blog that highlights the fabulous city of Lexington, the great state of Kentucky, and Southern living

don't tell us anything about how individuals actually speak. Rather, it simply indexes a supposed lack of literacy skills. Why would anyone purposefully use language that potentially suggests that they are ignorant or semi-literate (if not downright stupid)?

Text box 5: Welcome to Florence, y'all!

In Florence, Kentucky, located just south of Cincinnati, Ohio, there is a large water tower that says "FLORENCE Y'ALL" (see Figure 9.10). When it was built in the 1970s, the water tower said, "FLORENCE MALL" as it was built near a plot of land that would soon be home to a new area shopping mall. After the paint job was complete, the Bureau of Highways said it was illegal because it was advertising something that didn't exist yet (the water tower was painted with these words about two years before construction on the mall was complete). The mayor of Florence devised the cheap fix: just remove the vertical lines on the "M", add a stem under the remaining lines to make a "Y", then add an apostrophe. Since then, the water tower has become a symbol of Florence and northern Kentucky, ostensibly to both acknowledge the Southernness of Kentucky and to distinguish itself from Cincinnati, of which Northern Kentucky towns are considered like suburbs.

Figure 9.10 The Florence Y'all Water Tower

Source: courtesy of the Florence Y'alls

That identification became more fully realized in 2020 when the local minor league baseball team, the Florence Freedom, was renamed as the Florence Y'alls. You can read about them at the link in the QR code. Their mascot is a water tower, their colors are red, white, and blue (signifying the colors of the water tower against a baby blue sky), and even the shape of word in the logo is intended to reference the shape of the state of Kentucky (see Figure 9.11). On their website, they say, "We're taking ownership of the word. It's not our team, it's y'alls team."

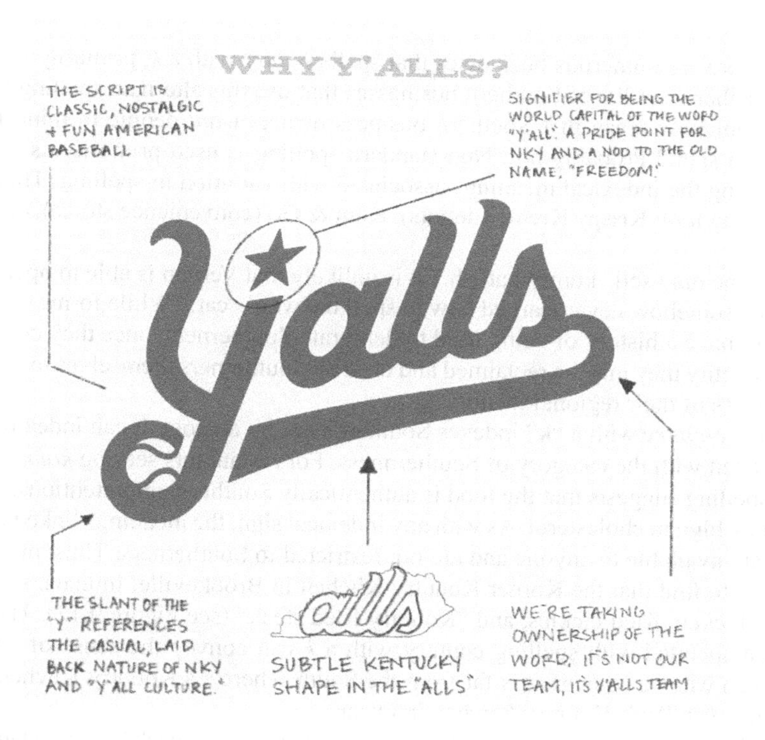

Figure 9.11 Description of the Florence Y'alls logo, courtesy of the Florence Y'alls

This is the question posed by the author of the "Open letter to Kuntry Kitchen" (quoted at the beginning of this chapter). In her letter, she tells the restaurant owner, "I saw your sign and was completely disgusted." She feels that the name of the restaurant reproduces the stereotype of rural Southerners as uneducated and illiterate and even suggests that the restaurant owner is making it more difficult for her children to learn to read. Not only does she think this spelling reflects ignorance and poor literacy skills, but she is also worried that this ignorance might be contagious.

Table 9.1 Southern businesses with *K(o)untry* in their names

Arlene's Kountry Kitchen	Corsicana, Texas
B & M Kuntry Kitchen	Richmond Hill, Georgia
Granny's Kuntry Kitchen	Clayton, Georgia
Klen's Kountry Kitchen and Katering	Tupelo, Mississippi
Kountry Kitchen and Seafood	Jeffersonville, Georgia
Kountry Kitchen Grille	Clarksville, Arkansas
Kountry Kitchen With Love	Vero Beach, Florida
Kuntry Kitchen Fried Chicken Joint	Pine Mountain, Georgia
Little Kuntry Kitchen	Moulton, Alabama
Mama's Kuntry Kafe	Inverness, Florida
The Original Kuntry Kitchen	Macon, Georgia
Vernon's Kuntry Katfish	Conroe, Texas

Indeed, there are numerous businesses that spell *country* with a *k*, primarily in the South. In Table 9.1 there is a list of Southern businesses that use this alternate spelling of *country*. Does this somehow mean that Southern business owners *want* people to think they don't know how to spell? Probably not. Non-standard spelling is used primarily as a marketing tool, exploiting the indexical meanings associated with variation in spelling. This is a common marketing tool: Krispy Kreme (donuts), Kum & Go (convenience stores), or Kids Kare (preschools).

Although he may sell "kuntry katfish," it is unlikely that Vernon is able to operate a small business but somehow never learned how to spell the word "cat." While forms of eye dialect like *kountry* have a history of being used to denigrate Southerners, once they come to index Southern identity they may be reclaimed and used by Southerners themselves to highlight the distinctiveness of their regional identity.

If spelling *country* with a "k" indexes Southernness, by analogy it can index other attributes associated with the category of Southernness. For restaurants serving *kountry* food, the alternate spelling suggests that the food is authentically Southern, unpretentious, traditional, and probably high in cholesterol. As with any indexical sign, the meanings linked to "country with a k" are available to anyone and are not restricted to Southerners. Thus, one would not be surprised to find that the Korner Kountry Kitchen in Brookeville, Indiana, serves barbecue, fried chicken, fried pickles, and "Kountry fried steak" (see Figure 9.12). The indexical meanings associated with spelling country with a *k* can convey the sense of "homestyle" cooking even when a restaurant is far from the South. There's a Kountry Kitchen in Kapaa, Hawaii, and even Ric's Kountry Kitchen in Qatar.

Despite the derogatory nature with which non-Southerners approach Southern language, it is clear that Southerners may take a different perspective. A sign that happens to index a negative stereotype for outsiders may serve as a badge of honor for Southerners themselves. The ways in which Southerners evaluate themselves and their speech is an important part of understanding the role of language as a marker of regional loyalties and the resistance to dialect leveling across space. Using these linguistic markers of identity in Southern linguistic landscapes serves to indicate these potential indexical meanings to those who encounter them.

What it means to sound Southern

In a survey of 798 adult residents of Georgia, individuals answered questions about what characteristics are associated with having a "Southern accent" and were subsequently asked

Figure 9.12 The Korner Kountry Kitchen in Brookville, Indiana

Source: photo by Anthony K. Webster

to evaluate their own language (the results are presented as "heavy" Southern or "no" accent as seen in Figure 9.13).

In any such direct inquiry, some people will underreport their own usage (claim to have no accent when in fact they do) and others will claim an accent when they are not local to an area and have not successfully acquired a new phonology. Thus, this type of poll is not able to tell us who actually has a Southern accent or how "heavy" peoples' accents might be, but it can tell us that people attach bundles of social attributes to varying degrees of sounding "Southern."

For that reason, such polls are useful in ways perhaps not anticipated by the persons who constructed them. In the selection of questions to be asked, the pollsters reveal much of the preconceived notions about connections between certain ways of life and language markers embodied in accent. But do these questions comprise a set of sociocultural distinctions truly relevant to the construction of definitions of "North" and "South"? Between "real" and "make-believe" Southern?

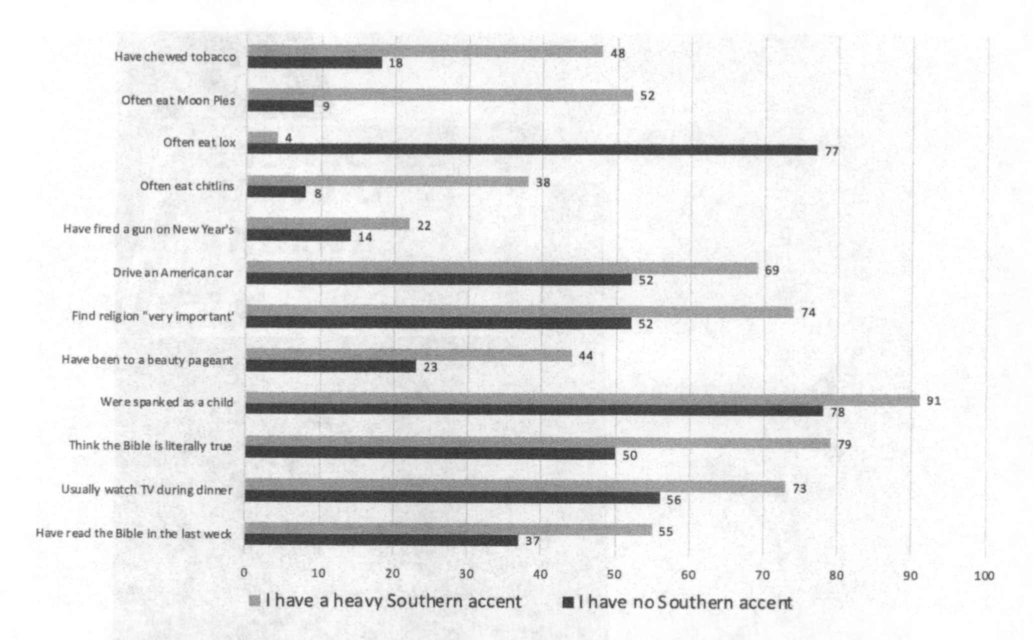

Figure 9.13 Southerners who claim different stereotyped traits of being Southern divided by whether they evaluate their own speech as accented

Source: adapted from Applied Research Center, Georgia State University, 1995

Questionnaires of this type inevitably reproduce stereotypes about the South. The researcher is looking for Southern/Non-Southern distinctions based on religious and cultural practices and beliefs. In choosing the questions themselves, the researcher likely imagined that "real" Southerners – those who will admit to having "strong" accents – are the ones who eat chitlins and Moon Pies and drive American cars to church on Sunday mornings. Of course, this presupposes that other, "less Southern" types are at home on Sunday eating "bagels and lox." Thus, the survey itself reproduces highly prejudicial views of the South. Not only does it erase the diverse experiences of Jewish Southerners, but it also portrays "authentic" Southerners as working-class evangelical Christians, thus also erasing the presence of other types of Christians and those from various class backgrounds. For many, it would be hard to imagine constructing a similar survey for Northerners. For such a survey to be conducted in Ohio, for example, what would serve as the equivalent of Moon Pies or beauty pageants?

Just as Southerners may embrace the negative stereotypes held by many non-Southerners, many Southerners are proud of their accents despite being well aware that their way of speaking may cause outsiders to view them negatively. Such situations where a local variety is viewed negatively by outsiders but has positive associations for locals are often described as involving *covert prestige*. Obviously, for speakers who take great pride in their unique way of speaking, the prestige of their native variety is not really covert at all. It is perhaps more accurate to describe such situations as involving competing language ideologies. While outsiders view undervalued Englishes as "wrong", for speakers of such varieties, their local dialect may be something that they treasure for its ability to index positive contexts of family, home, loved ones, and so on. In his work with Navajo poets, for example, Anthony

K. Webster (2015) finds similar positive evaluations of Navajo English despite the variety being negatively viewed by most outsiders. Communities often have deep emotions associated with particular local ways of speaking. Language that reminds us of home or indexes contexts that are culturally unique tends to trigger emotional responses. Webster calls these complex links between linguistic forms and emotional states *intimate grammars* because they reflect the emotional intimacy that forms of language variation can trigger. Speakers of non-standard varieties typically take great joy in their unique ways of speaking, regardless of whether the way of speaking indexes being Navajo, Muslim, Chicanx, or African American.

Perceptions meet strategies of condescension

In August 2018, President Trump said that he was dissatisfied with Attorney General Jeff Sessions because he didn't have an "Ivy League pedigree" and talked "like he has marbles in his mouth" (Beahm 2018). Sessions, a former senator from Alabama known for his distinctive drawl, would later be fired. Of course, his education and accent were widely known before Sessions was ever appointed, but in highlighting these two (supposedly negative) traits, the President was clearly suggesting that Sessions was unqualified because he is Southern. It also reproduces familiar language ideologies in which Southern accents index a lack of education (or pedigree) and an inability to make oneself understood to outsiders (like having marbles in one's mouth).

This idea that accent reflects intelligence linked to education, as promoted by the standard language ideology (see Chapter 3), serves as the basis for ideologies that view Southern language as deficient. People with "unacceptable" Southern accents are encouraged to get rid of them by enrolling in accent reduction or speech classes. Within this language ideology, people who use language variation to display their allegiance to a Southern home are expected to understand that, at least to their Northern neighbors, their accents mark them as inferior, both intellectually and culturally. The fact that the stereotypes that underlie this type of reasoning are imaginary formations is irrelevant; their power is still real, and they are effective. And the subordination process is most successful when the targets of these efforts become actively complicit and accept the belief that their own language is somehow deficient. Even when Southerners are not ashamed of their accents, they are usually aware of the risks their accent may pose in interactions with non-Southerners.

Consider, for example, the following quote from a foreign language professor native to the South:

> I got an interview with an extremely elite undergraduate college in the Northeast. They conducted the first substantial part of the interview in [another language] and it went well. When they switched to a question in English, my first answer completely interrupted the interview . . . they broke out laughing for quite a while. I asked what was wrong and they said they "never would have expected" me to have such an accent. They made a big deal about me having a [prestigious accent in the second language] and such a strong Southern accent. Of course, I had been aiming for bland Standard American English. After that, I got a number of questions about whether I'd "be comfortable" at their institution. Subtle, but to me it was not ambiguous.
>
> (Lippi-Green 1997)

This example demonstrates Northern discomfort when a link is drawn between intellectual authority and the South. A new PhD and a native speaker of English interviews for a faculty position in a foreign language department. He speaks that language fluently and with a prestigious accent. His experience, demeanor, and education have earned him an interview at a very elite school, which goes well until the interview switches to English. Whatever advantages he brought into the room are suddenly forgotten, and he is summarily rejected solely because of his Southern speech. He remains the same person, expressing the same range and quality of ideas, but his currency is suddenly devalued by linguistic features that index the lack of intelligence associated with the South.

The reaction of laughter is not unusual. Humor often highlights juxtapositions that highlight clashes between reality and expectations. Outsiders have long found humor in the idea that individuals who sound Southern might actually be competent, intelligent human beings. Consider the following journalistic attempts at humor while discussing Southern accents:

> Gov. Clinton, you attended Oxford University in England and Yale Law School in the Ivy League, two of the finest institutions of learning in the world. So how come you still talk like a hillbilly?
>
> (Mike Royko, "Opinion," *Chicago Tribune*, October 11, 1992)

> Federal law requires commercial airliners to carry infants trained to squall at altitudes above two hundred feet. This keeps the passengers calm, because they're all thinking, "I wish somebody would stuff a towel into that infant's mouth," which prevents them from thinking, "I am thirty-five thousand feet up in the air riding in an extremely sophisticated and complex piece of machinery controlled by a person with a Southern accent."
>
> (The Dave Barry 1995 Calendar, Tuesday, April 4, 1995)

In the first example, the juxtaposition is explicit: people who go to prestigious universities do not have Southern accents *and* Bill Clinton's Southern accent marks him as something other than what one should expect in a graduate of highly regarded institutions. One can further understand that the writer intends this excerpt to be understood as humorous because he has chosen constructions like *how come* and *hillbilly* instead of the less marked *why* and the more neutral-sounding *Southern.*

In the second example, Dave Barry jokes that people would rather hear crying babies than think about the fact that they may have a Southern pilot. Indeed, one might say Barry is psychic, as a recent study showed that passengers have a low level of confidence in the ability of pilots who possess Southern voices. A survey of more than 4,000 US flyers showed that 65% of respondents said they distrust pilots with Texan accents, instead preferring the voices of Midwestern and West Coast aviators (Erskine 2018).

There is no doubt that people use dialects and accents as cultural shorthand for stereotypes they would rather not mention directly. Whether it's a journalist describing the President or Disney·Pixar trying to portray the "sweet but stupid" Mater in the movie *Cars* (see Chapter 12), when people appropriate a "Southern" accent to make a joke, build a character, or emphasize a point, they are drawing on the set of stereotypes about Southerners that have been so carefully structured and nurtured. Southerners who do not assimilate to Northern norms are stereotyped as backward but friendly, kind but stupid, racist but somehow still polite, and obsessed with the past despite being largely ignorant of how to live in modern society.

Focusing on linguistic differences allows for symbolic revalorization in which the negative stereotypes of the South are conveyed in a way that escapes criticism for what would otherwise be seen as prejudiced and narrow-minded. Accent makes it possible for outsiders to draw attention to the South's need for redemption without specifically raising topics like economic inequality, which tend to make people uncomfortable.

Language ideologies continue to tie Southern speech to a wide variety of negative stereotypes that pressure Southerners to assimilate to Northern speech. Accent reduction courses taught by Northerners spring up in communities with strong Northern ties. Movies portray lazy and narrow-minded Southerners as speaking with twangs and drawls. Southern students who come north to attend college are taken aside and told that the phonology of their native language will be an impediment to true success. Job applicants are laughed at, and on the floor of Congress, reporters giggle and report not on a representative's position, but on their accent.

The South has resources to call on, ways to deflect these subordination tactics, and it seems that many Southerners are willing to take a stand:

> Notwithstanding the debate over [the South's] regional boundaries and the definition of its cultural ethos, it is safe to conclude that no region in the United States has a stronger sense of its identity. The increasing commodification of things Southern – from kudzu to speech – is ample testament of this persistent and intensifying awareness.
>
> (Wolfram 2003: 124)

Thus, although the institutions most responsible for the language subordination process try to coax Southerners toward the ultimate goal of cultural and linguistic assimilation, their efforts are often met with suspicion and defiance. What linguists believe about standard language matters very little to the majority of people, but the beliefs of non-linguists reflect their true experiences with linguistic subordination. In the lived experience of many Southerners, Northern stereotypes of Southernness matter more than scientific descriptions of linguistic realities that demonstrate that Southern dialects are just as legitimate as any other dialects of English. It is the job of sociolinguists to describe such cognitive realities by considering language attitudes and perception in addition to linguistic performance (Preston 1993: 26).

People in the American South are readily aware of the ways in which negative ideologies circulate and surface in meaningful ways. Many Southerners learn at a young age that they must walk a linguistic tightrope, balancing between the expectations of acceptability for Northern sensibilities and the feelings of comfort associated with their home life among other Southerners.

The realities of the linguistic tightrope

In teaching at a Southern university, the authors have often found that our local students find a great deal of comfort in talking about their home ways of speaking with us. They say that learning how their language works, learning that it does have structure and meaning, gives them more confidence. They often feel comfortable confiding in us the horror stories of interacting with others on campus or off campus – and not just their peers. One student said that a professor told her to change her speech because she "sounded poor," another said his professor told him he could never get a job "sounding like that," and another had the director of her graduate program tell her that the way she spoke made it seem like she was "a little slow." Another student said she had been scouted for a college softball scholarship, but when she talked to the coach, he told her he really wanted her for the team but just couldn't because she "sounded like such a rube." These are the real stories young people share with us about their struggles to embrace their own ways of speaking. After years of being told that you are unable to speak English correctly and that your language is a marker of ignorance and stupidity, it can be empowering to take linguistics courses and realize that your undervalued English is a regular, rule-governed language that in no way reflects any sort of "deficiency" on your part.

Developing an understanding about where people believe certain language varieties exist and the attitudes they have toward those ways of speaking gives linguists the on-the-ground perspectives that they must understand to conduct their research. But understanding not only how non-linguists perceive language use but also how they experience language in their day-to-day lives makes the power of language ideologies explicit – that which is perceived to be "less than" may simply not be granted space within a given linguistic landscape. On the other hand, that which is not present in the linguistic landscape may simply be invisible, making its presence appear odd and therefore unnatural. In true chicken-or-egg fashion, what people believe about language shapes how they view their world, and how they view their world shapes what they believe about language.

Discussion questions

1. Try the mental mapping activity yourself! Find a map of the United States and draw where you think people have a certain way of talking. Give each region you draw a label that reflects what you would call that variety. What kinds of labels did you choose? Are any of them overtly negative or positive? Are there parts of the country that you have left uncategorized? Why?
2. Get a list of all US states and rate them on a scale of 1–4 in terms of stereotyped levels of correctness and pleasantness, with 1 being the worst. Which states do you think would rank highly on correctness? Are they the same or different from the ones ranked as pleasant? Which stereotypes did you think of when you rated them in this way?
3. What kind of language varieties can you find in your own linguistic landscapes? Are there other languages present? Which ones? Are they serving informational or symbolic purposes? How do you know? Are there examples of linguistic features (like *maters*) or eye dialect (like *daze*) for the varieties of English used in your community? What do you think these variations index in these cases?
4. When other languages are seen on signs in your communities (even if only rarely), what kinds of reactions do people have? If you heard someone speaking a language other than English in your hometown, how would you respond? How are these reactions and responses connected to stereotypes about people who speak those languages?
5. Think about some of your favorite movies and television shows. Do any of the characters have a Southern accent? What other characteristics does the character have (e.g., type of clothing, job, hobbies)? How would you describe this character? Is it similar to the kinds of descriptions provided in this chapter? If not, what does having a Southern accent add to the character?

6. The intentional spelling of "country" with a *k* is just one example variation in spelling conventions. What other examples can you think of? What indexical meanings are associated with each way of spelling a particular word? For example, what indexical meanings are associated with each member of these pairs: *color/colour*, *boys/boyz*, *yes/yaaassss*?
7. Are you proud of the way you talk? If so, what makes you proud? Why? If you are not proud, what makes you so? Why? Do you ever feel like you are walking the linguistic tightrope?

10 A history of 'r' in the United States

Meaningful, important, and arbitrary

This chapter is essentially a case study for the themes and ideas presented in the preceding chapters through the lens of the single family of speech sounds represented by the letter 'r'. We begin this case study by repeating the apparent paradox at the core of this book: language and linguistic variation are simultaneously arbitrary and meaningful. Variation is meaningful both in the sense of conveying information – hearing a particular vowel or word can give the listener an idea where a person is from, who their friends are, whether English is one of their first languages, and so on – but also in the sense that it can limit or expand the opportunities people are willing to give themselves and each other. Linguistic variation is powerful. Sociolinguistic variation is culturally important. It is important but arbitrary in precisely the way that traffic lights are important but arbitrary. There is nothing (inherent) about a circle of red light that means "you must stop your car," but ignoring them and not doing so will nevertheless prove catastrophic; arbitrary, yes, but critically important. Think about how strange it would be if a referendum passed in your area that flipped the traffic lights: red will henceforth mean "go," green, from this day forward, will mean "stop," and yellow now means "the light will soon be green" instead of "the light will soon be red." It sounds ludicrous, but there is absolutely no reason this couldn't happen.

Color categories

Remember the discussion of the color *grue* in Chapter 2? Not all languages have the same color categories. Japanese used to be one such language with a single word 青 describing a grue category. This has since split into separate word, 青 (blue) and 緑 (green), but the blue name lingers in the descriptions of some objects that people from other cultures would probably call *green*. One such uniquely Japanese use of 青 is to describe traffic lights. In Japan, traffic light colors are 赤 (red), 黄 (yellow), and 青 (blue). And the actual traffic lights that mean *go* really are bluer than in other countries. The relationships between the colors and what they mean are arbitrary; what matters is that everyone agrees which color means what.

You may know that drivers in some countries drive on the left-hand side of two lane, bidirectional roads while drivers in other countries drive on the right-hand side. Visitors to

DOI: 10.4324/9781003332886-10

the United States from Japan, Indonesia, Ireland, and other left-side drive countries not only have to remember to drive on the right, rather than the left, but they must be especially careful to walk on the correct side of a sidewalk or to look in what feels like the wrong direction before crossing a street. Walking on the wrong side of a busy sidewalk will make you seem merely rude and thoughtless while stepping out into the road while diligently looking in the wrong direction for an oncoming bus can quite literally get you killed.

Which side of the road traffic moves on is arbitrary but, without any exaggeration of its importance, a question of life and death. It can also change. On September 3, 1967, on what is known in Swedish as Dagen H (short for *Högertrafikomläggningen*, the right-hand traffic diversion), the entire country of Sweden switched from being a left-side driving country, like Britain, to being a right-side driving country, like its contiguous neighbors Norway, Denmark, and Finland. Everyone's behavior and instincts had to begin to change literally in the blink of an eye. Behavior that had been proper, legal, and required one moment was improper, illegal, and wildly dangerous the next. This kind of change of the social value of an arbitrary, but important, rule happens in language with surprising regularity (albeit usually not on a particular day!).

In Geoffrey Chaucer's time (1343–1400), the "ks" pronunciation of what would become modern English *ask* as *axe* ['æks] was common and proper. The other pronunciation that has since gained primacy, ['æsk], was also in use, but that was not how Chaucer, an intellectual, said and wrote it. Nearly 200 years later, "aks" was still proper. The Coverdale Bible, published in 1535 as the first full translation of the Bible into English, includes, in Matthew 7:7, "Axe, and it shal be geuen you," which modern translations might present as, "Ask and it will be given to you." Living languages change. It's a central part of how language works and not some kind of corruption of modern civilization. One of the key ways scientists have found that language changes is that the social value associated with two variants already in use in a community, such as ['æks] and ['æsk] will flip. One variant that was widely normal will become less prestigious and another variant that was odd or even considered "incorrect" will replace it as standard. Often both usages will continue to co-exist, being used by different people or by the same people in different social situations, but with new social meanings and reversed social prestige.

Perhaps this seems outlandish. Throughout this book we have recognized that the forces of standard language ideology and prescriptivism that have likely been central to your education are a core tenet of membership in educated society. Once people are accustomed to a particular cultural phenomenon, however peculiar it might appear to outsiders or from the safe distance of historical reflection, it feels normal and natural. Any other way of being seems foreign, bizarre, or even impossible. It is intellectual heavy lifting to see the arbitrariness of the important social constructs active around us. As with traffic lights and road directions, there is no intrinsic meaning in the speech sounds, words, or syntactic structures used (except for iconic words and sounds; see Text Box 2 on p. 212).

The fact that this deeply meaningful, culturally important sociolinguistic variation is also arbitrary is difficult to see from within one's own culture. There is nothing inherent to a particular set of vowels, consonants, affixes, words, or syntactic structures that is, in any linguistic sense, lazy or intelligent or feminine or educated. But to really believe that this is true while listening to another person from within your own culture is extraordinarily difficult. These kinds of meanings become attached to a sociolinguistic variable through processes of social valuation and evaluation so that they *become* true for us, and they *become* necessary within a culture in ways that then seem inescapably and permanently correct.

This is not a new idea. George Philip Krapp, in his 1909 monograph *Modern English: Its Growth and Present Use*, writes this about language variation: "There is no objective system of language outside of the minds and experiences of the people who use and speak the language" (Krapp 1909: 155). His book, written more than 100 years, two World Wars, a Great Depression, a Great Migration, a Moon landing, a Civil Rights movement, an invention of computers, an invention of the internet, and two global pandemics ago, reads like a surprisingly modern struggle to reconcile this factual observation about language with the deep urge to recognize a single variety as properly and appropriately standard. Standard American English didn't exist then any more than it exists now, but there were already very real consequences for not using it. Krapp writes that by the middle of the 19th century in America (within "a few years" of 1828),

> the elegant pronunciation of [the vowel in words like *half* and *past*] became established as . . . the broad sound of a in *father*. This was undoubtedly due, in the main, to the influence of the speech of New England, particularly Boston, which, owing to its literary position during the lifetime of Longfellow, Emerson, Hawthorne, Lowell, and the other great figures of the first flowering period of American literature, was often regarded as the seat of culture in America. From Boston, where it was a normal and usual pronunciation, the broad sound a passed over by imitation to the speech of other communities. (132)

Try saying "half" and "past" with the vowel in *father* ([ɑ] rather than [æ] using the standard IPA transcriptions). Try saying it to your friends at a party and see how it goes. For most Americans this will sound humorously stilted (perhaps a bit "British" or "foreign"), but for Krapp writing in 1909, it was the established "elegant" pronunciation modeled on the speech of Boston. And it had been the elegant pronunciation, by his reckoning, for nearly 80 years!

For Krapp, what counted as the standard of pronunciation was a complex struggle between individuality and conformity, both of which he saw as deeply and necessarily democratic forces. He recognized that "educated" and "proper" were both arbitrary matters of opinion – and subject to change – but appears convinced that, to the extent that America had a standard pronunciation to aspire to, that standard, in vowels and consonants, would come from Boston and the Northeast. This was not only true for the situation Krapp describes of words like *half*. This was also true for the sound represented by the letter 'r'. At the dawn of the 20th century, the accepted American standard pronunciation for words like *horse* and *car* was, like Boston and New York City, with a long vowel and little or no 'r' sound at all.

Iconicity

One exception to the kind of arbitrariness described here is the use of iconicity in language. One can, for example, describe something as taking a *loooooong* time by extending the vowel. One can demonstrate that something was loud by yelling it or TYPING IN ALL CAPS. One might imagine that this iconicity extends to things like onomatopoeia (words formed in association with what they sound like), but English *buzz buzz* for a bee is *bhf bhf* (repeated [v] sounds) in Irish and, depending on what language(s) its owners speak, a cat might say *muwaa'* (Arabic), *miau* (Finnish), *miyav* (Turkish), *nyā* (Japanese), *yaong* (Korean), or many others.

The remarkable letter 'r'

A perfect example of the meaningfulness and arbitrariness of sociolinguistic variation can be demonstrated by even a partial history of the family of English sounds usually written down with the Latin letter 'r'. The members of this family of 'r'-like sounds are called *rhotics*. In the rest of this chapter, we are going to use the tools of phonetics, historical linguistics, dialectology, and sociolinguistics to provide what we hope will be an accessible introduction for non-linguists to one of the trickiest puzzles in linguistics: how 'r' works, at least in American English, to simultaneously create and communicate both linguistic and social meanings.

The English letter 'r' is part of the Latin alphabet because the people who first started writing English down tried their best to capture the sounds of English using letters borrowed from the Romans. Unfortunately for writing, there are no known occurrences of any two languages having exactly the same speech sound. English and French might both have a [p] sound and Mandarin and Russian might both have an [u] sound, but they're *different* from each other in sometimes quite remarkable and language-specific ways. Worse, for writing, cultures that borrow an alphabet often need to write down sounds that aren't even approximately like anything the alphabet was previously developed or modified to represent. English has sounds (like [θ] at the end of *with*, [ð] at the start of *there*, [ŋ] at the end of *king*, or [ʃ] at the start of *sheep*) that are spelled with two letters because the Latin alphabet didn't support them and required a work around.

Writing is a form of technology. It was developed to make language, which is inherently ephemeral, more permanent. Writing was, at one time, the absolute pinnacle of technology available to only a select, privileged few who were socially important (e.g., people who were wealthy, properly descended, or both) enough to be allowed access to it. English borrowed writing from the Romans, and the Romans borrowed it from the Etruscans who, in turn, had borrowed it from other Greeks who had ultimately borrowed it from the Phoenicians. Every language has its own, unique, set of sounds, though, so the alphabet had to be retrofitted for each new language to shoehorn a new set of sounds onto an old set of symbols. Writing is an astonishingly powerful cultural construct and tool, but the mapping of sounds to symbols is intrinsically messy. The sounds these letters were developed to represent are not the sounds English scribes originally used them to write down. And the sounds those scribes originally struggled to write down as something called "English" are, for the most part, no longer the same sounds used in English today. Perhaps there is no speech sound for which this is truer than for the sound represented by the letter 'r'.

Over the few hundred years that English speakers have lived out their lives in North America, the social meaning of the sounds represented by this letter has changed dramatically, multiple times, alongside changes in both American and British cultures. In the coming sections, we will describe some of this history as far as it is known, and we will see that, although the use of one mumbly, rumbling version of 'r' at the end of a syllable is now associated with education, wealth, and high status in America, this has not always been the case. In fact, the complete opposite was true at the dawn of the last century when "dropping" the 'r' sound after a vowel, as is now prestigious in Britain, was also the preferred correct American standard pronunciation for words like *standard*, *for*, and *words*.

Rhotics: variety, terminology, and symbols

Describing the variation present in English rhotic sounds requires some technical terminology from the field of phonetics to avoid the kind of desperate hand waving about "mumbly rumbling" and "dropping" that we were forced to engage with in the previous paragraph. Rhotic sounds fancy, but it is just an adjective meaning *R-like*. As a noun, it denotes a broad family of sounds that often have very little in common in the way they are pronounced or the physical sounds themselves. The rhotic sounds are grouped together as rhotics simply because they sound to listeners like they should be written down with the letter 'r'. There are exquisitely detailed descriptions of each of the apparently unrelated sounds that fall into this category, but a general definition isn't currently possible for the category itself. This is a uniquely difficult category of sounds for linguists to work with because most families of sounds will have some distinctive articulatory or acoustic feature that binds them together in the minds of speakers. Nasal sounds, like the [n], [m], and [ŋ] at the ends of the words "sun," "sum," and "sung" share a very clear set of features both as speech gestures and as sounds. The family of sounds called rhotics has no such common feature (Ladefoged & Maddieson 1996). There have been some efforts to improve upon this situation (see, for example, Lindau 1985), but for experts and non-experts alike, the word "rhotic" just means the sounds that, when written down, are usually written with the letter 'r'.

In most American English dialects today, the letter 'r' is used to represent a sound that phoneticians describe as an approximant. Approximants are the most vowel-like of the consonants in both the way they are produced in the mouth and in the way they vary from region to region. They are pronounced with a relatively open mouth so that the lips and tongue are not close enough together to cause any turbulence or to stop the air flow but still close enough together to add characteristic resonant qualities to the sound that comes out of the mouth.

You can think of your vocal tract (lips, tongue, the different regions of the roof of your mouth) as a kind of human musical instrument with a number of moving and non-moving articulators that most speakers learn to manipulate in earliest childhood (see Figure 10.1). To speak, one moves these parts around to dynamically change the sounds that the vocal tract produces. As active articulators move from position to position, each speech sound fluidly transforms into the next with no clear boundaries between them. There are no boundaries between speech sounds and no spaces between spoken words. Forcing air from your lungs while holding the tip of your tongue lightly against the bony ridge at the back of your top teeth, for example, will produce the turbulent airflow of the [s] sound at the beginning of words like *sea* or *cell*. These sounds are called "alveolar" (from the Latin word *alveus* for a little hollow or cavity) because that bony ridge behind your teeth that your tongue touches is a series of empty spaces that used to hold your adult teeth (or, depending on your age, may not be empty yet!). An [s] sound is described as an alveolar fricative: "alveolar" because of where the tongue typically touches the roof of the mouth and "fricative" because the sound is characterized by a turbulent, hissing noise.

There are many alveolar sounds in the world's languages, and English is no exception. You can vibrate your vocal folds while making an [s] sound to turn it into the [z] sound at the beginning of words like *zoo* or in the middle of *busy*. Try resting your hand gently on the front of your throat while switching between the sounds [s] "ssssss" and [z] "zzzzzz." That gentle vibration you feel during the [z] sound (and don't feel during the [s]) is the repeated flapping collision of your vocal folds called "voicing." "Voiced" sounds are sounds like [z] where the vocal folds are colliding while sounds like [s], without vocal-fold collisions, are "voiceless." Rhotic sounds are almost always voiced.

Starting a new [s] sound but pressing the tongue more firmly against the alveolar part of the roof of your mouth while still forcing air out of your lungs will cause all the airflow to stop and pressure to build up behind the tongue. Releasing this pressure produces the [t] sound in a word like *stand*. The voiced equivalent of a [t] is a [d]. With the velum lowered to

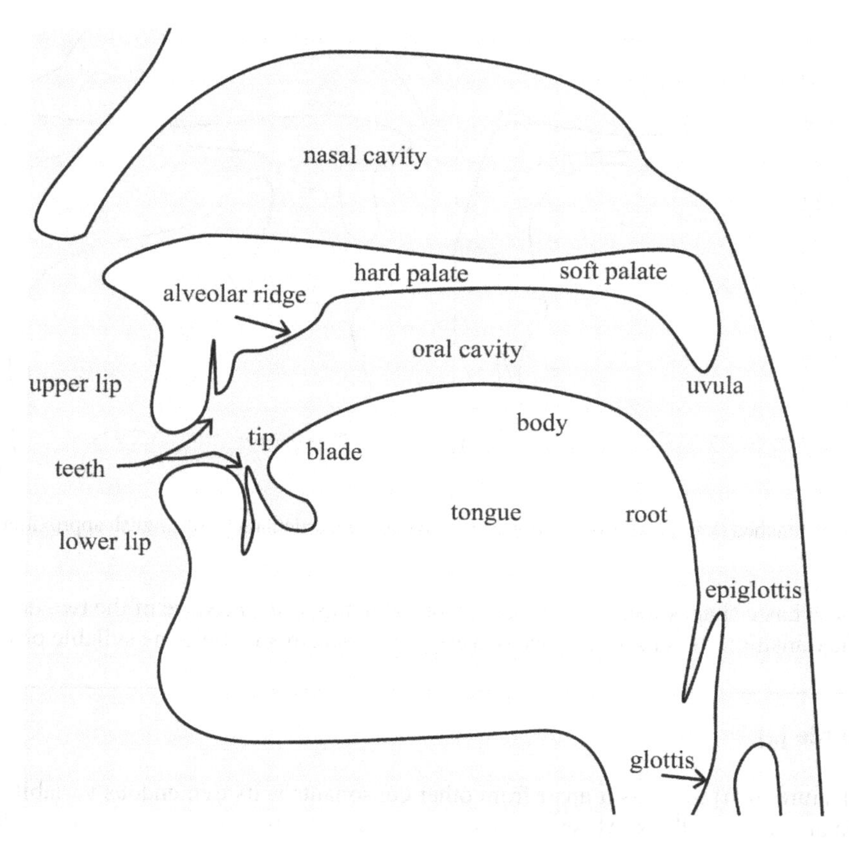

Figure 10.1 The human vocal tract labeled to indicate places of importance to speech articulation

connect the nasal passages to the rest of your vocal tract, it produces an [n] sound. Except for [n], you can't really hear these sounds without vowels (because the airflow is stopped), but if you put them each between a pair of [a] sounds, you can practice alternating between [ata], [ada], [ana]. Listeners pick up on the characteristic transitions from vowel into consonant and back into the next vowel to hear exactly where in the mouth your tongue is touching the roof. Not only is there no boundary between speech sounds, but the transitions between the sounds are essential to perception. As babies, hearing people also learn to use other constellations of cues to hear things like whether voicing is present, how the tongue is shaped, whether the lips are rounded, and many other features of this remarkable instrument.

Approximants involve moving the tongue or lips sufficiently far into the column of vibrating air in the mouth to change how it resonates without disrupting or stopping that flow of air. These sounds include the first and last sounds in words like *y'all* – the IPA symbols [j] and [l]. The American English approximant sound represented by the letter 'r' in words like *rat* or *carry* uses the upside-down IPA symbol [ɹ]. How Americans make this sound falls into two general tongue shapes that phoneticians refer to as *bunched* and *retroflex*. Figure 10.2 shows a schematic representation of a tip down, tongue body raised, bunched articulation on the left and a tip up, tongue body lowered, retroflex articulation on the right. You likely tend to use

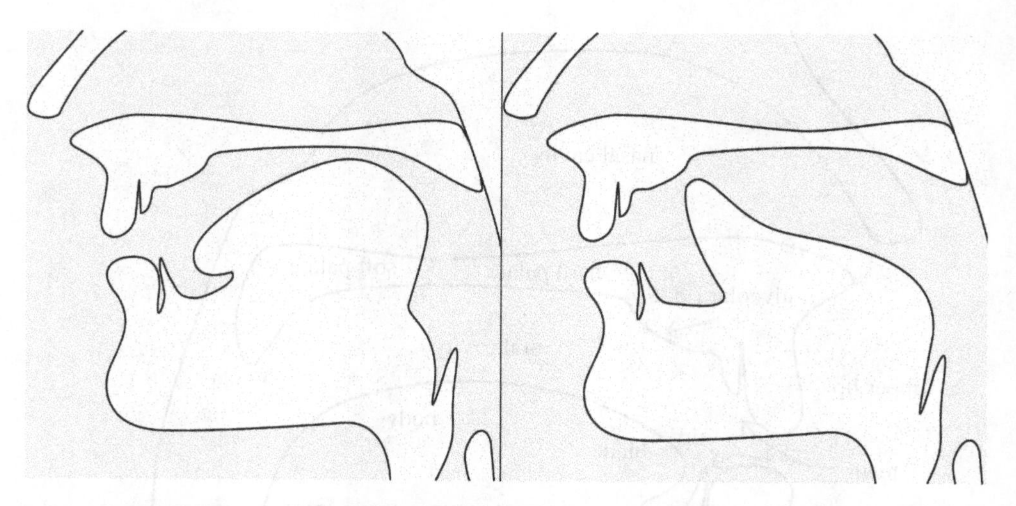

Figure 10.2 Bunched (left) and retroflex (right) are two common articulations of English approximant [ɹ]

one of these basic shapes without realizing it, but you may use a mixture of the two depending on the transitions to and from other vowels and consonants in the same syllable or word.

Variable [ɹ]

One feature of [ɹ] that sets it apart from other consonants is its tremendous variability within and across talkers. All speech sounds are variable. If you say them to yourself, you can feel the way that the [k] in *cat* is produced with the tongue farther back in the mouth than the [k] in *key* but farther forward in the mouth than the [k] in *car*. You can try saying these words to yourself and feel the way your tongue moves differently for each [k], the way it touches the soft part of your palate (the roof of your mouth) slightly differently, and the different way you hold your jaw to make each one. If you're careful you can say the [k] in isolation (or, better, download a piece of software like Praat and practice recording yourself and listening carefully to different speech sounds) and compare them.

[ɹ] does this too, but it is even more variable. Some people make an [ɹ] sound by bracing the tongue against the upper teeth and curling the tip of their tongue up and back toward the roof of the mouth for a ***retroflex*** [ɹ]. Some people make what functions as the same speech sound by pulling the muscles of their tongue together into a tight bunch in the middle of the mouth for what phoneticians call a ***bunched*** [ɹ]. Which gesture you do, when, and why when making the sound [ɹ] may possibly say something about who you are socially (Lawson et al. 2014), but the differences are so subtle that most people will never hear or feel them. You can try saying a word like ***arrow*** to yourself slowly to find out whether you use a retroflex [ɹ] or a bunched [ɹ], but if you're like most people, you won't be able to tell even with careful introspection.

It's also possible that you do both in different words. In our phonetics classes at the University of Kentucky we use an ultrasound system to let students watch their tongue move while saying different words to find out which type of [ɹ] they use in different words. Often students will be shocked to learn they do the opposite of what they had deduced based on careful introspection.

The final type of speech sound we will need for this discussion is a trill. Trills are produced by holding part of the vocal tract loosely against another non-moving part and forcefully exhaling to make the loose part pull away from and then slap back into the non-moving part, usually several times. Trills that are used in the world's languages can be made with the lips, with the tip of the tongue, and with the uvula (that punching bag-looking flesh structure hanging at the back of your throat; see Figure 10.1). The latter two, the alveolar trill (produced by flapping the tongue tip against the bony ridge of your hard palate) and the uvular trill are used as rhotics in the world's languages. Of these, only the alveolar trill is widely used in English. Thousands of languages use the alveolar trill, but perhaps the most famous alveolar trill in the American consciousness is the Spanish rolled 'r'.

The following descriptions serve to delineate the kinds of rhotics that will be useful for understanding 'r' in American English:

[r] the alveolar trill or trilled 'r': The right-side up symbol [r] denotes by far the most common rhotic sound in the world's languages, an alveolar trill (the so-called rolled r). This [r] trill is the Spanish *rr* sound in words like *perro* and *arroz*. Spanish has another sound that is written with a single *r*, but this sound is produced as a tap [ɾ] like the sound in the middle of American English words *water* or *ladder*. Although the tap occurs at the beginning and end of words, the trill does not, so that the two sounds only contrast, can only change the word's meaning, when they are used in the middle of words (compare *perro* "dog" and *pero* "but"). If they are used at the beginnings and ends of words, they can change how the word sounds but not what it *means*. Native speakers of Spanish may sometimes use the trill at the beginning or end of words to convey a variety of indexical meanings (as in saying *amorr* instead of *amor* "love" or *rrico* instead of *rico* "rich").

[ɹ] the alveolar approximant 'r': Among the world's rhotic sounds, American English [ɹ] is a notable, upside-down oddball. This alveolar approximant is a vowel-like consonant with no part of the tongue held near enough to the roof of the mouth to allow either the rumbling of a trill or the hissing of a fricative. We will not use the two symbols interchangeably in this book, but the right-side up [r] or /r/ transcription of this alveolar approximant sound is commonly used in other linguistics texts. It should be noted that, while uncommon in American English, [ɹ] can also be produced with the tongue held near enough to the bony ridge at the front of the mouth to produce a fricative sound. This alveolar fricative rhotic plays an important role in the history of non-rhotic Englishes and can still be heard in some English and Scottish accents.

(r) non-rhotic 'r': This right-side-up 'r' in parentheses is often used by sociolinguists who work on variable non-rhotic 'r'. This symbol is unlike the others in this section in that it does not represent a single speech sound but captures the fact that variation exists between speech sounds. When linguists use the symbol (r) it means that sometimes a word like "far" will be non-rhotic; it will have no audible 'r' sound at the end. For other people in that same community, and even for that same talker in different social contexts, though, "far" may still have some kind of audible 'r' sound such as [r] or [ɹ].

[ʀ] and [ʁ] uvular trill and voiced fricative: Although no longer widely used in English, these speech sounds are nevertheless common rhotics in the world's languages; this is the 'r' sound of modern standard French and most dialects of German. The uvular trill [ʀ] is produced by raising the back portion of the tongue into the back of the mouth/upper pharynx so that the otherwise passive uvula can be made to flap against it. The voiced uvular fricative [ʁ] is similar, but with the tongue held somewhat further from the uvula so the result is a turbulent, low-pitched hissing noise rather than the characteristic rumbling of a trill.

There are more rhotic sounds and symbols that could be included, but these are the ones that matter for the following discussion of 'r' in American English.

American [ɹ] is wei(r)d

One of the things Americans seem to just know about language, with no need for formal linguistic training, is that [ɹ] is weird. If you stop an American on the street and ask for an example of an accent, chances are that one of the first things you'll hear is that you may pa(r)k you(r) ca(r) in Ha(r)va(r)d Ya(r)d when near Boston or that you can "fuhgeddaboudit" in New York. People might also know that the Charleston in West Virginia is "Charleston" while the same city name a short way down the coast in South Carolina is "Chall'ston." Many speakers in these regions habitually speak without the [ɹ] sounds that appear syllable-finally in other, notably midwestern, varieties of American English.

Accents in which these [ɹ] sounds are pronounced are called *rhotic* (sometimes also called *r-ful*) because they have a distinct 'r' sound and speech where these syllable-final [ɹ] sounds are unpronounced or become vowel-like and add a bit of [ɹ] color to the vowel are called *non-rhotic* (or *r-less*). This use of (r), variable non-rhotic pronunciations, tends to be a highly salient sociolinguistic variable that speakers are aware of: people notice it, talk about it, and imitate it.

Stereotypical New England and New York speech is non-rhotic. Speech in places like Philadelphia, the Midwest, and the western states is rhotic. There seems to be a Northern stereotype that Southern US speech is non-rhotic, but this is generally not true. As we've said, coastal Southern speech, of the type you might hear in Charleston, South Carolina, is non-rhotic while modern inland Southern speech, of the type you might hear in Memphis, Tennessee, is rhotic. As is the Appalachian English you might hear in the mountains of eastern Tennessee, eastern Kentucky, western North Carolina, etc. Although the speech in many African American communities is non-rhotic, this also depends on where the speaker comes from and social class (Becker 2009). For example, the speech of African Americans in St. Louis is rhotic. The post-vocalic [ɹ] has come to index local St. Louis identity, as seen in songs by St. Louis rappers like Nelly (*Hot in Herre*) and Chingy (*Right Thurr*). Still, the non-rhotic stereotype exists for African American English; Eminem, who is himself a rhotic speaker from Detroit, will sometimes perform a hyper-white, nerdy persona by iconically over-pronouncing his [ɹ]s – making them louder and longer even than they naturally are.

Posh British speech is non-rhotic, while British pirates, in the collective imagination of many Americans, had so much excess [ɹ] that they apparently just stood around, looking rakish and saying *arrr* at one other. "Standard" American English is rhotic, but it hasn't always been. The "standard" pronunciation of 'r' in the United States switched during the second quarter of the 20th century from a Boston/Northeastern (non-rhotic) "standard" to a (rhotic) Midwestern/rural "standard." It is quite strange for the standard variety of a language to be modeled on the speech of a rural area like the Midwest rather than on the speech of a population and cultural center like New York City or Boston. How and why this happened provides key insight into the ways in which linguistic variation is arbitrary but meaningful (Bonfiglio 2002).

It is important to remember that individual speech sounds do not carry denotational meaning of their own. In the field of semiotics, *denotation* refers to the way the literal meaning of a word relates to the word itself. It is a foundational principle of linguistics that the individual sounds, the segments, of a word do not carry meaning of this type; that privilege is reserved for morphemes and words. The word *cat*, for example, is made of a [k], an [æ], and a [t] sound, but there is nothing about [k] that means "small, furry mammal," nothing about [æ] that means "lovingly contemptuous," and nothing about [t] that means "carries vicious concealed weapons in its adorable paws." These sounds together point, by the unconscious agreement of English speakers, to all of these characteristics and many more about cats, but the individual sounds themselves lack any aspect of this denotation. This truism does not hold exactly for social meaning. An individual speech sound, the way it is habitually employed by a talker, can communicate much about the identities of that person. These meanings are just as arbitrary and just as constructed through the (largely) unconscious agreement of English speakers, but they can attach not only to whole words (e.g., people who say *cool* may well be cool, but people who say *groovy* or *rad* are not) but to individual speech sounds themselves. Vowels often carry social meaning, but for American English, arguably no consonant sound carries more social meaning, across more varieties, more saliently, than 'r'.

Because [ɹ] is weird (salient, highly variable, a vowel-like consonant, and so forth) it is readily available for being enlisted to carry social meaning. Today, in the first half of the 21st century, "standard" English is a rhotic dialect. It is possible for non-rhotic dialects to sound prestigious as long as they also have other features that make them sound British (Sumner & Kataoka 2013) or, in the context of a particular city or region such as Charleston, SC, where non-rhotic speech is still the "uppity," "elegant" variety (Underwood 2019, radio broadcast). In contrast, most non-rhotic dialects with other features that mark them as distinctly American-sounding are not only associated with New York, Boston, or African American identities but are also typically associated with use by poor, socially disempowered speakers.

Where did American [ɹ] come from?

In the original cast recording of the musical *Hamilton*, Jonathan Groff, a rhotic American actor from Pennsylvania, does an exquisitely detailed and beautiful performance of an upper-class British accent portraying King George III in the song "You'll Be Back." All but one of the 'r' sounds at the beginning of words are the continuant [ɹ]. All of his (r) sounds after vowels are dropped, just like one would expect from a posh British accent. The only exceptions to this are the times when the following word begins with a vowel where Groff, very clearly, pronounces a so-called "linking" [ɹ] so that the line "For ever and ever and ever" has [ɹ] in "for," and the first two "evers," but, accurately to the modern ear, not in the last one. Groff does an absolutely perfect American impersonation of a posh British accent with the only problem being that it's probably entirely wrong. The only 'r' sound in the entire song that is probably what King George III would actually have sounded like is the short trilled [r] at the beginning of the word "remind" in the emphatically pronounced, threatening line, "To remind you of my love."

But Groff cannot be blamed for this historical inaccuracy. First, this is because there are no audio recordings from the 18th century, and very little explicit commentary seems to exist on King George III's 'r' sounds. Also, since his job was surely to embody a 21st century American idea of what it means to be (and, therefore, to *sound*) British, Groff deserves all of the praise he has received. In the American mind, British voices are, and have always been, non-rhotic. And more to the point of this chapter, American voices stereotypically have [ɹ] everywhere.

As recently as the late 18th century, though, the [ɹ] people think of as American 'r' was rarely heard. The 'r' in standard British speech at the time was the trill [r]. The non-rhotic sound people think of as quintessentially British was still a relatively new innovation gaining usage among London's elites but not yet established as "correct" pronunciation. To understand how the social meaning of [ɹ] has evolved and changed over the course of US history and what these changes can tell us about the creation and perception of social difference more broadly, it makes sense to look back to the earliest days of the British colonies in America.

The dominant 'r' of the Old English period was the alveolar trill [r] in all phonetic contexts: at the beginning of words, after vowels, and in consonant clusters like [tr] or [rʃ]. A very similar pronunciation of 'r' continues to be dominant in Scottish English; stereotypically appearing even in the name for this variety as "burr." There is a tendency among linguists and non-linguists alike to imagine that linguistic variation is a modern phenomenon. The Tower of Babel myth hinges on the ideology that human language was, at some point, fixed and perfect and that separate languages and language variation are just another kind of fall from grace. It is important, therefore, to bear actively in mind as we look back through the evidence of history that even though one can say a thing like "the dominant rhotic of the Old English period was an alveolar trill," there was surely meaningful, if arbitrary, variation present even then.

Written in 1597, *Romeo and Juliet* (Act 2, Scene 4) includes an exchange between a nurse and Romeo. The nurse asks Romeo if his name and Rosemarie don't both begin with the same letter. He replies that, yes, they both begin with 'R', and she says, "Ah, mocker, that's the dog's name." This little exchange, incomprehensible in modern pronunciations, is a low kind of humor in the English of Shakespeare's time. 'R', characteristically pronounced as the alveolar trill, was idiomatically referred to as "the dog's letter" because of the resemblance of this consonant to the sound of a dog's snarling growl. So despite evidence of the encroachment of a certain kind of weakening of the consonant at the ends of syllables, the accepted, standard, stereotypical 'r' in elegant British English in the earliest days of American colonization was an alveolar trill.

Commentary on this weakened, but still consonantal, 'r' in British English begins to appear not long before *Romeo and Juliet* in the latter part of the 16th century (Bailey 1996: 99). But there is evidence from the Middle Ages that this alveolar trill consonant had already begun to "weaken" in British usage. This weakening started particularly in consonant clusters before [s] and [ʃ] so at least some contemporary readers pronouncing the words "horse" or "worship" in Chaucer's *Canterbury Tales* had begun to do so with the alveolar trill [r] replaced with a fricative rhotic consonant. This fricative may have been alveolar or uvular, and both variants were likely in use. In his 1640 work *The English Grammar*, Ben Jonson describes word-initial 'r' as a trill, "jarring the tip of the tongue against the roof of the mouth near the fore teeth" but when pronounced after vowels, 'r' is "a vibration of the lower part of the tongue, near the root, against the inward region of the palate near the entrance to the throat." Such a phonetically lucid contemporary account of non-initial British 'r' as very possibly a uvular fricative [ʁ] in mid-17th- century London is important for understanding its history.

The year 1640 is of importance in the American story of 'r' because Jonson was writing only a little more than a decade after the founding of the Massachusetts Bay Colony in 1628. When the colonies were founded, non-rhotic (r) existed but was not yet part of prestigious British speech. The original alveolar trill had separated into two different speech sounds: the trill was retained at the beginnings of syllables but had been replaced with an alveolar or a uvular fricative after vowels.

British English retained its trilled [r] pronunciation at the beginnings of words well into the 20th century (Jones 1922: 47). There is evidence of a modern-like non-rhotic (r) pronunciation early in the 18th century (Jesperson 1913: 360, cited in Bailey 1996). Bailey notes that the result of this loss was to split words in common usage into pairs of rhotic and non-rhotic forms creating pairs like "burst, bust, curse, cuss, girl, gal, horse, hoss, parcel, passel." New England town records (court proceedings, deeds, etc.) show these non-rhotic spellings throughout the 18th century while this sound change was happening in prestigious British English.

Eeyore the . . . donkey?

In the Hundred Acre Wood, "Rabbit" is a rabbit, "Owl" is an owl, "Piglet" is a little pig, "Tigger" is a tiger, and "Winnie the Pooh's" proper name is "Edward Bear." Why then is the poor little donkey stuck with the apparently tacked-on (like his tail) name "Eeyore"? The answer is that the book's author, A. A. Milne, who was born in London in 1882, was a non-rhotic British speaker. The name "Eeyore," in such an accent, is an onomatopoeia for the sound donkeys make when they bray. The same sound, written down by speakers of American English, is usually *hee-haw*. A rhotic pronunciation of Eeyore, with the innovative spelling-based addition of an [ɹ] sound, masks the relationship between the animal sound and the donkey's name. To a non-rhotic reader, non-initial 'r' letters are essentially a mysterious silent letter like the "p" in *psychology* or the second "b" in *bomb*. The written letter 'r' is a marker of vowel length and, perhaps, vowel quality. A similar kind of spelling-based sound change has happened for modern speakers who have reevaluated the pronunciation of a word like *often* to include a [t] sound or *calm* to include an [l].

The rise of variable non-rhotic (r) after vowels in prestigious British English really takes off in the historical record at the end of the 18th century and proceeds in parallel in parts of the American colonies. It is important to note that, even from the beginning of prestigious non-rhotic speech, there are pockets of America where rhotic productions flourish. Boston and northern New England become non-rhotic during the 18th century, but Connecticut does not, and even Plymouth, Massachusetts, does not. New York City and much of New Jersey become non-rhotic but upstate New York and Pennsylvania, including the important metropolis of Philadelphia, do not. The coastal South (from Maryland to New Orleans) becomes non-rhotic, but the inland South and Appalachia do not. A similar pattern happens in the British Isles where southeastern England, chiefly centered around London, becomes rhotic, but Scotland, the west country, and (at least until the 20th century) the north of England (e.g., Liverpool, Manchester, and Lancashire) do not. The entire island of Ireland, from Cork on the southern coast to Derry and Belfast in Ulster and to the cultural hub of Dublin retain a traditional variety and do not become non-rhotic.

Another word for donkey?

Similar to the subject of Eeyore, the word *ass* for this ungulate quadruped is very old in Indo-European languages. The word is *assinus* in Latin and *asan* in Old Irish. The use of this spelling and the sequence of sounds it represents to mean "buttocks" in English is an example of language change that happened after variably non-rhotic speech emerged as a common variety of British English. As a result of this sound change, the previously distinct words *arse* and *ass* merged. *Arse* is the older Germanic form (cognate with *aars* in Dutch and *Arsch* in German) but has undergone reevaluation by English speakers since the merger. Following the usual pattern, the non-rhotic form has become the more informal (in this case vulgar) form while the rhotic form is considered more proper and more polite (see also pairs like *girl/gal*, *horse/hoss*, and *curse/cuss,* which have undergone the same reanalysis).

There have been many explanations given in the linguistics literature for why English speakers living in some parts of North America adopted a non-rhotic standard while others retained the older pattern of pronouncing non-initial 'r'. Some have simply stated that the distribution is due to "settlement patterns" from England (e.g., Kurath & McDavid 1961; Kurath 1971), but this has two major problems. First, many of these regions that become non-rhotic were colonized prior to the rise of a non-rhotic standard and much of what would become the rhotic regions of the United States was settled from the eastern seaboard westward after this rise. Second, this explanation of settlement patterns only pushes the same question back to England: why did some parts of the British Isles retain the older rhotic forms while prestigious London speakers adopted the new pattern that was to become standard?

Another explanation often given is that places like Boston, New York City, Richmond, and Charleston retained close cultural and economic ties to London after the American revolution and so developed (in the 18th century) and then entrenched (in the 19th century) a non-rhotic speech pattern along London norms. This scenario is difficult to reconcile with the actual patterns of economic activity in the United States before and after 1792. With whom did Philadelphia traders interact and how could it have been so different from New York City or, indeed, Trenton, New Jersey? As noted by Bonfiglio (2002), the Erie Canal, completed in 1825, quickly became the economic life blood of New York City and the source of much of its rise in wealth and cultural status during the remainder of the 19th century. The traders at the other end of the canal spoke a rhotic variety of English while New York City elites continued along the same non-rhotic trajectory as Londoners on the other side of the Atlantic with whom they had, comparatively at least, precious little in person contact.

It is not the role of a book like this one to advance new theories or to settle theoretical debates within the field. But it is appropriate, possibly essential, for a book about the ways in which linguistic variation is used to create and negotiate identities to observe that simple, mechanistic explanations involving geography or mere contact between groups of people risk under-appreciating the tremendous social value linguistic variation carries. London does not have an accent. New York City does not have an accent. Every individual person who speaks a language has an accent, and some of those people identify, at least in part, as Bostonians while others identify as Philadelphians. An explanation for how and why the subsequent patterns of variation emerged in the United States is surely rooted in the fact that these different 'r'-like speech variants came, over the course of the 18th and 19th centuries, to carry social meanings that meant "Boston" or "Charleston" or "Philadelphia" or "Chicago" to the ears of 18th and 19th century listeners. These variants were non-rhotic (for the first two cities) or rhotic (for the latter two cities), but the ways in which they were rhotic or non-rhotic were distinctly local. To say that one can look back into America's phonetic past and simply state why one region is rhotic while another region is non-rhotic is to imagine that one can solve some of the deepest and most perplexing questions of sociolinguistics with a mere fraction of the data available to modern researchers. So let's set questions of "why" aside for future study and just acknowledge that geographically and socially distributed patterns of 'r' usage emerged over the 18th and 19th centuries. If we have learned anything about the phonetics of 'r' in this chapter, it is that 'r' is highly variable and that these varieties have leant themselves to associate with social meanings.

These local meanings emerge alongside meanings like "prestigious," "educated," "polite," "effeminate," "Black," "foreign," and "urban" for the non-rhotic variants and "rural," "Irish," "Scottish," "strong." and "uncultured" for the rhotic variants. Bailey quotes an essay by educator Charles Remy (1900) in which Remy judged non-rhotic speech as "grossly inaccurate," saying that this pattern could be found in "the speech of the Harvard or Oxford professor, the farmer of New England, the professional man, the planter, the mountaineer, and the colored man of the South" (1900: 419). Each of these quite different character types was associated with the non-rhotic variant in ways that surely emphasized different aspects of the constellation of possible social meanings these varieties had accumulated.

The desires of people with different social alignments to include themselves or exclude themselves in these regional and social identities will surely be at the core of a successful understanding of how the geographic patterns of rhotic and non-rhotic speech became established before the turn of the 20th century (see, for example, Reed [2018] for an exploration of the role of "rootedness" in the retention or rejection of Appalachian speech patterns). Sometimes refusal to participate in the use of a variant or to participate in a change is itself a statement of identity (Babel 2016).

What can be said for certain is that as the United States and Britain entered the 20th century, both had adopted non-rhotic speech as the prestigious standard. On both sides of the Atlantic, non-rhotic speech was associated with large urban centers of economic and political importance and the more traditional rhotic forms persisted outside of these centers. As correctly noted in Bonfiglio (2002), "In reality, Standard British English does not have a parental, but instead a sibling relationship to American English." In both places, rhotic and non-rhotic forms were in daily use by different groups of people and carried, along with prestige and education, other meanings that would ultimately play out quite differently in the two countries in the 20th century.

From non-rhotic to rhotic: American sound change in the first half of the 20th century

As late as 1925, scholars still acknowledged variable non-rhotic (r) as the prestigious American pronunciation (Krapp 1925: 217). Interestingly, though, Krapp (1925) was also grappling with one additional English 'r' variant that we haven't needed to say much about yet. This is the extremely vowel-like approximant [ɹ] that a listener of today would identify as *the* stereotypically "American" 'r' sound. Krapp goes so far as to discard the possibility that this consonant is even a consonant because it is so unlike the proper trilled [r] or tapped [ɾ] rhotic that were historically English's standard rhotic variants.

So while what has been said so far about eastern New England, New York City and its environs, and the coastal South being areas of typically non-rhotic speakers is true, it is also true that the rest of the English-speaking portion of North America was inhabited by typically rhotic speakers; it's just that not all of those 'r's were the same 'r'. Grandgent (1920) describes the situation in much the way one might slow down to look in interested horror at a car accident on the highway:

> In a great part of the United States – a region, let us say, north of the Ohio and stretching from the Hudson to the Rockies – the retracting tendency is exaggerated and the tip of the tongue is curled up toward the middle of the root of the mouth, leaving a curiously shaped passage, which, though very wide, strikingly modifies the acoustic effect of the outgoing breath. A similar pronunciation may be heard in Kent [UK]. *This strange sound, which seems to afford its utterers an inexplicable satisfaction, does not convey in the least the impression of an r to anyone accustomed to either variety of the trill; it suggests merely an obstructed formation of the preceding vowel.* The Middle Western *par*, *court*, for example, impress the unpracticed ear rather as *pa*, *coat* spoken with one's mouth full.
>
> (Grandgent 1920: 36–37, quoted in Bonfiglio 2002, emphasis added)

Here there is a problem in the historical phonetic record that is not often, if ever, acknowledged in the existing research on the history of 'r'. Non-rhotic variable (r) is relatively easy to observe in the historic record because people who don't use 'r' sometimes leave it out of their spellings (e.g., *cuss* for *curse*) or add it in where it doesn't belong (e.g., *Bostorn* for *Boston*) because remembering where silent letters go is hard and, to a non-rhotic speaker, a non-initial 'r' like the one in *horse* is essentially a silent letter. But when someone has a different, but still distinctive, variant speech sound for the orthographic letter 'r', one must hope for an astute contemporary observer like Ben Jonson's 17th century observation of uvular [R], a sound-based literary joke like Shakespeare's dog's letter for alveolar trilled [r], or prescriptivist complaints like those of Krapp for whom approximant [ɹ] "is not a consonant" (Krapp 1925: 218) or Grandgent, for whom [ɹ] is a merely a homely, western American r-substitute to preserve traditional English rhoticism, albeit at the expense of the traditional, trilled English [r] sound.

What can be inferred from this historical record, existing research, and modern pronunciations is that, sometime during the 18th and 19th century, while the non-rhotic areas of the Americas were becoming non-rhotic in their distinctly local and yet distinctly American ways, the rhotic parts of the country were also seeing the rise of an 'r' variant that was also distinctly, if differently, American. It is surely the case that all and more of the rhotic variants described so far were in use in the United States in the first quarter of the 20th century.

A living language is a variable language. But commentaries from language scholars at the time agreed that the prestigious variety of American English was non-rhotic like the varieties of New York City, Boston, and the coastal South.

Evidence from Krapp (1925) suggests that non-rhotic speech was still the unquestioned standard in 1925. R-lessness continued to set the standard for prestigious speech in the United States through the late 1930s. Rhotic speech, by contrast, continued to be seen as less prestigious, less refined, and less educated but also, simultaneously, more rugged and healthier (Bonfiglio 2002). Queen (2015: 41) notes the example of the 1940 film *Philadelphia Story* in which rhoticity is used to help audiences recognize the class differences between Jimmy Stewart's earnest, rhotic everyman character Macaulay "Mike" Connor and Katharine Hepburn's wealthy, non-rhotic socialite character Tracy Lord. By the end of that same decade, though, the dominant position of non-rhotic speech and the less prestigious position of rhotic speech had flipped entirely. Almost as abruptly as Dagen H flipped the direction of travel on Swedish roads, the prestige of speaking a non-rhotic variety of American English was gone. Whether attitudes toward variable non-rhotic (r) shifted due to racial prejudice amid the Great Migration (see later in this chapter), anti-Semitism and an association of non-rhotic varieties with New York City, or growing American isolationism in the pre-war period (see Bonfiglio 2002 for a full exploration), the fact is that by the end of the 1940s non-rhotic speech was out in America, and rhotic speech was in.

Non-rhotic in Manhattan

One of the most famous and earliest studies of the connection between social identity and linguistic variation was William Labov's 1966 examination of syllable-final (r) in Manhattan (Labov 1972b). Labov observed that, in Manhattan, some people were non-rhotic and others were rhotic. He hypothesized that this variation was linked to social prestige and thus variation would pattern with observable, measurable socioeconomic factors. To test this hypothesis, he conducted a field study which took place at three department stores in Manhattan: Saks, Macy's, and Klein's. These department stores represented three distinct socioeconomic classes: Saks shoppers were wealthy; Macy's shoppers were middle class; and Klein's shoppers were working class. Crucially, they also all had at least four floors.

In each store, fieldworkers completed rapid and anonymous surveys with counter clerks at these stores in which the fieldworkers asked for directions to a department they already knew to be on the fourth floor (e.g., "Excuse me, where are women's shoes?"). Pretending not to hear or understand, the fieldworker would also ask the clerk to repeat the response (e.g., "Excuse me?). The clerk answered "Fourth floor" both times, the second one being more deliberate, and the fieldworker walked around a corner to note the results. They were interested in the production of both 'r' instances in the phrase and having the person repeat the answer allowed for the collection of casual and emphatic pronunciations. This methodology resulted in hundreds of tokens of the words "fourth floor" in both types of speech.

Using these data, Labov was able to pinpoint the effects of social class, prestige, style, gender, age, and other factors on the distribution of the use of [ɹ]. The more socially elevated an individual was (or strove to be), the more syllable-final [ɹ] sounds were retained in their speech. The simple conclusion would be that the lower the income level, the more non-rhotic the speech. But [ɹ] is never simple. The dramatic swapping of the prestigiousness of rhoticity happened only in America; in England of the 20th and early 21st centuries, for example, the exact opposite social meaning still holds. In that social context, the more non-rhotic one's speech, the more *posh*, or upper-class, the voice. There is nothing inherently prestigious about pronouncing or not-pronouncing [ɹ]s; this prestige is created in the mind and attitudes of the listener.

Prestige is a complex concept, precisely because it is so incredibly relative. What is prestigious to one person may be negative to the next person. More importantly, what is prestigious in one community may be a mark of disloyalty and highly stigmatized in the next, and thus the simplest truth about language variation: a speaker will gravitate to the variants tied to the community that is most important to them, despite possible negative repercussions.

Despite the presumptions of the Labov study cited previously, prestige is not always an issue of economics. Labov's study established that, for [ɹ], those who aspired, in the mid-1960s, to belong to the social upper crust in the United States were less likely to be non-rhotic (see Figure 10.3). Common sense alone should be enough to cast doubt on the idea that anybody in Manhattan who deletes syllable-final [ɹ] is without ambitions and disdainful of the trappings of social prestige. Donald Trump, a wealthy real estate developer, television personality, and former president of the United States, is generally a non-rhotic speaker. There are always people of all social and economic backgrounds trying to improve their lot in life; some people work three jobs, rack up huge school loans, buy lottery tickets, or invest in the latest widget. The fact is some people strive for economic success and socially upward movement but resist assimilation to the language habits of others who have successfully achieved that goal.

As is shown in Figure 10.3, studies since Labov's early work on the use of [ɹ] in Manhattan indicate that the rates of r-lessness continue to index social class in New York. However, younger speakers have much higher rates of r-maintenance across all social classes (Mather 2012). Speakers are still very sensitive to formality and style issues so that the more formal the situation, the more likely non-rhotic New Yorkers are to keep [ɹ] after vowels (Labov 1972b; Mather 2012).

The stability of the distribution of rhoticity in Manhattan is especially surprising when looking at other data on change over time. Elliott (2000) looked at films spanning most of the

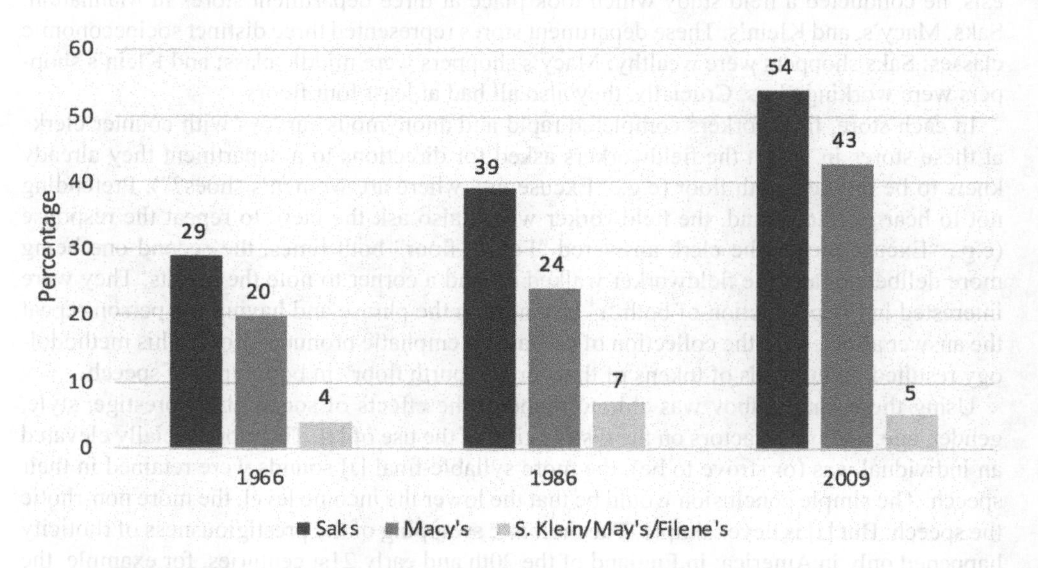

Figure 10.3 Percent overall non-rhotic responses in three classes of NYC department store

Source: adapted from Mather (2012: 314)

20th century, collecting data on an actor's use of [ɹ], along with information on the individual actor's original variety of American English (as mentioned earlier, Katharine Hepburn's native variety is non-rhotic; Ginger Rogers' is rhotic) and other demographic information. One clear finding was that non-rhotic speech was far more common earlier in the 20th century and that as the century progressed, actors moved rapidly toward r-fulness. Figure 10.4 indicates that both groups – actors whose native variety of English is non-rhotic and actors whose variety of English is rhotic – moved toward full r-fulness at about the same rate.

In the 1970s, Feagin undertook a similar investigation in Anniston, Alabama, and found a similar change in progress. Northerners tend to think of all Southerners as non-rhotic, but Feagin established that syllable-final (r) was creeping in quite steadily. Another ten years provided enough data and perspective for her to conclude that the South was moving from non-rhotic to rhotic in only three generations (Feagin 1990).

Elliott also found a great deal of stereotyping in the retention or deletion of [ɹ], often within the same film for the same actress. For example, Patty Duke's character in *Valley of the Dolls* starts out as a prototypical good girl, at which point she is non-rhotic no more than 9% of the time; by the end of the movie, she is a drug addict with no hope, and her r-less rate has risen to 29% (ibid.: 121–122). It is no surprise that an actor manipulates language in the process of trying to establish character, a topic that will come up again in the discussion of accent in children's animated film in Chapter 12.

There is a wide range of factors that play a role in this change in progress. In addition to place, age is a strong predictor – the younger the speaker, the more syllable-final [ɹ];

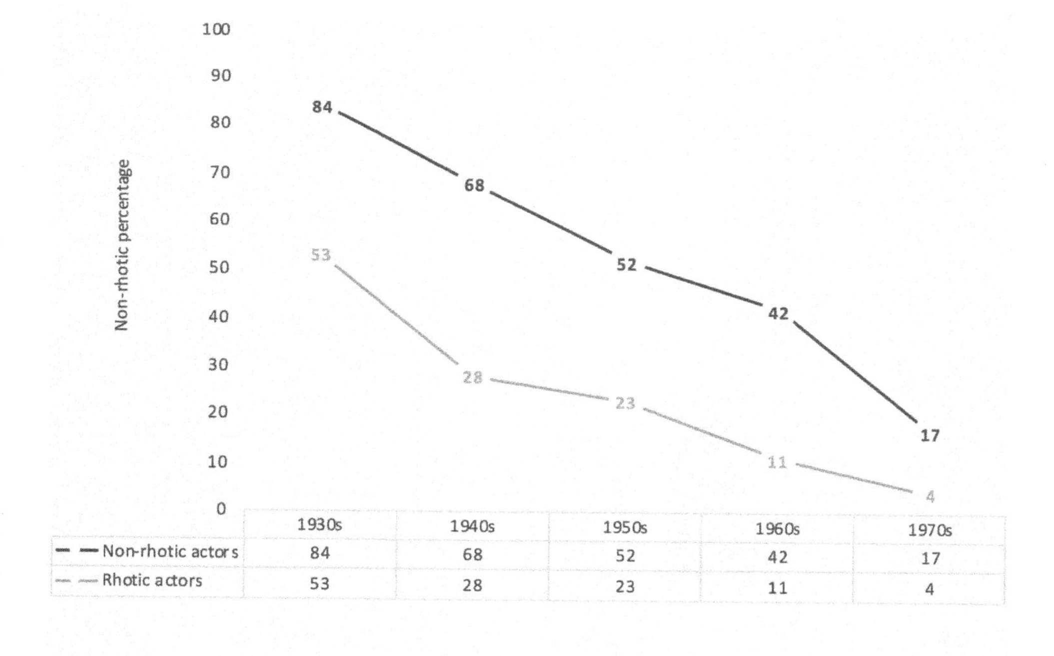

	1930s	1940s	1950s	1960s	1970s
Non-rhotic actors	84	68	52	42	17
Rhotic actors	53	28	23	11	4

Figure 10.4 Five decades of film and the rate of change from non-rhotic to rhotic, by actor's original rhoticity status whether rhotic or non-rhotic

Source: adapted from Elliot (2000: 105)

education is another strong predictor – people who have more formal education trend toward restoring (r). Race is more relevant still, as Labov (1972a) reports, "all other things being equal, African-American ethnicity lowers the frequency of (r) constriction by 32 percent."

African Americans tend to be non-rhotic wherever they live, whether in Iowa (where syllable-final (r) among speakers of the prestigious local variety is solid and categorical) or Alabama (where it is not). Figure 10.5 indicates that white speakers in New Hampshire are becoming more rhotic (there are no African American participants from NH in the original study), while both white speakers and AAE speakers in Boston are resisting this change (Nagy & Irwin 2010). Speakers of AAE are more persistently non-rhotic. The two groups' resistance to r-fulness may look similar on the surface, but the underlying motivations are certainly different.

This may be seen as following from many different factors, but the most important is likely the Great Migration. Between 1910 and 1940, roughly 1.5 million African Americans fled to the urban areas of the North to escape poverty and racism. After the interruption of World War II, another 1.5 million African Americans migrated North between 1940 and 1950, a trend that continued until about 1970. For communities of African Americans who migrated from, for example, rural South Carolina to take up work in Detroit, retaining syllable-final (r) in a region where rhotic speech was already established was most likely a way to emphasize their solidarity and common history.

Other linguists have argued for a more anthropological approach to the study of this kind of variation. Michael Silverstein (2003) proposed the concept of indexical order as an alternate way of studying language variation and change. Rather than assigning precise meanings to any given variable, for example, (r) deletion, it is more revealing and potentially more

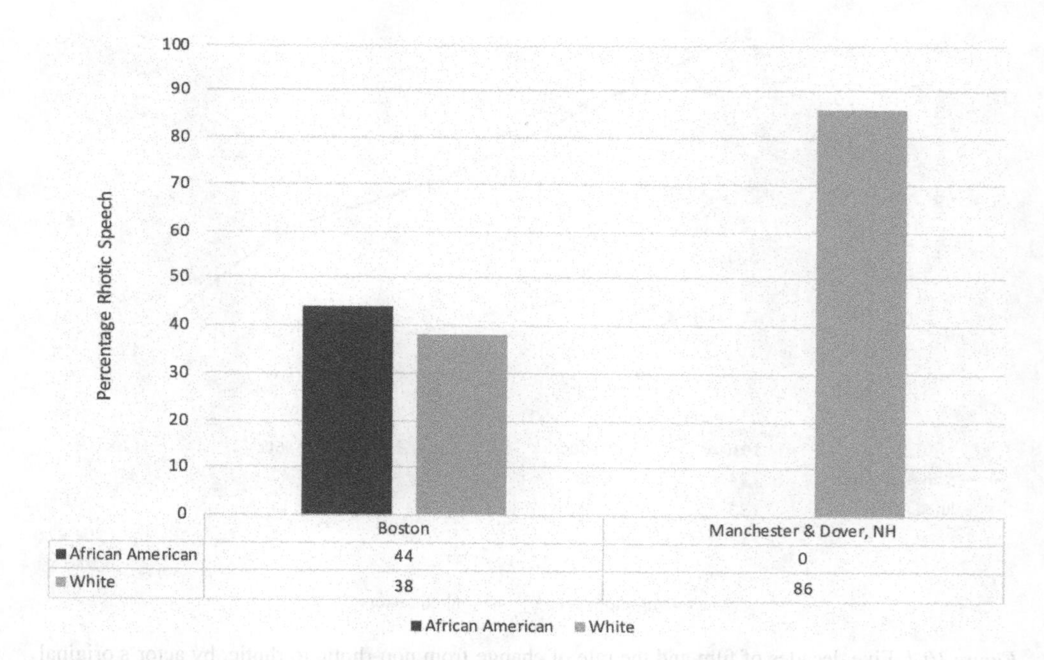

Figure 10.5 Percent syllable-final r-maintenance by age, location, and race

Source: adapted from Nagy and Irwin (2010)

useful to think of variables as existing within a pool or field of potential meanings. Eckert (2008: 454) has called this an indexical field, which is a "constellation of ideologically related meaning. . . . The field is fluid, and each new activation has the potential to change the field by building on ideological connections." In a traditional sociolinguistic study, data would be analyzed quantitatively, and the linguist would make observations. For example, the researcher might point to statistics to establish that the substitution of variant x for variant y is being propelled by adolescent males (or resisted by women of child-bearing age, etc.). The weakness of this approach is the way the focus on statistics has come to preclude study of less quantifiable aspects of language use. Thus, a statement like this change in progress is being led by middle-aged women says nothing about the kinds of behavior and ideologies that underlie these patterns, what kinds of meaning people attach to the conservative and innovative variant, who does and does not fit the pattern, and why (ibid.: 455).

Such a methodology would require a long period of observation to pinpoint those social categories which are truly relevant to the community in question, rather than simply trying to force the data into preconceived rubrics of class, ethnicity, race, etc. Eckert and Wenger point out that it is not social groups per se that are relevant to understanding distributions of data, but the "stances, activities and qualities" associated with those groups (2005: 584).

Non-rhotic speakers in the United States today have fewer social opportunities, work in more poorly paid jobs, and experience more negative interactions with police and the justice system. This chapter has been a case study for the themes and ideas presented in the preceding chapters through the lens of the single family of speech sounds represented by the letter 'r'. The prestigiousness of non-rhotic speech has not only changed dramatically in the relatively brief history of the United States, it has done so twice. It is important to remember that with this change of prestige meant real changes in the lives and prospects of the people who used the two varieties. Linguistic variation is not random, but it is arbitrary. From the perspective of the early 21st century it is easy for us to see that there is nothing inherently natural or superior about the once ubiquitous trilled [r] of the Old and Middle English periods. There is similarly nothing inherently "American" about [ɹ] or "British" about (r). All mappings of meaning, be they linguistic or social, to linguistic forms and variants are fundamentally arbitrary and ephemeral. Linguistic variation is simultaneously arbitrary and deeply, powerfully meaningful in the lives and opportunities of speakers.

Discussion questions

1. In addition to the color of traffic lights and what they mean, can you think of other examples from your culture of something that is arbitrary but also truly meaningful? How do you understand this idea of arbitrariness as connected to language? Give an example of arbitrariness in language beyond those discussed in this chapter.
2. Is your variety of English rhotic or non-rhotic? Have you ever visited a place that had a different status of 'r'? Did anyone comment on your 'r's or did you notice the 'r's of others in that place?
3. Do you speak a language that does something different with the letter 'r' than what has been described here? Try to describe to someone else how you think the letter 'r' is produced in your language using the descriptions of *bunched* and *retroflex* [ɹ] in the text as an example.
4. What regional varieties of American English do you think are prestigious today? How do you know? Are they rhotic or non-rhotic? What other linguistic features can you think of that separate the prestigious varieties from the less prestigious ones?

5. Later chapters in this book handle how speaking a variety other than "standard" American English can cause issues with employment, law enforcement, and education. Based on what you understand about rhoticity, how could you imagine, as we say near the end of this chapter, that "non-rhotic speakers in the United States today have fewer social opportunities"? What does this mean?

11 The communicative burden in education

The medium of instruction

Imagine trying to teach a child to read. How might you go about it? Some will begin by teaching the child the letters of the alphabet, what sounds they make, how they fit together. Others will begin by teaching children to recognize lists of common words by sight, reasoning that the child will associate the repeated forms with the sounds they represent and learn by analogy to extrapolate these memorized forms to new words. One might also combine these approaches and other methods to help the child learn to connect the language they speak naturally and have learned since birth with its artificial, written form. It may not seem like it anymore, but writing is advanced technology that has been invented probably not many more than four times in all of human history (in China, Sumer, Mesoamerica, and Egypt). Mapping one's spoken language to writing is a daunting task for any child, even those who seem to take to it with relative ease, and it is an essential one because literacy, as we will see, is the cornerstone of education. Critics of the primacy of literacy in educational contexts, which mark this specific kind of literacy as the necessary and sufficient conditions for economic success, call this the *literacy myth*, and in this chapter we'll see how its entanglement with the Standard Language Ideology spells trouble for speakers of undervalued Englishes.

Now imagine yourself trying to teach a child to read a language that they do *not* already speak. Imagine a French-speaking child has arrived in your English-medium classroom. If you do not speak French yourself or, worse, if you are convinced that speaking French is a choice and clear evidence of an inferior mind and limited intellectual potential, how successful is the child likely to be learning to read and write in English? Hand this child the same alphabet and list of sight words as the children sitting to their left and right, instruct them exclusively in your clearest, loudest English speech, reprimand them when they make mistakes or make a joke about their difficult-for-you-to-pronounce name. How successful will this child be?

Much of education, whether the subject is mathematics, physics, or literature, happens through the medium of language. Our thoughts are not, themselves, made of language, but language is the channel that allows us to move thoughts from one head to another. It is crucial, therefore, that teachers and students be able to understand one another. A tragic mistake that happens too often in the process of teaching and learning is confusing different meanings of *language*.

In the previous reading example, there are at least three distinct language varieties involved. First, there is written language, with its own particular rules and limitations (written language lacks gesture, for example, so spatial relationships that would be obvious in a conversation must be more laboriously specified). This written language is distinct

DOI: 10.4324/9781003332886-11

from the spoken language that is the medium of instruction (the language a teacher uses to explain concepts and ask questions and the language teachers typically expect students to respond in). There are also the native languages of the children (and the teacher) in the classroom. People often assume that the language used by the teacher and the different language varieties used by students will all be basically the same variety. And sometimes they are all very similar, especially when a middle-class white child walks into the average American classroom and the written standard, the language of instruction, and the child's native, or home, language are all likely to be closely related to one another. For children who speak undervalued Englishes, however, these understandings of "language" rarely align.

There may be benefits to having all these levels of language in instruction be related in this way, but there is no logical reason this must be the case. One can easily imagine a situation, for example, where the written variety is Latin, the language of instruction is French, and the children speak a variety of languages at home. In a situation like this, it would be clear that the children must be taught both Latin and its grammar along with the formal rules of writing and French with its grammar and the formal rules of speaking. Standard Language Ideology causes problems in American classrooms when it is assumed that 1) written English is just the standard spoken variety set in ink (it is not), 2) the language of instruction must logically be as close as possible to the written standard (it need not), and 3) children who speak a variety that differs substantially from the prescriptive standard are inferior, disadvantaged, or inexpert language users (they are not).

Children arrive at school already skilled participants in their native culture and adept users of their native language(s), with some rare exceptions (see specific language impairment and non-verbal autism in Chapter 3 and childhood access to signed languages in Chapter 8). The importance of this fact cannot be overstated: acquiring a language, signed or spoken, as an infant and toddler is an intrinsic capacity of human beings. What children are expected to do in school is to learn to read and write standard written English and to communicate with their teachers and classmates. As we have discussed throughout this book, "standard" written English may be similar to the child's home language or it may differ dramatically from it. In either case, reducing all of "language ability," "intelligence," and "potential" to the ability to read and write standard written English overlooks a tremendously complex negotiation of codes, culture, and modes of communication that will need to happen between the children and their teachers for instruction to be successful.

The situation described earlier, the French-speaking student arriving in an English-medium classroom and receiving no accommodation is not so far removed from the everyday lived experience of children who natively speak varieties of English that differ substantially from the imagined "standard" English. Often these children are met with bias from their teachers, bias from their classmates, and even bias from themselves and their own families (in the form of linguistic insecurity) simply based on their native variety of English.

Educators could make their own lives, and the lives of their students, much easier and better if they recognize two facts: 1) that "standard" English is just another variety of English that students can learn to add to their treasury of linguistic expertise, and 2) that students' home languages are logically-structured, valid forms of language that can be drawn upon to *connect* the student to the goals of the classroom rather than *exclude* them from those goals. Education requires mastery of new forms, not assimilation. The assumption that "standard" English is the default, correct, and basic form of communication reifies and exacerbates deep problems in the educational system that mirror and radiate out into deep problems in society.

Invisible ideologies go to school

According to the National Center for Education Statistics, 50.7 million, more than 90%, of children in the United States are educated in public schools (NCES 2020) where attendance is mandatory, and the curriculum is intended to prepare children to be competent, successful adults in civic, commercial, and cultural capacities. Furthermore, people hold schools responsible for turning the children in their care into productive citizens capable of critical thought. The ultimate goal of freely available, compulsory education is an informed electorate, one capable of electing and participating in a democratic government, participating in an economy, etc.

Malcolm X (1970) once said, "Education is our passport to the future, for tomorrow belongs only to the people who prepare for it today." By teaching students how to think and how to communicate, and by giving them a boost onto the shoulders of giants, teachers help prepare children to live fulfilled, engaged lives. Teaching is a particularly challenging way to make a living, undertaken by people who are deeply dedicated and truly wish to do well for the children in their charge. Faced with limited budgets, dedicated teachers regularly use their own pay to purchase supplies, books, and food for their students. As both an authority figure and a role model, a teacher has tremendous influence in a child's life.

When we write about education, we must keep in mind that teachers operate within the educational *system*, and, like all systems in our society, it is imbued with Standard Language Ideology. The focus, then, is on the system itself; when the system fails, it fails teachers and students. All of us have biases and expectations, and "standard" language ideology is by no means limited to educators. Our goal is to consider how inequality and disadvantage are perpetuated through language – for the most part unwittingly – when they emerge in the classroom and to explore ways in which these inequalities might be corrected.

There is a large body of research on the ways in which teachers' attitudes play out in the classroom. For example, Briggs and Pailliotet (1997) studied education majors who had had extensive coursework teaching writing. This coursework taught teachers to focus on writing as a creative, iterative process and to deemphasize the importance of "error correction" in that process. In this study, the education majors were asked to correct several essays, but despite their training and the framing of the task, the subjects were highly consistent in focusing on errors and attributing non-standard usage with carelessness, laziness, and incompetence. These findings supplemented Briggs' and Pailliotet's own observations on the power of language conventions and provided some insight into "how grammatical instruction remains a locus of power and control in English instruction at any level" (1997: 1). There is a crucial question without any clear answer: Most teachers are aware of the power and control they have, but how many of them realize how very influential their personal opinions are in student success? Ideology is most powerful when it is least visible; the invisibility of ideology also makes it much easier to propagate in a classroom.

Oh, bother!

A 2003 study asked non-academic professionals to evaluate 66 written sentences, each with one error (and a few with no errors, as a control). Their choices were "does not bother me," "bothers me a little," "bothers me a lot," or "no error." The researchers found that the professionals were very inconsistent and sometimes incorrect in their evaluations, and more interesting still, "while nonacademics are less bothered by usage errors, the errors that they find most bothersome are still common dialectical features" (Gray & Heuser 2003). Although the subjects had forgotten the grammatical rules they were taught in school, they retained language ideologies that denigrate undervalued varieties of English.

Language ideology in education is a multi-faceted and complex subject that cannot be addressed by means of a handful of academic studies. Instead, we focus here on two specific angles. First, we consider how children who speak stigmatized varieties of English (e.g., Appalachian English, Jamaican Patwa, Gullah, Chicanx English, Navajo English, etc.) cope or fail to cope with the implications of Standard Language Ideology. Second, we'll look at the language varieties spoken by the teachers themselves. When a teacher who grew up speaking a stigmatized variety is assigned to teach a first-grade class in their old neighborhood, what does institutional policy tell them about the kind of English they should use as the medium of instruction with those children? Do teachers in this position follow prescriptive usage rules, or do they simply use whichever language works best in reaching the children? How do they talk to children about their language? What advantages and disadvantages might there be to this?

The setting of goals

Figure 11.1 provides some insight into one of the most difficult and intractable problems in public education: there are large populations of children who do not learn to read. This

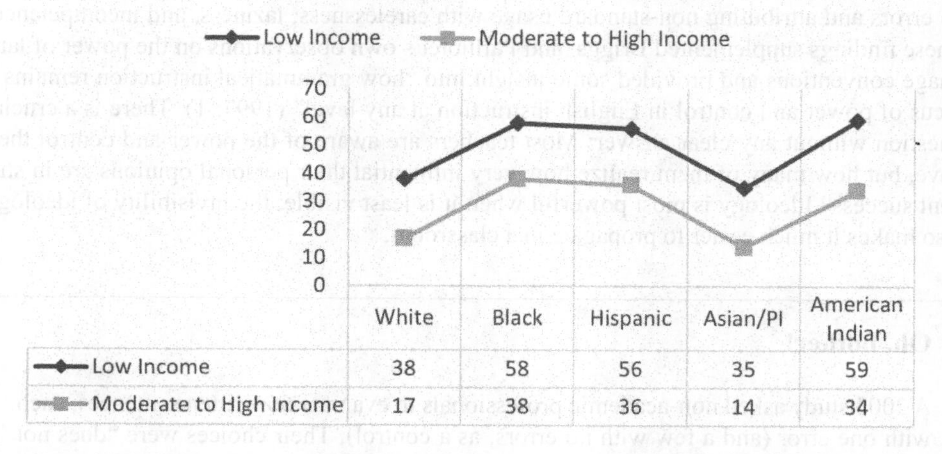

	White	Black	Hispanic	Asian/PI	American Indian
Low Income	38	58	56	35	59
Moderate to High Income	17	38	36	14	34

Figure 11.1 Percentage of fourth graders who scored less than "basic" reading skills, by race and income

Source: adapted from Fiester (2010)

disparity has been described for decades as the "reading gap." This not a new problem, but it is one that has evaded solutions. Educators, social scientists, government agencies, psychiatrists, and linguists spend a lot of time and ink trying to understand the reading gap and how to fix it. Meanwhile, whole generations of children leave school unprepared and, perhaps even worse, uninspired. A 2012 study suggests that children who do not read at grade level by the fourth grade are four times more likely to drop out of high school (Hernandez 2012). Even if a child does not end up dropping out of school, reading is the gateway to education. Math, science, social studies, technology, engineering, art, and music education all hinge critically on the student being able to read. There is even evidence that reading ability is positively correlated with empathy (Mar et al. 2009) and self-confidence (Hisken 2011).

When the subject of the reading gap comes into the public consciousness, it is almost always in connection with issues of race and ethnicity. Blame is also often attributed to bilingualism and stigmatized varieties of English; by which logic the reading gap is the fault of the linguistic backgrounds of the children who suffer because of it. One particularly insidious modern instantiation of this viewpoint is the so-called "Word Gap." According to Hart and Risley (1995, 2003), the social science researchers who perpetuated the idea in the late 1990s, the Word Gap (and subsequently the reading gap) was attributable to poor and working-class parents simply not speaking enough words to their children, as many as 30 million fewer words by age 3. This idea has been convincingly debunked by both linguists (see Baugh 2017) and educators. Sperry et al. (2019) report, after attempting to replicate the original "Word Gap" study under conditions more carefully controlling experimenter bias, the observer's paradox, and other methodological flaws:

> Not only did the Word Gap disappear, but also some poor and working-class communities showed an advantage in the number of words children heard, compared with middle-class communities. Our study also revealed a great deal of variation among communities within each socioeconomic stratum. . . . Our failure to replicate [Hart and Risley]'s findings when using their definition of the vocabulary environment raises the possibility that variation across communities within a particular social class is so great that it swamps variation across classes.
>
> (Sperry et al. 2019: 11)

Continuing to promulgate the "Word Gap" idea requires simultaneously a deep misunderstanding of how children acquire language and a willingness to use language as an excuse to blame the poor as somehow responsible for their poverty.

Word Gap?

The Word Gap argument goes something like this: "Some parents don't talk to their children enough and this causes most/all/some of the educational disparities." Like so much of Standard Language Ideology this beguiling idea is as powerfully harmful as it is simple. It allows dominant communities to feel absolved of any responsibility for low educational success among non-dominant groups because lack of success becomes their own fault. Adair et al. (2017) conducted a year-long video ethnography in two first-grade classrooms serving mostly children of Latinx immigrants. The teachers in these classrooms used dynamic teaching practices in which students "influenced and made decisions about how and what they learned in many different individual and collective ways." Children in these classes had more freedom to use their linguistic expertise and participate in learning instead of being told that they were somehow linguistically deficient. Three years later, 91% of these children passed the state assessments compared with an average of 60% passage rate for comparable children in three more standard learning environments.

To demonstrate the success of this methodology, Adair et al. produced and screened an 18-minute film demonstrating a typical day in these dynamic classrooms to 232 teachers, administrators, and first graders from schools serving a comparable immigrant population in five Texas schools in four separate districts. They found the teachers and administrators understood and approved of the practices in the film. However, because of Standard Language Ideology and the Word Gap, these professional educators were convinced that the immigrant children in their own classrooms could not benefit from such sophisticated learning experiences because they simply lacked enough vocabulary. They echoed the Word Gap myth that these children's parents didn't talk to them enough. They accepted the deficiency-based Word Gap argument despite the evidence before them and despite all their tremendous desire and efforts to help the children in their care succeed. And the children had learned the lesson of the Word Gap as well. When Adair et al. showed the same film to the first graders in these schools, they uniformly rejected the dynamic teaching practices as terrible. To learn, children need to "keep your mouth zipped, eyes watching and . . . and . . . and ears listening!", one boy interjected. The teachers in this scenario aren't to blame any more than the children are, but the Word Gap idea is dangerous to the very children it was intended to help.

The scientists who invented the Word Gap, like their eugenicist colleagues a century earlier, confused correlation with causation and bias with scientific reasoning. For the eugenicists, like famed statistician and geneticist Ronald Fischer, the mistake was believing the poor had more children than the elites because they were inherently inferior people. For Word Gap proponents, the mistake is believing that the poor speak to their children less (and the wealthy more) because the poor are somehow linguistically deficient. It also assumes that talking to children is a good measure of language acquisition, a point that was refuted in Chapter 7. Despite strong evidence that poverty is at the root of the reading gap and numerous other education challenges, the importance of poverty as a factor in educational inequality is rarely raised (but see Baugh 1999: 115 ff.). The imagined "poverty of words" has come to stand in for actual experiences of real-world poverty, deflecting attention away from the economic disparities at the root of educational inequalities.

Whose language?

In 1972, the executive committee of the Conference on College Composition and Communication, "the world's largest professional organization for researching and teaching composition, from writing to new media" (NCTE 2020) passed a statement on "Students' right to their own language." The statement was ratified by the membership in 1974 (and reaffirmed in 2003 and 2014).

> We affirm the students' right to their own patterns and varieties of language – the dialects of their nurture or whatever dialects in which they find their own identity and style. Language scholars long ago denied that the myth of a standard American dialect has any validity. The claim that any one dialect is unacceptable amounts to an attempt of one social group to exert its dominance over another. Such a claim leads to false advice for speakers and writers, and immoral advice for humans. A nation proud of its diverse heritage and its cultural and racial variety will preserve its heritage of dialects. We affirm strongly that teachers must have the experiences and training that will enable them to respect diversity and uphold the right of students to their own language.

Despite these clearly defined and articulated goals and a great many dedicated professionals who believe in the stated principles, more than 45 years have not seen much progress in terms of large-scale policies. Nevertheless, the discussion continues, and individuals have been working on ways to incorporate these goals into their research and teaching methodologies (Bruch & Marback 2005; Katz et al. 2009; Scott and National Council of Teachers of English 2009). Kinloch (2005) has taken an integrative approach, encouraging her colleagues

> [to] reimagine our educational commitments, our shared values, in ways that mobilize public and professional attitudes circulating around the education of monolingual and multilingual students. This mobilization, I believe, needs to be grounded in linguistic and cultural negotiation and not in a wrong language/right language debate.
>
> (2005: 94)

Consider that every child comes to school with a home language (sometimes more than one). They arrive fully fluent in that language. The child must now learn a series of concrete and abstract skills – reading and writing as well as an understanding of how and when different varieties are used to greatest effectiveness. But it is at this point that trouble arises. As discussed previously, many students find that their home language, the language of instruction, and the written standard are not aligned. This fact becomes painfully obvious when the teacher makes clear that the assumption of the classroom is that they are, indeed, aligned by discussing almost interchangeably the realities of all three varieties. The solid and reasonable arguments for literacy are now attached to the spoken language without discussion or pause. If Student A can learn to read and write, this mindset seems to go, then Student A can also learn to speak a different language variety. The two goals (mastering the standardized written language and replacing one spoken language with another) have different underlying motivations, and, in fact, they stand in opposition to each other. Instead of using children's expert mastery of their home language(s) to scaffold the acquisition of reading (as one might do with a French or German-speaking student arriving in an English-speaking classroom), the home language is devalued and stigmatized. For many American children, the opportunity to learn to read and write is often the first time they are told, in no uncertain terms, that something is fundamentally wrong with who they are.

What may seem minor in the first grade (reminding students to use a certain verb form) can mushroom across the curriculum into broad exclusionary practices that go beyond issues of spelling to the silencing of discourse, to the detriment of everybody (Gee 2007a [1996]: 221). This is an issue that is always close to the surface in African American communities in particular, in part because of what John Baugh has called educational malpractice stemming from educational apartheid (1999: 4). According to June Jordan (1989): "Black children in America must acquire competence in white English, for the sake of self-preservation. But you will never teach a child a new language by scorning and ridiculing and forcibly erasing his first language."

Appropriacy arguments

Professional organizations and educators often respond to the issue of language prejudice by arguing that although all dialects are equal, some varieties of English are simply "inappropriate" for the classroom. Such appropriacy arguments are typically tied to language segregation, with children being told that they should only speak their home language when they are physically at home. In addition to promoting racist views of language variation, such arguments confuse written and spoken standards. The National Council of Teachers of English (NCTE) and the International Reading Association regularly review, revise, and publish "Standards for the English Language Arts," a 12-point list which emphasizes reading and reading comprehension skills. The spoken language is mentioned only three times. A survey of language arts textbooks provides a similar picture, in which the focus is primarily the written language. In this view of education, children are potentially productive members of literacy communities rather than language communities (National Council of Teachers of English 1996: 3). Only a spoken variety that is as close as possible to the written variety is "appropriate" for use as the language of instruction. Therefore, any variety of English that is deemed to be too unlike the written standard can be targeted for culling with a ready-made but shallow set of appropriacy rationalizations as a matter of professional practice.

Tightly bound to the concept of linguistic appropriacy is that of communicative competence. Taken in its loosest form, communicatively competence refers to the ability to adjust one's language to fit specific social contexts (and the ability to recognize which contexts are associated with particular linguistic varieties). Communicative competence includes both learning the "appropriate" language to speak in the classroom and learning the "appropriate" ways to interact (such as raising your hand and waiting to be called on before speaking). In other words, communicative competence refers to the collection of indexical meanings that an individual recognizes. If communicative competence is taken as a speaker's ability to use language appropriately in social contexts, and we do not challenge the construction and implications of "appropriacy," then we have opened a back door to exclusion on the basis of another kind of "correctness" logic (see Cameron 1995: 234–235).

Appropriacy judgments cloak subjective, culturally bound judgments of "correctness." This might be made clearer by the contrast between two statements:

1. It is inappropriate for a law student to pose a question in Navajo English in the classroom.
2. It is inappropriate for a wife to contradict her husband.

While the second statement was once unremarkable, it would now evoke resounding criticism in most quarters. The first statement might still pass without comment, although the underlying issue, the silencing of voices considered unworthy or unequal, is the same. To challenge the first statement in the US educational system is to question the primacy of one language variety over all others.

At the same time, it is important to remember that ideologies and social strategies for the limitation of one language over another are not limited to one segment of the population. The following statements indicate that the concept of appropriacy has a wider and quite relevant place in the discussion of the distribution of language varieties over social space:

1. A child who is a native speaker of Navajo English may be criticized for using her home language rather than "standard" English in the classroom.
2. A child who is a native speaker of Navajo English may be criticized for speaking "school English" rather than her family's home language at the dinner table.

The varieties of English spoken in peripheralized communities persist because they are a primary way to establish solidarity and loyalty. Minority language community ideologies can be just as powerful as the ideologies and strategies of the dominant bloc institutions, and both are worthy of study. Individuals caught between competing ideologies must learn to deal with this "push-pull." As noted in Chapter 9, speakers of undervalued varieties of English are faced with a linguistic tightrope, maintaining balance between competing (and contradictory) language ideologies.

The argument put forth in support of "standard" English-only classrooms and schools generally sounds something like this:

> Student A must give up their home language in certain situations for their own good. This doesn't mean they have to give it up completely; there's no reason to deny that language. Instead, we should redirect the student's use of that language to environments and circumstances in which it is appropriate. At the same time, we should give the student another language ("standard" English) – for those situations in which it will be the only socially acceptable language. This is necessary if they are to pursue a career or education in the wider world where potential employers would otherwise reject them because of the variety of English they speak.

The NCTE guidelines for teaching the English language arts includes this very idea, but in different terms:

> All of us who speak English speak different varieties of English depending on whom we are communicating with, the circumstances involved, the purpose of the exchange, and other factors. Indeed, creative and communicative powers are enhanced when students develop and maintain multiple language competencies.
>
> Nonetheless, *some varieties of English are more useful than others* for higher education, for employment, and for participation in what the Conference on College Composition and Communication . . . in a language policy statement calls "the language of wider communication." Therefore, while we respect diversity in spoken and written English, we believe that all students should learn this language of wider communication.
>
> (National Council of Teachers of English 1996: 22–23; emphasis added)

The "appropriateness" argument is the basis for an approach to teaching "standard" English called "code-switching" (Swords & Wheeler 2006, 2010). The proponents of "code-switching" use the term only to mean *situational code-switching* (Blom & Gumperz 1972) or switching languages according to context (rather than using two languages in the same interaction). The code-switching approach is recommended for use in "urban classrooms" ("urban" serving potentially as a dog whistle indexing Blackness). The code-switching approach attempts to train children to recognize the differences between their speech and the "standard" to acquire the linguistic competence to use different varieties in different contexts. Of course, school-aged children already know how to adjust speech to contexts. The code-switching approach reduces language variation to two distinct varieties, one of which should be left at home when a child comes to school.

Teachers are directed to appreciate and respect the otherwise stigmatized languages of peripheral communities but, at the same time, reminded that those languages must be kept separate. This faux egalitarianism is well known to African Americans and others who fought for the reversal of the *separate but equal* doctrine. It is no coincidence that the "language of wider communication" is the primary language of white middle-class people. As has always been the case, the divide between socially stigmatized and socially sanctioned language runs along very predictable lines: certain vernacular varieties of US English should be restricted to the home and neighborhood, to play and informal situations, to the telling of folktales and stories of little or no interest to the wider world.

Variation in language socialization

Linguistic anthropologist Shirley Brice Heath examined patterns of language socialization in three communities in South Carolina. One community was primarily white and middle class, one was primarily African American and working class, and one was rural, white, and working class. The white middle-class homes tended to have many more books compared to the other communities. The parents in the homes socialized the children to interact with books in specific ways, typically having nightly bedtime stories where parent and child interact with the book together. During bedtime stories, parents typically ask the types of questions one might expect in a classroom context. Of course, not all parents have the resources to purchase books and spend large amounts of time with their children. Because the types of interactions and the use of books in school are based on white middle-class norms, white middle-class children will naturally find the culture of the classroom especially familiar.

With both feet firmly planted on the false assumptions of Standard Language Ideology and the literacy myth, a teacher may be adamant about the need to weed out the bad language and replace it with the good. This approach, which is mistakenly assumed to be in the best interest of the children involved, is built into the educational system at various levels (e.g., pedagogy, curricula, school rules). To give these children any chance for a better life, they must supply the children with a currency they don't have when they come to school: "standard" English, which is defined by default; it is not what these children speak. What is more destructive than this reliance on the idealized and imagined "standard," however, is the way in which these targeted varieties of English are devalued; the undefined "standard" is preferred, obligatory, appropriate, and widely used, while all other varieties of American English are narrow, inappropriate, unworthy of inclusion, and deserving of derision and ridicule. Indeed, in many cases, the push to change a child's language is part of a larger project attempting to make the child behave according to the norms of white middle-class culture.

Languagelessness

In addition to the belief that some children come to school speaking varieties of English that are "inferior," some educators go so far as to suggest that some children come to school with no language at all. This is particularly common with children who come to school speaking a language other than English. In his research in a high school in Chicago, Jonathan Rosa (2016, 2019) found that teachers often commented on the supposed "languagelessness" of students who were bilingual or were not native speakers of English. One of the teachers in Rosa's study described the bilingual *principal* of the school by saying, "Her English is horrible, and from what I hear, her Spanish isn't that good either."

The languages targeted for eradication from the classroom varies according to changing political climates. For example, during World War I, there were attacks on the use of German in the classroom. As noted in Chapter 7, US varieties of Spanish, French, and Chinese are often denigrated as "bad" or "broken" varieties. The same is true for the Englishes found in communities where other languages are spoken. The racist view that Chicanx, Puerto Rican, Dominican, and many Latinx Englishes and Spanishes are inferior creates obstacles for bilinguals. This racism is made worse by the prejudicial (and ignorant) belief that people code-switch because they cannot speak either language. In fact, most types of code-switching require fluency in two languages.

This view of languageless Latinxs aligns with racist stereotypes of Latinx people as backward, ignorant, and incapable of assimilating to broader American culture. The racist nature of these ideologies is reflected in this quote from a Massachusetts teacher discussing her Puerto Rican students:

> These poor kids come to school speaking a hodgepodge. They are all mixed up and don't know any language well. As a result, they can't even think clearly. That's why they don't learn. It's our job to teach them language – to make up for their deficiency. And, since their parents don't really know any language either, why should we waste time on Spanish? It is "good" English which has to be the focus.
>
> (Zentella 1997: 8–9)

This focus on "good" English erases students' home language and treats being bilingual as a problem that must be resolved. Indeed, the principal at the high school where Rosa conducted his research actually equated being "bilingual" with an inability to speak English: "They're bilingual. That means they don't know the language. The other ones just don't want to speak it" (Rosa 2019: 128). Of course, being bilingual means a person can speak two languages. The principal's attitude takes a bilingual's verbal skills and redefines them as part of a language deficit.

Perceiving emotion

Amy Halberstadt and her colleagues performed a study to see if race played a role in the ways that teachers interpreted children's emotional states (2018). Students in teacher training programs were shown images of children with facial expressions conveying a particular emotion (like in Figure 11.2). The future teachers were asked to note the emotion associated with the child's facial expressions. The researchers focused on the

Figure 11.2 How do we recognize a child's emotional states? Our judgments are often filtered through stereotyped assumptions about expected behaviors associated with the child's ethnic background

cases in which the subjects made mistakes and picked the wrong emotion. They found that, compared to white faces, the faces of Black children were more likely to be mistakenly marked as expressing anger. This effect was true for both Black girls and boys, but the pattern was especially strong when the face belonged to a Black boy. In other words, the mistakes demonstrated that the future teachers were prone to assuming that Black children (and Black boys in particular) are angry or hostile. Of course, this sort of bias ultimately results in different and unequal treatment of Black children.

Such attitudes impede learning and create additional obstacles for children who come to school speaking in a way that teachers neither respect nor recognize as language. Just as with any form of racism, Standard Language Ideology causes psychological damage to its victims, children who are reminded of their supposed inferiority every time they speak. As with other "deficit" explanations for social differences, the view of children as languageless allows educators to blame the children themselves for the failures of the educational system; the children don't learn "standard" English because they simply have no language at all or because they are lazy and "just don't want to speak it." Trying to keep a child's language out of school only increases the odds that the child will eventually leave school as well.

April Baker-Bell (2020) has called the prescriptive ideologies that dominate American classroom *anti-Black linguistic racism*. In working with African American students in Detroit, Baker-Bell found that her students had internalized racist attitudes toward their own ways of speaking, so she developed a pedagogical approach that incorporated lessons involving texts that use forms of Black language in order to shift the focus of lesson from using "proper" English to learning ways to analyze and interpret texts. Using works like lyrics from Tupac Shakur or novels like *The Hate U Give*, students learn literacy and rhetorical skills without implying that the language students speak is somehow inferior.

Education as cultural assimilation

One important aspect of elementary education in the United States involves teaching children to behave in ways that adhere to a specific set of cultural norms. This is often discussed in terms of instilling children with "citizenship" by training them to interact with others in specific ways: learning to wait your turn, not interrupting authority figures, keeping the volume of your speech within a specific range, and so on. Because these expectations for student behavior are based on middle-class white norms, some children will be familiar with those expectations before entering school. For others, however, being required to interact in unfamiliar ways is a form of forced cultural assimilation.

A child's learning begins long before they enter school so that children come to school with specific ideas about what learning entails and how it happens. There are many ways for a child to learn, and different approaches to learning vary widely across cultures. In her study of language socialization in three small towns in South Carolina, Shirley Brice Heath (1983) found that patterns of learning were quite different across communities. For example, the most common type of question used by African American parents was "analogy" questions (*What is that like? What does that remind you of?*). Analogy questions promote learning by encouraging children to make connections between their varied experiences in new and creative ways. However, in US elementary schools, analogy questions are quite rare. In contrast, the most common questions for middle-class white parents were questions that ask the child to provide an answer that is already known to the adult. An example of this sort of question would be pointing to a picture of a dog and asking the child, "What is that?" and expecting the child to say "dog." These questions do not emphasize new ways of thinking, but simply test whether the child has retained some piece of information.

Of course, these information-seeking questions are the most common form of questions used in classroom context. Such questions are the basis for the much of the testing that occurs in school, where the students are expected to demonstrate their knowledge by repeating back the information the teacher has given them. Thus, before entering school, white middle-class children are already primed for repeating back information in the way teachers usually expect. For children used to analogy questions, repeating back known information may be unfamiliar and unnatural: *Why do you want me to tell you something we both already know?* Responses expected for analogy questions are likely to be judged as simply "wrong." For example, if a child were shown a picture of a leopard and asked *What's this?*, an analogical answer (*It's like a tiger*) would not usually be recognized as a "correct" answer.

For children familiar with different cultural approaches to learning, the structure of classroom interactions can create an additional barrier to learning. This has been a persistent issue in the education of deaf children (as discussed in Chapter 8) and Native American children. As noted in Chapter 7, for almost a century, Native American children were taken from their homes and sent to boarding schools (see Figure 11.3) where they could learn English

Figure 11.3 In 1884, the Carlisle (Pennsylvania) Indian School had 375 students

Source: image from Cumberland County Historical Society and Carlisle Indian School Digital Resource Center

and become "civilized." The children were sent to boarding schools so that they could not be influenced by their parents or other members of their family. In addition to attempting to eradicate Native American languages, these schools forced children to "learn" in ways that were culturally unfamiliar and were counter to the ways they were used to interacting before they were sent to school.

Terrorizing Native American children

Pulling Native American children out of their communities not only denied them exposure to their own cultures; it also exposed them to new diseases and severe forms of corporal punishment. The children were kept in crowded quarters where diseases could spread easily. It is estimated than around 200 children died in the years the school operated (1879–1918). Among the dead were three Arapaho boys who were brought to the school in 1881. The school had its own cemetery to accommodate the children who died there. In 2016, the families of the three Arapaho boys petitioned to have the boys' remains returned to the Arapaho community. In 2017, the boys' remains were returned to the tribe for proper burial on Arapaho lands (Wenson 2017).

Although the boarding schools are now history, the role of schools in pushing children toward cultural assimilation continues. Consider, for example, the cultural norms associated with silence in Apache culture. As discussed in Chapter 6, it is usual for people who have just met to remain silent until they have gotten used to being around one another and have a sense of what the other person is like. Traditional Apache ways of teaching involve cultivating a learner's engagement with some aspect of their immediate environment. This may involve telling a story that uses some element of the current situation metaphorically. It may also mean that the teacher and learner sit together and remain silent. However, it does *not* involve lecturing or reprimanding children who are trying to learn.

In her work with Apache language revitalization efforts, Marybeth Nevins (2013) observed numerous examples demonstrating this approach to learning. For example, when Nevins asked a group of Apache women what the best way to learn the language would be, the women replied by saying that the best way to learn Apache would be to make bread. The reasoning is that in baking bread, Nevins would participate in a common activity where speakers used the language all around her. The process of baking produces the sort of interactional context conducive to learning Apache in a natural way. Of course, formal classroom teaching is typically quite different, with silence expected only from the children and only until they are called upon to speak (in which case failure to do so results in public embarrassment). Indeed, the "standard" American approach to education is often founded upon instilling children with fear; they will learn to avoid the public shaming associated with not knowing the answer when called upon. This approach differs drastically from the Apache approach of creating a context for learning one that is comfortable and natural.

In a study of education on the Warm Springs Reservation in Oregon, Susan Philips (1993) found a similar pattern. Philips found that the children were used to learning largely through observation. A child would observe an adult performing a task and then practice some small part of that task on their own before returning to the adult for advice about how to improve what they have done. Philips found that different types of classroom participation structures produced very different reactions from students. For example, the Warm Springs children rarely participated in contexts where the teacher would address the class, asking questions to individuals or to the class. In contexts where the teacher worked with a small group of students, such as to practice reading, the children refused to talk at all. The students' responses were best in cases where they worked alone and the teacher was available for help. Of course, this is the participation structure that would be most familiar to the students.

The teachers in Warm Springs did not recognize that the problem was due to different expectations for learning. Rather, they attributed the lack of participation to the children's natural "shyness." In cases where different cultural expectations lead to different ways of interacting, it is quite common for members of the dominant culture to interpret those differences in terms of stereotypes based on the presumed race of their interlocutor. This occurs for children entering school with different understandings of how learning occurs. Their behavior is often seen as a basic part of the child's personality, usually based on racial stereotypes (even if unconsciously). Native American and Asian children may be assumed to be naturally shy and quiet. African American and Latinx children may be stereotyped as being loud and angry. As we have seen so many other times, this is another example of blaming the child for the results of discourse structural racism. Children end up being written off as incapable of engaging in classroom culture, whether it is because they are wrongly perceived as being too shy, too loud, too disruptive, too lazy, too angry, too quiet, or simply unable to use any language properly.

Indexical bleaching is another aspect of cultural assimilation commonly found in educational contexts (Bucholtz 2016). As discussed in Chapter 7, boarding schools regularly gave Native American children new "English" names to use at school. Similarly, it was common for immigrant children to be given "American" names when they began school (see

Figure 11.4 April Lou, a teacher at PS 1 in New York with six immigrant children from Hong Kong and Taiwan. The children are holding up signs with their original name and the English name they were given for use in official school records

Source: photo by Fred Palumbo, *World Telegram & Sun*, Library of Congress

Figure 11.4). As discussed in Chapter 4, names continue to trigger forms of discrimination; identical schoolwork consistently receives lower grades when the student's name is associated with a minority group.

Zhao and Biernat (2017) tested what would happen if both names were linked to the same person by focusing on international graduate students. In higher education, international students continue to face pressure to adopt names that sound more "American." Zhao and Biernat sent out email messages to professors who were looking for graduate student researchers. All of the messages were from a student named *Xian Zhao* who openly identified as Chinese and requested a meeting with the professor to discuss their research program. Half of the messages contained the phrase *My name is Xian Zhao, you can just call me Xian* while the other half said *My name is Xian Zhao, but you can call me by my English name Alex*. The "Alex" messages were signed *Alex (Xian)* and were sent from an email account listed as belonging to Alex Zhao (rather than Xian Zhao). Even though "Alex" was clearly Chinese, the Alex messages were more likely to receive replies compared to the Xian messages. The authors of the study conclude that having an "American" name indexes a willingness to assimilate to American culture. In other words, the professors preferred students they believed to be more open to cultural assimilation. This bias demonstrates the importance of cultural assimilation in educational settings.

People expect education to mold children into good moral citizens. But this seems to presume a uniform cultural ideology of which behaviors are acceptable and which are likely to be sanctioned. It also presumes a single approach to learning, even if that approach is unnatural and alien to a subset of students. For such students, the classroom is a crucible of cultural assimilation: they must interact in new ways that reflect the norms of the dominant culture, their language is banned from the classroom, they must communicate in a language that they have never been explicitly taught, and the curriculum is overwhelming based on the culture and history of the dominant group. Efforts to create a multicultural curriculum help a great deal, but sanctions on language and interaction continue to make the classroom an unwelcoming place for too many students.

Ignoring Chicanx histories

In 1968, Chicanx high school students in East Los Angeles began a series of walkouts to protest the quality of education in their schools (see Figure 11.5). The school curriculum did not contain any material related to Chicanx history and few of the teachers spoke Spanish. Among the student demands were the introduction of bilingual education, teaching the students "standard" Spanish, and incorporating Chicanx topics into the curriculum. School funding was based on the number of students attending school each day. Roll was taken every afternoon in home room to produce the student count for the purposes of funding. The organizers of the Chicanx walkout had students leave

Figure 11.5 Pickets out front of Los Angeles Police headquarters protesting arrest of Mexican American student leaders, 1968

Source: *Los Angeles Times* Photographic Archive, UCLA Library

school immediately before home room so that they could not be counted, undermining the school funding process. It is estimated that some 20,000 students from different schools participated in the walkouts. Several of the organizers were arrested and were only released after further protest. The walkouts resulted in major changes in the Los Angeles school system and began an important era in the Chicanx civil rights movement (García & Castro 2011).

How teachers talk

Teachers are expected to speak the imaginary "standard" English. Each state has a complex administrative body which is responsible for reviewing and licensing teachers, and each publishes those guidelines openly. The guidelines for California, Michigan, New Mexico, and New York, for example, all have similar expectations for teachers to be speakers of "proper" English. For example, the New Mexico guidelines for evaluating teacher performance includes "grammar and vocabulary may be incorrect" as a marker of "unsatisfactory" teacher performance (Patterson 2019: 79).

Parents who encounter teachers with "accented" English are often afraid that their children will adopt the accent of their teacher. In linguistic terms, this fear has no foundation. Children learn the phonology of their language first from their families and then from their peers, a process that is largely stabilized by the time children enter school. Phonetics and phonology cannot pass from adult to children like viruses. A teacher helps students expand their vocabulary and stylistic repertoire, but these are additions to the basic grammar of language, which is well-established by age 6. By this age, children imitate their peers (other children) rather than parents or teachers. Other than possibly expanding their ability to understand accented speech (see later in this chapter), a teacher's accent in English has no real effect on their students' language abilities.

In 2002, after passage of the No Child Left Behind act, the state of Arizona began monitoring the speech of classroom teachers to ensure that all teachers were "fluent" in English. Teachers who spoke Spanish or used Spanish classroom materials were reported for breaking the state's "English Only" law, which prohibited the use of other languages by the state government. Monitoring teachers was part of a larger anti-immigrant movement in Arizona that specifically attacked Latinxs. Most of the teachers who were reported for "heavy accents" or "bad grammar" were teachers working in bilingual education classrooms. Students in bilingual classrooms had low scores on standardized tests, and Arizona state officials argued that the gap resulted from teachers who were not fluent in English or who used Spanish in the classroom. This, of course, is a highly unlikely explanation for the gap in test scores. Anyone unable to speak, read, and write in English would not be able to obtain teacher certification or make it through a job interview for a teaching position. Equally implausible is the idea that the children weren't learning English because their teachers occasionally used Spanish in the classroom. A much more likely explanation is that the "English Only" policy results in children being taught content (like math or science) in a language they do not speak. These "English Only" policies rob children of the educational foundation needed to do well on standardized tests. Attempting to eradicate Spanish from the classroom has the same effect as trying to force children to speak "standard" English (without teaching them this second dialect). It does little more than alienate and marginalize minority children.

The *Arizona Republic* newspaper reviewed the complaints filed against teachers in 2007. The examples of "heavy accents" resulting in teacher sanctions were largely features of Chicanx English. For example, teachers were reported for things like saying *lebel* instead of *level* and saying *mush* instead of *much.* Both "errors" are regular, predictable patterns found in Chicanx English. Spanish does not distinguish between the speech sounds /b/ and /v/. Although Spanish writing makes the distinction, these two sounds have long been merged in the spoken language with both pronounced with the sound /β/, which is a fricative like [v] but made with both lips like [b]. This merger between consonants has been borrowed into several English varieties used in Latinx communities. Similarly, the [ʃ] sound represented in English by the digraph "sh" does not occur in Spanish, so some speakers of Chicanx English substitute [ʃ] with [tʃ] (the sound represented in English by the digraph "ch").

Other examples of "bad grammar" were also regular patterns in Chicanx English. One teacher, for example, was reported for saying *What do we call it in English?* rather than *How do you say it in English?* The idea that this "error" reflects an inability to speak English is ludicrous. It would stand to reason that teachers who are able to speak the languages of their students would be more capable when it comes to communicating with these same students. Nevertheless, just as with students, teachers who use undervalued language varieties in the classroom are seen as unqualified and face language-based discrimination. None of the teachers reported for using Spanish or speaking "bad English" were fired, although some were transferred out of classrooms with English learners. Otherwise, teachers were reprimanded and highly encouraged to attend free English classes. Of course, this meant that teachers who were native speakers of English had to take courses on English as a second language to "learn" the language they have spoken their entire lives, just like the bilinguals discussed in Chapter 7. The results of teacher monitoring did nothing to help Arizona children who were learning English. The primary result was the discriminatory treatment, denigration, and humiliation of Latinx teachers.

According to federal guidelines, it is against the law to discriminate against non-native speakers of English because their English is "accented." For speakers of English as a second language (L2), accent discrimination is considered a form of discrimination based on national origin. In 2010, federal officials informed the Arizona government that the practice of monitoring teachers for "fluency" in English likely violated the 1964 Civil Rights Act for discriminating against Latinx and immigrant teachers. Working with the Departments of Justice and Education, Arizona officials rewrote their language policy so that it did not assess teachers based on "fluency." To comply with federal law, Arizona officials changed their policy so that local school districts were required to report on the fluency of their teachers. While the state policy was changed, Latinx teachers could still be subjected to language-based discrimination at the local level (Kossan 2011).

How graduate students talk

The resistance to teachers with unfamiliar accents is perhaps strongest in university settings. Most large research universities with graduate programs employ graduate students to teach, or assist in teaching, introductory courses in their areas of expertise and scholarship. This is an important part of training future professors and an economic necessity in larger universities. Many of these graduate students come from outside the United States and speak English as a second language. All universities have policies in place to ensure that graduate student instructors and teaching assistants have sufficient English fluency to effectively teach. Even so, students often complain about having to take courses from instructors with accented speech. Although universities recognize the importance of screening and training non-native speakers of English with teaching responsibilities, there is no parallel recognition of the need to educate undergraduates to discern between real communicative difficulties and those stemming not from language but from stereotype and bias.

The impact of student evaluations

In college, student evaluations play an important role in job security and salary determination. Evaluations continue to be widely used despite widespread evidence that they are fraught with bias (Heffernan 2022). As student evaluations are private school records, several researchers have analyzed evaluations posted on the RateMyProfessors.com website. Although the website data is somewhat outdated (the popularity of the site has greatly declined in recent years), it is the largest database of the language used in student evaluations. In comparing instructors with English-sounding names to those with Chinese or Korean-sounding names, Subtirelu (2015) found that (presumably) Asian instructors were much more likely to have comments focusing on their language, with words like *accent, understand,* and *English* all being significantly more frequent in evaluations of Asian-named instructors. In contrast, words that were more common in the evaluations of those with English-sounding names included *amazing, fun,* and *interesting*.

Evaluations are also known to contain widespread gender bias. In comparing evaluations of instructors with typically male names against typically female names, one can also see differences in the frequency with which particular words are used to describe instructors. Historian Ben Schmidt created a website that allows people to compare the frequency of different words according to gender and academic discipline. For example, words like *intellect, genius,* and *smart* are much more likely to be used in evaluations of (presumably) male professors. In contrast, female professors were more likely to be described using words like *bossy, strict, frumpy,* and *stylish.* Students evaluate professors of different genders and ethnicities according to different expectations based on social stereotypes.

Nicholas Subtirelu (2015) examined comments about instructors with Korean and Chinese-sounding names on the RateMyProfessors.com website. He found that, as a group, instructors with Korean or Chinese names received lower scores for both clarity and helpfulness. Instructors with Asian names were also less likely to be described with positive adjectives like *interesting* or *wonderful.* In a qualitative analysis of the comments, Subtirelu also found that negative evaluations of accents often assumed that the communicative burden falls entirely onto the non-native speaker in the interaction. In Chapter 4 we discussed the importance of sharing the communicative burden in producing successful communication. Often, native speakers of English fail to share any part of the communicative burden when interacting with someone they perceive as having a "foreign" accent. In looking at comments on the RateMyProfessors.com website, Subtirelu found that students often made comments absolving themselves from bearing any part of the communicative burden. Comments like *can't understand a word she says* or *don't take his course unless you speak Korean* suggest that there is no point in exerting any effort in trying to understand their instructor. Thus, while the issue involves two distinct problems, only one of those problems is addressed in trying to resolve the issue (see Table 11.1).

There is a growing body of research considering an individual's ability to distinguish between accents and make fair assessments of English proficiency (Baese-Berk et al. 2020). This work makes it clear that achieving success in communication between native and non-native speakers is far more complicated than one might assume.

Understanding speech is not a passive activity, and some people do it more accurately than others. The range of languages a listener knows or has studied, the range of dialects and varieties of these languages, phonological proficiency (flexibility hearing speech sounds), and even language attitudes have all been shown to play a role in predicting perceptual accuracy. Bent and Bradlow (2003) asked participants with different language backgrounds to transcribe sentences spoken by a mixture of native English and non-native Mandarin and Korean-accented speech. Their results demonstrate an "interlanguage speech intelligibility benefit" in which the non-native English speakers transcribed accented English more accurately than the native English speakers. This was true not only for participants who spoke Mandarin or Korean, whose language experience matched that of the talker, but for participants from other language backgrounds as well. Bent and Bradlow also found this benefit for non-native listeners who spoke a *different* first language than the talker in the experiment. Non-native listeners transcribed non-native and native speech with equal accuracy while native English listeners had more difficulty with the non-native speech.

In a similar study, native listeners of Cantonese, Japanese, Mandarin, and English listened to English spoken by native speakers of Cantonese, Japanese, Polish, and Spanish. These participants listened to the same set of recordings and, despite the differences in their native language experiences, tended to agree about which speakers were most or least intelligible (Munro et al. 2006). As in the Bent and Bradlow study noted earlier, native Japanese listeners in the study were slightly better able to understand Japanese-accented English, but Cantonese listeners show no such benefit for Cantonese-accented speech. Munro and his colleagues argue that this finding, along with similar discoveries since, suggests that both the properties of the speech itself and the native background of the talker are important factors in influencing how accurately accented speech is perceived. Although the properties of the speech itself and assumptions about a speaker's backgrounds are important, the deciding factor (particularly for native listeners) in producing successful communication may well be the language attitudes of the listener.

Attitudes can predict how well participants think an interaction went, independent of how successfully they actually communicated. Lindemann (2003) asked native English and

Table 11.1 Language conflict in the university classroom

Problem	*Proposed solution*
Graduate student speakers of English as a second language have special hurdles to deal with to become effective classroom teachers	Increased and more diligent screening and training of non-native English-speaking graduate student teachers
Undergraduates have stereotypes and biases which, if not put aside, interfere with a potentially positive and valuable learning opportunity	None

Korean-speaking students to collaborate on a task that required them to give each other directions from partial maps. Participants' ratings of the interaction were largely predicted by the native English-speaking students' attitudes toward Koreans. In her study, Lindemann found that participants with negative attitudes toward Koreans used interactional avoidance strategies that impeded the success of the interaction, such as failing to provide feedback or to ask questions even when there were obvious misunderstandings. This use of avoidance strategies reflects the language ideology expressed by students who make no effort to understand or communicate with instructors who are not native speakers of English.

Rubin and Smith (1990) found that native English-speaking students were not always able to distinguish between different levels of accentedness. Rather than reflecting actual levels of a teacher's accent, teacher ratings correlated with a student's *perceptions* of accent. Thus, if a student assessed an instructor with a very slight Cantonese accent as highly accented, the student also found that person to be a poor teacher. In another study that drew a great deal of attention, Rubin (1992) tested how perceptions of accent were tied to student attitudes and learning experiences. Undergraduate native speakers of English listened to a brief recording of a lecture on an introductory topic. While listening, the student saw a photograph meant to represent the instructor they were hearing. Both recordings heard were made by the same speaker (a native speaker of English from central Ohio), but there were two different projected photographs: half of the students saw a slide of a woman who appeared to be white, while the other half saw a woman who appeared to be Asian (the photographed women were otherwise dressed and styled similarly). After listening to the lecture, each student completed a test of listening comprehension and memory recall. Students were asked to rate the instructor's accent ("speaks with an American accent, speaks with an Asian accent"), ethnicity, and quality of teaching. Figure 11.6 show students' perceptions based on the slides they looked

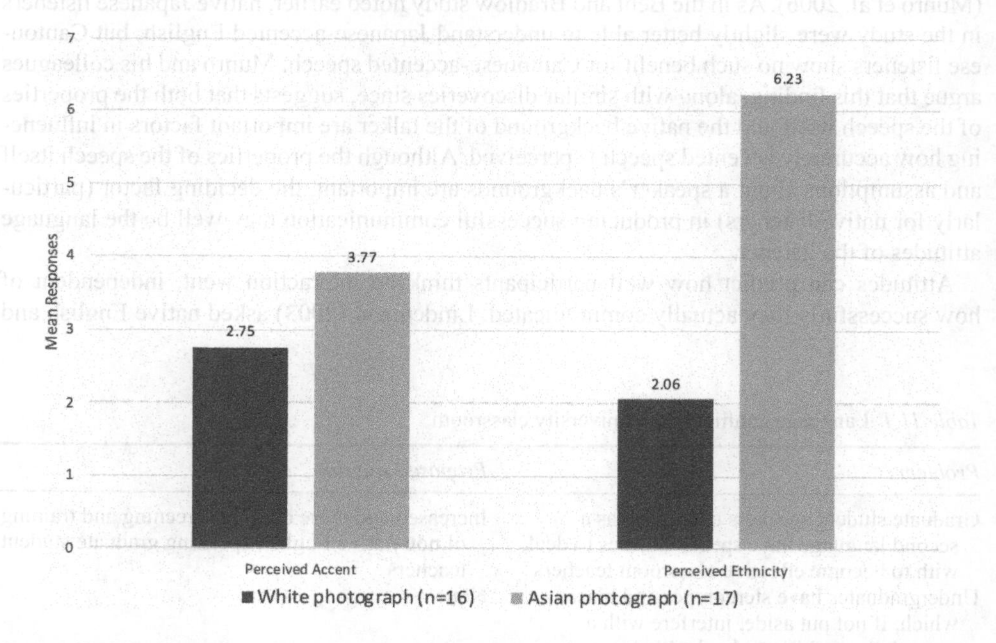

Figure 11.6 Student evaluation of lecturer's ethnicity and accent based on a recorded science lecture

Source: Rubin (1992: 516, Table 1)

at. These figures indicate that perceived ethnicity (based on the photographs) was a significant factor in student evaluations. The students who were shown the Asian face evaluated the same recordings as having more of an accent. One possible interpretation of these results suggests that some students who saw an Asian face were biased – incapable of hearing objectively. It can be stated with absolute certainty that the prerecorded language they listened to was native, Ohio-accented English. However, students looking at an Asian face were sometimes convinced that they heard a non-native accent. The students' negative preconceptions regarding Asians are clearly at work in accentedness ratings.

Overall, students remembered less of the lecture when they believed that the lecturer was Asian. When shown an Asian face, students were less able to retain the information they heard. The experiment was conducted with a lecture on a science topic and a lecture on a humanities topic. The decrease in scores associated with the Asian face was greater for the science lecture. Although it would be unwise to make broad generalizations from a single humanities lecture and a single science lecture, the study suggests that this effect might be stronger for Asian professors and graduate student instructors in STEM fields than for those in the humanities.

The actual mechanism by which a student's expectations lead to a communicative breakdown is not certain from the Rubin study alone. One possibility, endorsed by Rubin and previous editions of this book, is that listeners in this study see the Asian face, shirk their role in the communicative burden, and then simply pay less attention. This would explain both why participants report hearing a non-native accent that does not exist and why they tended to remember the words of the lecture less well. Rubin and colleagues have since named this effect Reverse Linguistic Stereotyping (Kang & Rubin 2009). The assumption behind this name is that listeners stereotype Asian speakers as "foreign" and subsequently hear an accent that does not actually exist.

However, it is equally possible, given the design and results of this and related studies, that when listeners are shown an Asian face of a graduate student instructor in an experimental context, they quite reasonably infer that this speaker may speak foreign-accented English. When this visual and social information is paired with central Ohio-accented English, the pairing is incongruous. At a social level, the participants believe the experimenters that the face provides reliable information about the identity of the talker, but at the level of speech perception – at the level where listening and comprehension occur – this social belief conflicts with the large amount of social information present in the voice (McGowan 2015, 2016; Babel & Russell 2015). A similar mismatch effect has been observed for Quechua/Spanish bilingual listeners in Bolivia when social information was provided in the instructions rather than visual cues (McGowan & Babel 2020). This incongruity hypothesis suggests that the problem results from a mismatch between listeners' expectations and the voice they are hearing.

To test this incongruity hypothesis, McGowan (2015) performed an inverted version of the Rubin (1992) listening experiment. Instead of playing native-accented American English paired with white and Asian faces, McGowan played Chinese-accented English. Listeners were instructed to look at the photograph of the speaker, listen carefully to Chinese-accented speech embedded in noise, and transcribe the sentence as accurately as possible. If Rubin's interpretation that listeners simply pay less attention because they've been shown an Asian face is correct, then the pattern of results should be identical regardless of whether listeners are hearing Ohio-accented or Chinese-accented speech.

McGowan's 2015 results are shown in Figure 11.7. Listeners in the "Chinese face" condition were significantly more accurate at transcribing Chinese-accented speech than listeners in the white face condition. This improvement was true regardless of experience level with Chinese-accented English. Listeners with more experience listening to Chinese-accented English did better on the task overall. In fact, this experiment also included a control condition where a third group of listeners heard the same voice as in the two experimental conditions but were shown only a rudimentary silhouette as the "face" of their talker. These results are displayed in the central column in Figure 11.7. It seems clear from these results that listeners in the Asian face condition were most accurate, listeners in the control condition were less accurate, and listeners in the "mismatched" white face + Chinese-accented English condition were the least accurate. Given that listeners generally performed well, and everyone performed *best* when Chinese-accented English was combined with a Chinese face, Rubin's interpretation that listeners simply shirk their part of the communicative burden and pay less attention when shown an Asian face simply cannot be correct.

So what can be learned from this thread of experimental research? Both studies suggest that whether an instructor needs further training in English may be irrelevant. The proposed rationale typically given for the rejection of instructors with foreign accents in teaching should be carefully examined. This rejection of non-native speakers presumes the following formula:

ACCENT → COMMUNICATIVE BREAKDOWN → POOR LEARNING EXPERIENCE

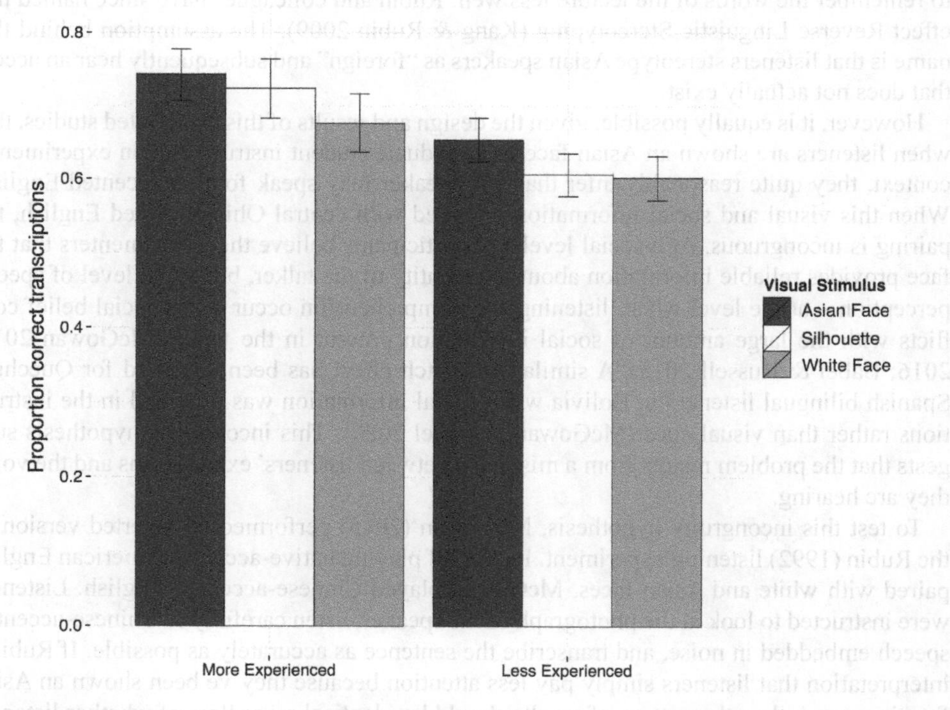

Figure 11.7 Proportion accuracy transcribing Chinese-accented speech when shown a Chinese face, silhouette, or white face for listeners with More and Less experience listening to Mandarin-accented English

Source: adapted from McGowan (2015)

Regardless of whether they are based on visual cues or emerge from bias, student expectations can have the dramatic effect on perception shown in both Rubin's and McGowan's studies. The mere *expectation* of hearing an accent may be enough to shift the communicative burden entirely from the student to the teacher. In this case, the formula takes on another dimension:

> INSTRUCTOR'S PERCEIVED ACCENT → STUDENTS' EXPECTATIONS → COMMUNICATIVE BREAKDOWN → POOR CLASSROOM EXPERIENCE

A second observation that can be taken from this pair of studies is that scientists are subject to the same biases and language ideologies as non-scientists. It seems clear that Rubin, in designing the matched guise study that paired different faces with a "Standard American English" voice is forgetting that an Ohio-accented voice carries just as much social information as a Chinese-accented (or any other accented) voice. Everyone has an accent, even people who speak the imagined standard. Pairing a face intended to lead listeners to expect foreign-accented English with a voice that is clearly not foreign-accented creates a mismatch effect. The effect of this is undone when McGowan pairs an Asian face with a genuinely Chinese-accented voice. Rubin and other researchers are making the same mistake discussed in the first half of this chapter when educators, administrators, and even parents argue that "Standard American English" is the only logical medium of instruction for the K-12 classroom. There can be no such concrete thing as "Standard American English" because there is no such thing as a linguistic variety that is devoid of social information. Children know this long before they come to school; college students know this and use this knowledge in their daily lives. When people open their mouths to speak, they reveal to the world not only what they think but who they are and where they come from. To devalue these "accented" voices is to devalue the real, living human beings who have them.

What Rubin does not get wrong, and what McGowan's study only reinforces, is that student complaints about instructor accentedness are usually about power and bias, not about language. Of course, sometimes unfamiliar accents really do make communication more difficult. It is possible that a true communicative breakdown may cause difficulties between a non-native speaker of English and a student. One important difference remains, though. A student new to the lecture hall has no way of knowing whether the person teaching the course is going to be a good communicator and dedicated teacher, and the native language of the instructor should be irrelevant to these questions. Native speakers of English are usually given the benefit of the doubt; some turn out to be good teachers and others do not. However, non-native speakers of English – especially speakers of non-European languages – may never be given a chance to show their excellence. Instead, they are predetermined to be "bad" teachers purely based on students' stereotyped expectations of "bad" English.

While universities and colleges across the country are trying hard to deal with the complicated issue of graduate student instructors who are not native speakers of English, it seems that policies to address the question of quality of classroom instruction must take a broader view. Foreign students need help in acclimating to a very different academic and social culture in a variety of matters. Language is of primary importance and deserves careful attention. In addition to the training of the foreign students, it is vitally important that native English-speaking students (and teachers) be similarly educated about matters of language and communication – both in and out of the classroom. People should be taught to take a reasonable amount of responsibility for their portion of the communicative burden and for their contributions to a successful educational experience.

What the science tells us

Arguments for the selection of one linguistic variety as somehow better or uniformly more useful than any other are circular arguments with no basis in the available evidence regarding how language works and how people learn. The insistence of a single "standard" as the best possible language variety for educational contexts does little more that create an additional burden for the least-privileged students and exclude potentially wonderful teachers from acceptance in the mainstream classroom. Educators have an incredibly difficult job. People want educators to provide children with a great variety of skills, from reading and writing to job training. Furthermore, people entrust them with teaching children the basics of good citizenship and responsible behavior as social beings; they are charged with occupying, entertaining, and teaching the next generation to think. On top of all these expectations, the teacher is asked to do the impossible and provide children that mythical unicorn of perfect spoken language called "standard" English, an imaginary language which is not only grammatically homogenous and accentless, but somehow has the power to eradicate racism, sexism, and many other forms of bias.

Expectations and biases can guide perceptions of foreign-accentedness even more than the accentedness of the voices themselves. Dedicated researchers in the study of language and education are themselves not immune to the effects of the Standard Language Ideology. There will always be a need for more carefully designed studies to fully understand not only what is wrong with debunked ideas like the Word Gap hypothesis of "standard" English but also to understand the social and psychological factors that make such bad ideas attractive to highly educated individuals.

Where does all the science leave us? Are people to allow, and even to encourage, the use of non-standard varieties of English in the classroom? Should college students be told to work harder as listeners when their instructor has an unfamiliar accent and to be aware that some of the difficulty they really, genuinely, are experiencing in understanding these instructors may be attributable to their biases and expectations and not to the instructor's accent? In a word, yes. Research has shown, in fact, that experience listening to different accents leaves the listener not only better able to understand the accents they have heard, but better able to understand any novel accents they might encounter as well. Baese-Berk et al. (2013) asked participants to listen to recordings of talkers from five language backgrounds. After this experience, these listeners could better understand talkers from both these and additional, unfamiliar accents. This learning suggests that exposure to foreign-accented speech prepares the student to be a generally more capable listener.

The primacy of "standard" English in the classroom appeals to habitual thought but does not stand up to rigorous reflection. The ideology of "standard" English limits the number of Americans who can benefit from education at all levels. It also limits the teachers who can provide the benefit of their experiences and professional standards. Education is intended to broaden the base of people who can participate in the American democracy, not limit it. Education is intended to broaden the experiences and thinking of the students participating in it, not limit them. Insistence upon "standard" English in the classroom fails all these tests.

Discussion questions

1. Write your own linguistic history. Where did your influences come from? What ideologies were you exposed to? Which did you accept and to what degree? Have you studied any world languages? Do you feel as though you could survive in a country where that language is spoken? What would it take?

2. Do you have any memories of being corrected for the way you said something? Who did the correcting? What reason was given, and how did you react?
3. Describe your own experiences in school. Were there speakers of stigmatized varieties of English in your classroom? Were you one of those speakers? How did perceptions make things easier or harder for them (or you)?
4. Search online in communities that discuss education and look for terms such as "standard English," "non-standard English," "dialect," "grammar," and "ugly." Was it easy or hard to find discussions of the issues covered in this chapter? What trends (if any) did you come across?
5. Interview a friend who has never taken a linguistics class. Ask that person for definitions of "standard" and "non-standard" English and be sure to ask for examples. Don't give away your thoughts or reactions, just record what your informant has to say, no matter how much you agree or disagree. Compare your findings with others in the class.
6. Consider this from the chapter:

   INSTRUCTOR'S PERCEIVED ACCENT → STUDENTS' EXPECTATIONS → COMMUNICATIVE BREAKDOWN → POOR CLASSROOM EXPERIENCE

   How accurate do you think this is? What might be missing?
7. Write a short list of guidelines you might go over with a biology class where all of the teaching assistants are non-native speakers of English. How can the students contribute to making communication work? Are there concrete steps to take when communication breaks down?
8. Interview a graduate teaching assistant or a professor or instructor who speaks English with an accent that contrasts with the average person on campus (e.g., someone with a Texas accent teaching in northern California, someone whose first language is Japanese teaching in Cincinnati). Ask what experiences they have had because of accent: positive, negative, neutral?

12 Language use, media stereotypes, and fake news

Storytellers, Inc.

Imagine the cry of a bald eagle (see Figure 12.1). Try to see, in your mind's eye, this majestic bird soaring on its seven foot wingspan and to hear, in your mind's ear, the noise it makes to warn a rival or to lure a mate. Chances are, if you are like most people, the sound you imagine is a piercing, threatening scream. It starts off high-pitched and pure with a sharp attack and descends into a raspy, warning rumble. The sound is instantly recognizable and majestic; it stirs patriotic pride in the hearts of Americans and, one imagines, terror in the hearts of rabbits and squirrels. The only problem with this image of the bald eagle's cry, its peal, is that it has been created in our collective imaginations by the careful work of generations of filmmakers and Foley artists.

Foley artists create the soundtracks for movies and tv, and their job – whether for a cartoon, a feature film, or a nature documentary – is to match sound effects to the images on screen. These sound effects need to fit audience expectations for what a movement or animal *should* sound like. The weak peal of a bald eagle, which sounds uncannily like the plaintive call of a seagull, is replaced with the cry of the comparatively diminutive but regal-sounding red-tailed hawk. These artistic decisions might initially be made for aesthetic reasons or to assist in the creation of a believable story or scene, but through repetition and exposure they come to replace the original, authentic sound in the minds of audiences. The manipulated pairing of sound to creature becomes the expected reality in the minds of the audience so that the genuinely chirpy call of an eagle come to sound strange or even comical.

People who create animated movies face a problem that moviemakers working with live beings do not – they must give personalities to inanimate objects like cars and candelabras, life stories to non-existent entities like unicorns, and voices to non-speaking beings like ducks, dogs, and mice. For decades, Disney has stood out among animators as the gold standard for making characters that are relatable and beloved or hated and reviled. How do they do it? How does Disney take a rusty old tow truck and turn it into Lightning McQueen's faithful but somewhat goofy sidekick Mater in the movie *Cars*? How do they make us know from the very beginning of *The Lion King* that this sulky, sullen, and pitiful lion known as Scar is the bad guy? Animators use lots of tricks to get viewers to follow their plots and understand their characters, but one particularly easy trick is to play into the stereotypes and prejudices that exist in the society within which the story is to be told. And the easiest way to do that is to use the stereotypes linked to language.

Teaching children how to discriminate

Stories are more than entertainment. Stories are essential to the species and "second in necessity apparently after nourishment and before love and shelter" (Price 1978: xiii). As

DOI: 10.4324/9781003332886-12

Figure 12.1 How do you imagine the sound of a bald eagle's cry?
Source: photo by Jennifer Cramer

all human beings dream, we also all think and structure our understanding of the world in terms of narrative. A child takes in his or her family's and community's stories and begins to experiment with storytelling at a young age. This process is crucial to socialization. In this section, we focus on the ways that children are systematically exposed to Standard Language Ideology by means of linguistic stereotypes presented in narrative form in film or television entertainment. And what better place to start than with the ubiquitous mouse! Indeed, Mickey Mouse's white gloves and body movements were originally modeled on blackface minstrel performers, and his first (1928) sound film included Mickey playing the song "Turkey in the Straw," which (under a different name) was a popular and openly racist minstrel standard at the time (Sammond 2005). Because representations from Disney have continued for so long, they have changed drastically over time. Even so, the racist undertones of past representations may persist long after they have been recognized as offensive.

Since the early 20th century, the broadcast media have steadily increased in importance as agents of socialization. While many tend to think of Disney as a magical kingdom (mostly because Disney has convinced us this is so), in fact it is first and foremost a large and complex corporation. As such, its primary concern is its shareholders, who are primarily interested in profit. To maintain and increase its customer base, Disney constantly reintroduces children to *their* worldview, evidenced most recently by the re-release of nearly every popular animated film in its repository as a live-action, CGI-intense blockbuster. Disney has been successful in winning its audience because, while there may be scattered protests about gender roles, racism, and historical inaccuracies in Disney films, such complaints never seem to have much of an impact on box-office numbers.

The purpose here is not to condemn Disney or any other producer of animated or otherwise child-focused material; Fisch (2005), for example, presents arguments for the constructive aspects of television viewing for children, who are exposed to positive role models and educational exercises in programming such as *Sesame Street*. Yet it is not reasonable to simply overlook, rationalize, or laugh off discriminatory and exclusionary behaviors, especially given the ubiquitous presence of such media in the lives of children. That is, while nothing may be gained by latching onto what seem to be trivialities, neither is any progress made by refusing to look more closely at systematic patterns that have a profound impact on the way children come to see the world. In what follows, we explore Disney's role as a case study in the role of child-directed media in the socialization of young children to demonstrate that their products (and likely the similar products made by other media companies) have a regular, systematic effect on children on a day-to-day basis and to reveal how children are influenced by the content of what they are seeing.

Why Disney?

Disney is the focus here because it holds such a large share of the market; for example, among its holdings in 2010 were five film studios in addition to a majority share in 20 different television stations (Giroux & Pollock 2010: 285). With its various other business partnerships, including entities like Pixar, Lucasfilm, and Marvel Studios, Disney has been involved in the production of hundreds of movies, television shows, and other media directly targeting the under-18 age group. The introduction of their streaming service, Disney+, in 2019 puts all of this content within easy grasp of a rather large audience, with over 116 million users worldwide as of summer 2021.

Most parents today use various safeguards to protect the youngest and most vulnerable from unhealthy or dangerous everyday items such as toys, food, and clothing. The broadcast entertainment industry is subject to the same kind of inspection but in a way that is far less consistent. Some producers of child-focused materials have an extraordinary amount of unquestioned access to children and relatively little or perfunctory oversight. Disney is probably the most prominent of the companies who rely on reputation and nostalgia to deliver a message. It is also true that a great deal of overtly discriminatory material has come out of all the animation studios from the earliest days of the industry. There is a large body of animated short films or cartoons that denigrate, trivialize, or mock the mentally ill, the handicapped, homosexuals, Native Americans, African Americans, Africans, Asians, Middle Easterners, Inuit peoples, Italians, Latinxs, Mexicans, Jewish people, the English, Irish, Scots, Russians, and just about every other nationality, ethnicity, and social group.

Uncle Remus at Disneyland

The discussion of African American voices in Disney animated films presented here does not include all African American actors who have had speaking roles in Disney animated films. For example, a thorough examination would require close study of *Song of the South*, a mixed live-action/animated film from 1946. *Song of the South* was based on Joel Chandler Harris' Uncle Remus stories. The film has been widely criticized for its portrayal of African American characters and for painting a positive image of slavery. Disney has never released the film on home media (in the United States), and it is not available on Disney+. However, the representations in the film long survived in the form of a ride found at several Disney parks called Splash Mountain. The ride has long included multiple scenes from *Song of the South* and is accompanied by music from the film. In 2020, Disney announced that the Splash Mountain ride would be redesigned so that it revolves around the 2009 film *The Princess and the Frog* instead of the more controversial older film.

Why is it so important to acknowledge the impact of media on children? Many argue that little kids don't really pay attention to details anyway, so they couldn't possibly be taking notes from cartoon characters on how to be prejudiced. But children – even very young children – are tireless observers of human behavior, and research indicates that they do indeed take in what they see and put it to use. Language acquisition is part of cognitive development more generally. While one part of the 4-year-old's mind is sorting through linguistic strategies for passive constructions (like "The vase <u>was broken</u>."), another part is working on categorization and category awareness. Categorization is a universal cognitive strategy, a tool that humans use to cope with the complexity of the world. It is also the very cornerstone of stereotype and, following from that, prejudice (Brown 2010).

Some aspects of learning to differentiate and categorize are not well understood, but children use similarity in this process. Furry creatures with four legs – dogs, goats, horses – are all "doggies" (or something similar) to 2-year-olds. By age 4, the same child can identify a dog (as distinct from a horse) reliably. The important thing to note is that children see patterns in the data the world presents on a daily basis, and those patterns, positive or negative, are put to use.

Children are not passive vessels who sit in front of the television and let stories float by them. What they take in is processed and added to the store of data on how things – and people – are categorized. Children absorb things both abstract and concrete. Rice and Woodsmall (1988) conducted an experiment in which 3- and 5-year-olds were shown two 6-minute animated television programs (see Figure 12.2). Included were 20 words which were not known to the children prior to the viewing in normal conversational context. After a single viewing of the two clips, 3-year-olds gained an average of 1.56 new words, while 5-year-olds retained 4.87 new words.

Given this general and vastly simplified information about children, language, cognition, and identity, consider the fact that by age 4 some children begin to exhibit prejudicial attitudes (Persson & Musher-Eizenman 2003: 531). In fact, numerous studies indicate that preschool

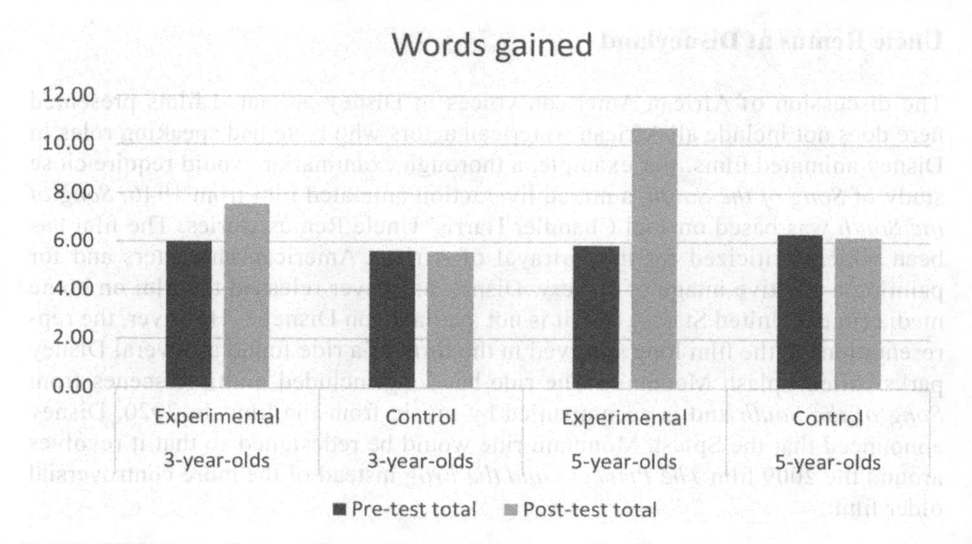

Figure 12.2 Words gained by 3- and 5-year-olds exposed to novel words (experimental) compared to a control group

Source: based on Rice and Woodsmall (1988)

children not only categorize by race; they also demonstrate bias (Aboud 2003, 2005; Katz 2003). Working with children between the ages 3 and 5 in a racially and ethnically-diverse day care center, Feagin and Van Ausdale (2001) found that the children used racial categories to identify themselves and others in conversation, to include or exclude others from activities, and to negotiate power in their own social/play networks.

Building on stereotypes

The use and manipulation of language variation to establish character are long-established practices in storytelling; Disney is by no means the first or only practitioner. When voice, stage, or screen actors use language or accent to create character quickly, building on well-established, preconceived notions associated with specific regions, ethnicities, races, or economic statuses, they use an age-old shortcut to characterization in which certain traits need not be laboriously demonstrated by means of a character's history and actions or an examination of motive. The blatant use of stereotype in any kind of storytelling (print, small or large screen, stage) may sometimes be used for satirical effect, but stereotypes can also indicate lack of imagination, laziness, bias, or some combination of the three on the part of the writer. The issue for us is not the quality of the storytelling; more important to the question of language-based discrimination is the way storytelling behaviors and reactions reflect and promulgate deeper beliefs and opinions. As we will see, stereotypes do not even have to be overtly negative to be problematic and limiting.

Any actor necessarily brings to a role their own native language. In many cases, the variety of English (we will focus here on film and theater in the United States) is irrelevant to the characterization and can be left alone. Some actors are infamous for never trying to portray an accent other than their own regardless of the nature of the story or the character. Ricky

Gervais, Aziz Ansari, and Diane Keaton (among others) have all made public statements about their unwillingness to attempt an accent other than their own. More often, however, the director and actor, working together (with an accent coach), will target a particular social, regional, or L2 accent, perhaps because it is intrinsic to the role and cannot be sacrificed. US audiences may or may not suspend disbelief when Robin Hood sounds like he grew up in Lynwood, California, but it would be harder to cast someone with an upper-class British accent as Ronald Reagan or Richard Nixon and not do serious harm to credibility, audience expectations, and reception.

In a similar way, non-native speakers of English who come to the United States to work as actors bring their L2 accents to their work. This accent may restrict the roles they can play, or they may have roles (re)written to suit the immutable nature of their accents. Arnold Schwarzenegger, Djimon Hounsou, Javier Bardem, Penelope Cruz, Chow Yun-Fat, Marion Cotillard, Benecio del Toro, and Juliette Binoche provide examples. American actors may undergo accent training of various kinds to learn to imitate what they need for a particular role, although there are many examples where this effort fails despite expensive and careful tutoring, even in the limited way it is asked of them during filming.

What is particularly relevant and interesting in this context, however, is the way that actors attempt to manipulate language as a tool in the construction of character, sometimes successfully, sometimes not (McGowan 2016). Educational programs for the training of actors for stage and screen often include classes on speech, dialogue, and the contrivance of accent. Simply put, with a lot of hard work and good editing, it may be possible to fool some of the people, some of the time.

In a film set in a country where English is not spoken, the writers and director have to come to an initial decision: they could hire actors who are native speakers of the language that is spoken in that setting and use subtitles; they could have the dialogue spoken in English, each actor using his or her native variety and simply abstracting away from the question of logical language spoken; or they could have native English-speaking actors speak English but sometimes take on the accent of the language they would logically be speaking in the time and setting of the story. This last choice has been the more common approach, at least in recent times.

If, for example, a French accent is meant to remind viewers that the story is taking place in France, then logic would require that all the characters in that story speak with a French accent. But this is not the case in animated or live action; for the most part, in movies set outside English-speaking countries, only a few actors will contrive the accent of that country. The decision about which actors will try to sound French in this example is not random, but typically follows logically from the dominant stereotypes. If one considers Disney's *Beauty and the Beast* (Trousdale & Wise 1991) as an example set in France (see Table 12.1), all of the major (protagonist) characters speak English with American or British accents with three exceptions: the sexy chamber maid (Fifi), the amorous butler (Lumière), and a temperamental cook (Chef Bouche). These are the only characters voiced by actors contriving French accents. When the film was remade in 2017 as a live-action film featuring Emma Watson as Belle and other big names in supporting roles, a similar tactic was used in choosing which characters would use French-accented English. In the remake, it is not the temperamental cook, who has very few lines in the new movie, but the operatic wardrobe who uses this accent, still playing into larger stereotypes, in this case, an obsession with fashion in 18th century France that is embodied in the wardrobe character. It is important to also note that none of the actors who use French-accented English are native speakers of French.

Table 12.1 Characters, actors, and accents portrayed in *Beauty and the Beast* (1991) and (2017) (three characters were given different names in the 2017 remake; in this table, the first name was used in the 1991 version, while the second name was used in the 2017 version)

Character	*Actor (1991)*	*Accent (1991)*	*Actor (2017)*	*Accent (2017)*
Belle	Paige O'Hara	American English	Emma Watson	British English
Beast	Robby Benson	American English	Dan Stevens	British English
Maurice	Rex Everhart	American English	Kevin Kline	American English
Mrs. Potts	Angela Lansbury	British English	Emma Thompson	British English
Chip	Bradley Pierce	American English	Nathan Mack	British English
Lumière	Jerry Orbach	French-accented English	Ewan McGregor	French-accented English
Cogsworth	David Ogden Stiers	British English	Ian McKellen	British English
Chef Bouche/ Cuisinier	Brian Cummings	French-accented English	Clive Rowe	British English
Fifi/Plumette	Kimmy Robertson	French-accented English	Gugu Mbatha-Raw	French-accented English
Wardrobe/Madame Garderobe	Jo Anne Worley	American English	Audra McDonald	French-accented English

While the storytelling is part of the equation, some voice actors are selected to voice a character simply because of name recognition. This was a new direction in casting that began in the 1960s with the production of Disney's *The Jungle Book* (Reitherman 1967, director), which was the first animated feature in which voice actors were cast based on public recognition and popularity. Actors and musicians who had already established a personality and reputation with the movie-going public were drawn, quite literally, into the animation and storytelling process so that the relationship between voice, popularity, language, and characterization in Disney film entered a new era.

In these cases, the character is fully embodied in the actor and the character traits that the individual brings. An extreme example of this, though potentially tied up with continuing a streak, is the fact that John Ratzenberger has had a voice role in almost every single Disney/ Pixar movie (e.g., Hamm in the *Toy Story* movies, Mack in the *Cars* movies). While such a practice might be less problematic in cases where the setting is not emphasized (e.g., *Toy Story* movies) or is made up (e.g., *Big Hero 6*) and potentially with non-human characters (e.g., the Genie in *Aladdin*), the choice of recognizable voice actors without reference to the story itself has caused some backlash.

Time and place must, however, be acknowledged. The stories Disney tells are quite often stories belonging to cultural traditions that they did not invent and do not own. In certain cases, Disney seems unconcerned with the setting and time and simply puts modern-day people and sensibilities in exotic places. *Tarzan* takes place in the Victorian era, somewhere on the African continent – which one must take on faith as there are no local (African) humanoids in speaking roles. *The Lion King* is set in Africa, but again the story does not involve human beings; here it is clear that it is Africa because the writers go out of their way to remind the audience. *The Jungle Book* is set in India, with a single human character – Mowgli – to establish that this story is set in a place meant to be considered "exotic" by audiences. In extreme cases, the filmmakers seem to want to draw on the atmosphere and cultural awareness associated with specific times and places, but the more pressing concern is how to engage the interest of the viewers by making the setting familiar and comfortable.

In these movies, the logical setting dictates a particular language or set of languages, but there is no attempt to try to build those social behaviors into the story. It makes a certain amount of sense to set aside issues of logical language use and simply tell the story in English, especially if the audience is very young and unable to read subtitles. However, in most cases, the directors or actors continue to draw on language-focused social differences to establish character.

The Emperor's New Groove (Dindal 2000) is probably an intense case of a disconnect between the proposed time and place and the way the story is told. The film is set in Incan Peru, a fact that is never explicitly named or identified in the film itself (Silverman 2002) but was spoken about freely when the creative staff were interviewed. Animators and producers talked at length about research into Incan culture and the fact that they went through many centuries of archeological artifacts to find those which appealed to them as supportive of a light-hearted, comedic plot. Silverman, an archeologist, estimates that as it is presented, the film contains elements that span 3,000 years and 275,000 square kilometers (171,000 miles) of space (ibid.: 309). As a result, "In Disney's hands, *Groove* so significantly departs and appropriates from the archaeologically known Inca Empire and other pre-Columbian civilizations of ancient Peru, that it is a textbook example of hyperreality and simulacra." That is, Disney's ancient Peru looks as though it is meant to be a copy of the original but in fact is created out of whole cloth. Add to this the choice of David Spade, an American comedian with a highly recognizable voice and a well-known slapstick, sarcastic, and over-the-top comedic style, for the voice of the main character, and the cultural and historical facts of Incan life are essentially dismissed altogether.

This is a case where all voice actors use their own varieties of English. There are no attempts at an accent that would evoke Incan culture because the story has nothing to do with that time and place. The goal seems to be to evoke other cultures only in so far as they will mesh with the expectations of an American audience. This is done by assimilation and objectification, and the result is a children's film which strips an entire culture of its history and trivializes what is left behind. *The Emperor's New Groove* accomplishes all of this in some 90 minutes. The unfortunate result is that most children who see this movie will retain Disney's version of Incan culture because it is the only version they will ever be exposed to. For these future adults, Disney's Incan culture *is* Incan culture. Few American students will have an opportunity to learn in more detail about the more complex – and interesting – history of the Incan people.

The use of entirely made-up aspects of culture and language is especially common in representations of Native Americans and indigenous peoples (such as the Inca). Linguistic anthropologist Barbra Meek (2006, 2011) has examined media representations of Native American language. In her research, Meek found that media representations of "Injun English" developed over time to become an identifiable and distinct variety that had absolutely no connection whatsoever to the actual speech of Native Americans. As noted in Chapter 7, representations of Native Americans typically involve imagined forms like saying "how" for "hello," using object pronouns as subjects, or adding -um to the end of verbs (as in "Me walkum long time"). Similarly, although there are a few exceptions, most representations of Native American languages have not actually used Native American languages. In Western films, it is common to find white actors made up in redface speaking to one another in gibberish as if it were an actual language.

Animated films offer a unique way to study how a dominant culture reaffirms its control over subordinate cultures and nations by re-establishing, on a day-to-day basis, their preferred view of the world as right, proper, and primary. A study of accents in animated cartoons over time reveals the way linguistic stereotypes mirror the evolution of national fears: Japanese and German characters in cartoons during World War II (Bugs Bunny starring in propaganda films for the United States), Russian spy characters in children's cartoons in the 1950s and 1960s (Natasha and Boris meet Rocky and Bullwinkle), Middle Eastern characters in the era of hostilities with Iran and Iraq (the soldiers in *Aladdin*). In the following discussion of systematic patterns found in a defined body of children's animated film, the hypothesis is a simple one: animated films entertain, but they are also a vehicle by which children learn to associate specific characteristics and lifestyles with specific social groups and to accept a narrow and exclusionary worldview.

Disney's worldview

A large-scale study was carried out for the first edition of this book in which 371 characters in 24 full-length animated Disney films were analyzed (everything available on VHS at the time). For the second edition, an additional 14 films were watched and analyzed, including only films that were fully animated, full-length, and produced by Disney (a full list is available in the book's website). This excludes films that were produced by Pixar but distributed by Disney, a step taken for the sake of consistency. Even a cursory look is enough to get a sense of the range of social and linguistic stereotypes Disney repeatedly presents to young children. Before the widespread availability of the VCR in the early 1980s, repeated viewings of *Cinderella*, for example, were unlikely for most children. Since the technology boom, however, Disney films can be rented or purchased, downloaded or streamed, and watched over and over again, so that the messages and morals become deeply ingrained and come to be part of a child's habitual thought patterns (Buescher & Ono 1996; Edgerton & Jackson 1996; Giroux & Pollock 2010; Lacroix 2004).

Stereotypes presented in these films are not subtle, ranging from *Lady and the Tramp*'s cheerful, musical Italian chefs to *Duck Tales*'s stingy, Scottish-accented Scrooge McDuck. Disney employs numerous stereotypes in portraying different character types; for instance, the stereotype of the sidekick as a scrappy inner-city tough guy with a heart of gold has been used by Disney time and time again across its collection. In this study, we examined how Disney uses stereotypes to portray characters by coding each character for a variety of language and characterization variables, creating a detailed linguistic description for each character.

What we discovered is that language and social characterizations dominate in Disney character development processes. Beginning by exploring how gender is portrayed, stereotypes abound. While male and female characters are equally distributed as major and minor characters in Disney films, female characters are rarely seen at work outside the home and family; where they do show up, they are mothers and princesses, devoted or (rarely) rebellious daughters. When they are at work, female characters are waitresses, nurses, nannies, or housekeepers. Men, conversely, are doctors, waiters, advisors to kings, thieves, hunters, servants, detectives, and pilots. The universe displayed to young children in these films is one with a clear division between the sexes in terms of lifestyle and life choices. Traditional views of the woman's role in the family are strongly underwritten, and in Disney films, from *Snow White* to *Meet the Robinsons*, the female characters see, or come to accept, their first and most important role in life as that of wife and mother. What does an examination of language use have to add to this observation?

Supermom!

Mothers (and some fathers) have it pretty bad in Disney movies. In many cases, the mother is absent or rarely, if ever, mentioned (as with Belle's mother in *Beauty and the Beast*, Ariel's mother in *The Little Mermaid*, Jasmine's mother in *Aladdin*, among others), dead prior to the events of the film (as in *Cinderella*, *Lilo & Stitch*, and *Big Hero 6*, among others), or dies during the movie (as in *Bambi* and *Frozen*). Some characters are orphaned early life (as in the case of the titular character in *Aladdin*), with the occasional single mother storyline (as in *The Princess and the Frog* and *Onward*), while others are raised by "bad guy" mother figures (as in *Tangled* and *Cinderella*). The treatment of mothers in Disney movies has even elicited numerous urban legends related to Walt Disney's own mother's death.

An example of an exception to the missing mother role can be found in the Disney·Pixar film *The Incredibles* (2004), a story that depicts the life of a not-so-typical nuclear family that happens to have superpowers. Mrs. Incredible, also known as Elastigirl or Helen Parr, is the mother, and her story, while less dire, still betrays the "mom does it all" struggle familiar to many working mothers. Indeed, the entire plot of the sequel (2018), and to some extent the original, focuses on how a mother can reconcile her family life with her superhero life. Such a struggle is rarely suggested for father characters in animated films.

The empirical work in this area confirms both Disney's use of gender stereotypes in its films and the ways in which that use tracks the evolution of these stereotypes in broader American culture. Karen Eisenhauer's work with Carmen Fought (2016, 2022) analyzed compliments given to female characters in 12 Disney movies released between 1937 and 2013. They divide this period into three "ages": Classics (1937–1959), Renaissance (1989–1999), and New Age (2009–2013). They then counted and analyzed compliments paid to female characters. Part of this analysis included dividing the basis of the compliment into the simple categories of "appearance" (e.g., emphasis on Snow White's beauty) and "skill" (e.g., fighting ability in *Mulan*).

As can be seen in Figure 12.3, compliments during the Classics era were 55% based on appearance and 11% on the basis of skill. During the Renaissance period, appearance-based compliments for female characters dropped to 38% while skill-based compliments rose to 23%. Finally, during the New Age period, appearance-based compliments fell even further to 22% with a corresponding rise in skill-based compliments to 40%. The trend is clear: female characters in Disney films have come to be evaluated more for what they can do than for what they look like. It is impossible to determine, from this correlation, whether Disney was following the market to change its characterizations of women to better reflect what the ticket-buying public wished to pay to see or whether this was an editorial decision by the company to lead by example. What is clearly the case, though, is that a child watching a New Age film like *Tangled* (2010) or *Brave* (2012) will receive a very different education in how women should expect to be treated by the world than a child watching only *Snow White* (1937) or even *The Little Mermaid* (1989). The use of stereotypical language by and about women in Disney's films both reflects and creates specific cultural expectations.

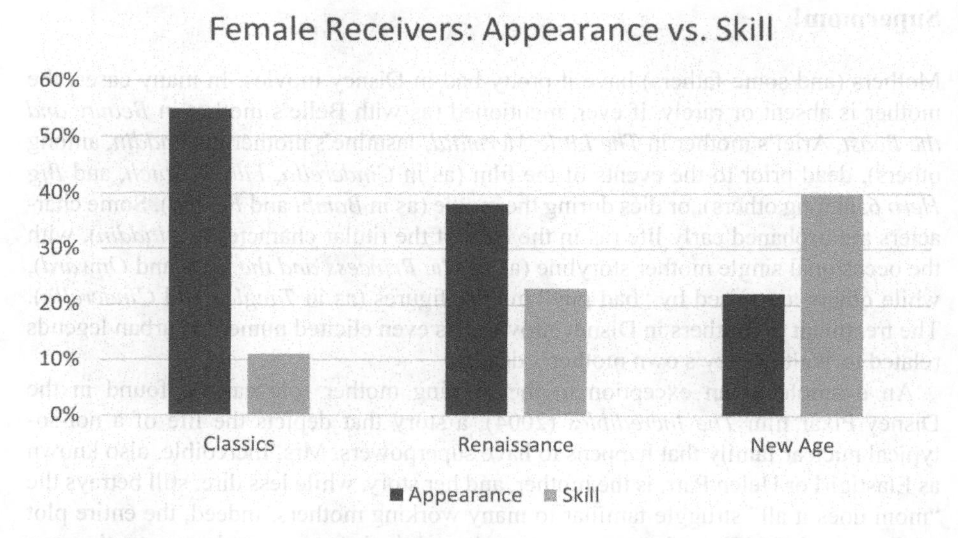

Figure 12.3 Comparing compliments received by female characters across three Disney film ages, appearance vs. skill

Source: adapted from Eisenhauer & Fought (2016)

Moving beyond gender stereotypes, one can examine Disney films for other kinds of identity representation. For the most part, the 371 characters analyzed for earlier editions of this book speak something approximating a standard variety of American English (43%). An even larger portion (91%) of the characters speak some variety of English (e.g., American, British, Australian) natively. Interestingly, though, a large proportion of the characters occur in roles where they would not logically be speaking English. Sometimes these are Americans abroad, as was the case in *Duck Tales*; sometimes these are characters who are not logically English-speaking, given their role and the story, as is the case for all the characters in *Aladdin*. Yet there are very few characters who speak English with a non-native accent.

Since a contrived foreign accent is often used to signal that the typical or logical language of the setting would not be English, it is not surprising to find that the highest percentage of characters with foreign-accented English occur in stories set in non-English-speaking countries. In fact, there are twice as many characters with foreign-accented English in stories set in places like France and Italy. Similarly, it is not unreasonable to assume that for stories set in Africa, the logical language would not be English. There is no acknowledgment of this fact in *Tarzan* (Buck & Lima 1999). And while some of the characters' names in *The Lion King* are derived from Swahili (e.g., the good-natured but dumb warthog is called "Pumbaa," or "simpleton"; "Shenzi," the name of the leader of the hyena pack, means "uncouth"), the only character who actually uses traces of Swahili and a contrived Swahili English accent is Rafiki (Swahili for "friend"), the wise and eccentric baboon who fulfills the role of spiritual guide.

It is also important to note that even more characters with foreign accents appear in stories set in the United States and England. In these cases, the stereotypes of interest have to do with the perceptions that Americans hold about non-native speakers of English as potential threats. In examining the variety used in relationship to the motivations and actions of the character's role, one can see that Disney's reliance on a good vs. evil storyline with a happy ending can be easily accomplished in constructing characters through pre-existing linguistic stereotypes. Of those characters who were analyzed as "bad guys," including the poacher and would-be child-murderer Percival McLeach in *The Rescuers Down Under* with his forced Southwestern accent and the whip-and-cleaver-wielding Stromboli of *Pinocchio* with his threats of dismemberment, incredible rages, and florid, contrived Italian English accent, they are still mostly native English speakers, not primarily "bad guys with foreign accents." However, when it comes to overall representation, it becomes clear that people with foreign accents are presented as far more negatively motivated than native speakers of English. Only about 20% of US English speakers are bad characters, while about 40% of non-native speakers of English are represented as evil, as can be seen in Figure 12.4.

Additional interesting patterns come forward when examining the representation of specific languages linked to national origin, race, or characterization. Race and ethnicity are particularly sensitive issues in all Disney animated films. The company has repeatedly offended different segments of the population. For example, despite efforts to reflect South Pacific culture more accurately in the 2016 hit *Moana* (Clements & Musker 2016), including traveling to the region, interviewing anthropologists and historians, and talking to locals, Disney found itself embroiled again in claims of racism for its depiction of Maui, the demigod who is well known in Polynesian mythologies. Critics panned the film for the stereotypical size of Maui because of high obesity rates in the South Pacific and for Maui's egotistical and foolish personality (driven at least partly by the selection of former WWE wrestling star Dwayne "The Rock" Johnson for the role) because it denigrates his hero status (Roy 2016). Add to this the embarrassing Maui Halloween costume Disney tried

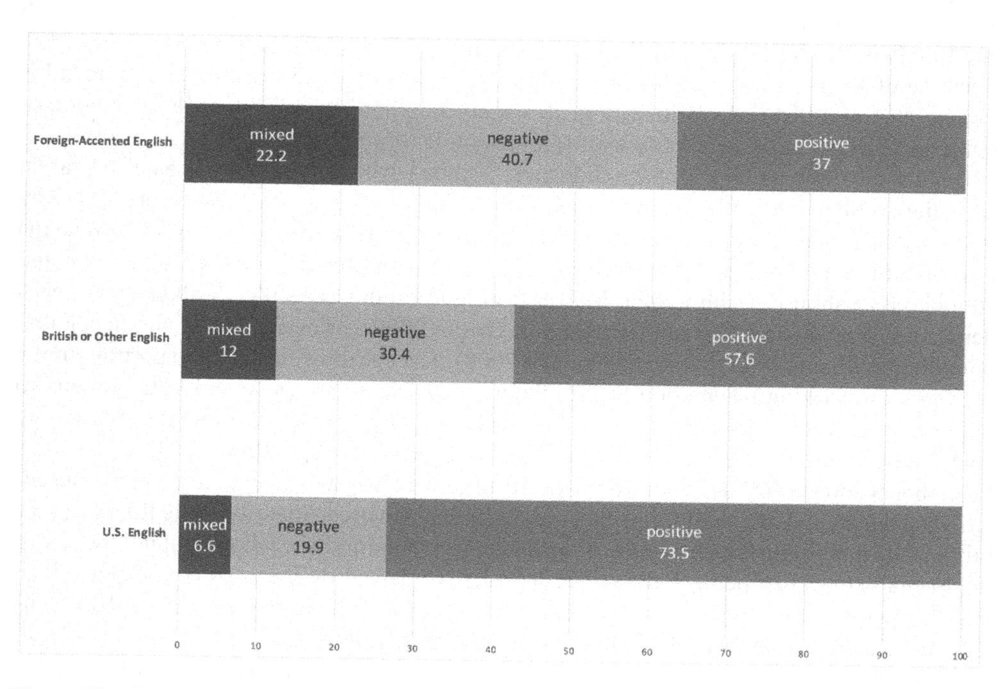

Figure 12.4 Percentage of animated characters with mixed, negative, or positive motivations, grouped by English accent

to market that essentially served as brownface (Rika 2016), and you have a recipe for a cultural misappropriation disaster.

Indeed, the most glaring missteps made by Disney have to do with the representation of African Americans and people of color more generally. Examples include irresponsible Latinxs and gregarious Italians (e.g., *Lady and the Tramp, Oliver and Company, The Lion King*); nefarious Asians (e.g., *Lady and Tramp, Mulan, The Aristocats*); smart-mouthed, lazy, disrespectful African Americans (e.g., *Dumbo, The Lion King, The Princess and the Frog*); and savage Native Americans (e.g., *Peter Pan, Pocahontas*). When considering the missteps made with respect to representations of African Americans in Disney films, it becomes apparent that it is not the presence of African Americans that is the problem; it is the problematic ways in which the film creators lean on generally negative stereotypes of African Americans and African American culture as a shorthand for the creation of characters who are meant to be perceived in a negative light.

The original analysis of African American characters in Disney films presented in earlier editions of this book analyzed 29 characters as representing African American personae, determined to be so because 1) the voice actor was African American, 2) the voice actor was most likely cast on the basis of voice recognition, regardless of race, 3) the animated character is Black either in actuality or symbolically, and/or 4) the animated character speaks English with some features found in African American Englishes.

For the sake of space, we will focus our attention on *The Lion King*, perhaps the most ideology-laden film examined in the earlier editions of this book. *The Lion King* is set in Africa, which may be the reason why some of the voice actors were African American. Of the three major roles (Simba, Scar, and Mufasa), only one is African American (Mufasa, Simba's father, voiced by the immediately recognizable James Earl Jones). Two of the voice actors for major characters are white (Simba, voiced by Jonathan Taylor Thomas as a cub and Matthew Broderick as an adult, and Scar, Simba's uncle, voiced by Jeremy Irons). The selection of Jeremy Irons for Mufasa's evil brother Scar is perhaps unsurprising though; his exaggerated and distinctly British English variety falls into a well-established practice of rendering evil geniuses as Brits (see also, for example, *Aladdin* and *Bolt*).

But it is the casting of the primary character – Simba – which stands out. As a cub and as an adult lion, Simba is voiced by white actors. That is, the prince, the son of characters played by African Americans (Sarabi, Simba's mother, is voiced by Jamaican actress Madge Sinclair) is white, a fact that did not go unnoticed by the critics and scholars who consider race and ethnicity (Benshoff & Griffin 2009; Martin-Rodriguez 2000; Sun 2008; Walker 1994), gender issues, sexuality and sexism (Benshoff & Griffin 2009), or class, power, and hegemony (Gooding-Williams 1995; Morton 1996; Sun 2008). The use of white actors to portray Simba is even more striking when compared to the use of African American and Latino actors to play the dangerous "bad guy" hyenas. The three primary hyenas who threaten Simba are composed of Shenzi (Whoopi Goldberg), Ed (Jim Cummings), and Banzai (Cheech Marin). Ed slobbers and grunts but has no language other than a Hollywood laugh that indexes insanity. Shenzi uses non-standard forms that index African American identity while Banzai uses a mix of Chicanx English with a touch of Spanish thrown in for those who might not recognize the hyena's dialect as being Latinx. The message conveyed by these voices is quite clear. People who speak in ways that are recognizable as African American or Latinx are dangerous and no different from those who suffer from severe mental illness.

Why not select an African American voice actor to play Simba? Why didn't Disney tap Eddie Murphy for the job? "Why Eddie Murphy?" you may be thinking. Let's first consider the criteria indicated previously. Eddie Murphy is African American, has a highly recognizable voice, would be able to represent a character that was intended as Black, and speaks with a variety of English easily heard as African American, thus meeting all four criteria.

Beyond that, though, he is clearly available for cartoon voice work; he voiced Donkey in the DreamWorks smash *Shrek* (and subsequent films/shows) and Mushu, the small, very scrappy guardian dragon sidekick, in Disney's own *Mulan*. He is also very good at this kind of work, most clearly indicated by not only the success of these two movies but also the fact that the illogic of a sidekick who speaks like a 20th-century African American in an imaginary fairytale forest and in ancient China seems to have been secondary to the need for this character type in both films. To top it off, in the (non-animated) movie *Coming to America*, which was released six years before *The Lion King*, the same actors who provided the voices for Simba's parents played the parents of Eddie Murphy's character.

A new lion king

For what it's worth, the 2019 live-action remake of *The Lion King* features even more African and African American voice actors, including Donald Glover as the voice of adult Simba, JD McCrary as young Simba, and Beyoncé as adult Nala (plus James Earl Jones reprises his role as Mufasa).

What the directors and producers were thinking when they cast the voice actors cannot be known; if notes on this process exist, they are not available to researchers, nor do the producers typically respond to requests for interviews. Nor is there any way to know which voice actors were considered for the role of Simba or whether any African American actors auditioned. It is unfortunate that so much of the process usually remains out of the public eye, as that information would provide invaluable insights.

More subtle is the stratification of characters voiced by actors who are recognizably African American. James Earl Jones (Mufasa) has a deep recognizable voice and employs articulatory and intonational patterns that are recognizable as indexing African American identity. However, Jones's speech uses grammar that would be considered "standard" English. Whoopi Goldberg, on the other hand, as the leader of the pack of hyenas who do Scar's bidding, shifts in and out of grammatical forms associated with African American English. Thus, the message is a familiar one: African Americans who speak non-standard English are dangerous and occupy the dark and frightening places. The non-standard English used by the hyenas indexes a context where Simba does not belong and should not be. Simba ought to be on the sunny savanna where "standard" English speakers like his father live.

Other types of entertainment media use these same strategies, of course, as bell hooks has observed:

> [It is the] current trend in producing colorful ethnicity for the white consumer appetite that makes it possible for blackness to be commodified in unprecedented ways, and for whites to appropriate black culture without interrogating whiteness or showing concern for the displeasure of blacks . . . white cultural imperialism . . . allows white audiences to applaud representations of black culture, *if they are satisfied with the images and habits of being represented.*
>
> (hooks 1996: 223, emphasis added)

An analysis presented in the first edition of this book found that all Disney characters using African American varieties of English before the mid-1990s appeared in animal rather than human form. Given the low overall number of characters voiced by African American actors, however, it is hard to draw any inferences from that fact. This correlation of African American to animal held true until *Atlantis: The Lost Empire* (Wise & Trousdale 2001) and the character of Dr. Joshua Strongbear Sweet. Dr. Strongbear Sweet is presented in human form and is clearly African American in appearance. Like Mufasa, Dr. Strongbear Sweet doesn't use non-standard English so that another indexical link is reinforced: powerful, educated = speaker of "standard" English.

Following *Atlantis*, Disney made some progress away from these racial stereotypes with *Lilo & Stitch. Lilo & Stitch* stands apart for its sensitive portrayal of *Hawai'i*, Hawaiian culture, and people of color. The difference had to do with the way the film was made: Chris Sanders and Dean DeBois were given "near-complete creative control as co-writers, storyboard artists and directors – a first for a Disney film" (Davis 2002). Lilo, her older sister, and her sister's boyfriend, David, have features that are not anglicized, and their lives are neither romanticized nor trivialized; they all speak using features of Hawaiian (Creole) English. While the actress who voiced Lilo (Daveigh Chase) is not of Hawaiian decent, both Nani (Tia Carrere) and David (Jason Scott Lee) are. The one African American character is Cobra Bubbles, a social worker who looks a great deal like a professional weightlifter. His looks are frightening and his voice – distinctly African American – is imposing, but this character is one of the good guys, sincere in his concern for the orphaned sisters. Unfortunately, Disney did not repeat this unusual arrangement, and the typical style of production oversight was restored for *The Princess and the Frog*.

The Princess and the Frog is set in New Orleans in the 1920s and features a young African American woman as the main character, one who has both father and mother as the story opens. The issue of language variety and accent was made somewhat easier for Disney because all the characters – humanoid and animal – speak a variety of English marked, at the very least, as Southern. It's important to recognize that the film makers tried to acknowledge the wide variety of language and language varieties spoken in and around New Orleans in the time: in addition to voices that are recognizable as African American, there are non-standard forms indexing white Southerner, Cajun/Creole, and Louisiana varieties of French. The language of the main African American characters is only slightly distinct from that of their white counterparts, in part because the voice actors restrict themselves to intonation patterns in marking ethnic difference. There are no non-standard grammatical constructions, words, or idioms that would make the white/African American linguistic differences more distinct. Indeed, one of the least "standard" speakers in the film – Tiana's father – dies before the story ever really starts.

Improving representations

The Princess and the Frog certainly represents an improvement over *The Lion King* in terms of stereotype and language markers, but other patterns are still there, if muted. Critics have questioned the fact that the young African American main character spends about three-quarters of the film as a frog:

> To make the first African American princess a frog, then, seems to literally conflate her with animality. Tiana, mixing her dreams of success with a lack of intelligence

> and reason, is a black girl who must hop around like a frog in the way early twentieth-century black actors had to don blackface and hop around like dogs.
>
> (Gehlawat 2010: 418)

The issue of language variety is sidestepped in the case of Prince Naveen, as well. The character, while charming and handsome, like all Disney princes, is also not American. Neither is he African American nor is he white. The voice actor (Bruno Campos) is a native of Brazil, which freed the writers and directors of dealing with the issue of the ethnic associations with different voices. Many critics and commentators took note of this equivocation, pointing out that by turning both prince and princess into frogs, the issue of color could be set aside. Some see this as a maneuver by Disney to anticipate and nullify the potentially explosive topic of miscegenation (Gehlawat 2010: 424). Others took a more sarcastic tone: "They say it ain't easy bein' green, but it's certainly a hell of a lot easier than being black" (Foundas 2009). Commentary on the web was often emotional and angry, with one commentator (Angela Bronner Helm) writing: "Disney obviously doesn't think a black man is worthy of the title of prince. His hair and features are decidedly non-black. This has left many in the community shaking their head[s] in befuddlement and even rage" (as quoted in Barnes 2009).

Film producers like Disney are primarily concerned with engaging the audience and filling theaters and theme parks. As one of the primary storytellers in the life of American children of all colors and ethnicities, Disney's films have a deep and long-lasting effect on socialization and the development of identity – for both self and other. There is a growing body of scholarship which looks at Disney in a wider context and without apologist rhetoric, and that work makes clear how systematically Disney animated films go in setting up conceptions of good and evil in ways that strongly correlate to race and ethnicity. The manipulation of accent is part of that process, and it works very well.

Information literacy: beyond cartoons

Disney both leans on and entrenches cultural stereotypes and biases as a shorthand way to create compelling characters. The discussion of Disney's role in this and the stories that people will happily pay to see recalls our discussion, from Chapter 2, of habitual and reflective thought. Putting the voice of a British man in the mouth of a cowardly lion to accentuate his villainy appeals to an individual's quick-moving, habitual brain. In the same way that cultures assign color words to some wavelengths and not others, "this is just what villains sound like," one might think to themselves if, indeed, they were thinking at all. But reflective selves are perfectly capable of recognizing that two brother lions growing up together on the savanna should, if they were to somehow acquire the power of speech, speak with strikingly similar accents. People tend to lean on stereotype and bias to understand stories they enjoy just as Disney leans on these devices to tell them. These devices become more insidious and worrying when one moves beyond the world of children's entertainment and consider the ways other forms of media – cable news, talk radio, podcasts, the internet – also lean on habitual thoughts in the same ways to sell not mere entertainment, but a version of reality that will maximally appeal to viewers' attention.

American mass media, and the news outlets in particular, have tremendous power to impact, shape, and even manipulate beliefs, attitudes, and behaviors seemingly at will (cf. McQuail 2010). There is a large, active community of academics and librarians who study the history, structure, and function of the media in all its forms. This work gives us the term *information literacy* to describe the set of skills a competent consumer of information should bring to any form of media. When people engage with media using only their habitual thoughts – browsing social media, letting cable news play, listening to a podcast – they are vulnerable to the many ways that the creators of that media use stereotypes and biases to provide a version of information that will excite and engage people's attention so it can be delivered to advertisers. Indeed, *people* are the product in these exchanges, and part of information literacy means trying to engage reflective thought, particularly when one finds themselves agreeing with a voice in the media, to ask questions like: What agenda does this media outlet have? How are they leaning on stereotype and bias to create a compelling product? What sort of questions am I not supposed to be thinking about right now? Information is a vast and important topic, but our focus in this book is specifically on how these media accept the language subordination model and Standard Language Ideology (presented in Chapter 4) in their role as the "voice of authority" to not only propagate stereotypes and control the presentation of the truth but more specifically as a means for imbuing "our lives with artificial perceptions and arbitrary values" (McLuhan 1964).

Beginning largely in the 20th century, American media companies came to see themselves as authorities of language and safeguards of the public discourse. Newspapers, radio, and later television broadcasters readily accepted the language ideology and saw themselves as defenders of that standard. This is a conscious, focused goal, as openly acknowledged in *The Art of Editing*: "The copy editor plays a major role in protecting the language against abuse" (from the chapter "Protecting the Language" in Baskette et al. 1986, cited in Cotter 1999: 175). But as we have seen over and over in this book, language and culture are inseparable, so an institution that takes on a role as language defender is necessarily adopting and defending a particular cultural perspective. When an institution sees itself as a protector and defender of the standard variety of the language, then that institution has taken on the role of defining and defending what it means to be a "standard" American. Standard Language Ideology makes it difficult to even see that the standard variety of a language is itself imbued with social meaning and connected to a particular kind of social identity that not only excludes other ways of being but makes them unacceptable, unreal, and substandard.

This role as protector and defender of the standard was codified in law through a series of pieces of legislation beginning in 1912 with legislation to regulate access to broadcast frequencies which was motivated, at least in part, by the tragic sinking of the *Titanic* earlier that year. This initial legislation, designed primarily to handle wireless telegraph communications, was replaced in 1927 to accommodate the rapidly expanding radio broadcast industry, and the Federal Communications Commission (FCC) was created in 1934 to regulate broadcast media as an interstate good.

Part of this regulation included attempting to ensure that the broadcast frequencies the FCC assigned to broadcasters could not then be used to manipulate and control public opinion. Lawmakers feared the ability of a small number of wealthy broadcasters to provide opinions and voting positions to vast swathes of the American voting public. Beginning in 1941, the FCC banned all editorial content on broadcast media. Broadcasters were to limit themselves to entertainment and the presentation of facts without commentary that might support any political view, party, or candidate. This position is, of course, impossible, and requires the tacit acceptance of the ideologies underpinning Standard Language Ideology.

Any presentation of information, however factual, necessarily makes decisions about what is "fit" to broadcast.

This untenable position was replaced, in 1949, by the FCC's fairness doctrine. The fairness doctrine required broadcasters both to air information about controversial topics relevant to public interests and to provide time (although not *equal* time) for dissenting viewpoints.

The fairness doctrine was law for almost 40 years and created a sense (among white people) that American television and radio news reporting was inclusive, fair, and balanced. Networks pitched their news teams as "the most trusted," and media consumers bought into this. This assumption of media authority only became possible through Standard Language Ideology. It is not uncommon, even now, for dialectologists and sociolinguists to hear from Midwesterners with quite distinct regional accents that their speech "sounds like newscasters" or to say that newscaster voices sound like them as a means of declaring their regional variant to be standard, authoritative, and pure.

The fairness doctrine was repealed in 1987 under the Reagan administration after arguments that it violated the First Amendment and was therefore unconstitutional. During the preceding decades, as the winning legal argument went, there had been such a proliferation of media outlets and voices with the advent of cable and satellite television that consumers could use the marketplace to achieve inclusion and the problem of requiring broadcasters to do this inclusion and fairness work themselves placed an undue burden on them. The repeal of the fairness doctrine almost immediately spurred the rise of one-sided talk radio news stations and eventually lead to the establishment of one-sided television news stations like Fox News and MSNBC. One-sided news sources continued to proliferate in precisely the way lawyers fighting the fairness doctrine had predicted, and today it is possible to consume one's news entirely through entities that appeal entirely to one's own political viewpoint or cultural identity. This creates an *echo chamber* in which one's existing beliefs are frequently amplified and rarely, if ever, challenged.

The result is a near complete blurring of the editorial and factual roles of news broadcasting without relinquishing the authority and gravitas imparted by the Standard Language Ideology. Martin and Yurukoglu (2014) looked at ideological phrases used on three prominent cable news networks: MSNBC, CNN, and Fox News. Martin's and Yurukoglu's analysis of the language used on these networks reveals that MSNBC viewers are increasingly exposed to purely Democratic party-leaning ideological spin, Fox News has always presented viewers with a conservative, Republican party-leaning ideological spin that has only increased, and CNN, which was established a decade before the end of the fairness doctrine, presented a fairly balanced ideological perspective with a noticeable shift to the political left during the early years of the Obama administration.

One can debate whether Martin's and Yurukoglu's phrases really represent these ideological positions, but the fact remains that all three networks assert the same authority, fairness, and centrality that viewers might have expected under the fairness doctrine, but no single network provides the diversity of opinions and perspectives that viewers continue to naïvely expect. This shift is perhaps even worse at the local news levels where large corporations with explicitly political agendas have quietly purchased television affiliate stations to replicate the ideological shift of cable news at the local level so that even viewers disenchanted with cable news as a source of unbiased information are unable to escape the echo chamber.

In terms of habitual and reflective thought, this change in broadcasting standards shifts the burden of skepticism and information literacy from the editorial staffs of broadcast networks and the FCC to the individual news consumer. To remain an informed consumer of information about the world through broadcast media, it is necessary to perform a degree of analysis and reflection that viewers, particularly those raised under the fairness doctrine, are ill-prepared to perform. By appealing to the authority granted to the media by Standard Language Ideology, media companies and viewers alike only make this skeptical reflection more difficult to achieve.

Language, with its intrinsic and functional variability, is far more deeply integrated into people's understanding of the world than any other external symbol of wealth or influence. Linguistic variation linked to social identity is far more subtle. One way to think about this is by means of what French sociologist Pierre Bourdieu (1987) calls the *linguistic marketplace*. In this theoretical model, an exchange between speaker and listener is about more than deciphering surface meaning. Sociolinguistic markers are "also signs of wealth, intended to be evaluated and appreciated, and signs of authority intended to be believed and obeyed" (Bourdieu & Thompson 1991: 66). Thus, when people hear "ain't" or "whom," they immediately know what they need to know about not only the speaker's language but also their likely levels of relative wealth and class (and a slew of other social "facts"). A speech act's value is based on power relations that have already been established, such as the mastery of class-marked linguistic competences.

Linguistic acts are always produced in particular contexts or markets, and the properties of these markets endow linguistic products with a certain "value" (ibid.: 18). It is important to note that there are multiple linguistic marketplaces, so that, in some contexts, a stigmatized variety of US English may in fact have more persuasive power and capital than the most capable National Public Radio reporter. This complexity was absent in the theory as Bourdieu first developed it, but other scholars – in particular, linguistic anthropologists – have refined it (Gal 2005; Seargeant 2009; Schieffelin et al. 1998; Woolard 2008).

Understanding linguistic marketplaces

Many Southerners learn at a young age, through their various entanglements with education, media, and the like, that Southern accents are "nice but dumb" in the minds of many non-Southerners. So when those Southerners go off to college outside the South, they quickly become the butt of the jokes. "Did you hear that? Say that again! It sounds so silly when you say 'pie' like 'paaaah'!" Those Southerners will often shift their speech to sound more like their collegiate counterparts to fit in because that linguistic marketplace does not value their native phonology. But when they return home for an academic holiday, the tables are turned. "Getting too big for your britches? Got your college-boy pants on now! You must think you're better than the rest of us, huh?" In the home marketplace, the lack of Southern sounds is noted and mocked, and those college students must switch back for the sake of acceptance. Throughout their lives, these bidialectal Southerners walk the linguistic tightrope between competing linguistic marketplaces.

Media representatives have claimed for themselves a spot as national role models in language. And, in fact, people allow them to chide them when their language differs from those varieties of English others speak or believe they speak. They have convinced people that they have the right to do this, and most do not challenge them. That unwillingness or inability to question such claims of authority does real damage. "The most successful ideological effects are those which have no need for words, *and ask no more than complicitous silence*" (Bourdieu 1987: 188, emphasis added).

A study of the various media outlets provides many examples of how media representatives see themselves and want to be seen. Sometimes the claims are very boldly stated, as in the following during a (2005) National Public Radio broadcast:

> NPR is considered by many to be the standard bearer for Standard American English. Listeners from around the country and around the world say that they find NPR English is the clearest and most comprehensible broadcast English available. They can hear that crisp American English on NPR member stations, on their Web sites, on line at npr.org or on the listeners' shortwave receivers.
>
> (Dvorkin 2005)

As is often the case when authority is claimed in public forums, the identity and credentials of the cited expert are left conveniently in the shadows. The passive construction "considered by many" could be considered a classic dodge in the tradition of "mistakes were made" (Broder 2007), leaving it to the reader to determine how many and whether those many are significant for them. Habitual thought leads us to rely on such superficial features as name recognition as a proxy; I know NPR, so it must be good! This line of argument is an appeal to authority and provides only the appearance of justification. A consumer engaging in proper information literacy – someone consuming media reflectively – must learn to spot vacuous phrases and argumentation like these to protect themselves from manipulation.

Extra, extra! Read all about it!

Newspaper headlines alone are sometimes quite sufficient evidence of a particular slant on language issues: "Bad English Spoken Here" (McKenzie 1992); "Language is the Guardian of Culture" (Nenneman 1992); "Black English Not Spoken Here" (Jarrett 1979); "Oy Gevalt! New Yawkese an Endangered Dialect?" (Sontag 1993); "Kardashians' 'vocal fry' drives grandma to distraction" (Dickinson 2018).

The most notorious style of media production that attacks language use is the editorial. Editorial opinions are not out of place in any kind of information media if they are clearly marked as such. The presentation of alternate interpretations is a public service, and an important one that can enhance information literacy. In recent years, however, the distinction between editorial commentary and news, between "news" and "entertainment," has been worn away to what has been called *infotainment* (Thussu 2007). The next step beyond that might be what has been called "fake news" (see Soll 2016 and later in this chapter), where editorial content is presented as fact, and facts are presented exclusively in support of a particular political or cultural viewpoint.

This erosion of the line between fact and editorial is perhaps most visible on social media, blogs, and related content where, very often, there is no attempt made to delineate fact from belief or, indeed, any evidence that the content creators understand that such a division is possible or desirable. But this erosion is not limited to online media. It used to be necessary to seek out media from another country to get a drastically different take on the events of the day. Now it is as simple as switching news channels; cable news outlets, like Fox News and MSNBC, and media giant Sinclair present such an editorialized, one-sided version of each days' events as fact that it can sometimes be difficult to tell they are describing the same event.

A new business venture may begin with a hole in the market – a real need which has not been filled – or with a need that has been placed in the mind of the public. Whiter, perfect teeth, for example, is a need which has been created through extensive promotion in mass media. Someplace along the way such a need for a better, more efficient, more elegant language was created in the minds of Americans. This followed not because speakers of English were suddenly no longer able to communicate with each other and required a solution but because they were made to feel inadequate or ashamed. Indeed, the media have been instrumental in creating this market need. And the parties sounding dire proclamations about the decline of spoken English are, not coincidentally, the ones with the cure to sell – those right-thinking and right-speaking individuals who are able to set the public on a straight and narrow path to the one true way of speaking.

Echo chambers and filter bubbles

Returning to the notion of "fake news," it is important to note that objectivity is a theoretical concept and hardly attainable in real-world communication, even by the best trained, widely experienced, and most professional and sincere journalists. Every exchange of information comes with a context that is relevant to understanding the speaker's intent. The purposeful lack or withholding of information is just as significant as the presentation of information as purported facts. It might be more useful to speak of a continuum from absolute, unvarnished truth to purposeful, unapologetic falsehood. Somewhere on this continuum is *spin*, or a kind of propaganda, one that might be seen as consisting of knowingly biased, deceptive, and persuasive half-truths. Spin sits somewhere between the center point and the purely subjective. There's spin when the public relations unit of a company must make a statement about a misbehaving CEO. There's spin when a company creates a bad product or makes a serious advertising blunder. The entire advertising enterprise might be described as spin. Commercials, internet ads, radio spots – they present to interested parties or captive audiences a vision of something that has but a small grain of truth. Mainstream media may be the biggest clearinghouse of spin:

> But the media are just a component of spin. So are advertising (a product unto itself), hype (sponsored exaggeration), lobbying (the persuasion of government officials), and polling (the analytical foundation of the spinformation society). So are direct mailing, grassroots campaigning, investor relating, media training, focus-group managing, jury consulting, opposition researching, issue managing, satellite uplinking, and speechwriting. Together with television and radio networks and stations, newspapers, magazines, and wire services, they constitute a veritable Media-Spindustrial Complex that appears to guide every image we receive, every decision we contemplate, every action we take.
>
> (Rothenberg 1996)

Everybody practices spin in communication. If someone does very poorly on a test, they might tell their friends by starting with the fact that they had the flu that day, or that everybody came in below the 70% mark, or that they were thinking of dropping anyway. One might not mention it at all. Someone might deny even taking a test. Or, if that person states the fact outright, "I flunked the last exam," the people they are talking to might provide the spin themselves and remind that person that they had the flu that week or that nobody did very well because the professor is a jerk. Spin, in these contexts, just feels like (and might even be) putting the facts of a situation in their appropriate context. The line between contextualization and spin can be blurry and subjective. One area of lived experience in which this kind of occasional, run-of-the-mill fuzzy spin accumulates to a way of life is on social media.

It only makes sense that when people go online, they might seek out people who are like themselves and topics that they are interested in. At the same time, when they post something online about themselves – a status update, a selfie, a video, or even an opinion – it only makes sense to publish the best version of this. People post about successes (e.g., a recent graduation, a new romance, a trip to Peru) and much less often will one post about failures or embarrassments (e.g., a clogged toilet, a missed rent payment, a failed test). On a micro scale, all these things are sensible. But on the massive scale of the internet, of walls and news feeds, the constant stream of others' successes can lead to a warped sense that one's own life compares negatively; people get to experience their own lives in all their richness and complexity, but viewers online only see the shiny highlights of others.

When this kind of filtering and selection occurs with one's information diet, the result is a *filter bubble*. A filter bubble is created when search, content, and advertising algorithms – intended to keep us consuming media for as long as possible – show us only the information and, crucially, the opinions individuals are likely to already agree with. Even without the overt presence of an editor as in traditional mass media, the result can be a one-sided, self-reinforcing echo chamber in which one's own views become the only sensible views, and those holding other views, speaking other languages, or practicing other customs are dehumanized.

Traditional and new media outlets claim to strive for objectivity, but study of practices over time provides evidence that bias is widespread. Society's comparatively short history with social media shows that, far from being ameliorated in these environments, bias is only distorted further and heightened online. Media outlets and social media sites are businesses like any others and must answer to corporate owners; this fact necessarily influences the context in which they do their work. What these types of media corporations have in common is also their most effective tool in forming public opinion: they control the flow of information – what people get to hear about, for how long, how a subject is framed, and in what detail. Not so long ago, the traditional media's ability to withhold, misrepresent, or trivialize potentially important or relevant news was a tool that could stop major legislation. The rise of the internet and the democratizing presence of social media platforms has made it much harder – and sometimes impossible – to bury a story. However, the media can still lift a story into the spotlight and keep it at the forefront for as long as it likes, and filter bubbles can still prevent a story that thoroughly captures the attention of one online community from crossing over into the awareness of others.

In recent years, as traditional media has faceted and been forced to share attention with social media, the fracturing and ideological isolation feared by proponents of the fairness doctrine has only proliferated. At the same time, though, voices that were never able to be heard or taken seriously before have been able to find a platform and an audience – be it in a podcast, on Twitter, or in a subreddit. While the American political landscape has become more bitterly divisive and vitriolic, voters have registered and struggled to turn out in record numbers to make their political voices heard. Objectivity is a theoretical concept, and one person's fair, reasonable context is someone else's bitterly partisan spin. These are particularly turbulent and difficult times to be a consumer of information, and there has probably never been more information for us to consume, filter, and be discerning about.

Bad is stronger than good

This discussion of information literacy began with a reminder about the usefulness of reflective vs. habitual thought and concludes with a cautionary note about another aspect of human cognition. Research in psychology and sociology has established beyond a doubt that negative and positive evaluations are not symmetrical (Baumeister et al. 2001). That is, it seems to be human nature to assign more weight and importance or validity to bad news than to good news. It is important to keep this in mind when considering the impact the media have on everything from how people think about current events to how parents raise their children to who citizens elect as politicians to what consumers place in their shopping carts. Bad news is far more interesting to people's brains than good news, from which follows the fact that bad news sells more papers, is given more broadcast coverage, and drives more likes and clicks than positive takes on the world. The allure of negative news is the source for the practice of *doomscrolling*, going through social media and news sources to get a deeper and deeper feeling that the world is falling apart.

When it comes to language in the media, everyone has a responsibility to themselves and to fellow citizens to be informed, reflective consumers. Knee-jerk, negative, and gut reactions feel wonderful – they literally release dopamine into our brains – but they are not conducive to long-term happiness. Remember that no one's life is as perfect as it seems in their online feed, no issue or idea is as simple and conclusive as it seems on Twitter, and "fake news" is only effective if the consumers of the news are willing to swallow it.

Discussion questions

1. Think about your favorite animated film. What kinds of speech varieties are presented? List the main characters (protagonists and antagonists), what you think the speech variety is, and why you think they chose that voice for that character. It may be useful to do some research online about the actors who voice those characters.
2. Pick any Disney movie and keep track of the following for one main female character: 1) how many times the character speaks, 2) what she speaks about, and 3) how many words she utters overall. If possible, do the same for a main male character. How do they compare? What does this tell you about these characters?
3. In the Disney movie *Frozen*, one of the bad guy characters speaks with a "standard" variety of American English (despite the Scandinavian setting). Why do you think Disney chose to break from the typical pattern here?
4. Make a list of the information/news websites or social media channels you engage in daily. Can you identify any bias in the information presented to you? If you were looking for unbiased information, where would you turn?
5. The term "fake news" became especially popular during Donald Trump's presidency. How did Trump use this term? How did his opponents use the term? Give an example of a recent "news" story that was eventually labeled fake. What are some of the main concerns with fake news and the existence of fake news outlets for information literacy?

13 Language in the workplace

Unwelcoming environments

In 2017, two African American women sued their employer, Fox News, for racial harassment by their supervisor, Judy Slater, comptroller for the company. Slater (who is white) regularly told African American employees that their "people" couldn't pronounce certain words correctly. During meetings with the payroll department, Slater would write the words *mother*, *father*, *month*, and *ask* on a whiteboard and ask African Americans to say each word out loud so that she could "correct" their pronunciation. This "correction" was for their own good so that they could "learn" to speak properly. There were many other instances where Slater behaved in a discriminatory manner. She asked one African American employee if her three children all had the same father, asked another why all Black men were "wifebeaters," and said that the payroll department had "too much afro" (Geier 2017).

In 2018, a Dunkin' Donuts franchise in Baltimore posted a sign asking customers to call and report any employees caught speaking in a language other than English (Shaffer 2018). The sign stated that customers who reported an employee would be rewarded with a free cup of coffee and a pastry of their choice. The sign was not on display for very long before it appeared on social media and began to receive negative attention. People called for a boycott of all Dunkin' Donut franchises. The company quickly made a statement clarifying that they did not have a policy requiring employees to speak only English. Indeed, having such a policy is often illegal, especially if the policy is not carefully written to make it clear that English is only required when it is necessary for conducting business. The owner of the Dunkin' Donuts franchise took the sign down, saying that a manager had posted it without his knowledge in an effort to deal with a complaint from a customer. In apologizing, the franchise owner emphasized that the sign's author did not intend to discriminate against employees who spoke other languages but that it was placed there as part of the effort to deal with the specific customer complaint. The manager probably should have realized that the problem was the complaining customer's racism and not an employee's use of a language other than English.

In 2019, Connie Cheung applied for a job at a Chicago employee recruitment firm. The email she received in response to her application contained only one sentence – "me love you long time." The message was between two of the company's male directors, but it was accidentally forwarded to Cheung. The phrase *me love you long time* (originally from the 1987 film *Full Metal Jacket*) is a racist/sexist slur directed specifically to sexualize and denigrate Asian women. The men involved admitted that the message was insensitive and apologized, but they maintained that the "joke" was simply a quotation from a movie and was not intended to be racist. The author of the message told a reporter, "It was an insensitive

DOI: 10.4324/9781003332886-13

comment, I realize that. It was a racist comment, I realize that. . . . I had no racist intentions. I'm not racist, I'm certainly not sexist" (Alani 2019).

In these cases, language ideologies serve as the basis for racist behavior that individuals attempt to absolve themselves of by claiming that the *intent* of their speech was not racism. The victims of racial harassment are treated as though their concerns are unfounded because they simply "took things the wrong way." But is the act of "correcting" another's pronunciation actually intended to help that person succeed? Is a racist joke between two white people somehow acceptable just because they didn't intend to harm the woman they were joking about? The concern over the intent of an action is part of Hill's *folk theory of racism*, where the problem of racial inequality is understood as resulting from the actions of individual racists. As discussed in Chapter 1, this theory does nothing to "explain" racism. Rather, it simply attempts to absolve those who cause harm by allowing them to argue that their racist acts are not an indicator that they are somehow part of the "racists" responsible for the problem. Particularly in the workplace, the "hunt for racists game" (Hodges 2016) serves to distract from the actual problems of structural racism and implicit bias.

A workplace can become unwelcoming in many ways. It may involve prohibiting the use of a particular language, using racist language to co-workers, making sexual comments to a co-worker, etc. Notice that all of these involve language. Language is crucial instrument involved in creating an unwelcoming environment. In this chapter, we will explore the ways in which the use of language in the workplace can result in exactly this kind of discrimination. Regulating the language used by employees can result in a violation of the Civil Rights Act (discussed later in this chapter). However, failing to regulate the language of an employee (who harasses others) can also produce workplace discrimination. While this chapter should not be considered legal advice (we are not lawyers), our hope is that it will provide you a clearer sense of how regular people doing their jobs encounter many kinds of issues related to language and foster an understanding of what it means to have inclusive, multicultural, and welcoming work environments for all.

Sorry not sorry

In her research on the workplace environments at advertising agencies, anthropologist Shalini Shankar (2020) found two basic ideologies and approaches for creating inclusivity in the workplace. Shankar refers to these distinct ideologies as *diversity* and *multiculturalism*. Following the folk theory of racism, the diversity approach assumes that the problem of racism is solved by having a diverse workforce combined with an absence of racist intentions. Workplaces following the diversity approach tend to assume that racism is resolved by having employees of different backgrounds. This means that outward appearances are critical for demonstrating a commitment to a diverse work environment and, in many cases, the appearance of a commitment to diversity becomes more important than actually creating an inclusive workplace. This is apparent when universities photoshop people of color into images of (otherwise entirely white) students (Prichep 2013).

In contrast, the multiculturalism approach is focused on incorporating the contributions from workers from diverse backgrounds to ensure that a variety of perspectives are always considered. In this approach, employees of different backgrounds are valued precisely because their different cultural experiences allow them to view a problem in multiple ways. Rather than being concerned with hiring individuals who fill "slots" in a checklist of visible diversity, workplaces using the multiculturalism approach focused on ensuring that their diverse employees were equal participants in the workplace culture.

Workplaces using Shankar's diversity approach were much more likely to experience public "gaffes" such as creating an ad campaign that people find racially offensive. In workplaces based in multiculturalism, this was not an issue, presumably because the varied perspectives of the workforce made it more likely for individuals to point out their discomfort with a proposal that might be considered racist. In cases where diversity-style workplaces resulted in public accusations of racism, the reaction was generally two-fold. First, directors would point out the number of people of color employed by the company as evidence of the absence of racism (even if those employees are in low-level positions with little opportunity for advancement). Second, the directors would emphasize that they did not *intend* to offend anyone. Indeed, some ad agencies argued that the intent of an advertisement was to demonstrate diversity by including a person of color (even though the person of color was presented in some denigrating and racist manner).

Both responses reflect the way in which the folk theory of racism serves to perpetuate racial inequality. The belief that racism is caused by individual racists makes it seem reasonable to attempt to focus on demonstrating a lack of racist intent. The logic here is that if an individual is not in the category of "racist," they are unable to discriminate and cannot be held responsible when people feel mistreated or insulted. For companies, this typically involves using the appearance of diversity as evidence for a lack of racist intent.

The argument typically goes like something like this: *I cannot be racist because I have Black employees; therefore, I could not have intended my comments to be racist so that anyone taking offense has either misunderstood or they are overly sensitive*. These responses are typically "false apologies"; they are structured to have the appearance of an apology but actually blame the victim for being offended (e.g., *I am sorry that you feel that way*; *I'm sorry if anyone misunderstood my words*; *I'm sorry that some people were offended*). This does nothing to correct or repair the harm caused by racism in the workplace. Instead, it helps maintain a racist work environment and makes minority employees feel that their concerns will not be taken seriously. The approach of demonstrating "diversity" in a workplace only serves to reproduce an environment where racial inequality not only persists, but it is likely to be the norm for workplace interactions.

The key to a multicultural workplace is to create an environment in which everyone feels welcome and knows that they belong and that their ideas, opinions, and feelings will be taken seriously. Simply hiring individuals who create the appearance of a diverse workplace is not enough to overcome an unwelcoming work environment. The term *unwelcoming environment* is used by the Equal Employment Opportunity Commission (EEOC) to describe workplaces marked by harassment. An unwelcoming (or hostile) work environment can take different forms, including ethnic slurs, workplace graffiti, physical violence, sexually inappropriate behavior, displaying offensive images, harassing a colleague outside of work, or a persistent failure to promote employees who belong to minority groups.

What is the EEOC?

The EEOC is the government agency responsible for enforcing federal laws that prohibit discrimination against employees or job applicants. The agency covers discrimination based on a person's race, skin color, religion, sex, national origin, age, disability, or genetic information. Discrimination based on sex includes gender identity, sexual orientation, and pregnancy status. The EEOC investigates charges against employees covered by various laws. This usually involves employers with at least 15 employees and may also include labor unions or employment agencies. An EEOC investigation assesses the allegations to determine if discrimination has occurred. In cases where an employer is found to have illegally discriminated, the EEOC will try to settle the case between an employer and the victims of discrimination. This usually involves a financial settlement paid to victims by the employer. In cases where a settlement cannot be reached, the EEOC has the authority to file a lawsuit to protect the rights of discrimination victims. Although the EEOC has the power to file lawsuits and represent victims, the agency only does so in a small percentage of cases. The EEOC determines which cases to litigate based on several different factors, including the strength of evidence, the severity of the discrimination, the number of people affected, and whether the case will set a legal precedent. Cases that might produce a legal precedent are those that deal with unsettled questions in discrimination law. Some relatively recent settled questions include things like whether sex discrimination includes sexual orientation or gender identity, do prohibitions against speaking Native American languages count as national origin discrimination, and does the law cover discrimination based on genetic information (such as refusing to hire someone because their DNA includes a genetic mutation that makes them prone to certain diseases).

The EEOC provides directives on national origin discrimination with multiple examples of what constitutes discriminatory behavior. Title VII of the Civil Rights Act was designed (in part) to protect workers from discrimination based on race, ethnicity, national origin, sex, age, and other protected categories, or traits directly linked to those categories. With the passage of the 1964 Civil Rights Act (Pub. L. 88–352, 78 Stat. 241), some types of discrimination in the workplace have been illegal under Title VII. In broad terms, Title VII makes it illegal to deny a person employment, promotion, or workplace advantages (benefits, use of facilities, etc.). The scope of the law is limited to protected categories (also referred to as *classes*): disability, genetic makeup, race, skin color, national origin, religion, and sex (including gender identity, sexual orientation, and sexual harassment). This protection extends to those with whom an employee has associations; for example, you cannot refuse to hire Asians nor can you refuse to hire someone who is married to an Asian.

"This is America, speak English!"

While it might seem reasonable to expect employees to speak English at work, rules requiring an "English-only" workplace are often more about discrimination than about business necessity. Here, we will consider some of the more common explanations for why one would want to restrict workers to only speak English (see Walters 2001). One common reason given is that having everyone speak English will reduce ethnic tension between speakers of different languages. Of course, this only makes sense from the perspective of those who are monolingual in English. A business owner could also reduce ethnic tension by only hiring white employees, but that would be (almost) universally recognized as racist and discriminatory. For the people prevented from speaking their native language, those who are being punished to appease their white co-workers, such policies would probably be seen as *increasing* ethnic tension.

The case of *EEOC v. RD's Drive-In*

Because of their proximity to the Navajo Nation, most of the employees (and customers) at RD's Drive-In were Navajo and spoke Navajo to one another at work. Although the owners of the restaurant did not speak Navajo, the restaurant had been part of the community since the late 1970s. In early 2000, the owners experienced a period of incredibly high employee turnover. In three months, they had hired 57 people who had quit their jobs shortly after being hired. One of the women who quit her job told the owners that she was leaving because a small group of employees was constantly using crude and vulgar language to insult other co-workers, customers, and the owners themselves. Because the owners were unable to know what employees were saying in Navajo, they had no way of knowing exactly when someone was intimidating other employees or being inappropriate in some other way. It seemed reasonable to require the employees to speak English at work so that their supervisors could better evaluate job performance and stop harassing behavior (Zachary 2005).

Although the owners of RD's Drive-In did not intend to discriminate against employees, the EEOC found that the way in which the policy was worded and implemented violated anti-discrimination laws. The owners' first policy simply said "No Navajo," but was quickly revised to better align with EEOC guidelines. From the EEOC's perspective, however, the new policy was overly broad. To avoid discrimination, such policies must be very specific about when English is required. The tone of a language policy can also be a factor in how such a policy is viewed by the EEOC. Employers must be extremely careful when drafting such policies to ensure that they are not in violation of the guidelines given by the EEOC.

Under the EEOC guidelines, prohibitions against using a particular language may (illegally) discriminate based on *national origin*. For an English-only policy to be legal, there must be a work-related necessity for speaking English. Asking a receptionist to answer the phone in English is fine. However, asking them to only speak English when they are taking a break or having lunch is likely to be illegal. Although one might *intend* to reduce workplace tensions with an English-only policy, it is often the case that the policy is part of a larger pattern of discrimination so that a workplace marked by "ethnic tension" is actually marked by racism.

Consider the case of *EEOC v. Central California Foundation for Health*, which involved Filipinx nurses who were prohibited from speaking Tagalog (or any other Filipino language). In 2006, the hospital held a special meeting only for Filipinx nurses who were told that they could not speak their native languages at work. The hospital enforced the policy by having security guards follow the nurses around the hospital and placing cameras at the nurses' station to catch them if they spoke the wrong language. This was part of a larger pattern of harassment of Filipinx employees. In one case, an employee sprayed air freshener all over a Filipina nurse's lunch because she said the food smelled bad. The hospital policy only applied to Filipino languages. There were nurses who were allowed to continue to speak Spanish, Hindi, Bangla, and so on (Do 2012). A workplace language policy that prohibits a single language but allows other languages (besides English) is going to be discriminatory. Directing the policy at a specific language demonstrates that English isn't required for the performance of the job (so that the problem isn't the use of some other languages). Such a policy is clearly illegal and is likely to result in a lawsuit. In this case, the hospital never admitted to discrimination but settled the lawsuit for $975,000

Another common argument in support of English-only policies is that they are intended to help workers who are native speakers of other languages learn the language more easily. Of course, being surrounded by a language you don't know in no way means that you will learn that language. It also assumes that workers who use other languages do so because they cannot speak English. By now, of course, you know that it is totally normal for bilinguals to alternate languages depending on context. Two Latinx employees who are native speakers of English are not speaking to one another in Spanish simply because that is the only language they know. The erasure of bilingualism is a basic part of the monolingual Standard Language Ideology in the United States. When the "helping them learn English" explanation is used, it is typically an afterthought to shift the focus to the intent rather than the effect of the policy (as in the case in the very first example in this chapter).

Consider another case involving the Duke University biostatistics graduate program. In 2019, two members of the faculty in that program went to the director of graduate studies to try to determine the names of Chinese graduate students they had observed speaking Chinese "very loudly" in the student lounge. The faculty members wanted the students' names so that they could avoiding having to advise or work with those students. The graduate director emailed the Chinese students to ask them not to speak Chinese, even in the student lounge when they were on break. In explaining the motivation for the policy, she wrote, "They were disappointed that these students were not taking the opportunity to improve their English and were being so impolite as to have a conversation that not everyone on the floor could understand." One would likely expect that anyone admitted to a graduate program in biostatistics at Duke ought to speak English fairly well already. It would also be quite awkward for two native speakers of the same language to have a casual conversation in some other language, regardless of whether some people nearby might not understand. The policy was quickly abandoned, and the director of graduate studies apologized to the students (Xu 2019).

Within the EEOC guidelines, it is discriminatory to prevent people from speaking other languages when they are on break, at lunch, or otherwise not directly engaged in work. English may only be required when it is deemed critical to job performance or in cases of emergency. You cannot forbid employees from speaking other languages just because someone is offended by hearing people speak something other than English. La Cantera Resort and Spa in San Antonio had an English-only policy directed at Latinx banquet employees at the resort who were told that they had to always speak English while at the resort (even on breaks). The resort owners settled the ensuing discrimination lawsuit in 2019 for $2.6 million (EEOC 2019a).

Another reason sometimes given for requiring all employees to speak English is that doing so improves the efficiency of the workplace. A policy that forbids other languages while on break does not improve efficiency. Indeed, English-only policies are just as likely to interfere with workplace efficiency. For example, in 2016, Leon's Frozen Custard in Milwaukee instituted a policy requiring employees to always speak English. Leon's is in an area of Milwaukee with a large Latinx population, and many of the employees and customers were bilingual (Mettler 2016). This English-only policy (which was quickly rescinded) gained widespread attention after a customer noticed that an employee was whispering (in Spanish) to anyone who ordered in Spanish to let them know that she was not allowed to speak to them in Spanish. If customers and employees both speak Spanish, requiring your employees to never speak Spanish is a very inefficient policy.

Inefficiency was also the result of an English-only policy for housekeepers at Colorado's Central Station Casino, which settled a discrimination lawsuit for $1.5 million in 2003 (EEOC 2003). Their policy was instituted after the human resources director expressed fears that the Latinx employees were talking about her in Spanish. Out of fear of being caught speaking Spanish, the housekeepers were meeting inside of closets to discuss work questions. Forcing your employees to find a place to hide from you to fulfill their work duties is anything but efficient.

Finally, it is sometimes argued that English-only policies are required for the purposes of workplace safety. Of course, if you were in a hotel hallway and the building were on fire, would you rather a monolingual housekeeper yell "*¡Fuego!*" immediately or have them wait to find a bilingual co-worker to ask how to say "fire" in English? In most cases, there is simply no need for an English-only policy for employees. Such policies are not created because employees are choosing to talk to English-speaking clients or customers in Spanish or Chinese. They are almost always put in place to appease those who take offense at people who speak other languages in public spaces. And actions against those who speak other languages are typically based on racism rather than having anything to do with work performance. In one case, a woman was fired for greeting a co-worker by saying *buenas dias* rather than *hello* or *good morning* (EEOC 2000). In another case, a custodian who had her job interview and her training conducted entirely in Spanish was fired for not being able to speak English (EEOC 2019b). Although English-only policies are typically intended to appease worker tensions or customer complaints, often they simply turn out to be forms of discrimination, and in some cases, can result in major lawsuits against companies with such policies.

"Nobody can understand those people"

Discrimination against speakers of English because of their accent is another common form of workplace discrimination. Like language choice, the EEOC views accent discrimination to be discrimination based on national origin. This means that native English speakers from the United States who are treated unfairly because they have a particular regional or ethnic accent are not able to bring discrimination cases to the EEOC. There have been cases of discrimination based on the English spoken by African American employees (as in the Fox News case at the opening of this chapter). In such cases, there are usually additional forms of racial discrimination that can serve as the basis for a lawsuit without considering language. Nevertheless, racial discrimination based on dialect or voice quality continues to be a problem, particularly in cases of linguistic profiling (discussed in Chapter 14), in which people racially discriminate over the phone based solely on the sound of someone's voice.

For white speakers who speak a regional dialect that is viewed negatively, there is no recourse for discrimination based on accent. Being from a particular area does not count as a protected class, so regional accents are not covered by civil rights laws. Unfortunately, deciding not to hire someone because they have an Appalachian or Boston accent is perfectly legal under current law. This is partially because the courts maintain the idea (which comes from Standard Language Ideology) that anybody who really wants to change their accent ought to be able to do so. Of course, like most of the Standard Language Ideology, this is simply not true. Believing it, however, allows accent-based discrimination to continue unabated.

An employer has some latitude in matters of language: "[a]n adverse employment decision may be predicated upon an individual's accent when – but only when – it interferes materially with job performance" (Civil Rights Act of 1964, §701 et seq., 42 U.S.C.A. §2000e et seq.). In other words, decisions like firing, disciplining, or not hiring regarding a non-native speaker of English because they have an accent may be illegal if the person's accent is not relevant for their ability to perform their job duties. Such decisions may discriminate based on national origin, particularly if a person's job does not require the use of English or if the person's accent is easy for the average English speaker to understand. For example, an employee who has been interacting with clients for many years cannot suddenly be disciplined for having an accent simply because a customer complains.

Discriminating on expectation

Because the perception of a non-native accent is influenced by expectations based on physical appearance, it is quite easy for decisions based on accent to also be instances of discrimination based on national origin. Discrimination against employees or job applicants because they speak English with a non-native accent is a form of national origin discrimination. An employee's accent may only be a factor if spoken English is required to perform job duties and the individual's accent interferes with their ability to communicate in English. Some things to consider about discrimination related to non-native accents in English:

- Requiring an employee to be fluent in written or spoken English is only allowed if the use of English is necessary for effective job performance. It is a form of national-origin discrimination to require fluency for employees who work in jobs where they do not interact with customers or clients.
- Employees must demonstrate that an individual's accent materially interferes with their ability to perform their job duties. If a person can satisfactorily perform their job when speaking accented English, it is illegal to discriminate on the basis of having a non-native accent.
- Customer complaints about an employee's accent may not be used as the basis for employment decisions unless there is evidence that the employee is unable to perform their job. If an individual's accent is understandable and does not interfere with job performance, the individual cannot be fire or punished simply because a customer was offended by having to interact with a non-native speaker. Complaints about having to interact with someone who is not a native speaker of English are typically no different from a customer complaining about an employee belonging to a particular race or religion.
- Where the evidence shows that an individual has a good command of spoken English or satisfactorily performs his job when speaking accented English, courts have ruled against employers for national origin discrimination.

The question of whether a person's accent interferes with their job performance depends upon distinguishing an accent that is discernable from one that interferes with the spoken communication skills the job requires. If an "unbiased" listener has no problem understanding a person's speech, then it is unlikely to interfere with job performance. The same is true for requiring fluency in English for employees who never have to use English to successfully perform their job duties. If, however, the job required using English, a fluency requirement is obviously appropriate. It is also acceptable to require employees to know some language other than English. For example, if a company wants an employee who can work with clients in both English and Spanish, it is perfectly legal to avoid hiring monolingual English speakers (who would not have the Spanish skills required to perform the job).

Whether it is prohibiting languages or discriminating against those with L2 accents, the important question is whether the employees involved speak in a way that makes it impossible for performing their job duties. It cannot be because other employees are uncomfortable hearing an accent or a foreign language or because a customer complains. If a person can perform their job successfully, the way that they happen to speak should be irrelevant. Otherwise, discrimination is likely to be involved.

"You sound so insecure when you talk the way I do"

In the 1930s, when commercial aviation began to expand as an industry, early airlines rejected the idea of using male stewards (like on trains) and decided to hire professional nurses to serve as stewardesses on their flights. The use of nurses had some important advantages. At the time, flights were not smooth so that air sickness was extremely common. The airlines realized that people in the throes of vomiting would feel more comfortable being helped by a nurse. These flight attendants wore nurses' uniforms in order to make travelers feel safer about flying. During World War II, when many nurses had joined the war effort, the airlines continued to hire only women as flight attendants (Barry 2007; Vantoch 2017; see Figure 13.1).

After the war, air travel became more common, especially for businessmen traveling for work. Stewardesses became part of a broad marketing scheme to make air travel attractive to male travelers on business. The airlines began to put restrictions on their female flight attendants to ensure that the women would be alluring to straight male travelers. The job requirements for stewardesses began to restrict those hired to very rigid physical standards. Stewardesses had to be of a certain height and weight, with regular weigh-ins to make sure none of the women were gaining weight. If you weighed more than the limit, you would lose your job. Stewardesses also had to be of a certain age. The airlines made it clear that the job was temporary and that employees when be let go when they reached a certain age (usually around 32). Some even presented this as a positive aspect of the job, claiming that with their many interactions with businessmen, a stewardess would likely find a husband and no longer need to work well before she reached the age limit placed upon employees.

In addition, stewardesses had to be unmarried, could not have children, and would be fired if they became pregnant. Through the 1960s and 1970s, airlines wanted stewardesses to appear sexually available to attract the male-dominated business market. Making stewardesses dress more like waitresses at Hooters (see later in this chapter) also masked the actual need for flight attendants in maintaining calm between passengers and being able to guide them should there be an emergency. To maintain the image of sexual availability, stewardesses were expected to appear happy, flirtatious, and carefree, regardless of their actual working conditions. Stewardess were valued for their ability to entice men, even though their job

Figure 13.1 Flight attendants for Pacific Southwest Airlines modeling the uniforms worn in the 1970s, which typically included miniskirts or other revealing features to highlight women's sexuality

was quite serious, involving making sure all that safety guidelines are followed, controlling passengers to ensure their safety, and being prepared to act in case of an emergency.

Presenting the losers

A good example of the attitudes toward "stewardesses" is the "Presenting the losers" ad campaign used by Eastern Airlines in the early 1970s, as seen in the QR code here. The "losers" were the "19 out of 20" women rejected for a job with the airline because they didn't meet their standards in terms of both physical attractiveness and ability to perform emotional labor. The advertisement portrayed the job application process like this:

> Sure, we want her to be pretty . . . don't you? That's why we look at her face, her make up, her complexion, her figure, her weight, her legs, her grooming, her nails and her hair. But we don't stop there. . . . We listen to her voice, her speech. We judge her personality, her maturity, her intelligence, her intentions, her enthusiasm, her resiliency, and her stamina. We don't want a stewardess to be . . . unconcerned about your needs.

In a classic study of the experiences of flight attendants, sociologist Arlie Hochschild argued that the job was a form of emotional labor in which the main purpose of the job was for the employee to project a particular emotional state (1983). In her research, Hochschild found that the one of the worst aspects of working as a stewardess was having to control your emotions and continue to appear cheerful while trying to deal with drunken outbursts and continuous forms of sexual assault. Hochschild found that many professions traditionally viewed as "women's work" were part of an economy of emotions involving the use of women to project particularly emotional states. Emotional labor is a central part of the work done by nurses, teachers in early grades, receptionists, restaurant servers, customer service representatives, and so on. Although much has changed since Hochschild's study, women in the workplace are still expected to perform more emotional labor than their male counterparts, regardless of the job involved. These expectations play a central role in how patterns of language use create forms of inequality in the workplace.

Although women have pushed back against their exploitation in the workplace, the assumption that women should be performing emotional labor continues to create unequal conditions in the workplace. This ideology is at the center of the double standard faced by many women in the workplace. If a female employee avoids public displays of emotion (just as many men in the workplace do), she is likely to be judged negatively, like some sort of cold-hearted "bitch." This is doubly true for women of color (see Hughes & Mamiseishvili 2014). However, women are also constantly judged based on an assumption of emotional display. Women's language use is often interpreted as indexing insecurity, a lack of assertiveness, or excessive emotional display. This is part of a much broader ideology concerning the differences between the way that men and women are socialized to speak.

It has long been recognized that women (especially white middle-class cisgender women) stereotypically tend to use forms of language that keep a conversation going and allow others a chance to speak (Lakoff 1975). This includes the use of more questions intended to promote conversation (rather than seeking information) and the use of backchannels, forms intended to let the listener know that you are paying attention, such as saying "uh-huh" every so often. It may also involve the use of rising intonation on statements (as opposed to only on questions), which indexes that the utterance isn't final and either the speaker or the listener should keep the interaction going. In other words, it indicates that although the utterance is ending, the discourse should continue (whether by the speaker or by the listener).

This linguistic phenomenon is sometimes called "uptalk" and is common in the speech of both men and women. Consider the case of text support instructions, which typically involve a series of utterances with rising intonation ("you need to go to your home screen [rise], and you should see an icon there [rise], and it should be shaped like an apple [rise]"). Young women studying business are often told to avoid using this intonation pattern because, they are told, it makes them sound insecure, weak, and unassertive. Of course, men use this pattern as well, and when they do, it almost always occurs without comment. This is just one of the ways in which women are criticized for speaking in ways that are also used by men. In Chapter 4, we also saw the case of creaky voice, a form typically associated with the speech of men but often stigmatized when used by women.

If women are socialized to use language in ways that encourage others to speak, men are typically socialized to do just the opposite and control the conversation as much as possible. In conversations involving only cis men, stereotypical language use may involve heavy amounts of interruption, conflicts over the direction of the conversation, and the use of insults and jokes to take control of the conversation from others. Many men hold the language ideology that they should use language to demonstrate competence and superiority by displaying knowledge or becoming the center of attention. For heterosexual men, feeling the need to index competence may be that much stronger when speaking to women. What may be intended to display competence by sharing knowledge will often come across as *mansplaining*. In many instances, however, men's interactional behavior goes well beyond attempting to show competence and becomes a means of silencing women in the workplace. This includes interrupting women, co-opting or taking credit for women's ideas, and dismissing women's suggestions or contributions. Such behaviors are often dismissed through evoking sexist stereotypes that women's speech is overly indirect, unclear, or indecisive.

Such sexist language ideologies are present in discourse regarding apologies. While there is no research demonstrating that women apologize more than men, there are seemingly endless articles, advice columns, and websites warning women about their tendency to apologize more than men. Women are encouraged to stop apologizing because it makes them look weak in the workplace. But there are serious problems with this idea. The assumption that women apologize more frequently is a stereotype rather than a fact. Much of what is pointed to (like "Sorry to bother you") are not actually apologies; they are types of politeness moves that serve to maintain relationships, not to admit to wrongdoing.

There is also the problem of assuming that apologies somehow "mean" that a person is weak. Research suggests that men who apologize are seen as more transformative leaders (Tucker et al. 2006). So when men apologize it is not viewed as a sign of weakness. Research also suggests that people typically view apologies from men as more sincere and more effective compared to apologies from women (Walfisch et al. 2013). So it is not the case that apologies suggest that a person is weak; it is only apologies *from women* that are interpreted as a sign of weakness.

The idea that women look weak because they apologize more is an example of how prejudice can influence the interpretation of one's speech. The stereotype that women are somehow always apologizing is widely circulating, and it influences the interpretation of apologies for both men and women. As we saw in Chapter 11, listener's expectations may influence the perception of the speech of others. A listener who anticipates an L2 accent is more likely to hear an accent, even when listening to a native speaker. In the same way, an apology coming from a woman is likely to be seen as expected and ordinary. It is more likely to seem insincere simply because it is what women are expected to do. An apology from a man is still judged through the lens of this stereotype, however, and since men are *not* expected to apologize, their apologies are seen as unexpected and, therefore, more sincere and more likely to be seen as a sign of leadership rather than as a sign of weakness. So the problem of women's speech in the workplace has nothing to do with the linguistic structure of women's speech. Men typically use the same forms. The problem is entirely about the *perception* of women's speech by others, and that perception is flawed because it is founded in sexist stereotypes and inaccurate understandings of language.

Silencing women

In a 1995 study examining interactions on two internet mailing list discussion groups, Susan Herring and her colleagues outlined four basic ways in which women's voices were silenced by male co-workers:

- *Avoidance* – simply ignoring women's comments, dismissing women's speech using humor or insult, and deflecting attention away from the issue a woman has raised
- *Confrontation* – rather than addressing the issue raised, creating a confrontation by starting an argument, criticizing the woman for speaking at all, or showing anger and threatening to leave
- *Co-option* – taking credit for women's ideas and contributions to a discussion, reconstructing events to portray oneself as an ally; men claiming the position of a "feminist" when acting in a sexist manner
- ***Interpretive control*** – trying to maintain control over how women's speech is interpreted, claiming that women mean something other than what they say, adopting a stance as the "true victim" (to criticism from "irrational" women)

Herring and her colleagues also outlined strategies that women used to successfully challenge efforts to silence their voices:

- *Persistence* – expect to be ignored, continue to speak up, and don't stop until you are heard
- *Consistent focus* – demand to be taken seriously, point out diversionary tactics, and return to the topic at hand
- *Solidarity* – there is power in numbers, so women should stand up for other women who are having their voices ignored or silenced
- *Awareness* – be conscious of silencing mechanisms, demonstrate their use by men, and make it clear that they are unacceptable (such as Kamala Harris' repeated use of "I'm still speaking" whenever she was interrupted during the 2020 vice presidential debate)

We have repeatedly seen that stereotyped assumptions and expectations about how someone will speak have a huge impact on how that person's speech will be interpreted and understood. The expectation for women to perform emotional labor means that women's speech is often evaluated based on emotional display rather than content. Women often find themselves walking that linguistic tightrope to avoid being judged as either cold-hearted and cruel or overly emotional and unprofessional. This double bind becomes even worse when women are victims of sexual harassment in the workplace, when displays of emotion can trigger retaliation or more severe harassment.

"You're so much prettier when you're not angry"

One of the most persistent forms of workplace discrimination is sexual harassment. In 2019, federal non-discrimination agencies filed charges of sexual harassment in more than 12,000 cases (EEOC 2021). This is only a small subset of all harassment complaints received and an even smaller subset of actual harassment (including complaints to state or local agencies and cases that go unreported). Just as with racial or ethnic discrimination, the persistence of sexual harassment is buttressed by millennia of representations that portray women as objects for men's sexual pleasure who should be subservient to men. For many men, histories of sexual conquest play a central role in the construction of a masculine social persona. The use of so-called locker room talk in conversations between men is often disregarded as "harmless" talk, but bonding between men through the mutual sexual objectification of women simply reinforces the indexical links that portray women as primarily existing to pleasure men.

The expectation for women to perform emotional labor is closely tied to this history of sexual objectification. Just as airlines decided that the sexualization of flight attendants would increase business travel from men, there are restaurants and bars that require female servers or bartenders to wear revealing uniforms intended to draw in and maintain male customers. Employees at strip clubs or restaurants specifically objectifying women (like Hooters) must agree not to file complaints of sexual harassment because it is simply expected to occur in those environments. Of course, sexual harassment is not limited to the workplace as women may be regularly subjected to harassment simply walking down the street. The pervasiveness of sexual harassment throughout society makes it especially difficult to control in the workplace (Debenport 2020).

#metoo

New York activist Tarana Brown began the MeToo Movement in 2006 (before there were hashtags). She began using the phrase on social media (on a site called MySpace) to let victims of sexual harassment know that they were not alone and had the support of others who had suffered forms of harassment. In 2017, the phrase became widespread after actress Alyssa Milano used it in reference to the sexual harassment case against (now convicted rapist and former movie producer) Harvey Weinstein. This led to many women sharing their experiences of harassment on social media, ultimately resulting in the exposure of a number of prominent men who had long histories of sexual harassment and sexual assault. This led to a global effort to raise awareness about sexual harassment.

The EEOC guidelines distinguish between two basic types of sexual harassment: quid pro quo cases and cases involving a hostile work environment. The term quid pro quo refers to when "submission to or rejection of such conduct by an individual is used as the basis for employment decisions affecting such individual" (EEOC 2021). In other words, it is illegal to require sexual favors as a condition of employment. A hostile environment refers to cases where harassment is pervasive and/or severe.

In some cases, the two types may co-occur or the line between the two types may be unclear. The main framework for evaluating cases of sexual harassment was established by the Supreme Court in the case of *Meritor Savings Bank v. Vinson* (1980). This case was the first to establish that unwelcome sexual behavior may be a form of sex discrimination. It also found that a company is responsible for sexual harassment by a supervising employee even if the director of the company was unaware that the harassment was occurring. This is one of the reasons why it is critical for employers to have a clear sexual harassment policy that includes guidelines for submitting complaints to the company. Employees must be aware of the policy and know how to report violations. If a company has no policy for dealing with cases of sexual harassment, it is unlikely that the courts will decide in their favor if a case comes to trial. In evaluating cases involving sexual harassment, the EEOC policy guidelines focus on three basic issues: determining whether sexual conduct was unwelcome, evaluating evidence of sexual harassment, and determining whether a work environment is hostile. These are the main questions that must be addressed in an EEOC evaluation of complaints of sexual harassment.

Because sexual conduct may be invited or uninvited-but-tolerated, it is important to establish whether the conduct was unwelcome. To be considered unwelcome, the conduct must be uninvited and be considered undesirable or offensive to the employee to whom it was directed. For this reason, it is important for victims of sexual harassment to openly state that the sexual conduct is unwanted and offensive. It is also important for victims (of any form of discrimination) to keep careful records of unwanted conduct and complaints to the offender or supervisors higher up in the company. Expressing that the conduct is unwelcome is an important step in trying to stop harassment before it becomes severe, but such complaints are not required, and an employer may still be found liable for harassment in cases where the victim did not openly complain. Here again, it is crucial for an employer to be sure that employees are aware of the process to safely report cases of sexual harassment. And for employees, it is important to respond to unwanted sexual conduct in a way that makes it clear that the behavior is offensive and undesirable. The determination of conduct as "unwelcome" may also consider the workplace behavior of the victim. If an individual has a history of initiating sexual banter with the accused harasser, it might suggest that the sexual conduct was not entirely unwelcome. However, the consideration of such factors must be specific to the case at hand. If an employee has a history of wearing revealing clothing, initiating sexual discussions, or flirting with co-workers, that history of conduct is irrelevant unless it specifically involved the individual currently accused of harassment.

Cases of sexual harassment often occur in private contexts where there are unlikely to be witnesses. Such cases often come to depend on the credibility of the victim's allegation. Again, it is useful for victims to keep a detailed record of unwelcome behavior and complaints to ensure that there is evidence to support their claim. Even so, in cases where there are neither witnesses nor a record of complaints, a victim's complaint can be found to be credible based on other evidence. For example, co-workers might witness a change in the victim's demeanor, particularly on occasions when harassment was said to occur. If a victim was clearly distraught after being alone with the harasser, observations by co-workers may be considered evidence. Similarly, a victim's conversations with friends and family may be used as corroborating evidence. If the victim discussed their problems with someone outside of work, this may be used to verify the victim's claims, especially concerning the timing of specific instances of unwelcome conduct.

The decision in the *Meritor Savings Bank v. Vinson* case determined that for sexual harassment to be discriminatory it must be sufficiently severe or pervasive that it creates a hostile, offensive, or intimidating working environment. In determining whether a given work environment is hostile, the EEOC considers several factors, including how frequently the conduct was repeated, if the conduct was patently offensive, if the harasser was a co-worker or a supervisor, and if there were multiple harassers or multiple victims.

In determining what is considered "patently offensive," the EEOC relies on a "reasonable person" standard based on whether a "reasonable person" would be offended by the conduct involved. For example, in a case where an employee invites someone to join a group of co-workers who regularly get together for drinks after work, one could expect that a reasonable person would not consider the invitation an example of unwelcome or hostile conduct.

Although the frequency of unwelcome sexual conduct is a factor in evaluating a work environment, it is possible for a single incident to be severe enough to be result in a hostile workplace. For example, a hostile environment can be established by a single instance of quid pro quo in which accepting a sexual advance is a condition of employment. In deciding whether a single instance of unwelcome conduct is severe enough to create a hostile environment, another factor is whether the harassment was verbal or physical. A single instance of unwanted touching may create a hostile environment and will be judged as more severe compared to verbal conduct. The regular use of sexually explicit language or the presence of pornography in the workplace do not necessarily create a hostile environment on their own, but such factors may be relevant in determining whether sexual conduct was pervasive enough to create a hostile environment.

Because of high profile cases involving powerful public figures, people tend to think of sexual harassment as somehow more common among men working in areas like entertainment, academia, or government. However, the women most likely to face sexual harassment in the workplace are those working in lower paying jobs, particularly jobs involving customer service. Because of the tendency for some businesses to exploit women's sexuality to attract male customers, men may somehow presume that women working in customer service somehow welcome sexual advances.

An example can be found in the case of *Barnhart et al. v. Safeway* (1991), which established that companies are responsible not only for preventing harassment between co-workers, but they must also prevent sexual harassment from customers. The case involved a grocery store where employees were expected to follow a particular script when interacting with customers. Grocery stores typically divide labor along gender lines with men typically performing jobs that require minimal interaction with customers such as working in the back of the store, stocking shelves, or bagging/sacking groceries while female employees work in positions involving constant interactions with customers, such as working as cashiers or at the customer service counter (see Figure 13.2). This division of labor is another product of the expectation that women should perform emotional labor. Employees working as cashiers are expected to maintain a pleasant demeanor even when a customer is being rude or offensive.

In the *Barnhart* case, the grocery store began using "secret shoppers" to determine if employees were following their assigned scripts in interactions with customers. An employee could be fired if a secret shopper reported them for not being sufficiently friendly. Because employees did not know which customers were secret shoppers, they had to maintain a pleasant demeanor regardless of how a customer behaved. Forcing female workers to be friendly toward customers who are offensive can easily lead men to misinterpret friendliness as a form of flirtation. The case was initiated by a female employee who was subjected to more and more severe forms of harassment from a customer who thought she had flirted with him. She was unable to reply that the conduct was unwanted for fear of offending a secret shopper

Figure 13.2 Women working in customer service positions are more likely to be subjected to sexual harassment because they may be victimized by customers in addition to co-workers

and losing her job. The company decided to reach a monetary settlement with the employees after the court determined that the company was responsible even though the harassment came from customers rather than other employees. In cases where employees have regular interactions with customers or clients, employers must ensure that their employees are not subjected to harassment from those working outside the company.

People also typically think of harassment as occurring between a male supervisor and a female employee, but sexual harassment may take many different forms. Sexual harassment doesn't always involve issues of sexual desire. It can also involve repeatedly berating another employee because of that person's sexual orientation or gender identity. For example, following a transgender employee to see which bathroom they use and harassing them because of their choice would be a case of sexual harassment. It is also possible to have sexual harassment cases where both the harasser and the victim are heterosexual men. This was established in the case of *Oncale v. Sundowner Offshore Services* (1998), which involved men who lived and worked on an oil rig in the Gulf of Mexico. A group of male workers persistently harassed one of their co-workers by claiming that he must be gay and subjecting him to forms of sexual humiliation and physical abuse including forcing a bar of soap into his anus. It was found that the abuse was a case of sexual harassment even though none of the harassers involved had any sexual attraction to the victim. Finally, a hostile work environment can result from actions taken outside of work. Stalking a co-worker outside work or sending them explicit texts or images would still be sexual harassment even if the unwelcome conduct occurred outside of work.

Given the complexity of sexual harassment, it is critical for employers to have a clear policy on harassment that provides employees with a safe and secure way to file complaints of harassment. The policy should include specific consequences that harassers should face because of their actions. It should also protect employees both from co-workers and from customers and clients. Everyone deserves to work in an environment where they feel safe and won't be regularly subjected to forms of conduct that are uninvited and unwelcome.

White men talking

There is a natural tendency for people to view a situation from one's own perspective even though those who from other cultural backgrounds may have very different understandings of the same situation. All employees must feel that they are valued and that their concerns will be heard and taken seriously. This sounds simple enough, but workplace discrimination continues to be a problem because forms of (implicit) bias often go unchecked or unrecognized. One cannot fix a problem if they don't even realize a problem exists.

Throughout their lives, individuals are flooded with representations that link social categories with indexical meanings. This inevitably leads people to sometimes focus their attention on some voices more than others. People are regularly exposed to myriad stereotypes and their reactions may be based on those stereotypes even if they aren't aware of it. With input from diverse perspectives, it becomes less likely that forms of bias persist to the point of creating an unwelcoming environment. It also helps avoid cases in which a company unintentionally "misfires" and does something that offends a subset of customers and clients.

There is a long tradition of workplaces being controlled by white men. It is not surprising, then, that the ways of behaving associated with a "professionalism demeanor" are also the ways of interacting that have been most used by white men. The discriminatory assumptions that result in workplace contexts are often those that have gone unrecognized by those in charge. For workers from marginalized groups, these assumptions may result in a workplace rife with *microaggressions*. Microaggressions are indirect, subtle, and often brief incidents that index hostile, derogatory, or negative attitudes toward some marginalized group. This includes things like complimenting an Asian American for their command of English or asking an African American why they don't sound Black. In a workplace where diverse perspectives are not considered, microaggressions may become so common that the workplace becomes unwelcoming for women or minorities. Of course, it is important to seek input from employees of different backgrounds without making individuals feel like they are being asked to represent their race. Telling someone "I want your input because you're Black" is just another microaggression that reduces an individual to nothing more than their designated racial category.

Microaggressions

While incidents that are clearly racist (microaggressions) are common, cases of microaggressions are ubiquitous. For many members of marginalized groups, microaggressions may be a regular part of daily life. Like many forms of discrimination, microaggressions rely on indexicality to make indirect reference to an individual's marginalized identity. Some examples include:

- asking a person who is Asian or Latinx, "Where are you *really* from?"
- asking about someone's ethnicity in a dehumanizing way, like, "What *are* you?"
- complimenting African Americans for being "articulate" or telling someone who was born in the United States that their "English is so good"
- asking female co-workers to perform tasks that wouldn't be asked of male co-workers (such as asking a woman to get you more coffee during a meeting)
- calling people by the wrong name but the same (or close) ethnicity: introducing Dr. Ramirez as "Dr. García" or referring to Dr. Chun as "Dr. Chung" or "Dr. Chong"
- inviting heterosexual spouses to an event without inviting those in same-sex marriages
- assuming that a person of color is a service worker, such as asking a co-worker (or supervisor) who isn't white if they can clean your office
- refusing to use someone's preferred pronouns
- repeated "compliments" that sexualize a co-worker but are subtle and indirect in ways that make it difficult to categorize as sexual harassment
- saying literally any of these statements:
  - "You're really pretty for a Black girl"
  - "You're pretty good at sports for a gay guy"
  - "How long has your family been in this country?"
  - "Why don't you speak Chinese (or Spanish or Korean or Vietnamese . . .)?"
  - "I don't really think of you as a Black (or Asian, Native American, etc.) person"
  - "I wouldn't know you were transgender; you could even pass for a 'real' woman"

In addition to resulting in problems like microaggressions, a failure to consider multiple cultural perspectives can also result in a failure to fully comprehend the attitudes and actions of co-workers. As we've discussed, perceptions can be influenced by stereotyped expectations based primarily on assumptions about an individual's identity. Culturally distinct ways of interacting are almost always interpreted in terms of stereotypes about members of particular social groups. Implicit bias is inherent not only in how one expects certain individuals to speak but also in the ways they interpret other people's behavior. When a group of African Americans is talking with one another in a movie theater, the response from white people is more likely to be "those people are rude" and not "watching a film is considered an interactive event in some cultures."

Stereotyped assumptions about an individual's intentions or motivations may have serious implications and create new forms of discrimination. An African American speaking at a higher volume (compared to white people) or a Latinx person speaking with higher emotional involvement (again, compared to white people) are rarely recognized as speaking in culturally distinct ways. Instead, individuals who speak in these ways are more likely to be labeled as violent, aggressive, and dangerous. Because culturally distinct ways of interacting go unrecognized, people of color regularly face false accusations of being "dangerous" simply because they speak in a manner that white people interpret based on racist stereotypes. In cases where employees are fired because of behaviors that are seen as dangerous or aggressive, it may just be that supervisors are simply unaware of the expected ways of interacting in different cultures. Of course, cases where management seriously misinterprets an employee's behavior are less likely to occur in a workplace where management includes people familiar with the employee's cultural norms for interacting.

Everyone deserves a workplace where they feel safe, valued, and appreciated regardless of their gender, age, ethnicity, or race. Approaches that emphasize creating the appearance of a diverse workforce but fail to include diverse perspectives cannot produce a truly welcoming working environment. Without actual input from multiple perspectives, the workplace will continue to view all employees through the lens of the white male culture entrenched in most American workplaces. And language ideologies play a key role in determining how the speech of employees is interpreted and understood; therefore, an atmosphere in which perceptions of language and cultural differences as promoting a healthy work environment can serve as one of the primary ways by which all employees feel safe and appreciated.

Discussion questions

1. Have you ever experienced a workplace environment like any of those described here? If so, did you personally feel discriminated against? Explain what the workplace was like and what you did about the discrimination. If you did not experience the discrimination but saw it happen to others, provide a description of what happened to the employee and the employer.
2. Most American universities maintain a public website where you can find information about the demographic makeup of the student population. Find this information for your university, then look for marketing materials showing students doing student things. Do the images reflect what the university numbers show? Or if you do not have numbers, do you think the images reflect your lived experience on campus? Explain what you think might be happening if you find a mismatch.
3. Have you ever been to a business (let's say a restaurant) where employees were speaking to each other (and even to some other customers) in a language that you did not speak?

How did you feel? Based on what you have read, do you think your feelings reflect stereotypes about people speaking different languages?

4. Listen to people in class, at work, and at home and count how many times you hear the word "sorry." Keep track of who says it and in what context. Who says "sorry" more – men or women? Are they always apologies? How do you know?
5. How do English-only policies work? Which ones are permitted (by the EEOC)? Can you think of specific jobs where English is likely to be necessary?
6. Think about the kinds of behaviors you have been told are "professional." Make a list and determine what kinds of stereotypes underlie those expectations.

14 Examining the American judicial system and housing

Language(s) and the law

By this point, it has likely become clear that language ideologies permeate every aspect of society. We have seen how Standard Language Ideology contributes to discrimination in different contexts in distinct ways. In the media (see Chapter 12) repeated representations influence assumptions and expectations about people who speak in different ways. In education (see Chapter 11) minority children are taught that their language is deficient and inappropriate, creating a type of language-focused double consciousness. In the workplace (see Chapter 13) non-native speakers of English may be put in situations where their accent serves as an excuse to discriminate even if their English is perfectly understandable. In this chapter, we consider discrimination in two other contexts: the justice system and housing. These contexts have their own unique relationships to Standard Language Ideology.

Law is an area where linguistics has unique (albeit underrecognized) relevance. The legal system has a specific language ideology in which all indexical meanings are erased so that language only serves to convey referential meaning. Within this legal language ideology, ambiguity is bad because it allows multiple interpretations of contracts, laws, or other legal documents. Dialectal differences are also bad because the standard is assumed to be less ambiguous. Witnesses who do not speak something close to "standard" English may find their speech "corrected" into the standard by court transcribers (Jones et al. 2019). Of course, dialectal variation may convey meanings other than those found in "standard" English (such as the use of habitual aspect in African American English or Navajo English). These distinctions are typically lost in the actual court proceedings, which are based entirely on the written court transcripts.

Consider the (hypothetical) case of a witness who says the phrase "We all know he be there," which is subsequently changed to "We all knew he was there" in the court record. Given the specific grammatical structure used by the witness, which carries habitual aspect in some African American Englishes, these two sentences mean very different things. Just because he *be* there, it doesn't mean he *was* there. The difference between the two becomes clear when another clause is added:

We all know he be there, but he ain't been there that day.
We all knew he was there, but he wasn't there that day.

Here, the first sentence makes sense (he is usually there but isn't there today), but the "standard" correction no longer makes sense (he was there, but he wasn't there).

Problems with the transcription of speech can also lead to misunderstandings with serious consequences. For example, Mary Bucholtz (1995) described a case in which a Spanish

DOI: 10.4324/9781003332886-14

speaker pronounced the word *sí* with rising intonation (like a question), but the transcriber did not add a question mark to the transcription. Thus, an interaction where the response to a question about drug sales was something close to "Really?" was entered into the record as "Yes." The difference in intention and meaning is clear in spoken language, but the reliance on the written transcript resulted in a serious misrepresentation of how the interaction had actually occurred.

The case of the missing comma

The importance of unambiguous and clear language in legal contexts is illustrated by *O'Connor v. Oakhurst Dairy* (2017), a case where the decision depended entirely on the absence of a single comma. The case involved delivery drivers for a diary in Maine who were not paid extra for working overtime because the dairy held that they were exempt from being paid "time and a half" under Maine law. The law that made some employees exempt from earning the extra overtime pay was written as follows:

> The canning, processing, preserving, freezing, drying, marketing, storing, packing for shipment or distribution of: (1) Agricultural produce; (2) Meat and fish products; and (3) Perishable foods.

The issue at hand, then, was whether the delivery drivers (who distributed perishable foods) were included in this group. The court found that the law was written in a way that didn't clearly include the delivery drivers. There would not have been ambiguity if the sentence had included a comma, so that the list of exempted employees read packing for shipment, or distribution of. The absence of the comma allowed for the interpretation where packing for shipment or distribution referred only to the packing of food (for distribution) and not to the distribution of the food itself. The legislature had intended for the law to include delivery drivers, but because they failed to include one comma, they accidentally excluded them from the law as it was written. Because of the missing comma in the law, the dairy lost the case and had to give the drivers back pay for any overtime they had worked.

Lost in translation

When languages other than English come into play, legal language ideology assumes that there is always a one-to-one correlation between words and idioms in different languages. Languages other than English have not always been welcome in the courtroom. Indeed, courts were not required to offer interpreters until 1970 when the courts overturned the conviction of a monolingual Spanish speaker in a trial that took place entirely in English. The use of interpreters did not change the language ideology of the legal system; so interpreting and translation are still presumed to produce exact correspondences between words in different languages.

In some cases, the language ideology of the courtroom leads to situations that produce legal forms of discrimination. For example, the Supreme Court found (in *Hernandez v. New York*, 1991) that in cases where a Spanish-speaking defendant is on trial, it is entirely legal to exclude all Spanish speakers from the pool of potential jury members. Indeed, a lawyer can eliminate potential jurors because they have Spanish surnames (and therefore might be able to understand Spanish to some degree). Obviously, in some cases, this would simply eliminate all Latinx potential jurors from serving in cases involving Latinx defendants. Yet many Latinx people are monolingual in English, so to be precise, the set of Spanish speakers is not the same group as the set of Latinx individuals. The logic behind excluding Spanish speakers is based entirely in the language ideology of the courts.

Juries are expected to base their decisions solely on the written transcript of the court proceedings. The details of *how* something is said are irrelevant (as legal language ideology rejects social-indexical meanings). Because the written record is the sole basis for decisions and because language in the written record is only in English, the details of the original Spanish (or Chinese, Thai, Choctaw, etc.) are irrelevant and may not be considered in jury deliberations.

Interpreters are not perfect, and there are many dialects of languages like Spanish, so the written record may include errors. If the interpreter makes a mistake or doesn't know how to translate something, the English written record will not be a true reflection of what was said in the courtroom. Even so, jurors must focus only on the written transcript. If a trial involves testimony in Spanish (or a specific variety of Spanish), and the interpreter makes an error (or speaks a different variety of Spanish), a Spanish-speaking juror cannot help but recognize that the written transcript contains errors. This means that they will be incapable of basing their decision entirely on the transcript (because they know it contains errors). So it only makes sense to exclude Spanish speakers because they are unable to follow the requirements of the courts and ignore the testimony that was given during the trial. This reasoning may be logical, but at every point, it relies entirely on a language ideology that is counter to everything linguists know about how language works. It also produces a result that is clearly discriminatory and may require jurors to base their decisions on a transcript that contains errors. This is how standard language ideologies work: they establish systems that privilege a single way of speaking, so that they exclude entire groups of people based on (assumptions about) how they (might) speak.

Another aspect of natural language that is unacceptable within legal language ideology is code-switching. Because it assumes that direct word-for-word translations are possible, moving back and forth between languages is both unnecessary and unacceptable. In a study of small claims courts in Queens, New York, Phillip Angermeyer (2014) found that the language ideology of monolingualism persisted even in courtrooms where almost all the participants are bilingual. Angermeyer examined cases where court arbitrators attempted to settle lawsuits rather than going to court. There were occasions where the court ran out of interpreters, delaying the entire process as arbitrators waited for interpreters to become available. In several cases, the arbitrators spoke Spanish themselves, and although one of the participants did not speak English, everyone in the room spoke Spanish. So, some arbitrators decided to conduct some of their proceedings entirely in Spanish. In such cases, the arbitrators would prohibit participants from code-switching or using an English word. Of course, for many US Spanish speakers, English borrowings may have replaced Spanish words so that "switching into English" may just involve using a single English word (as part of one's Spanish). So the language ideology of monolingualism prevailed and individuals were prohibited from speaking English in a US courtroom.

The case of Santiago Ventura Morales

Santiago Ventura Morales is a native speaker of Mixtec, a Mexican Indigenous language, who came to Oregon at the age of 14 in 1982. He lived in an Oregon community where practically everyone spoke Mixtec, and Ventura Morales was unable to speak either Spanish or English. In 1986, Ventura Morales was charged with murder after a young man was stabbed during a large party held by the community. The police were unable to communicate with many of those involved, and Ventura Morales was arrested primarily based solely on his demeanor and non-verbal behavior. Because he was from Mexico, a Spanish interpreter was used for the trial. Of course, Ventura Morales did not speak Spanish and did not understand the proceedings. Ventura Morales was found guilty and went to jail. His appeals were denied until his defense team found a witness who saw another man commit the crime. Once the actual perpetrator had confessed, Ventura Morales was released after spending five years in prison. He learned English and earned his GED in prison, and after he was released, he earned a full scholarship to the University of Portland, where he earned his degree in social work. After graduation he began working as an activist and social worker fighting for the rights of Indigenous immigrants.

A final component of Standard Language Ideology that impacts the legal system is the idea of *one nation, one language* meaning that each country should correspond to a single language. So in France they speak French, in Germany they speak German, and in Spain they speak Spanish. This ideology erases the true linguistic diversity found in the world. Yes, they speak Spanish in Spain, but they also speak Catalan, Galician, Asturian, Basque, and numerous other languages. Following this ideology, many people assume that all Americans speak English, all Chinese speak Mandarin, and all Mexicans speak Spanish. This ideology leads people to assume that an individual from Mexico will be a speaker of Spanish. However, in terms of languages, Mexico is very diverse, and there are many Indigenous languages that might be the only language some Mexicans (and Mexican Americans) speak on a regular basis. Because of ethnic violence and discrimination in Mexico and Central America, there are many Indigenous people who have come to the United States for safety. In the United States, they may live in isolated communities or with small groups of friends and relatives so that they have no need to use English or Spanish on a regular basis. When Indigenous immigrants find themselves in contexts where everything happens in English (e.g., hospitals, schools, courtrooms, etc.), it is common for them to be provided a Spanish interpreter even though they may not actually speak Spanish. As we saw in Chapter 7, this can have serious consequences, as in the case of Cirila Baltazar Cruz, who had her newborn child taken away unjustly.

The English used in legal context is often confusing and unclear for those who aren't lawyers and aren't familiar with the register of legal language. The language ideology of the courtroom requires exact correspondences between words in different languages. This ideology creates unique problems in situations that involve speakers of languages that do not have a large number of speakers. In a rural, Indigenous community in Central America, the justice system will be quite different from what is used in the United States. Because of the history of violence against Indigenous communities, people may avoid using a formal legal system that has only been used to discriminate against them. Thus, some communities continue to settle disputes according to traditional legal systems so that outside authorities do not become involved. This means that Indigenous immigrants from Mexico and Central America may have no idea how legal processes work in the United States. Speakers of Indigenous languages may not even be aware of concepts like guilty plea, settlement, restraining order, warrants, and so on. If a concept is entirely new to an individual, they probably don't have a word to describe it. But the language ideology of the courtroom requires that languages be equivalent so that interpreters may find themselves forced to use borrowings from Spanish or English that are unfamiliar to the participants involved. Such problems are common in interpreting for Indigenous languages, but they are especially common when the Indigenous person speaks enough Spanish to proceed without an interpreter but actually has never been exposed to the legal vocabulary used for court proceeding in Spanish.

The approach to language within the legal system builds on Standard Language Ideology in ways that create inequalities in how individuals are treated in legal contexts. This system ultimately excludes individuals who speak in ways that do not align with the narrow understanding of language within legal language ideology. Those who don't speak English are excluded from juries because English is the only language that is "appropriate" for jurors to use. Speakers of Indigenous languages go through court cases without ever having the legal process explained to them. Speakers of non-standard varieties find the subtle distinctions made in their dialect erased entirely. But for the most part, these things go unnoticed because they result from the "common sense" idea that there is a single correct and acceptable language variety that must be used in all contexts. Standard Language Ideology is so entrenched in American culture and cognition that it makes people unable to recognize clear forms of discrimination that would likely be upsetting and offensive if language were not a factor. What is more – when linguists present the opposing view, they are not always taken seriously.

Linguists as experts

It is hard to imagine a judge or jury simply refusing to believe testimony from a geneticist, biochemist, or physician. But language is deceptively approachable, and many individuals feel they have a good idea about how it works. While the idea that "If I speak a language, I ought to know how language works" is fairly common, few people would think that having a pancreas meant that one understands how a pancreas works. A judge may choose to believe an expert simply because they provide an opinion that very closely matches their own prior beliefs. It can be hard to accept the realities of linguistic prejudice when one is working within a legal context where Standard Language Ideology is a fundamental assumption.

While the legal system has long assumed that issues of language can simply be assumed, there is a growing field of *forensic linguistics* that focuses on issues of language and the law. The field provides a wide range of linguistic expertise in legal cases, including things like voice identification, determining authorship, addressing ambiguity in contracts and laws, and analyzing police interviews to determine if an individual was able to comprehend the interaction. Often, those working in forensic linguistics use specialized methods that can help solve crimes and resolve legal disputes. For example, the authenticity of a suicide note might be compared to a corpus of a million suicide notes to determine if it aligns with the features found in most suicide notes. Because there are many huge corpora of natural language data to use for comparative purposes, a linguist can look for unique trends in the speech of an individual and use that to determine if they were the likely author of a particular text. Insights into language variation, sociolinguistics, and linguistic anthropology are rarely sought out by lawyers, but these fields can make major contributions to understanding the legal process. Those contributions, however, may be ignored because they do not align with the prior beliefs of Standard Language Ideology that are the foundation of the legal system.

In Chapter 1, we discussed how language played a crucial role in understanding the trial concerning Trayvon Martin's murder. To illustrate the value of sociolinguistic research to courtroom discourse, we consider the way in which the testimony of Rachel Jeantel, Martin's friend, was received by the court. Jeantel was an important witness for the prosecution; from this side of the case, for Zimmerman to be found guilty, it was crucial that jurors see her as clear and trustworthy. Instead, she was seen as incomprehensible and not credible.

Which language experts?

Language is a complex phenomenon, and many different fields can provide some insight on how language works. Cognitive scientists and neurolinguists are interested in how language interacts with other brain functions. Language acquisition scholars can explain how children and adults grapple with learning the mechanics of their first, second, fifth, or nth language in sometimes similar, sometimes different ways. Speech pathologists, who tend to work in clinical conditions with a goal of helping patients attain specific linguistic goals (e.g., recovering from stroke, adjusting to hearing loss), can also bring interesting and relevant perspectives to court cases. The burden of determining which experts have the appropriate training to argue in a courtroom falls on the parties involved. However, when the required expertise challenges aspects of Standard Language Ideology of the courtroom, the expertise is much more likely to be disregarded.

In their analysis, Rickford and King (2016) painstakingly showed, as many linguists have time and again (e.g., Baugh 1973; Rickford 1999; Green 2002), that African American English, the variety of speech Jeantel was using, is systematic, rule-governed, and influenced by the varieties spoken in the community in which it is used (in Jeantel's case, Caribbean Englishes and Spanish). The graph in Figure 14.1 is a combination of some of the data from several similar graphs in Rickford and King (2016: 959–960), in which they compare Jeantel's use of various grammatical features associated with AAE to other studies involving African American youths. Within the rules of African American English, the presence of the /s/ (/z/) at the end of words is optional in certain contexts. The features that Rickford and King considered involved the presence or absence of /+s/ in particular contexts: third singular present tense verbs (*she work* vs. *she works*), possessive nouns (*her daddy's house* vs. *her daddy house*), and plural marking (*four chickens* vs. *four chicken*).

The analysis by Rickford and King made it clear that Jeantel spoke a regular, rule-based language that was like many other varieties and that the fact that she spoke this variety of English was in no way related to her intelligence or ability to serve as a witness. However,

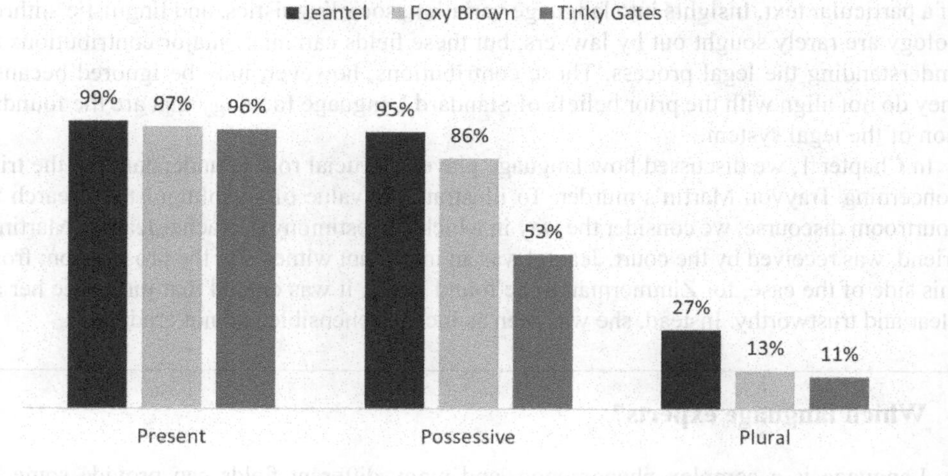

Figure 14.1 Comparing rate of absence of -s in third person present tense, possessives, and plural nouns of Rachel Jeantel to Foxy Brown and Tinky Gates, two African American teens analyzed in Rickford (1992)

Source: adapted from Rickford and King (2016)

journalists and jurors alike, as well as the public in the form of often virulent social media posts, decided that none of that matters. Jurors openly said that they disregarded her testimony because they had difficulty understanding her and therefore did not see her testimony as worthy of consideration. Linguists can do whatever systematic analysis they want, but the public need not listen. And in this case, they didn't. Rachel Jeantel was utterly humiliated and disregarded – as a person and as a witness.

Rickford and King's analysis of why Jeantel's testimony was essentially ignored by the courts has ramifications beyond this one trial. As they say,

> Not only was Jeantel's vernacular pivotal in the disregard of her critically important testimony in this case, but in numerous other cases in the United States and around the world in which witnesses or defendants use a vernacular rather than the mainstream variety, they tend to be misunderstood or discredited, and encounter dialect unfamiliarity or prejudice in courtrooms and potentially unfair judicial outcomes.
>
> (Rickford & King 2016: 950–951)

Thus, it shouldn't be surprising that many other court cases have seen similar outcomes. Whether it is the inaccuracies of courtroom transcribers (Lee 2015) or the ways in which lawyers and judges understand "plain language" as opposed to "legal language" in testimonies (e.g., Solan 1990; Cotterill 2003), there are numerous ways of misunderstanding. And linguistic misunderstandings can result in harsher penalties; Rengifo and colleagues showed that even the *use* of an interpreter for those with Limited English Proficiency (LEP) meant defendants would have higher cash bail and were less likely to be released on their own recognizance, suggesting that the partial insider status of interpreters (that is, since many interpreters are court-appointed, they may be more in line with the judges and lawyers than with the defendant they are supporting) causes major issues for the LEP defendants who depend upon them (Rengifo et al. 2020).

In the case of Jeantel, many of those misunderstandings likely arise from an underlying implicit racial prejudice. Sommers and Ellsworth (2003) explored white juror bias in the United States and found that white jurors show more bias when race is not salient in the context of the trial itself. While it is likely that race *was* salient in the context of Trayvon Martin's murder, it may not have been so salient in the moment when jurors were attending to Jeantel's testimony. Regardless, Jeantel's testimony was disregarded on the basis of how she spoke, so that the jury saw no problem totally ignoring the testimony of the only witness to the murder of Trayvon Martin. Just as with Jeantel's testimony, people who do not speak in a way that is recognized as "appropriate" and "standard" may themselves be tossed aside just because they learned a different type of English compared to middle-class white people.

Beyond examining real court cases, linguists have tested what might happen in a courtroom given some parameters. In so doing, they use a mock jury to test what impacts linguistic variation might have on an individual – usually a college undergraduate, but such people are eligible for actual juries, so their selection as test subjects is reasonable. Kurinec and Weaver (2019) conducted this kind of mock jury study to understand how race and dialect are intertwined in many American's perceptions. They found that speakers who used features of African American English were consistently rated as less professional and less educated (among other negative evaluations) compared to speakers who spoke with more standard features and sounded white. Similar findings have been discovered when examining how mock jurors perceive witnesses who require court interpreters (e.g., Berk-Seligson 2017), those who use many different non-standard varieties (e.g., Lippi-Green 1994), and those who have any number of linguistic features indexically associated with ethnicity (e.g., Frumkin 2007).

Of course, there can also be problems with misunderstandings related to gender. In Chapter 13, we discussed the ways in which evaluations of women's speech are influenced by stereotypes about gendered patterns of language use. The stereotype that women's speech is somehow overly indirect and purposefully unclear has serious implications. Wright and Hosman's (1983) work on stylistic variation in witness testimonies, for example, showed that female witnesses who used hedges and intensifiers in the courtroom were seen as less credible. More recently, similar gender biases have been seen on the other side of the courtroom; Lee (2015) showed that women attorneys are discriminated against by judges, jurors, and other attorneys, drawing on work by Hahn and Clayton (1996) that suggested that women attorneys are generally perceived to be less aggressive, the style that is most likely to win a case, and that use of a more aggressive style by a woman did not lend itself to the same outcome.

Susan Ehrlich (e.g., 2003) has done extensive research on the impact of language ideologies on the interpretation of women's speech in rape trials. Ehrlich found that, due to stereotypes of women's speech as insincere and indirect, rape survivors are frequently presumed to have not been sufficiently explicit in refusing sexual advances. Here again, the same cycle of language subordination is present: a stereotype about language use holds that the speech of women is somehow deficient > repeated instances of this stereotype make it part of habitual thought > women's speech is perceived and interpreted based on the stereotype > this conclusion is seen as validating the negative stereotype itself.

Juror's reactions

A great deal of attention was paid – in mainstream and social media – to what juror's thought about Jeantel's speech. In an interview on CNN, one juror explained that she thought Jeantel was "hard to understand" and "not credible." Other jurors claimed to be offended by her use of words like "creepy-ass cracker." In many ways, it ultimately amounted to simple misunderstandings, as in the transcript that follows, from Rickford and King (2016: 972); but the fact remains that those jurors seemed unable to separate their own misunderstandings from their ideologies and prejudices that resulted in their complete dismissal of Jeantel's testimony.

Rachel Jeantel (RJ): Yeah, now following him.
Bernie de la Rionda, prosecutor (BR): Now following him. Okay. What I want you to do, Rachel Jeantel –
Judge Nelson (THE COURT) [to a juror]: Just one second, please. Yes, ma'am?
A JUROR: He is now following me or – I'm sorry. I just didn't hear.
THE COURT: Okay. Can we one more time, please, give that answer again.
RJ: He said, he told me now that a man is starting following him, is following him.
A JUROR: Again or is still?
THE COURT: Okay. You can't ask questions.
A JUROR: Okay.
THE COURT: If you can't understand, just raise your hand.

Though one might, as Rickford and King do, attribute some of these kinds of problems to individual language variation, general dialect differences, or unfamiliarity with the varieties in question, what's really at play here is the true power of the Standard Language Ideology. It is so strong that people who are earnestly trying to do their part for justice (e.g., jurors) cannot even see that they are not being driven by facts. Instead, they make their decisions based in ideologies that connect "standard" language to the many kinds of things we've already established in this book – like power, wealth, and intelligence – and that link varieties that deviate from that standard as their opposites.

As these cases show, someone can be dragged in the court of public opinion *and* in the actual court, thus marking those people as "unsuitable witnesses." Ultimately, these kinds of discriminatory behaviors permeate every aspect of people's linguistic lives. Speakers of many kinds of American Englishes face backlash for their ways of speaking in so many facets of life – from the courtroom to the schools (see Chapter 11), from jobs (see Chapter 13) to housing – and it is this last one that we will explore in the remainder of this chapter. It is important to recognize that these same kinds of judgmental behaviors are indeed discriminatory and to acknowledge how Standard Language Ideology can even impact where you are allowed to work, to study, and to live.

American housing problems

In the period following World War II, one of the most pressing problems in the United States had to do with insufficient housing. In 1946, a report to the US House of Representatives indicated that there was a housing shortage: what existed was substandard, lacking in modern commodities like electric and plumbing, and could not facilitate the growing population and the large numbers of veterans returning from war. A Senate report at the same time called this state of affairs "a national tragedy." Additionally, the war had brought the construction of new housing to a standstill. There was a need to quickly build more than 3 million low or moderately priced housing units to adapt in the post-war era.

This plan seemed quite difficult for private industries, so the federal government got involved, passing the Veterans' Emergency Housing Act in 1946. The fallout from this, however, was not well-received by all. Private housing groups wanted the control to be in the market, not in federal mandates. White families, convinced developments in suburban areas were preferable to urban ones, essentially created segregated housing environments. And certain regulations established by the Federal Housing Administration made sure African American families had few choices. Property owners and managers, mortgage institutions, and insurance companies essentially participated in open discrimination against potential buyers or renters on the basis of color or ethnicity. It may be difficult to imagine, even now, that a coalition of real estate agents, banks, and insurance companies would fight – openly, unapologetically – for the right to discriminate against people of color. But this is precisely what happened across the country.

Redlining

One practice involving housing discrimination is called redlining, where poor or minority communities were marked in red on maps (like the one from Philadelphia in 1937 linked in the QR code) so that mortgage companies could discriminate against minority populations in the form of mortgage denial for certain neighborhoods. These efforts, which were often supported by the Federal Housing Administration, essentially labeled certain neighborhoods as riskier for mortgage loans, and the designation of high risk was usually dependent on the racial makeup of the neighborhood, resulting in continued residential racial segregation. Redlining is explicitly prohibited by the Fair Housing Act today, but other, perhaps even more insidious practices like predatory lending exist today to the further detriment of many African American families.

From the initial return of veterans, the housing boom, and these early days of discrimination, things reached a boiling point. In 1963, the California legislature passed the Rumford Fair Housing Act, which prohibited racial discrimination in housing practices. The California Real Estate Commission immediately started raising money to sponsor a referendum (referred to as Proposition 14) which called for a revision to the state constitution that would allow property owners to continue to discriminate any way they pleased:

> Neither the State nor any subdivision or agency thereof shall deny, limit or abridge, directly or indirectly, the right of any person, who is willing or desires to sell, lease or rent any part or all of his real property, to decline to sell, lease or rent such property to such person or persons as he, in his absolute discretion, chooses.
>
> (Noel & Cheng 2009)

That referendum passed with a 65% majority, thus nullifying the Rumford Act and "creating a California Constitutional right to discriminate against members of racial minority groups" (Oppenheimer 2010: 118). In turn, Proposition 14 was struck down when the California Supreme Court ruled it a violation of the 14th Amendment and thus unconstitutional (ibid.). The Equal Protection clause of the 14th Amendment requires that State governments provide equal protection under the law to all people within its jurisdiction, regardless of race or other protected category. In May 1967, the Supreme Court of the United States affirmed that decision.

David Oppenheimer's (2010) history of California's anti-discrimination legislation shows that the courts "acted with great courage, defying the will of the voters, to protect minority rights" (ibid.: 118). The courts were acting to countermand what founding father John Adams described as "the tyranny of the majority." The first US Congress anticipated such problems with the first ten amendments to the Constitution, the Bill of Rights, which together protect individuals even in the face of overwhelming public opinion.

Subsequent legislation (most notably the Civil Rights Act of 1968, Title VIII, of which is typically referred to as the Fair Housing Act) extended protections for the individual to include a wider range of discriminatory behaviors and protected classes. One move toward this kind of protection was the establishment of the Department of Housing and Urban Development (HUD) in 1965. It is a cabinet department of the executive branch of the US government, and it is administered by the Secretary of Housing and Urban Development.

As part of HUD, the Office of Fair Housing and Equal Opportunity (FHEO) describes its purpose as the office that administers and enforces federal laws and establishes policies that make sure all Americans have equal access to the housing of their choice. There are state organizations that perform similar functions, dozens of non-profit civil rights organizations, and a legion of fair housing advocates and activists who are deeply involved in the pursuit of equal housing for all.

Actions based on race, color, national origin, religion, sex, familial status, or disability that are specifically prohibited by law include the following:

- refusal to rent or sell housing or to negotiate for housing
- taking steps to making housing unavailable (e.g., a landlord or owner takes the property off the market to avoid potential renters or buyers on the basis of a protected category)
- setting different terms, conditions, or privileges for sale or rental of a dwelling (e.g., requiring people of a particular race to pay a larger security deposit)

HUD

The Department of Housing and Urban Development (HUD) was developed after a long history of housing legislation made it clear that a federal cabinet-level entity was necessary. Figure 14.2 is a timeline of the events leading to the establishment of HUD and the passage of the Fair Housing Act.

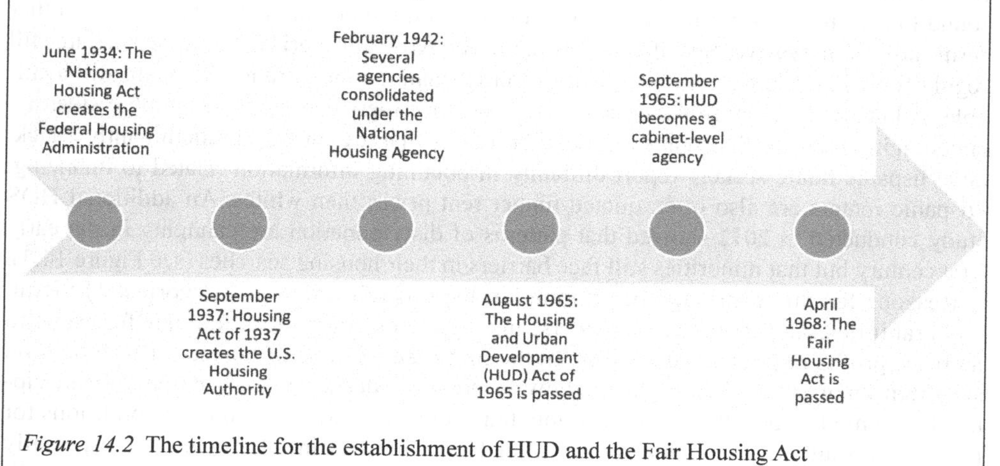

Figure 14.2 The timeline for the establishment of HUD and the Fair Housing Act

- limiting or providing different housing services or facilities (e.g., the landlord prohibits some renters from using the pool)
- falsely denying that housing is available for inspection, sale, or rental
- imposing different sales prices or rental charges for the sale or rental of a dwelling
- using different criteria, requirements, fees, analyses, or procedures for the sale or rental of a dwelling
- evicting or harassing a tenant or a tenant's guest
- failing or delaying performance of maintenance of property
- discouraging the purchase or rental of a dwelling
- for profit, persuading owners to sell or rent (blockbusting) or denying anyone access to or membership in a facility or service (such as a multiple listing service) related to the sale or rental of housing
- refusing to make a mortgage loan
- refusing to provide information regarding loans
- imposing different terms or conditions on a loan, such as different interest rates, points, or fees
- discriminating in appraising property
- refusing to purchase a loan
- setting different terms or conditions for purchasing a loan
- threatening, coercing, intimidating, or interfering with anyone exercising a fair housing right or assisting others who exercise that right

- advertising or making any statement that indicates a limitation or preference based on race, color, national origin, religion, sex, familial status, or handicap. This prohibition against discriminatory advertising applies to single-family and owner-occupied housing that is otherwise exempt from the Fair Housing Act

And still, housing discrimination today is widespread. The Housing Discrimination Study (HDS) undertaken in 2000, the third such study (with previous studies in 1977 and 1989), found that while some forms of discrimination are on the decline for certain groups, other forms are still pervasive. Specifically, Hispanic and African American home seekers are still regularly told units are unavailable when (non-Hispanic) whites are told they are still available. Additionally, African American home seekers experience more geographic steering, encouraging them to find homes in neighborhoods that are already predominantly Black, and Hispanic home seekers report difficulty in obtaining information related to financing. Hispanic renters are also often quoted higher rent prices than whites. An additional HDS study conducted in 2012 showed that patterns of discrimination are changing in the early 21st century but that minorities still face barriers in their housing searches (see Figure 14.3).

Reasons for this continued discrimination tend to fall into two categories: 1) victim vulnerabilities, and 2) property owners, managers, or contractors looking for ways to increase profits regardless of legality. In the first case, victims of housing discrimination are often unaware of their rights or how to pursue redress when rights have been violated. Jeannie Haubert Weil (2009) conducted a long-term study of housing conditions for Latinxs in Southern Louisiana shortly after Hurricane Katrina. Latinxs were especially vulnerable in the period following the disaster; when there was a lack of even rudimentary housing and tensions were high, employers – such as contractors who recruited Latinxs specifically to work on reconstruction projects – were also primarily responsible for the allocation of housing. Added to these factors was insufficient government oversight (ibid.: 491).

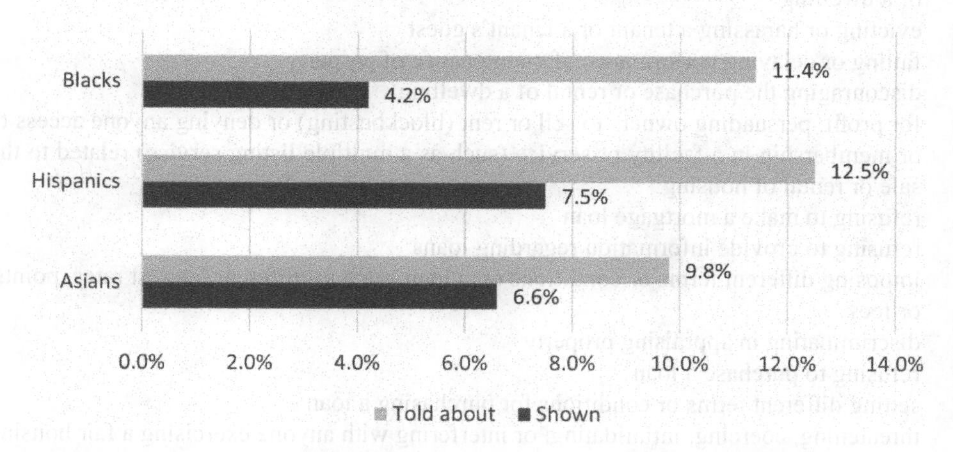

Figure 14.3 Minority rental unit seekers told about and shown fewer units available than their white counterparts

Source: based on data from the Executive Summary of HDS 2012: 5 (Figure 5)

A case in point is Natalia, a Latina teacher and a fluent speaker of English, who told Weil that prior to Katrina she had no basis for complaint: "If they felt like I was inferior, they didn't let me know. But I have never felt embarrassed or humiliated or slighted in any way as a Hispanic." Any reasonable interviewer, having established a good relationship with the informant, must take such information at face value. However, Natalia also took part in a discrimination audit which provided important additional data.

Government and non-profit agencies who track housing discrimination will often perform an audit when discriminatory practices are suspected. For example, if a Korean American person applies for a mortgage and is quoted an unusually high interest rate – and reports this – a white tester is sent in to apply for the same mortgage (supplying the same information on the application). This process may be repeated several times with different testers. If sufficient evidence can be documented, the bank or mortgage company may be charged with unlawful discrimination.

In Natalia's case, her experiences with rental agents were recorded and then compared to the experiences of a white, non-Latina shopper:

> Unbeknownst to [Natalia], she was discriminated against on several occasions; however, the discrimination was often masked by a friendly and seemingly accommodating voice . . . it is often difficult today for an individual to know whether he or she has been treated unfairly and, as a result, the vast majority of discrimination cases go unreported.
> (ibid.: 493)

With refinements of the laws, the dramatic changes to the housing market created by the internet (Wright 2019), and the widening of protections, property owners, landlords, bankers, and salespeople have become far more subtle in the techniques used to screen out renters or buyers whom they consider undesirable. The National Fair Housing Alliance pursues unethical real estate companies and rental agents because residential segregation "results in disparities in access to quality education, employment, home ownership and wealth accumulation for communities of color" (National Fair Housing Alliance 2009).

Traditionally, one of the more insidious ways that owners and managers have screened out applicants or buyers who are unwelcome is to do so over the phone, based on accent. In recognition of this fact, linguists have used their methods of analysis to determine whether linguistic profiling is "successful;" that is, can ordinary listeners tell the race or ethnicity of a potential buyer on the basis of voice alone?

Heard but not seen

John Baugh is a sociolinguist whose primary research areas have to do with the social stratification of English (especially in African American English) and with discriminatory practices toward individuals on the basis of how they speak. Baugh is himself African American; he grew up in urban Los Angeles and Philadelphia with parents who were both university professors and thus grew up comfortable communicating in a variety of language communities and with a range of spoken identities appropriate to those communities. All told, Baugh speaks (with native or native-like fluency) at least three varieties of English: a formal, academic register of English; African American English; and a California variety of Chicano English (see Purnell et al. 1999).

Some years ago, Baugh began looking for an apartment for himself and his family near Stanford University, where he was a professor. He began shopping, in what was then the usual way of things, by calling telephone numbers listed on real estate advertisements. In contacting landlords about advertised rental properties by phone, Baugh used his more formal, academic variety of English and was told that he could come see the apartment – only to be turned away with various excuses once the landlord saw him in person.

Baugh was the same person on the phone and off, but the perception of him had shifted; it is likely that the landlord perceived Baugh on the phone as a well-spoken, educated white person but that this perception shifted to something else (perhaps as a well-spoken, educated Black person) when he was met in person. And each time this shift occurred, the apartment Baugh had wanted to see was suddenly no longer available.

Baugh had experienced direct evidence that the language subordination model is built on deception. The ideology says: sound like us, and you'll *be* one of us. Yet Professor Baugh *does* command what people think of as Standard American English, and he is still discriminated against based on race. So, he endeavored to find out exactly what caused the initial perception – that Baugh was white – and to show how systematically landlords (and others) use these auditory perceptions to categorize and discriminate against individuals who come from specific racial and ethnic groups.

I had you at "hello"

In a long-term study funded by the Ford Foundation, Baugh and his associates looked at these issues closely. The initial question was a simple one, on the surface at least: Is it possible to tell a person's race and/or ethnicity based on an individual's speaking voice – without any visual clues at all? That is, are there specific phonological or phonetic features that are associated with a particular race and/or ethnicity, and if so, do specific traits trigger specific kinds of reactions?

Baugh and his colleagues (Purnell et al. 1999) designed a series of four experiments to better understand some of the most basic aspects of *linguistic profiling*, or the ways in which people use linguistic information to characterize individuals and discriminate against them based on that information. In the first stage of this study, Baugh collected the data himself by systematically calling landlords to inquire about advertised apartments, targeting five specific areas in the San Francisco Bay area (with the demographic breakdown indicated in Table 14.1) using each of the three varieties outlined in the previous paragraph as part of Baugh's repertoire. In every case, he used the same greeting: "Hello, I'm calling about the apartment you have advertised in the paper."

To avoid suspicion on the basis of idiosyncratic features, different return telephone numbers and (ethnicity-indexing) pseudonyms were used for each of the three calls to each landlord. As the authors indicated, this methodology was like the practices used by HUD when housing discrimination was suspected. Their hypothesis was that in communities where the

Table 14.1 Demographic makeup of the neighborhoods analyzed in Purnell et al. (1999) (based on their data in Table 2, p. 15, which comes from the 1990 US Census)

	East Palo Alto	*Oakland*	*San Francisco*	*Palo Alto*	*Woodside*
African American	42.9%	43.9%	10.9%	2.9%	0.3%
Hispanic	36.4%	13.9%	13.9%	5.0%	3.8%
White	31.7%	32.5%	53.6%	84.9%	94.7%

population was predominantly white, there would be fewer positive responses to inquiries made in AAE or Chicano English.

The second study was like the first in that the same sentence was used, but this time 20 individuals who were native speakers of one of the targeted varieties of English recorded the sentence in question. Baugh's three utterances were also recorded for the database. More than 400 students at Stanford took part in this experiment, in which they listened to the recorded segments and made note of their best guesses in terms of race, ethnicity, and sex.

The third and fourth experiments had to do with the measurement of very fine phonetic and acoustic detail to identify how sensitive listeners are to cues well below the level of consciousness. The methodology here involved isolating the single word *hello* from Baugh's three recordings. The reasons for limiting the experiment in this way are important:

> We have several reasons for examining one word. This allowed us to hold external factors to a minimum. Second, it also illustrates how little speech is needed for dialect identification. "Hello" is a self-contained utterance, making perceptual studies more natural. By focusing on one short word, we are able to hold utterance duration well below one second (x = 414 msec.), making it comparable to other studies already made. Student participants were again asked to identify race, ethnicity and sex on the basis of listening to that single variable.
>
> (Purnell et al. 1999: 13)

In each of these four experiments, the authors found that they had to reject the null hypothesis. That is, they began with the expectation that there would be no correlation between language features and discriminatory experiences. However, 70% of the time, listeners were able to accurately identify race, ethnicity, and sex based on an utterance less than a second long (ibid.: 14). After analysis of the four experiments, the authors came to four clear, statistically significant conclusions.

1. Dialect-based discrimination takes place.
2. Ethnic group affiliation is recoverable from speech.
3. Very little speech is needed to discriminate between dialects.
4. Some phonetic correlates or markers of dialects are recoverable from a very small amount of speech. (ibid.: 11).

A human failing

In the first experiment described in Purnell et al. (1999), Baugh targeted the five specific areas around the San Francisco Bay, described in Table 14.1, to see if the race/ethnicity distributions in those areas would serve as a predictor of linguistic profiling. The findings are laid out in Figure 14.4.

Recalling the race/ethnicity information provided in Table 14.1, there are some interesting patterns for which voices received confirmed appointments. East Palo Alto has approximately equal numbers of white people, Black people, and Chicanxs, with a slight majority in the white population. Palo Alto has very small populations of Chicanxs and Black people, and Woodside is even more exclusively white. Oakland has the largest proportion of Black people, while East Palo Alto has the largest populations of Chicanxs. What Figure 14.4 shows is that when Baugh spoke Chicano English, his inquiry calls were successful as few as 20% of the time. The best response to Chicano English inquiries came from East Palo Alto, which

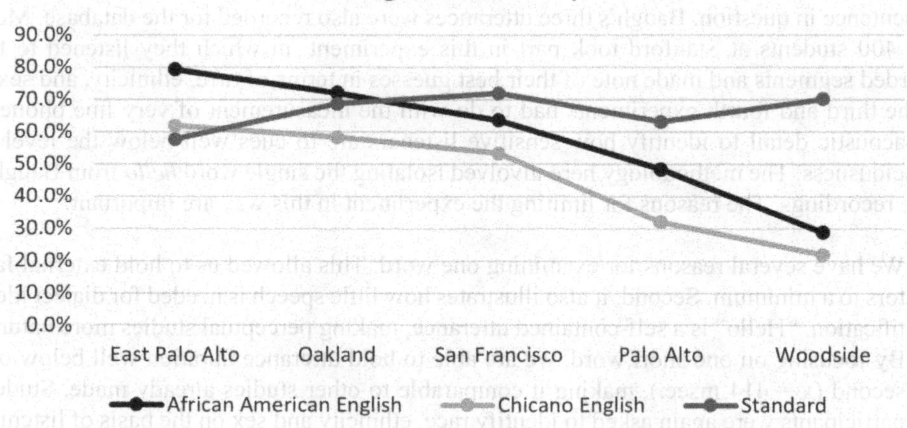

Figure 14.4 Appointments to see apartments confirmed, by race and ethnicity
Source: based on Purnell et al. (1999: 15)

is also home to the largest proportion of Chicanxs. However, even in East Palo Alto, Baugh's Chicano English inquiries were successful only 60% of the time. Corollary to this is the fact that even in the two areas where white people are outnumbered by people of color (Oakland and East Palo Alto), white callers still enjoy better success in booking these appointments.

This brings us back to the notion of housing discrimination as HUD sees it. HUD's National Fair Housing Alliance (NFHA) has been auditing suspected cases of housing discrimination linked to aural (rather than visual) traits with some success. Landlords advertising apartments, insurance companies offering low home insurance rates, banks eager to sell mortgages – in all aspects of the housing industry the NFHA continues to find evidence of linguistic profiling to the detriment of people of color and people who speak English as a second language.

The growing body of literature on linguistic profiling produced by scholars, government agencies, and non-profit civil rights organizations points to a simple conclusion: white renters are more likely to have calls returned; they hear a wider range of possibilities and may be offered monetary incentives; they are quoted better rates on insurance and mortgages before the persons making these decisions have ever checked references or credit ratings. But the investigation process is long, the legal system is slow, and the fines are too insignificant to have any lasting or long-term effect.

The first and best line of defense is to make sure that people are aware of their rights and how to protect those rights. Equally important is to make others aware of linguistic profiling. While the identification of social allegiances on the basis of language traits is a normal and natural practice for all human beings because variation is built into spoken language specifically to help people situate each other in social and geographic space, problems arise when individuals draw spurious conclusions from that variation and then use such conclusions to discriminate against and exclude individuals from normal activities on the basis of race, ethnicity, national origin, or any other protected category.

Just as Rickford and King (2016) do, we recall the words of Ferdinand de Saussure, a truly significant figure in 20th century linguistics, who said:

> [O]f what use is linguistics? . . . in the lives of individuals and societies, speech is more important than anything else. That linguistics should continue to be the prerogative of a few specialists would be unthinkable – everyone is concerned with it in one way or another. But . . . there is no other field in which so many absurd notions, prejudices, mirages and fictions have sprung up . . . the task of the linguist is . . . to dispel them as best he can.
>
> (Saussure 1966 [1916]: 7)

Discussion questions

1. We said that the legal language ideology assumes that there is always a one-to-one correlation between words across languages. Think about languages you have studied. Can you think of examples where there is no real translation of the concept into English without a lengthy explanation?
2. Thinking again about a language you have studied, do you think you would be prepared to provide testimony or otherwise participate in court in that language based on your training? Why or why not?
3. The Civil Rights Act of 1964 was enacted to end segregation based on race, religion, and national origin; barred discrimination by employers on those same grounds; and paved the way for other legislation aimed at providing equality across the country. What examples of linguistic discrimination have you encountered that seem contrary to this?
4. Watch the advertisement linked in the QR code. It was produced by the Equal Housing Authority on linguistic profiling and involves a white person making phone call after phone call about an advertisement for an apartment. With each call, he uses a different stigmatized accent. Asian and Middle Eastern accents are included, though, to our knowledge, no formal investigation of how such accents are profiled in day-to-day telephone interactions has been conducted. How might such an investigation look?

5. Imagine that you have a friend or co-worker who applied for an apartment and has been the victim of linguistic profiling, in your view of things. They are reluctant to register a complaint. Investigate the process and put together the information and forms that your friend will need to pursue the issue. Consider the following issues:

   a. Does this process strike you as reasonable or overly complicated?
   b. Why might an otherwise intelligent, well-established individual be reluctant to pursue equal treatment under the law?

6. Can you recall any instances of linguistic profiling over the phone, either by you or of you? What sort of judgments were made about/by the stranger on the other end? Reactions?

Epilogue

Teach your children well

Honesty & equality & respect & linguistic diversity

The sign in Figure 15.1, from the 2017 Women's March, links honesty, equality, respect, and grammar as some sort of positive ideals society should value. But one of these things is not like the others. While there are humans who are dishonest, disrespectful, and against equality, there aren't people who do not have grammar. As we have shown throughout this book, the grammar of our language(s) is a basic part of who we are, regardless of whether we are honest or respectful. Of course, the author of this sign adheres to Standard Language Ideology and is assuming that "grammar" means "proper grammar," that speaking "correctly" is a sign of honesty and respect, and that the world would be better if everyone spoke just like white, middle-class men from outside the South.

Imagine a sign that read, "Honesty & Equality & Respect & Whiteness." Such a sign would be recognized a racist, yet the inclusion of "Grammar" in place of "Whiteness" seems like common sense to many. The sign indicates, at least through the lens of Standard Language Ideology, that people who don't speak according to the norms found among white, middle-class Northerners are dishonest and disrespectful. Within Standard Language Ideology, the meaning of *grammar* is often amorphous and ambiguous. It is an abstract and relative concept like respectfulness or equality. Of course, what ought to be suggested by putting "grammar" and "equality" together is that all grammars are equally complex and capable of conveying complex thought, regardless of whether someone decides that the rules of that grammar are "right" or "wrong." All grammars are worthy of respect, and there is no relationship between the variety of English a person speaks and that person's ability to be honest or equitable.

The prescriptive idea of "correctness" is vague and hard to pin down, but this is exactly how it succeeds. A child watching cartoons may have never encountered people who speak in different ways, but the child still comes to learn that certain ways of speaking are tied to people who are dangerous, violent, unintelligent, or worthy of ridicule in some way, while other ways of speaking get linked to heroes and heroines, winners, and stars. The fact that the "bad" ways of speaking are the ones that are those found in minority communities goes unnoticed, and the child has acquired a new kernel of knowledge within discourse structural racism.

You've got to be carefully taught

History is ever with us. Even when people do not recognize it, the discourse that surrounds individuals every day is overrun with remnants of humanity's long history of moral failures.

DOI: 10.4324/9781003332886-15

Figure 15.1 Protesters at the 2017 Women's March on Washington
Source: photo by Ted Eytan

Although race has no scientific basis, it has come to be so central to the structure of American society that the imagined categories have become a basic part of many Americans' habitual thought. People unknowingly teach their children to sing old minstrel tunes that originated as a way of mocking Black people. People use words without being aware of their hateful histories. Just as individuals "know" the sound of an eagle's cry, they come to "know" and expect people to speak and act in particular ways based on the stereotyped representations in the wider world. People become trapped in a horrible cycle of prejudicial reproduction. They come to expect a person to speak a certain way based primarily on their appearance. Expectations for how someone will speak influence the way that individuals actually perceive that person's speech. So prejudicial representations draw individuals into a set of expectations that push their perceptions to match social stereotypes. All too often, the ways of speaking that one expects to hear are based on discriminatory histories and representations that link particular ways of speaking with negative traits.

A human's eyes tell their brains that their ears are going to hear someone who sounds a certain way, and their ears adjust to hear in that very way. When a police officer expects a young Black man to sound "dangerous" or "violent" and then proceeds to hear them in that very way, the fear that officer experiences is quite real regardless of whether there is actually any threat involved. The plethora of racist representations that permeate the world leads to a society where patterns of habitual thought create racially motivated fear in the absence of actual danger. Unconscious bias results from living in a world surrounded by discourse structural racism. Prejudice is unnatural and counter to the well-being of both individuals and society as a whole. Yet challenging forms of discrimination requires making the effort to reject the forms of prejudicial language ideologies that surround us.

The failure to question patterns of habitual thought result in cases where white people call the police to report innocuous behaviors like a Black birdwatcher walking through the park, Latinx children swimming in a community pool, or a woman wearing a hijab eating lunch at a sidewalk café. Taking a moment to step back and use a little reflective thought is key to preventing such ridiculous racial indignities. The failure to question patterns of habitual thought results in a society where it seems reasonable to force marginalized people to assimilate, a society where women are expected to perform emotional labor and accept sexual harassment, a society where Indigenous people and deaf people are denied use of their own languages. The failure to question patterns of habitual thought results in a society where people become indifferent to the killing of young people of color, a society where it takes more than 100 years to make lynching a federal crime, a society that continues to fail to recognize that Black lives matter.

The ideology of "standard" English marginalizes those who don't fit an imagined normative "correct" way of speaking and interacting. Exclusionary treatment of those who speak "incorrectly" begins when children learn the indexical associations between language variation and social stereotypes. In school, these associations come to be enforced by excluding children who are unable to communicate in a way that the teacher finds acceptable. Indexical meanings that become embedded into habitual thought can have detrimental and widespread implications.

The pervasiveness of Standard Language Ideology masks the myriad injustices that it produces. Inequalities stemming from beliefs in "standard" English are manifold: Southerners are not hired because their vowels happen to have negative indexical associations, people speaking another language are told to go back to where they came from, women are treated as "insecure" even when they use linguistic features common in the speech of men, and so on. Because the stereotypes in habitual thought may influence perceptions of the speech of others, the way individuals listen to others is driven by stereotypes of race, class, gender, age, and so on. Becoming a society based on honesty, equality, and respect requires shedding the instinctive tendency to let the patterns of habitual thought that have been inherited continue to regulate the ways in which individuals hear and see those who are different from themselves.

Our hope for you, dear reader

Language is the foundation of human sociality. In addition to making it possible for us to communicate with one another, language allows us to convey to others that we are unique individuals with distinct personal histories. Language is how the rest of the world comes to know who we are and where we come from. This is why rejecting entire groups of people because of the way they speak is no different from discriminating on the basis on skin color, gender, or ability.

Throughout this book you have seen how uninformed and misguided beliefs about language serve to preserve and reproduce social inequalities, silence minority voices, and attempt to legitimize myriad forms of discrimination. Ignorance not only makes us unable to see how actions can harm others, but it also robs people of countless opportunities to connect with others. Implicit bias is instilled in every one of us through an endless loop of representations that tell us to avoid those who are different from us. Discrimination is created through language, and it is only through language that social inequalities will be defeated. Ending prejudice requires learning to recognize and reject representations that reproduce the harmful stereotypes at the foundation of structural inequalities. Ending prejudice requires coming to know the individuals around you as unique and valuable human beings rather than seeing them as exemplars of some biased system of categorization.

When a child acquires language, it suddenly becomes possible for them to fulfill their insatiable curiosity about the wondrous world that surrounds them. Because no one has lived the same life, each person has their own unique ways of speaking and interacting that build upon distinct experiences of the world. These distinct experiences of life also mean that every other person you encounter knows something you have never learned before. Every other person on this planet has something to teach the world. When people are discounted because of who they are or how they speak, everyone is robbed of the joy of discovering something new about the incredible world we live in.

Our hope for you, dear reader, is that beginning to unlearn Standard Language Ideology offers you the opportunity to recapture the childlike wonder of the world by allowing you to learn from people you might have otherwise disregarded simply because of the way they looked or how they spoke. If you are willing to work to find the person behind the voice you hear, you will not only avoid inadvertently promoting discord and inequality, but you will also find yourself in a beautiful new world full of interesting and amazing people who can teach you about their unique perspectives on the world. We hope that you will not let language bias rob you of the chance to connect with other humans, so that you can learn from everyone you meet and come to live life to the fullest extent possible.

Bibliography

ABC7.com. 2019. Entire Massachusetts neighborhood learns sign language after family welcomes deaf baby. https://abc7.com/society/entire-neighborhood-learns-how-to-sign-with-deaf-baby/5129411/.

Aboud, F. E. 2003. The formation of in-group favoritism and out-group prejudice in young children: Are they distinct attitudes? *Developmental Psychology*, 39(1): 48–60.

Aboud, F. E. 2005. The development of prejudice in childhood and adolescence. In J. F. Dovidio, P. S. Glick, & L. A. Rudman (eds.), *On the Nature of Prejudice: Fifty Years After Allport*. Malden, MA: Blackwell, 310–326.

Ackerman, L., & Wallenberg, J. 2017. Categorization of gender, modulated by experience, can constrain coreference. *Formal Ways of Analyzing Variation*, 4.

Adair, J. K., Colegrove, K. S. S., & McManus, M. E. 2017. How the word gap argument negatively impacts young children of Latinx immigrants' conceptualizations of learning. *Harvard Educational Review*, 87(3): 309–334.

al-Rowais, H. 2012. Code switching between Arabic and English, social motivations and structural constraints. MA Thesis, Ball State University.

Alani, H. 2019. A Chinese-American woman applied for a job in Chicago. An employer responded: 'Me love you long time". *Block Club Chicago*, July 1. https://blockclubchicago.org/2019/07/01/a-chinese-american-woman-applied-for-a-job-in-chicago-an-employer-responded-me-love-you-long-time/.

Alfaraz, G. G., & Mason, A. 2019. Ethnicity and perceptual dialectology: Latino awareness of US regional dialects. *American Speech*, 94(3): 352–379.

Alim, H. S. 2006. *Roc the Mic Right: The Language of Hip Hop Culture*. New York: Routledge.

Alim, H. S., Rickford, J. R., & Ball, A. F. (eds.). 2016. *Raciolinguistics: How Language Shapes Our Ideas about Race*. New York: Oxford University Press.

Alim, H. S., & Smitherman, G. 2012. *Articulate While Black: Barack Obama, Language, and Race in the U.S.* New York: Oxford University Press.

American Bible Society. 2005. *De Nyew Testament (Gullah New Testament)*. New York, NY: American Bible Society.

Anderson-Clark, T. N., Green, R. J., & Henley, T. B. 2008. The relationship between first names and teacher expectations for achievement motivation. *Journal of Language and Social Psychology*, 27(1): 94–99.

Angermeyer, P. 2014. Monolingual ideologies and multilingual practices in small claims court: The case of Spanish-speaking arbitrators. *International Journal of Multilingualism*, 11(4): 430–448.

Austin, J. L. 1962. *How to do Things with Words*. Oxford: Oxford University Press.

Ayers, E. L. 1996. What we talk about when we talk about the South. In E. L. Ayers, P. N. Limerick, S. Nissenbaum, & P. S. Onuf (eds.), *All Over the Map: R American Regions*. Baltimore: The Johns Hopkins University Press.

Babel, A. M. 2016. Silence as control: Shame and self-consciousness in sociolinguistic positioning. In A. M. Babel (ed), *Awareness and Control in Sociolinguistic Research*. Cambridge UK: Cambridge University Press. 200–227.

Babel, A. M., & Russell, J. 2015. Expectations and speech intelligibility. *The Journal of the Acoustical Society of America*, 137(5): 2823–2833.

Baese-Berk, M. M., Bradlow, A. R., & Wright, B. A. 2013. Accent-independent adaptation to foreign accented speech. *The Journal of the Acoustical Society of America*, 133(3): EL174–EL180.

Baese-Berk, M. M., McLaughlin, D. J., & McGowan, K. B. 2020. Perception of non-native speech. *Language and Linguistics Compass*, 14(7): e12375.

Bailey, G., & Tillery, J. 1996. The persistence of Southern American English. *Journal of English Linguistics*, 24.

Bailey, R. W. 1996. *Nineteenth-Century English*. Ann Arbor: University of Michigan Press.

Baird, B. O., Marcos, R.-M., & Cating, C. 2018. Perceptions of lexically specific phonology switches on Spanish-origin loanwords in American English. *American Speech*, 93: 1.

Baker-Bell, A. 2020. *Linguistic Justice: Black Language, Literacy, Identity, and Pedagogy*. New York: Routledge Press.

Baldwin, J. 1979. If Black English isn't a language, then tell me, what is? *The New York Times*.

Baranowski, M. 2007. *Phonological Variation and Change in the Dialect of Charleston, South Carolina*. Durham, NC: Duke University Press.

Barbieri, F. 2009. Quotative be like in American English: Ephemeral or here to stay? *English World-Wide*, 30(1): 68–90.

Barnes, B. 2009. Her prince has come. Critics, too. *The New York Times*, May 29.

Barrett, R. 2006. Language ideology and racial inequality: Competing functions of Spanish in an Anglo-owned Mexican restaurant. *Language in Society*, 35(2): 163–204.

Barrett, R. 2008. Is it any way might you could tell me how come am I not a English speaker? Subject- auxiliary inversion and introspective methodologies in linguistics and anthropology. Plenary address, Arizona Linguistics and Anthropology Symposium. University of Arizona, Tucson, AZ, May 9, 2008. http://linguistics.arizona.edu/podcasts/direct_pods.php.

Barrett, R., Cruz, H., & García, M. L. 2016. Difficult interpretations: Linguistic anthropology and access to social services. *Anthropology News*, 57(8): 110–112.

Barrie, J. M., Sears, T., Penner, E., Peet, B., Hibler, W., Rinaldi, J., Banta, M., Wright, R., & Cottrell, W. (writers). 1953. *Peter Pan*. Burbank, CA: Disney Studios.

Barry, Dave. 1995. *The Dave Barry 1995 Calendar*. April 4.

Barry, K. 2007. *Femininity in Flight: A History of Flight Attendants*. Durham, NC: Duke University Press.

Bartelt, H. G. 1980. *Language Transfer of Navajo and Western Apache Speakers in Writing English*. Tucson, AZ: University of Arizona Press.

Basso, K. H. 1970. "To give up on words": Silence in western Apache culture. *Southwestern Journal of Anthropology*, 26(3): 213–230.

Baugh, J. 1973. *Black Street Speech: Its History, Structure and Survival*. Austin: University of Texas Press.

Baugh, J. 1999. *Out of the Mouths of Slaves: African American Language and Educational Malpractice*. Austin: University of Texas Press.

Baugh, J. 2017. Meaning-less differences: Exposing fallacies and flaws in "the word gap" hypothesis that conceal a dangerous "language trap" for low-income American families and their children. *International Multilingual Research Journal*, 11(1): 39–51.

Bauman, H. D. L., & Murray, J. J. 2010. 14 deaf studies in the 21st century: "Deaf-gain" and the future of human diversity. In M. Marschark & P. E. Spencer (eds.), *The Oxford Handbook of Deaf Studies, Language, and Education* (Vol. 2). New York: Oxford University Press, 210–225.

Bauman, Richard and Charles Briggs. 2003. *Voices of Modernity: Language Ideologies and the Politics of Inequality*. Cambridge, UK: Cambridge University Press.

Baumeister, R. F., Bratslavsky, E., Finkenauer, C., et al. 2001. Bad is stronger than good. *Review of General Psychology*, 5: 323–370.

Beahm, A. 2018. Trump's latest criticism of sessions: His Southern accent, Alabama education. *Al.com*. www.al.com/news/2018/08/trump_mocks_sessions_southern.html. Accessed 23 June 2020.

Becker, K. 2009. /r/ and the construction of place identity on New York City's Lower East Side. *Journal of Sociolinguistics*, 13(5): 634–658.

Bell, A. G. 1884. *Memoir: Upon the Formation of a Deaf Variety of the Human Race*. Washington, DC: National Academy of Sciences, 1–88.

Benor, S. B. 2009. Do American Jews speak a "Jewish language"? A model of Jewish linguistic distinctiveness. *The Jewish Quarterly Review*, 99(2): 230–269.

Benor, S. B. 2010. Ethnolinguistic repertoire: Shifting the analytic focus in language and ethnicity 1. *Journal of Sociolinguistics*, 14(2): 159–183.

Benshoff, H. M., & Griffin, S. 2009. *America on Film: Representing Race, Class, Gender, and Sexuality at the Movies*. Malden, MA: Wiley-Blackwell.

Bent, T., & Bradlow, A. R. 2003. The interlanguage speech intelligibility benefit. *The Journal of the Acoustical Society of America*, 114(3): 1600–1610.

Berk-Seligson, S. 2017. *The Bilingual Courtroom: Court Interpreters in the Judicial Process*, 2nd Ed. Chicago, IL: University of Chicago Press.

Blasi, D., Michaelis, S. M., & Haspelmath, M. 2017. Grammars are robustly transmitted even during the emergence of creole languages. *Nature Human Behaviour*, 1: 723–729.

Blom, J-P., & Gumperz, J. 1972. Social meaning in linguistic structures: Code switching in Northern Norway. In J. Gumperz & D. Hymes (eds.), *Directions in Sociolinguistics: The Ethnography of Communication*. New York: Holt, Rinehart, and Winston, 407–434.

Blum, H. 2016. Totally fried. *The ASHA Leader*, February 1, 2016. https://leader.pubs.asha.org/doi/full/10.1044/leader.FTR2.21022016.50. Accessed 9 June 2020.

Bonfiglio, T. P. 2002. *Race and the Rise of Standard American*. Berlin: Mouton De Gruyter.

Bonilla-Silva, E. 2003. *Racism without Racists: Color-Blind Racism and the Persistence of Racial Inequality in the United States*. Lanham, MD: Rowan and Littlefield.

Bounds, P., Cramer, J., & Tamasi, S. 2020. *Linguistic Planets of Belief: Mapping Language Attitudes in the American South*. New York: Routledge.

Bourdieu, P. 1987. *Outline of A Theory of Practice*. Cambridge, UK: Cambridge University Press.

Bourdieu, P., & Thompson, J. B. 1991. *Language and Symbolic Power*. Cambridge, UK: Polity.

Bourhis, R. Y., Montaruli, E., & Amiot, C. E. 2007. Language planning and French-English bilingual communication: Montreal field studies from 1977 to 1997. *International Journal of the Sociology of Language*, 185: 187–224.

Briggs, L., & Pailliotet, A. W. 1997. A story about grammar and power. *Journal of Basic Writing*: 46–61.

Britt, E. 2011. "Can the church say amen": Strategic uses of black preaching style at the State of the Black Union. *Language in Society*, 40(2): 211–233.

Broder, J. M. 2007. Familiar fallback for officials: "Mistakes were made." *The New York Times*, March 14.

Brown, B. 1986. Cajun/English code-switching: A test of formal models. In D. Sankoff (ed.), *Diversity and Diachrony*. Amsterdam: Benjamins, 399–206.

Brown, R. 2010. *Prejudice: Its Social Psychology*, 2nd Ed. Malden, MA: Wiley-Blackwell.

Bruch, P., & Marback, R. (eds.). 2005. *The Hope and the Legacy: The Past, Present, and Future of "Students' Right to their Own Language."* Cresskill, NJ: Hampton Press.

Bruns, R. 2014. *Zoot Suit Riots*. Santa Barbara, CA: ABC-CLIO.

Bucholtz, M. 1995. Language in evidence: The pragmatics of translation and the judicial process. In M. Morris (ed.), *Translation and the Law*. Amsterdam: John Benjamins, 115–129.

Bucholtz, M. 1999. "Why be normal?": Language and identity practices in a community of nerd girls. *Language in Society*, 28(2): 203–223. Chicago.

Bucholtz, M. 2016. On being called out of one's name. Indexical bleaching as a technique of deracialization. In H. S. Alim, J. R. Rickford, & A. F. Ball (eds.), *Raciolinguistics: How Language Shapes Our Understanding of Race*. New York: Oxford University Press, 273–289.

Bucholtz, M., & Lopez, Q. 2011. Performing blackness, forming whiteness: Linguistic minstrelsy in Hollywood film. *Journal of Sociolinguistics*, 15(5): 680–706.

Buck, C., & Lima, K. (directors). 1999. *Tarzan*. Burbank, CA: Walt Disney Studios.

Buescher, D. T., & Ono, K. A. 1996. Civilized colonialism: Pocahontas as neocolonial rhetoric. *Women's Studies in Communication*, 19: 185–212.

Burdin, R. S., Holliday, N., & Reed, P. E. 2018. Rising above the standard: Variation in L+H* contour use across 5 varieties of American English. In *Proceedings of the 9th International Conference on Speech Prosody*. Baixas, FR: International Speech Communication Association, 354–358.

Burkette, A., & Kretzschmar Jr, W. A. 2018. *Exploring Linguistic Science: Language Use, Complexity, and Interaction*. Cambridge, UK: Cambridge University Press.

Bybee, J. L., & Slobin, D. I. 1982. Rules and schemas in the development and use of the English past tense. *Language*, 58(2): 265–289.

Byrd, S. 2010. Immigrant sues over lost custody of child in Miss. *Mississippi Clarion Ledger*, August 12.

Cameron, D. 1995. *Verbal Hygiene*. New York: Routledge.

Campbell-Kibler, K. 2007. Accent, (ING), and the social logic of listener perceptions. *American Speech*, 82(1): 32–64.

Cargile, A. C., Maeda, E., Rodriguez, J., & Rich, M. 2010. "Oh, you speak English so well!": US American listeners' perceptions of" foreignness" among nonnative speakers. *Journal of Asian American Studies*, 13(1): 59–79.

Cenoz, J., & Gorter, D. 2006. Linguistic landscape and minority languages. *International Journal of Multilingualism*, 3(1): 67–80.

Chambers, J. K., & Trudgill, P. 1998. *Dialectology*. Cambridge, UK: Cambridge University Press.

Chang, J., & Le, T. N. 2010. Multiculturalism as a dimension of school climate: The impact on the academic achievement of Asian American and Hispanic youth. *Cultural Diversity and Ethnic Minority Psychology*, 16(4): 485–492. https://doi.org/10.1037/a0020654.

Charity Hudley, A. H., Mallinson, C., Bucholtz, M., Flores, N., Holliday, N., Chun, E., & Spears, A. 2018. Linguistics and race: An interdisciplinary approach towards an LSA statement on race. *Proceedings of the Linguistic Society of America*, 3(1): 8–11.

Chen, J. M., de Paula Couto, M. C. P., Sacco, A. M., & Dunham, Y. 2018. To be or not to be (black or multiracial or white) cultural variation in racial boundaries. *Social Psychological and Personality Science*, 9(7): 763–772.

Chen, L. 2013. Motivation for code-switching in the Chinese Christian Church in the United States. *SALSA XXI/Texas Linguistic Forum*, 56: 1–11.

Cheryan, S., & Bodenhausen, G. V. 2000. When positive stereotypes threaten intellectual performance: The psychological hazards of "model minority" status. *Psychological Science*, 11(5): 399–402.

Chomsky, N. S. 1957. *Syntactic Structures*. The Hague: Mouton.

Chomsky, N. S. 1959. Review of B. F. Skinner, verbal behavior. *Language*, 35.

Chun, E. W. 2004. Ideologies of legitimate mockery: Margaret Cho's revoicings of Mock Asian. *Pragmatics*, 14(2–3): 263–289.

Chun, E. W. 2016. The meaning of Ching-Chong: Language, racism, and response in new media. In H. S. Alim, J. R. Rickford, & A. F. Ball (eds.), *Raciolinguistics: How Language Shapes Our Understanding of Race*. New York: Oxford University Press, 81–96.

Clements, R., & Musker, J. (directors). 2016. *Moana*. Burbank, CA: Walt Disney Studios.

Comas-Diaz, L. 2001. Hispanics, Latinos, or Americanos: The evolution of identity. *Cultural Diversity and Ethnic Minority Psychology*, 7(2): 115.

Conrod, K. 2020. Pronouns and gender in language. In K. Hall & R. Barrett (eds.), *The Oxford Handbook of Language and Sexuality*. New York: Oxford University Press.

Copeland, B. J., & Pillsbury III, H. C. 2004. Cochlear implantation for the treatment of deafness. *Annual Review of Medicine*, 55: 157–167.

Cotter, C. 1999. Language and the news media. In R. S. Wheeler (ed.), *Workings of Language*. London: Praeger, 165–180.

Cotterill, J. 2003. Language and power in court. Houndmills, Basingstoke: Palgrave Macmillan.

Cramer, Jennifer. 2016. Contested Southernness: The linguistic production and perception of identities in the borderlands. *Publication of the American Dialect Society 100*. Durham, NC: Duke University Press.

Cramer, J., & Preston, D. R. 2018. Introduction: Changing perceptions of Southernness. *American Speech*, 93(3–4): 337–343.

Crampton, J. W. 2011. *Mapping: A Critical Introduction to Cartography and GIS*. Hoboken, NJ: John Wiley & Sons.

Cruz, C. B. 2010. Complaint: Cruz v Mississippi department of human services, singing river health system. Justice Department U.S. District Court for the Southern District of Mississippi, August 12.

Dailey-O'Cain, J. 2000. The sociolinguistic distribution of and attitudes toward focuser like and quotative like. *Journal of Sociolinguistics*, 4(1): 60–80.

Davis, A. Y. 1981. *Women, Race & Class*. New York: Vintage Books.

Davis, P. 2002. Disney Goes Hawaiian. *Hana Hou!* 5(2).

De Mente, B. 2011. *The Mexican Mind! – Understanding & Appreciating Mexican Culture*. Burlington, VT: Phoenix Books.

Debczak, Michele. 2018. 5 ways to define a sandwich, according to the law. *Mental Floss*, November 3. https://www.mentalfloss.com/article/501011/5-ways-define-sandwich-according-law.

Debenport, E. 2020. Sexual harassment, speech acts, and public secrets in US higher education. In K. Hall & R. Barrett (eds.), *The Oxford Handbook of Language and Sexuality*. New York: Oxford University Press.

DeGraff, M. 2005. Linguists' most dangerous myth: The fallacy of Creole Exceptionalism. *Language in Society*, 34: 533–591.

Dickinson, A. 2018. Kardashians' 'vocal fry' drives grandma to distraction. *Detroit Free Press*, March 7. https://eu.freep.com/story/life/advice/2018/03/06/vocal-fry-drives-grandma-distraction/377355002/.

Dilley, L., Shattuck-Hufnagel, S., & Ostendorf, M. 1996. Glottalization of word-initial vowels as a function of prosodic structure. *Journal of Phonetics*, 24: 423–444.

Dindal, G. (director). 2000. *The Emporer's New Groove*. Burbank, CA: Walt Disney Studios.

Do, A. 2012. Filipino nurses win language discrimination settlement. *Los Angeles Times*, September 18. www.latimes.com/health/la-xpm-2012-sep-18-la-me-english-only-20120918-story.html.

DuBois, W.E.B. 1903. *The Souls of Black Folk*. Chicago, IL: A. C. McClurg and Co.

Dvorkin, J. 2005. Pronunciamentos: Saying it right. *National Public Radio*, November 8.

Eckert, P. 2008. Variation and the indexical field. *Journal of Sociolinguistics*, 12(4): 453–476.

Eckert, P., & Wenger, É. 2005. Communities of practice in sociolinguistics. *Journal of Sociolinguistics*, 9(4): 582–589.

Edgerton, G., & Jackson, K. 1996. Redesigning Pocahontas: Disney, the "white man's Indian," and the marketing of dreams. *Journal of Popular Film and Television*, 24(2): 90–98.

EEOC. 2000. EEOC reaches landmark "English only" settlement; Chicago manufacturer to pay over $190,000 to Hispanic workers. *Press Release*, September 1. www.eeoc.gov/newsroom/eeoc-reaches-landmark-english-only-settlement-chicago-manufacturer-pay-over-190000.

EEOC. 2003. Central station casino to pay $1.5 million in EEOC settlement for national origin bias. *Press Release*, July 18. www.eeoc.gov/newsroom/central-station-casino-pay-15-million-eeoc-settlement-national-origin-bias-0.

EEOC. 2019a. EEOC sues Blackstone Consulting, Inc. for national origin discrimination. *Press Release*, December 16. www.eeoc.gov/newsroom/eeoc-sues-blackstone-consulting-inc-national-origin-discrimination.

EEOC. 2019b. La Cantera resort and spa to pay Over $2.5 million to settle EEOC national origin discrimination suit. *Press Release*, October 31. www.eeoc.gov/newsroom/la-cantera-resort-and-spa-pay-over-25-million-settle-eeoc-national-origin-discrimination.

EEOC. 2021. www.eeoc.gov/laws/guidance/policy-guidance-current-issues-sexual-harassment.

Ehrlich, S. 2003. *Representing Rape: Language and Sexual Consent*. New York: Routledge.

Eisenhauer, K., & Fought, C. 2016. A quantitative analysis of gendered compliments in Disney princess films. Linguistic Society of America. Marriott Marquis, Washington, DC, January 17. Conference Presentation.

Elliott, N. 2000. A study in the rhoticity of American film actors. In R. Dal Vera (ed.), *Standard Speech and Other Contemporary Issues in Professional Voice and Speech Training*. New York: Applause, 103–130.

Erard, M. 2007. *Um: Slips, Stumbles, and Verbal Blunders, and What They Mean*. New York: Pantheon Books.

Erskine, C. 2018. "Hey y'all" – passengers don't trust pilots with Southern accents nearly as much as Midwestern pilots. *Los Angeles Times*, September 21. https://www.latimes.com/travel/la-tr-airline-pilots-accents-20180921-story.html.

Fader, A. 2009. *Mitzvah Girls: Bringing Up the Next Generation of Hasidic Jews in Brooklyn*. Princeton: Princeton University Press. https://doi.org/10.1515/9781400830992.

Feagin, C. 1986. More evidence for major vowel change in the South. *Diversity and Diachrony*, 83: 96.

Feagin, C. 1990. The dynamics of a sound change in southern states English: From R-Less to R-full in three generations. In J. A. Edmondson, C. Feagin et al. (eds.), *Development and Diversity: Language Variation Across Time and Space*. Dallas, TX: Summer Institute of Linguistics, 129–146.

Feagin, C. 2003. Vowel shifting in the southern states. In S. J. Nagle & S. L. Sanders (eds.), *English in the Southern United States*. Cambridge: Cambridge University Press, 126–140.

Feagin, J. R., & McKinney, K. D. 2005. *The Many Costs of Racism*. Lanham, MD: Rowman & Littlefield Publishers.

Feagin, J. R., & Van Ausdale, D. 2001. *The First R: How Children Learn Race and Racism*. Lanham, MD: Rowman & Littlefield Publishers.

Fiester, L. 2010. *Early Warning! Why Reading by the End of Third Grade Matters*. Kids Count Special Report. Baltimore, MD: Annie E. Casey Foundation.

Filppula, M. 2000. Inversion in embedded questions in some regional varieties of English. *Topics in English Linguistics*, 31: 439–454.

Fisch, S. M. 2005. Children's learning from television. *Televizion*, 18: 10–14.

Foss, K. A. 2014. Constructing hearing loss or "deaf gain?" Voice, agency, and identity in television's representations of d/deafness. *Critical Studies in Media Communication*, 31(5): 426–447.

Fought, C. 2002. *Chicano English in Context*. Basingstoke: Palgrave Macmillan.

Fought, C., & Eisenhauer, K. 2022. *Language & Gender in Children's Animated Films*. Cambridge: Cambridge University Press.

Foundas, S. 2009. Disney's Princess and the Frog can't escape the ghetto. *The Village Voice*, November 24. http://Goo.Gl/BU717.

Freeman, A. 2017. Milk, a symbol of neo-Nazi hate. *The Conversation*, August 30, 2017. https://theconversation.com/milk-a-symbol-of-neo-nazi-hate-83292.

Freeman, M. 2006. Reconsidering the effects of monosodium glutamate: A literature review. *Journal of the American Academy of Nurse Practitioners*, 18(10): 482–486.

Fridland, V. 1998. The southern vowel shift: Linguistic and social factors. PhD Thesis, Michigan State University, East Lansing, MI.

Fridland, V. 2001. The social dimension of the Southern vowel shift: Gender, age and class. *Journal of Sociolinguistics*, 5(2): 233–253.

Frumkin, L. 2007. Influences of accent and ethnic background on perceptions of eyewitness testimony. *Psychology, Crime & Law*, 13(3): 317–331.

Gal, S. 2005. Language ideologies compared: Metaphors of public/private. *Journal of Linguistic Anthropology*, 15(1): 23–37.

García, M. T., & Castro, S. 2011. *Blowout! Sal Castro and the Chicano Struggle for Educational Justice*. Chapel Hill, NC: University of North Carolina Press.

Gee, J. P. 1999. *An Introduction to Discourse Analysis: Theory and Method*, 4th Ed., 2014. London: Routledge.

Gee, J. P. 2015. Discourse, small d, big D. In C. Ilie & T. Sandel (eds.), *The International Encyclopedia of Language and Social Interaction*, Malden, MA: John Wiley & Sons, 1–5.

Gee, J. P. 2007 [1996]. *Social Linguistics and Literacies: Ideology in Discourses*. New York: Taylor and Francis Group.

Gehlawat, A. 2010. The strange case of the princess and the frog: Passing and the elision of race. *Journal of African American Studies*, 14(4): 417–431.

Geier, T. 2017. Fox news sued by 2 black women charging 'top-down racial harassment'. *The Wrap*, March 29.

Giles, H., Taylor, D. M., & Bourhis, R. Y. 1977. Dimensions of Welsh identity. *European Journal of Social Psychology*, 7(2): 165–174.

Giroux, H. A., & Pollock, G. 2010. *The Mouse that Roared: Disney and the End of Innocence*. Ukraine: Rowman & Littlefield Publishers.

Gobl, C., & Chasaide, A. N. 2003. The role of voice quality in communicating emotion, mood and attitude. *Speech Communication*, 40: 189–212.

Goldgeier, K., & Mcleskey, M. 2018. 30 Years after Gallaudet students demanded a deaf president, it's a 'typical University'. *WAMU*, March 12, 2018. https://wamu.org/story/18/03/12/30-years-gallaudet-students-demanded-deaf-president-typical-university/.

Gooding-Williams, R. 1995. Disney in Africa and the inner city: On race and space in the lion king. *Social Identities*, 1: 373–379.

Goodman, A. H., Moses, Y. T., & Jones, J. L. 2019. *Race: Are We So Different?* Malden, MA: John Wiley & Sons.

Gordon, M. J. 2000a. Phonological correlates of ethnic identity: Evidence of divergence? *American Speech*, 75(2): 115–136.

Gordon, M. J. 2000b. Tales of the Northern cities. *American Speech*, 75: 412–414.

Gordon, M. J. 2001. *Small-Town Values and Big-City Vowels: A Study of the Northern Cities Shift in Michigan*. Durham: Duke University Press.

Gould, P. R., & White, R. 1992. *Mental Maps*. Boston: Allen and Unwin.

Grandgent, C. H. 1920. *Old and New*. Cambridge, MA: Harvard University Press.

Gray, L. S., & Heuser, P. 2003. Nonacademic professionals' perception of usage errors. *Journal of Basic Writing*, 50–70.

Green, L. J. 2002. *African American English: A Linguistic Introduction*. Cambridge: Cambridge University Press.

Grenoble, L. A., & Whaley, L. J. 2005. *Saving Languages*. Cambridge, UK: Cambridge University Press.

Grieve, J. 2019. *Regional Variation in Written American English*. Cambridge: Cambridge University Press.

Grieve, J., Nini, A., & Guo, D. 2018. Mapping lexical innovation on American social media. *Journal of English Linguistics*, 46(4): 293–319.

Grimes, J. 2019. Hate, conflict, and public space: Stand your ground laws and potential immunity for hate crimes. *Journal of Hate Studies*. 15.83.10.33972/jhs.163.

Groce, N. E. 1985. *Everyone Here Spoke Sign Language: Hereditary Deafness on Martha's Vineyard*. Cambridge, MA: Harvard University Press.

Grosjean, F. 1982. *Life with Two Languages: An Introduction to Bilingualism*. Cambridge, MA: Harvard University Press.

Hahn, P. W., & Clayton, S. D. 1996. The effects of attorney presentation style, attorney gender and juror gender on juror decisions, *Law and Human Behavior* 20(5): 533–534.

Halberstadt, A. G., Castro, V. L., Chu, Q., Lozada, F. T., & Sims., C. M. 2018. Preservice teachers' racialized emotion recognition, anger bias, and hostility attributions. *Journal of Experimental Social Psychology*, 54: 125–138. DOI: 10.1016/j.cedpsych.2018.06.004.

Harari, H., & McDavid, J. W. 1973. Name stereotypes and teachers' expectations. *Journal of Educational Psychology*, 65(2): 222.

Harmon, A. 2018. Why white supremacists are chugging milk (and why geneticists are alarmed). October 17, 2018. www.nytimes.com/2018/10/17/us/white-supremacists-science-dna.html.

Hart, B., & Risley, T. R. 1995. *Meaningful Differences in the Everyday Experience of Young American Children*. Baltimore, MD: Paul H Brookes Publishing.

Hart, B., & Risley, T. R. 2003. The early catastrophe: The 30 million word gap by age 3. *American Educator*, 27(1): 4–9.

Haubert Weil, J. 2009. Finding housing: Discrimination and exploitation of Latinos in the post-Katrina rental market. *Organization & Environment*, 22(4): 491–502.

Haviland, J. B. 2003. Ideologies of language: Some reflections on language and U.S. law. *American Anthropologist*, 105(4): 764–774.

Haycock, G. S. 1933. *The Teaching of Speech. Stoke-on-Trent*. England: Hill and Ainsworth, LTD.

Heath, S. B. 1983. *Ways with Words: Language, Life and Work in Communities and Classrooms*. Cambridge, UK: Cambridge University Press.

Heffernan, T. 2022. Sexism, racism, prejudice, and bias: A literature review and synthesis of research surrounding student evaluations of courses and teaching. *Assessment & Evaluation in Higher Education*, 47(1): 144–154.

Henton, C. G., & Bladon, A. 1988. Creak as a sociophonetic marker. In L. M. Hyman & C. N. Lee (eds.), *Language, Speech and Mind: Studies in Honor of Victoria A. Fromkin*. London: Routledge, 3–29.

Hernandez, D. 2012. *How Third-Grade Reading Skills and Poverty Influence High School Graduation*. Baltimore, MD: The Annie E. Casey Foundation.

Herring, S., Johnson, D. A., & DiBenedetto, T. 1995. "This discussion is going too far!": Male resistance to female participation on the internet. In M. Bucholtz & K. Hall (eds.), *Gender Articulated: Language and the Socially Constructed Self*. New York: Routledge, 67–96.

Hill, J. C. 2015. Language attitudes in deaf communities. *Sociolinguistics and Deaf Communities*, 146–174.

Hill, J. H. 1993. Is it really "No Problemo?" Junk Spanish and Anglo-Racism. In R. Queen & R. Barrett (eds.), *SALSA I: Proceedings from the first Symposium about Language and Society – Austin*, 1–12.

Hill, J. H. 1998. Language, race, and white public space. *American Anthropologist*, 100(3): 680–689. https://doi.org/10.1525/aa.1998.100.3.680.

Hill, J. H. 2008. *The Everyday Language of White Racism*. Malden, MA: Wiley-Blackwell.

Hinton, L. 2001. The master-apprentice language learning program. *The Green Book of Language Revitalization in Practice*, 217–226.

Hisken, L. J. 2011. The correlation between self-esteem and student reading ability, reading level, and academic achievement. Master thesis. Postgraduate School, University of Central Missouri.

Ho, E. 2011. Y'all talk funny: Regional accents may be getting stronger, expert says. *Time Magazine*. http://newsfeed.time.com/2011/09/13/yall-talk-funny-regional-accents-may-be-getting-stronger-expert-says/. Accessed 22 September 2017.

Hochschild, A. R. 1983. *The Managed Heart: Commercialization of Human Feeling*. Berkeley and Los Angeles: University of California Press.

Hodges, A. 2016. Hunting for "racists": Tape fetishism and the intertextual enactment and reproduction of the dominant understanding of racism in US society. *Journal of Linguistic Anthropology*, 26(1): 26–40.

hooks, b. 1996. *Reel to Real: Race, Sex, and Class at the Movies*. New York: Routledge.

Hoyert, D. L. 2021. *Maternal Mortality Rates in the United States, 2019*. Health E-Stats. Hyattsville, MD: National Center for Health Statistics.

Hughes, C., & Mamiseishvili, K. 2014. Linguistic profiling in the workplace. In M. Y. Byrd & C. L. Scott (eds.), *Diversity in the Workforce: Current Issues and Emerging Trends*. New York: Routledge, 249–265.

Hult, F. M. 2014. Drive-thru linguistic landscaping: Constructing a linguistically dominant place in a bilingual space. *International Journal of Bilingualism*, 18(5): 507–523.

Instituto Cervantes. 2019. *El español: Un lengua viva, informe 2019*. Madrid: Instituo Cervantes.

Irvine, J. T. 1989. When talk isn't cheap: Language and political economy. *American Ethnologist*, 16(2): 248–267.

Jacobsen, K., & Thompson, K. F. 2020. "The right to lead": Navajo language, dis-citizenship, and Diné presidential politics. *Journal of Sociolinguistics*, 24(1): 35–54.

Jarrett, V. 1979. "Black English" Not Spoken Here. Chicago Tribune, August 17.

Johnson, K. 2006. Resonance in an exemplar-based lexicon: The emergence of social identity and phonology. *Journal of Phonetics*, 34(4): 485–499.

Johnstone, B. 2006. Mobility, indexicality, and the enregisterment of "Pittsburghese." *Journal of English Linguistics*, 34(2): 77–104.

Johnstone, B. 2013. *Speaking Pittsburghese: The Story of a Dialect*. New York: Oxford University Press.

Jones, D. 1922. *An Outline of English Phonetics*. Leipzig, Germany: BG Teubner Verlag.

Jones, J. 2003. African Americans in Lansing and the northern cities vowel shift: Language contact and accommodation. PhD dissertation, Michigan State University, East Lansing, MI.

Jones, T. 2015. Toward a description of African American vernacular English dialect regions using "Black Twitter". *American Speech*, 90(4): 403–440.

Jones, T., Kalbfeld, J. R., Hancock, R., & Clark, R. 2019. Testifying while black: An experimental study of court reporter accuracy in transcription of African American English. *Language*, 95(2): 216–252.

Jordan, J. 1989. *White English/Black English: The Politics of Translation. Moving Towards Home: Political Essays*. New York: Basic Books, 29–40.

Kachru, B. B. 1992. Teaching world Englishes. *The Other Tongue: English Across Cultures*, 2(2): 355–365.

Kaiser, L., Rosenfield, S., & Gravois, T. 2009. Teachers' perception of satisfaction, skill development, and skill application after instructional consultation services. *Journal of Learning Disabilities*, 42(5): 444–457.

Kang, O., & Rubin, D. L. 2009. Reverse linguistic stereotyping: Measuring the effect of listener expectations on speech evaluation. *Journal of Language and Social Psychology*, 28(4): 441–456.

Katz, L., Cobb Scott, J., & Hadjioannou, X. 2009. Exploring attitudes toward language differences: Implications for teacher education programs. In J. Cobb Scott, D. Y. Straker, & L. Katz (eds.), *Affirming Students' Right to their Own Language: Bridging Language Policies and Pedagogical Practices*. New York: Routledge, 99–116.

Katz, P. A. 2003. Racists or tolerant multiculturalists? How do they begin? *American Psychologist*, 58(11): 897–909.

Kawai, Y. 2005. Stereotyping Asian Americans: The dialectic of the model minority and the yellow peril. *The Howard Journal of Communications*, 16(2): 109–130.

Kelsey, G. 2011. An open letter to Kuntry Kitchen (blog post). http://ginkelsey.blogspot.com/2011/06/open-letter-to-kuntry-kitchen.html.

Kinloch, V. 2005. Revisiting the promise of students' right to their own language: Pedagogical strategies. *College Composition and Communication*, 57(1): 83–113.

Kossan, P. 2011. Arizona teacher accent scrutiny halted. *The Arizona Republic*, September 12. http://archive.azcentral.com/arizonarepublic/news/articles/20110912arizona-teacher-accent-scrutiny-halted.html.

Krapp, G. P. 1909. *Modern English: Its Growth and Present Use*. New York: Charles Scribner's Sons.

Krapp, G. P. 1925. *The English Language in America* (Vol. 1). New York: Century Company.

Kroskrity, P. V. 2018. On recognizing persistence in the Indigenous language ideologies of multilingualism in two native American communities. *Language & Communication*, 62: 133–144.

Kurath, H. 1971. Mourning and morning. In J. V. Williamson & V. M. Burke (eds.), *A Various Language. Perspectives on American Dialects*. New York: Holt, Rinehart & Winston, 417–423.

Kurath, H., & McDavid, R. 1961. *The Pronunciation of English in the Atlantic States*. Ann Arbor, MI: University of Michigan Press.

Kurinec, C. A., & Weaver III, C. A. 2019. Dialect on trial: Use of African American Vernacular English influences juror appraisals. *Psychology, Crime & Law*, 25(8): 803–828. DOI: 10.1080/1068316X.2019.1597086.

Kwachka, P. 1991. The effect of language shift on the acquisition of orientational systems, Choctaw and English. *Linguistics and Education*, 3: 169–185.

Kwok, R. H. M. 1968. Chinese-restaurant syndrome. *New England Journal of Medicine*, 278: 796.

Labov, W. 1972a. *Language in The Inner City; Studies in The Black English Vernacular*. Philadelphia, PA: University of Pennsylvania Press.

Labov, W. 1972b. *Sociolinguistic Patterns*. Philadelphia, PA: University of Pennsylvania Press.

Labov, W., Ash, S., & Boberg, C. 2006. *The Atlas of North American English: Phonetics, Phonology, and Sound Change: A Multimedia Reference Tool*. Berlin: Walter De Gruyter.

Lacroix, C. 2004. Images of animated others: The orientalization of Disney's cartoon heroines from the Little Mermaid to the Hunchback of Notre Dame. *Popular Communication*, 2(4): 213–229.

Ladefoged, P., & Maddieson, I. 1996. *The Sounds of the World's Languages*. Oxford: Blackwell.

Lakoff, R. T. 1975. *Language and Woman's Place*. New York: Harper Colophon Books.

Lance, D. M. 2003. The pronunciation of Missouri: Variation and change in American English. *American Speech*, 78(3): 255–284.

Landry, R., & Bourhis, R. Y. 1997. Linguistic landscape and ethnolinguistic vitality: An empirical study. *Journal of Language and Social Psychology*, 16(1): 23–49.

Lawson, E., Scobbie, J. M., & Stuart-Smith, J. 2014. A socio-articulatory study of Scottish rhoticity. In *Sociolinguistics in Scotland*. London: Palgrave Macmillan, 53–78.

Lee, C. 2015. Gender bias in the courtroom: Combating implicit bias against women trial attorneys and litigators. *Cardozo Journal of Law & Gender*, 22: 229–252.

Lee, K. E. 2016. The perception of creaky voice: Does speaker gender affect our judgments? *Theses and Dissertations – Linguistics*, 17. https://uknowledge.uky.edu/ltt_etds/17.

Lee, S. J. 1994. Behind the model-minority stereotype: Voices of high-and low-achieving Asian American students. *Anthropology & Education Quarterly*, 25(4): 413–429.

LeMaster, B. 2006. Language contraction, revitalization, and Irish women. *Journal of Linguistic Anthropology*, 16(2): 211–228.

Leonard, W. Y. 2008. When is an "extinct language" not extinct? Miami, a formerly sleeping language. In K. King, N. Schilling-Estes, L. Fogle, J. Lou, & B. Soukup (eds.), *Endangered and Minority Languages and Language Varieties: De-fining, Documenting and Developing*. Washington, DC: Georgetown University Press.

Lien, Pei-Te, Margaret Conway, M., & Wong, J. 2003. The contours and sources of ethnic identity choices among Asian Americans. *Social Science Quarterly*, 84: 461–481.

Lillo-Martin, D., Quadros, R. M. de, & Chen Pichler, D. C. 2016. The development of bimodal bilingualism: Implications for linguistic theory. (Invited keynote paper for epistemological issue.) *Linguistic Approaches to Bilingualism*, 6(6): 719–755.

Lindau, M. 1985. The story of /r/. *Phonetic Linguistics: Essays in Honor of Peter Ladefoged*: 157–168.

Lindemann, S. 2003. Koreans, Chinese or Indians? Attitudes and ideologies about non-native English speakers in the United States. *Journal of Sociolinguistics*, 7(3): 348–364.

Lindemann, S. 2005. Who speaks "broken English"? US undergraduates' perceptions of non- native English. *International Journal of Applied Linguistics*, 15(2): 187–212.

Lippi-Green, R. 1994. Accent, standard language ideology, and discriminatory pretext in the courts. *Language in Society*, 23(2): 163–198.

Lippi-Green, R. 1997. *English with an Accent: Language, Ideology, and Discrimination in the United States*, 1st Ed. New York: Routledge.

Losin, E. A. R., Woo, C. W., Medina, N. A., Andrews-Hanna, J. R., Eisenbarth, H., & Wager, T. D. 2020. Neural and sociocultural mediators of ethnic differences in pain. *Nature Human Behaviour*, 4(5): 517–530.

Lucy, J. A. 1992. *Language Diversity and Thought: A Reformulation of the Linguistic Relativity Hypothesis*. Cambridge, UK: Cambridge University Press.

Manring, M. M. 1998. *Slave in a Box: The Strange History of Aunt Jemima*. Charlottesville, VA: University of Virginia Press.

Mar, R. A., Oatley, K., & Peterson, J. B. 2009. Exploring the link between reading fiction and empathy: Ruling out individual differences and examining outcomes. *Communications: The European Journal of Communication Research*, 34(4): 407–428.

Markowicz, H. 1972. Some sociolinguistic considerations of American sign language. *Sign Language Studies*, 1(1): 15–41.

Martin, G. J., & Yurukoglu, A. 2014. *Bias in Cable News: Real Effects and Polarization*. Cambridge, MA: National Bureau of Economic Research.
Martin-Rodriguez, M. 2000. Hyenas in the pride lands: Latinos/as and immigration in Disney's the Lion King. *Aztlán: A Journal of Chicano Studies*, 25(1): 47–67.
Mather, P. A. 2012. The social stratification of /r/in New York City: Labov's department store study revisited. *Journal of English Linguistics*, 40(4): 338–356.
Matsuda, M. J. 1991. Voices of America: Accent, antidiscrimination law, and a jurisprudence for the last reconstruction. *Yale Law Journal*: 1329–1407.
McCaskill, C., Lucas, C., Bayley, R., & Hill, J. 2011. *The Hidden Treasure of Black ASL: Its History and Structure*. Washington, DC: Gallaudet University Press.
McGowan, K. B. 2015. Social expectation improves speech perception in noise. *Language and Speech*, 58(4): 502–521.
McGowan, K. B. 2016. Sounding Chinese and listening Chinese: Awareness and knowledge in the laboratory. In A. M. Babel (ed), *Awareness and Control in Sociolinguistic Research*. Cambridge UK: Cambridge University Press.
McGowan, K. B., & Babel, A. M. 2020. Perceiving isn't believing: Divergence in levels of sociolinguistic awareness. *Language in Society*, 49(2): 231–256.
McGurk, H., & MacDonald, J. 1976. Hearing lips and seeing voices. *Nature*, 264(5588): 746–748.
Mckenzie, J. N. 1992. Bad English spoken here. *The Wall Street Journal*, April 27.
McLendon, S. 2003. Evidentials in Eastern Pomo with a comparative survey of the category in other Pomoan languages. *Typological Studies in Language*, 54: 101–130.
McLuhan, M. 1964. *Understanding Media: The Extensions of Man*. New York: McGraw-Hill. [This quote is on p. 199 of the 1994 reprint, published by MIT Press].
McQuail, D. 2010. *McQuail's Mass Communication Theory*. Los Angeles: Sage Publications.
Meek, B. 2006. "And the Injun goes 'How!'": Representations of American Indian English in white public space. *Language in Society*, 35(1): 93–128.
Meek, B. 2011. Failing American Indian languages. *American Indian Culture and Research Journal*, 31(2): 43–60.
Mettler, K. 2016. 'We can't be the United Nations': Milwaukee frozen custard shop defends 'English only' policy. *Washington Post*, May 19. www.washingtonpost.com/news/morning-mix/wp/2016/05/19/we-cant-be-the-united-nations-milwaukee-frozen-custard-shop-defends-english-only-policy/.
Milroy, J., & Milroy, L. 1985. Linguistic change, social network and speaker innovation1. *Journal of Linguistics*, 21(2): 339–384.
Monmonier, M. 1991. *How to Lie with Maps*. Chicago, IL: University of Chicago Press.
Morgan, M. 2001. "Nuthin' but a G thang": Grammar and language ideology in Hip Hop identity. In S. Lanehart (ed), *Sociocultural and Historical Contexts of African American English*. Amsterdam: John Benjamins: 187–210.
Morrison, Toni. 1975. Black Studies Center public dialogue (public lecture), March 30. Portland, OR: Portland State University.
Morrison, Toni. 1992. *Playing in the Dark: Whiteness and the Literary Imagination*. Cambridge, MA: Harvard University Press.
Morton, J. 1996. Simba's revolution: Revisiting history and class in *The Lion King*. *Social Identities: Journal for the Study of Race, Nation, and Culture*, 2(2): 311–317.
Mufwene, S. 2004. Gullah: Morphology and syntax. In B. Kortmann & K. Burridge (eds.), *A Handbook of Varieties of English: A Multimedia Reference Tool* (Vol. 2). Berlin, Germany: Mouton de Gruyter, 356–373.
Munro, M. J., Derwing, T. M., & Morton, S. L. 2006. The mutual intelligibility of L2 speech. *Studies in Second Language Acquisition*, 28(1): 111–131.
Muysken, P. 1997. Code-switching properties: Alternation, insertion, and congruent lexicalization. In M. Pütz (ed.), *Language Choices: Conditions, Constraints, and Consequences*. Amsterdam: Benjamins, 361–381.
Nagy, N., & Irwin, P. 2010. Boston (r): Neighbo(r)s Nea(r) and Fa(r). *Language Variation and Change*, 22(2): 241–278.

National Center for Education Statistics (NCES). 2016. Projected number of participants in educational institutions, by level and control of institution: Fall 2016. https://nces.ed.gov/programs/digest/d15/tables/dt15_105.10.asp Accessed 28 March 2022.

National Center for Education Statistics (NCES). 2020. The Condition of Education 2020. https://nces.ed.gov/pubsearch/pubsinfo.asp?pubid=2020144

National Council of Teachers of English (NCTE). 1996. *Standards for English Language Arts*. Urbana, IL: National Council of Teachers of English.

National Fair Housing Alliance. 2009. 2009 Fair Housing Trends Report. https://nationalfairhousing.org/resource/2009-fair-housing-trends-report/

National Geographic Society and Council on Foreign Relations. 2016. *What College-Aged Students Know About the World: A Survey on Global Literacy*. Washington, DC: National Geographic Society.

Nenneman, R. A. 1992. Language is the guardian of the culture. *The Christian Science Monitor*, July 8.

Nesbitt, M. 2021. The rise and fall of the Northern Cities Shift: Social and linguistic re- organization of TRAP in 20th century Lansing, Michigan. *American Speech*, 96(3): 332–370. https://doi.org/10.1215/00031283-8791754.

Nevins, M. E. 2013. *Lessons from Fort Apache: Beyond Language Endangerment and Maintenance*. Malden, MA: Wiley-Blackwell.

Nguyen, T. P. 2012. English-Vietnamese bilingual code-switching in conversations: How and why. Hawaii Pacific University. *TESOL Working Paper Series*, 10: 40–53.

Noel, A., & Cheng, P. 2009. Through struggle to the stars: History of California's fair housing law. *California Real Property Journal*, 27(4): 3–12.

Ochs, E., & Schieffelin, B. B. 1984. Language acquisition and socialization: Three developmental stories and their implications. In R. Shweder & R. Levine (eds.), *Culture Theory: Essays on Mind, Self and Emotion*. Cambridge: Cambridge University Press, 276–320.

Olney, J. W. 1969. Brain lesions, obesity, and other disturbances in mice treated with monosodium glutamate. *Science*, 164(3880): 719–721.

Oppenheimer, D. B. 2010. California's anti-discrimination legislation, proposition 14, and the constitutional protection of minority rights: The fiftieth anniversary of the California fair employment and housing act. *Golden Gate University Law Review*, 40. https://digitalcommons.law.ggu.edu/ggulrev/vol40/iss2/1.

Padden, C. 2010. Sign language geography. In G. Mathur & D. J. Napoli (eds.), *Deaf Around the World*. Oxford, NY: Oxford University Press, 19–37.

Patterson, N (committee chair). 2019. *New Mexico's Three-Tiered Licensure Performance Evaluation Handbook*. Santa Fe, NM: New Mexico Public Education Department.

Persson, A., & Musher-Eizenman, D. R. 2003. The impact of a prejudice-prevention television program on young children's ideas about race. *Early Childhood Research Quarterly*, 18(4): 530–546.

Pfaff, C. 1979. Constraints on language mixing: Intrasentential code-switching and borrowing in Spanish/English. *Language*, 55(2): 291–318.

Philips, S. U. 1993. *The Invisible Culture: Communication in Classroom and Community on the Warm Springs Indian Reservation*. Long Grove, IL: Waveland Press.

Pittam, J. 1987. Discrimination of five voice qualities and prediction to perceptual ratings. *Phonetica*, 44: 38–49.

Podesva, R. J. 2011. The California vowel shift and gay identity. *American Speech*, 86(1): 32–51.

Podesva, R. J., & Callier, P. 2015. Voice quality and identity. *Applied Linguistics*, 35: 173–194.

Pratt, R. H. 1892. Official report of the nineteenth annual conference of charities and correction (1892), 46–59. Reprinted in Richard H. Pratt. 1973. *"The Advantages of Mingling Indians with Whites," Americanizing the American Indians: Writings by the "Friends of the Indian" 1880–1900*. Cambridge, MA: Harvard University Press, 260–271.

Preston, D. R. 1989a. *Perceptual Dialectology: Nonlinguists' Views of Areal Linguistics (Topics in Sociolinguistics)*. Berlin, Germany: Mouton De Gruyter.

Preston, D. R. 1989b. Standard English spoken here: The geographical loci of linguistic norms. In U. Ammon (ed.), *Status and Function of Languages and Language Varieties*. Berlin: Walter De Gruyter, 24–354.

Preston, D. R. 1993. Two heartland perceptions of language variety. In T. C. Frazer (ed.), *Heartland English: Variation and Transition in the American Midwest*. Tuscaloosa, AL: University of Alabama Press, 23–47.

Preston, D. R. 1996. Whaddayaknow? The modes of folk linguistic awareness. *Language Awareness*, 5(1): 40–74.

Preston, D. R. 1999. *Handbook of Perceptual Dialectology*. Philadelphia: John Benjamins.

Price, R. 1978. *A Palpable God*. New York: Atheneum.

Prichep, D. 2013. A campus more colorful than reality: Beware that college brochure. *Weekend Edition Sunday, Nationalo Public Radio*, December 29. www.npr.org/2013/12/29/257765543/a-campus-more-colorful-than-reality-beware-that-college-brochure.

Purnell, T., Idsardi, W., & Baugh, J. 1999. Perceptual and phonetic experiments on American English dialect identification. *Journal of Language and Social Psychology*, 18: 10–30.

Pyne, M. T., McCormick, C. H., Shirmer, R. E., McKenney, F. D., McAlpin, D. H., Evans, F, Farrand, M., Pease, L. F., & Dennis, A. L. P. 1894. *Carmina Princetonia: The University Song Book*, 8th Ed. Newark, NJ: Martin R. Dennis & Co.

Quadros, Ronice Müller de, Lillo-Martin, Diane, & Chen Pichler, Deborah. 2016. Bimodal bilingualism: Sign language and spoken language. In M. Marschark & P. Elizabeth Spencer (eds.), *The Oxford Handbook of Deaf Studies in Language: Research, Policy, and Practice*. Oxford, UK: Oxford University Press, 181–196.

Queen, R. 2015. *Vox Popular: The Surprising Life of Language in the Media*. Hoboken, NJ: John Wiley & Sons.

Queen, R. 2019. Linguists often talk the talk but how can we also walk the walk. University of Kentucky Linguistics Department Colloquium Series. Lexington, KY. November 7, 2019.

Queen, R., & Boland, J. E. 2015. I think your going to like me: Exploring the role of errors in email messages on assessments of potential housemates. *Linguistics Vanguard*, 1(1): 283–293.

Ramírez, N. F., Lytle, S. R., & Kuhl, P. K. 2020. Parent coaching increases conversational turns and advances infant language development. *Proceedings of the National Academy of Sciences*, 117(7): 3484–3491.

Rampton, B. 1995. Language crossing and the problematisation of ethnicity and socialisation. *Pragmatics*, 5(4): 485–513.

Reed, P. E. 2018. The importance of Appalachian identity: A case study in rootedness. *American Speech: A Quarterly of Linguistic Usage*, 93(3–4): 409–424.

Reitherman, W. (director) 1967. *The Jungle Book*. Burbank, CA: Walt Disney Studios.

Remy, C. F. 1900. Where the best English is spoken. *The School Review*, 8(7): 414–421.

Rengifo, A. F., Rouzbahani, D., & Peirce, J. 2020. Court interpreters and the political economy of bail in three arraignment courts. *Law and Policy*, 42(3): 236–260.

Rice, M. L., & Woodsmall, L. 1988. Lessons from television: Children's word learning when viewing. *Child Development*, 59(2): 420–429.

Rickford, J. R. 1992. Grammatical variation and divergence in Vernacular Black English. In M. Gerritsen and D. Stein (eds.), *Internal and External Factors in Syntactic Change*. Berlin, Germany: Mouton de Gruyter, 174–200.

Rickford, J. R. 1999. *African American Vernacular English: Features, Evolution, Educational Implications*. Malden, MA: Wiley-Blackwell.

Rickford, J. R., & King, S. 2016. Language and linguistics on trial: Hearing Rachel Jeantel (and other vernacular speakers) in the courtroom and beyond. Language, 948–988.

Rickford, J. R., & Rickford, R. J. 2000. *Spoken Soul: The Story of Black English*. New York: John Wiley & Sons, Inc.

Rickford, J. R., Wasow, T., & Zwicky, A. 2007. Intensive and quotative all: Something old, something new. *American Speech*, 82: 3–31.

Rika, A. T. T. T. 2016. How did Disney get Moana so right and Maui so wrong? *BBC*. www.bbc.com/news/world-europe-37430268.

Roeder, R. V. 2006. *Ethnicity and Sound Change: Mexican American Accommodation to the Northern Cities Shift in Lansing*. Michigan: Michigan State University.

Rosa, J. 2016. Standardization, racialization, languagelessness: Raciolinguistic ideologies across communicative contexts. *Journal of Linguistic Anthropology*, 26(2): 162–183.

Rosa, J. 2019. *Looking Like a Language, Sounding Like a Race*. New York: Oxford University Press.

Rothenberg, R. 1996. The age of Spin. *Esquire*. http://classic.esquire.com/article/1996/12/1/the-age-of-spin.

Roy, E. A. 2016. Disney depiction of obese Polynesian god in film Moana sparks anger. *The Guardian*. www.theguardian.com/world/2016/jun/27/disney-depiction-of-obese-polynesian-god-in-film-moana-sparks-anger.

Royko, M. 1992. Here's a debate worth watching. *Chicago Tribune*. October 8: 3.

Rubin, D. L. 1992. Nonlanguage factors affecting undergraduates' judgments of nonnative English-speaking teaching assistants. *Research in Higher Education*, 33(4): 511–531.

Rubin, D. L., & Smith, K. A. 1990. Effects of accent, ethnicity, and lecture topic on undergraduates' perceptions of nonnative English-speaking teaching assistants. *International Journal of Intercultural Relations*, 14(3): 337–353.

Sakoda, K., & Siegel, J. 2003. *Pidgin Grammar: An Introduction to the Creole English of Hawai'i*. Honolulu, HI: Bess Press.

Samant, S. 2010. Arab Americans and sound change in southeastern Michigan. *English Today*, 26(3): 27–34.

Sammond, N. 2005. *Birth of an Industry: Blackface Minstrelsy and the Rise of American Animation*. Durham, NC: Duke University Press.

Santa Ana, O. 1999. "Like an animal I was treated": Anti-immigrant metaphor in US public discourse. *Discourse & Society*, 10(2): 191–224.

Saussure, F. de. 1966 [1916]. *Course in general linguistics*, Charles Bally and Albert Sechehaye (eds.), W. Baskin (trans.) New York: McGraw-Hill

Scancarelli, J., & Hardy, H. K. (eds.). 2005. *Native Languages of the Southeastern United States*. Lincoln, NE: University of Nebraska Press.

Schieffelin, B. B., Woolard, K. A., & Kroskrity, P. V. (eds.). 1998. *Language Ideologies: Practice and Theory*. New York: Oxford University Press.

Schulz, W. A. 2020. Gullah Geechee voices. Doctoral dissertation, University of West Georgia.

Scott, J., & National Council of Teachers of English. 2009. *Affirming Students' Right to their Own Language: Bridging Language Policies and Pedagogical Practices*. New York: Routledge and National Council of Teachers of English.

Seargeant, P. 2009. Language ideology, language theory, and the regulation of linguistic behaviour. *Language Sciences*, 31(4): 345–359.

Shaffer, J. 2018. Baltimore Dunkin' Donuts removes sign asking patrons to report employees shouting in foreign languages. *Baltimore Sun*, June 18. www.baltimoresun.com/business/bs-md-dunkin-donuts-english-sign-20180618-story.html.

Shankar, S. 2020. Nothing sells like whiteness: Race, ontology, and American advertising. *American Anthropologist*, 122(1): 112–119.

Shuck, G. 2006. Racializing the nonnative English speaker. *Journal of Language, Identity & Education*, 5(4): 259–276.

Shulist, S. 2018. Signs of status: Language policy, revitalization, and visibility in urban Amazonia. *Language Policy*, 17(4): 523–543.

Siegel, M. E. A. 2002. Like: The discourse particle and semantics. *Journal of Semantics*, 19(1): 35–71.

Silverman, D. A. 2005. *Faith and Boundaries: Colonists, Christianity, and Community among the Wampanoag Indians of Martha's Vineyard, 1600–1871*. Cambridge: Cambridge University Press.

Silverman, H. 2002. Groovin' to ancient Peru: A critical analysis of Disney's the emperor's new groove. *Journal of Social Archaeology*, 2(3): 298–322.

Silverstein, M. 2003. Indexical order and the dialectics of sociolinguistic life. *Language & Communication*, 23: 193.

Sledd, J. 1988. Product in process: From ambiguities of standard English to issues that divide Us. *College English*, 50(2): 168–176.

Slobe, T. 2018. Style, stance, and social meaning in mock white girl. *Language in Society*, 47(4): 541–567.

Smitherman, G. 1994. *Black Talk: Words and Phrases from the Hood to the Amen Corner*. Boston, MA: Houghton Mifflin.

Solan, L. 1990. *The Language of Judges*. Chicago: University of Chicago Press.

Soll, J. 2016. The long and brutal history of fake news. *Politico Magazine*. www.politico.com/magazine/story/2016/12/fake-news-history-long-violent-214535.

Sommers, S., & Ellsworth, P. C. 2003. How much do we really know about race and juries? A review of social science theory and research. *Chicago-Kent Law Review*, 78(3): 997–1031. https://repository.law.umich.edu/cgi/viewcontent.cgi?article=2582&context=articles.

Sontag, D. 1993. Oy Gevalt! New Yawkese an endangered dialect? *The New York Times*, February 14.

Sperry, D. E., Sperry, L. L., & Miller, P. J. 2019. Reexamining the verbal environments of children from different socioeconomic backgrounds. *Child Development*, 90(4): 1303–1318.

Squires, L. 2014. From TV personality to fans and beyond: Indexical bleaching and the diffusion of a media innovation. *Journal of Linguistic Anthropology*, 24(1): 42–62.

Stokoe, W. C. 1960. Sign language structure (Studies in Linguistics. Occasional paper, 8.

Stuart-Smith, J. 2007. The influence of the media. In C. Llamas, L. Mullany, & P. Stockwell (eds.), *The Routledge Companion to Sociolinguistics*. London and New York: Routledge, 140–148.

Subtirelu, N. C. 2015. "She does have an accent but . . .": Race and language ideology in students' evaluations of mathematics instructors on RateMyProfessors. com. *Language in Society*, 44(1): 35–62.

Sumner, M., & Kataoka, R. 2013. Effects of phonetically-cued talker variation on semantic encoding. *The Journal of the Acoustical Society of America*, 134(6): EL485–EL491.

Sun, C. F. 2008. Always on top of the food chain – "circle of life," the lion king, and hegemony. In K. S. Sealey (ed.), *Film, Politics, and Education: Cinematic Pedagogy Across the Disciplines*. New York: Peter Lang, 125–146.

Sutherland, George. 1923. *Opinion: United States v. Bhagat Singh Thind 261 U.S. 204*. Washington, DC: U.S. Supreme Court.

Swords, R., & Wheeler, R. S. 2006. *Code-switching: Teaching Standard English in Urban Classrooms*. Urbana, IL: NCTE.

Swords, R., & Wheeler, R. S. 2010. *Code-switching Lessons: Grammar Strategies for Linguistically Diverse Writers: Grades*. Portsmouth, NH: Firsthand Heinemann, 3–6.

Tabak, J. 2006. *Significant Gestures: A History of American Sign Language*. Westport, CT: Greenwood Publishing Group.

Tagliamonte, S., & D'Arcy, A. 2004. He's like, she's like: The quotative system in Canadian youth. *Journal of Sociolinguistics*, 8: 493–514.

Talbot, M. 2018. The myth of whiteness in classical sculpture. *The New Yorker*, October 22, 2018. www.newyorker.com/magazine/2018/10/29/the-myth-of-whiteness-in-classical-sculpture.

Taylor, D. B., & Morales, C. 2020. Professor who asked student to 'anglicize' her name is put on leave. *The New York Times*, June 21, 2020. www.nytimes.com/2020/06/21/us/phuc-bui-diem-nguyen-laney-college.html.

Thussu, D. K. 2007. *News as Entertainment: The Rise of Global Infotainment*. London: Sage.

Tracy, S. E. 2016. Delicious: A history of monosodium glutamate and umami, the fifth taste sensation. Doctoral dissertation, University of Toronto, Canada.

Trousdale, G., & Wise, K. (directors). 1991. *Beauty and the Beast*. Burbank, CA: Walt Disney Studios.

Tucker, S., Turner, N., Barline, J., Reid, E. M., & Elving, C. 2006. Apologies and transformational leadership. *Journal of Business Ethics*, 63: 195–207.

U.S. Census Bureau. 2007. American community survey: Language statistics. https://www.census.gov/library/publications/2010/acs/acs-12.html

U.S. Census Bureau. 2016. 2009–2013 American community survey: Language statistics. www.census.gov/data/developers/data-sets/language-stats.html.

Underwood, T. 2019. South Carolina is home to several charming Southern accents. *South Carolina Public Radio*. www.southcarolinapublicradio.org/sc-news/2019-09-27/south-carolina-is-home-to-several-charming-southern-accents.

Valli, C., & Lucas, C. 2000. *Linguistics of American Sign Language: An Introduction*. Washington, DC: Gallaudet University Press.

Vantoch, V. 2017. *The Jet Sex: Airline Stewardesses and the Making of an American Icon*. Philadelphia: University of Pennsylvania Press.

Walfisch, T., Van Dijk, D., & Kark, R. 2013. Do you really expect me to apologize? The impact of status and gender on the effectiveness of an apology in the workplace. *Journal of Applied Social Psychology*, 43: 1446–1458.

Walker, J. M. 1994. Disney's policy? No black people, please. *New York Amsterdam News*, July 23.

Walters, K. 2001. English-only rules in the workplace and the courts' response. *University of Pennsylvania Working Papers in Linguistics*, 7(3): 295–309.

Webster, A. K. 2012. "Don't talk about it" Navajo poets and their ordeals of language. *Journal of Anthropological Research*, 68(3): 399–414.

Webster, A. K. 2015. The poetry of sound and the sound of poetry: Navajo poetry, phonological iconicity, and linguistic relativity. *Semiotica*, 207: 279–301.

Wenson, K. 2017. 'Long time coming': Army returns remains of Arapaho children who died at assimilation school. *The Washington Post*, August 9. www.washingtonpost.com/news/morning-mix/wp/2017/08/09/a-long-time-coming-army-returns-remains-of-arapaho-children-who-died-at-assimilation-school-in-1800s/.

Wieling, M., Grieve, J., Bouma, G., Fruehwald, J., Coleman, J., & Liberman, M. 2016. Variation and change in the use of hesitation markers in Germanic languages. *Language Dynamics and Change*, 6(2): 199–234.

Wilson, C. R., & Ferris, W. R. 1989. *Encyclopedia of Southern Culture*. Chapel Hill, NC: University of North Carolina Press.

Winawer, J., Witthoft, N., Frank, M. C., Wu, L., Wade, A. R., & Boroditsky, L. 2007. Russian blues reveal effects of language on color discrimination. *Proceedings of the National Academy of Sciences*, 104(19): 7780–7785.

Wise, K., & Trousdale, G. 2001. *Atlantis: The Lost Empire*. Burbank, CA: Walt Disney Studios.

Wolfram, W. 1974. The relationship of white southern speech to vernacular Black English. *Language*, 50: 498–527.

Wolfram, W. 1993. Ethical considerations in language awareness programs. *Issues in Applied Linguistics*: 292–313.

Wolfram, W. 1998. Language ideology and dialect: Understanding the Oakland Ebonics controversy. *Journal of English Linguistics*, 26: 108–121.

Wolfram, W. 2002. *The Development of African American English*. Malden: Blackwell Publishers.

Wolfram, W. 2003. Reexamining the development of African American English: Evidence from isolated communities. *Language*: 282–316.

Wolfram, W. 2004a. *Social Varieties of American English*. New York: Cambridge University Press.

Wolfram, W. 2004b. The grammar of urban African American vernacular English. In E. W. Schneider & B. Kortmann (eds.), *A Handbook of Varieties of English: A Multimedia Reference Tool*. Berlin: Moulton De Gruyter.

Wolfram, W. 2007. Sociolinguistic folklore in the study of African American English. *Language and Linguistics Compass*, 1: 292–313.

Wolfram, W. 2008. Language diversity and the public interest. In K. A. King (ed.), *Sustaining Linguistic Diversity: Endangered and Minority Languages and Language Varieties*. Washington, DC: Georgetown University Press.

Wolfram, W. 2011. The African American English canon in sociolinguistics. In A. Curzan (ed.), *Contours of English and English Language Studies*. Ann Arbor, MI: University of Michigan Press.

Wolfram, W. 2018. Changing ethnolinguistic perceptions in the South. *American Speech* 93(3–4): 344–373.

Wolfram, W., Daugherty, J., & Cullinan, D. 2014. On the (in) significance of English language variation: Cherokee English and Lumbee English in comparative perspective. *University of Pennsylvania Working Papers in Linguistics*, 20(2): 22.

Wolfram, W., Hazen, K., & Ruff Tamburro, J. 1997. Isolation within isolation: A solitary century of African-American vernacular English. *Journal of Sociolinguistics*, 1: 7–38.

Wolfram, W., Reaser, J., & Vaughn, C. 2008. Operationalizing linguistic gratuity: From principle to practice. *Language and Linguistics Compass*, 2: 1109–1134.

Wolfram, W., & Thomas, E. 2008. *The Development of African American English*. Malden, MA: John Wiley & Sons.

Wong, A. W. M., & Hall-Lew, L. 2014. Regional variability and ethnic identity: Chinese Americans in New York City and San Francisco. *Language & Communication*, 35: 27–42.

Woodrow, K. M., Friedman, G. D., Siegelaub, A. B., & Collen, M. F. 1972. Pain tolerance: Differences according to age, sex and race. *Psychosomatic Medicine*, 34(6): 548–556.

Woolard, K. A. 2008. Why dat now? Linguistic-Anthropological Contributions to the explanation of sociolinguistic icons and change. *Journal of Sociolinguistics*, 12: 432–452.

Woolard, K. A., & Schieffelin, B. B. 1994. Language ideology. *Annual Review of Anthropology*, 23(1): 55–82.

Wright II, J. W., & Hosman, L. A. 1983. Language style and sex bias in the courtroom: The effects of male and female use of hedges and intensifiers on impression information. *Southern Speech Communication Journal*, 48(2): 137–152. DOI: 10.1080/10417948309372559.

Wright, K. E. 2019. Experiments on linguistic profiling of three American dialects. MA Thesis, University of Michigan. https://deepblue.lib.umich.edu/handle/2027.42/163508.

X, M. 1970. *By Any Means Necessary: Speeches, Interviews, and a Letter*. Atlanta, GA: Pathfinder Press.

Xu, Y. 2019. Duke professor is sorry for urging Chinese students not to speak Chinese. *National Public Radio*, January 19. www.npr.org/sections/goatsandsoda/2019/01/29/689660523/duke-professor-is-sorry-for-urging-chinese-students-not-to-speak-chinese.

Young, R., & Morgan, W. 1987. *The Navajo Language*. Albuquerque: University of New Mexico Press.

Young, V. A., Barrett, R., Rivera, Y. Y., & Lovejoy, K. B. 2014. *Other People's English: Code Meshing, Code Switching and African American Literacy*. New York: Teacher's College Press.

Yuasa, I. P. 2010. Creaky voice: A new feminine voice quality for young urban-oriented upwardly mobile American women? *American Speech*, 85(3): 315–337.

Zachary, M.-K. 2005. More than the law: Perspectives on an English-only case in Navajo country. *Labor Law Journal*, 56(1): 5–29.

Zappa, M. U. 1982. *Valley Girl*. (7-inch single). North Hollywood, CA: Barking Pumpkin Records.

Zentella, Ana Celia. 1997. *Growing Up Bilingual: Puerto Rican Children in New York*. Malden, MA: John Wiley & Sons.

Zhao, X., & Biernat, M. 2017. "Welcome to the U.S." but "change your name"? Adopting Anglo names and discrimination. *Journal of Experimental Social Psychology*, 70: 59–68.

Index

Note: Page numbers in *italics* refer to figures; numbers in **bold** refer to tables.

AAE *see* African American English (AAE)
accents: of animated characters 262–266, 268–273, *269*; differences in 53–54; foreign-sounding 45; French 263, **264**; of instructors 252–255, *252*, *254*; Japanese 53; of native English speakers 53; of nonnative English-speaking actors 263; perceived 255; perceptions of 53; prosodic features 49; as reflection of intelligence 205–208; regional 218; second language 52, 263, 288; segmental features 49; Southern American English 197, *198*, 202–205, *204*, 276, 322; Spanish 53; stigmatized 65; use by actors 262–263
African American English (AAE): absence of -s in *308*; additional meanings in 109–110, **110**; appropriation of 155; aspectual markers 113, 116–117, **117**, 125, 302; fluency in 315; and the language of education 237–238; literary representations of 115; in mock jury trials 309; as non-rhotic 218, 228; racial stereotypes of 125; role in housing discrimination 314–319; sentence structure 111–112, 117; similarity to Southern English dialect 79, 83; symbolic valorization of 118, 120; as systemic and rule-governed 307–308; used by Disney characters 270–272; variations in grammar 105–106; variations in pronunciation 110–111, 300; viewed as less professional 309
African Americans: actors 270–273; and Blackness 2, 4, 5, 38, 111, 125, 127, 239, 271; children 6, 16, 17, 245; and chronic pain 121–122; dehumanizing Discourse against 15–16; discrimination against 281, 287; emotional states of 242; English variations of 105–106; in films and cartoons 260, 270–273; housing discrimination against 314–319; and hypertension 26; men/young men 2–3, *3*, 14, 125, 128, 307; migration of 83, 111, 225, 228; older terms used for 39–40; representations of 6, 14, 105; speech of 105–106, 300; stereotypes of 104–105; violence against 13–17; volume of speech 120; women 14, 125, 281; *see also* African American English (AAE); Gullah/Geechee English; people of color
African diaspora 117
African languages 114, 115, 117; *see also* Swahili language; Yoruba language
Africans 26, 260
Aladdin (Disney film) 264, 270
Alsatian language 136
American English: Appalachian/Ozark 52, 77, 100, 112, 197, 218, 223, 234, 287; in Boston 52, 212, 218, 219, 221, 222, 223, 225, 228, 287; "correctness" of 191, *191*; in Disney films 268; erosion of regional differences 79; in New England 212, 218, 221–222, 225–229; in New York 83, 212, 218, 219, 221, 222–225, 226; "r" sound in 19, 199, 214, *216*, 218–229; regional varieties of 81–100, 218; regional word choice variations 84–87; Southern varieties of 19, 82, *82*, 218, 222; Standard 56–57, 255, 277; *see also* African American English; Southern accents
American Sign Language (ASL) 107, 161–162, *162*, 166–167, *168*, 169–170, *169*, 185; in Canada 167; and ethnic identity 170; as marker of social identity 184; name signs 179
Angelou, Maya 197
Angermeyer, Phillip 304
Ansari, Aziz 263
anti-Semitism 58
Anzaldúa, Gloria 60
Apache language 245
apartheid 17; educational 238
apologies 68, 69, 292–293
Appalachian/Ozark English 52, 77, 100, 112, 197, 218, 223, 234, 287
appropriacy arguments 238–240
Arabic language 131, 141, 146
Arapaho language 152
Aristocats, The (Disney film) 270

Armenian language 146
Arnold, Bob 165
Arnow, Harriett 60
Art of Editing, The 274
Asian Americans 33, 62, 136, 153, 154, 299
Asians 260; stereotypes of 104–105, *104*
ASL *see* American Sign Language (ASL)
ASL Slam 165
aspectual marking 114–116, **115**, **116**
assemblages 12, 19
Asturian language 136
Atlantis: The Lost Empire (Disney film) 272
Atlas of North American English 80, *81*
audism 181, 183
Aunt Jemima 125, *126*
Austen, Jane 11
Australia 53
Ayers, Edward L. 196

baby talk 136–138
Baker-Bell, April 243
bald eagles 259, *260*
Baldwin, James 129
Bambi (Disney film) 152, 267
Bardem, Javier 263
Barnhart et al. v. Safeway 297
Barry, Dave 206
Basque language 136, 194, 305
Bassa language **23**
Baugh, John 238, 315–316, 318
Beauty and the Beast (Disney film) 263, **264**, 267
Bell, Alexander Graham 177–178, 181
Bell, Alexander Melville 178
Bell, Eliza Grace 178
Bell, Mabel Hubbard 178
Bengali language 146
Benor, Sarah 109
Berenstain Bears, The (television show) 152
Beyoncé 271
bias 323; and language variation 9
Big Hero 6 (Disney film) 264, 267
bilingualism 19, 107, 130–132, 139, 142–143, 153, 159; in Bolivia 253; in education 247–248; embracing 158–159; and languagelessness 241; native 134; in signs 194
Binoche, Juliette 263
Birth of a Nation, The (film) 14
Black American Sign Language (Black ASL) 107
Black language 7, 123, 125; *see also* African American English (AAE)
Black Lives Matter (#BlackLivesMatter) 5–6, 16
Black people: binary opposition to whiteness 2; enslavement of 13
blackface 127, 273
Blackness 4, 38, 111, 125, 239, 271; indexing 127; opposition to 2, 5
Boland, Julie 56
Bolt (Disney film) 270
Bonilla-Silva, Eduardo 76
Booker, Cory 130, 158
Boomers 11
Boston American English 52, 212, 218, 219, 221, 222, 223, 225, 228, 287
Bourdieu, Pierre 276
Braidwood Academies 178
Brave (Disney·Pixar film) 267
Brazil **27**, 29–30, 32
Breakfast at Tiffany's (film) 153
Breton language 136
British Sign Language (BSL) 170, *171*, 185
Broderick, Matthew 270
Brown, Foxy *308*
Brown, Tarana 295
brownface 155, *155*, 270
BSL (British Sign Language) 170, *171*, 185
Bucholtz, Mary 127, 302–303
Burmese language 146
Buttigieg, Pete 130, 158

Cajun French 140, 197, 272
California Real Estate Commission 311–312
California Vowel Shift (CVS) 91, *91*
Caló (Spanish) language 133
Campos, Bruno 273
Canada: English spoken in 53, 80, 91, 140, 151; ASL in 167; French spoken in 140
Canterbury Tales (Chaucer) 220
Cantonese language 116, 131, 134, 251, 252
Cape Cod 171–174, *172*
Carlisle Indian Industrial School 148, *244*
Carrere, Tia 272
Cars (Disney·Pixar film) 206, 258, 264
Carter, Byron *3*
Castro, Joaquin 131
Castro, Julián 130, 131, 133, 139, 158
Catalan language 136
categorization 32–35, 39
"caught/cot" merger 88
chain shift 90
Chase, Daveigh 272
Chatino language 146–148
Chen, Jaqueline 32
Cherokee language 35, *195*, 197
Cheung, Connie 281
Chicago Manual of Style 10, 11
Chicanx English 108, 112, 234, 249, 270
Chicanx persons 33, 133; protests by 247–248, *247*; in the San Francisco Bay Area 317–318
Chichewa language 35
Chickasaw language *195*
Chinese Americans 111

Chinese Exclusion Act 29, 105, 152
Chinese languages 146; Cantonese 116, 131, 134, 251, 252; Mandarin 132, 141, 145, 251; spoken in the US 241; varieties of 134
Chinese laundry 104
Chinese restaurant syndrome 102, *103*, 105, 117
Chinese virus 106
ching-chong 153–154
Chinglish 139
Chingy 218
Choctaw language 141, 197
Chomsky, Noam 44, 59
Chow Yun-Fat 263
Chun, Elaine 153
Cinderella (Disney film) 266, 267
Civil Rights Act 282, 284, 312, 319
Clerc, Laurent 178, 180
Clinton, William J. "Bill" 206
clothing, indexical meanings of 118, *119*, 120
cochlear implant hearing 184
code-switching 139–140, 160, 239–240, 304; examples 140–141; intrasentential 139–140, 142; situational 239–240
cognitive categories 32–35
cognitive scientists 307
color terms 23, **23**, 210; grue 23, 210
Color Purple, The (Walker) 57
"Come by Here" (song) 114
Coming to America (film) 271
Communicative burden: mutual responsibilities of 65–67; between speakers of different English varieties 72–73
Conference on College Composition and Communication 236–237
Conrod, Kirby 11
Corsican language 136
Cotillard, Marion 263
counter poetry 165
covert prestige 204–205
COVID-19 106
creaky voice 68–70, *68*, 77–78, 120
Creoles 53, 115; French-based 197
critical race theory 58
crossing 127
Cruz, Cirila Baltazar 146–148, 305
Cruz, Penelope 263
Cruz, Rubi 147–148
Cuban Spanish 133
cultural appropriation 127
cultural assimilation 243–248
Cummings, Jim 270

Dagen H (Högertrafikomläggningen) 211, 225
dairy products 40
DARE (Dictionary of American Regional English) 80
Darwin, Charles 81
Davis, Angela 14
Davis, Jordan 118
deaf community: and American Sign Language 161–162; and audism 181, 183; cultural model of deafness 164–166, 183; and education 243–245; education in 177–178; ideologies within 180–184; late-deafened 184; medical model of deafness 183; musicians 164; oral deaf 184; oralism vs. manualism 174–180, 181, 183; poets 165; and signed languages 19, 131; use of assistive devices within 184; *see also* American Sign Language (ASL); signed languages
Deaf President Now (DPN) movement 182–183, *182*
DeBois, Dean 272
del Toro, Benecio 263
Department of Housing and Urban Development (HUD) 312, *313*
derogation 155–156
Deschene, Chris 151
dialect literature 128
dialect maps 188–191, *190*, *198*
dialectology 80, 84, 186; perceptual 51, 186, 188–191
dialects 49; of American English 81–82; of English 80; ethnic 122–123, 133, 153; hierarchies of 237; NORMs 79–80; regional 79, 287; of sign languages 180; in the US 190–192
Diaz, Natalie 152
Dictionary of American Regional English (DARE) 80
DiMarco, Nyle 183
diphthongization 89, 90
diphthongs 52, 85, 89, 91, 111
discourse markers 97–99; quotative 98–99, *99*
discourse/Discourse 5–7; dehumanizing 15–16; and the idea of racial difference 106; and language ideologies 71; public 72; racial 5–7, 16, 38, 77, 129; racist 17, 29, 38–39, 106; of social difference 19; in the work environment 283–284
discourse structural racism 5–6, 19, 105, 106, 107, 117; *see also* racism
discrimination: against African Americans 287; based on national origin 285, 285–287, 288; dialect-based 317; and discourse 7; in housing and zoning *137*; in housing issues 310–319; language-based 12, 322; linguistic 42, 73; linguistic profiling 316–317, 318, 319; racial 40; against stigmatized accents 65; in the workplace 285–289
Disney: cultural stereotypes in 273; market share of 260; racist representations by 259; representations of women by 266–267, *268*;

and Uncle Remus 261; use of stereotypes by 262–266; worldview of 266–273
diversity 282–283; ethnolinguistic 196–197; linguistic 320–323
Dominican Spanish 133
donkeys 221, 222
doomscrolling 280
double consciousness 17, 71
double negatives 95
DPN (Deaf President Now) movement 182–183, *182*
Du Bois, W.E.B. 17, 71
Duck Tales (Disney film) 266, 268
Duke, Patty 227
Dumbo (Disney film) 270
Dunkin' Donuts 281
Duolingo 152

Eastern Pomo language 21–22, 45
Ebonics 123–124; *see also* African American English (AAE)
echo chambers 275, 278–280
Eckert, Penelope 38
education: bilingual 247–248; as cultural assimilation 243–248; English-only 239, 248; funding for 4; goals in 234–236; language and 230–234; and Latinx teachers 248–249; of Native Americans 148–149, 243–244, *244*; and the speech of teachers 248–249; and standard language ideology 240; in urban classrooms 239–240; and the use of non-standard English 256
EEOC *see* Equal Employment Opportunity Commission (EEOC)
EEOC v. Central California Foundation for Health 285–286
EEOC v. RD's Drive-In 285
Ehrlich, Susan 309
Eisenhauer, Karen 267
Ellison, Ralph 16
Eminem 218–219
emotional states 241–242
Emperor's New Groove, The (Disney film) 265
Encyclopedia of Southern Culture 197
English Grammar, The (Jonson) 221
English language: accented versions of 50–54, *51*, 58, 248, 249–250; appropriacy arguments 238–240; borrowed words 46; British 53; in Canada 53, 80, 91, 140, 151; Chicano/Chicanx 108, 112, 234, 249, 270, 315, 317; Chinese-accented 52; color terms 23–24, **23**; dialect regions of *81*; dialects of 19, 47, 49, 80; ethnic varieties of 118, 123, 128–129; ethnicity-indexing 117; Google search for grammar terms **54**; Gullah/Geechee 114–116, **115**; Hawaiian 116, **116**, 272; Hollywood Injun 154–155, 158; Indian 111–112; "inferior" varieties of 241; inversion in **113**; Irish 116–117; Italian American 110; Jamaican/Patwa 114, 234; Jewish 108, 109, 110; Latinx 109, 110, 117; learning a second dialect of 60; linguistic variables in 47–48; as majority native language 53; Native American 110; Navajo 108, 111, 113–114, 128, 205, 234, 238, 239, 302; Newfoundland 117; non-standard varieties of 256; and noun marking 22; as official language 145–146, *145*; Old English 94–95, 96, 220; signed 167; "standard" 4, 7, 42–43, 54–58, 60, 62, 67, 70, 93, 109, 232, 239, 248, 256; Standard British 223; standard language privilege 67, 117; stigmatized varieties of 234; use of "like" 98–99; used by Disney characters 270–272; and verb markings 21–22; *see also* African American English (AAE); American English
"English Only" laws 248
English people 260
engma 45
Equal Employment Opportunity Commission (EEOC) 283–284, 285; lawsuits 285–287; on sexual harassment 295
ethnic enclaves *137*, 192–195
ethnicity 29–31; and linguistic variation 107–109; in the US Census **31**
eugenics 29, 236
euphemism 156
eye dialect 199–200

Fair Housing Act 311–312, 312–314, *313*
fairness doctrine 275
fake news 277, 278–280
Farsi language 136
Faulkner, William 197
Federal Communications Commission (FCC) 274
Federal Housing Administration 311
femininity 37, 41
feminism 58
FHEO (Office of Fair Housing and Equal Opportunity) 312
Filipino Americans 33
Filipino languages 285–286; *see also* Tagalog language
Filipinx people 285–286
filter bubbles 278–280
fingerspelling 179
Florence Y'all water tower 200–201, *200*
Florence Y'alls baseball team 200–201
Forbes, Sean 164
forensic linguistics 306–307
Fought, Carmen 92, 267
Fox News 275, 278, 281, 287
Foxworthy, Jeff 197
France, languages spoken in 136

French Creole 197
French language 132; in the African diaspora 117; Cajun 197, 272; in France 197; Louisiana varieties of 272; negation in 95; spoken in Canada 140; spoken in the US 134, 146, 241
French Sign Language *(langue des signes française*, LSF) 178, 185
Friday (film) 153
Frisian language 35, 194
Frozen (Disney film) 267, 280
Full Metal Jacket (film) 281

Galician language 136
Gallaudet, Edward Miner 179, 180
Gallaudet, Thomas Hopkins 178–179, 180
Gallaudet University 167, 169, 179, 181; candidates for president 182, *182*, 185
Gates, Tinky *308*
Gen Xers 11
gender 9–11; and identity 37, 298; and language use 309
gender-neutral words 9–12, 20
Generation Alpha 11
Generation Z 11
genocide 13, 15
German language 132, 134, 152
Gervais, Ricky 262–263
Glass, Ira 70
Glennie, Evelyn 164
Glover, Donald 271
Goldberg, Whoopi 270, 271
Goodman, Alan 24
grammar: correcting *57*; descriptive 56; Google search for terms **54**; intimate 205; missing commas 303; prescriptive 55–56, 57, 60, 62, 93, 95, 98, 105–106, 186, 211; proper 321; rules of 58
Grammarly.com *61*
grammaticality 59
Great Migration 111, 225, 228
Green Book, The 5
Griffith, D. W. 14
Groff, Jonathan 219–220
Gujarati language 146
Gullah/Geechee English 114–116, **115**, 234

habitual aspect marking 116–117
habitual thought 23
Halberstadt, Amy 241
Hall-Lew, Lauren 111
Hamilton (stage play) 219–220
Harris, Joel Chandler 115, 261
Hartford school 178
Harvard Crimson 9–10
Harvey, Mandy 164
Hawai'i 272
Hawaiian English 116, **116**, 272
Hawaiian language 116, 152
HDS (Housing Discrimination Study) 314
healthcare access 5
hearing, physiology of 162–164
hearing loss 164; *see also* deaf community
Heath, Shirley Brice 240, 243
Hebrew language 109
Helm, Angela Bronner 273
Hepburn, Katherine 225, 227
Hernandez v. New York 303–304
Herring, Susan 293
high rising terminal (HRT) intonation 70
Hill, Jane 1, 128, 155–156, 282
Hindi language 146
hip hop identity 128
Hispanics 31, 33; *see also* Latinx people
Hochschild, Arlie 291
Hodges, Adam 2
Hokkien language 132
Hollywood Injun English 154–155, 158
Hollywood Protective Society sign *18*
Hmong language 146
hoodies 118, *119*
hooks, bell 271
Hounsou, Djimon 263
housing discrimination 310–319; against African Americans 314–319; appointments to see apartments *318*; demographic makeup of neighborhoods in study **316**; Fair Housing Act 311–314, *313*; against Latinx people 314–315; percent fewer rental units compared to whites *314*
Housing Discrimination Study (HDS) 314
HRT (high rising terminal) intonation 70
HUD (Department of Housing and Urban Development) 312, *313*
Hurricane Katrina 314–315
Hurston, Zora Neale 60, 197
hyperanglicization 155, 156
hypercorrection 48, 50
hypertension 26

"I am a man" mural 16, *16*
iconicity 212
icons 35
immigrants: American names for 245–246, *246*; Chinese 102; English fluency of 107; European 123; Indigenous 305–306; Irish 112; Japanese 17; from Latin America 148; Latinx 15, 235–236; Scottish 112; Ukrainian 86
immigration laws 152
Incredibles, The (Disney·Pixar film) 267
indexical bleaching 109, 125, 127–128, 245–246
indexical meanings 9, 40, 302; of clothing 118, *119*, 120; and code switching 140, 142–143; indexical fields 229; of languages other than

English 158; of spoken language 62; and the use of Spanish 130; of written language 60
indexical signs 35–38, 73–74; types of 38
indexicality 73–74
Indian English 111–112
Indigenous languages 305–306; Mayan 136; from Mexico 146–148; in the US 146; *see also* Native American languages
Indonesian language 146
inequalities: and language ideologies 19; structural 322
information literacy 273–278, 280
infotainment 277
"Inner Circle" countries 53
Interactional styles 120
International Phonetic Alphabet (IPA) xii, 44–45
International Reading Association 238
interpretation 304
interpreters 146–148, 303–304, 305, 306, 308–309
interruptions 69
intimate grammars 205
Inuit peoples 260
Invisible Man (Ellison) 16
IPA (International Phonetic Alphabet) xii, 44–45
Irish Americans 123
Irish English 116–117
Irish language 112, 117, 260
Irons, Jeremy 270
Irvine, Judith 9
isoglosses 80, 84
Italian American English 110
Italian Americans 120, 123, *124*
Italians 260

Jamaican Patwa 114, 234
Japanese language 53, 116, 146, 251; color terms 210
Japanese Americans 33, 152
Jeantel, Rachel 2, 4, 7, 19, 307–308, *308*, 309, 310
Jewish English 108, 109, 110
Jewish people 15; Americans 107, 109, 120, 145; in films and cartoons 260
Jim, Rex Lee 152
Jim Crow laws 17
"jive" 123–124
Johnson, Dwayne "The Rock" 269
Johnson, James Weldon 13
Jones, James Earl 270, 271
Jonson, Ben 221
Jordan, I. King 182–183
Jordan, June 238
Jungle Book, The (Disney film) 264

Kachru, Braj 53
Kalaallisut language 35
Kaluli culture 137
Keaton, Diane 263
Kelsey, Gin 186
Khmer language 134, 146
K'iche' (Maya) language 23, **23**, 35; neologisms in 46–47
K'iche' Maya Language Academy 46
Kilpatrick, James 55
King, Martin Luther Jr. 16
King, Sharese 4
King James Bible 10
Klassen, Mari 165
Konglish 139
Korean language 134, 146
Korenglish 139
"K(o)untry" spelling 186, 201–202, **202**, *203*, 209
Krapp, George Philip 212, 224–225
Kroskrity, Paul 12
Ku Klux Klan 14
"Kumbayah" (song) 114
Kuntry Kitchen 186, 201–202
Kwok, Robert Ho Man 102

Labov, William 225–226
lactose intolerance 40
Lady and the Tramp (Disney film) 266, 270
Lakota language 152
language(s) 73–74; in court testimony 302–304; differences in interactional styles 121; and education 230–234; errors in 233–234; and ethnic inequality 120–123; in films 260; "foreign" 131–132; gendered patterns of use 309; heritage speakers of 131, 139, 143; and human sociality 322; impact of media on 79; Indigenous 152, 305–306; informal forms of 20; and the law 302–319; master-apprentice programs 151; mechanisms for categorizing people 24–33; minority 194; mock representations of 153–154; morphosyntactic variations 92–96; myths about 40–41, 42, 70, 79, 136; native 232; native speakers of 131; natural 304; privileged varieties of 71; and race 3–4; and racialization 38–41; racism and 4; racist 123; regional variations in 99–100; "sleeping" 150; social/indexical meanings 9; spoken 232; spoken at home 237, 239; standard 77; stereotypes linked to 259; structural properties of 22–24; students' right to their own 236–238; subordination of **73**; symbolic revalorization of 12, 42, 118, 120, 206; in university classrooms 249–253, **251**, *252*; used in textbooks 64–65; variations and similarities between 43; variations in 7, 8–9, 81; vernacular varieties of 74–77; written 60, 230–231

language acquisition 18, 43–47, 323; and baby talk 136–138; in different cultures 138; in Native American communities 151–152; scholars of 307; and second language proficiency 180; words gained by 3- and 5-year-olds *262*
language appropriation 123–129, 128
language disorders (LDs) 44
language ideologies 7–13, 9–12; of "appropriate" speech 192; as assemblages 12, 19; confronting 75–77; of the courts 303–304; within the deaf community 180–184; and discourse structural racism 19; in education 233–234; and English public space 152–158; and ethnic dialect 120; and geography 187; and hip hop identity 128; and ideologies of race 121; and the interpretation of women's speech 309; and the media 274–275; one nation, one language 305; prejudicial 321–323; and pronoun envy 10, 17; sexism in 292–293; standard 65, 70–75, 236, 240, 275, 302, 305–307, 322, 323
language nests 151–152
language socialization 240
languagelessness 241–243
langue des signes française (LSF) 178, 185
Lao language 146
laryngealization 68–70, *68*
Latin America 33, 148
Latinx English 109, 110, 117
Latinx people 15, 31, 33, 120, 139, 286–287, 304; children 245; deportation of 152; English speaking 107–108; in films and cartoons 260; housing conditions for 314–315; as immigrants 235–236; "languageless" 241; racist stereotypes of 157; speech of 300; use of Spanish by 130–131
LD (language disorder) 44
Lee, Jason Scott 272
LEP (Limited English Proficiency) 308–309
l'Épee, Abbé de 178, 180
Lethal Weapon 4 (film) 154
lexical havoc 128
Lilo & Stitch (Disney film) 267, 272
Limited English Proficiency (LEP) 308–309
linguistic anthropology 42, 276
linguistic assimilation 77
Linguistic Atlas Project 80, 84
linguistic landscapes 187, 192–195, 198–199
linguistic marketplace 276
linguistic profiling 316–317, 318, 319
linguistic tightrope 207, 209, 239, 276, 294
linguistic variation 47, 60, 77; and ethnic dialects 122–123; ethnicity-indexing (sentences and meanings) 111–117; ethnicity-indexing (words and sounds) 109–111; in literature 128; parameters of 100; and race and ethnicity 106, 107–109; and social stereotypes 19
linguistics: forensic 306–307; historical 18; subfields of 18
linguists 56, 58; as experts 306–310
Linnaeus, Carolus 27
Lion King, The (Disney film) 258, 264, 268, 270–271; 2019 live-action remake 271
lip-reading 175–176, 177, 179
literacy 139, 237, 238, 243; and education 231, 243; information 273–278, 280
literacy myth 231, 240
literacy skills 37, 60, 81, 200, 201
Little Mermaid, The (Disney film) 267
Lou, April *246*
Lovelace, Marcellous *16*
Loving v. Virginia 17
LSF (*langue des signes française*) 178, 185
Lucy, John 22
Lushootseed language *195*
lynchings 13–15

Magic Washer 104–105, *104*
Magnetic Resonance Imaging (MRI) 180
malaria 25–26
Malayalam language 35
Mandarin (Chinese) language 132, 141, 145, 251
mansplaining 292
manualism 174–180
Māori language 152
mapmaking 188–191
Marin, Cheech 270
marriage, interracial 17
Martha's Vineyard Sign Language (MVSL) 171–174, 178–179, 181
Martin, Trayvon 2, *3*, 4, 5, 307, 309; and discourse 6–7
mascots 39, 49–50, *50*
Massieu, Jean 178, 180
master-apprentice language programs 151
Matsuda, Mari 58
Mayan languages 136; *see also* K'iche' (Maya) language; Yucatec (Maya) language
McCrary, JD 271
McGurk Effect 175–176
media: engagement with 274–278; impact on regional variations 79, 82; influence on children 261–262; and negative news 280; news broadcasting 275–276; newspaper headlines 277; objectivity in 279–280; from other countries 278; and spin 278–279; *see also* social media
Meek, Barbra 265
Meet the Robinsons (Disney film) 266
mental mapping *189*, *190*, 208

Meritor Savings Bank v. Vinson 295–296
MeToo Movement 295
Mexican Americans 123; *see also* Chicanx people
Mexicans 260
Mexico 132–133; before the Texas Revolution *132*
Meyer, Robert 152
microaggressions 74, 299–300
Middle Easterners 260
Mien language 146
Milano, Alyssa 295
Millennials 11, 37
Milne, A. A. 221
minstrel shows 127
Minstrelese 125
Mitchell, Blackhorse 60, 128, 158
Mixtec language 305
Moana (Disney film) 269
Mock Asian 153–154, 158
Mock Ebonics 125, 127
Mock Spanish 155–156, *155*, 158, 194
Modern English: Its Growth and Present Use (Krapp) 212
Mojave language 152
Mongolian language 146
monodialectalism 19
monolingualism 19, 107, 131, 143, 187; in the US 136, 192–194, 304
monophthongization 82, 86, 90, 91, 92, 111, 114
monophthongs 52, 85
monosodium L-glutamate (MSG) 102–103, 105, 117
Moon Unit Zappa 98
More, Thomas 10
Morgan, Marcyliena 128
morphology 18; regional variations in 92–96
Morrison, Toni 2, 71
Motherese 136
MRI (Magnetic Resonance Imaging) 180
MSG (monosodium L-glutamate) 102–103, 105, 117
Mulan (Disney film)267, 270, 271
multiculturalism 247, 282–283
multilingualism 143–144, 158, 187; in signs 192–195, *193*
Murphy, Eddie 270–271
myths: about Black people 121; of the Black rapist 14, 15; about language 40–41, 42, 70, 79, 136; literacy 231, 240; one nation, one language 136, 187; of race 13, 15, 24, 41; of standard English 54, 56, 58, 62–63, 237; suspect bilingual 139, 154; Tower of Babel 220; white South 197; Word Gap 236
names: American 245–246, *246*; ASL signs for 179; and discrimination 246; foreign/ethnic 128, 129; of instructors 250; pronunciation of 128
National Council of Teachers of English (NCTE) 238–239
National Fair Housing Alliance (NFHA) 318
National Public Radio (NPR) 277
Native American English 110
Native American languages 21–22, 107, 146, 149–151, 152, 187, 195, 196; Apache 245; Arapaho 152; Cherokee *195*, 197; Chickasaw *195*; Choctaw 197; Lakota 152; Lushootseed *195*; Mojave 152; Navajo **113**, 152, 285; Osage *195*; poetry in 152; regional variations 99; signs in *195*; Tohono O'odham 152
Native Americans 13, 15; Apache 244–245; in California 151; education of 148–149, 243–244, *244*; film representations of 154; in films and cartoons 260; Haudenosaunee (Iroquois) Confederacy 152; Kanien'kehá:ka (Mohawk) 152; Lakota 152; Myaamia (Miami) 151; Navajo **113**; Navajo Nation 151; Seneca 152; stereotypes of 104; Supaman (Lakota) 152; Tunica 151; Wampanoag 148, 151, 171; Western Apache 121
Navajo English 108, 111, 113–114, 128, 205, 234, 238, 239, 302
Navajo language **113**, 152, 285
Navajo Nation 151, 285
Navlish 139, 142
NCS (Northern Cities Shift) 88–89, *88*, 92
NCTE (National Council of Teachers of English) 238–239
Nelly 218
neologisms 46, 150; in K'iche' 46–47
Nepali language 146
"nerd" identity 127
neurolinguists 307
Nevins, Marybeth 245
New England American English 212, 218, 221–222, 225–229
New York American English 83, 212, 218, 219, 221, 222–225, 226
New Zealand 53, 152
Newfoundland English 117
Newman, Edwin 55
news broadcasting 275–276
NFHA (National Fair Housing Alliance) 318
No Child Left Behind Act 248
"No Dogs, Negroes, Mexicans" sign *15*
Norman, Jason 165
Northern Cities Shift (NCS) 88–89, *88*, 92
NPR (National Public Radio) 277

Oak Ridge National Laboratory 72
obscenities 69
Occitan langauge 136
O'Connor v. Oakhurst Dairy 303
Office of Fair Housing and Equal Opportunity (FHEO) 312
Oliver and Company (Disney film) 270
Oncale v. Sundowner Offshore Services 298
O'Neal, Shaquille 153
onomatopoeia 35
Onward (Disney·Pixar film) 267
Oppenheimer, David 312
oralism 174–180, 181, 183
O'Rourke, Beto 130, 158
Osage language *195*
"Outer Circle" countries 53
Ozawa, Takao 29

Pachuco (Spanish) language 133
Parentese 136
Patwa 114, 234
"pen/pin" merger 82, *83*, 88, 111
perceptual dialectology 51, 186, 188–191
performativity 36–37
Perlmutter, David M. 167
perpetual foreigner syndrome 134, 136
Peter Pan (Disney film) 154, 270
Philadelphia Story (film) 225
Phillips, Susan 245
phonation 68, 69
phonetics 18, 81, 213, 217, 223, 248
phonology 18, 45, 49–50, 51, 62, 81, 90, 203, 207, 248; of ASL 167; native 52–53, 276; Spanish 158
Ping, Chae Chan 29
Pinocchio (Disney film) 269
Pirahã language 44
Pittsburghese *84*, 85–87
Plessy v. Ferguson 32
plural marking 22, 111, 156, 307
Pocahontas (Disney film) 154, 270
Podesva, Rob 91–92
poetry: and the deaf community 165; in Native American languages 152, 204–205
Polish language 251
Portuguese language 116
poverty 5, 235–236
pragmatic variations 96
pragmatics 18
Pratt, Richard 148
prejudice 7; and categorization 39; against deaf community 179; and English varieties 53; and informal language forms 20; and language ideologies 321–323; linguistic 72; racial 225, 309
presbycusis 164
prescriptivism 57, 59–60, 123, 211; *see also* grammar, prescriptive
prescriptivists 55–56, 57
Preston, Dennis 186, 189, 191
Princess and the Frog, The (Disney film) 261, 267, 270, 272–273
pronominal forms 94
pronoun envy 10, 17
pronouns: and gender 9–12; gender-neutral 11–12; singular "they" 10–12
prosodic features, in lip-reading 176
Provençal language 136
psycholinguistics 18
Puerto Rican Spanish 133
Punjabi language 146

Quebec 143–144
Quechua language 253
Queen, Robin 56, 67

race: as factor in medicine 121–122; language and 3–4; and linguistic variation 107–109; myth of 13, 15, 24, 41
racial categories 24–25, 27–31, **27**, *28*; in Brazil 32; and cognition 32–33; and indexical meanings 40; stereotypes of 39; and the US Census **31**, 33
Racial Discourse 5–7, 16, 38, 77, 129; *see also* discourse/Discourse
racial identifications 3
racial profiling 5; *see also* housing discrimination
racial violence 13–14
racialization 38–41, 105
racism: in America 1–2, 4, 29, 283; anti-Asian 281–282; anti-Black linguistic 243; anti-Latinx 157; and "bad"/"broken" English 70–71; in caricatures 53; in child's play 127; "color-blind" 1, 76; and COVID-19 106; discourse structural 5–6, 19, 105, 106, 107, 117; folk theory of 1, 7, 282; "joking" 123–124, 281–282; and language 4; and mob violence 14–15; racist slurs 3; structural 2, 3, 4–7, 17, 19, 54, 58, 120, 131, 158; systemic 70–71; *see also* stereotypes, racist
racists 1–2, 283; hunt for 3, 6, 282
Ramsey's Diner *199*
RateMyProfessors.com 250–251
Ratzenberger, John 264
reading: active 65; of textbooks 64–65; and the reading gap 234; *see also* literacy
reading skills *234*, 238; and education 234–236
Red Summer 13
redlining 311
reflective thought 23
Remy, Charles 223

Rescuers Down Under, The (Disney film) 269
Reverse Linguistic Stereotyping 253
rhotic sound 62; by age, location, and race 228–229, *228*; alveolar approximant "r" 217; alveolar trill 217, 220–221; "American" 224–229; in British English 219–221; in court testimony 302–303; in films 219–220, 225, 226–227, *227*; non-rhotic "r" 218, 224–225, *226*; and social class 225–226, *226*; uvular trill and voiced fricative 218; variable "r" sound 216–217
rhotics 213–218
Rickford, John 4
Ridloff, Douglas 165
Rischer, Ronald 236
Rogers, Ginger 227
Romeo and Juliet (Shakespeare) 220
Rooney, Mickey 153
Rosa, Jonathan 241
Rosch, Eleanor 34
Rosetta Stone 152
Rowland, Dick 13
Rumford Fair Housing Act 311–312
Russian language 23, 145, 146
Russians 260

Salinas, Maria Elena 130
salt 102–103
Sanders, Chris 272
sandwiches 34–35
Santa Ana, Otto 15
SCD (Sickle Cell Disease) 25–26, *26*
Schmidt, Ben 250
schwa raising 48
Schwarzenegger, Arnold 156, 263
Scots 260
second language learners 53
secret shoppers 297–298
segregation: ending 319; language 238; racial 107, 311; residential 311, 315; in South Africa 17; in the US 17, 40
semantics 18, 167
semiotics 35–38, 219
Sesame Street (television show) 260
Sessions, Jeff 205
sexism 58, 69, 270; in language ideologies 292–293
sexual harassment 294–298, *297*
sexual orientation 298
Shakespeare, William 11, 220, 224
Shankar, Shalini 282
Shona language 23
Shrek (DreamWorks film) 271
Sicard, Abbé 178, 180
Sickle Cell Disease (SCD) 25–26, *26*
signed languages 19, 131, 162, *162*, 169–170, 177; British (BSL) 170, *171*, 185; French (LSF) 178, 185; and poetry 165; Women's Irish Sign Language 107; *see also* American Sign Language (ASL)
Silverstein, Michael 228
Simon, John 55
Sinclair, Madge 270
skin color 25–26, 32, 40; *see also* prejudice
Slater, Judy 281
slavery 4, 13, 15, 261
Snow White (Disney film) 266
social categorization 19, 20, 52, 73, *73*, 75, 107
Social Darwinism 29–30
social discourse, patterns of 123
social inequality 41, 106
social meanings 9
social media 2, 4, 7, 59, 79, 152, 186, 192, 274, 277, 279–280, 281, 295, 308, 310; and the Travon Martin shooting 2, 4
Song of the South (Disney film) 261
South Africa 17, 53
South Asian Americans 120
Southern Accent Reduction 72
Southern American English 19, 82, *82*, 218, 222; accents 197, *198*, 202–205, *204*, 276, 322; in comic strips 199; in movies 208; Southern dative 96
Southern Poverty Law Center 148
Southern US states 187, 190–191, 195–197, 202
Southern Vowel Shift (SVS) 80, 88, 90–91, *90*
Southernness 52, 83, 91, 111, 187, 200, 202–205, 207
Spade, David 265
Spain: languages spoken in 136; racial categories in Spanish colonies 27, *27*
Spanglish 139
Spanish language 22, 52, 107–108, 112, 136, 141, 146; appropriation of by white speakers 155; Caló or Pachuco 133; Caribbean 133; Chicanx 133; Mock 155–157, *155*; native speakers of 251; as "official" language 136; regional variations in 99; spoken by US candidates 130–131, 134; spoken in Latin America 134, 136; spoken in the US 130–131, 132, 134, 139, 146, 241; "standard" 133
Spanish Influenza 106
specific language impairment 44, 232
speech deficits 69
speech pathologists 307
speech therapy 122
speech-reading 175–176, 177
spelling variations 60
Spilman, Jane Bassett 182
St. Rita's School *166*
standard English privilege 67
Standard Language Ideology 146; *see also* language ideologies

Standards for the English Language Arts 238–239
Star Wars (film) 152
stereotypes: of African Americans 6; about Black language 123–124; about women 309; of the American South 197, 199–200, 204, 206–207; and clothing style 118, *119*, 120; cultural 273; of deaf people 161; of femininity 37; "gangsta/thug" 125; gender 266–267; linked to language 259; negative 12; racial 125; of racial categories 39, 42; racist 104–105, 106, 118, 154, 157, 241; in storytelling 262–266; of white men 298–300; of women 292–293, 294
stereotyping: racial 73; racist 102–104; and the rhotic sound 227
Stewart, Jimmy 225
Stokoe, William 169, 179–180, 181
storytelling 258–262; accents of animated characters 268–273, *269*; stereotypes in 262–266
structural inequalities 322
Subtirelu, Nicholas 250
Supaman 152
SVS (Southern Vowel Shift) 80, 88, 90–91, *90*
Swahili language 35, 132, 268
symbolic revalorization 12, 42, 118, 120, 206
symbols 35
syntax 18, 76, 81, 180; regional variations in 92–96
Syriac language 146

Taa language 44
Tagalog language 52, 116, 134, 143, 146, 285
Tamil language 146
Tangled (Disney film) 267
Tannen, Deborah 120
Tapahonso, Luci 152
Tarzan (Disney film) 268
Taste of Dahntahn *84*
Telugu language 146
Terminator, The (film) 156
Texas Revolution 132–133
texting 62
Thai language 146
they (singular) 11
Thind, Bhagat Singh 29, *30*
This American Life (radio show) 70, 78
Thomas, Angie 60
Thomas, Jonathan Taylor 270
To'Haali, Hastiin (Tom Torlino)148, *149*
Tohe, Laura 128, 152
Tohono O'odham language 152
Toy Story (Disney·Pixar film) 264
transgender persons 11, 12, 298
translation 304
transphobia 58
Treaty of Guadalupe Hidalgo 132
Trump, Donald 157, 205, 226, 280
Tucker, Chris 153
Twain, Mark (Samuel Clemens) 115

Uncle Remus stories 261
United States vs. Thind 29
uptalk 69, 70, 77–78, 292
Urdu language 146
US Census 29–31, **31**, 33, 41; on English proficiency 134, *135*; Native American languages 149–150
US Constitution: First Amendment 152, 275; Tenth Amendment 145; Thirteenth Amendment 4, 179; Fourteenth Amendment 312
UV (ultraviolet) radiation 25

Valley of the Dolls (film) 227
Ventura Morales, Santiago 305
verb forms 94; modals 96; stative verbs 96; strong/weak 94–95, **95**; syntactic patterns 95–96
Veterans' Emergency Housing Act 311
Vietnamese Americans 33, 45, 196
Vietnamese language 128, 134, 141, 146, 193, *193*
voter suppression 4–5
Voting Rights Act 146, *147*
vowel shifts 88; California Vowel Shift (CVS) 91–92, *91*; chain shift 90; Northern Cities Shift (NCS) 88–89, *88*, 92; Southern Vowel Shift (SVS) 88, 90–91, *90*
vowels: changes in pronunciation 91–92; variations in pronunciation of 87–92, *88*

Walker, Alice 57
Walloon language 136
Warm Springs Reservation 245
Webster, Anthony K. 204–205
Weil, Jeannie Haubert 314
Weiner, Fred 183
Weinstein, Harvey 295
West African languages 117
Western Apache language 121
White City v. PR Restaurants 34
white juror bias 309
white privilege 117
white public space 128, 133, 194
white supremacy 5, 40, 148
Williams, Serena 122
Williams, Tennessee 197
women: African American 125; Asian 153–154; of color 32, 292; in Disney films 266–267, *268*; exploitation in the workplace 289, 289–298; and femininity 37, 41; as flight attendants 289, *290*, 291; and sexual harassment 294–298, *297*; silencing of

293–294; speech of 309; stereotypes of 292–293, 294; use of "creaky voice" by 68–70, 77–78; use of language by 69–70
Women's Irish Sign Language 107
Women's March on Washington *321*
Wong, Amy 111
Wong, Jimmy 153–154
Word Gap 235–236
work environment: controlled by white men 298–300; discrimination in 283–284; English-only 284, 286–287, 301; exploitation of women in 289–298; hostile 295, 296; multiculturalism and diversity in 247, 282–283; unwelcoming 281–283

X, Malcolm 233
xenophobia 146, 158
!Xóõ language 44

y'all 82, 93, 94, 96
Yao Ming 153
Yiddish language 86, 107, 109, 110, 144–145, *144*
Yoruba language 132
Yucatec (Maya) language 22

Zepeda, Ofelia 152
Zimmerman, George 2–3, 5, 6–7
zoot suits 118, *120*